Macroeconomics

THE HARBRACE SERIES IN BUSINESS AND ECONOMICS

Macroeconomics

Robert L. Crouch

University of California at Santa Barbara

(805) 893-8000
2152 - Office
3670 - Department

Harcourt Brace Jovanovich, Inc.

New York Chicago San Francisco Atlanta

ISBN: 0-15-551255-2

Library of Congress Catalog Card Number: 75-176489

Printed in the United States of America

To my parents
Jane and Reginald Charles Crouch

Preface

This book developed from a set of notes that I have used for some time in the intermediate course in macroeconomics for undergraduate majors. In fact, it was the positive response of my students which persuaded me to expand the notes into a textbook. In its present form, *Macroeconomics* is a comprehensive survey of the current state of comparative static macroeconomic theory, and it is designed to bridge the gap between the crude analysis of the introductory course and macroeconomics as practiced by professionals. Since the book is intended for undergraduate economics majors, the predominant form of exposition is the traditional blend of literary and graphical analysis. The student whose mathematical preparation includes high school algebra and geometry will have no difficulty following the discussion. In general, mathematical manipulations are kept to a minimum since the emphasis is on the logic used in finding a solution.

My experience has been that most students emerge from their principles of economics course with the impression that economics is a house divided between microeconomics, with one mode of analysis, and macroeconomics, with its own separate mode of analysis. Unfortunately, this dichotomy is frequently reinforced by intermediate textbooks. It is usually virtually impossible to detect anything in common between the analytical techniques of an intermediate microeconomics text and an intermediate macroeconomics text. In this book I have made every effort to make it clear, as professionals are well aware, that economics is not a schizophrenic subject but a unified and cohesive discipline. In fact, that is the main purpose of Part I on the *Microeconomic Foundations of Macroeconomics,* where the value-theoretic underpinnings of macroeconomics are developed. After completing that portion of the book, students should be completely persuaded that the subject matter of macroeconomics, just like that of microeconomics, is the interaction of transactors on certain *markets*. The reader will also have learned that the unique features of macroeconomics are simply, first, the transactors and the markets are highly aggregated and, second (unlike microeconomic partial equilibrium analysis), explicit allowance must be made for the interdependence of these macroeconomic markets because feedback effects exist among them. By the time the student finishes Chapter 6, *The Complete Macroeconomic Model,* he should understand that macroeconomics emerges naturally from microeconomic theory as a special case of general equilibrium analysis—special in that it is a highly aggregated form of general equilibrium analysis. Those already acquainted with macroeconomics will recognize immediately that the intellectual bloodlines of this book are Hicks–Modigliani–Patinkin out of Keynes.

Our model consists of four goods (labor, commodities, money, and bonds) and three transactors (households, firms, and government). The market for each good has a separate chapter devoted to it where an aggregate demand and supply function for that good is derived. These component aggregate demand and supply functions are all put together in Chapter 6. In Part II, *Neoclassical Macroeconomics,* we put the model through its paces in the light of *neoclassical assumptions.* These assumptions are: all (three) prices are flexible, no money illusion exists in any supply or demand function, expectations are unit-elastic, and distribution effects are absent (or are unimportant). In addition, we consider the validity of such famous neoclassical comparative static propositions as: "full employment is always guaranteed," "money is a veil," "the price level is proportional to the supply of money," and "fiscal policy changes the mix of income between public and private goods, not the level of income."

In Part III, *Neo-Keynesian Macroeconomics,* we operate the model in the light of neo-Keynesian assumptions. These assumptions are that: one (or more) of the prices is inflexible, money illusion exists in one (or more) of the supply and demand functions, expectations are not unit-elastic, and distribution effects exist (and are important). The important neo-Keynesian comparative static propositions which we demonstrate include: "permanent unemployment is quite possible," "money is not a veil," "money may not matter," and "fiscal policy changes the level of income as well as its mix between public and private goods."

Since the student will see the *same* theory generate either neoclassical propositions or neo-Keynesian propositions, depending upon which ground rules are used, he should come away from this book fully aware that macroeconomists are separated only by the assumptions they make concerning price flexibility, money illusion, expectations, and distribution effects. Therefore, to the extent that macroeconomists are divided into factions, they are divided over empirical questions and not the theory.

A final chapter on *Macroeconomic Disequilibrium* incorporates into a textbook (for the first time, I believe) Clower and Leijonhufvud's more recent reinterpretation of Keynes as, primarily, a macroeconomic disequilibrium theorist.

I would like to thank Professors William J. Baumol and Robert W. Clower, who read a preliminary version of the manuscript in its entirety. The multitude of helpful suggestions they made improved the final version immeasurably. What faults remain are, of course, my responsibility.

This manuscript was typed by a succession of students too numerous to mention individually. It is, perhaps, more appropriate to thank the federal government—their collective benefactor, and mine, through its Educational Opportunity Program.

If the first shall be last, my greatest debts are to my wife, Janet, and son, Gregory. As every economist who has written a book knows, the externalities of authorship, which are all costs, fall on his family. Mine bore up under them stoically.

Robert L. Crouch

Contents

Part I

The Microfoundations of Macroeconomics

1

The Unity of Economic Theory

1 Microeconomics and Macroeconomics

The prefix *macro-* comes from the Greek word μακρο meaning "large." Thus, freely translating, *macro*economics means "economics in the large." This is in contrast to *micro*economics which can be interpreted to mean "economics in the small" (since *micro-* comes from the Greek word μικρο meaning "small"). To shed further light by example, when we analyze the output, and the price of that output, for a single *firm* (or *industry*) we are engaged in microeconomic analysis. Similarly, analysis of the level of employment and the wages paid to workers in a certain firm (or industry) is, again, microeconomic analysis. By way of contrast, analysis of the level of output for the *whole economy,* the (average) wage of *all* workers employed throughout the economy, and so on, is the stuff of macroeconomics. Essentially then, macroeconomic analysis is the analysis of *economywide,* or *aggregate,* variables.

Hence, we observe that there is no difference *in principle* between microeconomics and macroeconomics—it is simply that macroeconomics deals with variables that are highly aggregated. Thus, these two branches of economics differ only in *degree;* namely, the degree of aggregation involved. We cannot stress too strongly that the analytical tools of microeconomic theory, especially the supply and demand approaches, are equally applicable (indeed, indispensable) to the elucidation of macroeconomic problems. There is not one branch of economics, microeconomics, which uses supply and demand analysis and another branch of economics, macroeconomics, which uses some other apparatus. Both microeconomics and macroeconomics are concerned with the interaction of transactors on *markets* and, as a result, each is amenable to analysis with the same tools.

2 Partial, General, and Quasi-General Equilibrium Analysis

A typical microeconomic problem would be concerned with the price and output behavior of a particular commodity in what is called a *partial equilibrium* setting. A partial equilibrium setting means we assume constant (that is, ignore) everything occurring in the economy outside the market in which we are immediately interested. Adoption of such an attitude is legitimate if the market under examination comprises an insignificant part of the total economy. Then what happens in the market being studied has no important impact on the rest of the economy as a whole and, hence, no change which might have feedback effects on the original market is induced in the rest of the economy. One might say that microeconomics looks at markets in splendid isolation. This method of analysis was pioneered by Alfred Marshall.

At the other extreme to partial equilibrium analysis there exists what is called *general equilibrium* analysis. In this approach, far from markets being treated as though they existed in splendid isolation, everything depends on everything else. If, for example, it is confirmed that cigarettes cause lung cancer, the resulting switch in preferences away from cigarettes to, let us say, bourbon will lower the price and sales of cigarettes and raise the price and sales of bourbon. There will be less employment offered at lower wages in Virginia and the Carolinas and more employment offered at higher wages in Kentucky. People will move from the former to the latter, so that real estate prices will fall in the South Atlantic Coast states and rise in the Middle Border states. The fall in factor prices (land and labor) in tobacco-producing areas and rise in factor prices in bourbon-producing areas will affect the situation of *other* industries in these regions; for example, cotton in the former and racehorses in the latter. This influence will trigger readjustments in these industries, which will lead to repercussions in still different industries. In short, the original disturbance will permeate the *whole economy*. In the last analysis, it is conceivable that a disturbance to the equilibrium price and quantity in one market could lead to a disturbance in the equilibrium prices and quantities of *all* other markets (of both products and factors of production).

The example above shows that in a general equilibrium analysis a change in one market induces changes in other markets which are assumed (contrary to partial equilibrium analysis) to have feedback effects on the original market. The nature of the interrelationships between all markets frequently is not obvious, and it is difficult to determine what effects a change in one variable in the system will have on the final equilibrium values of all the other variables. General equilibrium analysis was pioneered by Leon Walras, whose formularization of the problem is one of the great intellectual *tour de forces* of economics. In all honesty, though, the practical payoff of the theory has been strictly limited to date. However, this is not so surprising if one notes that Einstein revealed $E = mc^2$ a generation before the first mushroom cloud appeared on the horizon.

Between the two polar extremes of partial and general equilibrium analysis lies macroeconomic analysis. Macroeconomics does not concern itself, on the one hand, only with a single market as in partial equilibrium analysis nor, on the other hand, try to deal simultaneously with the behavior of all markets as in general equilibrium analysis. Macroeconomics occupies the middle ground. Vast numbers of individual markets are aggregated and only then do we proceed to examine the interdependence among this reduced number of markets.

For example, all the household demand functions on individual markets for all consumption goods are added together (that is, aggregated) to derive the aggregate demand for consumption goods. Similarly, all firms' demand functions for individual investment goods are added together to derive the aggregate demand for investment goods. And again, all the individual household demand functions for bonds are added together to obtain the aggregate demand for bonds. This aggregation process continues and the result is that the markets with which we have to concern ourselves are reduced from the astronomical number implied by the Walrasian general equilibrium system (one market for each good traded) to a manageable number. The interrelationships among this reduced number of markets are what characterize macroeconomics. Thus, macroeconomics might be said to be the application of *quasi-general equilibrium analysis* to economic problems.

3 The Historical Record of Some Macroeconomic Variables

As we have just noted, macroeconomic analysis is concerned with the interrelationships among a relatively small number of key aggregate variables. These aggregate variables typically include employment, real income, consumption, investment, government expenditure and taxes, the wage rate, the price level, the supply of money, and the interest rate—to name just a few. The purpose of this book is to construct a general macroeconomic model which will elucidate the nature of the relationships among these and other variables. Before we turn to this task, however, it is of some interest to examine the historical record of the variables themselves without attempting to explain the nature of the interdependencies between them. The time paths followed in the United States by some of the most interesting aggregate economic variables are plotted in Figures 1–6 for each year from 1929 to 1969. (The data was obtained from *The Economic Report of the President 1970*. These annual *Reports* are an excellent secondary source of macroeconomic information.)

Consider Figure 1 where we have plotted three time series labeled Y_m, Y, and P. The series labeled Y_m is the *dollar value* (equivalently, *money* or *nominal* value) of all final goods and services produced in each year. Essentially, Y_m is obtained by multiplying the number of units of each final good and service produced in a year by their prices in that year and summing. Thus, one obtains the *total* dollar value of the goods and services produced

FIGURE 1 Nominal Income Y_m, Real Income Y, and Prices P

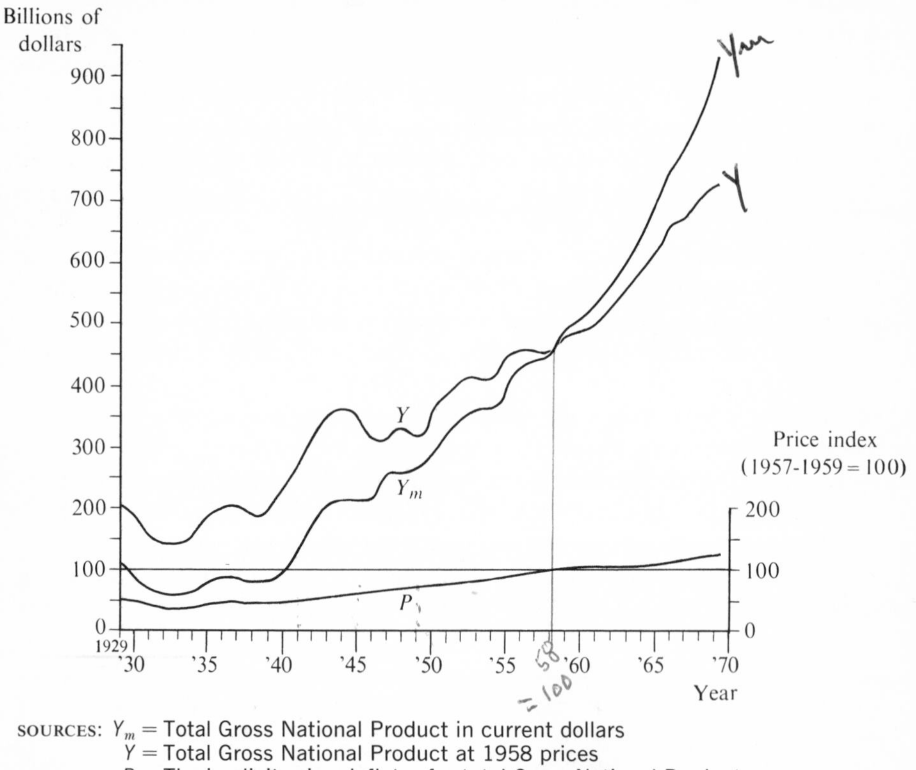

SOURCES: Y_m = Total Gross National Product in current dollars
Y = Total Gross National Product at 1958 prices
P = The implicit price deflator for total Gross National Product
All from *Economic Report of the President 1970.*

measured in terms of the prices prevailing in that year. Since this figure indicates the dollar value of the goods and services produced and at our collective disposal, it shows the *income* our productive efforts generated each year measured in that year's prices. Because it measures our annual income in terms of the goods and services which were produced, we have symbolized it Y_m (Y is the common symbol for income used by economists, and the subscript m indicates it is in *money, nominal,* or *current dollar* terms).

This series does not necessarily give a good indication of how our *real* income has changed. Suppose that the number of units of each final good and service produced remains the same, but, on the average, the prices of these goods and services rise. Then the total *money* value of the goods and services produced shows an increase, while the total *number* of units of goods and services remains unchanged. Clearly, we are no better off collectively, since there are no more goods and services to go around. To overcome this problem, we can calculate the value of goods and services produced each year *always* using the prices of those goods and services which prevailed in some base year. Thus, to calculate our *real* income Y (or our income measured in *constant dollars*) in any year, multiply the number of units of each good and service produced in that year by their *base year prices*. Essentially, this is how series Y is obtained using 1958 (actually the average prices prevailing from 1957 to 1959) as the base year for prices. Y is, perhaps, the most absolutely crucial macroeconomic variable. If Y increases, we know the total quantity of goods and services which our productive efforts have generated, and which are at our collective disposal, has increased, and we may conclude that we are indubitably better off (in material terms); if Y decreases, the quantity of goods at our disposal has decreased, our real income is down, and we are worse off collectively (again, in material terms).

The Y series has some notable highlights. It declined catastrophically in the great economic collapse of 1929 to 1933, which signified the onset of the depressed thirties. It only picked up slowly throughout the rest of that decade (with 1938 being an off year). Real income rose rapidly during the Second World War until 1946, when it fell sharply as adjustment to a peacetime economy was in full swing. There was hardly any increase between 1948 and 1949; but, then, when the Korean war got under way, the increase became rapid. Since that time real income has increased annually, except in the recession years of 1954 and 1958.[1] Real income Y will figure prominently in the macroeconomic model that we will construct as the book proceeds.

Another important variable for our later studies is the price level. An index of the average price of all final goods and services is plotted in the lower half of Figure 1 and labeled P.[2] Notice how prices fell during the onset of the Depression from 1929 to 1933. They rose slightly until 1937, after which they fell for two more years. During the Second World War, prices rose rapidly (despite, we may remark, price controls on many goods). They continued to rise until 1948 (while most price controls were being dismantled), after which they fell slightly for one year, which was the last time they did. Since 1949 prices have risen continuously—more rapidly in some years than in others, but always continuously. The macroeconomic model we shall develop is capable of explaining this ubiquitous postwar inflation.

In Figure 2 we have plotted real income Y again together with the three most important categories of aggregate expenditure which, jointly, comprise the total demand for goods and services (that is, the demand which generates income Y). These are the demand for consumer goods C, the demand for investment goods I, and the demand for goods by government G. All are plotted in *real* terms, i.e., in constant (1958) dollars. Notice how investment is relatively much more variable than consumption. Using the macroeconomic model we shall develop, it is possible to explain the relative variability

[1] Economists commonly define a recession as a decline in real income which persists for two or more *quarters*. If the data used to plot Y in Figure 1 had been quarterly (instead of annual) data, we could also identify recessions in 1960–61 and 1966–67. We might dispose of some lay definitions here: a *recession*, when your neighbor loses his job; a *depression*, when you lose your job; and a *catastrophe*, when your wife loses her job.

[2] The actual series which has been plotted is the so-called implicit price deflator for Gross National Product (GNP). What this means exactly need not concern us here. Suffice it to say that the series is an index of the average price of all goods and services with base year 1958 = 100. This series can be calculated by dividing Y_m by Y and multiplying by 100, that is, $P = (Y_m/Y)$ 100.

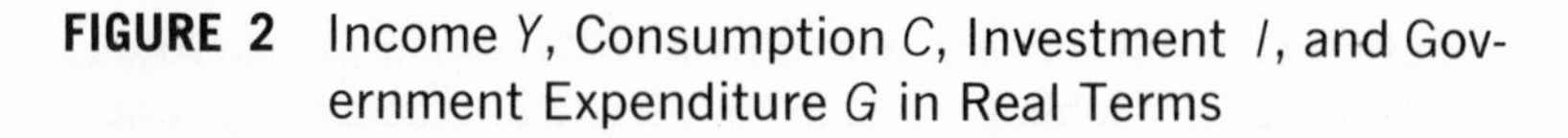

FIGURE 2 Income Y, Consumption C, Investment I, and Government Expenditure G in Real Terms

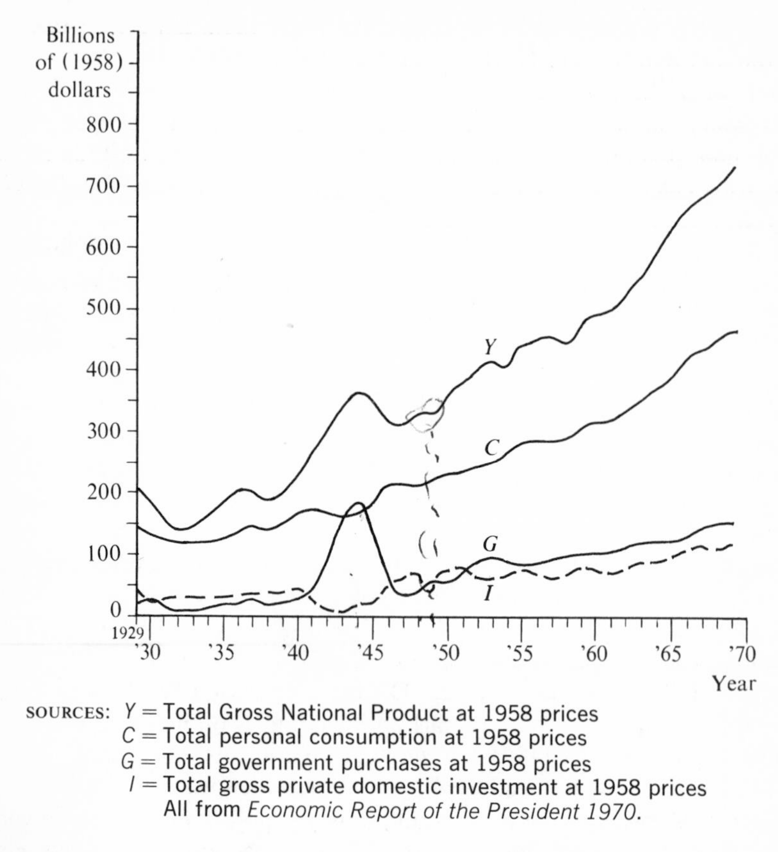

SOURCES: Y = Total Gross National Product at 1958 prices
C = Total personal consumption at 1958 prices
G = Total government purchases at 1958 prices
I = Total gross private domestic investment at 1958 prices
All from *Economic Report of the President 1970.*

of investment and the extremely important repercussions that such variations have on the other variables of the model such as income, consumption, prices, employment, and so on.

Figure 3 shows another extremely interesting group of aggregate variables. These are the total civilian labor force F, the number of these who are employed N, and those unemployed U, expressed as a percentage of those employed. The total civilian labor force F has grown continuously since 1929; not so employment N, which fell precipitously from 1929 to 1933. Employment also fell significantly in 1949 and the 1954 and 1958 recessions and very slightly in 1961. The level of employment (and, of course, unemployment) is another prominent variable which will be included in our macroeconomic model.

Having looked at employment and unemployment, let us now inquire about the remuneration for work. In Figure 4 we have plotted the average hourly wage rate W (paid by manufacturing industries), measured in current dollars. This is the *money,* or *nominal,* wage rate. It increased almost sixfold over the period, but not smoothly. Like practically every other statistic (except unemployment), it fell at the onset of the Depression from 1929 to 1933. From 1933 it has risen continuously—rapidly during the Second World War and more moderately, in fits and starts, since then. Especially interesting is the fact that the hourly wage measured in current dollars (the *money,* or *nominal,* wage rate) rose even in the recession years 1954 and 1958.

Although money wages measured in current dollars have risen, this is no guarantee that employees are better off. If prices rise faster than money wages, for example, employees are worse off, since the wage they receive buys fewer goods and services. To see whether the *purchasing power* of wages has changed over time, we need to adjust for changes in the prices of goods and services. This can be done by recalculating the wage rate in dollars of constant purchasing power to get the *real* wage rate. The process is straightforward. Simply divide (or *deflate*) the money wage by an index of prices. The real wage W/P obtained by dividing the money wage W by the consumer price index P (and multiplying by 100) also is plotted in Figure 4. We can see that although the real wage fell from 1929 to 1933, it did not fall by nearly as much as the money wage. Notice the behavior of the real wage immediately after the Second World War, too. We previously remarked that

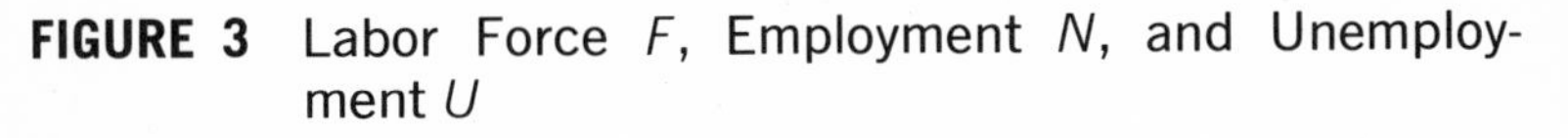
FIGURE 3 Labor Force F, Employment N, and Unemployment U

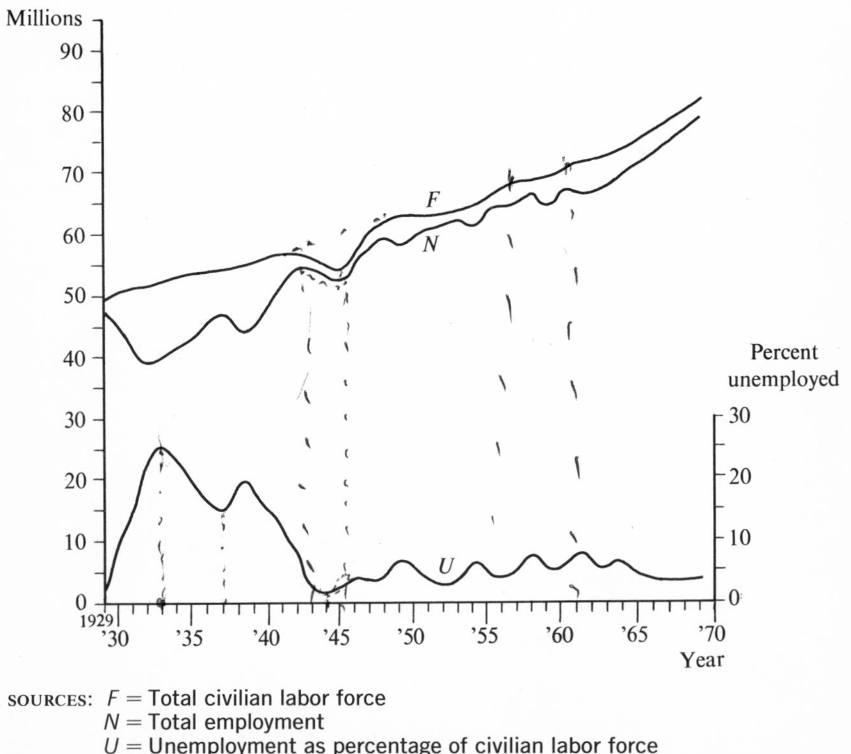

SOURCES: F = Total civilian labor force
N = Total employment
U = Unemployment as percentage of civilian labor force
All from *Economic Report of the President 1970.*

FIGURE 4 Nominal Wages W, Prices P, and Real Wages W/P

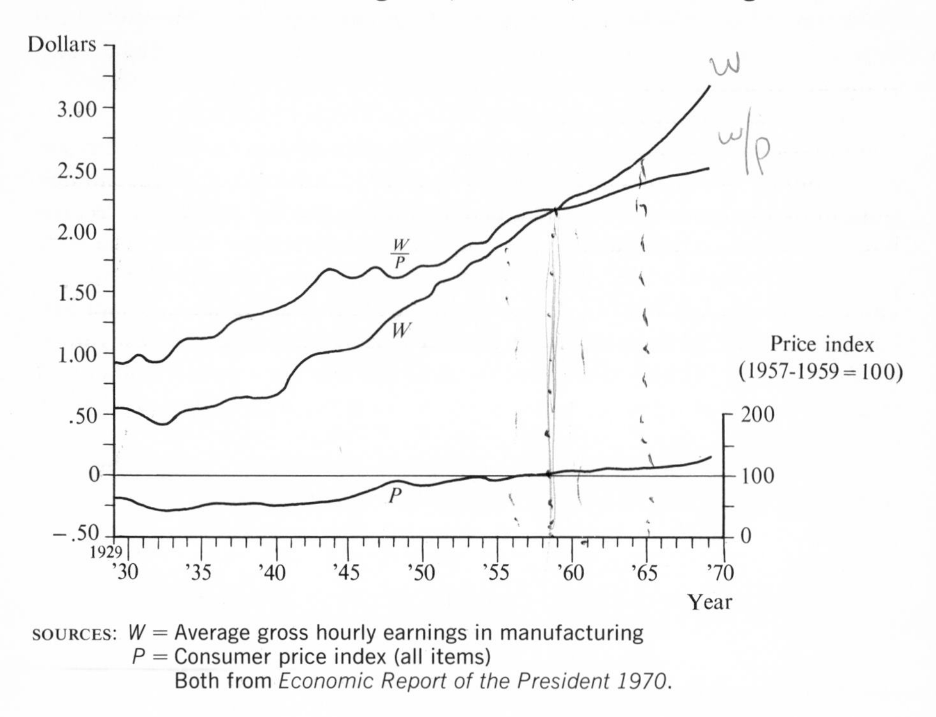

SOURCES: W = Average gross hourly earnings in manufacturing
P = Consumer price index (all items)
Both from *Economic Report of the President 1970.*

the money wage rose continuously during this period. However, the real wage fell from 1945 to 1947 because prices were rising so much more rapidly than money wages. Also interesting is the recession year of 1958. Even though the money wage rose, prices rose almost as rapidly so that the real wage hardly increased. The model that we shall construct is also capable of explaining changes in money and real wages.

The government's *fiscal* activities (by which we mean government taxing and spending policies) have an important impact on macroeconomic variables, and will also be integrated into our model. Government expenditure on goods and services G and tax receipts T have been plotted in Figure 5 along with the difference between the two, $T - G$. When the government's tax receipts exceed its spending, it is said to have a *budget surplus* (+); and when the reverse is true it is said to have a *budget deficit* (−). Perhaps the single most obvious feature about G is the marked increase that it has undergone since 1929. Clearly, too, the government has, overall, run larger deficits, and for longer periods of time, than it has run surpluses. This is reflected in Figure 6 where the government has to *borrow* (sell securities and increase its debt) when it has a budget deficit; the fact that its total debt B has increased throughout the overall period indicates that the government has, on net, run deficits. Of course, the really massive increase in the debt occurred during the Second World War when the government's expenditure obligations far outstripped its capacity to finance them through taxation.

When the government has a surplus (tax receipts in excess of its expenditures) it can, and in general does, redeem (buy back) its debt. Notice how the surpluses generated immediately after the Second World War led to a decline in the government's debt outstanding.

The final two macroeconomic variables which we wish to draw attention to now are the money supply M^s and the interest rate r plotted in Figure 6. The money supply declined from 1929 to 1933, after which it rose moderately until 1937, when it declined again slightly. During the Second World War it doubled, after which it declined a little. Since 1949 it has increased in every year except 1957 and 1960, but this increase has not been steady. The gain was small in 1953 and again in 1966; it was particularly large in 1951 and 1968. Finally, consider the behavior of a typical interest rate r (represented here by the yield on high-grade corporate bonds). It declined only slightly during the catastrophe from 1929 to 1933, after which there

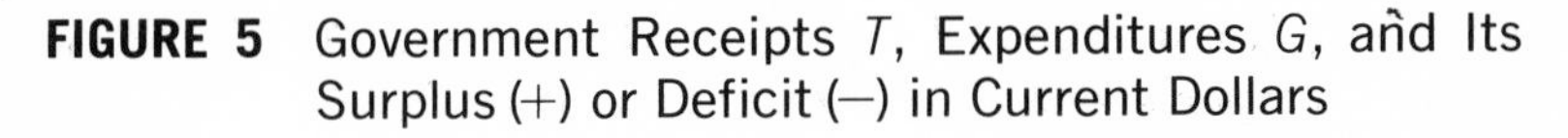

FIGURE 5 Government Receipts T, Expenditures G, and Its Surplus (+) or Deficit (–) in Current Dollars

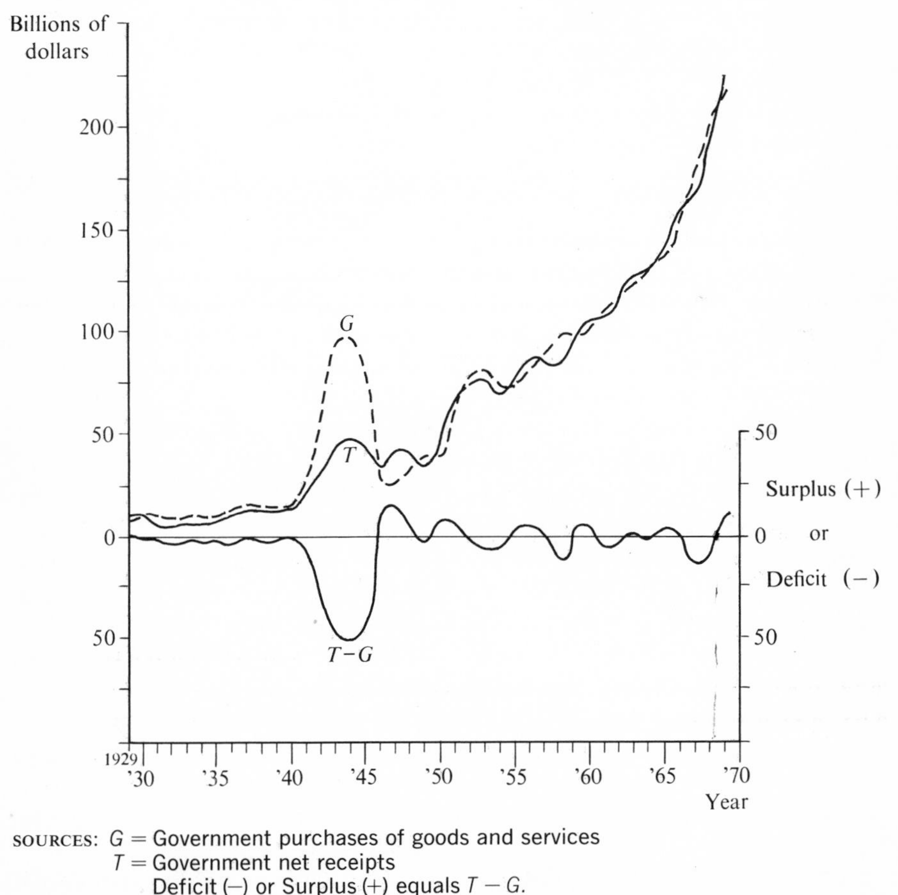

SOURCES: G = Government purchases of goods and services
T = Government net receipts
Deficit (–) or Surplus (+) equals $T - G$.
Both from *Economic Report of the President 1970.*

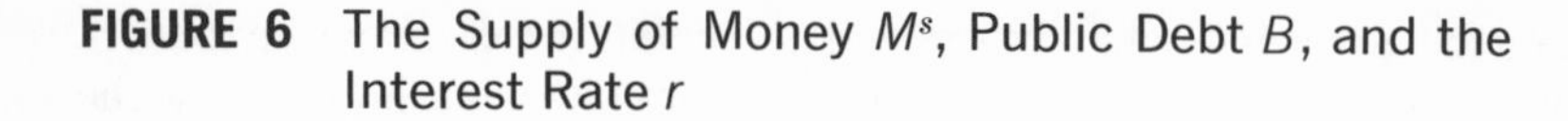

FIGURE 6 The Supply of Money M^s, Public Debt B, and the Interest Rate r

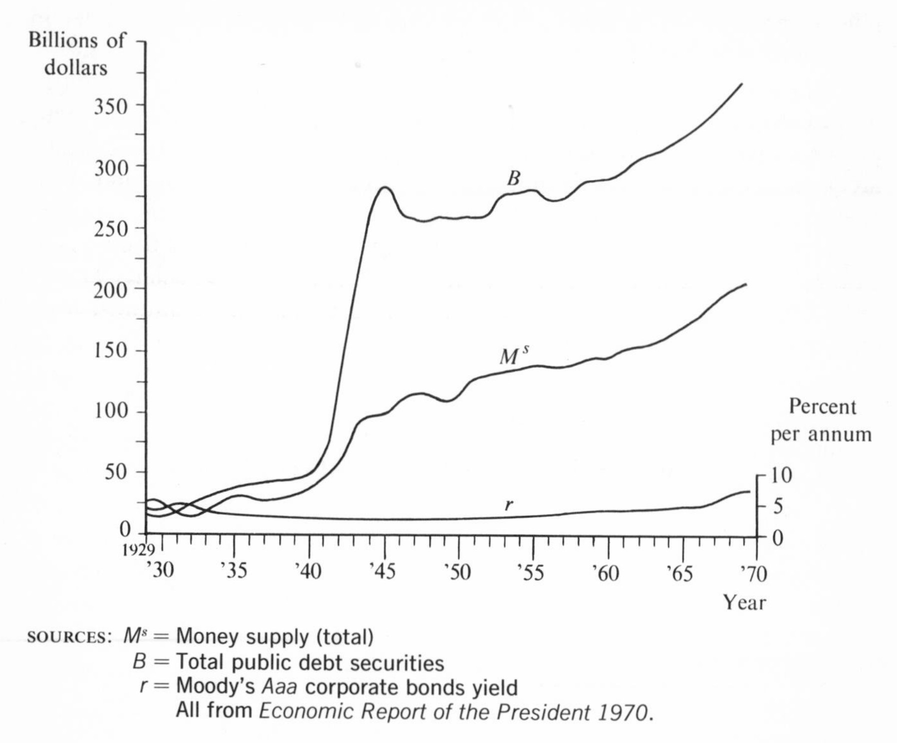

SOURCES: M^s = Money supply (total)
B = Total public debt securities
r = Moody's *Aaa* corporate bonds yield
All from *Economic Report of the President 1970.*

ensued a period of progressive decline until the beginning of the Second World War. It then became more or less stable around a low level until 1950, and from then on the trend of this typical interest rate clearly has been upwards. This increase was particularly marked at the end of the period. The money supply and the rate of interest will play an important role in the macroeconomic model we shall develop.

This concludes our brief review of the recent historical record of some of the more important macroeconomic aggregates. At the end of the previous section we noted that macroeconomics is quasi-general equilibrium analysis and is concerned with the interrelationships existing among variables whose values are determined in the relatively small and, therefore, manageable number of markets obtained after heroic aggregation of the component supplies and demands. In the following section, we are more precise about the degree of aggregation which underlies the macroeconomic model we shall construct.

4 The Four Macroeconomic Markets

It is convenient to aggregate up to just four markets, and that is what we propose to do in this book. We shall work with a model consisting of the commodity market, the labor market, the bond market, and the money "market."

The Commodity Market

We shall assume that only one commodity is produced in the economy. This commodity can be consumed *or* imbedded in the capital stock, where in combination with the other factor of production, labor, it can be used to produce more of the same commodity. Thus, the same standard commodity is consumed and invested. Furthermore, the invested commodity is capable of producing more of the same commodity. The obvious name for a commodity with such properties is, of course, "a shmoo"—after cartoonist Al Capp's well-known all-purpose little creatures which can reproduce themselves as well as be worn, eaten, ridden, and kicked about. Hence, our model may be described as that of a "shmoo-good economy." There is a splendid tradition in economics of shmoo-good macroeconomic analysis. It is not just a quirk of our own. In fact, perhaps 90 percent of macroeconomic analysis is carried on in such a context for convenience and simplicity. As soon as one begins to increase the number of commodities, one is starting down the path to general equilibrium analysis. Thus, we emphasize that all commodities are identical, or homogeneous. One is as good as another for both consumption and investment purposes. The market for commodities will be characterized by a supply function, a demand function, and a price of commodities.

In terms of the variables discussed in the previous section's historical survey, the total supply of commodities is equivalent to real income Y, and the *aggregate* demand for commodities is equal to the *sum* of consumption demand, investment demand, and government demand for commodities (i.e., $C + I + G$). The price of commodities is equivalent to P.

The Labor Market

We shall assume that only one type of labor service can be performed in our economy; namely, commodity making. All commodity-makers are assumed to be equally talented. Like the commodity they make, commodity-makers, too, are identical in every respect—they are homogeneous. One is as good as another. Together with commodities that have been invested and become imbedded in the capital stock, commodity-makers are the only other factor of production. So far, we have what is described succinctly as a "one-commodity/two-factor model." The one commodity is shmoos, the two factors of production are labor and capital (that is, commodities that have been invested and imbedded in the capital stock where, in combination, with labor they can turn out more commodities).

Our model will further assume that, for all practical purposes, the *only* variable factor of production is labor. The time period for which our model is designed to be relevant is too short for changes in the capital stock to be noticeable. The stock of capital is inherited from the past, and although investment may occur during the time period with which we are concerned, this investment is assumed to be small *relative to the existing stock of capital.*[1] Thus, investment which occurs in the current period does not substantially alter the total outstanding stock of capital. Notice that investment is the flow of commodities in the period which is added to the stock of capital at the end of the period. Since this investment flow is assumed to be small relative to the stock, current investment does not alter materially the existing capital stock and, thus, our capacity to produce more commodities. This assumption is clearly tenable only when the time period is kept short enough so that the investment which occurs does not lead to a material augmentation of the capital stock. Our model is only relevant for such a time period.

Effectively, then, the production decision is reduced to deciding how much labor should be hired to work the fixed stock of capital at our disposal. That decision is elucidated through analysis of the labor market. This market will be characterized by a demand function, a supply function, and a price of labor (or wage). In terms of the variables discussed in the previous section, the supply of labor is equivalent to the total labor force F, the demand for labor is equivalent to the level of employment N, and the price of labor is equivalent to the real wage W/P.

The Bond Market

The markets for commodities and labor together comprise what is described as the "real sector" of our model. Our model will also contain two financial assets; namely, bonds and money. The bond is a variable-priced financial asset, while money is fixed in price. The markets for these two assets comprise the financial, or monetary, sector of the model. There are no distinctions between long bonds and short bonds, risky bonds and safe bonds, and so on. All bonds are identical, or homogeneous. The bond market will be characterized by a demand function, a supply function, and a price of bonds.

The Money "Market"

When speaking of money, we put the word "market" in quotation marks advisedly, since there is *not* a market for money in the usual sense of that word. It is simply false to say that there is a *marketplace* for money where a transactor can go to supply money or demand it, like the marketplaces where transactors can go to supply or demand commodities, labor, and bonds. Money is a good which has no market of its own. *The* distinguishing characteristic of money is that it is *the* good which is exchanged against all other goods in *their* markets. For example, if a transactor goes to the commodity market as a demander, he offers to buy commodities *in exchange for money;* and if he goes there as a supplier, he offers to sell commodities *in exchange for money*. The same is true of supply and demand transactions on the bond and labor markets.

Nonetheless, there is a certain supply of money in existence which must

[1] Not necessarily small in *absolute* amount, though it might be.

be *held* by transactors collectively. Every dollar of currency and checking deposits in existence must be held by someone at any moment in time. The time paths of the total supply of money in existence each year from 1929 to 1969 were plotted in Figure 6. Similarly, there is a collective demand for money to *hold.* This depends on what transactors judge their money requirements to be in order to consummate their transactions in *other* markets efficiently plus any demand transactors may have for money to hold as an *asset* (money can be held as an asset just like bonds). When the supply of money that must be held is equal to the demand for money to hold (as an asset and for transactions purposes), then we say (speaking disgustingly loosely, but, nonetheless, following convention) that the money "market" is in equilibrium.

We will *not* develop a supply function for money, since we shall assume throughout that it does *not* depend on any other variables in the model but is set by act of government policy.[2] We shall, though, develop a demand function for money to hold. The price, or (opportunity) cost, of *holding* money is the interest rate, since that is what one *loses,* or foregoes, for every dollar of money held.

The price of a unit of money itself is always fixed at unity, since it always takes just one dollar to buy one dollar, and you can always get one dollar, and only one dollar, if you choose to sell a dollar for dollars. This is because money, being the medium of exchange, is the good which is chosen to be *numeraire,* or, in English, the good in which we choose to measure the prices, or exchange ratios, of all *other* goods. If you have *four* goods in a model (as we do: commodities, labor, bonds, and money), then you only have *three* independent prices or rates of exchange; so many dollars per unit of commodity, so many dollars per unit of labor, and so many dollars per unit of bonds. There is always just one dollar per unit of money, i.e., per dollar.

That completes our discussion of the *market structure* which we shall assume underlies our macroeconomic model. At several points we have mentioned transactors. Let us now examine who the various economic transactors on the economic stage are.

5 The Three Transactors

Who are the suppliers and demanders of the four goods in our model? We shall assume that there are three classes of transactors: households, firms, and the government. The transactions which these groups engage in may be conveniently summarized in the transactions matrix, or flow of funds diagram, illustrated by Table 1.

The diagram indicates the market relationships which the three groups of transactors have with each other. Moving across a row one sees what

[2] Money is what economists call an *exogenous* variable. What this means exactly need not concern us at the moment. The meaning of exogenous (and its opposite, *endogenous*) is explained in detail in Chapter 6. Suffice it to say that an exogenous variable is one whose value is *given* and, thus, does *not* need explaining.

TABLE 1 Transactions Matrix or Flow of Funds Diagram

		Transactors Buy down Columns			
		HOUSEHOLDS	FIRMS	GOVERNMENT	
Transactors Sell across Rows	HOUSEHOLDS	1.	2. Labor services Retired bonds	3. Retired bonds	4. Total inflow of money to households (or households' sources of money) Sum of 2 and 3
	FIRMS	5. Consumption commodities New bonds	6. Investment commodities	7. Collective consumption and investment commodities	8. Total inflow of money to firms (or firms' sources of money) Sum of 5, 6, and 7
	GOVERNMENT	9. New money New bonds Collective commodity services (for taxes)	10. New money	11.	12. Total inflow of money to government (or government's sources of money) Sum of 9 and 10
		13. Total expenditure of money by households (or households' uses of money Sum of 5 and 9	14. Total expenditure of money by firms (or firms' uses of money) Sum of 2, 6, and 10	15. Total expenditure of money by government (or government's uses of money) Sum of 3 and 7	

one transactor sells to the other transactors; moving down a column one sees what one transactor buys from the other transactors. It is instructive to go through this matrix cell by cell.

Cell 1 indicates that households do not sell anything to other households.

Cell 2 shows that households sell labor services to firms, and they also sell bonds to firms when those firms choose to retire them.

Cell 3 reveals that households sell bonds back to the government when the government chooses to retire them. When we discuss the bond market in detail, we will explain that the homogeneous bond, issued by firms and the government, is an irredeemable bond, or what is called a perpetuity (or, in England where such things do exist, a consol). All this means is that the issuer never guarantees to redeem the security at any date in the future. If the issuer wishes to retire his bonds, as he certainly may, he merely goes to the market, buys his own bonds, and tears them up. His motive would be, of course, to save the interest he pays on them.

Cell 4 is the sum of cells 2 and 3. It indicates the total inflow of money to households. All the money which flows into households must come from the sale of labor services to firms or the sale of bonds back to firms or the government as either of these transactors retire some of their bonds. Note that, *as a group,* households cannot derive an inflow of money from the sale of bonds to each other.

Cell 5 shows that firms sell commodities for consumption purposes to households, and they also sell newly issued bonds to households. Note that firms do not derive any money from the transactions involving their already existing bonds among households. Only the sale of *new* bonds generates an inflow of money.

Cell 6 indicates that firms sell investment commodities to other firms to be added to the capital stock. One might like to visualize some firms who produce commodities for consumption and other firms who produce commodities for investment purposes, even though all commodities are identical.

Cell 7 reveals that firms also sell commodities to the government. These commodities are either collectively consumed or added to the communal capital stock. This acknowledges the fact that the competitive market mechanism breaks down as a resource allocation device in certain instances. Some goods just cannot be produced or consumed privately in an efficient way. Either a producer cannot collect payment for the good he provides, or a consumer cannot prevent the rest of the community enjoying the commodity he payed for. These cases are described in the theory of public finance as *spillover, third-party, externality,* or *neighborhood* effects. The classic example is provided by lighthouses. If you build a lighthouse, it is difficult for you to collect payment from the users of the service you provide. Ships steal silently by in the night. Or we, as shipowners, would hesitate to pay for the services of a lighthouse ourselves when we cannot prevent other piratical shipowners from enjoying the service we paid for.

Goods which have the above property are called *public goods*. One way (*not* the only one) of dealing with the dilemma these goods pose for a competitive economy is to have the government provide the good without direct charge [which does not mean "free"—see cell 9]. If the good would not be provided in a competitive environment, the government purchases it for the community and makes it available to the community without direct charge. This is the solution adopted for such goods as defense, lighthouses, and so on. Hence, some of our all-purpose commodities are sold to the government for such collective enjoyment.

Cell 8 indicates that the total inflow of money to firms comes from the sale of commodities to the three potential purchasers—households, firms, and government—and the sale of newly issued bonds to households.

Cell 9 shows that governments make available to households the services of the public-good commodities discussed for cell 7 without direct charge. Government is assumed not to sell these services, since it is not able to identify or catch the individual beneficiaries. But the government needs money to finance its public-good purchase program. It obtains these funds by collecting taxes, selling *new* bonds, and issuing *new* money. Note that the government is the only issuer of money. There is no privately issued money. We shall relax this assumption, however, later in the book.

Cell 10 has only one entry, "New money." The government may finance part of its commodity purchase program by paying firms with some of its new money issues. Notice that it does *not* issue new bonds to firms or collect taxes from them, since firms are assumed not to hold (i.e., demand) bonds and all taxes are assumed to be collected from households.

Cell 11 is empty, since the government engages in no transactions with itself.

Cell 12 indicates that the total inflow of money to the government is comprised of the sum of the items in cells 9 and 10.

Cells 13, 14 and 15 are the sums of the respective columns above them. Just as moving down a column indicates the purchases that the relevant transactor is making, these sums show the transactor's total money expenditure. For example, households spend money on consumption commodities, on new bond acquisitions, on taxes, and on additions to their money holdings. Broadly similar observations hold for the purchases of firms and the government.

For much of the early part of this book we shall find it convenient to simplify the model even more by assuming the nonexistence of a government. When this is the case, the third row and third column of this transactions matrix become redundant. This causes no complications of a substantive nature. We merely then assume that the economy's money is a commodity money (like gold) which is not produced or consumed. When monetary policy experiments are performed on our model under such circumstances we resort to highly artificial manipulations such as having money drop from the sky (and, therefore, *not* being produced) if we want to increase the money stock, or disappear into thin air (and, therefore, *not* being consumed) if we want to decrease the money stock. Believe it or not, there is a long tradition of such legerdemain in economic theory.

This tour of the transactions matrix has served to pinpoint the transactors on each of our four markets. The information gathered is summarized in Table 2. The only vaguely unusual feature of this table is the appearance of firms as both suppliers and demanders of commodities. The latter is due, of course, to the appearance of firms as demanders of their own commodity output for investment purposes. The same information is revealed more immediately by the graphic representation of the four markets in Figure 7, which represents each of the four markets separately and attaches to the demand and supply curves the names of the transactors from whom they are derived.

The information displayed in this diagram is all readily comprehendible except for the appearance of "the reciprocal of the interest rate" on the price axis of the bond market. It will be shown in Chapter 3 that this is what the price of bonds in our model turns out to be equal to.

Figure 7, more than pages of words, should serve to further impress two things which we have already stressed at some length. The first is the quasi-general equilibrium nature of macroeconomic analysis (which, for us, describes a gross version of full general equilibrium analysis). The economy has been heroically reduced to four markets and we will have economywide equilibrium only when all these markets are in equilibrium. Moreover, all these markets will also prove to be interdependent, so that what happens in one market will usually affect the other markets, which will, more often than not, have feedback effects on the original market. We shall be genuinely concerned, then, with problems of general equilibrium even if only on a fairly gross scale. Second, this figure serves to indicate heuristically the unity of microeconomic and macroeconomic theory; there are markets, supply curves, demand curves, and prices. That, basically, is what microeconomic theory is all about and that, we shall strive to show, is what macroeconomic theory is all about, too.

TABLE 2 The Transactors as Suppliers and Demanders

TRANSACTOR \ MARKET	COMMODITY	LABOR	BOND	MONEY
HOUSEHOLDS	Demanders	Suppliers	Demanders	Demanders
FIRMS	Demanders Suppliers	Demanders	Suppliers	Demanders
GOVERNMENT	Demander		Supplier	Supplier

FIGURE 7

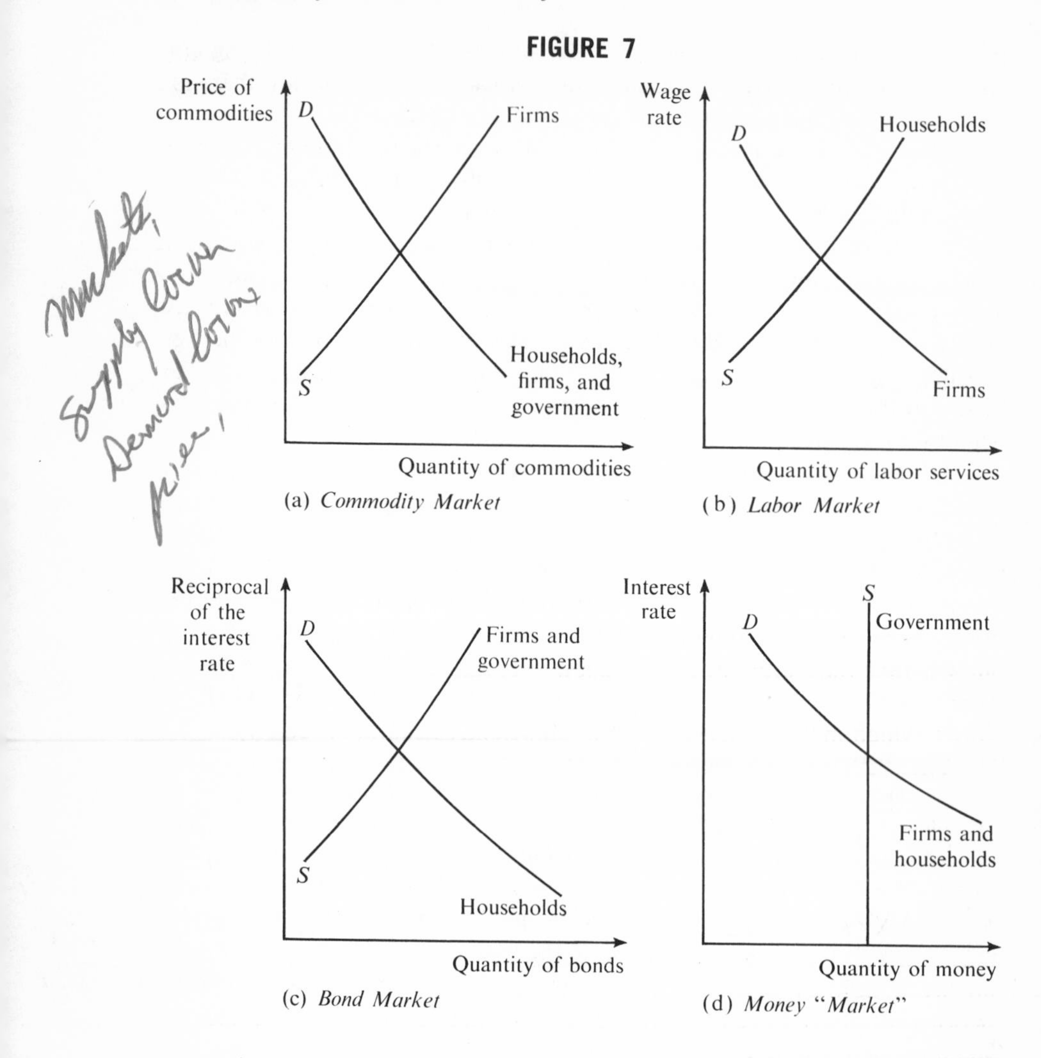

(a) *Commodity Market* (b) *Labor Market*

(c) *Bond Market* (d) *Money "Market"*

6 Some Methodological Observations

The skeptical reader is possibly already laughing inwardly at the ludicrously simplified and overwhelmingly abstract nature of the macroeconomic model we propose to build. Is it possible, he may be asking, that such a model will be useful as an analytical framework in which to discuss the real world macroeconomic problems we face? What earthly good can a model be which assumes that there exists only one commodity which you apparently can use to eat, wear, sleep, commute on, and, better yet, accumulate whereupon it miraculously reproduces more of the same?

However, we urge you to suspend judgment. What, if anything, is remarkable about our macroeconomic model is the large number of predictions we can make from it about observable phenomena in the real world which apparently are not refuted by observations of these real world events. The model is powerful notwithstanding that it is simple. Crippled as it may appear, it can still explain such important macroeconomic phenomena as the causes of unemployment, changes in real income, inflations, and many, many others.

The purpose of economic theory is to develop hypotheses which abstract the essential features of complex reality. An economic theory is judged good, or bad, according to whether it does, or does not, have good predictive capacity for the class of phenomena it is designed to explain. In particular, it is especially futile to assay theories by the extent to which their assumptions conform to "reality." A theory is an abstraction and should not even try to reproduce reality. If it did, it would be worthless, for its complexity would render it incomprehensible. Good theories *must,* therefore, be descriptively false in their assumptions. In the words of Solow, "All theory depends on assumptions which are not quite true. That is what makes it theory."[1] Or, equivalently, to quote from a famous article on methodology by Friedman, ". . . the relevant question to ask about the 'assumptions' of a theory is not whether they are descriptively 'realistic,' for they never are, but whether they are sufficiently good approximations for the purpose in hand. And this question can be answered only by seeing whether the theory works, which means whether it yields sufficiently accurate predictions."[2]

The crucial test of the usefulness of a theory, then, is whether it works for the class of phenomena it is designed to explain and not the "reality" or "unreality" of its assumptions. As this is basically a textbook of macroeconomic *theory,* the student will finish it without any real knowledge of the various theories' predictive capacities. They are empirical questions and their answer would take us much too far afield. Thus, the student will not know whether the theory he has been exposed to is useful or not. We give our word now that, broadly speaking (though not in every detail), the theories we shall develop (outrageous assumptions and all) are the sort which applied macroeconomists began with. True, those theories have been refined, and frequently complicated, to improve their predictive capacity, but, by and large, their origins can be traced back to the sort of grotesquely simple model we are about to construct.

7 Stocks and Flows

In §3 we discussed the historical performance of some of the most interesting macroeconomic variables which will be incorporated into our model. Before we proceed, it is worth taking a moment to draw attention to

[1] R. M. Solow, "A Contribution to the Theory of Economic Growth," *Quarterly Journal of Economics,* February, 1956, p. 65.

[2] M. Friedman, "The Methodology of Positive Economics," in *Essays in Positive Economics,* University of Chicago Press, 1955.

what is, unfortunately, a common problem in economics; namely, a confusion between *stock* variables and *flow* variables.

The basic distinction between a stock variable and a flow variable is that a stock variable is a quantity measured at a *point* (or *moment,* or *instant*) *in time,* and a flow variable is a quantity which can only be measured in terms of a *specific period of time.* Thus, although both stock variables and flow variables are dated, stock variables only have a *time reference* associated with them, while flow variables have a *time dimension.* If a variable has magnitude at a *point* in time, it is a stock variable; if it has magnitude only when time is allowed to run for some *period* (or *interval*), it is a flow variable.

Let us consider some examples. If you were asked what your assets were at any point (which is, for mathematical purposes, an *infinitesimally* small interval) in time, you could answer meaningfully. Your answer might be 100 dollars in money, 200 dollars in bonds, 300 dollars in physical assets—or 600 dollars worth of assets in total. Clearly, all these assets have magnitude at any point in time and, thus, they are stock variables. But suppose you were asked what income you earned, or how much you consumed, or how much work you did at that point (infinitesimally small interval) in time? You could not answer or, rather, would have to answer zero. Income is earned only over a *period* of time, consumption occurs only over a *period* of time, and work occurs only over a *period* of time. These, then, are obviously flow variables, since a time dimension is associated with them. It would be easy to answer the questions: how much money did you earn last *year* (an interval of time), how much did you spend on consumption last *year,* and how much did you work last *year?* You might answer 4,800 dollars *per annum,* 3,600 dollars *per annum,* 2,400 hours *per annum,* respectively.

Notice, now, that the time period over which a flow variable is measured is extremely important. Taking the previous example, if you were asked how much you earned *per month,* how much you consumed *per month,* or how much you worked *per month,* you would answer 400 dollars, 300 dollars, and 200 hours *per month,* respectively. These figures are obtained by dividing the per annum figures by 12 to put them on a per month basis. The process assumes, of course, that you earned, consumed, and worked at a constant rate through the year. When this assumption is made, a flow variable measured over one interval can easily be converted into its measure over a different interval by appropriate division or multiplication.

With this discussion of the distinction between stock and flow variables in hand, let us consider the stock or flow status of the macroeconomic variables introduced in §3. GNP is a flow variable, since it measures the total gross output of goods and services *per annum.* Consumption C, investment I, and government expenditure G also are all flow variables. They, too, are measured *per annum.* The civilian labor force F and the number of these employed N are both stock variables. At any point in time a certain number of people may be regarded as being in the labor force and, similarly, a certain number are employed. Government tax receipts T are a flow variable.

Its tax receipts are so much *per annum*. Since we have already seen that government expenditure G is a flow variable, it follows that the government's surplus or deficit $T - G$ is also a flow variable. The government has a surplus or deficit of so much *per annum*. This should serve to remind us, too, that operations on variables such as addition and subtraction are only legitimate when their dimensions are commensurable. It is all right to add and subtract flow variables when they are measured for the same time interval. It is not legitimate, however, to perform such operations when they are measured for different time intervals. And, a fortiori, it is *never* legitimate to add or subtract a flow variable and a stock variable, since the former *always* has a time dimension and the latter *never* has a time dimension. The total public debt B is a stock variable. This is the value of the government's liability for the securities it has issued; and, clearly, this liability can be measured at any point in time. Finally, another stock variable is the supply of money M^s, which indicates our monetary assets at any point in time.

8 Some Macroeconomic Applications and Theoretical Controversies

Macroeconomic analysis is interesting from both a *practical* and a *theoretical* point of view. We shall be able to bring our macroeconomic model to bear on a whole host of practical applications and theoretical controversies. From a practical policy-oriented point of view, for example, our model will tell us what the impact will be of any of the following list of events (which is by no means exhaustive) on the crucial variables which comprise the model such as GNP, employment (and unemployment), the price level, wage rates, consumption, saving, investment, the fiscal position, the interest rate, and so on:

1. A change in government expenditure or taxation policy.
2. A change in monetary policy.
3. A change in entrepreneurs' expectations about the profitability of investment.
4. A change in households' attitudes towards thrift.
5. A change in international trading relationships such as the impact of the imposition (or removal) of tariffs or quotas on foreign goods.
6. A change in the foreign exchange rate.
7. A change in the supply of labor.
8. A change in the productivity of labor.
9. Increases in wage rates achieved by collective bargaining on the part of organized labor.
10. Increases in prices achieved by monopolizing firms.

In general, when any of these (and many other) events occur, we shall be able to use the macroeconomic model to *predict* what happens to the variables in the model in *qualitative* terms—by which we mean that we shall be able to predict whether any variable included in the model will increase, decrease, or not change.[1] Thus, the qualitative model enables us to predict the *direction* of change of any variable, if the variable changes at all, but not the size of that change.

Our model can also be pressed into service to resolve some intensely interesting theoretical controversies which have tested the ingenuities of macroeconomic theorists from time to time. For example:

1. Will a competitive free-enterprise capitalist economy generate enough jobs so that everyone who wants one can get one? That is, will it *automatically* generate full employment? Alternatively, will a mature competitive free-enterprise capitalist economy *stagnate?* That is, will chronic unemployment plague such economies unless the government takes discretionary action (e.g., with respect to its own spending) to counteract this congenital tendency?
2. Does a change in the supply of money *only* affect the price level (and other *nominal* variables), or does it *also* affect *real* variables such as GNP, employment, and, especially, the interest rate? This is the famous (some would say, notorious) question, is money *neutral* or *not neutral?*
3. Can organized labor impose inflation by collectively bargaining continuous increases in wages? That is, are unions to be blamed for inflation?
4. If the economy is dominated by a handful of firms, can they, and will they, continuously raise their prices and force inflation on us? That is, is inflation caused by the pricing practices of a few monopolistic firms which dominate the economy?

We shall use the model to shed light on all these, and several other, theoretical controversies as the book proceeds. We shall pay particular attention to the first two because they were the twin themes of the great debate between Keynes and the Classics which broke out in the wake of the publication of Keynes' magnum opus, *The General Theory of Employment, Interest, and Money,* in 1936 (the year, by the way, in which it would not be too far wrong to say modern macroeconomics was invented). This book's impact on economics in the twentieth century has been as profound as the impact of Adam Smith's *The Wealth of Nations* was on the economics of the nineteenth century.

Before we proceed to a resolution of the practical problems and theoretical controversies in Parts II and III, however, there is further preparatory spadework to be done. We must lay the microeconomic foundations of the macroeconomic model we shall construct. This will occupy us for the remainder of Part I, Chapters 2–5. We devote one chapter to each of the four markets—labor, commodities, money, and bonds—in that order.

[1] To be able to make *quantitative* predictions (that is, to be able to predict the *size* of the change in any variable), we would need numerical estimates of the model's coefficients or parameters. This quantitative discussion we shall eschew, since it would force us too far into the field of econometrics, and that would require another book.

Summary

Macroeconomics is "economics in the large" as opposed to *microeconomics,* which is "economics in the small." *Partial equilibrium* analysis is when one market is treated in isolation and any repercussion which that market has on the rest of the economy is assumed to be so small that there is no *feedback* effect from the rest of the economy to that market. *General equilibrium* analysis is when *all* markets are treated together and the interactions among them, or feedbacks, are explicitly allowed for. Macroeconomics is, in effect, *quasi-general equilibrium* analysis. The number of markets implied by a full general equilibrium model is reduced by massive *aggregation,* and then interactions among this reduced number of markets are examined.

We shall construct a macroeconomic model to explain the behavior of many crucial economic aggregates such as GNP, employment (and unemployment), the price level, the interest rate, the wage rate, consumption, saving, investment, the government's fiscal position, and so on. In §5 the historical record of these variables was reviewed briefly from 1929 to 1969.

The quasi-general equilibrium macroeconomic model we propose will involve *four markets:* commodities, labor, bonds, and money. There are assumed to be *three transactors:* households, firms, and the government. The relationships between these three transactors and the four markets are summarized by the transactions matrix presented in Table 1 (and in Table 2 and Figure 7). The model will be relevant to relatively *short-run* analysis.

Although the model to be developed is clearly "unrealistic" in its underlying assumptions, models cannot legitimately be criticized on the basis of the "realism" or "unrealism" of their assumptions. All theory is based on assumptions which are not quite true. Models must be accepted or rejected on the basis of their predictive capacity for the class of phenomena they are designed to explain.

All economic variables are dated. However, *stock* variables only have a *time reference,* whereas *flow* variables have a *time dimension.*

When the microeconomic foundations of the macroeconomic model have been laid, we shall press the model into service to solve many applied macroeconomic problems (some of which are listed in §8) and resolve some theoretical controversies (such as will a competitive free-enterprise capitalist economy be plagued by unemployment unless the government takes discretionary action, and is money neutral?).

Questions

1. What is the basic distinction between microeconomics and macroeconomics? What is the basic similarity?
2. Discuss the distinction between partial, general, and quasi- (or aggregate) general equilibrium analysis.

3. Between 1929 and 1933 the GNP fell from $204 billion to $142 billion (when measured in 1958 prices, or *real* terms). This is a decline of approximately 30 percent. Do you now have any idea why this occurred? If you do, jot your ideas down and see whether they are the same when you have finished this book.
4. What is a "public good"? Why are they frequently provided by the government in an otherwise predominantly free-enterprise capitalist economy?
5. In what sense is it technically erroneous to speak of a money "market"?
6. Economists usually assume that firms conduct their affairs so as to maximize their profits. However, when surveyed, nine out of ten businessmen deny this. Therefore, the corpus of economic theory erected on the assumption of profit maximization is virtually useless. Do you agree with this inference? If so, why; if not, why not? What would lead you to regard an economic theory as useless?
7. Discuss the distinction between stock and flow variables. Is investment a stock or flow variable? What stock variable is investment intimately related to?
8. Jot down what you think are the correct answers to the theoretical macroeconomic controversies mentioned in §8. See if your answers are the same when you have completed this book.

SELECTED READINGS

1. D. W. Bushaw and R. W. Clower, *Introduction to Mathematical Economics,* Irwin, 1957, chapter 2. An authoritative discussion of the distinction between stocks and flows.
2. *Economic Report of the President,* Government Printing Office, annual. An excellent secondary source of macroeconomic data. Also contains a macroeconomic analysis of the year past and some predictions for the year to come. It is cheap and worth buying the current issue.
3. M. Friedman, "The Methodology of Positive Economics," in *Essays in Positive Economics,* University of Chicago Press, 1955. An excellent discussion of economic methodology.
4. D. Patinkin, *Money, Interest, and Prices,* 2nd ed., Harper & Row, 1965, chapter 9, section 1. Sets up a macroeconomic model like the one we shall construct.

FURTHER READINGS

5. E. Nagel, "Assumptions in Economic Theory," *American Economic Review, Proceedings,* May, 1963. A philosopher-logician's approach to methodological questions.
6. P. A. Samuelson, "Problems of Methodology – Discussion," *American Economic Review, Proceedings,* May, 1963. Together with Nagel [5], presents some telling counterarguments to Friedman's position [3] on methodology.

2

The Labor Market

We have decided to aggregate the economy into four markets: the labor, commodity, bond, and money markets. The first market we shall examine is the labor market.

In this market, firms appear as buyers, or demanders, of labor services and households appear as sellers, or suppliers, of labor services. Note that it is the services of labor which are sold in this market and not the laborers themselves. So many man-hours of labor services are exchanged, not so many men. Moreover, we are concerned with a flow of labor services. That is to say, there is a time dimension attached to the man-hours of labor exchanged such as per day, per week, or per year. Thus, we shall be concerned with the demand for man-hours of labor per time period and the supply of man-hours of labor per time period. The time period actually chosen can be that which is most convenient for the purpose in hand. In what follows you may wish to fix on the week as a suitable time period.

1 The Demand for Labor

Let us look first at the demand for labor. Labor is demanded by firms and, hence, its analysis requires some discussion of the production function of firms.

The Production Function

Our assumption has been that firms are engaged only in the production of the one commodity existing in our model economy. All firms are also thought of as homogeneous, or identical in *all* respects; for example, they are all equally well managed or mismanaged, they all face the same technology, and so on. This means that if we focus our attention on *one* firm we can be certain that the information we discover also applies to every other firm. Clearly, this simplifies our task. Better yet, when we want to know what all firms in total are doing, we can just aggregate them, as they are all identical in every respect.

It is also assumed that all firms operate in perfectly competitive markets for both their product and the factors of production, labor and capital (i.e., investment commodities), which they buy. This means that the firms themselves have no influence, let alone control, over either the price of their product or the prices of their factors of production, no matter how much nor how little of their product they sell or factors of production they buy. Both the price of its product and the prices of its factors of production are given parameters for the individual firm quite independent of its influence. All firms are what is described as *price-takers* in all the markets in which they operate.

Typically, firms can produce commodities with a variety of combinations of the two factors of production, labor and capital, included in the model. These technologically feasible levels of output for various combinations of the two inputs are illustrated by the production function in Figure 1. For example, Q_1 units of the commodity per week could be produced by using N_1 man-hours of labor (services) per week in combination with K_1 capital (services) per week. (What is meant by "capital services" will be explained in detail in Chapter 3 when we discuss investment.) Equally, Q_1 units of output could be produced with N_2 man-hours per week and K_2 capi-

FIGURE 1

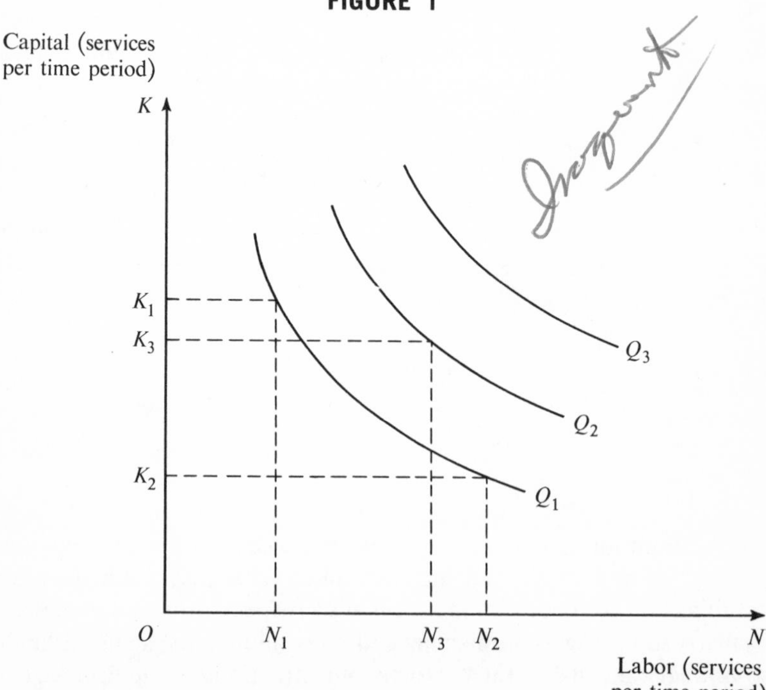

FIGURE 2

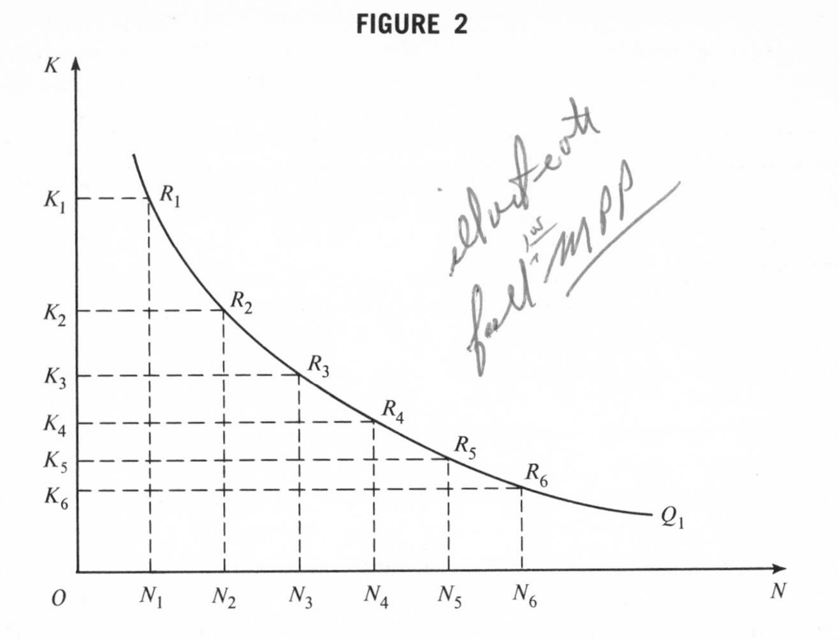

tal services per week, or, in other words, more labor and less capital. The curve labeled Q_1 is constructed to join all capital and labor combinations which can produce Q_1 units of the commodity. This is the well-known *isoquant* which, interpreted, is the locus of all input combinations capable of producing the same level of output.

There is an isoquant for every level of output. Some other examples of these have also been drawn in Figure 1 and labeled Q_2 and Q_3 where $Q_3 > Q_2 > Q_1$. For example, the level of output Q_2 could be produced with N_3 labor and K_3 capital or with any other combination of factor inputs represented by the curve Q_2. Clearly, to produce the level of output Q_2, which exceeds Q_1, you need more labor or more capital or more of both. In economics, too (perhaps one should say, especially), nothing is for nothing.

Observe that all the isoquants in Figure 1 have been drawn convex to the origin. This implies that, to maintain output at a set level when a unit of one factor is given up, the size of the increase needed in the input of the other factor will be greater for smaller initial (before a unit is given up) amounts of the first factor than for larger ones. To elaborate, in Figure 2, consider the level of output Q_1. This can be produced by any combination of inputs shown by K_1 and N_1, K_2 and N_2, and so on. The labor axis has been marked off in units where each unit represents one man-hour.

Start with the factor combination N_6 and K_6. If one unit of labor is given up, then to maintain output at Q_1, $K_5 - K_6$ more units of capital are required. If, however, we had started out with much less labor and much more capital (the combination N_2 and K_2, say) and then given up one more unit of labor, the increment in capital required to maintain output at Q_1 would be much greater; namely, $K_1 - K_2$. You will see that as you move from R_1 toward R_6 the quantity of capital necessary to compensate for the loss of one unit of labor declines progressively when the isoquant is convex to the origin. This illustrates the phenomenon that economists call a *diminishing (marginal) rate of technical substitution;* the less of an input you have to begin with, the more of a second input you require to compensate for the loss of one more unit of the first input. The less easy it is to substitute one factor for another in the productive process, then the more convex to the origin are the isoquants and, of course, the more rapidly does the marginal rate of technical substitution decline.

A diminishing marginal rate of technical substitution of one factor of production for another in the productive process is a widely observed technological fact of life. We shall assume it to be characteristic of the production process of our firms and, thus, draw isoquants that are convex to the origin.

One other feature revealed by the slope of an isoquant is worth recording. The slope at any point on the curve is the ratio of the marginal physical products of the factors at that point. This can be seen quite easily. Consider Figure 3. Assume that you are at R_1. Output could be increased from Q_1 to Q_2 by keeping the input of capital constant at K_2 and increasing the input of labor by ΔN. The resultant increase in output ΔQ would be equal to the increase in labor N times the marginal physical product of labor MPP_L, which is defined in the usual way as the increase in output resulting from employing one more unit of labor. Thus,

$$\Delta Q = \Delta N \times MPP_L \tag{1}$$

Equally though, starting from R_1 again, output could be increased from

FIGURE 3

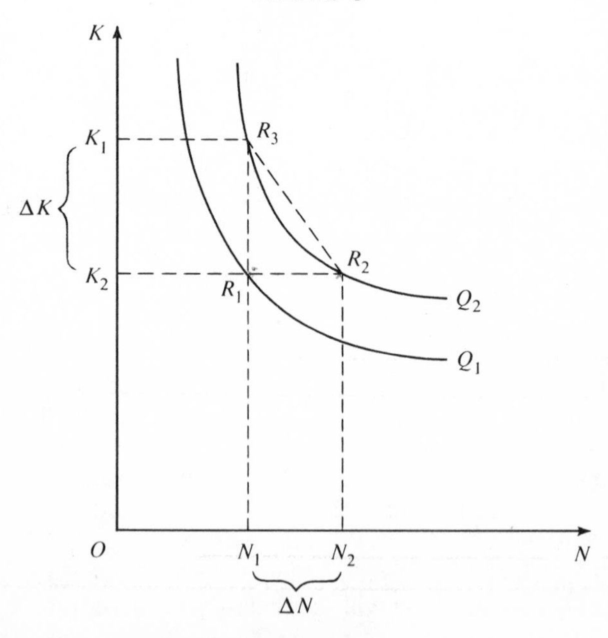

Q_1 to Q_2 by holding the labor input constant at N_1 and increasing the input of capital from K_2 to K_1. The increase in output (which is ΔQ again because R_3 is on the same isoquant as R_2) this time is equal to the increase in capital ΔK times the marginal physical product of capital where that is defined in an analogous manner to the marginal physical product of labor.

That is,

$$\Delta Q = \Delta K \times MPP_K \tag{2}$$

But clearly (1) and (2) are equal. So

$$\Delta N \times MPP_L = \Delta K \times MPP_K \tag{3}$$

From which it follows that

$$\frac{\Delta K}{\Delta L} = \frac{MPP_L}{MPP_K} \tag{4}$$

But when the appropriate negative sign is inserted, the left-hand side of (4) is simply the slope of the hypotenuse of the triangle $R_1R_2R_3$ which, when the changes in labor and capital (and, therefore, output) are small enough, approximates fairly closely the tangent of the isoquant. And, of course, the tangent of the isoquant at any point reveals the slope of the isoquant at that point. Thus, it follows from (4) that the slope of the isoquant gives the ratio of the marginal physical products of the factors $-(MPP_L/MPP_K)$.[1]

Profit Maximization and the Demand Curve for Labor

We shall assume throughout this book that the stock of capital available to firms is fixed in quantity. Implicitly, we confine ourselves to short-run analysis. Firms have accumulated a certain stock of capital in the past and they must live with it. In the short run which we consider, there is no way they can change their capital stock. Although they can acquire new capital by investing (or allow their existing capital to be reduced via depreciation), such investment (or depreciation) is assumed to have no substantive effect on the stock of capital available to them. Investment (or depreciation) in the short run is small relative to the existing stock of capital, so, for all practical purposes, the stock of capital may be thought of as constant. We may assume, then, that the capital stock is fixed at $\bar{K}$.

In Figure 4, this means that the *feasible* factor combinations that the firm may choose in order to produce output are indicated by the ray $\overline{KK}$. The firm's capital stock is fixed at $\bar{K}$, thus it can only change its output by changing the quantity of the variable input, labor, it uses. If the firm wishes to produce Q_1 output it does so with its capital stock $\bar{K}$ and the quantity of labor N_1; if it wishes to produce Q_2 it uses its capital stock $\bar{K}$ and N_2; and so on. Hence, labor is the only variable input.

[1] This is all we need to say about the properties of isoquants. Readers who are interested in the other commonly assumed features are referred to the appropriate chapter of any intermediate microeconomic textbook. Try, for example, C. E. Ferguson's *Microeconomic Theory*, Irwin, 1969, rev. ed., Chapter 6.

FIGURE 4

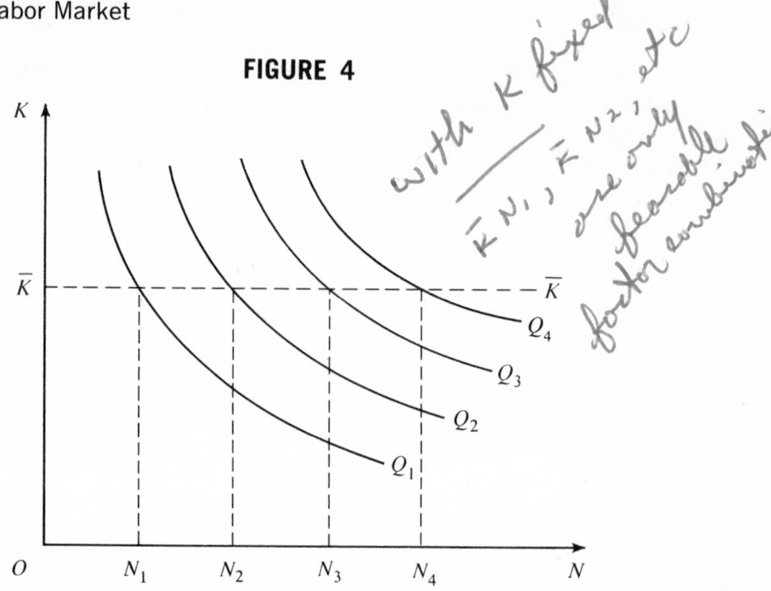

We saw in the first part of §1 that the slope of an isoquant is equal to the ratio MPP_L/MPP_K. Observe the slope of the isoquants as they cross $\overline{KK}$. These slopes decrease (in absolute value). The slope of Q_1 at $\overline{KK}$ is greater than the slope of Q_2 at $\overline{KK}$, which is greater than the slope of Q_3 at $\overline{KK}$, and so on. Thus, it follows that as you move out along $\overline{KK}$ to higher isoquants the marginal physical product of labor declines. This is due to diminishing returns. As you move out along $\overline{KK}$, more and more labor is being combined with the same amount of capital. In effect, when more workers are hired, each worker has less and less capital to work with. Thus, the addition to output obtained by adding one more worker declines as more and more workers are hired. And this, of course, is equivalent to saying that the marginal physical product of labor declines as more workers are hired.

If the marginal physical product of labor is plotted as a function of the level of employment, we would obtain a downward-sloping curve like that shown in Figure 5. When N_1 are employed, the marginal physical product of labor is MPP_L (1); when N_2 are employed it declines to MPP_L (2).

Of all the alternative outputs a firm can produce, which one should it choose if it plans to maximize its profits? It is well known that profits are maximized when that level of output is produced at which marginal cost MC is equal to marginal revenue MR. Since our firm is a perfect competitor, marginal revenue is equal to price P. Thus, a perfectly competitive firm maximizes profits when it produces the output where

$$MC = P \tag{5}$$

It is convenient for our purposes to reformulate this profit maximizing condition in a different way. Marginal cost is, by definition, the increase in cost incurred by increasing output by one unit. The only variable factor for our firm is labor. So if the firm wants to increase output it must hire more labor. If one more unit of labor services is hired, costs are increased by the price per unit of that service; namely, the nominal wage rate W. The output is increased by the marginal physical product of labor MPP_L. It follows that the increase in costs incurred by increasing output by one unit, or the marginal cost, is equal to W/MPP_L. To rephrase this, when one more worker is hired costs go up by W and output by the MPP_L; thus the additional cost per unit of output is the marginal cost W/MPP_L.

We may, therefore, rewrite the profit maximization condition (5) as

$$\frac{W}{MPP_L} = P \tag{6}$$

which is equivalent to

$$\frac{W}{P} = MPP_L \tag{7}$$

The variable on the left-hand side of (7), the ratio of the money wage rate to the commodity price level, is known as the *real wage* rate. It has the dimension "commodities per man per time period." This can be seen by noting that W has the dimension "dollars per man per time period" and P has the dimension "dollars per commodity." So

$$\frac{W}{P} = \frac{\dfrac{\$/\text{man}}{\text{time}}}{\$/\text{commodity}} = \text{commodity/man/time period}$$

The real wage is the return for work in terms of commodities. Equivalently, it is the real, or commodity-purchasing power of the money wage.

The profit maximization condition (7) has intuitive appeal. It says hire

FIGURE 5

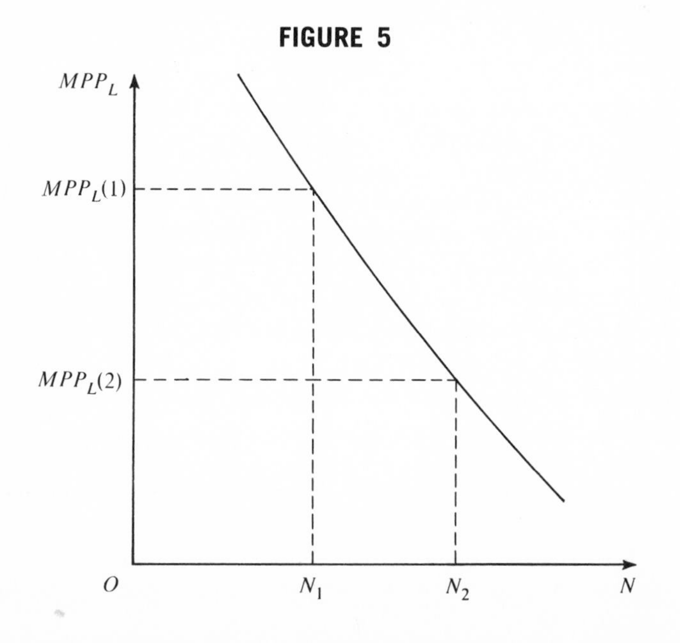

workers to produce output until the real purchasing power you have to turn over to them is equal to the addition to real product that occurs when the last, marginal, worker is hired. Consider Figure 6 which reproduces the marginal physical product of labor curve described in Figure 5, but now both the MPP_L and the real wage are plotted vertically. This is permissible, since they both have the same dimension, namely, "commodities per man per time period."

Suppose the real wage is $(W/P)_1$. This is a parameter to the firm, since both the nominal wage rate and the commodity price level (and therefore, their ratio) are beyond its control (recall that we have assumed that the firm is a price-taker in both factor and commodity markets). Given that the firm is confronted by this real wage, how many men should it employ? Condition (7) tells us it should employ N_1, since that is the level of employment at which the MPP_L is equal to the real wage $(W/P)_1$. Now, if the real wage falls to $(W/P)_2$, condition (7) indicates that N_2 should be employed, and so on. What do we have here? The combinations $(W/P)_1$ and N_1 and $(W/P)_2$ and N_2 indicate prices of labor and quantities of labor that would be demanded. They are, therefore, points on a demand curve for labor. But we have just seen that they lay along the MPP_L curve. Thus, we conclude that the demand curve for labor is identical to the MPP_L curve. Notice that by operating in accordance with such a demand curve the firm is observing condition (7) and, thus, is maximizing its profits.

If the firm had a larger capital stock, the demand curve for labor would increase because, for any given level of employment, the marginal physical product of labor is higher when the capital stock is larger. This, of course, is due to the fact that, at any given level of employment, each worker has a

FIGURE 6

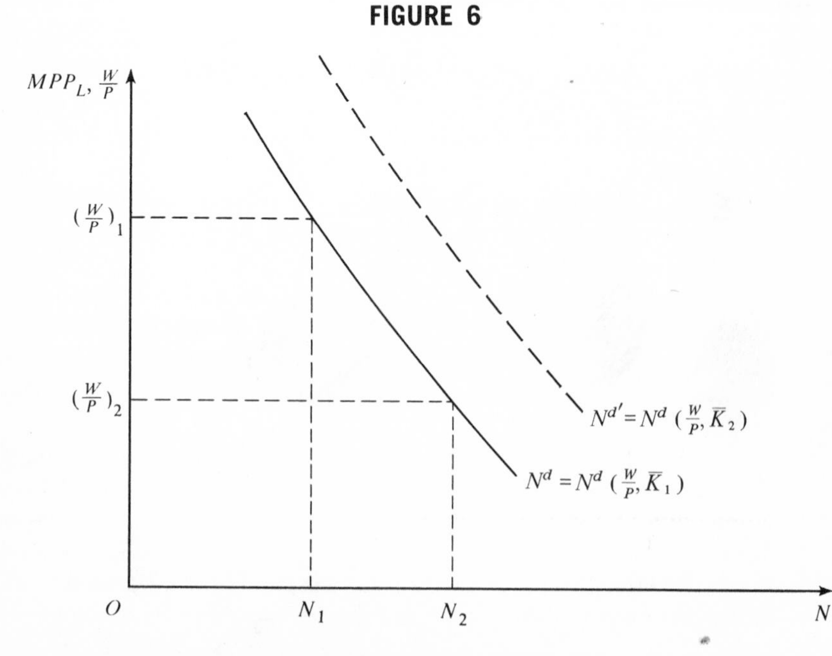

larger share of the capital stock to work with when the size of the capital stock increases. In Figure 6, the dashed curve labeled $N^{d'}$ is that associated with the larger capital stock $\bar{K}_2$.

We may write what we have just established in the form of an equation

$$N^d = N^d\left(\frac{W}{P}, \bar{K}\right), \; N_1^d < 0 \tag{8}$$

which states that the firm's demand for labor is a function of the real wage and its capital stock. Since we are assuming that the capital stock is constant in our model (signified by the bar over K), changes in the demand for labor will never be the result of changes in the capital stock. Thus, variations in the demand for labor will result only from changes in the real wage rate. And, as we have seen, the two are inversely related. This latter information is summarized compactly by the statement $N_1^d < 0$. This should be read "the derivative of the demand for labor function with respect to the real wage is negative" because N_1^d represents the derivative of the function with respect to the first argument (variable) in the parentheses.

2 The Supply of Labor

The sources of labor services in our model are the individuals who comprise the households. These individuals are all commodity-makers. Thus, the only type of labor service supplied is the services of commodity making. As functioning economic units, these households have to make several decisions including the following:

1. How much of the total time at their disposal should they offer to firms and how much should they retain for their own enjoyment? This is the *work/leisure* decision, or how much labor service to supply.
2. How much of the income they eventually receive should they consume and how much should they save? This is the *consumption/saving* decision. (This is discussed in Chapter 3.)
3. How much of their accumulated savings should they hold in the form of bonds and how much should they hold in the form of money? These are the only two assets that households can hold in our model, but this question amounts to the general *portfolio balance* decision. (This is discussed in Chapter 4.)
4. [In a more general model than ours in which more than one commodity exists, households also have to decide what quantities of each commodity to consume. This is the *consumption pattern* decision. In our model, this is redundant; it is "the standard commodity" or nothing at all with the income that the households have decided to allocate to consumption. Hence, we put this decision in brackets.]

In this section, we shall be concerned with the households' work/leisure decision. How the other two relevant decisions are made will be dealt with in the indicated chapters.

An individual is assumed to derive utility from both income and leisure. He would like as much of both as he can get. Figure 7 illustrates an individual's utility function. Hours of leisure are measured along the X axis, and real income (which is a number of commodities) is measured along the Y axis. Both of these are flow variables, since their measurement involves a time period.

The curves labeled U_0, U_1, U_2, . . . (the three dots to indicate these are only three of the infinite number which jam this space) are *indifference curves*. Each curve shows various combinations of income and leisure that provide the same level of utility to the individual. For example, the combination of Y_1 income and L_1 leisure is just as appealing a combination of "goods" to the individual as the combination Y_2 income and L_2 leisure. In fact, the curve labeled U_1 is the locus of all combinations of income and leisure which provide the same level of utility to the individual. Naturally, these curves are negatively sloped because less income has to be compensated for by more leisure or, conversely, less leisure has to be compensated for with more income if the same level of utility is to be maintained. But we impose a further restriction on the shape of these curves—we assume that they are convex to the origin. This implies that there is a diminishing marginal rate of substitution between the two alternatives. What does that mean? It means to maintain utility at any level when a unit of one good is given up, a greater increase

FIGURE 7

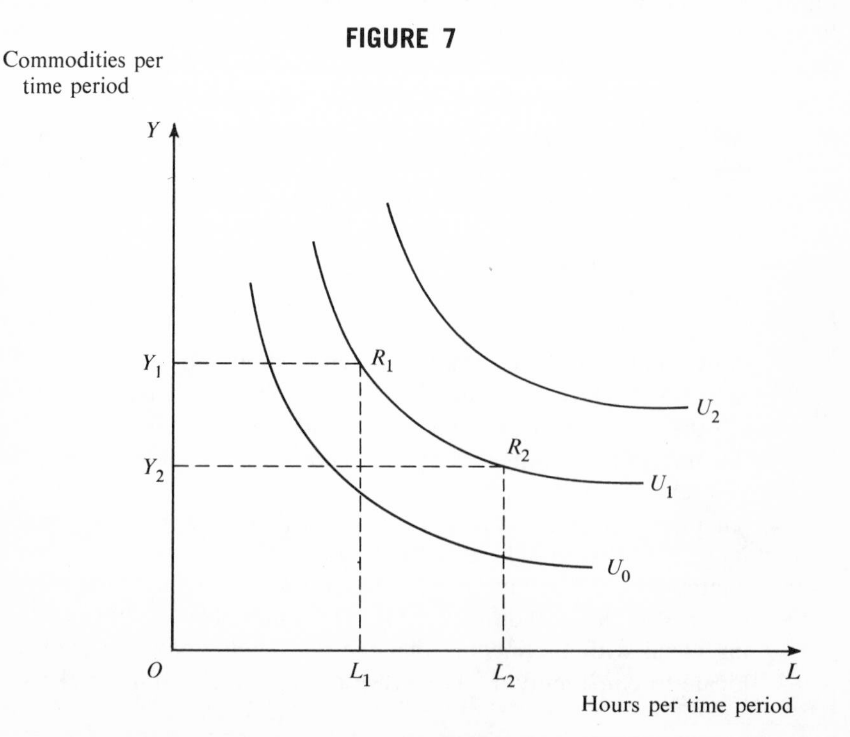

FIGURE 8

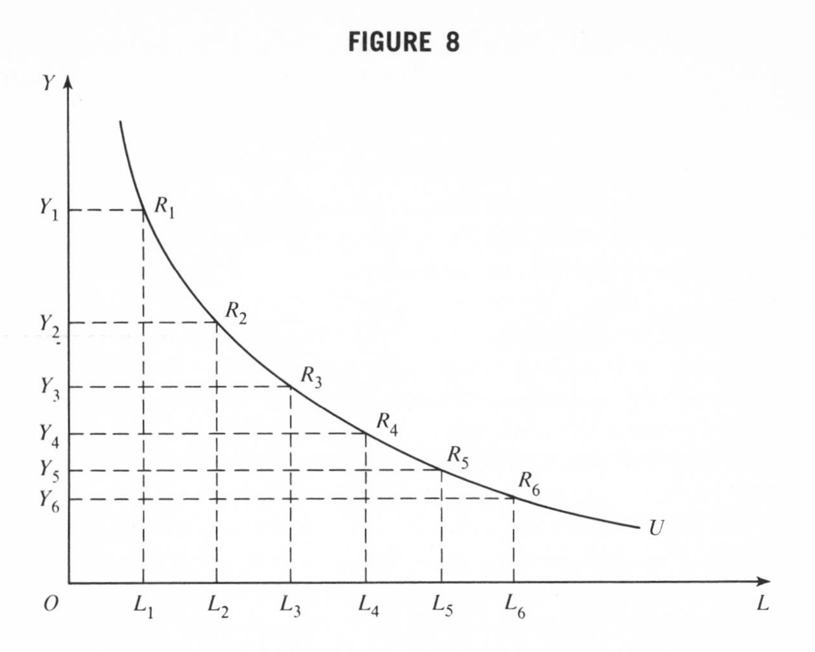

in the quantity of the other good is necessary for smaller initial (before you decided to give up a unit) amounts of the first good than for larger amounts. This is analogous to the situation we encountered when substituting factors of production.

As an example, consider the single indifference curve illustrated in Figure 8. The leisure axis has been marked off in equal amounts. Assume that the individual is initially enjoying Y_6 income and L_6 leisure. If he is to be induced to give up one more unit of leisure without being made worse off, this individual requires an additional $Y_5 - Y_6$ income. But now consider the situation if the individual originally had only L_2 leisure and Y_2 income (much less leisure and more income than before). Then if he were to be induced to part with one more unit of leisure he would require $Y_1 - Y_2$ income, a larger amount than before, in compensation if he were not to be made worse off. Clearly, the income needed to compensate for the loss of one more unit of leisure declines progressively as we move from R_1 to R_2 to R_3 . . . to R_6. This is what is meant by a diminishing marginal rate of substitution of income for leisure and is represented only by indifference curves that are convex to the origin. They are, in fact, drawn that way because it seems reasonable to assume such a diminishing marginal rate of substitution. Be introspective for a moment. If you were working your fingers to the bone (enjoying very little leisure), would you not demand much more income to part with one more hour of leisure and still not be made worse off than the amount of income you would require to compensate for parting with one more hour of leisure if you were loafing most of the day? If you agree, you have a diminishing marginal rate of substitution for leisure. If you do not agree we are reluctant to believe you, for you would be saying that the less leisure you have the more you are willing to give up for equal increments to your income. Note that we are only reluctant to believe you, not that we refuse to believe you. Such an attitude is possible. It describes someone who is addicted to income. The more income he has, the more he wants. And as income in our model takes the form of commodities, it means you are hooked on commodities. This, we concede, is a possibility. However, we do not wish to incorporate individuals with a commodity habit in our model, so we must insist that individuals do have the assumed diminishing marginal rate of substitution between income and leisure.

As we have already remarked, the indifference map illustrated in Figure 7 shows only three of the potentially infinite number of indifference curves jamming that space. Among these indifference curves, those curves that are further from the origin are preferred to those curves that are closer to the origin. So, for example, U_2 is preferred to U_1 and U_0 is less preferred than U_1.

An individual is assumed to be a utility maximizer. That means he wants to get onto the highest indifference curve possible—loafing as much as he can while still acquiring as much of the commodity as possible. But the individual is constrained in two ways: first, by the wage rate at which he can sell his labor services and, second, by the fact that he only has a finite amount of labor services of which to dispose. How do these constraints impinge on him?

Assume that our individual is deciding how many hours of his commodity-making services to make available, or supply, on the labor market *per week*. Then in Figure 9, he has the option of putting himself at point M, where he enjoys M hours of leisure and receives no income. The distance M is equal to 168 hours (= 7 days × 24 hours). (We are including sleep as leisure.)

Alternatively, an individual could, by working all the hours God made, take no leisure (or sleep) at all. After such a decision, he would clearly be

FIGURE 9

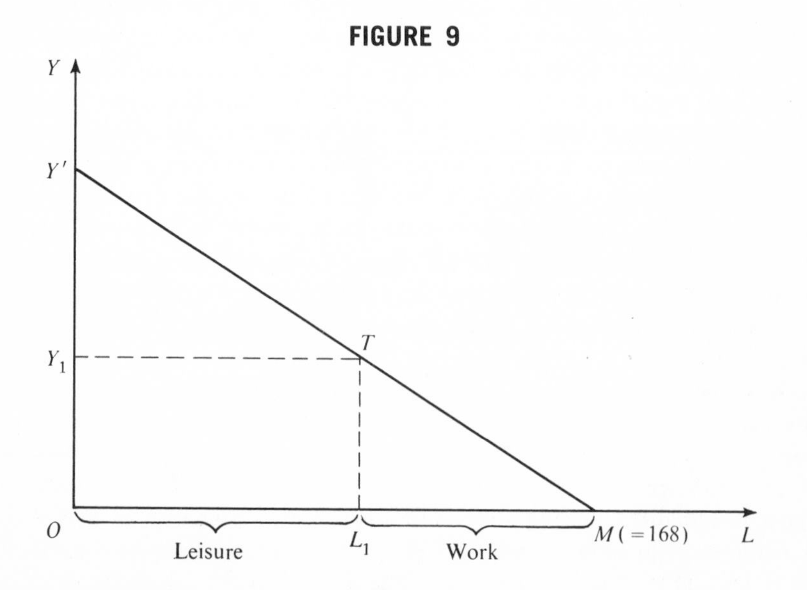

FIGURE 10

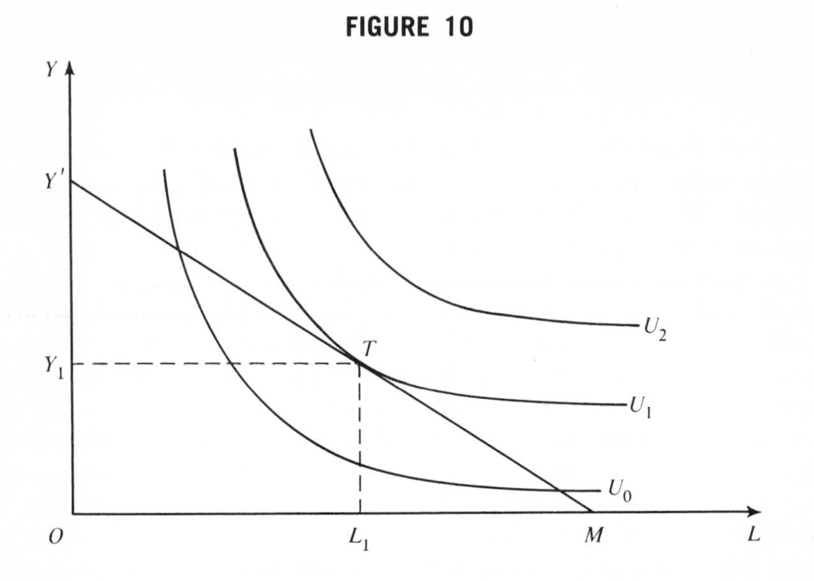

somewhere on the Y axis. Let us assume that the point is Y'. Now join Y' and M. The slope of this line is equal to the real wage. Why? If you work for M hours, you get Y' income in the form of commodities, or Y'/M commodities per hour. But the number of commodities received per hour for working is equal to the real wage. The reader will recall that W/P, the real wage or the purchasing power of the money wage, was shown to have the dimension "commodities per man per time period." Thus Y'/M, which is the slope of the line joining Y' and M, is equal to the real wage. Obviously, the supplier of labor services is not bound to points such as M or Y'. He can enjoy any combination of income and leisure shown by line $Y'M$ if, as we shall assume, the real wage is independent of the amount of labor any individual offers. This assumption keeps the slope of $Y'M$ constant whatever the individual's decision is. It amounts to the same thing as saying that he sells his labor in a perfectly competitive market. For example, the individual could put himself at point T. Here he receives Y_1 income (in exchange for ML_1 work) while enjoying L_1 leisure. Note that leisure is measured from O along the X axis and M hours is the maximum weekly leisure possible. Therefore, if he takes only L_1 hours of leisure, he must work for ML_1 hours. Thus, work is measured on the X axis from M toward O, and leisure is measured on the X axis from O toward M.

Given the time at his disposal, the real wage with which he is confronted, and the individual's preference map for income and leisure, we are now in a position to observe how many hours of labor he will supply. Consider Figure 10 where the indifference map and the constraints are combined.

The individual's aim is to maximize his utility, that is, get onto the highest possible indifference curve, subject to the constraint $Y'M$. Clearly, this occurs at the point T where $Y'M$ is tangent to indifference curve U_1.

At T the individual is receiving Y_1 income (in exchange for ML_1 work) and is enjoying L_1 leisure. At points on $Y'M$ to the left or to the right of T the individual is on lower indifference curves, in a less preferred situation than at T. Thus, T is preferred to all these other *feasible* points.

We are particularly concerned with the supply curve of labor. That is to say, we wish to know about the quantities of work that individuals plan to supply at different real wages. Thus, let us change the real wage to various levels and observe how the individual's offers of work changes. The outcome of the experiment is illustrated in Figure 11.

In this diagram the real wage is variously set at the slopes of $Y'M$, $Y''M$, $Y'''M$, and so on. At each of these real wages the individual offers the amount of work at which the relevant wage is tangent to an indifference curve. As a result we see that when the real wage is equal to the slope of $Y'M$, the individual offers ML_1 hours of work; when the real wage rises to the slope of $Y''M$, the individual offers ML_2 hours of work, and so on. The curve $MT_1T_2T_3T$ is the locus of all points of tangency between different real wage rates and indifferent curves. It is quite easy to construct the familiar supply curve of labor from Figure 11, and this is done in Figure 12. From Figure 11 we can see that as the real wage rises from $(W/P)_1$ [the slope of $Y'M$] to $(W/P)_2$ [the slope of $Y''M$], the quantity of labor supplied by the individual rises from ML_1 to ML_2. It is readily appreciated that the supply curve of labor obtained from an individual whose preference map looks like that in Figure 11 will be a monotonically increasing function of the real wage like that shown in Figure 12(a).

However, it is possible (we say no more than possible) that the curve $MT_1T_2T_3T$ shown in Figure 11 should bend back upon itself once a certain real wage has been reached. Such a situation is shown in Figure 13.

FIGURE 11

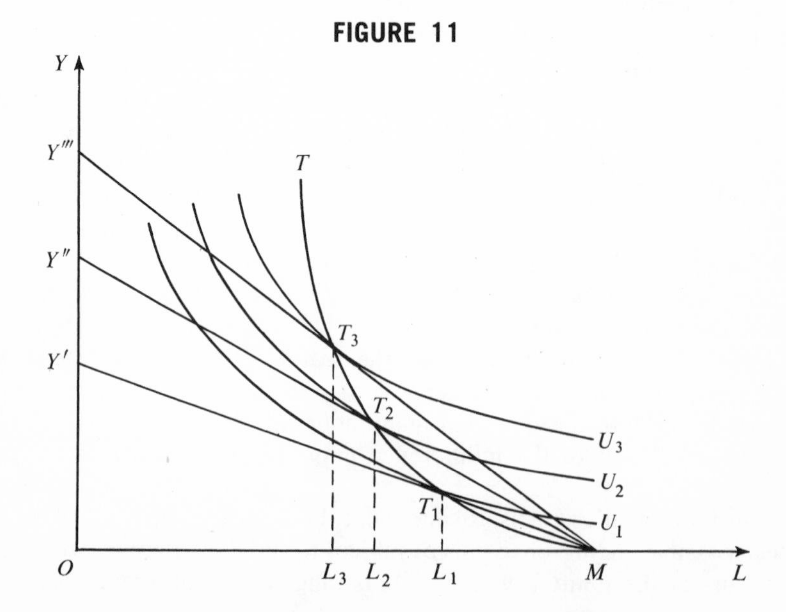

FIGURE 12

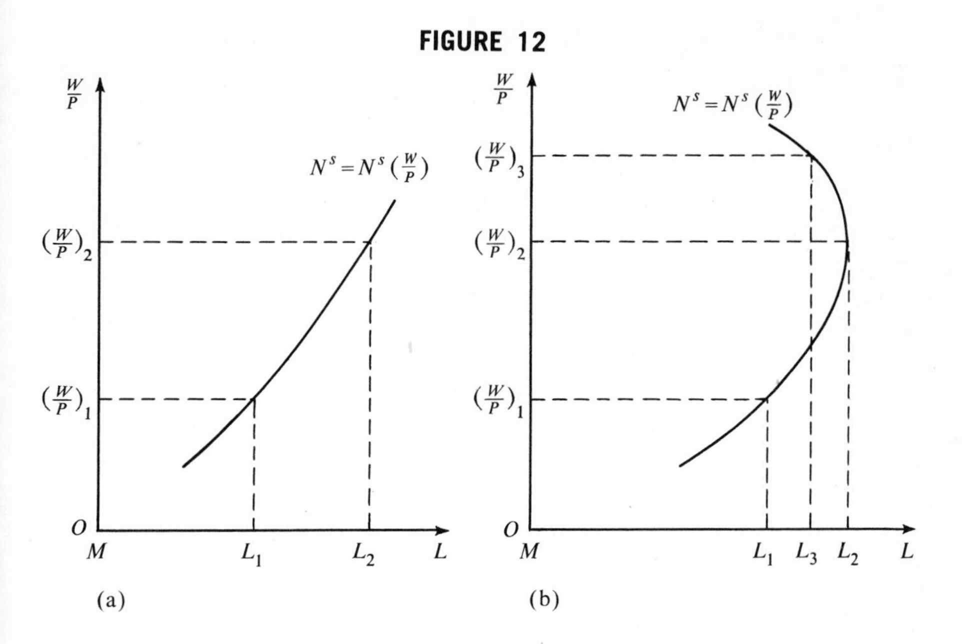

This individual supplies more labor as the real wage rises from the slope of $Y'M$, $(W/P)_1$, to the slope of $Y''M$, $(W/P)_2$; but when the real wage rises beyond that to the slope of $Y'''M$, $(W/P)_3$, he begins to offer *less* labor services, not more. At $(W/P)_1$ he supplies ML_1; at $(W/P)_2$ he supplies ML_2; and at $(W/P)_3$ he supplies ML_3. This individual's supply of labor is illustrated explicitly in Figure 12(b). This is the well-known *backward-bending supply curve of labor.* Clearly, whether or not individual supply of labor

FIGURE 13

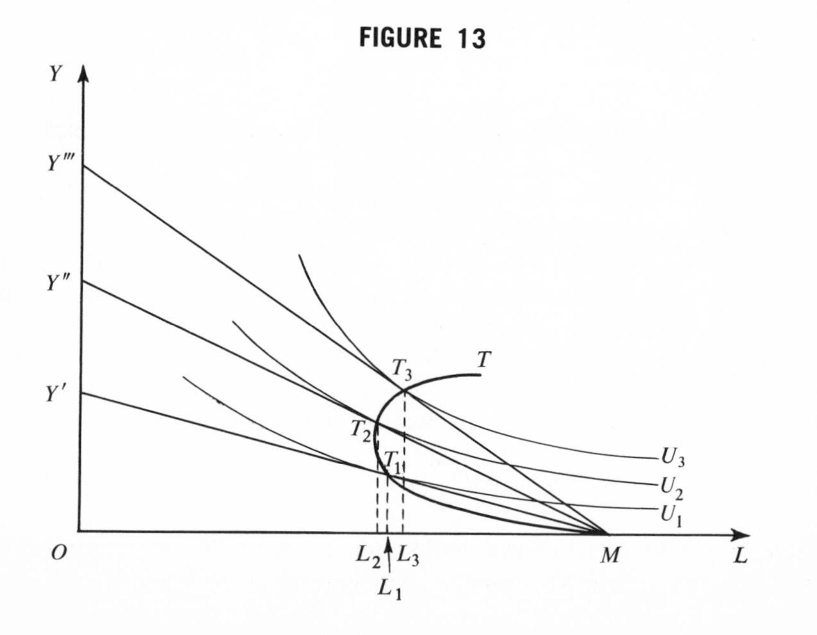

curves bend backwards depends on the nature of the individual's income/leisure preference map. It has been alleged that miners and plantation workers have backward-sloping supply curves of labor. Beyond a certain wage, miners are supposed to put in less effort at the mine and more effort at the track, and plantation workers to put more time in the bush and less on the plantation. Needless to say, these arguments are advanced by mine and plantation owners, not miners and workers. Be that as it may, we assume that it is *not* true of the commodity-makers in our model. Hence, these individuals have continuously upward sloping supply curves of labor as a function of the real wage. That is,

$$N^s = N^s\left(\frac{W}{P}\right), \qquad N_1^s > 0 \tag{9}$$

Again, N_1^s represents the derivative of the function with respect to the first argument in the parentheses.

Plausible arguments can be marshaled to the effect that the supply of labor is not solely a function of the real wage. It is also for example, some people will say, a function of wealth. The wealthier a person is, so this argument runs, the less labor he is willing to supply at any given real wage; the less wealthy he is, the more labor he is willing to supply at any given real wage. This merely amounts to saying that the supply curve of labor shifts to the left when wealth increases and to the right when it decreases. This certainly seems plausible. Casual empiricism seems to confirm it too. All sorts of White Russian émigré aristocrats were driving taxicabs in Paris after October, 1917, whereas they had not been known to have contributed noticeably to the supply of labor while previously in Mother Russia. In any event, our assumption here is that such wealth effects on the supply of labor are of no importance, and we shall make the supply of labor a function *only* of the real wage as in (9).

3 The Market Demand, the Market Supply, and the Price of Labor

So far, we have derived the firm's demand for labor curve as a function of the real wage and the (fixed) capital stock, and the individual's supply of labor curve as a function of the real wage. The market demand curve is merely the horizontal summation of all the firms' demand curves. Consequently, it will look exactly like Figure 6 except that the scale of the horizontal axis will be much larger. Clearly, the market demand for labor function will depend on the same variables as the individual firm demand functions. Thus, we may write the market demand function as

$$N^d = N^d\left(\frac{W}{P}, \bar{K}\right) \qquad N_1^d < 0 \tag{I}$$

where N^d represents the *total* market demand for labor, $\bar{K}$ the *total* capital stock of all firms, and N_1^d is its slope with respect to the real wage. This is the first of the sixteen equations that will eventually comprise our complete macroeconomic model.

Similarly, the *market* supply of labor curve is obtained by the horizontal summation of all the individual workers' supply curves. It will look just like Figure 12(a) except that the horizontal scale will be much larger. It is obvious that the market supply function of labor will depend only on the same variables as the individual supply function. Thus, we may write the market supply function as

$$N^s = N^s\left(\frac{W}{P}\right), \qquad N_1^s > 0 \tag{II}$$

where N^s is the total market supply of labor.

The third basic equation of the macroeconomic model that we are developing is an *equilibrium condition.*

$$N^d = N^s \tag{III}$$

That is, when our model is in equilibrium, the quantity of labor demanded must be equal to the quantity of labor supplied. In terms of the familiar supply and demand diagram of Figure 14, this occurs only at the real wage $(W/P)^*$. At this wage, the quantity of labor demanded is equal to the quantity of labor supplied—and both are equal to the equilibrium level of employment N^*.

If, for some reason, the real wage happened to exceed $(W/P)^*$, there would be an excess supply of labor. For example, if the real wage was $(W/P)_1$ more labor services would be offered than were being demanded. As a result some people who were looking for work (offering their labor services) at that wage, would not find it. In such circumstances, until we assume the contrary, these individuals would be induced to lower their

FIGURE 14

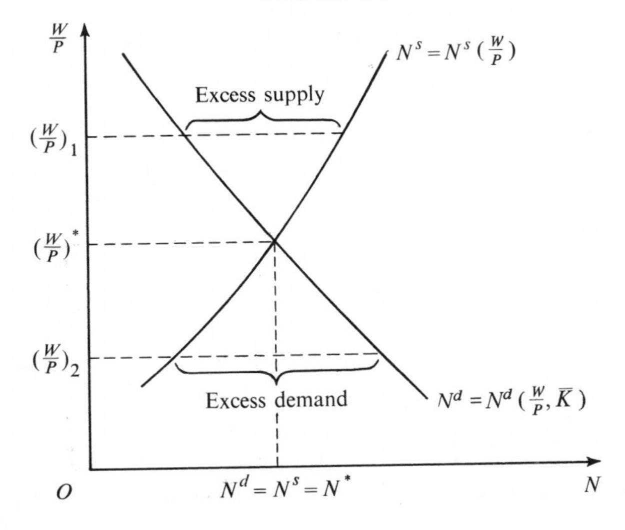

asking price. This would mean that W, the nominal wage, would fall. As W falls the ratio (W/P) clearly falls, too, assuming P is constant. And as the real wage decreases, the quantity of labor demanded increases and the quantity of labor supplied decreases. Thus, eventually, equality between the two will be brought about, in particular, when (W/P) has fallen to $(W/P)^*$.

Conversely, if the real wage happened to be less than $(W/P)^*$, there would be an excess demand for labor. For example, suppose the real wage happens to be $(W/P)_2$. At this wage, the quantity of labor demanded exceeds the quantity of labor supplied. There is then, by definition, excess demand. In these circumstances some firms who are looking for workers are not able to hire them. These frustrated employers will therefore offer to pay more. That is, they will bid against each other by raising the nominal wage W. As the nominal wage W rises so, clearly, does the real wage W/P, assuming P is constant. Eventually, the nominal wage will rise until the real wage reaches $(W/P)^*$. At this real wage the excess demand will disappear. Notice that the rise in the real wage eliminates the excess demand for employment in two ways. First, the quantity demanded decreases as the real wage rises. We move back, so to speak, up the demand curve. Second, the quantity supplied increases, and we move back up the supply curve.

The foregoing analysis assumed that P was constant and that only W varied to establish the market-clearing real wage $(W/P)^*$. However, when unemployment prevails, for example, it is unreasonable to suppose that P will remain constant, since the demand for commodities will decrease and P will tend to fall. This problem is discussed at length in later chapters. At the moment, it will suffice to point out that when the real wage is above $(W/P)^*$ and unemployment exists, this unemployment will be removed if W and P both fall, so long as W falls further than P. Conversely, if the real wage is below $(W/P)^*$ and an excess demand for labor exists, this excess demand will also be removed if W and P both rise, so long as W rises more than P.

This brings to an end our discussion of the first of the four markets which comprises our macroeconomic model. In Chapter 3, we shall discuss the market for commodities.

Summary

Using our knowledge of the microeconomic theory of the firm, we showed that a profit-maximizing firm's demand curve for labor is identical to the MPP_L curve. As long, therefore, as the MPP_L decreases as employment increases (which it will do when diminishing returns exist), the demand curve for labor will slope down. The aggregate demand for labor curve, which is obtained by aggregation of the individual firm's demand curves, will have a similar configuration.

Similarly, on the basis of the microeconomic theory of consumer behavior, we were able to derive a household's supply of labor from its underlying income/leisure preferences by having the individual maximize its utility subject to the time at its disposal and the prevailing wage rate. The result was that an individual's supply curve of labor did not have an unambiguously positive slope. Therefore, the aggregate supply of labor curve (which is obtained by aggregation of the individual supply curves) may not have an unambiguously positive slope either. However, this problem was *assumed* away and, in what follows, we shall at all times assume that the supply curve of labor does slope up from left to right.

Finally, we found that given competitive behavior on both sides of the market (that is, both firms and households act as price-takers), a unique equilibrium real wage will emerge at which the demand for, and supply of, labor are equal and, thus, by definition, full employment will prevail.

Questions

1. Prove that when a competitive labor market is in equilibrium:
   " I. *The* [real] *wage is equal to the marginal* [physical] *product of labor.*
   II. The utility of the [real] wage when a given volume of labor is employed is equal to the marginal disutility of that amount of employment."[1]
2. Show that the slope of an isoquant is equal to the ratio of the marginal physical products of the inputs at that point.
3. Assuming that a firm has a fixed capital stock, show that it will maximize its profits by hiring labor until the marginal physical product of labor is equal to the real wage. Is this consistent with the other well-known profit-maximizing condition, namely, producing the output at which marginal cost and marginal revenue are equal?
4. From an individual's income/leisure preference map, derive a labor supply curve which bends backwards.

SELECTED READINGS

1. C. E. Ferguson, *Microeconomic Theory,* rev. ed., Irwin, 1969, chapters 5, 6, and 13.
2. J. M. Keynes, *The General Theory of Employment, Interest, and Money,* Macmillan, 1936, chapter 2.
3. D. Patinkin, *Money, Interest, and Prices,* 2nd ed., Harper & Row, 1965, chapter 9, section 2.

FURTHER READING

4. A. C. Pigou, *Theory of Unemployment,* London, 1929.

[1] These are described as "the classical postulates I and II" by J. M. Keynes, *The General Theory of Employment, Interest, and Money,* Macmillan, 1936, p. 5.

3

The Commodity Market

With the labor market behind us, we can now turn to an analysis of the other market which also comprises the "real" sector of our macroeconomic model, namely, the market for commodities. The remaining two markets (money and bond) comprise the financial sector of the model and will be discussed in Chapters 4 and 5.

1 The Supply of Commodities

There is both a supply of and a demand for commodities in our model. It turns out that the supply of commodities is much simpler to handle than the demand for commodities so we shall discuss supply first.

Most of the groundwork for our discussion here was laid in the previous chapter. The supply of commodities comes from firms. Consider the production function of the individual firm illustrated in Figure 1 and its demand curve for labor illustrated in Figure 2. In Figure 1, the firm is restricted to the ray $\overline{KK}$ due to our assumption of a constant capital stock. It can only vary its output by varying the quantity of labor N it combines with the fixed stock of capital $\bar{K}$. If the real wage is $(W/P)_1$, we see from Figure 2 that the firm will hire N_1 labor services. At that employment level the marginal physical product of labor MPP_L is equal to the real wage. Furthermore, the firm's output—its supply of commodities—is Q_1, as we see from Figure 1. If the real wage falls to $(W/P)_2$, the firm will hire N_2 units of labor service. That quantity of labor then has to be employed before the MPP_L will decline to equal the new, lower real wage. And with N_2 employed, the supply of commodities the firm produces is Q_2. Similarly, if the real wage is $(W/P)_3$, N_3 labor services will be employed and Q_3 commodities supplied. It should be obvious that the level of employment determines the supply of commodities.

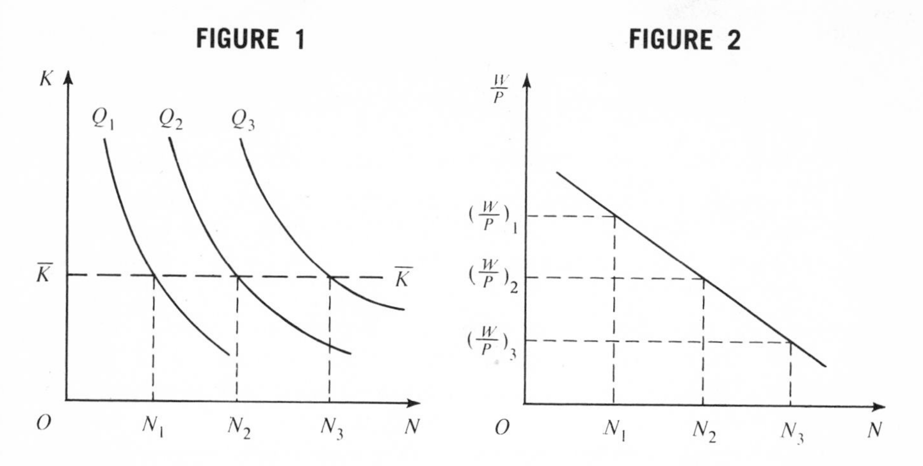

It is convenient to plot this relationship specifically. This is done in Figure 3, where we have aggregated all firms together. If the output of each firm depends on the quantity of labor it individually employs, then the output of all the firms will depend on the quantity of labor they all hire together. The level of employment is plotted horizontally and the level of output, now relabeled Y^s, vertically. This relabeling has been introduced because in economics the common symbol for *real income* is Y (the superscript s indicates supply). And it must be pointed out that *the supply of commodities produced by all firms is equal to our real income*. This is the pie that we can carve up among ourselves. There is nothing else. This real income will be shared among the workers, bond holders, and entrepreneurs; in what proportions, we will find out in Chapter 6. *Output, the supply of commodities,* and *real income* are all synonymous terms. We remark, too, that the supply of com-

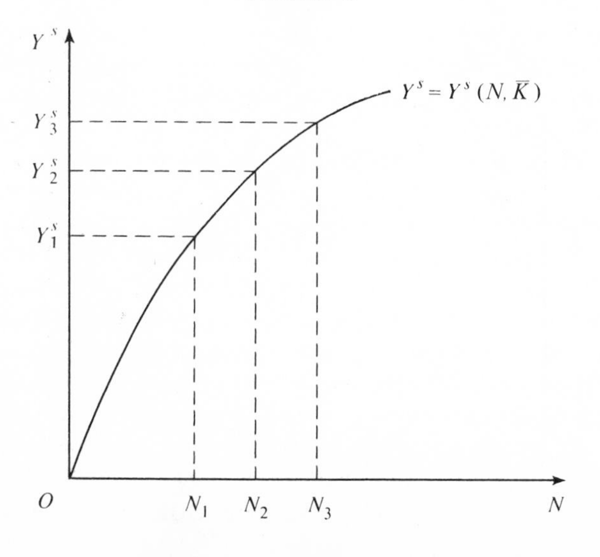

modities, or real income, is a *flow* variable. There are so many commodities produced, so much real income generated, per time period.

The relationship between output and the level of employment in Figure 3 has a special feature worth noting; namely, it is concave to the horizontal axis. This illustrates the ubiquitous phenomenon of diminishing returns. When employment is increased by equal increments, the resultant increase in the supply of commodities diminishes. For example, when employment increases by $N_2 - N_1$, output goes up by $Y_2^s - Y_1^s$; however, when employment increases by $N_3 - N_2$ $(= N_2 - N_1)$, output goes up by only $Y_3^s - Y_2$ $(Y_3^s - Y_2 < Y_2^s - Y_1^s)$. Thus, equal increments in employment give a diminishing return. This, of course, is due to the fact that as more and more labor service is employed, each unit of labor has less and less of the fixed factor (capital) to work with.

Figure 4 illustrates the dependence of the supply of commodities on the level of employment determined in the labor market. If the solid curves indicate the original position, the labor market would be in equilibrium with the real wage $(W/P)_1^*$ and level of employment N_1^*. This quantity of labor service combined with the fixed stock of capital $\bar{K}$ generates a supply of

FIGURE 4

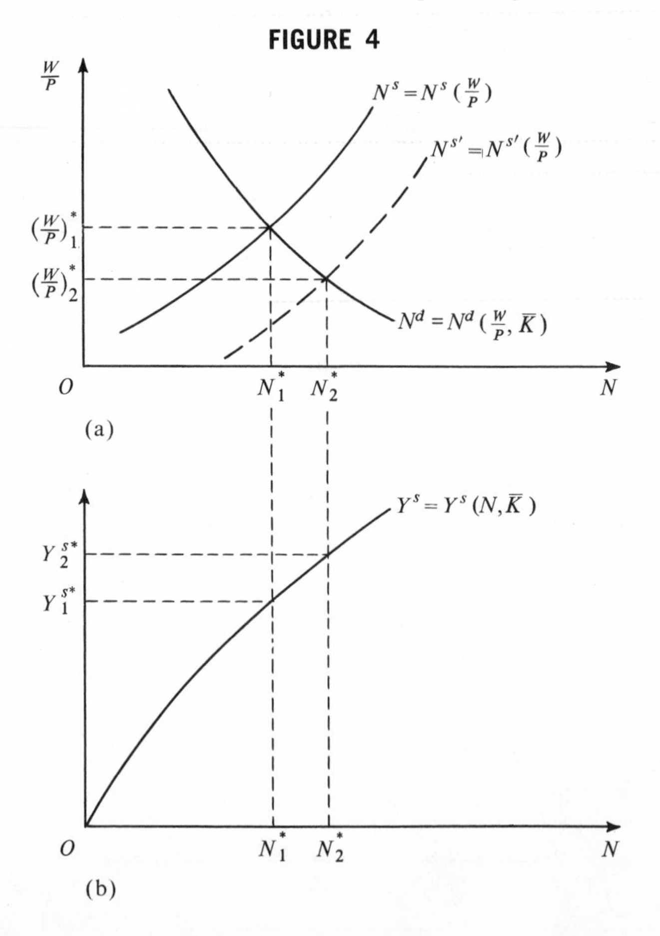

commodities equal to Y_1^{s*}. If, now, the supply curve of labor shifted to $N^{s\prime}$ (suppose, for example, a more tolerant immigration policy was introduced), the equilibrium real wage would fall to $(W/P)_2^*$ and employment would rise to N_2^*. With this level of employment, the supply of commodities rises to Y_2^{s*}. Basically, then, we have the following situation. The level of employment is determined in the labor market and generates a certain supply of commodities through the production function. Variations in the level of employment may, of course, arise in numerous ways. We are not restricted to shifts in the supply curve of labor. Nonetheless, however changes in the level of employment arise, they will lead to changes in the supply of commodities.

Algebraically, the dependence of the supply of commodities on the level of employment can be written

$$Y^s = Y^s(N, \bar{K}), \qquad Y_1^s > 0 \tag{IV}$$

This is the fourth equation of our complete macroeconomic model. In equation (IV) the supply of commodities has also been shown to depend on the level of the capital stock. *If* the capital stock increased, so would the supply of commodities. The supply of commodities is directly dependent on both the level of employment *and* the stock of capital. However, for our purposes we are assuming that the stock of capital is constant. Consequently, changes in the supply of commodities in our model occur *only* through changes in the level of employment. This functional relationship between the supply of commodities and the level of employment has been appended to the output curve in Figure 4(b).

2 The Demand for Commodities

We shall study the three components of the overall, or aggregate, demand for commodities separately in the following order: the demand for commodities for consumption purposes, the demand for commodities for investment (that is, commodities which are to be added to the stock of capital), and the demand for public-good commodities, which the government makes available to us for our collective enjoyment. This final demand will not be discussed until Chapter 9, when the government is introduced into the model as a taxing and spending agent.

The Demand for Commodities to be Consumed

The demand for commodities to be consumed comes from *households*. In §2.3 we saw how households made their income/leisure decision. As a result of this decision, households have a certain real income coming in from the work (or effort) they have elected to supply. They are then faced with a second important decision; namely, what part of real income should they spend on consumption and what part should they save? We are involved now in the households' *consumption/saving* decision. Before we proceed to analyze the factors on which this consumption/saving decision will depend, we can state one thing straightaway—all the income which households receive is either used for purchases of commodities which are consumed C, or it is saved S. There are no other alternatives. Algebraically, real consumption plus real saving are equal to real income or

$$Y^s = C + S$$

Equivalently,

$$S = Y^s - C \qquad \textit{(definition of saving)} \qquad \text{(XIV)}$$

Equation (XIV) in our complete macroeconomic model is merely a definition of saving.[1] All income *not* consumed is saved. It follows immediately from the above definition that when a household decides what to spend on consumption, it is at the same time making its decision on what to save. Clearly, what it consumes it cannot save, and what it does not consume it *must* save. Thus, although we are concentrating mainly on the factors affecting the household's consumption decision, we are also elucidating as a by-product the factors affecting its saving decisions.

For simplicity, let us divide the household's planning period into two parts: the present and the future, respectively, t and $t + 1$. Households wish to maximize their utility over the whole period. Utility flows from consumption, which is of two varieties: current consumption of present commodities and future consumption of commodities available only later. Consider Figure 5. Quantities of present commodities are measured vertically and of future commodities horizontally. Indifference curves fill the space. A household is, for example, indifferent among all the different combinations of present and future commodities represented by I_1. If it was enjoying combination Q_1 and was then asked to give up AB in present commodities, it would require CD future commodities in order to remain on the same indifference curve. Naturally, I_2 would be preferred to I_1, and I_3 to I_2. Notice, too, the assumed diminishing marginal rate of substitution between present and future commodities illustrated by the indifference curves drawn convex to the origin. As you move down any given indifference curve towards the right, you are only willing to give up smaller and smaller amounts of present commodities in return for a given increment of future commodities the smaller is your level of present commodity consumption. Figure 5 illustrates the household's preferences. What are the constraints it works under in its attempt to maximize these preferences? They are as follows:

1. The household's present and expected future *money* income, Y_t and Y_{t+1}. (We have omitted the s superscript to indicate *money* income.)
2. The current price of commodities and the expected future price of commodities P_t and P_{t+1}.
3. The interest rate r.
4. The household's original asset holdings. These we assume to be zero

[1] When we present the complete system of equations representing the entire model (see Chapter 6), it is convenient to include the definition of saving given here as the fourteenth equation. That is why we give it the seemingly odd number (XIV) here.

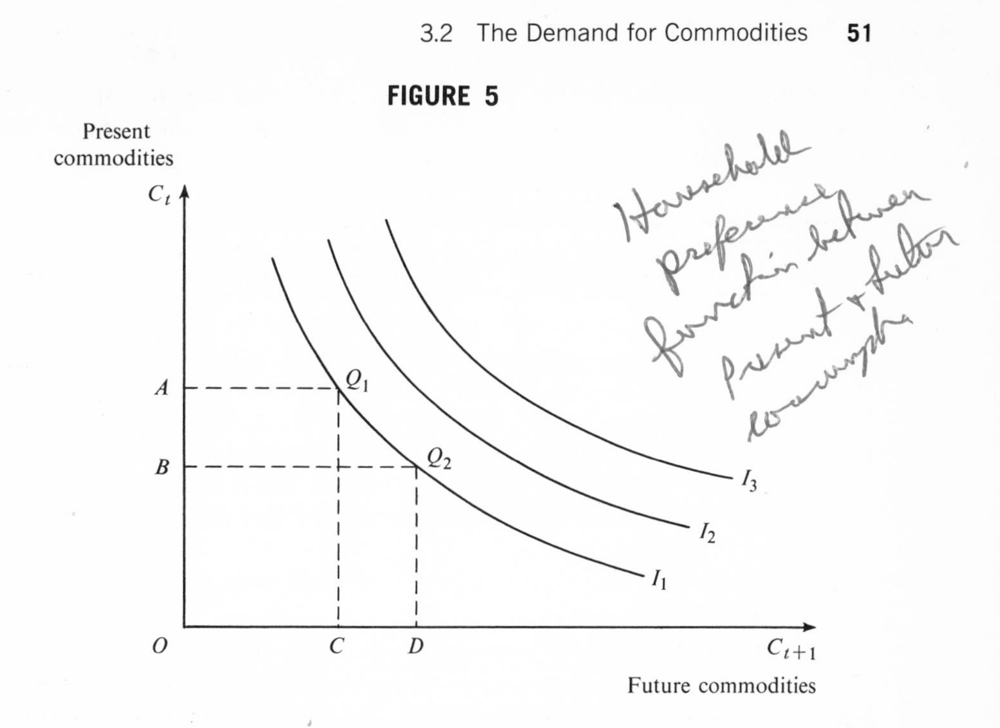

FIGURE 5

for the moment. We shall take up the influence of asset holdings on consumption in a later section of this chapter.

Taking all these variables as given, what options in terms of present and future commodity consumption are open to the household? If the household consumed no present commodities at all and used all its current and future income to consume future commodities, the amount of money it would have available to purchase future commodities would be $Y_{t+1} + Y_t + Y_t r = Y_{t+1} + Y_t(1 + r)$, i.e., the sum of its future income plus its current income plus the interest on that current income. Given the expected future price of commodities P_{t+1}, we may calculate the quantity of future commodities this sum would buy. In Figure 6, suppose the household's future income enables it to buy OA future commodities $(= Y_{t+1}/P_{t+1})$ and his current income plus interest allows him to buy AB commodities $(= Y_t(1 + r)/P_{t+1})$. Thus, if the household does *all* its spending in the future, it can obtain OB future commodities where

$$OB = \frac{Y_{t+1} + Y_t(1 + r)}{P_{t+1}} \tag{1}$$

Conversely, if the household consumed no future commodities and used *all* its current and future income to purchase present commodities, the amount of money it would have available to purchase present commodities would be $Y_t + [Y_{t+1}/(1 + r)]$, i.e., its current income plus the discounted value of its future income. The discounted value of its future income is equivalent to the amount the household could borrow in the present against its future income to purchase commodities now.[2] Given the current price of commodities, we can calculate the quantity of current commodities this amount of money would buy. Referring again to Figure 6, the household's current income would buy OC $(= Y_t/P_t)$ present commodities and the money it could borrow against its future income would buy CD $[= Y_{t+1}/P_t(1 + r)]$ present commodities. Thus, if the household does all its spending in the present, it could get OD present commodities where

$$OD = \frac{Y_t}{P_t} + \frac{Y_{t+1}}{P_t(1 + r)} \tag{2}$$

Now the line DB represents all the options between current and future commodity consumption available to the household. This line passes through all combinations of present and future commodities the household can enjoy, given its current and expected future income, current and expected future prices, and the interest rate.

If (1) is divided into (2) the slope of this line is seen to be equal to

$$-\frac{P_{t+1}}{P_t(1 + r)} \tag{3}$$

The equation of DB represents current commodity consumption C_t as a function of future commodity consumption C_{t+1} and is equal to

$$C_t = \left[\frac{Y_t}{P_t} + \frac{Y_{t+1}}{P_t(1 + r)}\right] - \frac{P_{t+1}}{P_t(1 + r)} C_{t+1} \tag{4}$$

The intercept in square brackets was obtained from (2) and the slope from (3).

The household's preferences and its budget constraint have been combined in Figure 7. Obviously, the household will maximize its utility if it adopts the present/future commodity consumption pattern represented by R

[2] Let us clarify this briefly. If you borrow against your next year's income Y_{t+1} in order to consume now you could not borrow the full amount, Y_{t+1}, of that income. Why? All you can pay back next year is the amount Y_{t+1} (that is, *all* next year's income). So, if someone loaned you Y_{t+1} now, that is all he would be able to get back from you next year, too. But if he loaned Y_{t+1} in the market he would have $Y_{t+1} + rY_{t+1}$ at the end of one year; clearly more than he receives from you.

How much would he lend you, then? You agree to pay him back Y_{t+1} in one year. In this case, he would lend you now an amount, call it PV, which, with interest accumulated at the market rate would equal Y_{t+1} in one year. The amount he could obtain from the market by loaning PV and waiting for one year is $PV + PVr = PV(1 + r)$. So if we form the equation

$$PV(1 + r) = Y_{t+1}$$

and rearrange we get

$$PV = \frac{Y_{t+1}}{1 + r}$$

where PV is the present value of your next year's income or, equivalently, what you could borrow against it. Frequently, discounted value is used as a synonym for present value.

We shall have more to say about evaluating future income in the next section. This explanation has been very terse.

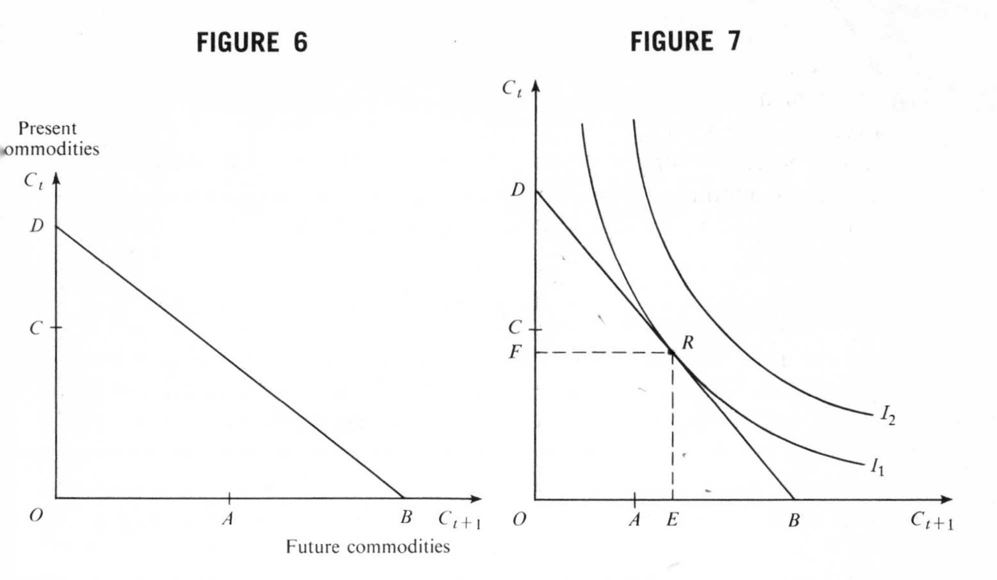

where its budget constraint is just tangent to indifference curve I_1. The household plans to consume OF present commodities and OE future commodities.

Since we have seen above that the household's current income would have purchased OC present commodities and it, in fact, consumes only OF, it must plan to currently save an amount of money equal to $CF \times P_t$ with which it purchases bonds. In the future, the household plans to use its expected future income Y_{t+1} to purchase OA commodities and to cash its bonds plus accumulated interest to buy AE commodities. This household plans to save in the present and dissave in the future. Naturally, AE is greater than CF due to the interest accumulated between the present and the future.

How will present consumption vary when the factors on which it depends vary? We shall make some simplifying assumptions. First, household preferences vis-à-vis present and future commodities are assumed constant; that is, the indifference map does not shift. Second, we assume current and expected future prices are equal. The household expects the current price level to prevail. It has what are called *static price expectations*. If the current price level rises, expected future prices rise in the same proportion. Third, we assume that current and expected future income are the same. The household expects to earn the same income in the future as it does now. Hence, it has *static income expectations*. If its current income rises, its expected future income rises in the same proportion.

Consumption and Income Since we have assumed $P_t = P_{t+1}$ and $Y_t = Y_{t+1}$, the budget constraint equation (4) can be simplified to

$$C_t = \frac{Y_t}{P_t}\left[1 + \frac{1}{1+r}\right] - \frac{1}{1+r} C_{t+1} \tag{5}$$

An interesting feature of this equation is that the slope coefficient has the limiting value of −1 (minus one) when the interest rate is zero. At all positive interest rates the slope of the budget constraint is less than unity in absolute value.

The relevant question now is, how will current consumption change when the parameters of (5) change? We are especially interested in the relationship between current real consumption C_t and current real income (Y_t/P_t), and the relationship between current real consumption C_t and the interest rate r. We deal with the consumption/income relationship first.

Consider Figure 8. If real income rises from $(Y_t/P_t)_1$ to $(Y_t/P_t)_2$, it is apparent that the intercept of (5) rises without a change in the slope. The budget constraint shifts out parallel from DB to $D'B'$ and the household adopts the R' consumption pattern. Its current consumption has risen from OF to OF'. We have, then, a direct relationship between the household's current real consumption C_t and its current real income (Y_t/P_t). Such a relation is plotted directly in Figure 9. (The 45°-line, which has a unit slope, is introduced solely for convenience.) This is the famous *consumption function.* It has been drawn with a slope less than unity. When real income increases, real consumption increases but by a smaller amount. This restriction is apparent from Figure 8. When income increases by $DD' = RT$, consumption increases by $FF' = RU$, which is clearly less than the associated increase in income RT.

It later turns out that the slope of the consumption function has important implications so it is given a special name, which is the *marginal*

FIGURE 8

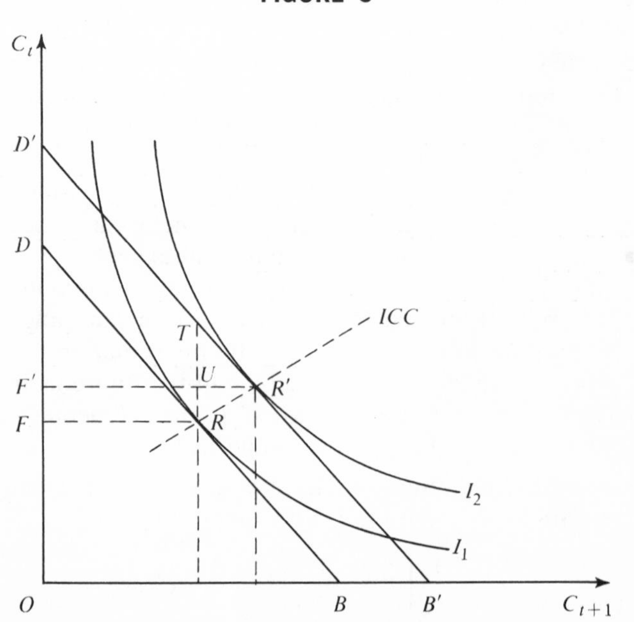

FIGURE 9

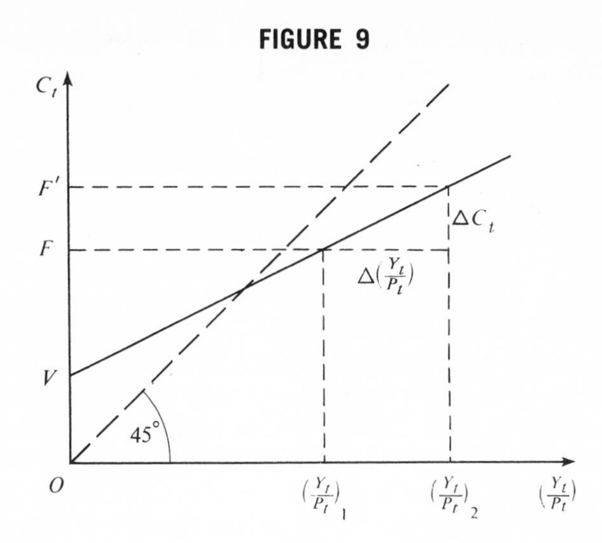

propensity to consume (*mpc*). By definition, the *mpc* is equal to the ratio of the change in consumption associated with a given change in income:

$$\frac{\Delta C_t}{\Delta(Y_t/P_t)} = \text{marginal propensity to consume} \qquad (mpc)$$

This amounts to saying the *mpc* is the change in consumption per unit change in income. By inspection of Figure 9, it can be seen that this ratio is, indeed, equal to the slope of the consumption function. The *mpc* is assumed to be greater than zero and less than unity, $0 < mpc < 1$. It is greater than zero because when income increases so does consumption; it is less than unity because when income increases so does consumption, but not by as much.

The consumption function illustrated in Figure 9 has also been drawn with a positive intercept which indicates that when current income is zero consumption is positive. Again, this can be inferred from Figure 8. If we set current income (Y_t/P_t) equal to zero, then OD, the intercept of the constraint, would simply equal $Y_{t+1}/P_t(1 + r)$, see equation (4). In general this constraint would be tangent to some indifference curve indicating that current consumption is positive, even though current income is zero. In such a situation, the household must be either *borrowing* against its future income or *running down its assets* (if it has any). Both activities are described as *dissaving*. In Figure 9, when current income is zero, consumption equals OV and this is what is being dissaved. With $(Y_t/P_t) = 0$, we have $0 = C_t + S_t$ or $-S_t = C_t$.

We have now effectively identified the relationship between current real consumption and current real income; real consumption and real income are directly related. What of the relationship between current real saving and current real income? This is easily dealt with. Consider Figure 10. We know that current income not consumed must be saved. When income is $(Y_t/P_t)_1 = OA = AC$ (through the properties of the 45°-line), consumption is AB. But the difference between income (AC) and consumption (AB) is saving BC. Similarly, when income is $(Y_t/P_t)_2 = OD = DF$, consumption is DE. The difference between income (DF) and consumption (DE) is saving (EF). It will be seen immediately that saving at various levels of income is always equal to the vertical distance between the consumption function and the 45°-line at that level of income. The quantity $(Y_t/P_t)_b$ is a *break-even* income, i.e., that level of income at which consumption is equal to income and saving is zero.

The relationship between current real saving and current real income, known as the *saving function,* is plotted directly in Figure 11; real income and real saving are directly related, as can be inferred also from Figure 8. When income increases by $DD' = RT$, consumption increases by $FF' = RU$. Therefore, since any increase in income not consumed must be saved, saving increases by TU. The slope of the saving function is described as the *marginal propensity to save* (*mps*). By definition, the *mps* is equal to the ratio of the change in saving associated with a given change in income:

$$\frac{\Delta S_t}{\Delta(Y_t/P_t)} = \text{marginal propensity to save} \qquad (mps)$$

This is equivalent to saying that the *mps* is the change in saving per unit change in income. By inspection of Figure 11, it can be seen that this ratio is, indeed, equal to the slope of the saving function. Since the *mps* is the slope of the saving function, the *mps* is between zero and unity, $0 < mps < 1$. The *mps* is greater than zero because when income increases so does saving; and it is less than unity because when income increases so does saving, but not by as much. This restriction is also implied by Figure 8. When income in-

FIGURE 10

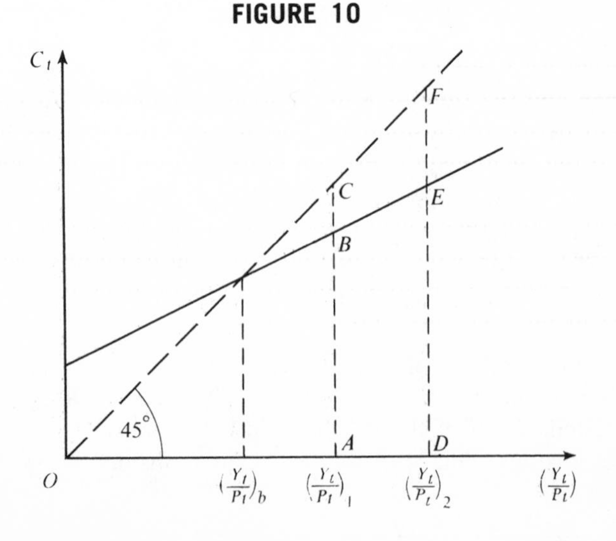

FIGURE 11

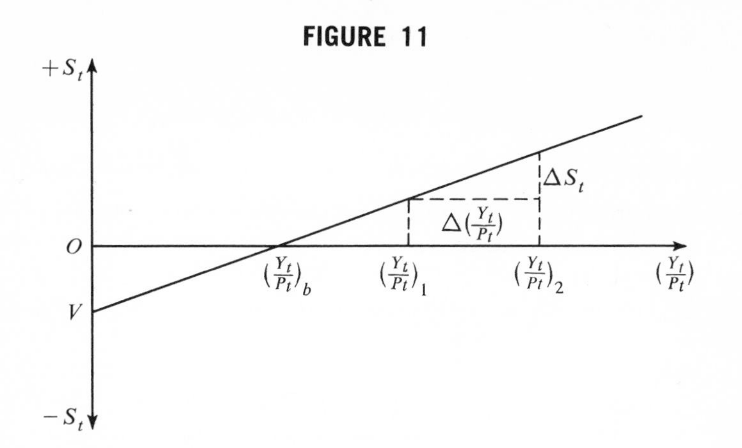

creases by $DD' = RT$, saving increases by TU, which is clearly less than the associated increase in income.

The intercept in Figure 11, OV, is the amount of negative saving, or dissaving, which occurs when current income is zero. It corresponds to OV in Figure 9.

We have seen that both the *mpc* and the *mps* are restricted between zero and unity. It is also easy to show that they *sum* to unity. We know that current real income either must be consumed or saved. Thus,

$$(Y_t/P_t) = C_t + S_t$$

It follows that any change in income must lead to a change in consumption or a change in saving or, in general, a change in both. So,

$$\Delta(Y_t/P_t) = \Delta C_t + \Delta S_t$$

Dividing through by $\Delta(Y_t/P_t)$, we obtain

$$1 = \frac{\Delta C_t}{\Delta(Y_t/P_t)} + \frac{\Delta S_t}{\Delta(Y_t/P_t)} = mpc + mps$$

which is what we wished to prove.

Consumption and the Interest Rate Having established the relationship to be expected between consumption (saving) and income, we now turn our attention to the relationship between consumption (saving) and the rate of interest.

The key to this relationship again lays in the impact of a change in the rate of interest on the budget constraint (5). You will notice that the interest rate appears in both the intercept and the slope of that equation. A decrease in the rate of interest raises both the intercept and the slope (in absolute value) and vice versa. Consider Figure 12. With the original rate of interest r the budget constraint was DB and the household chose the consumption pattern R where it consumed OF and saved CF. (You will recall that the household's current income *could* buy OC commodities, but it chooses only to purchase OF. Therefore it must save the difference FC.)

FIGURE 12

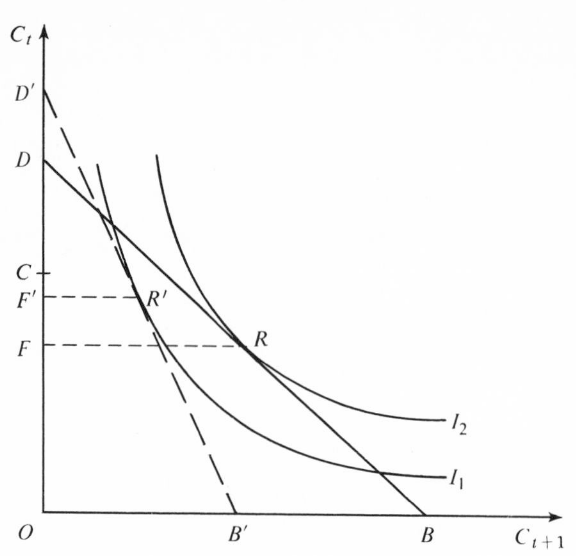

When the interest rate falls to r', the budget constraint shifts to $D'B'$ and the household adopts the consumption pattern R'. Its consumption has increased to OF' and its saving has fallen to CF'. This follows from the fact that its current income *could* still buy the same amount of commodities OC, so if its consumption increases to OF' its saving must fall to CF'.

We have seen then that, other things being equal, real consumption is inversely related to the rate of interest and real saving is directly related to the rate of interest. Typical relationships are plotted explicitly in Figures 13 and 14. Such relationships are *not,* however, inevitable. Depending on the nature of the household's preference map, consumption and saving both may

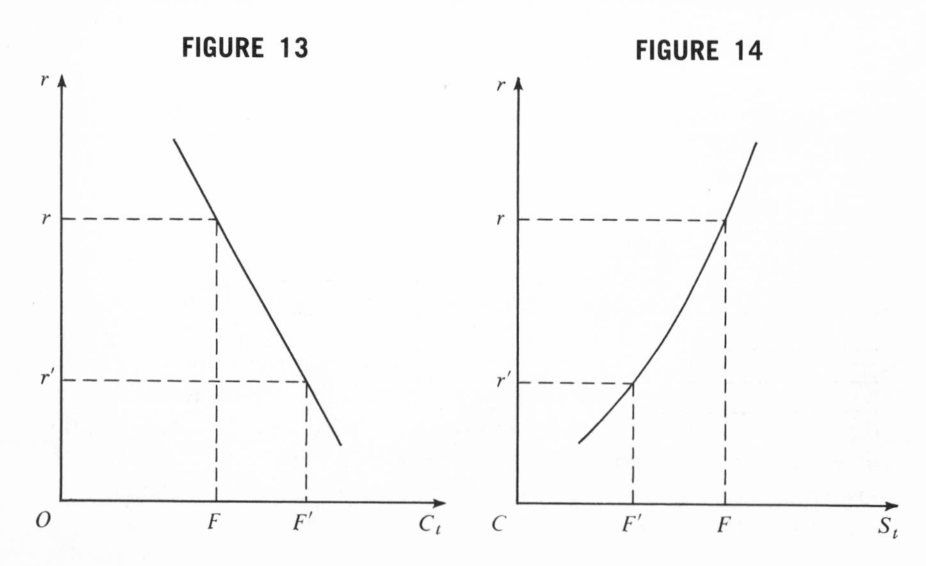

be independent of the interest rate or the relationships illustrated above may be reversed. Consider Figures 15 and 16. In the former, when the interest rate falls and the budget constraint shifts from DB to $D'B'$, the household's consumption pattern switches from R to R'. But at R' its current consumption is still OF and its current saving is still CF, and thus, these variables are independent of the interest rate. In terms of Figures 13 and 14, we would have vertical straight lines in both diagrams. Consumption and saving would be perfectly inelastic with respect to the interest rate. Households whose preference maps generate this sort of situation might be described as *target consumers.* No matter what the interest rate, they are going to currently consume OF. Of course, this means that when the interest rate falls, their *future* consumption will suffer and decline from OE to OE'. This is reasonable since they are buying the same quantity of bonds, which now yield a lower rate of interest. Therefore, the purchasing power they carry over to the future must be less.

In Figure 16, when the budget constraint shifts to $D'B'$ because of the fall in the rate of interest and the consumption pattern adopted switches to R', current consumption actually *falls* from OF to OF' and current saving rises to CF'. Consumption here is directly related to the rate of interest and saving is inversely related to the rate of interest. Thus, the slopes of the curves of Figures 13 and 14 would be reversed; the consumption curve would have a positive slope and the saving curve a negative one. Households whose preference maps generated this sort of outcome might be described as *target savers.* You will notice that they maintain the same level of *future* consumption OE after the interest rate falls. In order to do this, they must save *more* now that the interest rate has fallen and the interest they earn from their bonds is not so large if they are to carry over the appropriate amount of purchasing power. Figures 15 and 16 illustrate, of course, two limiting cases where current consumption and future consump-

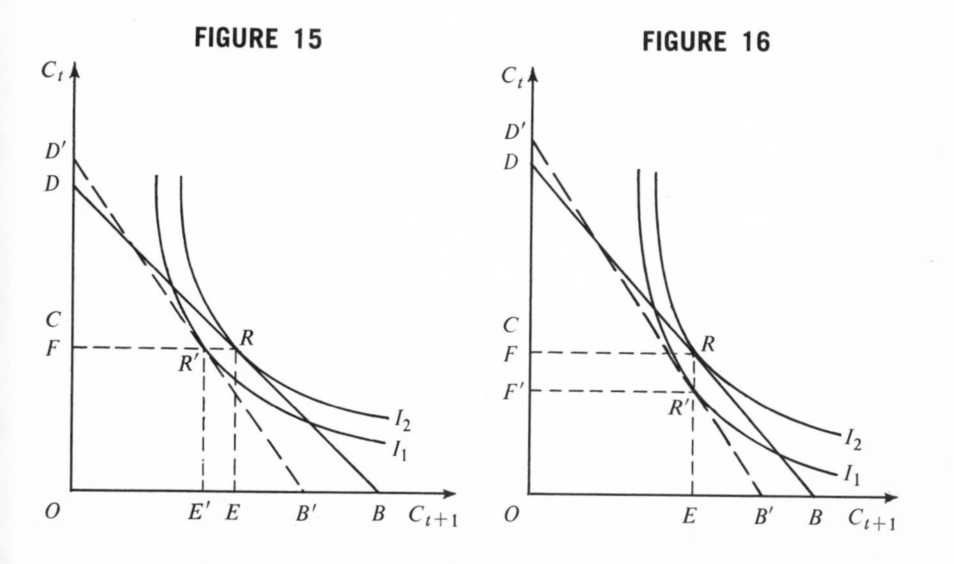

tion, respectively, are constant notwithstanding the interest rate. However, R' can lie anywhere to the lower left of R along $D'B'$ depending on the precise configuration of the preference map.

In general, then, we cannot establish through pure theoretical reasoning what effect a change in the rate of interest will have on consumption and saving. For the most part we shall *assume* that it is as shown in Figures 13 and 14 while bearing in mind, when the need arises, that it may not be.

Consumption and Assets We now wish to examine the influence of assets on consumption. In our model there are two assets: noninterest-bearing money and interest-bearing bonds.

Let us assume M is the nominal value of the transactor's money holdings and B is the number of bonds the transactor holds. The question now presents itself: What is the nominal value of these bonds? To find the answer, we need to know the price of a bond. When we do, we can multiply the number of bonds by their price to find their nominal value.

In our model there is only one type of bond; namely, consols. These bonds are supplied by firms (and, later, the government) and are held by households. As we mentioned briefly in Chapter 1, consols are a special type of security. First, they are perpetuities, which means they have no redemption date. Second, they confer on the holder the right to receive (and, thus, impose on the issuer the obligation to pay) a payment at the *end* of each period (year) fixed in nominal amount. We shall assume that this nominal payment that the holder has the right to receive, and the issuer is obliged to pay, is fixed at one dollar. These fixed one-dollar yearly payments are the *coupon yield* of the bond. Thus, to hold a bond in our model is to hold the title, or right, to one dollar per annum in perpetuity. We must now ask, what would a transactor pay for the right to receive one dollar per annum forever? We need to calculate the value of this income stream

$$\$1.00_1 + \$1.00_2 + \$1.00_3 + \cdots + \$1.00_\infty$$

where $\$1.00_1$ represents one dollar due at the end of one year, $\$1.00_2$ represents one dollar due at the end of two years, . . . and $\$1.00_\infty$ represents one dollar due at the end of an infinite number of years.

What would you pay for one dollar due in one year? Clearly, not one dollar. Why? Because if you took your dollar and loaned it out at the going rate of interest, at the end of one year you would have $\$1.00 + \$1.00 \times r = \$1.00(1 + r)$, which is obviously better than just one dollar. The most you would pay now for one dollar due in one year is an amount PV_1 (dollars) which, if loaned at interest, would be equal to one dollar at the end of one year. You would be indifferent between one dollar at the end of one year and PV_1 now because if you loaned PV_1 now it would itself be worth one dollar in one year. Setting $PV_1 + PV_1 \times r$ equal to $1.00, we can calculate PV_1 when r is known. Thus,

$$PV_1(1 + r) = \$1.00$$

and

$$PV_1 = \frac{\$1.00}{(1 + r)}$$

The amount PV_1 is the *present value* of one dollar due in one year. It is what you would pay for one dollar due in one year. Equivalently, PV_1 is said to be the discounted value of one dollar due in one year, and $(1 + r)$ is the discount factor.

Now what would you pay for one dollar due in two years? Clearly, an amount PV_2 such that, if loaned at interest for two years, it would equal one dollar. Then you would be indifferent between one dollar at the end of two years and PV_2 now, because, if you loaned PV_2 now, it would itself just be worth one dollar in two years. In one year, PV_2 is worth $PV_2 + PV_2 \times r = PV_2(1 + r)$; in two years it is worth $PV_2(1 + r) + PV_2(1 + r)r = PV_2(1 + r)^2$. Thus, if you set $PV_2(1 + r)^2$ equal to \$1.00, you can calculate PV_2 when you know r. Therefore, we have

$$PV_2(1 + r)^2 = \$1.00$$

and

$$PV_2 = \frac{\$1.00}{(1 + r)^2}$$

PV_2 is the present value of one dollar due in two years, or, equivalently, the discounted value of one dollar due in two years. By analogous reasoning, you can show that the present value of (what you would pay for) one dollar due in three years is equal to $\$1.00/(1 + r)^3$; and the present value of one dollar due at the end of an infinite number of years is $\$1.00/(1 + r)^\infty$. [This latter amount is very small since $(1 + r)^\infty$ is very large.] You can see that the present value of one dollar due further and further into the future declines as the discount factors rise.

If you would pay $\$1.00/(1 + r)$ now for one dollar due in one year, $\$1.00/(1 + r)^2$ now for one dollar due in two years, . . . , and $\$1.00/(1 + r)^\infty$ now for one dollar due in an infinite number of years, it should be obvious that the present value of (what you would pay for, or your demand price for) a bond yielding such a stream of income is equal to the *sum* of these present values. That is

$$P_b^d = \frac{\$1.00}{(1 + r)} + \frac{\$1.00}{(1 + r)^2} + \cdots + \frac{\$1.00}{(1 + r)^\infty} \tag{6}$$

where P_b^d (dollars) is the demand price of such a bond. It is already clear from (6) that a household's demand price for bonds will rise when the interest rate falls, and vice versa. But there is an even more interesting relationship. We can show that the demand price of such a bond is a unique function of the interest rate. Multiply (6) by $(1 + r)$ to obtain

$$P_b^d(1 + r) = \$1.00 + \frac{\$1.00}{(1 + r)} + \cdots + \frac{\$1.00}{(1 + r)^{\infty - 1}} \tag{7}$$

Now subtract (6) from (7). The result is

$$P_b^d(1 + r) - P_b^d = \$1.00 \tag{8}$$

from which

$$P_b^d = \frac{\$1.00}{r} \tag{9}$$

This means that the demand price for one of the bonds in our model depends only on the market rate of interest, since its coupon yield is always (by assumption) fixed at one dollar. It is obvious by inspection that the price of bonds rises when the interest rate falls, and vice versa. The price of bonds is merely equal to the reciprocal of the interest rate. Given this unique relationship between the price of bonds and the interest rate, if we know one then we know the other. A numerical example might help here. If the interest rate were 10 percent (0.10 in decimal terms), the price of bonds would be 1/0.10, or \$10.00. If the interest rate *fell* to 5 percent (0.05 in decimal terms), the price of bonds would rise to 1/0.05, or \$20.00.

Now we are armed with the information necessary to calculate the nominal value of a transactor's bond holdings. This is equal to the *number* of bonds he holds B multiplied by the price of one bond $1/r$, which is clearly B/r. (Observe that B is a simple number, since it is merely the number of pieces of paper the individual holds each one of which entitles him to a one-dollar perpetual income stream.) Hence, we now know that the nominal value of a transactor's money holdings are equal to M and the nominal value of his bond holdings are equal to B/r.

As we refer to Figure 17, let us recall from the previous section that the maximum possible current consumption available to the household which has no assets is

$$OD = \frac{Y}{P} + \frac{Y}{P(1 + r)}$$

when we assume $Y_t = Y_{t+1}$ and $P_t = P_{t+1}$. If the household also has M dollars in money and B/r dollars in bonds, it could now acquire an additional M/P commodities if it spent all its money in the current period (= DJ) and an additional B/rP commodities if it cashed all its bonds and spent the proceeds in the current period (=JK). Thus, if it confined its consumption to the current period, the maximum quantity of commodities it could buy would be

$$OK = \frac{Y}{P} + \frac{Y}{P(1 + r)} + \frac{M}{P} + \frac{B}{rP} \tag{10}$$

What if the household went to the opposite extreme and consumed nothing in the current period and deferred all its consumption to the future? We saw in the previous section that the maximum possible future consumption the household which has no assets can enjoy is

$$OB = \frac{Y}{P} + \frac{Y(1 + r)}{P}$$

FIGURE 17

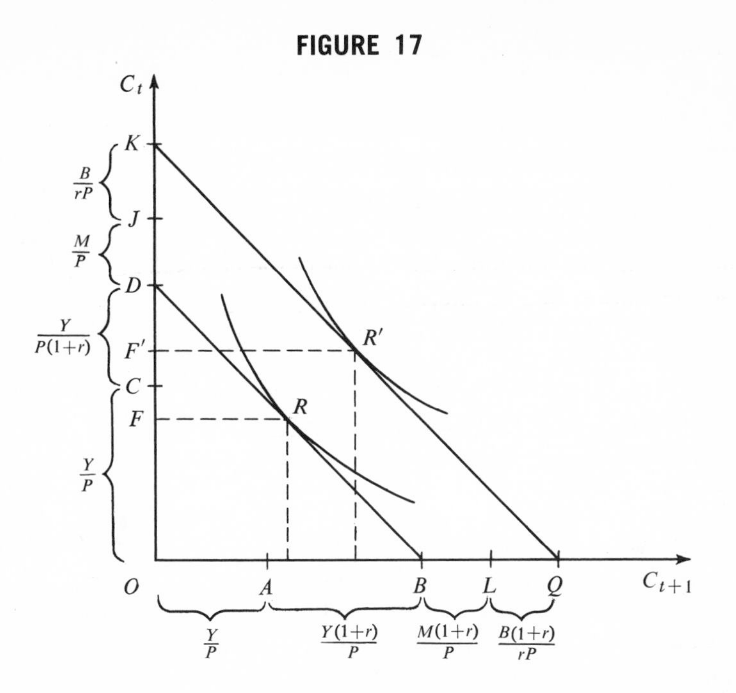

when $Y_t = Y_{t+1}$ and $P_t = P_{t+1}$. Now, though, it can carry its money balance and its bond holdings through to the future as well. If it does so, the money balance will then be worth $M(1 + r)$ dollars and will buy $M(1 + r)/P$ units of commodity in the future (= BL). This assumes that the household converts its money balance into bonds so as to earn interest on them when it decides to carry its money balance over into the future. If it carries all its bonds over into the future, these will be worth $B(1 + r)/r$ dollars and will buy $B(1 + r)/rP$ units of commodity in the future (= LQ).

Thus, if the household confined its consumption to the future, the maximum quantity of commodities it could buy would be

$$OQ = \frac{Y}{P} + \frac{Y(1 + r)}{P} + \frac{M(1 + r)}{P} + \frac{B(1 + r)}{rP} \tag{11}$$

The line KQ represents all the options between current and future commodity consumption available to the household when it has asset endowments of M dollars in money and B/r dollars in bonds. If (11) is divided into (10), the slope of this line is seen to be equal to

$$-\frac{1}{1 + r} \tag{12}$$

which is the same slope for the budget constraint when we assume the household held no assets (and $P_t = P_{t+1}$). All that the inclusion of assets has done, then, is shift the budget constraint out parallel. The complete equation of KQ representing current commodity consumption as a function of future commodity consumption is given by

$$C_t = \left\{\frac{Y}{P}\left[1 + \frac{1}{1+r}\right] + \frac{M}{P} + \frac{B}{rP}\right\} - \frac{1}{1+r}\, C_{t+1} \tag{13}$$

It is clear from (13) that an increase in either M or B increases the intercept and shifts the budget constraint out, and vice versa.

Referring to Figure 17, if initial asset holdings were zero, the consumption pattern adopted is represented by R; if assets are increased by DK, the consumption pattern adopted is R', which involves *increased* current consumption. Notice, too, that this implies *decreased* current saving. Prior to the increase in assets, saving was equal to CF. After the increase, consumption actually exceeds current income and the household is *dissaving* CF'. This, of course, is an extreme exaggeration imposed on us by the exigencies of geometry. But, in general, increased assets will lead to a reduction in saving.

One other phenomenon is worth drawing attention to now that assets have been included among the factors affecting consumption. You will recall from equation (5) and Figure 12 that when assets were *not* included, if the interest rate fell, for example, the intercept and the slope of the budget constraint both increased (in absolute value). When assets are included, we get the same sort of result. If you examine (13), the slope clearly increases in absolute value when r falls. But in this case the intercept increases on two counts. First, the term $1/(1 + r)$ rises; second, the value of the bond portfolio B/rP also rises.

We may summarize our discussion to this point with the following two equations:

$$C = C\left(\frac{Y}{P}, r, \frac{A}{P}\right), \qquad C_1 > 0, C_2 < 0, C_3 > 0 \tag{14}$$

$$S = S\left(\frac{Y}{P}, r, \frac{A}{P}\right), \qquad S_1 > 0, S_2 > 0, S_3 < 0 \tag{15}$$

Equation (14) states that an individual household's real consumption is a function of its real income, the interest rate, and the real value of its asset holdings (real money balance plus real bond holdings, i.e., $M/P + B/rP = A/P$). Both real income and real asset holdings affect real consumption directly, while the interest rate and real consumption are indirectly related. Equation (15) states that an individual household's real saving is a function of the same variables. However, its real saving is directly related to its real income and the interest rate, while its real asset holdings affect its real saving indirectly.

The household consumption function (14) leads straight to the aggregate consumption function (V), which is the fifth equation in our complete macroeconomic model,

$$C = C\left(Y^s, r, \frac{V}{P}\right) \qquad C_1 > 0, C_2 < 0, C_3 > 0 \tag{V}$$

with C now representing *aggregate* consumption, Y^s *aggregate* real income, and V/P real *net* assets. What this last variable is equal to exactly will be explained in §5.4.

Geometrically, equation (V) is illustrated in Figure 18. The solid curve labeled C shows consumption as a function of income for *given* values of r and V/P. If r falls to r' *or* real assets rise to $(V/P)'$ the whole consumption function shifts up to, say, C'; if r rises to r'' *or* real assets fall to $(V/P)''$ the whole consumption function shifts down to, say, C''.

Finally, we should mention how changes in the community's attitude towards "thrift" affect the consumption function. If our collective "tastes" vis-à-vis present and future consumption change in favor of present consumption we are said to have become less thrifty, if they change in favor of future consumption more thrifty. Such a change in tastes for an individual household would, of course, be reflected in its preference map. In terms of Figure 7, less thriftiness would make the indifference curves rotate somewhat counterclockwise, and more thriftiness would make them rotate clockwise. Thus, with an unchanged budget constraint, in the former case the point of tangency P would slide up the budget constraint (more present consumption, less future consumption), and, in the latter case P would slide down the budget constraint (less present consumption, more future consumption).

A change in thrift shows up in equation (V) as a change in the *form* of the function represented by the *functional* C preceding the parentheses. If the community became less thrifty and planned to consume more—even though real income, the interest rate, and real net assets were unchanged—we would write $C' = C'(Y^s, r, V/P)$. Geometrically, in Figure 18, the consumption function would shift up, even though real income, the interest rate, and real net assets were unchanged. Of course, if the community became more thrifty, the opposite would occur.

Alternative Theories of Consumption The consumption function which we shall use throughout the remainder of this book is given by equation (V).

FIGURE 18

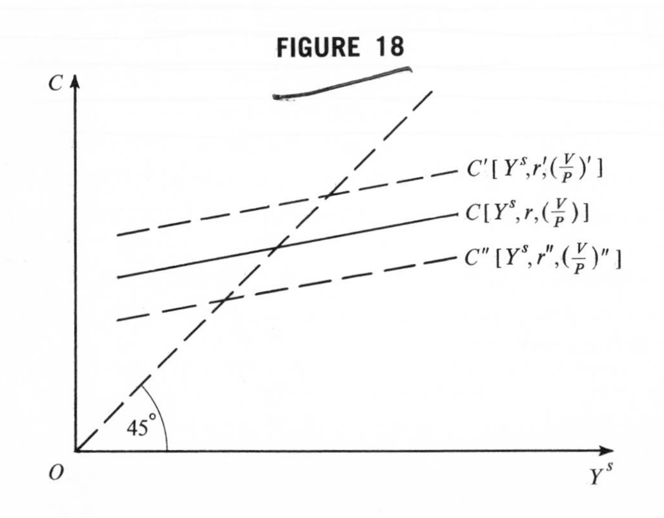

However, the theory of the consumption function has proved to be a very fertile and very controversial field of research and we should indicate that there are a number of other famous theories of household consumption behavior. Of these, we should particularly mention Duesenberry's *relative income* hypothesis; Friedman's *permanent income* hypothesis; Modigliani, Brumberg, and Ando's *life-cycle* hypothesis; and Clower and Johnson's *endogenous income* hypothesis.[3] Although it would have been too complicated to incorporate these alternative hypotheses into the remainder of this book the student may wish to explore them on his own. Because the original sources are often quite difficult, he might like to consult simultaneously either Johnson or Shapiro as a sort of student's guide.[4]

The Demand for Commodities for Investment

The second component of the demand for commodities consists of the demand for commodities to be added to the capital stock, or what is called *investment demand.* This demand for commodities for investment purposes comes from firms. We wish to show that investment is inversely related to the interest rate, directly related to the level of real income, and dependent upon the expectations of entrepreneurs.

Investment and the Interest Rate The *stock* of capital (which, in our simple model, is a *number* of machines) is capable of yielding a *flow* of capital services per time period. The whole stock of capital is not used up in any given time period, only the flow of services yielded by the capital stock in that period. We shall assume that the flow of services from the stock of capital is *proportional* to the stock of capital. Referring to Figure 19, if the stock of capital is K_1, the flow of capital services will be k_1; if the stock of capital is $2K_1$, the flow of capital services will be $2k_1$. Thus, given a certain stock of capital there will be a unique flow of capital services available to a firm.

Now consider the production function of a particular firm illustrated in Figure 20. You will recall that the isoquant Q_1 illustrates the various combinations of capital and labor services which may be employed to produce the level of output Q_1, and similarly for the other isoquants Q_2, Q_3, and so on. Given that any particular level of output can be produced with a variety of factor combinations, what is the best (that is, *least-cost*) way of producing that level? To answer this question, one needs information about the prices of the factors of production; in our model this corresponds to the price of a

[3] See J. S. Duesenberry, *Income, Saving, and the Theory of Consumer Behavior,* Harvard, 1952; M. Friedman, *A Theory of the Consumption Function,* National Bureau of Economic Research, 1957; F. Modigliani and R. Brumberg, "Utility Analysis and the Consumption Function: An Interpretation of Cross-section Data," in S. Harris (ed.), *Post-Keynesian Economics,* Rutgers, 1954; A. Ando and F. Modigliani, "The Life Cycle Hypothesis of Saving: Aggregate Implications and Tests," *American Economic Review,* March, 1963; R. Clower and M. B. Johnson, "Income, Wealth, and the Theory of Consumption," in N. Wolfe (ed.), *Value, Capital, and Growth,* University of Edinburgh, 1968.

[4] See: E. Shapiro, *Macroeconomic Analysis,* 2nd ed., Harcourt Brace Jovanovich, 1970, chapters 9 and 10; M. B. Johnson, *Household Behavior: Consumption, Income, and Wealth,* Penguin, 1970.

FIGURE 19

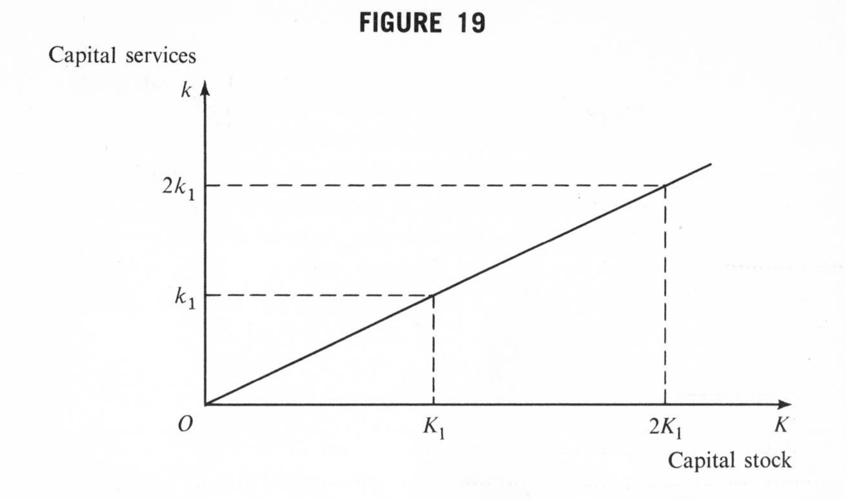

unit of labor services (the wage rate) and the price of a unit of capital services.

What is the price of a unit of capital services? Let us assume that our machines have a useful working life of n years. That is, they yield capital services over an n-year period after which they are worked out and worthless. (Thus we assume they have no scrap value.) Let the price of one of these machines be P_m.[5] This price is determined in the market for machines, which is assumed to be a competitive market. Thus, the price of machines determined there is beyond the control of any one firm. Each firm, then, is a price-taker on the market for machines.

A firm which buys one of these machines either has to borrow the money to pay for it by selling the appropriate amount of bonds on the bond market at the market rate of interest, or it has to use its own money to buy the machine in which case it *foregoes* earning the market rate of interest on that money which it could have earned by buying an equivalent amount of bonds in the bond market. Whichever way you look at it, then, the interest cost *per period* (either explicit or foregone) is equal to the price of the machine times the market rate of interest, i.e., $P_m r$. This is one part of the cost of buying the machine's productive service. But it is not the whole cost.

This machine wears out, or *depreciates,* over its n-year lifetime, and the entrepreneur has to allow for such depreciation when calculating the price of the capital services the machine is yielding him. When the machine eventually wears out after n years the entrepreneur wants to be able to replace it. He wants to have set aside each period an amount of money d which will, at at the end of n years, have accumulated to the replacement price of the machine. Thus, apart from the interest cost per period $P_m r$ already discussed, there is a depreciation cost per period d to be calculated. How do you calculate d?

[5] Since our model is only a one-commodity model (the standard commodity is used for consumption *and* investment) there is only *one* price for commodities. Thus, strictly speaking, P_m and P (the symbol used for the price of commodities) are *always* equal. However, there is some convenience in using the subscript m when we are talking about the price of machines.

FIGURE 20

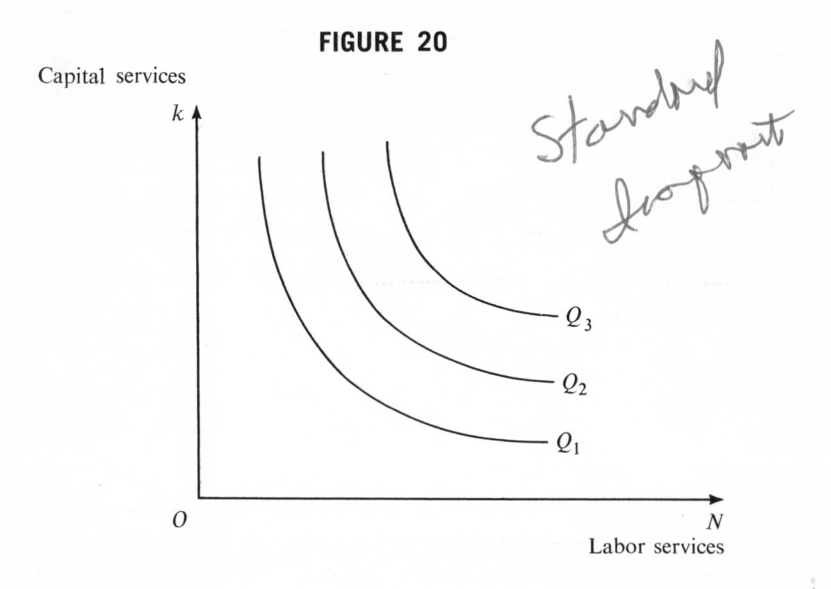

If a sum of money d is set aside each period, this money could be used to buy bonds so that interest would be earned. After n years the value of the bonds held is planned to be equal to the price of the machine. Let us suppose that the sum d is set aside at the end of each period. Thus, the sum d set aside at the end of the first year will earn interest for $n - 1$ years; the sum d set aside at the end of the second year will earn interest for $n - 2$ years, and so on.

Now a sum d loaned for one year will be worth $d + dr = d(1 + r)$ at the end of that year, since $d(1 + r)$ represents the sum loaned plus the interest on that sum. If this sum is loaned for a second year, at the end of the second year it will again earn interest and will be worth $d(1 + r) + d(1 + r)r$. By factoring out $d(1 + r)$, we see this expression is equal to $d(1 + r)(1 + r) = d(1 + r)^2$. By similar reasoning, if *this* sum is loaned for a third year, it will be worth $d(1 + r)^3$ at the end of three years. In general, then, a sum d loaned for n years will be worth $d(1 + r)^n$; if loaned for $n - 1$ years it will be worth $d(1 + r)^{n-1}$; and so on.

We have assumed that the first sum d set aside is loaned at the end of the first year. Thus it will earn interest for $n - 1$ years and will be worth $d(1 + r)^{n-1}$ when the machine is worn out. The sum d set aside and loaned at the end of the second year will only earn interest for $n - 2$ years and will be worth $d(1 + r)^{n-2}$; and so on. If d is set aside and loaned at the end of every year, the *total* sum of bonds accumulated will be equal to

$$d(1 + r)^{n-1} + d(1 + r)^{n-2} + \cdots + d \qquad (16)$$

(Note that the sum d set aside at the end of the last year earns no interest.) Now we wish to set aside each year a unique amount d such that the *total* accumulated at the end of n years is just sufficient to replace the machine. That is, we wish (16) to equal P_m. So setting (16) equal to P_m we obtain

$$d(1+r)^{n-1}+d(1+r)^{n-2}+\cdots+d=P_m \tag{17}$$

Assuming that the life of the machine n, its price P_m, and the interest rate r are known to the entrepreneur, he can solve (17) for d, the depreciation charge per machine per period. The solution may be obtained as follows: Multiply both sides of (17) by $(1+r)$ to obtain

$$d(1+r)^{n}+d(1+r)^{n-1}+\cdots+d(1+r)=P_m(1+r) \tag{18}$$

Now subtract (17) from (18) to obtain

$$d(1+r)^{n}-d=P_m[(1+r)-1] \tag{19}$$

which yields

$$d=\frac{P_m r}{(1+r)^n-1} \tag{20}$$

Expression (20) is the depreciation cost that must be incurred per period if the price of the machine is to be recouped over its working life. If we add to this the interest cost per period $P_m r$ incurred by buying the machine, we obtain

$$P_{cs}=\frac{P_m r}{(1+r)^n-1}+\frac{P_m r}{1} \tag{21}$$

which is equal to

$$P_{cs}=\frac{P_m r(1+r)^n}{(1+r)^n-1} \tag{22}$$

In the above equations P_{cs} is the total price to the firm of the capital services provided by one machine per period. Just as W is the price of the services of one unit of labor per period, so P_{cs} is the price of the services of a unit of capital per period.

The price of capital services is also described as the *rental price* of a unit of capital. It is the amount a firm would have to pay in a competitive market if it hired or rented a machine *from* someone else, or the amount the firm would get if it rented a machine it owned *to* someone else. Also, if the firm owned a machine and did not hire it out to someone else but used it itself, the price is the *implicit* rental price (or opportunity cost) of the services of that machine to the firm. The dimension of P_{cs} is "dollars per machine per time period." To see this, substitute the dimensions of P_m (dollars per machine) and r (a pure number per time period) in (22). As an example, if the price of a machine is \$1,000, the machine has a two-year life, and the interest rate is 0.05, the rental price of the machine would be (approximately) \$540 per time period. This is the price a firm would have to pay per period to get the use of such a machine from its owner, or, if the firm owned the machine, the price it could charge per period for the use of such a machine.

We can divide (22) by the commodity price level to find the real rental price of a unit of capital per time period. This quantity has the dimension of "commodities per machine per time period," since

$$\frac{\dfrac{\$/\text{machine} \cdot \#/\text{time} \cdot \#/\text{time}}{\#/\text{time}}}{\$/\text{commodity}} = \text{commodity/machine/time period}$$

The real rental price of a unit of capital per time period has the nature of a "commodity rate of interest." Since our machines are themselves commodities, what we have calculated is the return in commodities per unit of commodity per time period. Thus, the commodity rate of interest is also frequently described as the "own-rate" of interest. As we saw in Chapter 2, the real wage is the commodity rate of return to labor services per time period; similarly, the real rental price of capital is the commodity rate of return per unit of capital (i.e., per machine or per (capital) commodity) per time period. It is the number of commodities per time period a firm would have to pay to rent a machine from someone or the number of commodities the firm would receive per time period if it rented a machine to someone else.

A perfectly competitive profit-maximizing firm will acquire units of capital (machines) until the real rental price of a unit of capital is equal to the marginal physical product of capital; that is, until

$$\frac{P_{cs}}{P} = MPP_k$$

This follows since, as is well-known, a profit-maximizing firm produces that output where its marginal costs MC equal the price of its product P. That is,

$$MC = P$$

But when the firm varies the amount of capital it owns MC, the addition to costs per unit-increase in output is equal to the cost of a unit of capital's services P_{cs} divided by the marginal physical product of capital MPP_k. So the profit-maximizing condition for a firm is equivalently

$$\frac{P_{cs}}{MPP_k} = P$$

or

$$\frac{P_{cs}}{P} = MPP_k$$

However, we have just seen that the variable on the left-hand side is equal to the real rental price of capital. Thus, a profit-maximizing firm acquires capital until the real rental price of a unit of capital is equal to the marginal physical product of a unit of capital. Intuitively, this seems eminently reasonable. If the MPP_k (which is the addition to output from an extra unit of capital per time period) exceeded the real rental price of capital (which is the commodity cost of an extra unit of capital per time period), a firm would clearly increase its profits (in terms of commodities) by acquiring more capital. By adding capital, it adds more to its output of commodities than it has to pay in commodities to acquire that capital; and vice versa if

MPP_k was less than the real rental price of capital. Clearly, then, the firm benefits by acquiring capital until the addition to output of commodities is equal to what it has to pay in commodities to acquire the services of a unit of capital – no more and no less.

It is apparent that the firm's decision vis-à-vis capital is completely analogous to its decision vis-à-vis labor discussed in Chapter 2. There, you will recall, we found that a profit-maximizing firm hired labor until the marginal physical product of labor MPP_L was equal to the real wage W/P. Now we find that such a firm also acquires capital until the marginal physical product of capital MPP_k is equal to the real rental price of capital P_{cs}/P.

The marginal physical product of capital as a function of the size of the capital stock has been graphed in Figure 21 (for a given labor force $\bar{N}$). MPP_k is inversely related to the size of the capital stock due to diminishing returns. Apart from measuring MPP_k vertically, we can also measure the real rental price of capital P_{cs}/P. If the real rental price of capital is $(P_{cs}/P)_1$, the optimal capital stock will be K_1, since this is where the marginal physical product of capital is equal to the real rental price of capital (which, we have just seen, is the optimum, or profit-maximizing, capital stock). Analogously, if the real rental price of capital falls to $(P_{cs}/P)_2$, the optimum capital stock will rise to K_2. However, $(P_{cs}/P)_1$ and K_1, and $(P_{cs}/P)_2$ and K_2 are price-quantity combinations defining points on the demand curve for capital. But we have just seen they lie along the MPP_k curve. We therefore conclude that the demand curve for capital is *identical* to the MPP_k curve. (In Chapter 2 we also found that the demand curve for labor was identical to the MPP_L curve.)

It is obvious from (22) that the price of the services of a unit of capital per period P_{cs} is dependent upon the price of machines P_m and the interest rate r. By inspection, it is clear that the price of such services increases when the price of the machine increases, and vice versa. However, it is not so

FIGURE 21

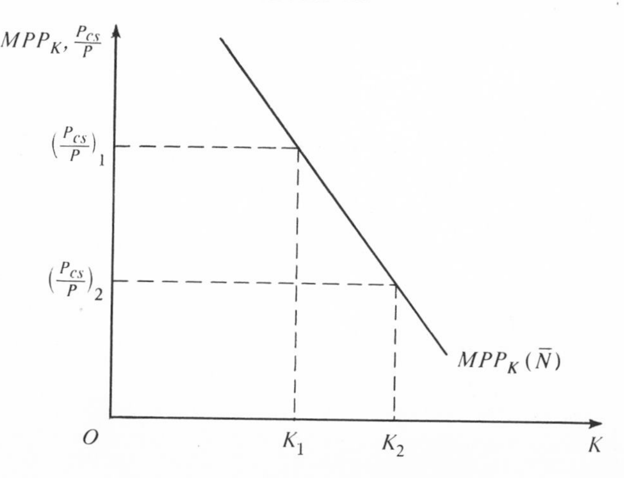

clear how the price of such services varies with r. The derivative of (22) with respect to r is equal to

$$\frac{\partial P_{cs}}{\partial r} = \frac{P_{cs}}{r} - \frac{nP_{cs}}{(1+r)[(1+r)^n - 1]} > 0$$

which, as indicated, is strictly positive.[6] Thus, when the interest rate rises, the price of the services of a unit of capital per period rises, and vice versa.

Since the price of capital services is directly related to the rate of interest and we know (see Figure 21) that the optimum stock of capital is inversely related to the price of capital services, it follows that the optimum stock of capital is also inversely related to the rate of interest. When interest rates rise, the price of capital services rises and the optimum stock of capital falls.

It can be shown that P_{cs} has three interesting limiting values. First, when the interest rate tends toward zero, P_{cs} tends toward P_m/n. There is an appealing intuitive explanation for this. When r is zero the per period interest cost of the money borrowed to buy the machine is clearly zero. Moreover, the sums d put aside to cover depreciation each period also earn no interest. Therefore, the sum d put aside each period should be set equal to the price of the machine divided by its life. Second, when the interest rate tends towards infinity, P_{cs} also tends towards infinity. That is, with very high interest rates the price of the services of a unit of capital per period becomes prohibitively expensive. The intuitive explanation of this is not so obvious, but you might find appealing the suggestion that if r is infinite the per period interest cost of borrowing the money to buy the machine in the first place also will be infinite.[7] Third, when capital never wears out or, equivalently, is infinitely durable, the price of capital services is $P_m r$. The intuitive explanation is quite straightforward. If capital never wears out there is no need to put aside any money to cover depreciation. The only cost associated with acquiring the machine is the interest cost of its purchase $P_m r$. The same result can be obtained formally by dividing the numerator and denominator of (22) by $(1 + r)^n$. We obtain

$$P_{cs} = \frac{P_m r}{\dfrac{(1+r)^n}{(1+r)^n} - \dfrac{1}{(1+r)^n}} = P_m r \text{ as } n \to \infty$$

Clearly, as n tends towards infinity (which is what infinitely durable capital means) the first term in the denominator tends towards 1 and the second term to zero. Thus, the whole expression tends towards $P_m r$.

An interesting relationship that prevails in equilibrium between the bond rate of interest and the marginal physical product of capital is worth exploring and can be illustrated quite simply. Consider a transactor with one dollar. If he is of a mind to acquire an income earning asset for one period,

[6] We omit the rather tedious derivation of this derivative and the proof that it is strictly positive. Those skilled in the calculus may check it out for themselves. It is a tough exercise.

[7] The interested reader may derive these limits formally by appeal to L'Hôpital's rule.

he has two options in our model; he can acquire a bond or a machine. If he acquires a bond, holds it for one period, then sells it, he would have earned r dollars in interest. If, on the other hand, he acquires a machine, holds it for for the period, then sells it, his earnings would be

$$\frac{1}{P_m} P_{cs} - \frac{1}{P_m} d$$

This follows since one dollar purchases $1/P_m$ machines and each such machine earns P_{cs} per period (its rental price). His gross earnings from the machines will, therefore, be $(1/P_m)P_{cs}$. This is the first part of the above expression. However, when he goes to sell the $1/P_m$ machines he has bought, each of them will have depreciated by d. The total depreciation on his machine holdings will, therefore, be $(1/P_m)d$, which is the second part of the above expression. His net return from holding machines is clearly going to be the difference between the gross earnings and the depreciation—which is exactly what we have above. Now for asset holders not to be flooding either the bond market or the machinery market with their money (that is, for equilibrium to exist), it is apparent that what you can get by using one dollar in the bond market for a period must equal what you can get by using one dollar in the machinery market for one period. That is, we must have

$$r = \frac{P_{cs}}{P_m} - \frac{d}{P_m}$$

However, P_{cs}/P_m is the real rental price of capital. In equilibrium we know that this is equal to the marginal physical product of capital MPP_k. In equilibrium then

$$r = MPP_k - \delta$$

where $\delta = (d/P_m)$ and is described as the *depreciation rate*. Thus, in equilibrium, the bond rate of interest is equal to the marginal physical product of capital minus the depreciation rate of machines. In the special case of infinitely long-lived machines (equivalently, nondepreciating), δ is equal to zero because d is equal to zero, and the rate of interest and the marginal physical product of capital are equal.

Now that we have information on the price of capital services and the price of labor services, we are in a position to discuss the manner in which a firm will decide to combine these factors of production to produce any given level of output at least cost.

If a firm employs N units of labor service at W and k units of capital service at P_{cs}, its total costs TC would be

$$TC = WN + P_{cs}k \tag{23}$$

which can be rewritten

$$k = \frac{TC}{P_{cs}} - \frac{W}{P_{cs}} N \tag{24}$$

Our firms are price-takers on *all* markets; therefore, W and P_{cs} (which, remember, is a function of P_m and r) are given constants, or parameters, to the firm. Thus, if we assign an arbitrary constant value to TC, (24) becomes a linear equation in the two variables k and N. The intercept value of this equation is TC/P_{cs} (note that this is a number of units of capital services, since both TC and P_{cs} are denominated in dollars); and its slope is equal to $-(W/P_{cs})$. This linear equation in k and N is plotted in Figure 22. What does the graph show? It shows various combinations of k and N that can be acquired when a given level of costs TC are incurred and the price of labor services and the price of capital services are kept constant at W and P_{cs}, respectively. Manifestly, the curve will have a negative slope because if total cost is held constant at TC, then it follows that if more labor services are hired, less capital services must be used. This common-sense conclusion has already been confirmed by the observation that the slope of this line is equal to $-(W/P_{cs})$. Such lines have special names. They are called *isocost lines.* An isocost line is the locus of capital and labor service combinations which can be employed at any given cost, in this case TC, when the price of the services are constant.

If we are prepared to incur a higher cost, say, TC', we clearly could hire larger quantities of capital and labor at the same prices, P_{cs} and W. What quantities specifically? Clearly, the quantities available to us are shown by the isocost line whose equation is

$$k = \frac{TC'}{P_{cs}} - \frac{W}{P_{cs}} N \tag{25}$$

which differs from equation (24) only in the value of its intercept. The slopes (the coefficient of N) are the same. This isocost line is also shown in Figure 22 by the dashed line.

It now becomes obvious that for any given level of cost we choose to specify there is an associated isocost line. When W and P_{cs} are held constant, these lines will all be parallel. Thus in principle, the space in Figure 22 can

FIGURE 22

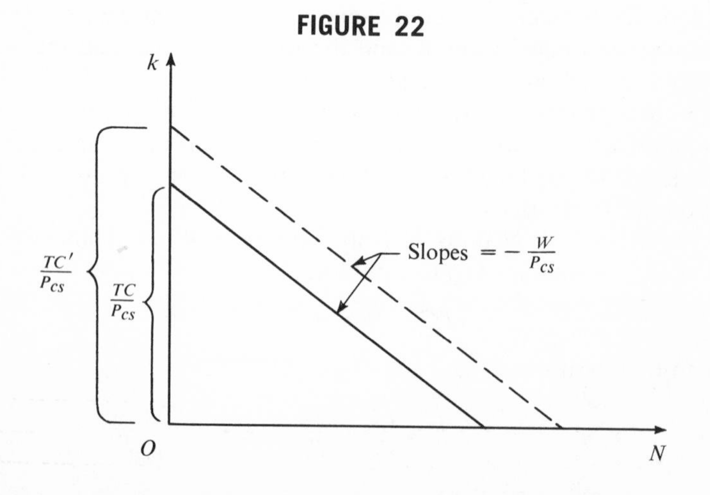

FIGURE 23

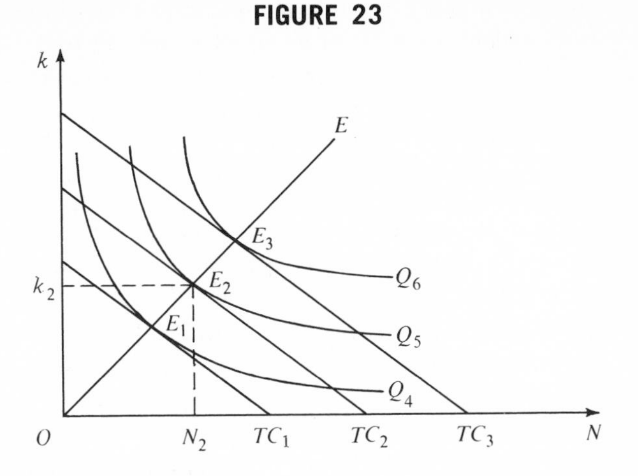

be jammed full of parallel isocost lines—one for each conceivable level of cost we might wish to incur. These lines would be parallel because, for the moment, we are assuming that the price of labor services and the price of capital services are constant, which keeps their ratio and, hence, their slope constant. Naturally, the further away from the origin these parallel isocost lines are, the higher the level of cost they represent.

In principle, too, the space in the production function of Figure 20 is also jammed full of isoquants convex to the origin—one isoquant for every conceivable level of output. A few of these isoquants and some of these isocosts (of the very large numbers of both that exist in principle) have been reproduced in Figure 23. We shall use this diagram to illustrate the answer to the question, what combination of factor inputs should the firms use to produce any particular level of output?

Naturally, the firm should produce any chosen level of output for the least possible cost. Assume, for the moment, that the level of output that the firm has decided to produce is Q_5. What is the least-cost combination of factors that can be employed to produce this output? It is N_2 of labor services and k_2 of capital services, the combination represented by point E_2. Why? Put yourself anywhere you like on the Q_5 isoquant and, by moving along it, see if you can get onto a lower isocost line than that represented by TC_2. You cannot. As you approach E_2 (where the Q_5 isoquant is tangent to the TC_2 isocost) from the lower right, you keep crossing on to lower and lower isocost lines. If you carry on past E_2 along Q_5 you start crossing on to higher and higher isocost lines. It is apparent that the lowest cost at which Q_5 can be produced is where the Q_5 isoquant just touches, or is tangent to, an isocost. This is the point marked E_2. And at E_2 it is seen that K_2 of capital and N_2 of labor are employed.

By analogous reasoning, if Q_6 is to be produced it can be produced at a minimum cost with the combination of factors implied by point E_3. This is the combination of factors at which the Q_6 isoquant is tangent to an isocost line, in this case the TC_3 isocost line. It is now obvious that the least-cost method of producing any output is that method which uses the combination of factor inputs at which the relevant isoquant is tangent to an isocost. All such points have been joined to comprise the curve labeled E which is described as the *expansion path.* Recall that only a few of the isoquants and isocosts have been included in Figure 23 for expository convenience. Thus, there are many more points of tangency not included in the diagram. The expansion path E has been drawn to go through the lot—both included and excluded points of tangency. The expansion path represents the locus of factor combinations from which any level of output can be produced at least cost.

We have seen earlier that the slope of an isoquant is equal to the negative of the ratio of the marginal physical products of the factors, and that the slope of an isocost is equal to the negative of the ratio of the factor prices. However, when the isocosts and the isoquants are mutually tangent, these slopes are equal. Therefore, along E, the locus of all such points of tangency, the following condition holds

$$-\frac{MPP_L}{MPP_K} = -\frac{W}{P_{cs}}$$

and

$$\frac{MPP_L}{W} = \frac{MPP_k}{P_{cs}} \tag{26}$$

Formulation (26) should have intuitive appeal. It states that the least-cost productive process is that where the marginal physical product per dollar spent on labor services is equal to the marginal physical product per dollar spent on capital services. This is an eminently reasonable cost-minimizing rule. Consider the position when this equality does not prevail. Say, for example,

$$\frac{MPP_L}{W} > \frac{MPP_k}{P_{cs}}$$

That is, suppose the marginal physical product per dollar spent on labor services exceeds the marginal physical product per dollar spent on capital services. Obviously, it would pay to transfer expenditure from capital services to labor services. This means you use less capital services and more labor services, or, equivalently, labor services are substituted for capital services. As expenditure is shifted in this fashion, the marginal physical product of labor will fall and the marginal physical product of capital will rise. Thus, sooner or later, equality (26) will come to pass. Referring to Figure 24, assume that the firm is originally in equilibrium at E_1 using N_1 labor services and k_1 capital services to produce output Q_1.

If k_1 is the optimal quantity of capital services this implies that the optimal stock of capital the firm can own is K_1 (see Figure 19). As long as this situation prevails, the firm would keep its capital stock constant at the op-

FIGURE 24

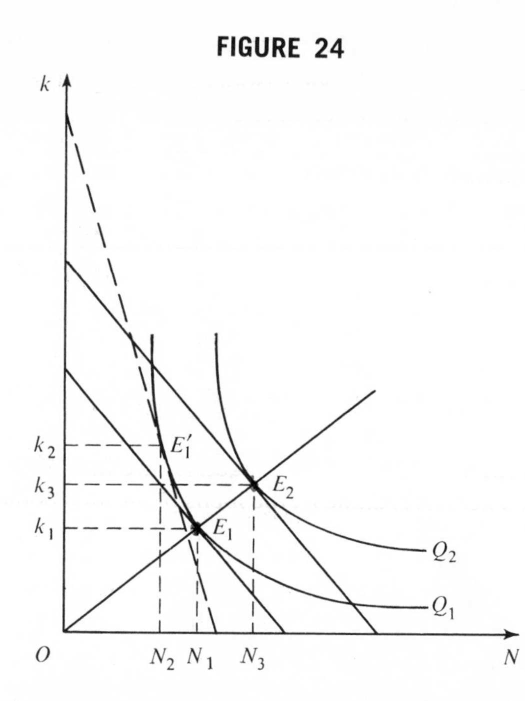

timal level K_1. That is, it would neither add to its capital stock nor allow its capital stock to run down by failing to replace worn-out machines.

Now we must define investment. There are two varieties: gross and net. *Gross investment* is defined as the purchases of capital goods *per time period.* This can be positive or zero. It is zero when purchases are not being made and, thus, worn-out machines are not being replaced. A firm that is trying to reduce its capital stock would undertake zero gross investment and the rate at which its capital stock declines will equal the rate at which its machines are wearing out. A firm that is trying to *maintain* its capital stock would undertake gross investment at the same rate at which its machines are wearing out. Finally, a firm which is trying to increase its capital stock would undertake gross investment which exceeds the rate at which its machines are wearing out. The difference between a firm's purchases of capital goods per time period (gross investment) and the rate at which its machines wear out per time period (depreciation) is defined as its *net investment* per time period. That is,

$$\text{Net investment } (I_n) = \text{gross investment } (I_g) - \text{depreciation } (D) \quad (27)$$

Net investment I_n can be positive, zero, or negative. It is positive if the firm's purchases of capital per time period I_g exceeds the rate at which its capital is wearing out per time period D; it is zero if I_g equals D; and it is negative if I_g is less than D. The maximum negative value of I_n is equal to D, since I_g cannot be less than zero. Net investment is the rate at which the capital stock is changing per time period (it is, therefore, a flow variable). At E_1 in Figure 24, the firm's optimal capital stock is K_1 (implying the level of capital services k_1). As long as things remain the same this firm would be happy with the same stock of capital K_1. Thus, its purchases of machines per time period (gross investment) would be equal to the rate at which they are wearing out per time period (depreciation), and the additions to its capital stock per period (net investment) would be zero. How will this firm react to a change in any of the circumstances on which this equilibrium is predicated? We are particularly interested in the impact of a change in the rate of interest and the level of real income.

We shall consider a change in the rate of interest first. Let us assume that a decrease occurs. When r decreases, the price of capital services decreases, which means the ratio W/P_{cs} rises (in absolute value). Thus, the slope of the isocosts also increases in absolute value; let us assume the new value is illustrated by the dashed lines in Figure 24. With these new isocosts, if the firm were to produce the *same* output Q_1 in the least-cost way, the optimal quantities of labor and capital services that it should employ would be N_2 and k_2. The latter implies that the firm's optimal capital stock would now be K_2. When it has achieved this new optimum, the firm's net investment would again be zero, since it would merely continue to replace its capital stock as it wore out. That is, its gross investment would be equal to the rate of depreciation. Thus, it is apparent that *although the size of the optimal capital stock for a firm is inversely related to the rate of interest, the level of net investment is not*. In equilibrium, net investment is zero at both the original interest rate and the new interest rate. Consequently, at the level of the comparative static theory of the individual firm a function relating the rate of net investment to the rate of interest *does not* exist. Nonetheless, we shall proceed to show that *although the individual firm's net investment is independent of the rate of interest, the level of aggregate, economywide investment is inversely related to the rate of interest in the short run.*

To show this, we will change the direction of our approach slightly. Consider Figure 25. The solid curve labeled D_m shows the quantity of machines that a firm would want to own at various prices (at a given rate of interest r_1). Note that the price of a unit of capital (one machine) is plotted vertically; this does *not* denote the price of a unit of capital services. The curve D_m slopes down from left to right indicating that more machines would be held at the lower prices, and vice versa. There are at least two reasons why this should be so. First, a lower machine price means a lower price of capital services and, as we have seen, this encourages a more capital-intensive production process. Capital is substituted for labor when the price of capital declines. Because of diminishing returns, the marginal profitability of additional capital falls as the number of machines held increases. Thus, if more machines are to be held, their price must fall. Second, when additional machines are installed some disruption of the production process is likely. These disruption costs can be offset, and the installation made, if the price of machines is lower.

Having rationalized the slope of this demand curve, we ask on what will its position depend? To answer this question, we need to discuss the factors

FIGURE 25

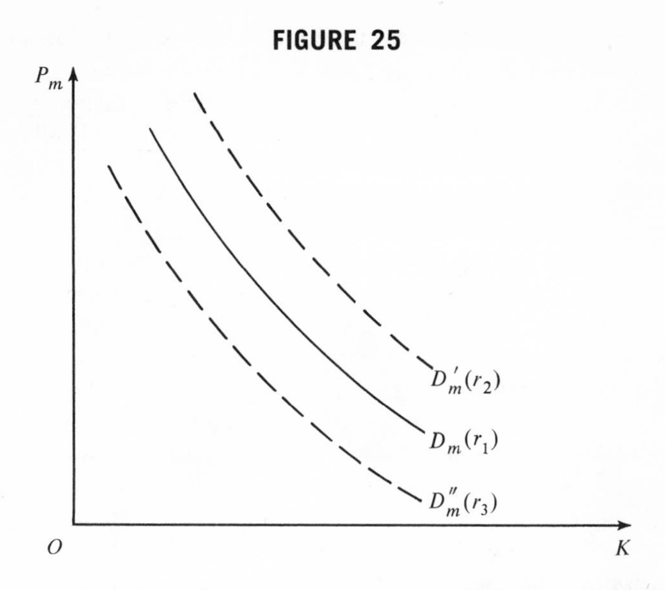

which influence the firm's demand price for machines (or, in other words, what determines the amount a firm would pay for a machine). Machines do not yield income in only one period, they yield a *stream of income* over several periods. If they have an n-year life, they yield a stream of income lasting n years. Let a machine have a net yield of R_1 (dollars) in year one, R_2 in year two, . . . , and R_n in year n. These net yields are obtained by subtracting all the operating costs (for example, labor costs, raw material costs, capital service charges, and so on) from the gross revenue obtained by selling the machines' output. The question reduces, then, to discovering what a firm would pay for the following n-year stream of income:

$$R_1 + R_2 + R_3 + \cdots + R_n$$

We shall assume that these net yields all appear at the *end* of each year.

When we discussed the calculation of a household's demand price for bonds earlier in this chapter, we found that one dollar due in one year had a present value of $1/(1 + r)$, one dollar due in two years had a present value of $1/(1 + r)^2$, . . . , and so on. It should be immediately obvious, then, that R_1 (dollars) due in one year has a present value of $R_1/(1 + r)$, R_2 due in two years has a present value of $R_2/(1 + r)^2$, . . . , and so on. Consequently, the present value of (what you should pay for) a machine yielding such a stream of income is equal to the *sum* of these present values, that is,

$$P_m^d = \frac{R_1}{(1+r)} + \frac{R_2}{(1+r)^2} + \cdots + \frac{R_n}{(1+r)^n} \qquad (28)$$

Demand Price

where P_m^d (dollars) is the demand price of such a machine. It is clear from (28) that a firm's demand price for machines will rise when the interest rate falls, and vice versa. Referring back to Figure 25, if the interest rate falls to r_2, the firm's demand curve for machines shifts up to the right to D'_m; if the interest rate rises to r_3, the firm's demand curve for machines shifts down to the left to D''_m. These shifts in the demand curve for machines which occur when the interest rate changes merely reflect the fact we established before—the optimal capital stock rises when the interest rate falls and falls when the interest rate rises.

Now in Figure 26(a), the curve labeled D_m has been obtained by horizontal aggregation of the demand curves for machines of *all* individual firms (of which D_m in Figure 25 is typical) when the interest rate is r_1. Similarly, D'_m and D''_m in Figure 26(a) are obtained by horizontal aggregation of all individual firms' demand curves for capital where the interest rate is r_2 and r_3, respectively. Thus, these demand curves show the aggregate demand for capital at various interest rates. Now, in the short run, the supply of machines in existence is fixed at $\bar{K}$. This is illustrated by the perfectly inelastic supply curve at that stock of capital. In Figure 26(b) the supply curve of the capital good–producing industry is illustrated by S.[8] All firms producing capital goods are assumed to be perfect competitors. It is well known that the supply curve of a perfectly competitive *firm* is identical to its marginal cost curve (above minimum average variable cost) and that the *industry* supply curve is obtained by horizontal aggregation of these individual firm supply curves. Thus, if all firms produce under conditions of increasing marginal costs (as they do, by assumption), the industry supply curve will be upward sloping just like the individual marginal cost curves. The curve labeled S in Figure 26(b) represents the quantities of *new* machines that the capital good–producing industry will be willing to supply per time period at various prices for their product P_m. The output of new machines per time period is, by definition, gross investment I_g and the horizontal axis in Figure 26(b) has been so labeled.

Let us assume that the initial interest rate is r_1 and that all firms are in equilibrium at points such as E_1 in Figure 24. The aggregate demand for capital is shown by D_m in Figure 26(a), and the price of machines will be P_m. In equilibrium, net investment is zero, and gross investment is equal to the rate at which machines are wearing out. Thus, the output of the capital good industry is equal to this rate, or I_g in Figure 26(b). Figure 26(c) shows the level of net investment I_n (which may be positive or negative) at various interest rates. In the initial equilibrium position when the interest rate is r_1 no firms plan to change their capital stock, so I_n is equal to zero.

Now assume that the interest rate falls to r_2. The optimal factor combination for firms is now E_2 (in Figure 24). Hence, firms plan to add to their stock of capital. The aggregate demand curve for machines shifts to D'_m. But, in the short run, the supply of machines in existence is fixed at $\bar{K}$. Thus, an excess demand for machines prevails at P_m, and the price of machines is bid up to P'_m. At this price for its output, the capital good–producing industry is willing to produce I'_g new machines and this is the rate at which

[8] Although *all* firms in our model produce the *same* commodity it is convenient to assume that some produce it for consumption and others produce it for firms to invest. By this arrangement we can speak about a "capital good–producing industry."

FIGURE 26

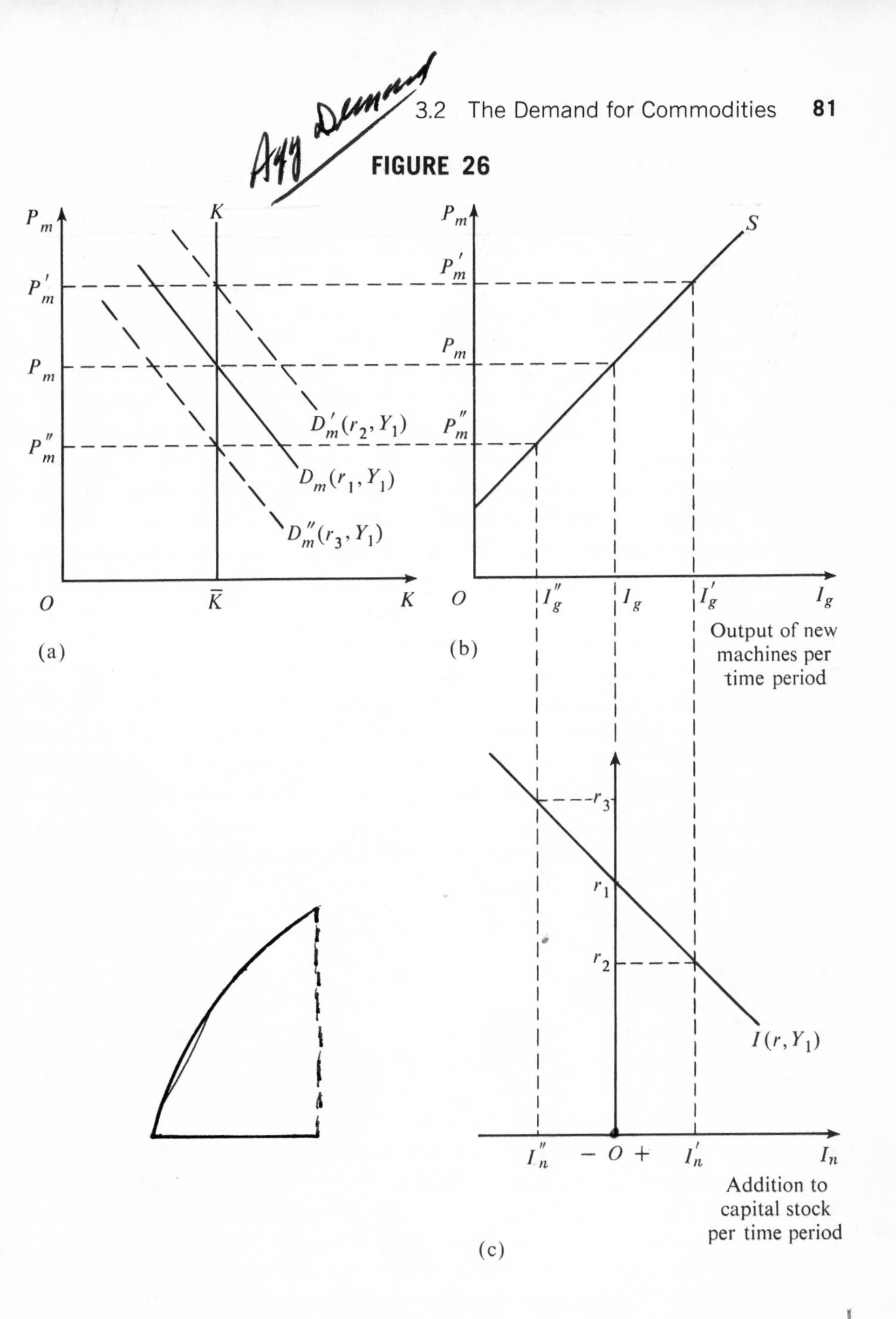

gross investment proceeds. This rate of gross investment implies the rate of net investment I'_n. *The interest rate has fallen and net investment has risen.* We now emphasize three very crucial points.

1. When the interest rate changed, all firms' optimal capital stocks became K_2 and this is what they aimed for. However, simply knowing what the new optimal capital stock is does *not* tell us anything about the *rate* at which firms will acquire new capital per period to achieve the optimum. There is

nothing in the comparative static theory of the firm that tells us what the optimal rate of net investment at various interest rates is. The actual rate at which investment proceeds depends upon supply conditions in the capital good-producing industry. The output of new machines was I'_g when the interest rate fell to r_2 because that is the rate of output which the capital good-producing industry is willing to supply at P'_m.

2. Throughout this analysis we have assumed that the actual stock of capital is fixed at $\overline{KK}$. But the reader undoubtedly has observed that if net investment is occurring at the rate I'_n the stock of capital *must* be increased by a like amount. This is certainly true. However, we have assumed, and shall continue to assume, that the existing stock of capital is large relative to the rate at which net investment is occurring, so that in the short run the stock of capital is, for all practical purposes, fixed at $\overline{KK}$.

Nonetheless, the reader may still be interested in what happens if we lengthen our time horizon and follow the process of adjustment to the point where the new optimal stock of capital has been acquired. We shall do this *only* for interest's sake. After this exercise is through, we shall revert to the short run where we take the capital stock to be fixed at $\overline{KK}$.

Consider Figure 27. When the interest rate falls from r_1 to r_2, the first-period gross investment and net investment occur at the rates I'_g and I'_n, respectively. Thus, at the end of the first period the capital stock has increased to KK'. This lowers the price of machines to P''_m. As a result, in the second period, even though the interest rate is unchanged at r_2, gross and net investment proceed at the rates I''_g and I''_n, respectively.

At the end of the second period the capital stock has increased from $K'K'$ to $K''K''$ (a shift equal to I''_n). Thus, the price of machines will fall to P'''_m, and gross and net investment will proceed in the third period at the rates I'''_g and I'''_n, respectively. In Figure 27(c) the I' curve has shifted to I''. The analysis continues along these lines with P_m falling and I_g and I_n occurring at lower and lower rates until the new optimal capital stock K^*K^* is acquired. The new equilibrium price of machines will be P^*_m and gross investment will equal I^*_g. This new equilibrium level of gross investment I^*_g is greater than the original equilibrium level of gross investment I_g because the new equilibrium stock of capital K^*K^* is higher than the original equilibrium stock of capital $\overline{KK}$ and, thus, depreciation will be higher. This implies a higher rate of gross investment for replacement purposes. For the capital good industry to produce this higher output the final equilibrium price of machines P^*_m must exceed the original equilibrium price of machines P_m. When the new equilibrium stock of capital K^*K^* prevails, net investment again must be zero. Thus, the vertical axis in Figure 27(c) now must be relocated directly under I^*_g. This has been shown by shifting the whole axis to the right.

A major point of this discussion is that although a reduction in the interest rate leads to an increase in net investment in the short run (as we saw earlier), in the long run net investment is zero *no matter what the interest rate*. This serves to drive home the idea that if we rely on an inverse relation-

FIGURE 27

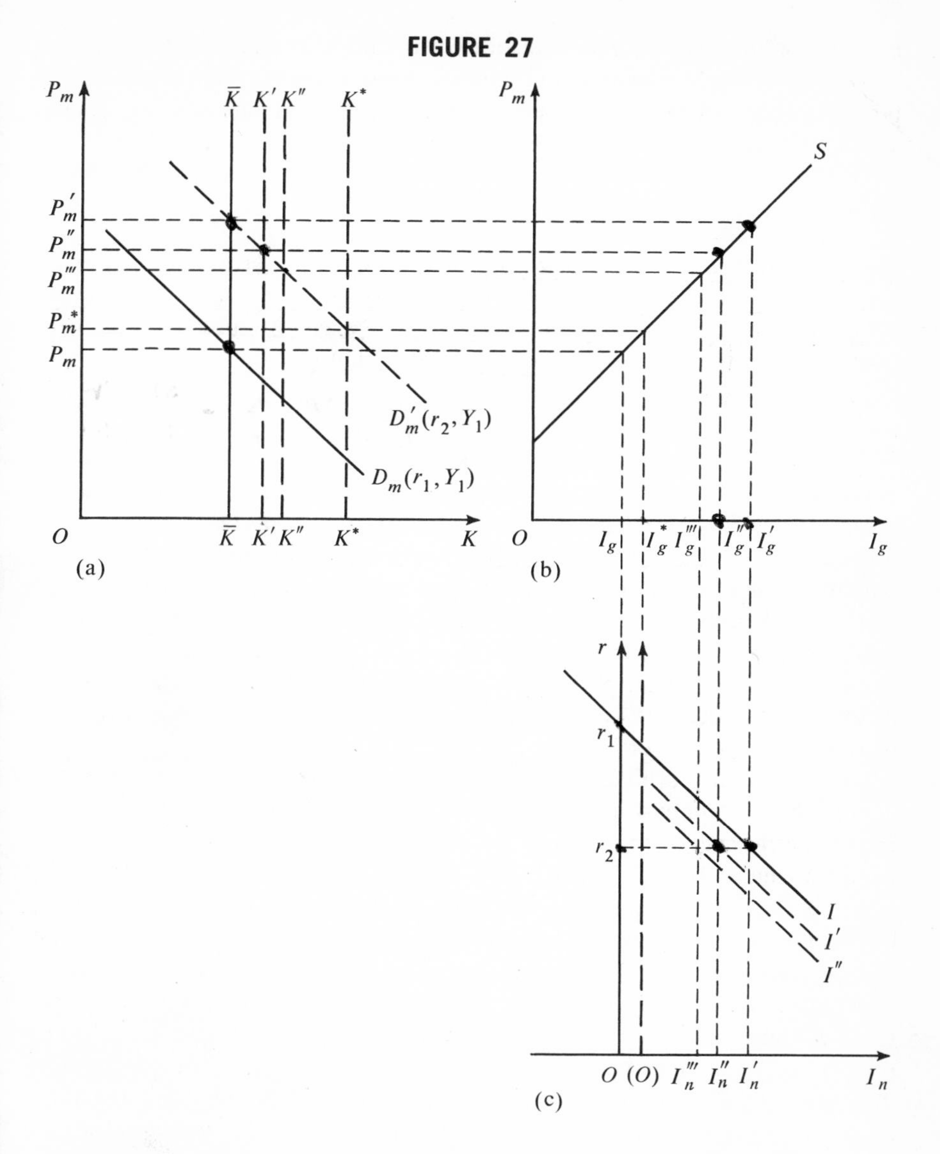

ship between the interest rate and net investment, we must restrict ourselves to the short run.

So far we have considered only the impact on investment of a reduction in the interest rate. We showed that in the short run a fall in the latter variable induces a rise in the former. Analogously, it can be shown that, ceteris paribus, a rise in the interest rate which occurs when all firms are in equilibrium will cause a reduction in the optimal capital stock, a fall in the price of machines, and a fall in gross investment, so that net investment becomes negative and the capital stock is reduced to the new lower optimum level.

3. At several points throughout the rest of this book we shall have occasion to discuss the responsiveness of investment to changes in the rate of

interest, or the interest elasticity of investment $e(I, r)$. It is in order to say something about it now. The interest elasticity of investment is, by definition, the proportional change in investment associated with a given proportional change in the interest rate. Symbolically,

$$e(I, r) = \frac{(\Delta I/I)}{(\Delta r/r)} = \frac{\Delta I}{\Delta r} \cdot \frac{r}{I}$$

According to the theory we have just developed, this interest elasticity is the product of two other elasticities: the elasticity of the demand price of machines with respect to the interest rate and the elasticity of investment with respect to changes in the price of machines. That is,

$$e(I, r) = \frac{\Delta I}{\Delta r} \cdot \frac{r}{I} = \left(\frac{\Delta P_m}{\Delta r} \cdot \frac{r}{P_m}\right)\left(\frac{\Delta I}{\Delta P_m} \cdot \frac{P_m}{I}\right) \qquad (29)$$

(You will observe that appropriate cancellations on the right-hand side of (29) reduce it to the left-hand side.) Thus, the interest elasticity of investment depends (directly) on these two other elasticities. In terms of our diagrammatic analysis, a large elasticity of the demand price of machines with respect to the interest rate [the first part of the right-hand side of (29)] means that the demand curve in Figure 26(a) is very sensitive to changes in the interest rate. Thus, small changes in that rate bring about large shifts in the position of the demand curve and, consequently, large changes in the price of machines. The reverse occurs if this elasticity is small.

The elasticity of investment with respect to changes in the price of machines [the second part of the right-hand side of (29)], is simply the elasticity of the supply curve of the capital goods–producing industry, i.e., the supply curve in Figure 26(b).

Clearly, for investment to be elastic with respect to the rate of interest, the demand curve in Figure 26(a) should be responsive to changes in the rate of interest, *and* the supply of machines from the capital goods–producing industry should be elastic. Conversely, investment will be inelastic with respect to the rate of interest if *either* the demand curve in Figure 26(a) is unresponsive to changes in the rate of interest *or* the supply of machines from the capital goods–producing industry is inelastic. It is quite probable that the reader arrived intuitively at such conclusions during the earlier discussion of Figure 26.

Can we say anything a priori about these two component elasticities of the interest elasticity of investment? Consider the elasticity of the supply of capital goods first. This obviously depends on the cost conditions in the industry. If diminishing returns set in rapidly, marginal costs rise fast and the supply curve will be inelastic, and vice versa.

Now let us examine the elasticity of the demand price of machines with respect to the interest rate? One factor that is crucial in this analysis is the lifetime of machines. This may be illustrated by an example. Consider two machines that both have net returns each period of 10 dollars, but let machine 1 have a life of just two years while machine 2 has an infinitely long life. If the interest rate is 5 percent the demand prices of these two machines will be

$$\text{machine 1} \qquad P_m^d = \frac{10}{1.05} + \frac{10}{(1.05)^2} \approx \$18.60$$

$$\text{machine 2} \qquad P_m^d = \frac{10}{.05} = \$200$$

These demand prices can be obtained by solving equation (28) after substituting the properties of the given machines. However, the demand price for machine 2 is obtained even more simply. Since it has an infinite life, it is just like a perpetual consol bond with a 10-dollar coupon rate. We learned earlier in this chapter that the demand price for a perpetuity with a 1-dollar coupon rate is $1/r$. Analogously, the demand price for a perpetuity with a 10-dollar coupon rate is $10/r$.

Now let us double the interest rate to 10 percent keeping everything else the same. The demand prices of the two machines become

$$\text{machine 1} \qquad P_m^d = \frac{10}{1.10} + \frac{10}{(1.10)^2} \approx \$17.40$$

$$\text{machine 2} \qquad P_m^d = \frac{10}{.10} = \$100$$

We see that a 100 percent change in the interest rate has had a very small effect on the demand price of the short-lived machine and a very large effect on the demand price of the long-lived machine. Specifically, the elasticities of the demand price of the two machines with respect to the interest rate can be calculated from the formula $(\Delta P_m/\Delta r)(r/P_m)$. We find

$$\text{machine 1} \qquad \frac{-1.20}{.05} \times \frac{.05}{18.60} \approx -0.06$$

$$\text{machine 2} \qquad \frac{-100}{.05} \times \frac{.05}{200} \approx -0.5$$

Thus, the elasticity of the demand price of the long-lived machine with respect to the interest rate is about eight times as large as the elasticity for the short-lived machine, even though the only difference between the two machines is in the length of their lives. We may conclude, therefore, that the interest elasticity of investment will depend crucially on the length of the useful life of capital. If capital is short-lived, the interest elasticity of investment will inevitably be small; if capital is long-lived, the interest elasticity of investment may be large. (We only say "may be" because this elasticity also depends on the supply elasticity of machines from the capital goods–producing industry.)

One argument frequently advanced to suggest that the interest elasticity of investment is generally on the low side is the following. It is argued that entrepreneurs have a "fixed payoff period" in mind for machines which is short, notwithstanding that the physical working life of the machine may be long. In effect, entrepreneurs arbitrarily truncate the R_i stream in equation (28) at some fixed (and fairly short) period, say, between 5 to 10 years. The justification advanced is that estimates made beyond such a period are so clouded by ignorance and uncertainty that they are useless. Demand conditions might change, machines might become technologically obsolescent, and a host of other developments could occur to make estimates of the R_i more than 5 to 10 years into the future fall hopelessly wide of the mark. Consequently, entrepreneurs do not make them. In effect, capital is assigned a short *economic* life even though its *physical* life may be much longer. If such a procedure is followed by entrepreneurs, de facto, all capital becomes short-lived. And this, we know, lowers the interest elasticity of investment, ceteris paribus.[9]

Investment and the Level of Income We now wish to establish the relationship between investment and the level of income, ceteris paribus. Assume that factor prices are constant and that their ratio is such that the solid isocost curves in Figure 24 prevail. Moreover, assume that the firm's optimal output is Q_1. Thus, it will utilize N_1 units of labor service and k_1 units of capital service (implying that its optimal capital stock is K_1). As long as nothing disturbs this equilibrium, the firm's net investment is zero and its gross investment equals the rate at which its machines are wearing out, so that its capital stock is kept at the optimal level K_1.

Now let the firm's optimal output rise to Q_2, ceteris paribus. As we already know, an increase in the output of all firms is equivalent to an increase in the supply of commodities or an increase in real income. When a single firm's output is Q_1 the aggregate level of real income is Y_1^s; when a single firm's output is Q_2 the aggregate level of real income is Y_2^s. With no change in factor prices, the solid isocost lines continue to apply, and firm's least-cost factor combination becomes N_3 and k_3. The increased input of capital services k_3 implies the new, higher optimal capital stock K_3. Once this larger cap-

[9] We may conclude this section by explaining why we have said that the elasticity of the demand price of machine 2 with respect to the interest rate calculated above is only equal to −0.5 "approximately." This is due to the discrete nature of that calculation. In the limit, the interest elasticity of the price of a perpetuity (whether bond or machine) is *always* equal to −1.0. This can be seen as follows for machine 2:

$$P_m^d = \frac{10}{r}$$

and

$$\frac{\partial P_m^d}{\partial r} = -\frac{10}{r^2}$$

But the limiting value of the elasticity of the demand price with respect to the interest rate is by definition

$$\frac{\partial P_m^d}{\partial r} \cdot \frac{r}{P_m^d} = -\frac{10}{r^2} \cdot \frac{r}{(10/r)} = -1.0$$

The reader may wish to prove to himself that the elasticity of the demand price of the perpetual consol bonds in our model is also equal to −1.0.

ital stock has been acquired (through net investment), it will be maintained. Thus, gross investment will equal depreciation and net investment will fall to zero. As in the case of a change in the interest rate, then, we see that *for the individual firm the level of net investment is independent of the level of output*. In equilibrium, net investment is zero when output is Q_1 (and real income is Y_1^s), and net investment is also zero when output is Q_2 (and real income is Y_2^s). Just as we showed that there is nothing in the comparative static theory *of the firm* indicating a functional relationship between the rate of interest and the rate of investment, we have also shown that there is nothing in that theory indicating a functional relationship between the level of output and the rate of investment.

However, there was a short-run relationship between the rate of interest and aggregate investment. We shall show now that there is a similar short-run relationship between aggregate real income and aggregate investment. In Figure 28(a), the curve $\overline{KK}$ shows the stock of capital in existence which is the equilibrium stock when income is Y_1. The original aggregate demand curve for capital when the interest rate is r_1 and real income is Y_1^s is shown by D_m. The price of capital is P_m. At this price, the output of new machines is I_g, which is just equal to the rate at which machines are wearing out. Thus, net investment is zero and the capital stock is maintained constant at $\overline{KK}$.

Now when real income rises to Y_2^s, all firms wish to add to their capital stock because they want to achieve the new optimal capital stock K^*. The aggregate demand curve for capital shifts right to D_m'. Referring to equation (28), the demand price for machines has risen because the R_i have risen because of the increased demand for the firms' products resulting from the rise in income. This forces the price of machines up to P_m' and induces the capital good–producing industry to increase its output to I_g'. Gross investment proceeds at this rate, and net investment proceeds at the rate I_n'. *Thus, a rise in income has led to a rise in the level of net investment in the short run*. Clearly, the larger the rise in real income, the larger the rise in P_m and the larger the rate of gross and net investment which generates a curve like that labeled I in Figure 28(c).

In the long run, the additions to the capital stock caused by positive I_n will progressively shift $\overline{KK}$ towards K^*K^*. This will lower P_m and lead to progressively lower rates of gross and net investment as the new optimal capital stock K^*K^* is approached. An analysis along these lines (omitted here) would proceed in exact analogy to the long-run adjustment discussed when the rate of interest fell (see Figure 27 and its accompanying discussion). However, as we have mentioned many times before, we shall only utilize our model in a short-run context and, therefore, bypass the long-run adjustment. The interested reader can grind it out for himself.

Our discussion of the factors influencing the *aggregate* level of demand for commodities for investment purposes in the short run can be summarized algebraically by

$$I = I(Y^s, r), \qquad I_1 > 0, I_2 < 0 \tag{VI}$$

FIGURE 28

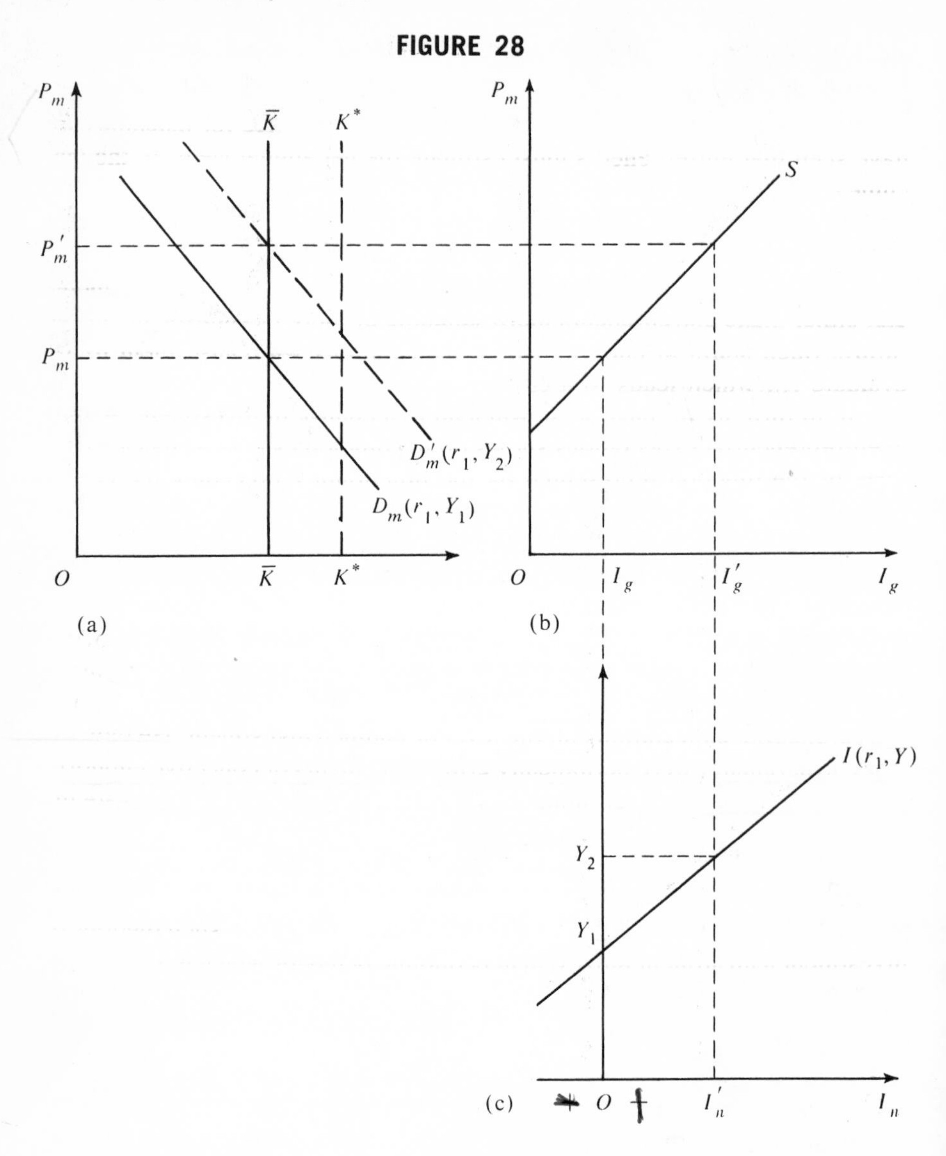

which is the sixth equation in our complete macroeconomic model. Investment is directly related to the level of real income and indirectly related to the level of the interest rate.

Equation (VI) is illustrated geometrically in Figure 29. When income is Y_1^s, net investment will be I_n if the interest rate is r_1. If the interest rate falls to r_2, net investment will rise to I_n', even though income remains at Y_1^s; if the interest rate rises to r_3, net investment will fall to I_n'', even though income remains at Y_1^s. In short, reductions in the interest rate cause the whole curve to rise, and increases in the interest rate cause the whole curve to fall.

Investment and Entrepreneurs' Expectations The final factor whose influence we must take account of as a determinant of investment is entrepreneurial expectations. In calculating their demand price for machines we have seen that entrepreneurs must estimate the net annual yields of the machine over a number of years into the future—R_i in equation (28). Until now we have assumed that entrepreneurs arrive at unique and certain estimates of R_i. However, such estimation is obviously a very tricky business subject to all sorts of vagaries and uncertainties. Unanticipated new developments can either make entrepreneurs more sanguine or more pessimistic about the future. Such shifts in entrepreneurial expectations will cause them to re-evaluate R_i, which leads to a change in their demand price for machines, which, in turn, as we have seen, will lead to a change in investment. A shift in entrepreneurial expectations shows up in equation (VI) as a change in the *form* of the function represented by the *functional* I preceding the parentheses. If entrepreneurial expectations became more optimistic and they planned more investment, even though real income and the interest rate were unchanged, we would write the new equation $I' = I'(Y^s, r)$. Geometrically, in Figure 29, the investment curve would shift up, even though income and the interest rate were unchanged. And, of course, the reverse would occur if entrepreneurial expectations became more pessimistic. We might mention here that Keynes attached particular importance to the impact of changing entrepreneurial expectations on the level of planned investment. He thought that entrepreneurs were periodically gripped by flights of collective euphoria punctuated by bouts of self-doubt. As a result, Keynes felt the aggregate investment schedule was hopelessly unstable.

In concluding our discussion of investment we should mention one glaring omission. We refer to *accelerator* theories of investment whereby investment is made a function of the *change* in income. However, such theories of investment lead straight into *cyclical* economic behavior which is a topic outside the scope of this book.

FIGURE 29

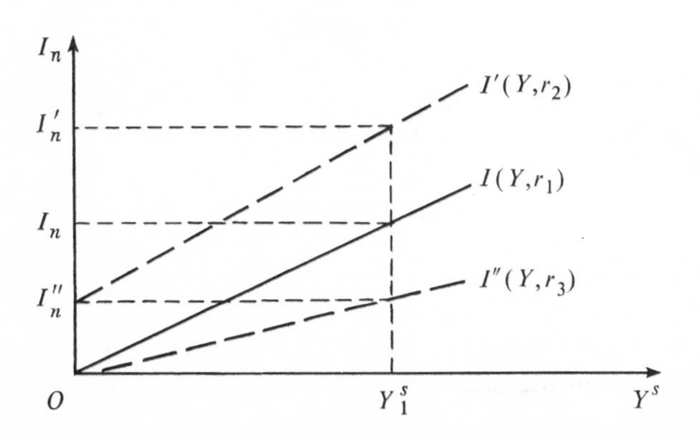

FIGURE 30

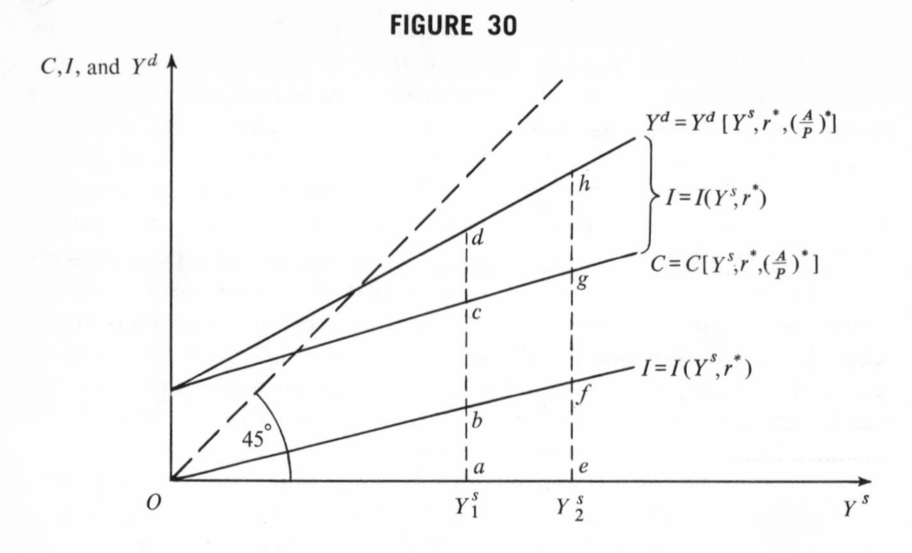

3 The Aggregate (Market) Demand for, and the Aggregate (Market) Supply of, Commodities

Aggregate commodity demand is equal to the sum of consumption demand and investment demand.[1] Thus, aggregate commodity demand is defined by

$$Y^d = C + I \tag{VII}$$

which is the seventh equation in our complete macroeconomic model. Aggregate commodity demand is obviously going to be a function of the variables which affect consumption and investment so we may write

$$Y^d = Y^d\left(Y^s, r, \frac{V}{P}\right), \qquad Y^d_1 > 0, Y^d_2 < 0, Y^d_3 > 0 \tag{30}$$

Aggregate commodity demand will be directly related to real income (because C and I are), indirectly related to the interest rate (because C and I are), and directly related to real net assets (because C is).

It is customary in macroeconomics to geometrically illustrate aggregate commodity demand as a function of the level of real income (not, as with the other markets, as a function of some price). We shall follow this practice. Consider Figure 30. Consumption and investment as a function of income are represented separately by the curves C and I, respectively, which are taken from Figures 18 and 29. Aggregate commodity demand Y^d is merely the sum of the two. Thus, if income were Y^s_1, investment would equal ab, consumption would equal ac, and aggregate demand would equal ad (= $ab + ac$); if income were Y^s_2, investment would equal ef, consumption would equal eg, and aggregate demand would equal eh (= $ef + eg$). From this construc-

[1] When government is not included in the model.

tion it is clear that investment is always equal to the vertical difference between the aggregate commodity demand curve and the consumption function, as has been indicated in the diagram. This is a salient fact to bear in mind as it will come in useful later.

The aggregate supply of commodities is, we know, equal to real income. In the usual 45°-line diagram this is measured from the origin along the horizontal axis. But from the properties of the 45°-line itself, the aggregate supply of commodities so measured is also equal to the distance measured vertically above that point to the 45°-line. Thus, in Figure 31 if the aggregate commodity supply (real income) is Y_1^s, aggregate commodity supply is also equal to Y_1^sA; if aggregate commodity supply (real income) is Y_2^s, aggregate commodity supply is also equal to Y_2^sB. Consequently, you can always observe aggregate commodity supply at a given real income as the vertical distance from that income point to the 45°-line.

Now, for the commodity market to be in equilibrium, aggregate commodity demand must equal aggregate commodity supply. That is

$$Y^d = Y^s \qquad \text{(VIII)}$$

This is the eighth equation in our complete macroeconomic model.

Aggregate commodity demand and supply have been combined in Figure 32. These two are equal and, therefore, the commodity market is only in equilibrium when they intersect on the 45°-line. When the aggregate supply of commodities is Y^{s*} (= *ab*), the aggregate demand for commodities is Y^{d*} (also = *ab*) and, thus, commodity market equilibrium prevails.

If the aggregate commodity supply were Y_1^s (= *ce*), aggregate commodity demand would only be *cd* and, thus, there would be an excess supply of commodities equal to *ed*; if aggregate commodity supply were Y_2^s (= *fg*), aggregate commodity demand would be *fh* and, thus, there would be an excess demand for commodities equal to *gh*. How disequilibrium in the commodity market (i.e., an excess supply of, or demand for, commodities) is

FIGURE 31

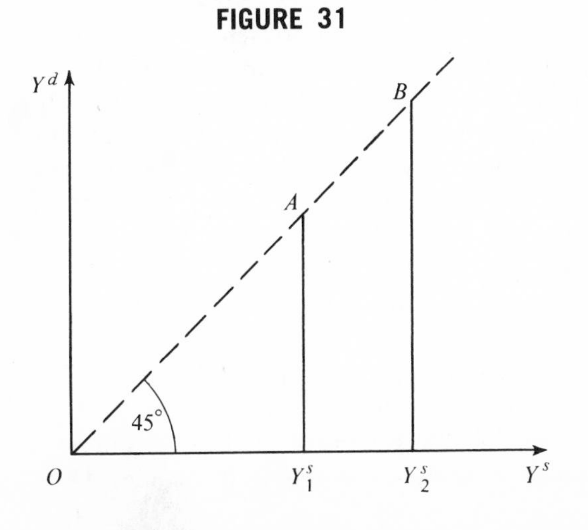

FIGURE 32

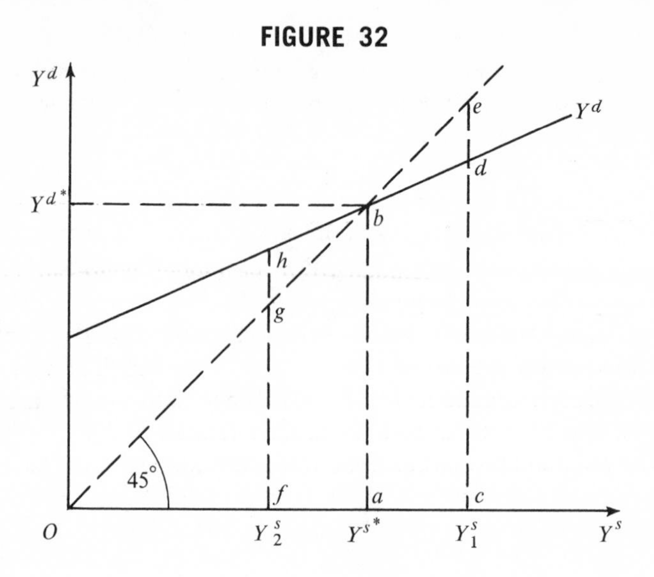

removed will interest us greatly throughout the rest of this book. Depending on the assumptions under which the model is being operated (for example, neoclassical or neo-Keynesian), equilibrium is brought about by price and interest rate changes or real income changes. But elaboration on these matters must wait until Parts II and III.

Summary

In this chapter we showed that the aggregate supply of commodities (real income) depends *solely,* and directly, on the level of employment when the capital stock is fixed. That is, $Y^s = Y^s(N, \bar{K})$ with $Y_1^s > 0$.

The demand for commodities is comprised of three components: consumption demand, investment demand, and government demand.

Consumption. On the basis of household preferences vis-à-vis present and future commodities and given the constraints imposed on them by current and expected future income, current and expected future prices, their assets, and the interest rate, we found that consumption is directly related to current income, inversely related to the interest rate (by assumption only), and directly related to the household's assets. That is, $C = C(Y^s, r, V/P)$ with $C_1 > 0$, $C_2 < 0$, $C_3 > 0$. The change in consumption per unit change in income was defined as the *mpc* (marginal propensity to consume); it was shown to equal the slope of the consumption function (i.e., current consumption plotted as a function of current income).

Investment. Our analysis demonstrated that although a *firm's* investment is unrelated to either the interest rate or its level of planned output, *aggregate* investment is inversely related to the interest rate and directly related to the level of aggregate output (real income). Thus, $I = I(Y^s, r)$ with

$I_1 > 0, I_2 < 0$. In addition, we saw that the interest elasticity of investment is the product of the elasticity of the demand price of machines with respect to the interest rate and the elasticity of investment with respect to changes in the price of machines. If *either* of these component elasticities is small (zero), the interest elasticity of investment will be small (zero).

Government. The demand for commodities by government is not discussed until Chapter 9.

When government is excluded from the model, aggregate commodity demand is equal to consumption demand plus investment demand: $Y^d = C + I$. Aggregate commodity demand is a function of the variables which affect C and I, so we may write $Y^d = Y^d(Y^s, r, V/P)$ with $Y_1^d > 0$ (since both C and I are directly related to Y^s), $Y_2^d < 0$ (since both C and I are inversely related to r), and $Y_3^d > 0$ (since C is directly related to V/P).

For the commodity market to be in equilibrium we must have $Y^d = Y^s$. Geometrically, this occurs *only* where the aggregate supply curve and the aggregate demand curve intersect on the 45°-line.

Questions

1. Show that with W and P flexible and a fixed capital stock $\bar{K}$, the aggregate supply of commodities (real income) depends only on the real wage. In such circumstances, what would happen to real income if a law were passed prohibiting anyone over fifty from working?
2. How would an increase in expected future prices P_{t+1}, ceteris paribus, affect current consumption?
3. Assume that an individual was robbed of half of his money balance, ceteris paribus. How would it affect (a) his current consumption, (b) his future consumption?
4. Show that the *mpc* and *mps* sum to unity.
5. Why did Keynes think that changes in the interest rate have little or no effect on aggregate current consumption one way or the other?
6. Assume that machines sell for P_m and they have n-year working lives, after which they are worth J as junk. If the interest rate is r, what would you have to pay to rent such a machine for one year?
7. Show that a cost-minimizing firm will employ factors in amounts such that the marginal physical products per dollar it spends on them are equal.
8. Show that although individual firms' net investment is independent of the rate of interest, the level of aggregate, economywide investment *is* (inversely) related to the rate of interest in the short run.
9. Show that although individual firms' net investment is independent of their level of output, the level of aggregate, economywide investment *is* (directly) related to the level of output (income) in the short run.
10. Discuss the factors on which the interest elasticity of investment depends.
11. Some economists are described as "interest elasticity pessimists"; that is, they think that neither C nor I are very responsive to changes in the interest rate. Make the best case you can for them.

SELECTED READINGS

1. R. W. Clower, "An Investigation into the Dynamics of Investment," *American Economic Review,* March, 1954. The original version of the approach to investment taken in this chapter.
2. J. M. Keynes, *The General Theory of Employment, Interest, and Money,* Macmillan, 1936, book III. This outlines Keynes' theory of the consumption function. Before this, the consumption function did not exist.
3. D. Patinkin, *Money, Interest, and Prices,* 2nd ed., Harper & Row, 1965, chapter 9, section 3.
4. J. G. Witte, "The Microfoundations of the Social Investment Function," *Journal of Political Economy,* October, 1963. Witte's elaboration and extension of Clower's article [1].

FURTHER READINGS

Consumption

5. A. Ando and F. Modigliani, "The Life Cycle Hypothesis of Saving: Aggregate Implications and Tests," *American Economic Review,* March, 1963. The source for the life-cycle hypothesis, together with [13].
6. D. Brady and R. Friedman, "Saving and the Income Distribution," *Conference on Research in Income and Wealth,* Vol. 10, National Bureau of Economic Research, 1947. The seminal work on cross-section, or short-run, consumption functions, which shows that such functions have positive intercepts that increase with time and, thus, in the short run, consumption is not proportional to income.
7. R. W. Clower and M. B. Johnson, "Income, Wealth, and the Theory of Consumption," in N. Wolfe (ed.), *Value, Capital, and Growth,* University of Edinburgh, 1968. The source for the endogenous income hypothesis.
8. J. S. Duesenberry, *Income, Saving, and the Theory of Consumer Behavior,* Harvard, 1952. The source for the relative income hypothesis.
9. R. Ferber, *A Study of Aggregate Consumption Functions*, National Bureau of Economic Research, Technical Paper No. 8, 1953. Together with [14], an excellent summary of prior empirical results on the consumption function.
10. M. Friedman, *A Theory of the Consumption Function,* National Bureau of Economic Research, 1957. The source for the permanent income hypothesis.
11. M. B. Johnson, *Household Behavior: Consumption, Income, and Wealth,* Penguin, 1970. A lucid and elementary guide to the various theories of the consumption function.
12. S. Kuznets, *National Product since 1869,* National Bureau of Economic Research, 1946. Provided the first indication that the average propensity to consume does not decline secularly and that in the long run consumption is proportional to income (i.e., the long-run consumption function has zero intercept).
13. F. Modigliani and R. Brumberg, "Utility Analysis and the Consumption Function: An Interpretation of Cross-section Data," in S. Harris (ed.), *Post-Keynesian Economics,* Rutgers, 1954. Together with [5], the source for the life-cycle hypothesis.
14. E. Shapiro, *Macroeconomic Analysis,* 2nd ed., Harcourt Brace Jovanovich, 1970, chapters 9 and 10. Another useful guide to the various theories of consumption.
15. D. Suits, "The Determinants of Consumer Expenditure: A Review of the Present Knowledge," in *Impacts of Monetary Policy,* Commission on Money and

Credit, Prentice-Hall, 1963. Together with [9], an excellent summary of prior empirical results on the consumption function.

16. J. Tobin, "Relative Income, Absolute Income, and Savings" in *Money, Trade, and Economic Growth,* Macmillan, 1951. Argues that the upward shift in the short-run consumption function which occurs with time may be explained by the inclusion of assets as an additional explanatory variable.

Investment

17. R. Eisner and R. H. Strotz, "Determinants of Business Investment," in *Impacts of Monetary Policy,* Commission on Money and Credit, Prentice-Hall, 1963. A good account of received investment theory with extended references.
18. J. Hirshleifer, *Investment, Interest, and Capital,* Prentice-Hall, 1970. A good account of received capital theory developed in a Fisherine framework plus Hirshleifer's extension to a world of uncertainty.
19. J. M. Keynes, *The General Theory of Employment, Interest, and Money,* Macmillan, 1936, chapters 11 and 12. Discussion of the investment decision which introduced the concept of the marginal efficiency of capital.
20. A. D. Knox, "The Acceleration Principle and the Theory of Investment: A Survey," *Economics,* August, 1952. A good article on the principle of acceleration—a concept *not* integrated into the text of this book.
21. A. Leijonhufvud, *On Keynesian Economics and the Economics of Keynes,* Oxford, 1968, chapter 3, section 3. Argues that Keynes himself was not an "investment interest elasticity pessimist."
22. A. P. Lerner, *The Economics of Control,* Macmillan, 1944, pp. 330–338. Introduced the notion that aggregate investment is limited by the capital goods sector's willingness to supply rather than by some finite rate at which investing firms demand to augment their capital stock.
23. J. E. Meade and P. W. S. Andrews, "Summary of Replies to Questions on Effects of Interest Rates," *Oxford Economic Papers,* October, 1938. Triggered the debate on the interest elasticity of investment—conclusions pessimistic.
24. J. R. Meyer and E. Kuh, *The Investment Decision,* Harvard, 1957. Makes the case for investment being critically dependent on firms' financing abilities.
25. W. H. White, "Interest Elasticity of Investment Demand," *American Economic Review,* September, 1956. A notable contribution to the debate on the interest elasticity of investment, with references to other contributors.

4

The Money Market

The previous two chapters have dealt with the components of the *real sector* of our model – the labor market and the commodity market. In this and the succeeding chapter we turn to the *financial sector*, which consists of the money market and the bond market. We discuss the supply of money first, then proceed to a discussion of the demand for money and the demand for bonds. (Since the demand for these two assets is intimately related, we will discuss them jointly.) The chapter concludes with a discussion of the overall money market.

1 The Supply of Money

The money supply arrangements in our model are very simple. There are two varieties of money: *fiat money,* which is a liability of the government, and *deposit money,* which is a liability of *the* bank. We assume that there is only *one* bank and that it is *owned* by the private sector, but *controlled* by the government. That is to say, if the government tells the bank to engage in an open-market operation to change the supply of deposit money, the bank does as it is told. This means that the total supply of money is completely at the mercy of the government. The government controls the supply of fiat money because it issues that, and it controls the supply of deposit money because the bank always obeys the government. The total money supply, then, is set at a particular level $\bar{M}^s$ as an act of government policy. It is, therefore, an exogenous variable. We shall have more to say about the distinction between exogenous and their opposite, endogenous, variables in Chapter 6. Suffice it to say for the moment that the values of exogenous variables are set "outside the model." This means they are not dependent in any way on the values of the other variables in the model. In the present context, for example, the government, acting through its creature the monopoly bank via open-market operations, sets the nominal supply of money at a certain amount $\bar{M}^s$ and that is that. Once chosen by the government, a particular $\bar{M}^s$ does not change in response to changes in any of the other variables in the model. Consequently, we do not need an equation to explain its behavior. Another exogenous variable we have encountered is the stock of physical capital $\bar{K}$. This is not set as an act of policy, but is, nonetheless, fixed at a constant level, namely, that level inherited from the previous period.

2 The Demand for Money and Bonds

The purpose of this section is to show that the demand for real money balances and real bonds is a function of real income, real assets, and the interest rate. The demand for both real money balances and real bonds turns out to be directly related to real income and real assets, while the influence of the interest rate is indirect on the demand for real money balances and direct on the demand for real bonds.

Real Income and the Demand for Money and Bonds

We saw in §3.2 that the nominal value of a transactor's asset portfolio A is equal to the sum of his nominal money balance M plus his nominal bond holdings B/r. That is,

$$A = M + B/r \tag{1}$$

It is convenient to discuss a transactor's demand for assets in real terms, so we divide both sides of (1) through by the price level P to obtain

$$\frac{A}{P} = \frac{M}{P} + \frac{B}{rP} \tag{2}$$

In words, equation (2) states that the real value of the asset portfolio is equal to the sum of real money balances M/P and real bonds B/rP. The real value of the asset portfolio is dimensioned in *commodities*. This follows, since A is dimensioned in dollars, P is dimensioned in dollars per unit of commodity, and "dollars" divided by "dollars per commodity" is equal to "commodities." Real assets are also a *stock* variable because it makes sense to say the asset portfolio is worth so many units of commodity at an instant of time. The real asset portfolio represents "command over commodities"—if it was converted into commodities, that is how many you would get.

Figure 1 illustrates an individual's indifference system between *holding* real assets and *consuming* commodities. These indifference curves have the usual properties: they are convex to the origin (a diminishing marginal rate of substitution), they do not cross, and the further they are from the origin the higher level of utility they indicate. The latter implies, quite reasonably, that more assets and more consumption are preferred to fewer assets and less consumption.

FIGURE 1

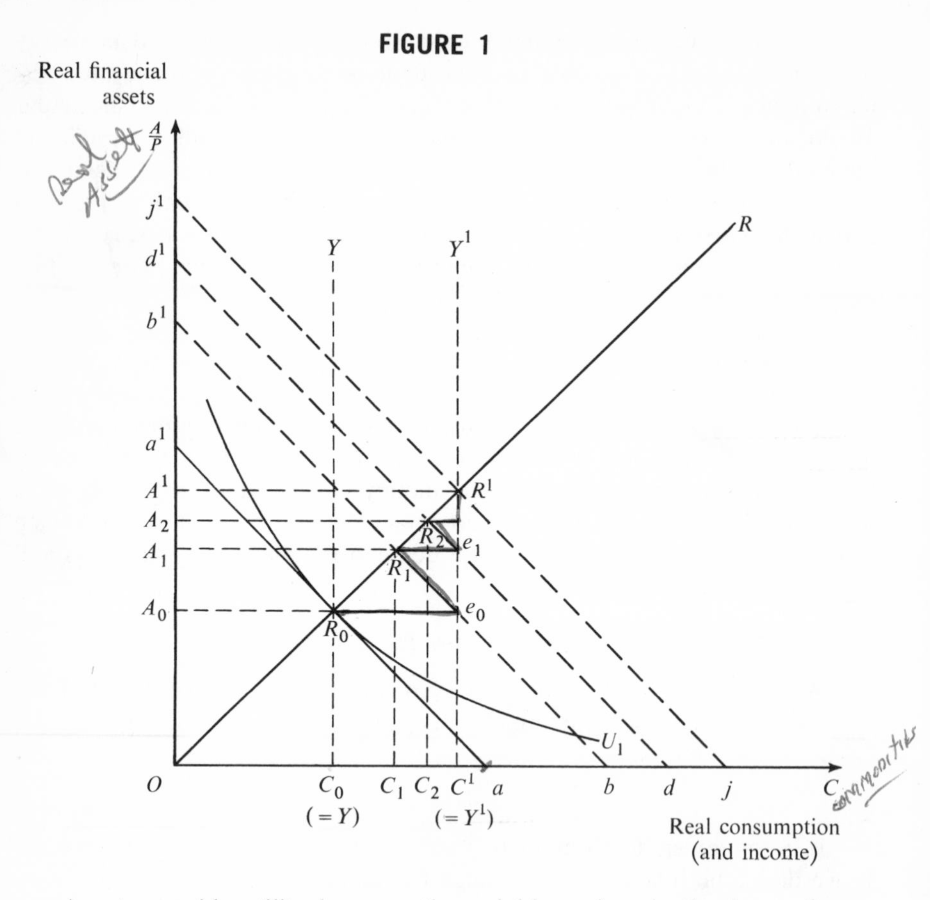

Assets provide utility because they yield services in the form of convenience, security, and (from bonds) interest income. The convenience yield of the money component of the asset portfolio is worth drawing particular attention to. It would be highly inconvenient not to hold any money balance. One would be forced to synchronize one's expenditure completely to one's income, an extremely burdensome arrangement. As soon as income flowed in it would have to be spent. If, as is usual, income is received only periodically, expenditure can be distributed throughout a period only if a money balance is held during the time between the receipt of income and the time of planned expenditure. Money held for such a reason is described as being held for *transaction purposes*. Holding some money for transaction purposes makes life much more convenient, since it obviates the necessity to synchronize income and expenditure.

A money balance also provides a measure of security against the occurrence of both calamitous and fortuitous events. For example, an individual may experience some temporary incapacitation. If he has a money balance, he may use it to tide himself over the period of misfortune without being forced to disrupt his bond portfolio. Conversely, should the opportunity to make a fortuitous unplanned purchase arise, he can take advantage of it if he has some money over and above his regular, planned transaction requirements. If, indeed, the individual has this extra money, then he has the security of knowing that he is protected, to some extent, against the slings and arrows of outrageous fortune, and that he is also in a position to capitalize on any of life's breaks. Money held in such a context is said to be held for *precautionary purposes* and provides utility in terms of security.

We have said enough about the transactor's preferences. What, now, can we say about the constraint facing him? It always has a very simple configuration; namely, a unitary (negative) slope. This follows from the fact that one unit of "actual commodities" (real income) can always be converted into one unit (no more, no less) of "command over commodities" (real assets). In Figure 1, note that if a transactor had a commodities he *could* consume them all and not acquire any assets (in which case he would remain at point a), or he *could* convert all these commodities into an equivalent amount of real assets and enjoy a^1 assets and no consumption. Clearly, $a^1 = a$ and any combination of consumption and assets along aa^1 is an option open to him.

A transactor is in equilibrium when his constraint is tangent to an indifference curve. Let us examine such a transactor at R_0. (The ray OR is the locus of points of tangency between all indifference curves and constraints in Figure 1, but to keep the diagram simple only one indifference curve U_1 has been illustrated.) At R_0, the transactor's asset portfolio and his consumption are optimal. It follows that his consumption C_0 must equal his income Y. If it does not (suppose his income exceeded his consumption), he is inevitably acquiring bonds or adding to his money holdings. In either case, he is adding to his asset portfolio which, therefore, cannot be described as optimal. Consequently, when the transactor is in *full* equilibrium his consumption is equal to his income and his asset portfolio is constant.

What happens if, for some reason, the transactor's real income rises to Y^1 and remains constant at this higher level. We must follow the analysis through several periods. When income rises to Y^1, the budget constraint in the first period shifts to bb^1. Why? The individual's income is now Y^1, but he has carried over A_0 assets from the previous period. These assets must be added to his income to get the maximum current consumption he *could* enjoy. Thus, b equals Y^1 plus A_0. (Note that $A_0 = e_0 = Y^1b$, since bb^1 must have a unitary negative slope.) Given this first period constraint, the transactor goes to R_1 where the constraint is tangent to an indifference curve (not shown). He consumes C_1 and acquires the asset portfolio A_1. The addition to his asset portfolio $A_1 - A_0$ is equal to the excess of his current income over his current consumption $Y^1 - C_1$. But R_1 is only a position of *short-run equilibrium*. If income remains at Y^1 in the second period (as we are assuming), the second-period constraint is dd^1. Why? At the end of the first period the asset portfolio is A_1. This has to be added to income Y^1 to determine the maximum possible second-period consumption. Adding distances $A_1 = e_1 = Y^1d$ to Y^1 we obtain d. Given this constraint, the second-period optimum is R_2, where consumption is C_2 and the asset portfolio A_2. In the third period the constraint shifts out to the right again (not shown), and we proceed with the analysis as for the previous periods. It is clear that this

Stop Across

process continues with ever smaller adjustments and converges on R^1, where the transactor is in *full equilibrium*. His consumption C^1 is equal to his income Y^1 once more, and, thus, his asset portfolio remains constant at A^1. Consequently the constraint remains fixed at jj^1. Full equilibrium in this context corresponds, for the household, to the classical "stationary state," where consumption is equal to income and, consequently, saving is zero. The analogue for the firm is when its capital stock is optimal and, thus, net investment is zero. As we have mentioned many times before, we are much more interested in short-run problems where saving and net investment are both occurring (though both may be negative). In the short run we can have a comparative static equilibrium without having a completely stationary state. Short-run comparative static equilibrium points (such as R_1) are the grist of this book's mill, rather than full equilibrium stationary state points (such as R^1). It is apparent that the increase in income from Y to Y^1 leads to an increase in the asset portfolio from A to A_1 in the short run (and from A to A^1 in the long run). We do not know for sure, however, whether *both* components of the asset portfolio have risen. Nonetheless, we shall assume they have. This amounts to assuming that both money and bonds are "superior assets," that is, they are assets for which the demand increases when income increases, other things being equal. This is reasonable, since it seems plausible to assume that an individual would hold a larger money balance for both transaction and precautionary purposes when his income has risen, and one certainly would expect his bond holdings to increase when his income has increased.

Naturally, the opposite result occurs when real income declines. Holdings of real assets (both components) decline. As an exercise, the reader may wish to start the transactor in full equilibrium and trace out the adjustment process in this case.

The preceding analysis contains one defect which we should point out. When income increased from Y to Y^1 we assumed it remained constant at this level. This, however, cannot be strictly true. The reason is that the transactor is adding to his bond portfolio by, let us assume, an amount ΔB. But each additional bond he purchases gives him one dollar of additional income. Thus, these additions to his bond portfolio increase his real income by $\Delta B/P$. Consequently, real income increases beyond Y^1 by this amount, and to ignore this repercussion is strictly illegitimate. However, the simplification we have adopted avoids some (even more) complicated geometry without losing anything substantive. Basically, all that happens is that the final levels of Y^1, C^1, and A^1 are higher and R^1 is further out along the ray OR.

Assets and the Demand for Money and Bonds

Having established the direct relationship between real income and the demand for both components of the real asset portfolio, we now wish to examine how a change in the transactor's real assets affects these demands.

Once again, we start with a transactor in full equilibrium as illustrated by point R_0 in Figure 2. Now let his real money balance be increased from M/P to M^1/P. This means that his total real asset portfolio will also increase from A_0 to A^1 and his constraint will shift from aa^1 to bb^1. The distance A^1b^1 is equal to Y, since $A^1b^1 = A^1e_0 = Y$. Given this increase in his real assets, the first-period (short-run) optimum for the transactor is at R_1 where he retains the asset portfolio A_1 and consumes C_1. Notice that his consumption C_1 exceeds his income (which is constant at Y). He finances the consumption in excess of his income by running down his asset portfolio by A^1A_1 ($= C_1Y$). In the first period, then, his demand for assets to hold and his consumption increase when his asset portfolio is increased. However, in the second period the transactor's constraint shifts to dd^1 because his asset portfolio is now only A_1 and his income is constant at Y. The distance $A_1d^1 = A_1e_1 = Y$. Then the transactor's second-period optimum is R_2, where he retains the asset portfolio A_2 and consumes C_2. The latter is again in excess of his income and he has financed this excess ($= C_2Y$) by running down his asset portfolio by A_1A_2. In running down his asset portfolio, the transactor shifts his third-period constraint in again (not shown) and his optimum to R_3. It is clear that the transactor is converging in the saw-toothed path on R_0. When this point is reached, he retains the portfolio A_0 and his consumption is again equal to his income.

From this analysis we see that, in the short run (periods prior to the re-establishment of full equilibrium), the demand to hold real assets increases when the transactor's endowment of real assets increases. (We shall assume that this increased demand applies to both components of the asset port-

FIGURE 2

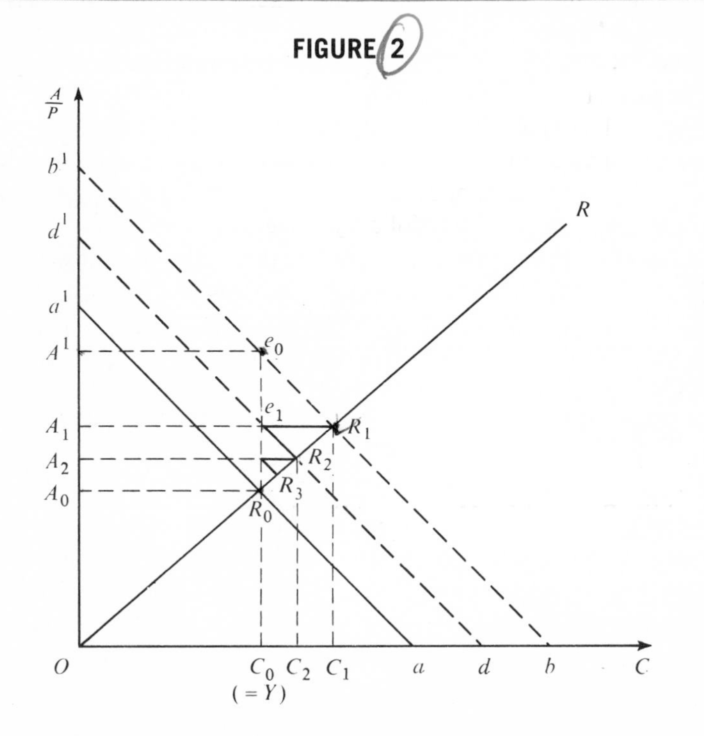

folio.) The reader can easily show himself that if the transactor's initial endowment of assets had decreased his short-run demand to hold real assets would also decrease. Thus may be established the direct functional relationship between a transactor's asset endowment and his demand to hold real assets (in the short run), for which we have been looking.

In the long run, however, when the transactor returns to full equilibrium, his asset portfolio will return to its original level. He runs down his asset portfolio gradually to A_0 again over several periods by consuming in excess of his income.

The Interest Rate and the Demand for Money and Bonds

Having established in the previous two parts of §2 that both the demand for money and the demand for bonds are increasing functions of the transactor's real income and his asset endowment, we turn now to an examination of the influence of the interest rate on the demand for money and bonds. We shall show (on various grounds) that the interest rate influences the demand for money indirectly and the demand for bonds directly. Various explanations of this relationship have been advanced. We shall discuss three of them, namely, the hypotheses developed by Tobin, Keynes, and Baumol, in that order.

We are engaged now in a discussion of the third major decision facing transactors, namely, the *portfolio balance* decision. We assume transactors have accumulated a certain asset portfolio consisting of money and bonds and must now decide how to allocate this portfolio between the two (hence, the portfolio balance decision). You may recall that the two other major decisions we have discussed are the income/leisure decision (in Chapter 2), and the consumption/saving decision (in Chapter 3).

Uncertainty and Risk[1] Money is not only a medium of exchange but also an asset, which permits an individual to accumulate wealth in the form of money balances. However, money is sterile. It generates no pecuniary yield. The question immediately presents itself, then: Why should anyone accuulate wealth in this form (after he has enough to satisfy his transaction and precautionary money requirements) when alternative *interest-bearing* assets like bonds exist? In general, an individual accumulates a certain quantity of financial assets which, in our model, he can hold in the form of money or bonds. Our purpose here is to explore the way in which he will allocate his financial assets between these alternatives and, in particular, to show how his allocation will depend on the interest rate. Every transactor is obliged to hold some money for transaction purposes, given that income and expenditure are imperfectly synchronized. We shall show, however, that a transactor will not necessarily hold all his financial assets over and above his transaction requirements in the form of bonds. He may choose to hold some of his assets, in excess of his transaction requirements, in the form of

[1] This section and the next rely heavily on James Tobin's seminal article, "Liquidity Preference as Behavior towards Risk," *Review of Economic Studies,* February, 1958.

money, even though money is sterile. In short, it is rational to demand money as an asset as well as to demand money for transaction purposes.

Money and bonds are distinguished by the fact that the former is fixed in price,[2] while the latter varies. This implies that wealth held in the form of money has a capital value which is nominally *certain*, while wealth held in the form of bonds is uncertain in value. When an individual holds one unit of money, he always has one dollar; when he holds one bond, he is not certain what its nominal value will be at any moment. The price of the bond can vary (inversely, with the rate of interest, we have seen). Consequently, if he holds bonds he can benefit from a capital gain (if their price rises) or be stuck with a capital loss (if their price falls). Thus, bonds expose the holder to *risk*, and the larger the proportion of wealth held in bonds, the larger this risk of capital gain or loss. On the other hand, the larger the proportion of wealth held in bonds, the larger is the interest income earned. Hence, the asset holder is confronted with the choice between interest income and risk: to go after more interest income he must accept more risk; and to reduce his risk he must forego interest income. In other words, the more risk he accepts the more interest income he will earn; the less risk he is willing to bear, the less interest income he will earn. Interest income and risk, then, are positively related. Let us see if we can make this notion more precise.

A bond holder observes a particular current bond price. But he is *uncertain* about future bond prices; they may go higher or lower—he does not know. Whichever way they move, the percentage capital gain (or loss, if negative) g that he will experience is given by

$$g = \frac{\frac{1}{r_f} - \frac{1}{r}}{1/r} \tag{3}$$

which is to say the difference between the future price of bonds $1/r_f$ and the current price $1/r$ divided by the current price. Simple algebraic manipulation reduces this to

$$g = \frac{r}{r_f} - 1 \tag{4}$$

Now the nominal value of an asset portfolio A is equal to the sum of the money M and bonds B/r held in it. That is,

$$A = M + B/r$$

from which

$$1 = \frac{M}{A} + \frac{B/r}{A}$$

and

$$1 = A_1 + A_2$$

[2] Money is always fixed in *price*, even though its *value* changes if the commodity price level changes. In this section, we avoid the problem of changes in the value of money by assuming that the commodity price level is constant.

FIGURE 3

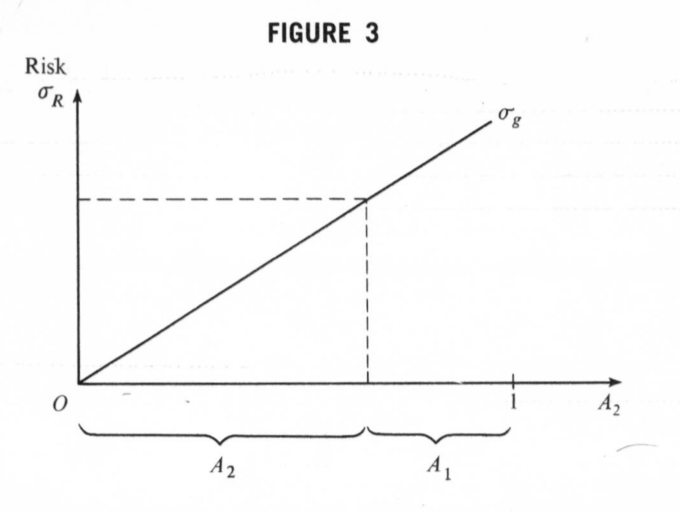

where A_1 is the *proportion* of the asset portfolio held in money and A_2 the *proportion* held in bonds. Clearly, both A_1 and A_2 are individually constrained between zero and unity and always sum to unity. Notice that the initial size of the total portfolio is *given*. Given the size of his portfolio of financial assets, the asset holder must still decide how to allocate it between money and bonds. Obviously, a decision on the proportion of the total portfolio to be held in bonds A_2 immediately implies A_1 (the proportion to be held in money), since $A_1 = 1 - A_2$.

The return R on a given portfolio will be

$$R = A_2 (r + g) \tag{5}$$

which is to say the proportion of the portfolio held in bonds multiplied by the interest rate plus the capital gain. The *expected* return $E(R)$ is, however, only

$$E(R) = A_2 r \tag{6}$$

because the *expected* value of g is zero. This requires some explanation. Although g is *calculated* by (3), its *expected* value is zero to asset holders because they are *uncertain* whether future rates will be higher or lower than present interest rates. They have no firm convictions about the direction interest rates will move in in the future. Instead, all asset holders are assumed to associate with g a *probability distribution* which has an expected (mean) value equal to zero for the above reasons and a standard deviation (which is a measure of g's *variability*) equal to σ_g. We also assume that the probability distribution is independent of the level of the interest rate r. This means that asset holders feel that a doubling (or halving), for example, of the interest rate is just as likely when the interest rate is 5 percent as when it is 2 percent—which is, of course, a strong assumption by Tobin.

The standard deviation, or variability, of g, σ_g, is an index of the risk associated with holding one bond. The risk σ_R associated with the whole portfolio is

$$\sigma_R = \sigma_g A_2 \tag{7}$$

Since σ_g is constant by assumption, (7) indicates that the total risk σ_R is a linear function of A_2, the proportion of the portfolio held in bonds. Such a relationship is shown in Figure 3 where A_2 is plotted along the horizontal axis from the origin. The maximum value of A_2 is unity; since $A_1 = 1 - A_2$, the distance along the horizontal axis between A_2 and the unit point represents A_1. The slope of this line is equal to σ_g.

From (6) and (7) it can be seen that for a given interest rate r, the proportion of the total asset portfolio held in bonds A_2 determines *both* the expected return and the risk of that portfolio. Under our assumptions, the relationship between expected return and risk can be obtained by substituting (7) into (6) to yield

$$E(R) = \left(\frac{r}{\sigma_g}\right) \sigma_R \tag{8}$$

Now σ_g is constant by assumption, so that the ratio in parentheses is a constant for a given interest rate. Thus, it is obvious from (8) that expected return is a linear function of risk. Not only are expected return and risk positively related (which we established intuitively above) but they are *linearly* related. This is illustrated in Figure 4. Expected return is plotted vertically and risk horizontally. The slope of the solid line is equal to r/σ_g. Obviously, if interest rates rise the slope of this line increases; for a given risk, there will be a higher expected return. This is shown by the dashed curve labeled r_1/σ_g in Figure 4. It follows that a fall in the interest rate would reduce the slope. These curves are described as *opportunity loci.* As increased risk is incurred the opportunity for expected returns increases. This is the *constraint* which faces the asset holder.

If we rotate Figure 3 in a clockwise direction 90° and superimpose it on Figure 4, we obtain Figure 5. This figure shows how risk and expected return are related to the proportion of the total portfolio held in bonds. When

FIGURE 4

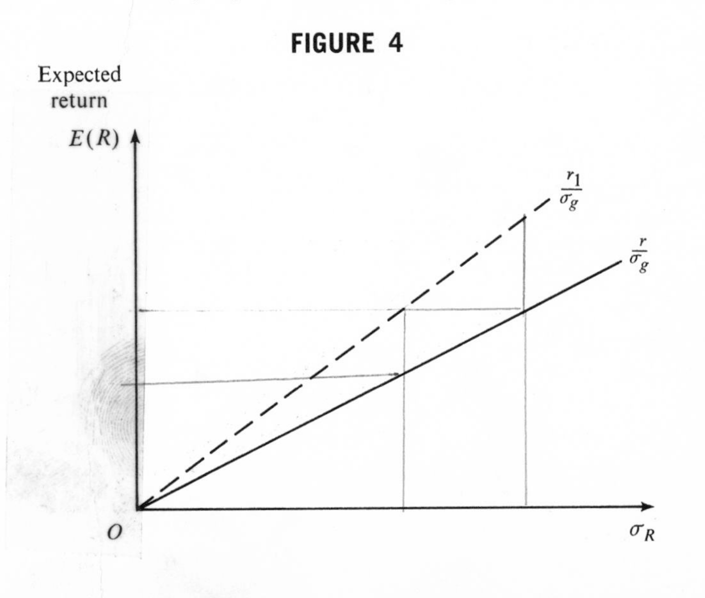

FIGURE 5

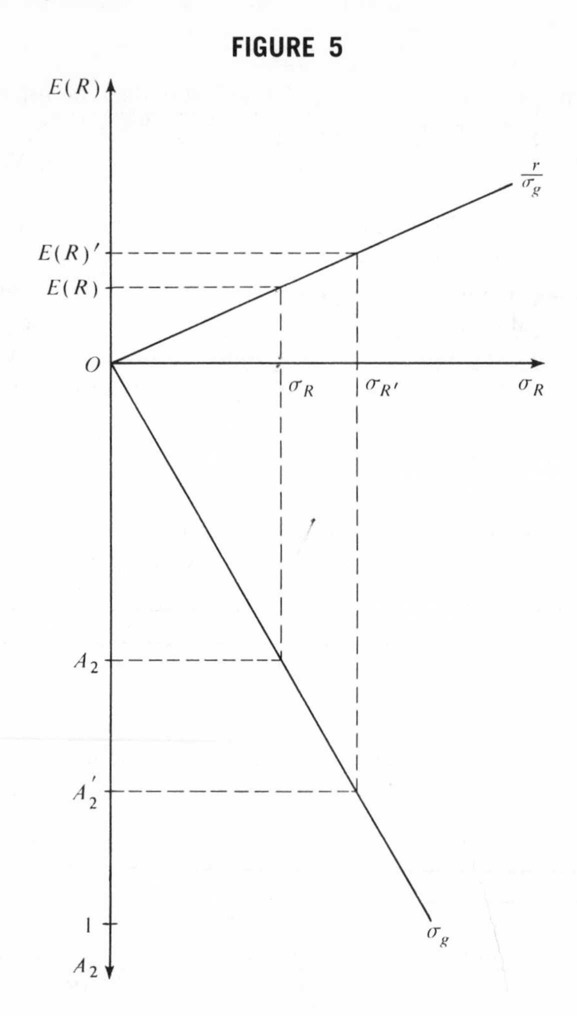

this proportion is A_2, risk is σ_R and expected return is $E(R)$; when the proportion held in bonds is increased to A_2', risk is σ_R' and the expected return is $E(R)'$.

This concludes our outline of the constraints which face the asset holder. What will determine his optimum portfolio A_2^*? To answer we need information about his preferences.

A family of indifference curves which indicate the asset holder's preferences between expected return and risk are illustrated in Figure 6. They have been drawn with a positive slope which indicates that asset holders require a higher expected return if they are to assume more risk and, at the same time, not be made worse off. This is a preference map for what is called a *risk-averter;* to stay on the same indifference curve, increased risk must be offset by a higher expected return.[3]

[3] The positive slope of these indifference curves *is* only an assumption. It is certainly possible that some asset holders are "risk-lovers." That is to say, they would accept a *lower* expected

FIGURE 6

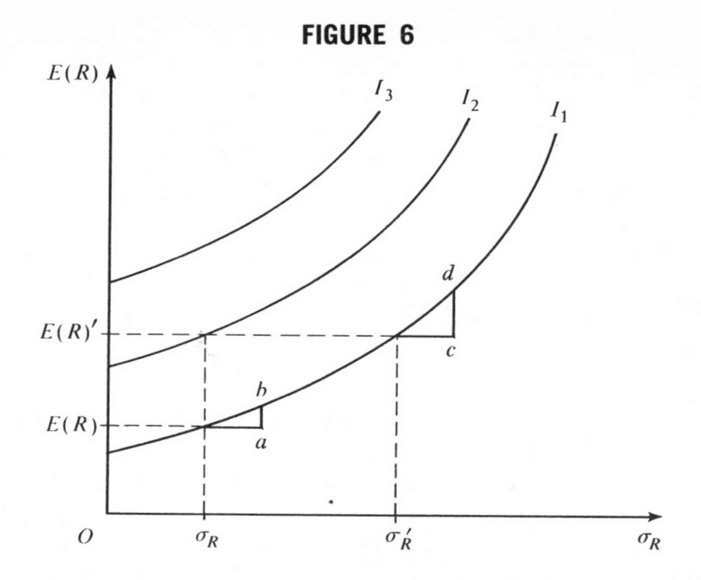

These indifference curves have also been drawn concave from above. The increase in expected return required to keep the asset holder on the same indifference curve rises per unit increase in risk as the level of risk rises. For example, on I_1, when the level of risk is σ_R, a unit increase in risk will be offset by an increase in expected return of *ab*; but when the level of risk is σ'_R a unit increase in risk will be offset only by an increase in expected return equal to *cd*. Clearly, *cd* exceeds *ab*. This again implies risk aversion: the higher the level of risk, the greater the increase in expected return required to offset the assumption of additional risk. An asset holder is assumed to be indifferent among all points on any one indifference curve such as I_1. He is just as well off at any point on I_1 as at any other point on I_1. Similarly, any point on I_2 is as good as any other point on I_2 as far as he is concerned. However, he prefers any point on I_2 to any point on I_1, since for any given risk σ_R the expected return on I_1 is only $E(R)$, whereas on I_2 it would be $E(R)'$; and a larger expected return is preferred to a smaller one when risk is constant. Looking at it the other way, for a given expected return $E(R)'$ the lower risk σ_R associated with I_2 is preferred to the higher risk σ'_R associated with I_1. This, again, is characteristic of risk-aversive preferences. Naturally, I_1, I_2, and I_3 are only a small subset of the asset holders' complete indifference map. Conceptually, the space in Figure 6 is jammed full of indifference curves with positive slopes and concave from above.

We can now put the asset holder's constraints and preferences together to determine how he decides on his optimal asset portfolio. This is done in Figure 7. Begin by assuming that the asset holder's entire portfolio is held in money ($A_2 = 0$) and that the interest rate is equal to r. He is at the origin in

return in exchange for exposure to the possibility of a larger capital gain (risk). Such persons would have indifference curves with a negative slope. In the text we ignore risk-loving behavior. The interested reader is referred to Tobin, *op. cit.*, for the application of his analysis to risk-lovers.

the diagram (on I_0). What happens if he decides to buy some bonds and, thus, increases the proportion A_2 in his portfolio? As A_2 increases, we see from the lower quadrant that risk increases. Given the opportunity locus r/σ_g, as risk increases so does the expected return. The asset holder is moving out along r/σ_g from zero. When will he stop increasing A_2? Clearly, when the opportunity locus is tangent to an indifference curve. In the figure, this occurs at A_2^*. Either a smaller or a larger value of A_2 would leave him on a lower indifference curve. Once A_2^* is decided upon, so is A_1^*, since $A_1^* = 1 - A_2^*$. Moreover, since

$$1 = \frac{M}{A} + \frac{B/r}{A}$$

when the second ratio is determined in the manner outlined above, so is the nominal quantity of bonds demanded $(B/r)^*$, since A is given. With $(B/r)^*$ thus determined and A given, the *quantity* of money demanded M^* is also uniquely determined.

What will happen to the quantity of bonds and money demanded when the interest rate rises? In this case the slope of the opportunity locus increases. Figure 8 includes two opportunity loci associated with an increase in the interest rate from r to r_1. Given the shape of the indifference curves, these loci indicate that as the interest rate rises the optimal A_2-ratio increases from A_2^* to $A_2^{*\prime}$. When r rises, B/r and A both fall. But the percentage de-

FIGURE 7

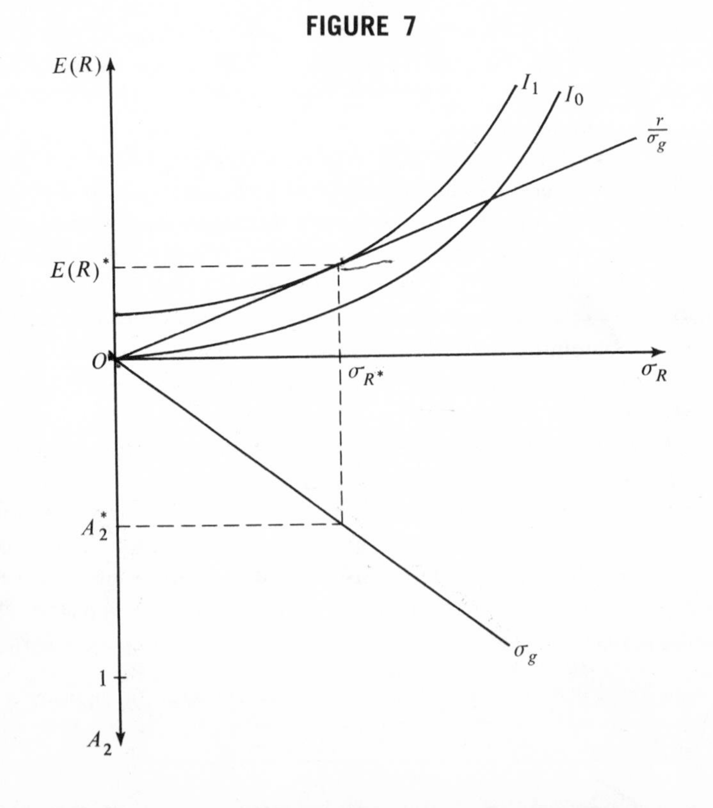

FIGURE 8

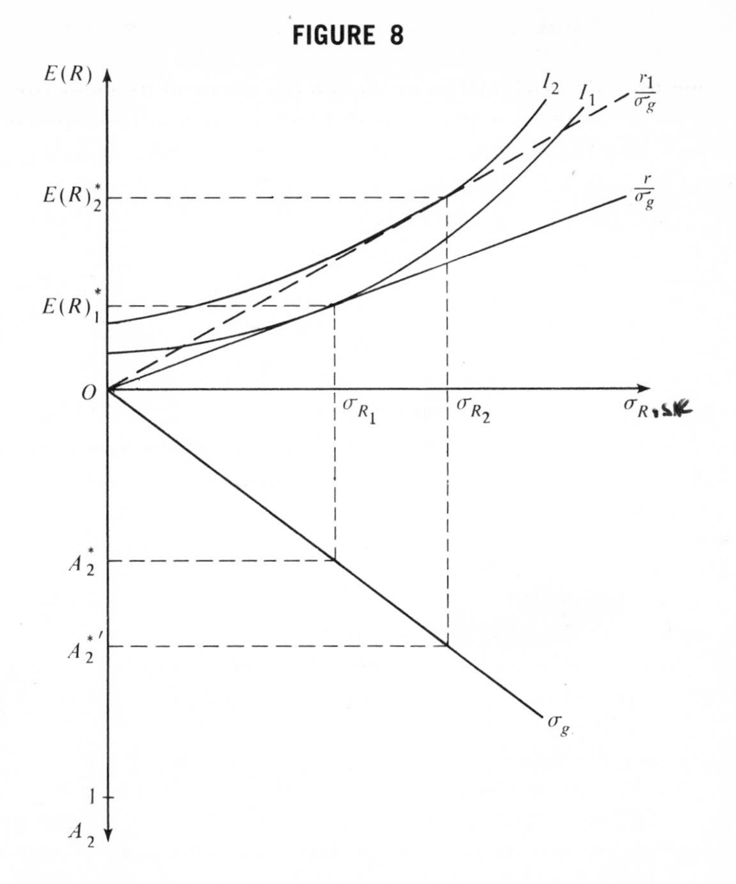

cline in B/r exceeds the percentage decline in A, since $A = M + B/r$ [and M is unchanged]. Thus, the impact effect of a rise in r is to *reduce* the A_2-ratio. We have seen, however, that the transactor wishes to *raise* the A_2-ratio. He must, therefore, want to hold a larger number of bonds, say, B_1^d, when r rises to r_1. If he holds a larger number of bonds when r rises, he must wish to hold a smaller money balance, say, M_1^d. With this preference map the number of bonds demanded increases and the quantity of money demanded decreases, when the interest rate rises.[4] These conclusions are illustrated in Figures 9 and 10.

The reciprocal of the interest rate (the price of bonds) is plotted on the vertical axis in Figure 9 and the number of bonds demanded B^d is on the horizontal axis. When the interest rate is low at r, the price of bonds is high and the number demanded is B^d; when the interest rate rises to r_1, the price of bonds falls and the number demanded rises to B_1^d. In Figure 10, at the high interest rate r_1, the quantity of money demanded is M_1^d; at the lower interest rate r the quantity demanded is M^d. If the demand curves of all individual

[4] It is *possible* to draw a preference map such that the points of tangency between opportunity loci of increasing slope and indifference curves occur at smaller and smaller values of A_2—contrary to what we have just concluded. We ignore such possibilities. The interested reader is referred to Tobin, *op cit.*, p. 185.

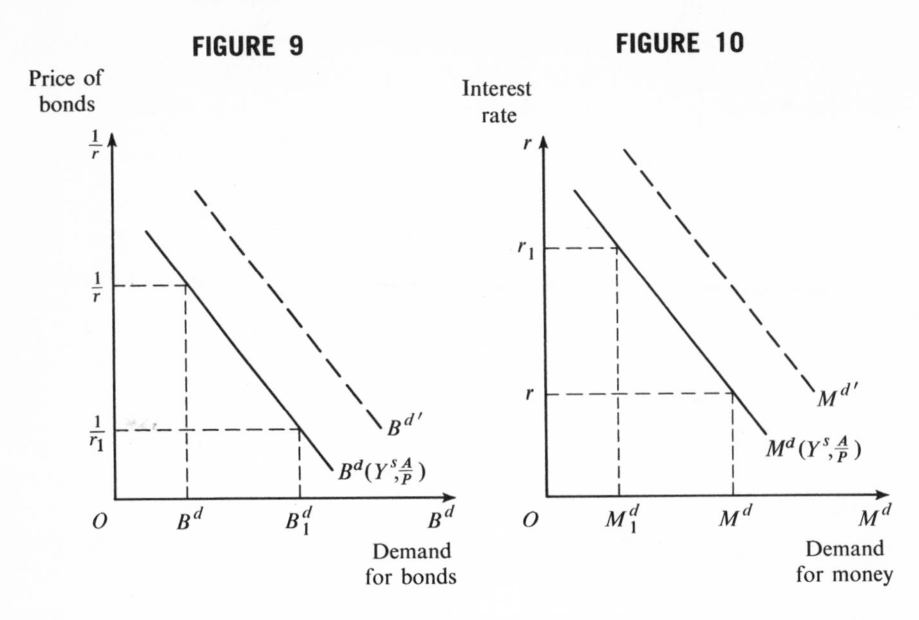

asset holders for bonds and money have these negative slopes then so must the market demand curves, which are merely the sum of the individual demand curves.

We remark that the solid curves in Figures 9 and 10 are drawn for a *given* level of real income and a *given* initial asset portfolio. In the first two sections of this chapter we have shown that a rise in real income or a rise in the transactor's asset endowment increases both the demand for real money balances and real bonds. If either of these events should occur, both demand curves would shift right as illustrated by the dashed curves in Figures 9 and 10. Conversely, a decrease in real income or the transactor's asset endowment would shift the solid curves to the left.

Inelastic Bond Price Expectations In the previous section we showed that it is possible to derive a demand for money function that is responsive to interest rate changes if we merely assume that asset holders are *uncertain* about future bond prices. The purpose of this section is to demonstrate that an interest-responsive demand for money function can also be based on *inelastic bond price expectations*. This was the explanation Keynes himself provided when he introduced his famous liquidity preference function in the *General Theory*.

Consider a transactor deciding how to hold his wealth in the coming period (say, the year). As before, the choice is between money and bonds. At the end of the period he expects with certainty the price of bonds to be $1/r_f$. The capital gain he expects to make is, therefore,

$$g = \frac{\frac{1}{r_f} - \frac{1}{r}}{\frac{1}{r}} = \frac{r}{r_f} - 1 \tag{9}$$

(This is, of course, negative if r_f is greater than r; he expects a capital loss if he holds bonds.) We should remark on the difference in emphasis in the treatment of (9) by Tobin and Keynes. According to Tobin, although g will have a certain *realized* value when the future arrives, it has a zero *expected* value because transactors expect, or believe, current bond prices to prevail. According to Keynes, transactors hold firm expectations about r_f. Thus, for him, g has a definite *expected* value. The *total* return he expects to receive if he holds bonds is equal to the current interest rate plus the expected capital gain. That is,

$$r + \frac{r}{r_f} - 1 \gtreqless 0 \tag{10}$$

This expression may be positive, negative, or zero depending on the relationship between r and r_f. If this expression is positive, the transactor will gain during the period by holding *all* his assets (over and above his minimim transaction and precautionary requirements) in bonds; if it is negative he will lose by doing so and, therefore, should hold all his assets in money; finally, if it is zero he will neither gain nor lose and, presumably, should sit tight and do nothing (that is, he keeps the same portfolio he already has). This type of transactor is described as a "plunger." If (10) is positive he goes completely into bonds; if it is negative he goes completely into money. By simple algebraic manipulation of (10) we can find this transactor's decision in terms of the current interest rate:

$$r \gtreqless \frac{r_f}{1 + r_f} = r_c \tag{11}$$

If the current interest rate exceeds the middle expression in (11), the plunger goes completely into bonds; if it is less, he goes completely into money; if they are equal, he stays put. Notice that the only variable in the middle expression in (11) is r_f, the interest rate the transactor expects with certainty to prevail at the end of the period. He is, therefore, capable of calculating a *critical* current rate of interest from it, r_c. Now, then, if the actual rate of interest he observes in the market r exceeds the critical value r_c that he has calculated he goes completely into bonds; if the actual interest rate is less than the calculated critical rate, he goes completely into money.

What will this transactor's demand for money as a function of the market rate of interest look like? Consider Figure 11. The transactor has calculated r_c from (11). As long as r exceeds r_c he holds no money no matter what the level of r; this gives us the heavy section of his demand curve *RS* coincident with the Y axis. As long as r is less than r_c he holds only money no matter what the level of r; hence, we get the heavy section of his demand curve *TU*.

We have assumed so far that the expectations transactors form about the future interest rate r_f are quite independent of the current level r. This need not be the case. Keynes, in particular, thought that the two were closely related. He argued that expectations about future interest rates were what

FIGURE 11

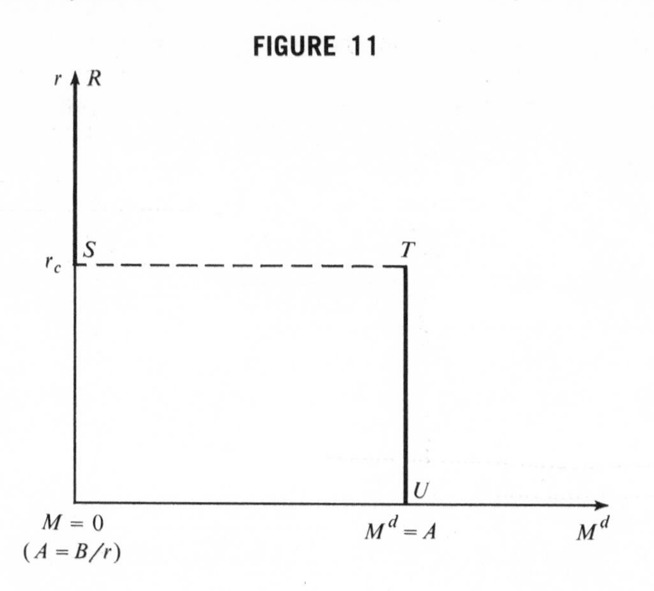

is called "regressive," or inelastic. That is, if the current interest rate rises, transactors do not expect the future interest rate to rise as much. This is because transactors have a "normal," or "safe," interest rate in mind. Consequently, when the current interest rate rises, it diverges from this normal rate. Since transactors consider the normal rate more likely to prevail, the interest rate they expect in the future will be less than the current rate—that is, they expect future interest rates to regress down toward normal. The same thing happens in reverse. If transactors see the current interest rate fall below their idea of the normal rate they do not expect this condition to prevail in the future. Rather, they expect a more normal interest rate to be reestablished. Therefore, they expect the interest rate in the future to be higher than the current rate. They expect future interest rates to regress up toward normal. When the percentage change expected in future interest rates is less than the percentage change in the current interest rate, transactors are said to have *inelastic* interest rate expectations; when the two are equal, they have *unit-elastic* expectations; and when the percentage change in future interest rates is greater than the percentage change in current rates, transactors are said to have *elastic* interest rate expectations. Basing his argument on the notion of a normal interest rate, Keynes believed that transactors had inelastic interest rate expectations. When they saw the current rate rise, they did not expect the future rate to be as high. (From the discussion of Tobin's hypothesis in the previous section, it is apparent that he assumes transactors have unit-elastic expectations. He always expects the established interest rate to prevail. Therefore, when the current interest rate changes, future interest rates expected must change in the same proportion.)

We can depict the relationship that Keynes believed to exist between current interest rates and expected future interest rates graphically (Figure 12). The current interest rate is plotted horizontally and the interest rate expected to prevail in the future vertically. A 45°-line has been introduced purely for convenience. The relationship between r_f and r is assumed linear for simplicity. If the current interest rate is r_1, the future interest rate expected is r_f (which, from the properties of a 45°-line is, by inspection, less than r_1). What happens if the current rate increases from r_1 to r_2? The expected future interest rate rises by less; namely, from r_f to r_f'. This is what is meant by inelastic interest rate expectations. Clearly, the percentage change in r_f will always be less than the percentage change in r as long as the function $r_f = \phi(r)$ cuts the 45°-line from above moving from left to right (or, equivalently, has a positive intercept). Analogously, if the current rate falls from r_1 to r_3, the expected future interest rate again falls proportionately less, namely, from r_f to r_f''. Note that at any interest rate above r_0, future interest rates expected would be lower; at any interest rate below r_0, the future interest rate expected would be higher.

If r_f is a function of r, it follows that $r_f/(1 + r_f)$ is also a function of r. This function will merely have a lower level than the function $r_f = \phi(r)$ (Figure 13). We know from (10) that when the current rate r exceeds $r_f/(1 + r_f)$, the transactor goes completely into bonds; when it is less, he goes completely into money. The critical interest rate where he goes from one decision to another is r_c in Figure 13. That is the only interest rate where r is equal to $r_f/(1 + r_f)$ [from the properties of the 45°-line].

In the discussion prior to Figure 11, we showed that a transactor who has *definite expectations* about future interest rates would have the sort of demand curve for money depicted in that diagram. We have just finished showing that a transactor who has *definite and inelastic expectations* about future interest rates will have a similar demand curve. There is a critical level of the current interest rate above which he plunges into bonds and be-

FIGURE 12

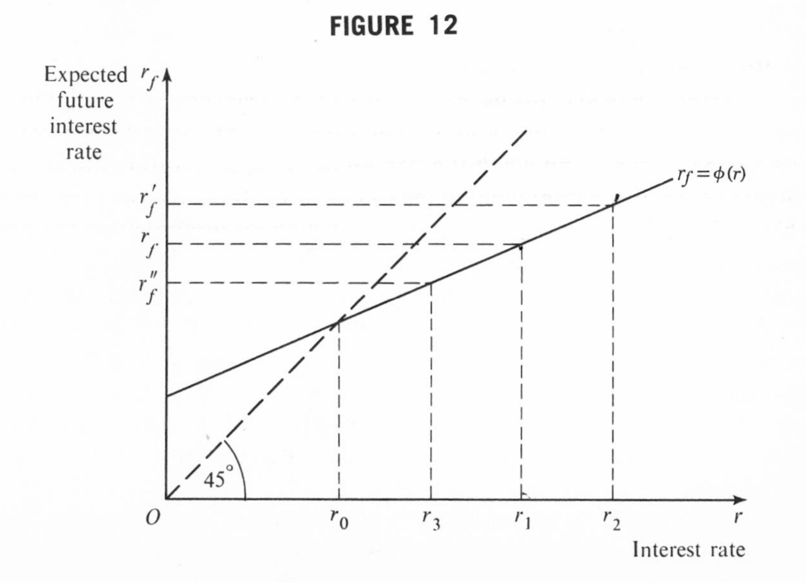

FIGURE 13

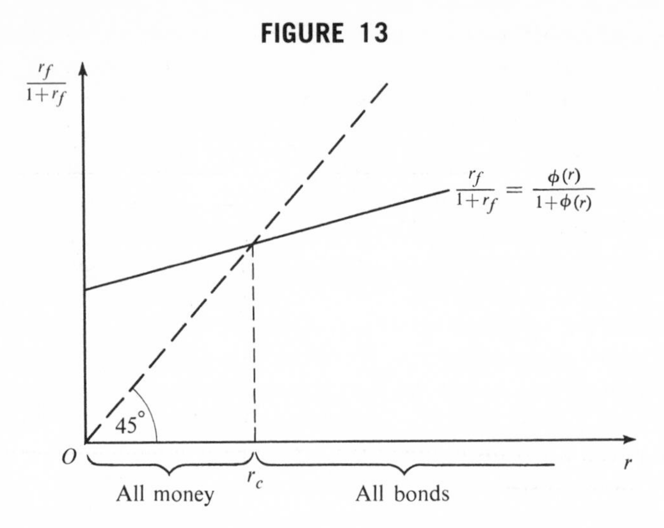

low which he plunges into cash. Figure 11 shows, then, the sort of *individual* transactor demand curve for money obtained when the sort of interest rate expectations asserted by Keynes exists.

How, then, is the usual smooth, downward-sloping liquidity preference function obtained? The answer is perfectly simple. Individual transactors are assumed to have definite expectations about future interest rates, but *different ones*. Through (11) this gives each transactor a different critical value of the current interest rate r_c. Thus, even though each individual's demand curve is stepped at r_c, the steps occur at different values. When a very large number of functions stepped at different levels are aggregated horizontally, the resulting function will have a smooth outline. Thus, the total market demand for money function will appear just like that illustrated in Figure 10. Similarly, the market demand for bonds function will appear like that illustrated in Figure 9.

An Inventory-Theoretic Approach[5] In the last two sections we found that there are plausible theoretical reasons to suppose that the demand for money to hold as an asset is inversely related to the rate of interest. Now we propose to show that, theoretically, the demand for money to use for transactions may also be inversely related to the rate of interest. An interesting by-product of the analysis will be the "economies of scale" to be found in the transaction demand for cash. That is, when the volume of transactions increases, the optimal quantity of cash demanded for transaction purposes increases less than proportionately.

Consider an individual who receives an inflow of money at the beginning of the year (period) equal to T (dollars) and who plans to spend the whole amount during the year at a constant rate. The time profile of his ex-

[5] This section (which may be omitted at a first reading without loss of continuity) relies heavily on W. J. Baumol's seminal article "The Transactions Demand for Cash: An Inventory Theoretic Approach," *Quarterly Journal of Economics*, November, 1952.

penditure and money balance will appear as in Figure 14. At the beginning of year t_1 he receives an inflow of money equal to $T(= OO')$. He spends all this money during the year at a constant rate so that at the end of year t_1 his total expenditure will be T and his money balance will be zero. At the beginning of year t_2 he receives another inflow, and so on. Clearly, his *average* money balance during the year is equal to $T/2$.

Notice that this individual holds money because his income and expenditure are not synchronized. His income occurs at discrete intervals, while his expenditure is continuous. If income and expenditure were completely synchronized, he would have no reason to hold any money for transaction purposes. Some of the money received at the beginning of the period is only used for transactions later in the period—in the interim it lays idle. Might it not occur to this individual to purchase securities with this idle money until it is required for transactions? If he does he will have converted a sterile asset into an interest-bearing one for some part of the year. This should be an appealing prospect.

Of the T (dollars) he receives at the beginning of the period, let him invest I (dollars) in securities and retain R (dollars) in money. Thus,

$$T = I + R \tag{12}$$

Clearly, the money he has invested in securities cannot stay invested for the whole year because eventually he has to use *all* of T for his year's transactions. He will, therefore, sell some of his securities periodically throughout the year to get money to complete the transactions coming due. Let him sell securities (convert them back into money) in lots (or batches) of C (dollars) at even intervals throughout the year. If C is large in relation to T, the number of times he has to sell securities in the year will be small; if C is small, the number of times he has to sell securities in the year will be large. Notice that if buying and selling securities is *costless* he would engage in a very large number of security transactions. At the beginning of the period he would invest all of T except the first day's expenditure and then sell securities every day in an amount equal to the day's expenditure. That way he would clearly maximize his interest earnings from securities. It follows

FIGURE 14

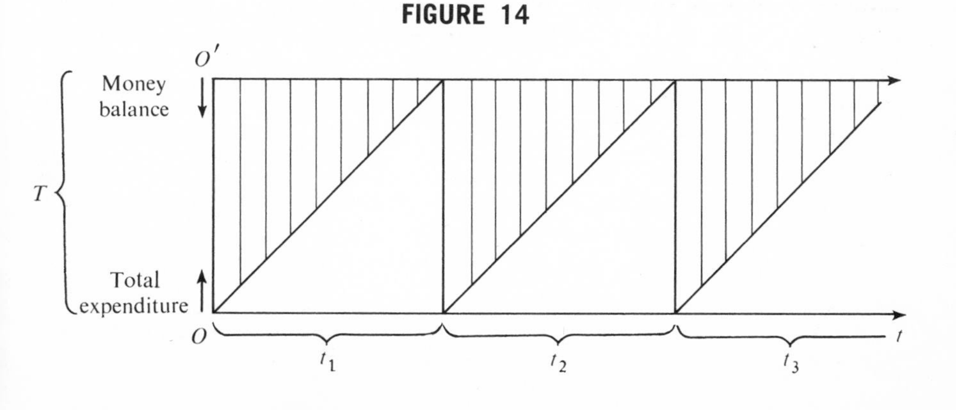

that C would be equal to a day's expenditure, and he would sell securities daily.

A diagram may prove helpful here to illustrate what the transactor is doing. Consider Figure 15. The time profile of his expenditure is unchanged. However, when he receives T (dollars) at the beginning of the period he buys securities in an amount I and only retains R money, which he uses to finance the first part of the year's transactions. When this runs out he sells off securities at equal intervals over the rest of the year in equal amounts C. Thus, the time profile of his money balance has the uneven saw-toothed shape shown. Clearly, the sum of the Cs equals I, as the dashed guidelines reveal by inspection.

However, it is in fact the case that both buying securities and selling them is *costly*. What are these security "dealing costs"? They are many. As you will be aware if you have ever owned a security, there is a psychic cost (you can go gray with worry); the dealing is costly in terms of time and energy; there are mailing and telephone costs; there are bookkeeping costs; and, finally, there are brokerage fees. Let us assume that there are some costs which depend on the size of the security transaction (for example, the brokerage fee) and some costs which are fixed, or independent of the size of the security transaction (for example, the telephone call). Specifically, we shall assume that the cost of investing I dollars in securities is given by the linear function $b_d + k_d I$ and the cost of withdrawing C dollars in cash from the security market is given by the linear function $b_w + k_w C$, where b and k are different constants.

The first thing we must do now is derive the cost associated with the decision, made at the beginning of the year, to invest I dollars in securities and retain R dollars in money; second, we must determine the costs associated with the decision to withdraw several batches of dollars at later periods of the year.

FIGURE 15

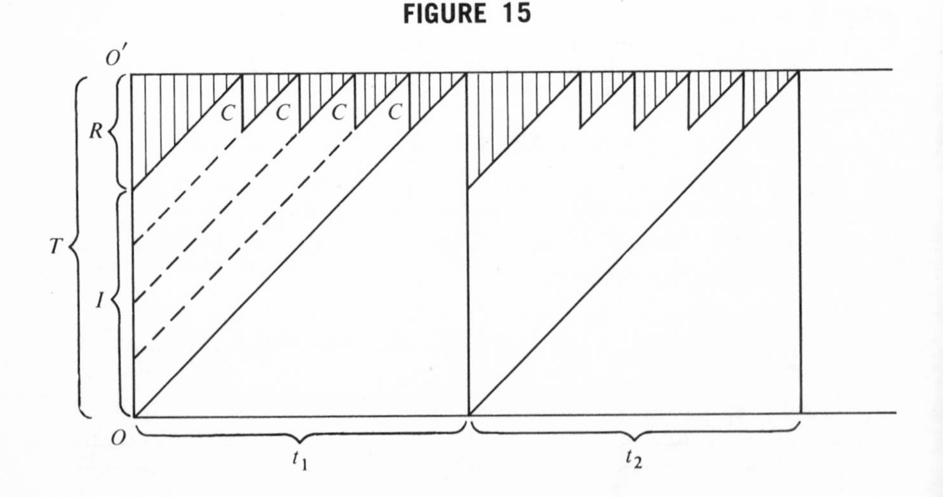

That amount of money R which is not invested at the beginning of the year will serve to cover expenditure needs for a fraction of the year given by $R/T = (T - I)/T$ [from (12)]. [It follows that if you spend 100 dollars in a year and retained 10 dollars in money at the beginning of the year (having invested the other 90 dollars), that 10 dollars would cover your expenditure for 1/10 of a year.] During this fraction of the year, your average money holding would be $R/2 = (T - I)/2$. Thus, if the annual rate of interest is r (assumed constant), the opportunity cost in terms of foregone interest of the decision to keep R dollars in money at the beginning of the year is given by

$$\frac{T-I}{2}\left(r\frac{T-I}{T}\right) \tag{13}$$

which is the average balance multiplied by the annual rate of interest and the fraction of the year it was held.

At the beginning of the year when the individual decided to keep R dollars in money, he also decided to invest I dollars in securities. The cost of this decision was

$$b_d + k_d I \tag{14}$$

Now let us examine the costs incurred in that part of the year when withdrawals are being made. If I dollars originally were invested and C-dollar batches are periodically withdrawn, the number of withdrawals is obviously I/C. If we multiply the given cost of each withdrawal by this we obtain

$$(b_w + k_w C)\frac{I}{C} \tag{15}$$

These are the costs specifically associated with the withdrawals. But during this part of the year opportunity costs, in terms of foregone interest, also are being incurred. They will be equal to the average balance held during this part of the year $C/2$ multiplied by the interest rate r and the fraction of the year this average balance was held I/T, or

$$\frac{C}{2}\left(r\frac{I}{T}\right) \tag{16}$$

The fraction of the year during which the average balance held was $C/2$ is equal to I/T because, as we saw earlier, the other fraction of the year during which $R/2$ was held was $(T - I)/T$; and $1 - [(T - I)/T]$ equals I/T.

Thus, the total cost K of the individual's cash operations for the year is equal to the sum of (12)–(15):

$$K = \frac{T-I}{2}\left(r\frac{T-I}{T}\right) + b_d + k_d I + (b_w + k_w C)\frac{I}{C} + \frac{C}{2}\left(r\frac{I}{T}\right) \tag{17}$$

We now wish to find the optimum size withdrawal C (that C which minimizes K). To do this, differentiate (17) partially with respect to C, set the result equal to zero, and solve for C. Thus,

$$\frac{\partial K}{\partial C} = -\frac{b_w I}{C^2} + \frac{rI}{2T} = 0$$

$$C = \sqrt{\frac{2Tb_w}{r}} \tag{18}$$

From (18) we observe that the optimum C and, therefore, the average balance $C/2$ held later in the year when securities are being sold to finance transactions, is inversely related to the rate of interest: when r rises C falls.

How do we determine the optimal size of R? This, you will recall, is the portion of the initial money balance which was held to finance expenditure in the early part of the year without first being invested. The technique is the same as above. First rewrite (18) in terms of R by substituting R for $T - I$ and $T - R$ for I, then partially differentiate with respect to R, set the result equal to zero, and solve for R. Thus,

$$\frac{\partial K}{\partial R} = \frac{Rr}{T} - k_d - \frac{b_w}{C} - k_w - \frac{Cr}{2T} = 0$$

$$R = \frac{C}{2} + \frac{b_w T}{Cr} + \frac{T(k_d + k_w)}{r} \tag{19}$$

It is clear from (19) that the size of R and, therefore, its average $R/2$ is inversely related to the rate of interest, too. Thus, if both the average balance initially retained at the beginning of the year $R/2$ and the average balance maintained through the rest of the year when $R/2$ is used up (i.e., $C/2$) are inversely related to the rate of interest, then it follows that the average balance held throughout the year will be similarly related. Thus, we have shown that there is a good theoretical basis to suppose that an individual's demand for money for transaction purposes is inversely related to the rate of interest. This implies, of course, that his demand for bonds is directly related to the rate of interest. When the individual demand curves for bonds and money are aggregated, we would once more obtain market demand curves similar to those shown in Figures 9 and 10.

Finally, we draw attention to another implication of these results, namely, that *economies of scale* exist in the transaction demand for money. From the result in (18) it is apparent that $C/2$ does not increase in proportion to T, but *in proportion to its square root*. Since $C^2 = 2Tb_w/r$ from (18), the second term in (18) is equal to $C^2/2C$; and (18) may be rewritten as

$$R = C + T\,\frac{k_w + k_d}{r} \tag{20}$$

Examination of (20) reveals that one part of R, given by the second term, varies in proportion with T, while the other part varies with C. But we have already seen that C varies in proportion with the square root of T. Thus, overall, R will also vary less than in proportion to T. Consequently, the transaction demand for money as a whole will vary in less than proportion to T and economies of scale are said to exist here.

3 The Market Demand and Supply of Money

Our analysis of the demand for real money balances and real bonds by an individual transactor allows us to write

$$\frac{M^d}{P} = L\left(Y^s, r, \frac{V}{P}\right), \qquad L_1 > 0, L_2 < 0, L_3 > 0 \tag{XII}$$

and

$$\frac{B^d}{rP} = B^d\left(Y^s, \frac{1}{r}, \frac{V}{P}\right), \qquad B_1^d > 0, B_2^d < 0, B_3^d > 0 \tag{IX}$$

as the aggregate demand functions for these two financial assets. In these equations V/P is real *net* assets (see §5.4). These are the twelfth and ninth equations in our complete macroeconomic model. We shall continue our discussion of the demand for real bonds in the next chapter along with an analysis of the supply of real bonds function. For the moment, we now concentrate on the demand for money balances. It is convenient to express this relationship geometrically in nominal terms so we multiply both sides of (XII) by P to obtain

$$M^d = P \cdot L\left(Y^s, r, \frac{V}{P}\right) \tag{21}$$

For given values of real income Y^s, real *net* assets V/P, and the price level, money demand appears as the solid curve labeled M^d in Figure 16. Here the nominal demand for money is plotted as a function of the interest rate.

As we began by noting, the supply of money $\bar{M}^s$ is an exogenous variable whose amount is completely controlled by the government and, as such,

FIGURE 16

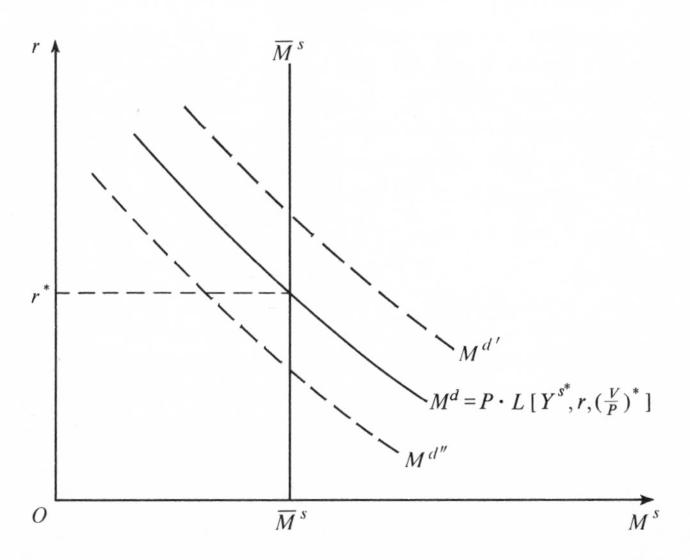

is unresponsive to changes in any of the other variables in the model. We do not, therefore, need an equation to explain its behavior. Diagrammatically, it appears as a vertical line in Figure 16.

The thirteenth basic equation in our complete macroeconomic model is the money market equilibrium condition

$$M^d = \bar{M}^s \tag{XIII}$$

This equation merely states that in equilibrium the nominal quantity of money demanded must equal the nominal quantity of money supplied. In Figure 16, this occurs at r^*; at interest rates above r^* there would be an excess supply of money and downward pressure on r, and at interest rates below r^* an excess demand for money and upward pressure on r. From our preceding analysis we know that if Y^s or V/P increases the M^d curve will shift right to $M^{d'}$, thus raising the equilibrium interest rate. Furthermore, if Y^s or V/P decreases this curve will shift left to $M^{d''}$, thus lowering the equilibrium interest rate. It remains to discuss the influence of changes in P on this curve, other things being equal. We see by inspection of equation (21) that when P increases, for example, so will M^d; when the price level increases, the demand for nominal money balances must increase proportionately if the same level of *real* balances is to be maintained. However, transactors will *not* wish to maintain the same level of real balances when the price level rises, since their real net assets V/P are thereby reduced and this, we know, reduces the demand for money. Consequently, we may conclude that when the price level increases, while other conditions do not change, the demand for nominal money balances increases but less than proportionately. The opposite result occurs, of course, for a decrease in the price level; that is, the demand for nominal money balances decreases but less than proportionately, since an increase in V/P tends to raise the demand for real money balances. In terms of equation (21), the change in P outside the parentheses is inducing a proportionate change in M^d, but the change P induces on the term V/P inside the parentheses makes the change in M^d less than proportionate. Therefore, a rise in the price level would increase M^d to a position such as $M^{d'}$, forcing the equilibrium interest rate to go higher; a fall in the price level would shift M^d to a position such as $M^{d''}$, thus lowering the equilibrium interest rate.

The final factor influencing M^d that we must discuss is a change in *liquidity preference*. With *no* change in either real income, the interest rate, or real net assets, transactors may just decide that they wish to hold more money and fewer bonds. In such a case, their *preferences*, or "tastes," vis-à-vis the two assets have changed and they are said to have experienced an increase in liquidity preference. Analogously, a decrease in liquidity preference means that transactors' preferences vis-à-vis money and bonds have changed in favor of bonds because of a shift of tastes towards the latter (with *no* change in real income, the interest rate, or real net assets). A shift in liquidity preference shows up in equation (21) as a change in the *form* of the function represented by the functional L preceding the parentheses. If liquidity preference increases, we would write the equation $M^{d'} = P \cdot L'(Y^s, r, V/P)$. Diagrammatically, the whole curve would shift right to a position such as $M^{d'}$ in Figure 16 and the equilibrium interest rate would rise. And, of course, the opposite would be true for a decrease in liquidity preference.

In summary, M^d will be shifted right by an increase in Y^s, V/P, P, or liquidity preference (and the interest rate will rise); and M^d will be shifted left by a decrease in Y^s, V/P, P, or liquidity preference (and the interest rate will fall).

Before concluding this discussion we should repeat our caveat from Chapter 1 concerning the loose way in which we, along with almost everybody else, talk about the money "market." We have already explained that there is no market for money in the usual sense of the word. A place where transactors go to supply and demand money simply does not exist in the way that a place where transactors can go to supply and demand labor, commodities, or bonds does. Money is *the* good which is exchanged against all other goods in their markets – money does not have a market of its own. Nonetheless, there is a certain supply of money which must be held and a demand for money to be held. When the quantity of money which transactors are willing to hold and the supply of money which must be held are equal, we say the money "market" is in equilibrium.

This completes our investigation of the money market which is the third market of our macroeconomic model. It remains for us to discuss the bond market in Chapter 6.

Summary

The supply of money, whether it is of the fiat or bank variety, is assumed to be under the direct control of the government. The total supply of money $\bar{M}^s$ is, therefore, described as an exogenous variable.

On the basis of microeconomic theoretical reasoning, we showed that the demand for money and bonds are directly related to real income and, in the short run, to transactors' asset endowments. The dependence of the demand for money and bonds on the interest rate was then discussed. We considered three alternative hypotheses which rationalize an inverse relationship between the demand for money and the interest rate and a direct relationship between the demand for bonds and the interest rate. These were *Tobin's* hypothesis based on transactor's attitudes toward *risk and uncertainty*, *Keynes'* hypothesis based on transactor's *inelastic bond price expectations*, and *Baumol's* hypothesis based on *optimal inventory holdings*. We found that the demand for real money balances could be written $M^d/P = L(Y^s, r, V/P)$ with $L_1 > 0$, $L_2 < 0$, and $L_3 > 0$; while the demand for real bonds could be written $B^d/rP = B^d(Y^s, 1/r, V/P)$ with $B_1^d > 0$, $B_2^d < 0$, and $B_3^d > 0$.

Questions

1. Using microeconomic theory as a basis, explain why the demand for money and the demand for bonds are directly related to the level of income.
2. The demand for money and the demand for bonds are directly dependent on transactors' asset endowments in the short run, but independent of them in the long run. Explain, using microeconomic foundations.
3. Explain why when the price level increases and other conditions remain the same, the demand for nominal money balances increases but *less* than in proportion to the change in the price level. Assume that the demand for real money balances is given by $M^d/P = L(Y^s, r, V/P)$ with $L_1 > 0$, $L_2 < 0$, $L_3 > 0$.
4. Explain Keynes' rationalization of an inverse relationship between the demand for money and the interest rate.
5. Explain Tobin's rationalization of an inverse relationship between the demand for money and the interest rate.
6. Explain Baumol's rationalization of an inverse relationship between the demand for money and the interest rate.

SELECTED READINGS

1. G. C. Archibald and R. G. Lipsey, "Monetary and Value Theory; A Critique of Lange and Patinkin," *Review of Economic Studies,* October, 1958. Showed that *in the long run* the demand for money and bonds is independent of transactors' asset endowments. Critical of Patinkin's inclusion of real balances in demand and supply functions. However, Patinkin's position still holds in the short-run or non-stationary states. An interesting followup to this article is "A Symposium on Monetary Theory," *Review of Economic Studies,* October, 1960.
2. W. J. Baumol, "The Transactions Demand for Cash: An Inventory Theoretic Approach," *Quarterly Journal of Economics,* November, 1952. Using optimal inventory control theory, Baumol shows that the transactions demand for cash should be inversely related to the interest rate.
3. R. W. Clower, "A Reconsideration of the Microfoundations of Monetary Theory," *Western Economic Journal,* December, 1967. Critical of the notion of a money "market." Argues that money's distinguishing characteristic is that it is traded in all other markets and is without a market of its own.
4. J. M. Keynes, *The General Theory of Employment, Interest, and Money,* Macmillan, 1936, chapters 13 and 15. Argues that the demand for money (liquidity preference) is inversely related to the interest rate via inelastic bond price expectations. The first attempt to rationalize such an inverse relationship. Also introduces the famous distinction between transactions, precautionary, and speculative money balances.
5. D. Patinkin, *Money, Interest, and Prices,* 2nd ed., Harper & Row, 1965, chapter 9, sections 4 and 5.
6. J. Tobin, "Liquidity Preference as Behavior towards Risk," *Review of Economic Studies,* February, 1958. Rationalizes an inverse relationship between the demand for money and the interest rate based on transactors' attitudes toward risk and uncertainty.

FURTHER READINGS

7. D. Laidler, *The Demand for Money: Theories and Evidence,* International, 1969. A short book which surveys the theory and evidence on the demand for money.

Finds that the evidence for an inverse relationship between the demand for money and the interest rate is overwhelming. Contains an excellent bibliography which makes the inclusion of further references here redundant.

8. J. Tobin, "The Interest Elasticity of Transactions Demand for Cash," *Review of Economics and Statistics,* August, 1959. Like Baumol [2], uses inventory theory to rationalize an inverse relationship between the demand for money and the interest rate.

5

The Bond Market

This chapter will be brief, since most of the groundwork has already been laid in previous chapters, especially the analysis of the demand for real bonds. Hence, we dispense with this first, then move on to a discussion of the supply of real bonds, and, finally, investigate how the demand for and supply of bonds interact to determine the price of bonds (and, implicitly, the rate of interest).

1 The Demand for Bonds

We have already established that the demand for real bonds, which emanates exclusively from the household sector, may be summarized by the ninth equation of our model:

$$\frac{B^d}{rP} = B^d\left(Y^s, \frac{1}{r}, \frac{V}{P}\right) \qquad B_1^d > 0,\ B_2^d < 0,\ B_3^d > 0 \qquad \text{(IX)}$$

The left-hand side of this equation represents real bonds demanded. This is equal to the *number* of bonds demanded B^d multiplied by the price per bond $1/r$ (which gives the nominal value of the bonds) divided by the price of a unit of commodities P which gives the real value of bonds demanded. The factors on which the demand for real bonds depends are real income Y^s, the price of bonds $1/r$, and real net assets V/P. When real income increases, more saving is planned and, thus, more bonds are demanded, and vice versa. Thus, the influence of real income on real bonds demanded is a direct one. When the price of bonds rises (i.e., the interest rate falls) two factors which tend to reduce the demand for bonds come into play. First, less saving is planned and, second, transactors switch from bonds to money (for reasons discussed in Chapter 4). When the price of bonds falls, an opposite situation prevails. Thus, the influence of the price of bonds on the quantity demanded is an inverse one. However, when real net financial asset holdings rise the demand for real bonds increases (in the short run), and vice versa. Thus, the relationship between the demand for real bonds and real financial assets is a direct one.

Geometrically, it is convenient to plot the number of bonds demanded B^d as a function of their price $1/r$. To see how B^d is affected by the factors on which it depends, multiply both sides of (IX) by rP to obtain

$$B^d = rP \cdot B^d\left(Y^s, \frac{1}{r}, \frac{V}{P}\right) \tag{1}$$

How will B^d react to a ceteris paribus change in the interest rate? The interest rate r appears in equation (1) twice. Its appearance outside the parentheses with a positive sign indicates a direct relationship; when the interest rate rises (the price of bonds falls), the number of bonds demanded rises. Its appearance inside the parentheses, we have already learned, reflects a similar functional relationship. When the interest rate rises (the price of bonds falls), the number of bonds demanded rises. Thus, if we plot the number of bonds demanded as a function of their price we obtain an unambiguously downward-sloping demand curve such as that labeled B^d in Figure 1(a). Note that the number of bonds demanded is a *stock* variable; it indicates the demand to hold a certain number of bonds at an instant of time.

If real income increases to Y_1^s, ceteris paribus, we know the demand for real bonds increases. Thus, since we are talking about a ceteris paribus increase in income, the number of bonds demanded B^d must increase. It follows that an increase in real income would shift curve B^d to the right to, let us say, $B^{d'}$ in Figure 1(a). Similarly a decrease in real income to Y_2^s would shift B^d left to $B^{d''}$.

How will a ceteris paribus change in the price level affect B^d? The price

FIGURE 1

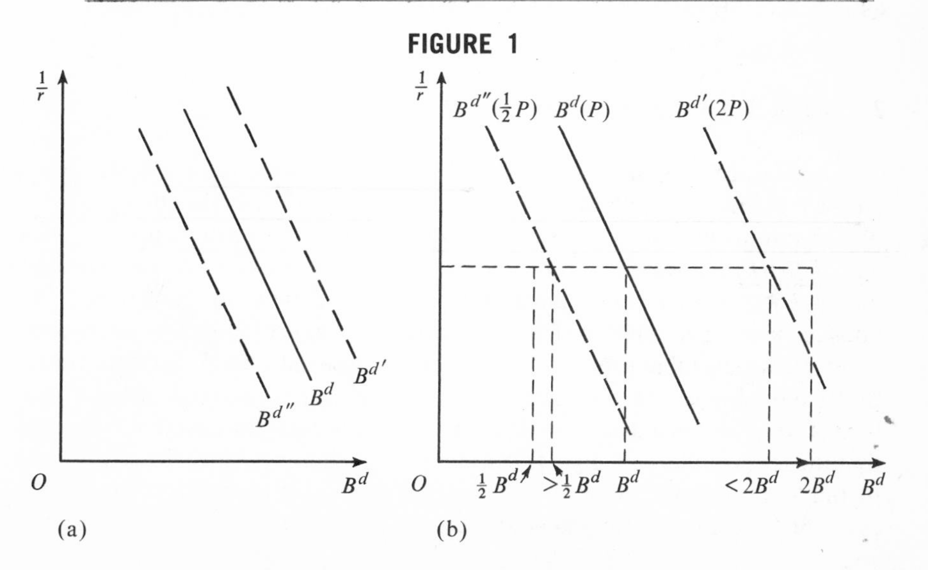

level P also appears in equation (1) twice. Its appearance outside the parentheses with a positive sign indicates that an increase in the price level will result in a *proportional* increase in B^d. Thus, if P appeared only there, then, for example, when the price level doubled the number of bonds demanded would also double. However, P also appears inside the parentheses in the denominator of the real net financial asset term V/P. So when P rises V/P falls if, as we assume, V is constant. We know a fall in V/P reduces the number of bonds demanded. Consequently, the influence of P outside the parentheses (which, by itself, would tend to cause a proportionate increase in the number of bonds demanded) is attenuated by the influence of P in the term V/P. Thus, we may conclude that when P rises B^d will rise, *but less than proportionately*. For example, if the original price level is P and the original quantity of bonds demanded is B^d, then if the price level doubles to $2P$ the number of bonds demanded should rise, but to something less than $2B^d$. [See the curves B^d and $B^{d'}$ in Figure 1(b).] If we reverse our assumptions we come to the same sort of conclusion. The first appearance of P indicates a proportionate fall in B^d when P falls. However, the decrease in P also increases real financial assets V/P and this tends to increase B^d. Thus, overall, the fall in P reduces B^d, *but less than proportionately*. If the original price level is P and the original quantity of bonds demanded is B^d, then halving the price level to $1/2\ P$ would cause the number of bonds demanded to fall but not as low as $1/2\ B^d$. [See curves B^d and $B^{d''}$ in Figure 1(b).] To summarize the effects of a change in P on B^d we offer the following important conclusion: *When P changes B^d changes in the same direction but* **less** *than proportionately*.

Finally, let us discuss the influence of a ceteris paribus change in net financial assets. This is quite straightforward. When financial assets increase, V/P and B^d increase. The curve B^d in Figure 1(a) would shift right to $B^{d'}$. If net financial assets decrease, V/P and B^d decrease. Then B^d in Figure 1(a) would shift left to $B^{d''}$.

2 The Supply of Bonds

Bonds are supplied by firms. The real supply of bonds is equal to the *number* of bonds supplied B^s multiplied by the price of a bond $1/r$ divided by the commodity price level P or, algebraically, the real supply of bonds equals B^s/rP. On what does this quantity depend? When firms supply bonds they are borrowing. The question reduces itself, then, to what factors influence firms' borrowing? If firms borrow to finance the plant and equipment on which their production activities are based, then what determines the size of their plant and equipment?

During our discussion of firms' investment plans in Chapter 3 we saw that the level of planned investment in plant and equipment is directly related to the level of real income. Thus, when real income changes, firms' investment plans change in the same direction. This induces a parallel change in firms' borrowing requirements, that is, the real bonds they plan to supply. Consequently, we may conclude that there is a direct relationship between the supply of real bonds and real income.

We also saw in Chapter 3 that the level of planned investment is inversely related to the rate of interest. When the rate of interest declines (bond prices rise), for example, planned investment rises. The additional financing required to augment the capital stock will induce an increase in borrowing. Thus, the real supply of bonds will increase when the rate of interest falls (bond prices increase), and vice versa. We conclude, then, that the real supply of bonds is directly related to the price of bonds.

The final factor which affects the quantity of real bonds firms will supply has not been discussed previously. We refer to firms' real money balances M/P. Firms have a demand to hold real money balances to finance their transactions. A firm which has an inadequate money balance will be forced either to default on some of its contractual obligations or to make hurried and, therefore, costly borrowing arrangements. The larger the firm's real money balance, the greater is the security it affords the firm against such embarrassments and inconveniences. However, the *marginal* value of the security against embarrassment and inconvenience provided by the real money balance decreases as the size of the balance increases. There comes a point where the marginal value of the security provided by the real money balance just equals the interest saving that could be achieved if the firm used some of its real money balance to reduce its outstanding debt. At this point, the firm is holding an optimal money balance. If its money balance should *rise* above this optimum, it would benefit the firm to use some of it to *reduce* its outstanding debt, that is, *reduce* its real supply of bonds; if its money balance should *fall* below this optimum, it would be to the firm's advantage to *increase* its money balance, that is, borrow, or *increase* its real supply of bonds. Thus, starting with all firms at an optimum, an increase in real balances will induce a reduction in the real supply of bonds, and a reduction in real balances will lead to an increase in the real supply of bonds.

The foregoing discussion implies the following equation for the real supply of bonds:

$$\frac{B^s}{rP} = B^s\left(Y^s, \frac{1}{r}, \frac{M}{P}\right) \qquad B_1^s > 0,\ B_2^s > 0,\ B_3^s < 0 \tag{X}$$

This is the tenth equation of our complete macroeconomic model. By multiplying both sides of (X) through by rP we obtain

$$B^s = rP \cdot B^s\left(Y^s, \frac{1}{r}, \frac{M}{P}\right) \tag{2}$$

which shows the *number* of bonds supplied as a function of the variables on which it depends. How will this quantity vary with the interest rate (the price of bonds)? The answer is ambiguous, since the interest rate appears twice in equation (2). Considering the term $1/r$ inside the parentheses, we may infer that a fall in the interest rate (a rise in bond prices) induces firms to borrow more in order to invest in more plant and equipment and therefore increases the number of bonds they wish to supply. So, if we are plotting B^s as a function of bond prices as in Figure 2(a) we would get a positively sloping curve. However, the interest rate also appears outside the parentheses with a positive sign indicating that if r falls (bond prices rise) B^s falls. This means that B^s as a function of bond prices has a negative slope. We shall assume that this negative relationship is dominated by the former positive relationship and, thus, that overall the B^s curve has a positive slope. (The basic economic reason for a component of the supply of bonds involving the inverse relationship discussed is that when bond prices rise the number of bonds which has to be issued to raise a given amount of finance declines because each bond supplied raises more money.)

By inspecting equation (2) we can see that the B^s curve in Figure 2(a) will be shifted right to a position such as $B^{s\prime}$ if real income Y^s increases, and left to $B^{s\prime\prime}$ if real income decreases.

Now let us discuss the influence on B^s of a ceteris paribus change in money balances. When M increases, M/P increases and firms use some of their additional real money balances to redeem some bonds. Thus B^s shifts left to $B^{s\prime\prime}$ in Figure 2(a). If M falls, M/P falls and firms wish to rebuild their real money balances by issuing more bonds. Thus, B^s shifts right to $B^{s\prime}$ in Figure 2(a).

The influence of a change in prices on the B^s curve is slightly more complicated, since P appears twice in equation (2). Its first appearance with a positive sign indicates that B^s changes proportionately to the price level. For example, if P is doubled, B^s also doubles. However, P also appears inside the parentheses in the term M/P, so that when P rises M/P falls. A fall in M/P induces firms to issue *more* bonds to rebuild their money balances. Consequently, an overall increase in P leads to a *more than proportionate*

FIGURE 2

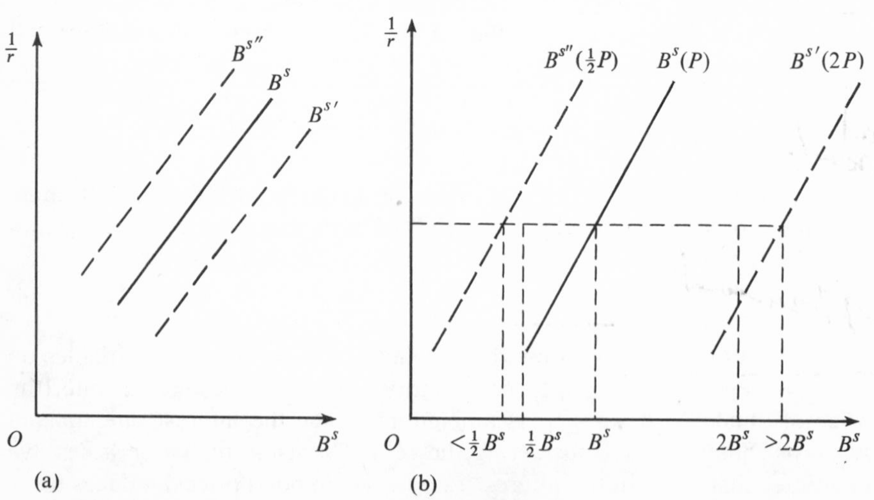

increase in B^s. This is illustrated in Figure 2(b), where, after P doubles, the B^s curve shifts right by more than double to $B^{s\prime}$.

Similarly, a more than proportionate reduction in B^s occurs when P falls. The first appearance of P in equation (2) indicates a proportionate reduction in B^s when P falls. But when P falls M/P rises and firms use some of the increase in real balances to redeem more bonds. This is illustrated in Figure 2(b) where, after P is halved, the B^s curve shifts left to $B^{s\prime\prime}$, which is less than half B^s. To summarize the effects of a change in P on B^s we offer the following important conclusion: *When P changes B^s changes in the same direction but **more** than proportionately.*

We should mention here that the change in P outside the parentheses in equation (2), which leads firms to change the number of bonds they plan to supply in proportion to the change in P, is explained in two rather shaky ways. True, the change in prices means that a proportionate change in the number of bonds outstanding is called for to finance the same level of real activity, but

> there is an implicit assumption here that all the firms' capital equipment must be replaced during the period in question. Alternatively, we can assume that [in the event of a price rise] firms immediately write up their capital equipment in accordance with its increased value, and pass on the implicit capital gains to their entrepreneurs. Conversely, in the event of a decrease in prices, entrepreneurs must make good the implicit capital loss, and firms then use these funds to retire bonds. In this way the nominal amount of bonds outstanding can always be kept equal to the current value of the firms' assets.[1]

A Critical Aside on "Money Illusion"

Both of the above explanations probably strike the reader as somewhat far-fetched in that they are demonstrably not true of the "real" world. We are in the process of constructing a short-run macroeconomic model, so that it is unreasonable to suppose that all the firms' capital must be replaced during the period in question. (In the case of nondepreciating consol capital this assumption is palpably false!) Similarly, it is uncommon, to say the least, for entrepreneurs to write up the value of their capital equipment when prices rise, issue a quantity of bonds equal in amount to the increased value of the equipment, and take the proceeds as a capital gain. (If prices fall, we assume according to the reasoning from Patinkin, that entrepreneurs write down the value of their capital equipment, make good the capital loss to the firm from their own resources, and then have the firm use this money to buy back its bonds in order to keep them equal to the lower value of the capital equipment.)

However, an important issue is raised when entrepreneurs do *not* respond in this way to increases or decreases in the price level, but behave with what is described as *money illusion* vis-à-vis their supply of bonds. In general, a transactor has money illusion if the amount he demands or sup-

[1] D. Patinkin, *Money, Interest, and Prices*, 2nd ed., Harper & Row, 1965, p. 217, fn. 13.

plies of *any* real good (whether commodities, labor, bonds, or money) varies in response to some change in circumstances which does not affect his real income (current or future), relative prices, the interest rate, or his real assets.

To illustrate this proposition, consider the real bond supply function in the form of equation (X). Now assume P increases and the firm's money holdings increase proportionally to P. This keeps M/P constant. We assume that everything else (e.g., Y^s and $1/r$) is constant. Thus, there is no change in the real circumstances confronting the firm. Now if B^s on the left-hand side of equation (X) is *not* increased by the firm (in the "unrealistic" manner explained in the penultimate paragraph) in exactly the same proportion that P has increased, the real supply of bonds B^s/rP *must* change (actually, decrease). As a result, we would have the supply of real bonds changing with no change in the real variables on which it depends—Y^s, $1/r$, and M/P. The firm would, then, be reacting with money illusion.

Another example of a money illusion–dominated function will help clarify the nature of the phenomenon. Assume (for this example *only*) that the real supply of labor N^s is given by the function $N^s = N^s(W)$; $N_1^s > 0$. This states that the real supply of labor is an increasing function of the *nominal* wage. To see that this function contains money illusion, assume an increase in P and a proportional increase in W. This keeps the real wage constant (which is the relative price of labor in terms of commodities); and everything else is assumed to be constant in ceteris paribus. Nonetheless, according to the function postulated above the real supply of labor *will* increase merely because W has increased. None of the *real* circumstances surrounding the transactor have changed, and yet he is responding by changing his real supply of labor. This is therefore defined as a money illusion response.

In the grand neoclassical tradition of economics, transactors are all perfectly rational *homo oeconomici,* and it is anathema to allow them to behave irrationally. Nevertheless, supply and demand functions containing money illusion responses are certainly indicative of transactor irrationality because, as we have just seen, a transactor makes a real economic response when none of the real circumstances confronting him have changed. In keeping with the neoclassical tradition of completely rational behavior by *all* transactors, in Part II when we discuss the properties of our complete macroeconomic model in detail in a neoclassical context, we *exclude* money illusion from *every* supply and demand function. Consequently, we must, for example, make the supply of labor a function of the real wage and also adopt an assumption vis-à-vis a firm's supply of bonds like the one discussed above—namely, that when the price level rises entrepreneurs write up the value of their firm's capital, issue a quantity of bonds equal in amount to the increased value of the equipment, and take the proceeds themselves as a capital gain (and vice versa when the price level falls).

Neo-Keynesian macroeconomics is not so wedded to the concept of the perfectly rational *homo oeconomicus.* Thus, in Part III when we discuss neo-Keynesian macroeconomics in detail, we are not adverse to allowing money illusion to creep into some of our basic functions. After all, Keynes himself argued that the quantity of labor supplied reacted to changes in *money* wages (see the excerpts from the *General Theory* quoted at the beginning of Chapter 10). In Part III we will not shrink, therefore, from admitting money illusion into the labor supply function (Chapter 10) and into the bond supply function (Chapter 12). When we do so, we shall take pains to compare the overall properties of our macroeconomic model when it involves some functions containing money illusion with its properties in a neoclassical context, which totally excludes money illusion from every function (the neoclassical view is developed in Part II).

We should make one final comment about the bond supply function before proceeding to a discussion of the bond market as a whole. The ability of firms to supply bonds must be limited in some way which we have not yet discussed. If firms' ability to supply bonds were *not* restricted, bonds would be supplied in unlimited amounts, which would enable a firm to exert an unlimited claim on the economy's real resources of labor and commodities. Notice that the obligation to pay interest on its bonds would *not* effectively restrain the firm's willingness to supply bonds. All the firm need do would be to supply even more bonds to raise the money to pay the interest. The accepted method of coping with this dilemma is to assume that some "imperfection" in the bond market prevents any firm from issuing an unlimited quantity of bonds. We shall adopt this convention.

3 The Bond Market

The equations characterizing the bond market so far consist of the number of bonds demanded [equation (1)] and number of bonds supplied [equation (2)]; this system is completed by the bond market equilibrium condition

$$B^d = B^s \tag{XI}$$

This is the eleventh equation in our complete macroeconomic model. It simply states that in equilibrium the number of bonds demanded must equal the number of bonds supplied.

The bond market as a whole is illustrated in Figure 3. For given levels of real income Y^s, the price level P, and real net assets A/P (for households) and M/P (for firms), the equilibrium price of bonds would be $(1/r)^*$. If real income changes, both B^d and B^s change in the same direction. We shall make the *special assumption* that they also change by the same amount. Thus, the equilibrium price of bonds (and the interest rate) is *invariant* against changes in real income. An increase in real income, for example, from Y^s to Y_1^s would shift B^d and B^s to $B^{d\prime}$ and $B^{s\prime}$, respectively, in Figure 3(a), leaving bond prices unchanged at $(1/r)^*$.

If the price level changes, we know that both B^d and B^s change in the

FIGURE 3

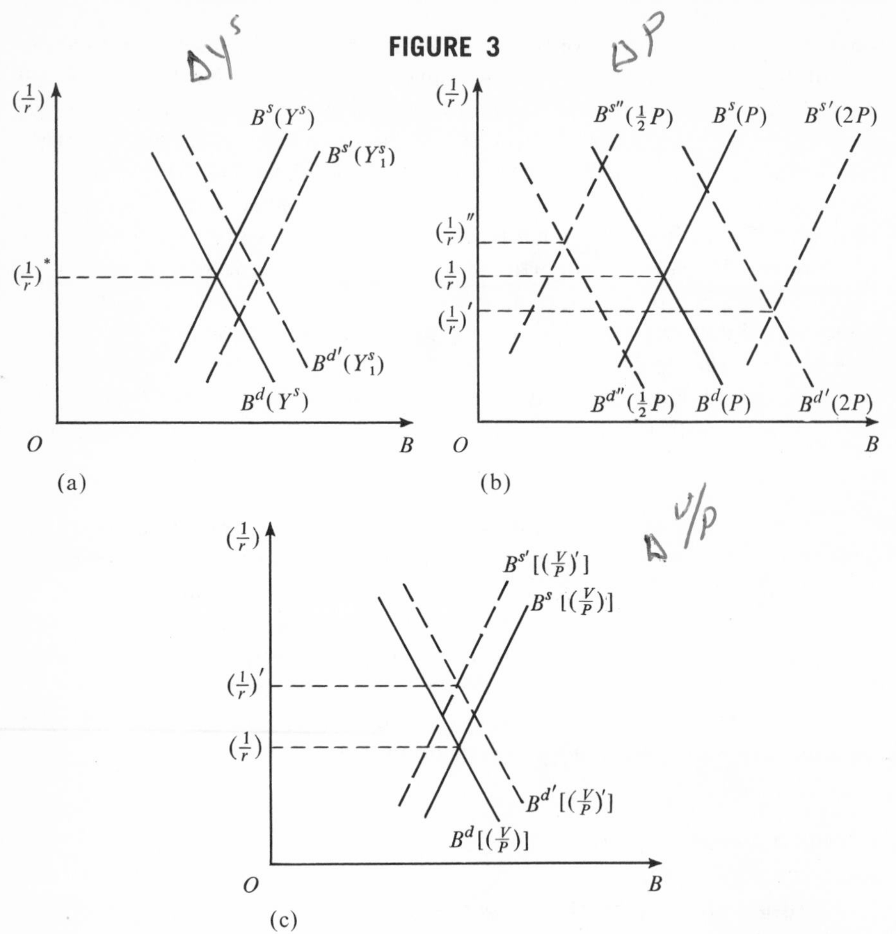

same direction. We also know that B^s changes more than proportionately and B^d changes less than proportionately. So, if P rises, both B^d and B^s move to the right, but B^s shifts more than B^d. Consequently, the two curves intersect at a lower bond price (implying a higher interest rate). This is illustrated by curves $B^{d'}$ and $B^{s'}$ in Figure 3(b). If P falls, both B^d and B^s shift to the left, but B^s shifts more than B^d. Thus, the curves intersect at a higher bond price (implying a lower interest rate). This is illustrated by curves $B^{d''}$ and $B^{s''}$ in Figure 3(b). We may summarize the impact of a ceteris paribus change in the price level, then, by stating the following important conclusion: *A rise in prices raises the interest rate; a reduction in prices reduces the interest rate.*

If real *net* financial assets change, ceteris paribus, the interest rate changes in the opposite direction. For example, if real money balances *increase* then the B^d curve shifts right to $B^{d'}$ [Figure 3(c)] and B^s shifts left to $B^{s'}$. Thus, the equilibrium price of bonds rises to $(1/r)'$ as r falls to r' (and vice versa).

The final aspect of the bond market which we must discuss is the impact of a change in liquidity preference. You will recall from §3.3, that a change in liquidity preference is said to occur when there is a change in transactors' tastes vis-à-vis money and bonds, although there is *no* change in real income, the interest rate, or real net assets. A change in liquidity preference changes the *form* of the demand for money function (signified by attaching a prime to the functional L preceding the parentheses). Similarly, such a change must alter the form of the bond demand *and* supply functions, since the change in tastes occurs vis-à-vis money and bonds. It is obvious that the form of the bond demand function must change as household basic preferences shift between money and bonds. The reason that the form of the bond supply function will also be different when liquidity preference changes is that in general, firms' preferences vis-à-vis money holding and debt issuing will also change. Thus, when liquidity preference *increases* we would write equation (1) as

$$B^{d'} = rP \cdot B^{d'}\left(Y^s, \frac{1}{r}, \frac{V}{P}\right)$$

and equation (2) as

$$B^{s'} = rP \cdot B^{s'}\left(Y^s, \frac{1}{r}, \frac{V}{P}\right)$$

Geometrically, the B^d curve shifts *left* (fewer bonds are demanded by households), and the B^s curve shifts *right* (firms want to hold more money so they raise it by issuing more bonds). The result is an unambiguous fall in bond prices (rise in the interest rate). Conversely, when liquidity preference *decreases* the B^d curve shifts *right* (more bonds are demanded by households), and the B^s curve shifts *left* (firms do not want to hold as much money so they use some of it to retire their bonds). The inevitable result is a rise in bond prices (fall in the interest rate). These conclusions are, of course, consistent with our earlier analysis of liquidity preference in Chapter 3, where we found an increase in liquidity preference raised the interest rate and a decrease in liquidity preference lowered it.

4 Net Assets, Net Worth, and Net Wealth

At several points in Part I we have had occasion to mention that the private sector's (households and firms) behavior is influenced by its net asset position. You will recall that consumption, the demand for money, the demand for bonds, and the supply of bonds are all functions of the private sector's asset position. Yet we never did precisely define the term *net assets*. This must be done before we continue.

To identify the private sector's *net asset* position (equivalently, its *net worth*, or *net wealth*), we need information about the balance sheet positions of these transactors. These are shown in Figure 4. Some brief commentary is in order on the non-self-explanatory entries. The household sector holds, as an asset, two types of money: fiat money and deposit money. In the lit-

FIGURE 4

HOUSEHOLD SECTOR'S BALANCE SHEET

Assets		Liabilities	
1. Fiat (*outside*) money	M_o^h	1. Net worth of households	V^h
2. Deposit (*inside*) money	M_i^h		
3. Private bonds	B_f^h/r		
4. Government bonds	B_g^h/r		

FIRM SECTOR'S BALANCE SHEET

Assets		Liabilities	
1. Fiat (*outside*) money	M_o^f	1. Private bonds	B_f/r
2. Deposit (*inside*) money	M_i^f	2. Net worth of firms	V^f
3. Physical assets	$P\bar{K}$		

BANKING SECTOR'S BALANCE SHEET

Assets		Liabilities	
1. Fiat (*outside*) money	M_o^b	1. Deposit (*inside*) money	M_i
2. Private bonds	B_f^b/r	2. Net worth of banks	V^b
3. Government bonds	B_g^b/r		

erature, these are also described, respectively, as *inside* and *outside* money.[1] Briefly, outside money is money which appears as an asset for someone in the private sector and *not* as a liability for someone else in the private sector. If you glance over the balance sheets, you will see outside money held as an asset by households, firms, and the bank (M_o^h, M_o^f, and M_o^b, respectively), but it does not appear as a liability anywhere in these balance sheets. (It is, of course, a liability of the government who issues it.) In contrast, inside money is money which appears as an asset for someone in the private sector *and* as a liability for someone else. For example, inside money held as an asset by households and firms (M_i^h and M_i^f), also appears as a liability of the banks M_i.

The net worth of households is equal to the sum of their inside and outside money holdings *plus* the sum of their private and government bond holdings.

Firms also hold both inside and outside money. Their only other asset is the stock of capital (the economy's physical assets), whose nominal value is equal to the number of units $\bar{K}$ times the price per unit P. The net worth of firms is equal to the sum of these assets *minus* the bonds they have issued.

[1] The terminology was introduced by J. G. Gurley and E. S. Shaw in their seminal work, *Money in a Theory of Finance,* Brookings, 1960, pp. 72–73.

The banking sector holds some outside money (as a reserve) and some private and government bonds. Against these assets, it incurs deposit money liabilities. The net worth of the bank is equal to the *difference* between its assets and its liability for deposit money.

We now wish to calculate the private sector's total net worth, that is, $V^h + V^f + V^b = V$. The balance sheet identities imply that

$$V = M_o^h + M_i^h + \frac{B_f^h}{r} + \frac{B_g^h}{r} + M_o^f + M_i^f + P\bar{K} + M_o^b + \frac{B_f^b}{r} + \frac{B_g^b}{r} - \frac{B_f}{r} - M_i \quad (3)$$

Since total outside money $M_o = M_o^h + M_o^f + M_o^b$, total inside money $M_i = M_i^h + M_i^f$, and $B_f/r = (B_f^h/r) + (B_g^h/r)$, equation (3) simplifies to

$$V = M_o + \frac{B_g}{r} + P\bar{K} \quad (4)$$

If we now convert the nominal wealth of the private sector into real terms by dividing through by P, we obtain

$$\frac{V}{P} = \frac{M_o}{P} + \frac{B_g}{rP} + \bar{K} \quad (5)$$

In words, equation (5) says that the private sector's net worth (equivalently, its net assets or net wealth) is equal to its real *outside* (i.e., fiat) money balances, its real *government* bond holdings, and its physical capital. Notice that *private* bonds and *inside* money do not appear. They "wash out" (that is, cancel) when the private sector's total net worth is calculated because they appear as an asset for one group and a liability for another group.

Since the stock of physical capital in our model is always fixed at $\bar{K}$, the private sector's real net assets are, for practical purposes, *only* a function of its real outside money holdings and its real government bond holdings. Moreover, when government is *excluded* from the model except as an issuer of outside money (as we have done so far), the private sector's real net assets are *only* a function of its real outside money holdings. Symbolically,

$$\frac{V}{P} = \frac{M_o}{P} \qquad \textit{(government excluded)} \quad (6)$$

$$\frac{V}{P} = \frac{M_o}{P} + \frac{B_g}{rP} \qquad \textit{(government included)} \quad (7)$$

We should now point out that the notion that inside money is not a component of the private sector's wealth since it washes out in the balance sheet consolidation process has recently been attacked by Pesek and Saving.[2] However, the controversy continues, the situation is fluid, and the issues are not yet resolved. Therefore, we shall proceed on what was once, at least, the conventional wisdom; namely, that inside money does wash out and is not, therefore, a legitimate component of the private sector's net worth.

[2] B. P. Pesek and T. R. Saving, *Money, Wealth, and Economic Theory,* Macmillan, 1967.

This completes our discussion of the microfoundations of the basic supply and demand functions which comprise our complete macroeconomic model. In the next chapter, we put together all our findings. In succeeding chapters we observe the model in operation under various assumptions. Part II concentrates on the predictions of the model when various disturbances are imparted to it under neoclassical assumptions; Part III concentrates on the predictions of the model when similar disturbances are imparted to it under neo-Keynesian assumptions.

Summary

In the previous chapter we found that the demand for real bonds was directly related to the level of income, the interest rate, and transactors' asset endowments. Thus, we may write $B^d/rP = B^d(Y^s, 1/r, V/P)$ with $B_1^d > 0$, $B_2^d < 0$, and $B_3^d > 0$. In this chapter we proceeded to show that when the price level changes, ceteris paribus, the number of bonds demanded B^d changes in the same direction, but *less* than proportionately. This is a crucial point to remember.

Next, our discussion pointed up two important relationships; first, that the real supply of bonds is directly related to the level of real income and, second, that it is indirectly related to the interest rate and firms' real money balances. Thus, $B^s/rP = B^s(Y^s, 1/r, M/P)$ with $B_1^s > 0$, $B_2^s > 0$, and $B_3^s < 0$. We also saw that when firms act without money illusion vis-à-vis their supply of bonds, the number of bonds they supply B^s changes in the same direction as the price level when it changes, other things being equal, but *more* than proportionately. This is another crucial point.

When the price level changes, ceteris paribus, the number of bonds demanded changes in the same direction but *less* than proportionately, while the number of bonds supplied changes in the same direction but *more* than proportionately; thus, it follows that when the price level decreases (again, ceteris paribus), bond prices rise (the interest rate falls), and vice versa. The student must master an understanding of these important relationships now or much of what follows will be unclear to him.

The final concept discussed was that of net wealth (net assets or net worth). The private sector's net real wealth is equal to the sum of its capital stock, its *outside* money holdings, and its holdings of *government* bonds. Thus, $V/P = \bar{K} + M_o/P + B_g/rP$. *Inside* money and *private* bonds do not appear as part of the private sector's net wealth, since they wash out in the balance sheet consolidation process one performs to arrive at net wealth.

Questions

1. What will happen to the price of bonds (the interest rate) if there is an increase in the private sector's net wealth, ceteris paribus?

2. Why does the number of bonds demanded change in the same direction as the price level but less than proportionately?
3. Why does the number of bonds supplied change in the same direction as the price level but more than proportionately?
4. Why do bond prices fall (the interest rate rises) when the price level increases, ceteris paribus?
5. Why do bond prices rise (the interest rate falls) when the price level falls, ceteris paribus?
6. Explain why a rise in bond prices (a fall in the interest rate), with no change in other factors, *might* lead to a smaller, rather than a larger, number of bonds being supplied by firms. (In the text we assume this does *not* occur, but it is a possibility.)
7. Explain why private bonds and *inside* money do not appear as a component of the private sector's net wealth.
8. Define money illusion. Explain why it is contained in the following functions:

$$C_n = a_1 + b_1 Y_n \qquad \textit{(consumption function)}$$

$$M^d = a_2 Y_n - b_2 r \qquad \textit{(money demand function)}$$

where C_n and Y_n are *nominal* consumption and income, respectively, and a_i and b_i are fixed coefficients. (*Hint:* Write everything in *real* terms by dividing through by P, then assume a change in P. What happens, according to these equations, to real consumption C/P and the demand for real money balances M^d/P?)

SELECTED READINGS

1. J. G. Gurley and E. S. Shaw, *Money in a Theory of Finance,* Brookings, 1960. Introduces the distinction between inside and outside money and the notion that the former washes out when the private sector's net wealth is calculated.
2. D. Patinkin, "Money and Wealth," *Journal of Economic Literature,* December, 1969. A critique of Pesek and Saving's critique [4] of Gurley and Shaw [1].
3. D. Patinkin, *Money, Interest, and Prices,* 2nd ed., Harper & Row, 1965, chapter 9, section 4.
4. B. P. Pesek and T. R. Saving, *Money, Wealth, and Economic Theory,* Macmillan, 1967. Challenges Gurley and Shaw's thesis [1] that inside money washes out and argues that it is, therefore, a legitimate component of the private sector's net wealth.

Part II

Neoclassical Macroeconomics

6

The Complete Macroeconomic Model

1 The Variables and the Equations

En route to this point in the discussion we have developed a demand function, a supply function, and a market clearance (equilibrium) condition for each of the four goods with which we are concerned. Now we are in a position to draw all the threads together and present the complete macroeconomic model exclusive of the government sector. This model has some interesting and useful properties which we want to develop and discuss without the clutter which inclusion of a government sector would inevitably involve. We shall certainly modify this basic model in due course (the end of Chapter 7) to incorporate a government sector. We give the algebraic version of the model first in Table 1 and then offer the geometric equivalents of these equations.

It will be helpful to briefly define again the variables which comprise this model and to classify them first as endogenous or exogenous variables and, then, as flow, stock, or price variables.

I. Endogenous Variables
   A. Flow variables
      1. N^d, demand for labor (labor services per time period).
      2. N^s, supply of labor (labor services per time period).
      3. Y^s, real income (total output of commodities per time period).
      4. C, real consumption (commodities consumed per time period).
      5. I, real investment (commodities invested, added to the capital stock, per time period).
      6. Y^d, real aggregate demand (total demand for commodities per time period).
      7. S, real saving (output of commodities *not* consumed per time period).

TABLE 1 Equations for the Complete Macroeconomic Model (excluding a Government Sector)

	EQUATION	NAME	MARKET
(I)	$N^d = N^d\left(\frac{W}{P}, \bar{K}\right)$	Labor demand function	Labor market
(II)	$N^s = N^s\left(\frac{W}{P}\right)$	Labor supply function	
(III)	$N^d = N^s$	Labor market clearance condition	
(IV)	$Y^s = Y^s(N, \bar{K})$	Production (or commodity supply) function	Commodity market
(V)	$C = C\left(Y^s, r, \frac{V}{P}\right)$	Commodity demand function for consumption (the consumption function)	
(VI)	$I = I(Y^s, r)$	Commodity demand function for investment (the investment function)	
(VII)	$Y^d = C + I$	Total (or aggregate) commodity demand function	
(VIII)	$Y^d = Y^s$	Commodity market clearance condition	
(IX)	$\frac{B^d}{rP} = B^d\left(Y^s, \frac{1}{r}, \frac{V}{P}\right)$	Bond demand function	Bond market
(X)	$\frac{B^s}{rP} = B^s\left(Y^s, \frac{1}{r}, \frac{V}{P}\right)$	Bond supply function	
(XI)	$B^d = B^s$	Bond market clearance condition	
(XII)	$\frac{M^d}{P} = L\left(Y^s, r, \frac{V}{P}\right)$	Money demand function	Money market
(XIII)	$M^d = \bar{M}^s$	Money market clearance condition and (exogenous) money supply function	
(XIV)	$S = Y^s - C$	Definition of saving	Definitions of useful supplementary variables
(XV)	$Y^s_m = PY^s$	Definition of money income	
(XVI)	$V = P\bar{K} + \bar{M}^s$	Definition of money wealth (net assets or net worth)	

8. Y_m^s, money income (money value of total output of commodities per time period).

B. Stock variables
1. B^d, demand for bonds (number of bonds demanded to hold).
2. B^s, supply of bonds (number of bonds planned to be outstanding).
3. M^d, demand for nominal money (number of dollars demanded to hold).
4. V, nominal wealth, or net worth (dollar value of real assets and money).

C. Price variables
1. P, the absolute, or nominal, price level (the price of commodities).
2. W, the absolute, or nominal, wage level (the price of labor or wage rate).
3. $1/r$, the absolute, or nominal, price of bonds.

II. Exogenous Variables

A. Flow variables

None.

B. Stock variables
1. $\bar{K}$, the real capital stock (the number of commodities that have been accumulated up to the beginning of the present time period).
2. $\bar{M}^s$, the supply of nominal money (the number of dollars available to be held).

C. Price variables

None.

We have been careful to distinguish among stock, flow, and price variables in our earlier discussion, but we should now make some additional clarifying remarks about the distinction between endogenous and exogenous variables.

Exogenous variables are variables whose values are *not* determined by the model. In the present model there are only two exogenous variables—the capital stock $\bar{K}$ and the supply of money $\bar{M}^s$. The value of the former is inherited and is the cumulative total of all *past* investment. The latter is a *policy variable* (the only one in this elementary model which does not include a government sector), which means that it can be set at any level the monetary authority wishes. These exogenous variables determine the values of one or more of the remaining endogenous variables, but they themselves are not determined or influenced in any way by the endogenous variables.

An *endogenous variable* not only helps to determine the value of the other endogenous variables in the model but also has its own value determined by the other endogenous variables. In other words, these variables are mutually dependent. Endogenous variables have the dual role of determining *and* being determined in the system. The endogenous variables are those

FIGURE 1

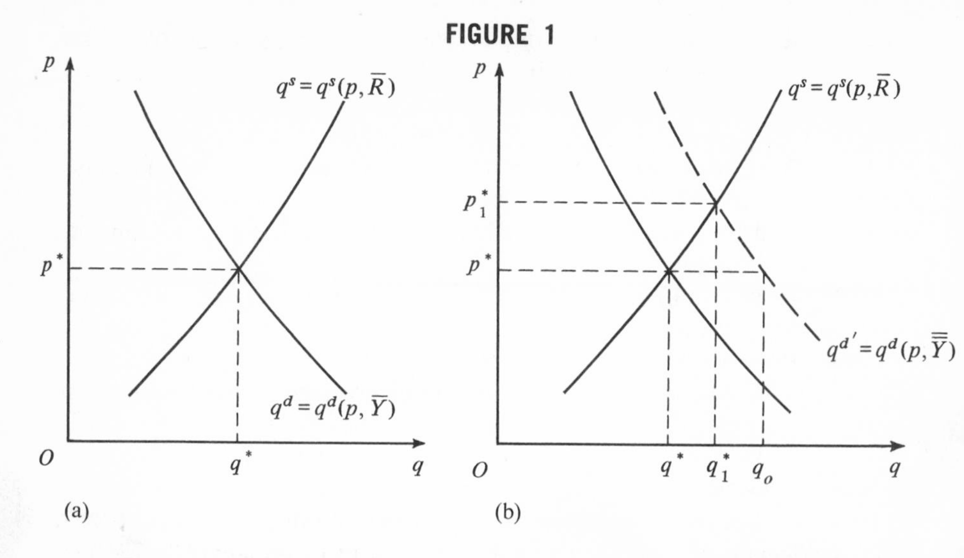

(a) (b)

variables whose equilibrium (or solution) values are explained by the model. This difference between exogenous and endogenous variables can be driven home by resorting to a simpler model. Consider the system

$$q^d = q^d(p, Y) \qquad (\textit{demand function})$$
$$q^s = q^s(p, R) \qquad (\textit{supply function})$$
$$q^d = q^s \qquad (\textit{market clearance condition})$$

where q^d is the quantity demanded, q^s is the quantity supplied, p is price, Y is income, and R is rainfall. This is a model of the market for an agricultural commodity in a partial equilibrium setting. The three equations of the model are sufficient to determine the equilibrium values of the three endogenous variables (q^s, q^d, and p) for given values of the exogenous variables (Y and R). Consider the geometry of the model. Figure 1(a) shows the market in equilibrium for given values of the exogenous variables $\bar{Y}$ and $\bar{R}$. Now let the exogenous variable $\bar{Y}$ increase to $\bar{\bar{Y}}$. At the original price level p^* the quantity demanded would be q_0. But at this price there is excess demand. Therefore the price begins to rise to p_1^*. This is the impact of the change in the exogenous variable from $\bar{Y}$ to $\bar{\bar{Y}}$ on the endogenous variable p. But now observe that the change in p has an effect on q^*. The rise in p from p^* to p_1^* raises q to q_1^*. Here we see one endogenous variable determining another endogenous variable. Hence, this little example brings out the mutual dependence—the joint-determination—among the endogenous variables quite succinctly.

Finally, the equations which relate all the variables in our complete macroeconomic model are listed, in order, in Table 1.

2 Walras' Law

If the reader counts the number of equations and the number of endogenous variables he will find sixteen of the former and fifteen of the latter, or one more equation than there are unknowns. What is happening here? Have we made a mistake? Fortunately, the answer is no. The answer is simply that one of those equations is redundant—it is not an independent equation in its own right. The equation is not genuine in the sense that once fifteen of our equations hold it can be shown that the sixteenth equation *must* hold, or alternatively, once fifteen of the equations are determined the sixteenth just has to fall into line.

How do we know this? The proof proceeds as follows. Imagine an economy in which there are n goods (n in our model is equal to four: commodities, labor, bonds, and money). Now, *whether or not prevailing market prices are such as to equate demand with supply for each good,* the money value of all goods demanded at a given point in time by any individual transactor (i.e., a household, a firm, or the government) must be equal to the money value of all goods offered for sale by him at the same time. For example, if an individual plans to *purchase* 200 dollars worth of goods (let us say, 50 commodities at 2 dollars per commodity and 2 bonds at 50 dollars per bond), then, simultaneously, he must also plan to *sell* goods in amount of 200 dollars (for example, 40 hours of labor at 4 dollars per hour and 40 dollars from his money balance).

Reverting from the particular to the general, the money value of what the jth individual transactor plans to purchase can be written symbolically as

$$P_1D_{1j} + P_2D_{2j} + \cdots + P_nD_{nj} = \sum_{i=1}^{n} P_iD_{ij}$$

where $P_1, \ldots, P_n$ are the prices of the n goods, and $D_{1j}, \ldots, D_{nj}$ are the quantities of those goods that the jth individual plans to purchase. Similarly, the money value of what the jth individual plans to sell can be written symbolically as

$$P_1S_{1j} + P_2S_{2j} + \cdots + P_nS_{nj} = \sum_{i=1}^{n} P_iS_{ij}$$

where $S_{1j}, \ldots, S_{nj}$ are the quantities of the n goods that the jth individual plans to sell. Since the money value of all the goods that the jth individual plans to buy *must* always be equal to the money value of all the goods he plans to sell, we may write

$$\sum_{i=1}^{n} P_iD_{ij} \equiv \sum_{i=1}^{n} P_iS_{ij} \tag{1}$$

We have written this condition as an identity (an identity is a proposition which is true by definition), since we assume that no individual transactor in our model will be so misguided as to suppose that he can acquire something for nothing. (Tacitly, our model assumes that transactors are not thieves, extortioners, embezzlers—or philanthropists!) This being so, (1) is, in effect, a statement of the budgetary *constraint* under which individuals formulate their purchase and sales plans.

Granted that each individual's planned market transactions in goods satisfy condition (1), it follows as a matter of simple arithmetic that the money value of the quantities demanded by *all* individuals must be equal to the money value of the quantities offered for sale by *all* individuals. Therefore, summing condition (1) over all individuals we obtain

$$\sum_{j=1}^{m} \sum_{i=1}^{n} P_i D_{ij} \equiv \sum_{j=1}^{m} \sum_{i=1}^{n} P_i S_{ij}$$

when we assume that there are m individual transactors. Factoring out the price variables from this expression yields

$$\sum_{i=1}^{n} P_i \left(\sum_{j=1}^{m} D_{ij} \right) \equiv \sum_{i=1}^{n} P_i \left(\sum_{j=1}^{m} S_{ij} \right)$$

However, the expression in parentheses on the left-hand side is simply the *total market demand* for the ith good, since it is the sum of the individual transactors' demands for that good. We write this market demand D_i. Similarly, the expression in parentheses on the right-hand side is simply the *total market supply* of the ith good, since it is the sum of the individual transactors' supplies of that good. We write this market supply S_i. Thus, we arrive at the conclusion

$$\sum_{i=1}^{n} P_i D_i \equiv \sum_{i=1}^{n} P_i S_i$$

which is a proposition known as *Walras' identity*. Verbalized, it states that the money value of planned market purchases are identically equal to the money value of planned market sales.

As indicated by our derivation, Walras' identity is valid whether or not market prices equate demand with supply for each good. However, now do the following. Assume that a set of prices has been established which will equate demand with supply in every market *except* the nth market. Since $n - 1$ markets are in equilibrium, we are sure that

$$D_1 = S_1, D_2 = S_2, \ldots, D_{n-1} = S_{n-1}$$

Next, multiply through by the set of prices that put these $n - 1$ markets in equilibrium. Then

$$P_1 D_1 = P_1 S_1, P_2 D_2 = P_2 S_2, \ldots, P_{n-1} D_{n-1} = P_{n-1} S_{n-1}$$

and summing, we obtain

$$\sum_{i=1}^{n-1} P_i D_i = \sum_{i=1}^{n-1} P_i S_i$$

If this is now subtracted from Walras' identity we obtain

$$P_n D_n = P_n S_n$$

and

$$D_n = S_n$$

which implies immediately that the nth market is also in equilibrium. To recapitulate verbally what we just did (using Walras' identity), we showed that *if all but one of the markets in an economy are in equilibrium, then that other market also must be in equilibrium.*

The statement in italics above is *Walras' law*. It is this law which makes one of the market clearance conditions included in the equations of our complete model otiose. We can get along without it. Thus, we can cast out one of the market clearance conditions, since it is implied by the remaining ones. The particular condition which we discard is immaterial. Walras' law is quite general – if $n - 1$ markets are clearing, the nth must be too; and it does not matter which markets are included among the $n - 1$ clearing markets and which market is left out as the nth.

We have just seen that it is possible to appeal to Walras' law to reduce the apparent number of equations in our model by one and thus equalize the number of endogenous variables and the number of *independent* equations. In certain circumstances this is enough to allow the system of simultaneous equations to have a solution. However, equality between the number of equations and the number of unknown (endogenous) variables is not, in fact, either a necessary or a sufficient condition for such a solution to exist. (We expand briefly on this problem in the appendix to this chapter.) Having acknowledged this problem, we ignore it and *assume* that our system of fifteen independent equations in fifteen unknown variables does have a solution.

3 The Geometric Version of the Model

The geometry of the individual markets has been presented during our construction of the overall model. However, it will prove helpful if we take this opportunity to present the full model geometrically. Hence, consider Figure 2. The asterisks attached to the variables indicate that they are equilibrium values. These are the solution values of the endogenous variables of our equation system. You will notice that there are fourteen altogether. Every one of the endogenous variables is accounted for except Y_m^*, but that, we know, is merely equal to P^*Y^{s*}. Figures 2(a), 2(b), 2(d), and 2(e) represent the four basic markets (labor, commodities, bonds, and money, respectively), while Figure 2(c) provides a convenient geometric rationale of the transition from the level of employment determined in the labor market to the level of real income (commodity supplies) available in the commodity market as determined by the production function. In fact, the labor market in the full macroeconomic model is self-contained and forms what is described as a *determinate subsystem*. All this means is that there are enough equations in the labor sector (three) to provide a solution for the three endogenous variables which appear in that sector of the model (W/P, N^d, and N^s). Thus, the three equations determine the real wage at which the demand and supply of labor are equal.

The reader can easily confirm that of the four markets that comprise the model only the labor market is self-contained, or what economists call

FIGURE 2

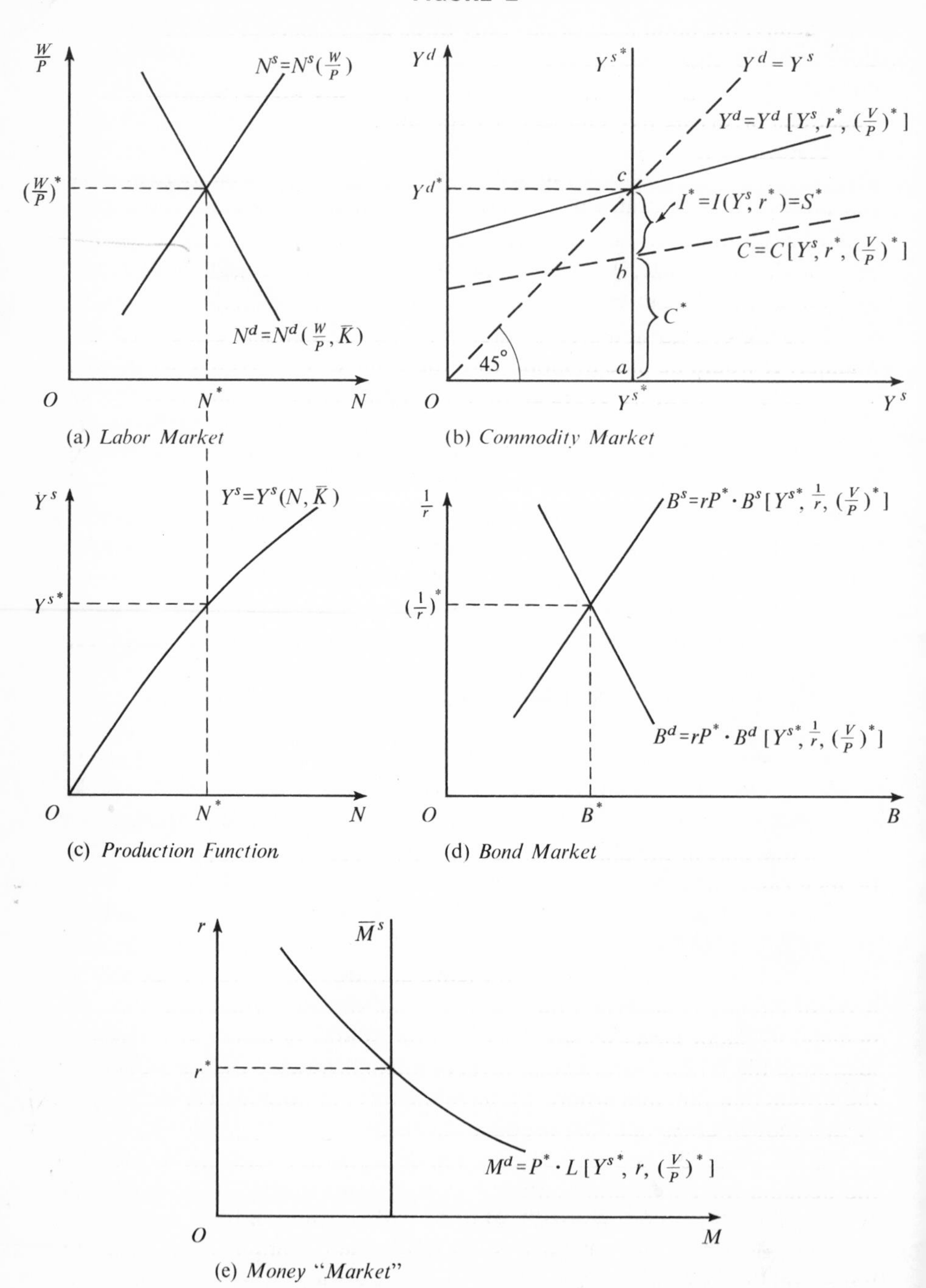

(a) *Labor Market*

(b) *Commodity Market*

(c) *Production Function*

(d) *Bond Market*

(e) *Money "Market"*

separable, in this way. None of the other three markets has enough equations to solve for the endogenous variables included in the equations forming it. Specifically, the bond market has only three equations, but these three equations involve eight endogenous variables; the commodity market has four equations and eight endogenous variables; and the money market has two equations involving five endogenous variables.

Returning to the self-contained labor market, we see that once the equilibrium level of employment is determined there, it immediately determines the level of real income Y^{s*} available to the community, since the production function tells us what the total output of commodities can be, given a certain level of employment N^* and the available capital stock $\bar{K}$. However, as soon as the level of real income is determined by the labor market this is as far as we can go in a step-by-step (or what economists call a *recursive*) manner. It would be nice if, along with the value of Y^{s*} given to us from the production function, we could go to the commodity market and solve for the value of one more endogenous variable. It would be nice, but unfortunately it is not possible. The rest of the model has to be solved simultaneously because, as we have just seen, none of the remaining markets—and that includes the commodity market—are independent of the others. Individually, each of them has more unknown endogenous variables than equations, although when all four are combined the result is exactly the same number of equations as unknowns.

Recall that our discussion of Walras' law showed that we can be certain our fourth market is in equilibrium if the other three markets are clearing. This means that one of Figures 2(a), 2(b), 2(d), or 2(e) is superfluous or redundant and could be omitted without a loss. In fact, most macroeconomic models ignore the bond market. Therefore when we ignore one market, this is the one we shall ignore. However, experience has shown there is a certain pedagogic payoff to following the analysis of all four markets, even though one part of the analysis is technically redundant. The procedure may be inelegant, but it is usually worthwhile.

Observe that this simple diagrammatic representation of our model illustrates most of the major macroeconomic variables which we are concerned with in the "real" world. In Figure 2(a) we find the real wage and the level of employment. When this market is not in equilibrium and, thus, the demand for labor is, let us say, less than the supply of labor, we are also illustrating the (vitally interesting) level of unemployment. Figure 2(c) shows the production function where we have the level of output (real income) or, in this model, gross national product (GNP). In Figure 2(b) we see how the GNP is allocated by households between consumption and saving and how the demand for goods consists of household consumption demand and the demand by firms for investment goods. In Figures 2(d) and 2(e) we see how bond prices and/or the interest rate are determined. Simple as the model is, therefore, most of the crucial macroeconomic variables are represented. The only variable not directly illustrated in this simple graphic arrangement is the price level. However, we shall see that we can always infer what happens to the price level when the model's equilibrium is disturbed in one way or another.

4 The Functional Distribution of Income

This is an appropriate point to draw attention to the *functional distribution of income* implied by our model. By this last phrase we mean the amount of income which goes to each factor of production. Economists usually work with four factors of production: land, labor, capital, and enterprise. However, our model only incorporates two of these: labor and capital. Land and enterprise are not incorporated. It is tacitly assumed that the entrepreneurial function is performed by a "head commodity-maker" who is willing to carry out his duties for the same real wage as the ordinary commodity-makers, and that no land is utilized in the production of commodities. The omission of an entrepreneur in the formal structure of the model is not that serious. It is well known that in equilibrium under perfect competition, profits are always "normal." The functional distribution of income which concerns us is that between "labor" and "others." How the "others" carve up their piece of the pie between rentiers, capitalists, entrepreneurs, and so on is of a second order of importance. These preliminaries aside, the total quantity of real income available for distribution between labor and others is obviously Y^{s*}. Remember that this is a number of commodities. Of this total, labor receives as its share $N^*(W/P)^*$, or, verbally, the quantity of employment times the real wage (which, we know, is the commodity rate of reimbursement for working). Naturally, this leaves $Y^{s*} - N^*(W/P)^*$ commodities for the "others." Since the only remaining factor payment in the model is interest, it follows that what is paid to the others must equal what is paid in interest. The real value of the total interest payments made is equal to B^*/P^*. This is so because there are B^* bonds outstanding, each one of which pays 1 dollar. Therefore, the total nominal interest payment is $B^* \cdot 1$ dollars and the total real income paid in the form of interest is B^*/P^*. Thus we may write

$$\underbrace{Y^{s*}}_{\text{total real income}} = \underbrace{N^*\left(\frac{W}{P}\right)^*}_{\text{labor's share}} + \underbrace{\frac{B^*}{P^*}}_{\text{others' share}}$$

Hence, it is clear from the above expression that total money income is comprised of the money wage bill plus money interest payments made to others. That is,

$$\underbrace{Y_m^{s*}}_{\text{money income}} = P^*Y^{s*} = \underbrace{N^*W^* + B^*}_{\text{wage bill + interest payments}}$$

(Of course, all quantities are in terms of dollars.)

The functional distribution of income can be shown diagrammatically by using the labor market figure. Consider Figure 3. From what we have said

FIGURE 3

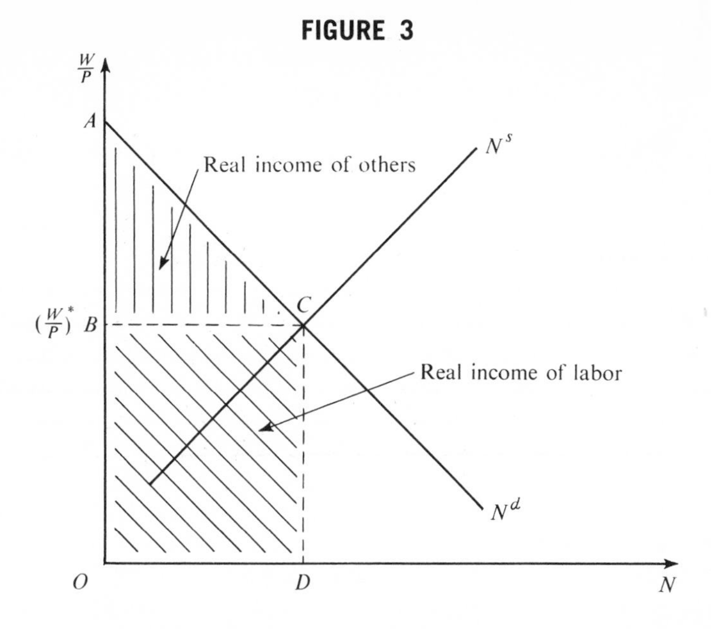

already, it is quite obvious that labor's real income is equal to the area of the rectangle $OBCD$, since that is equal to $N^*(W/P)^*$. It is not so immediately obvious though that the others' real income is equal to the area of triangle ABC. To see this is true, note that the area of the quadrilateral $AODC$ is equal to total income. This follows from the fact that the shaded area under the demand curve which comprises this quadrilateral is equal to the sum of the marginal physical products of the N^* units of labor services employed. As labor is the only variable factor of production, the sum of the marginal physical products is equal to the total product—which, in turn, is equal to total real income. We remind you that the shaded area is equal to the sum of the marginal physical products of labor in the following way.

Consider Figure 4. It was shown in Chapter 2 that profits will be maximized if labor is hired until the marginal physical product of labor is equal to the real wage. Thus, if the real wage were $(W/P)_1$, then ON_2 workers would be hired. By then the marginal physical product of labor would have fallen to $(W/P)_1$. If the real wage were only $(W/P)_2$, however, ON_n labor would be hired. Not until that many were employed would the marginal physical product of labor fall to equality with the real wage $(W/P)_2$. It is apparent then that the demand curve for labor is a locus of points representing the marginal physical product of labor at various levels of employment. Consequently, the total product when ON_1 are employed is equal to $ON_1 \cdot a_1N_1$, that is, employment times the marginal physical product of each employed worker; when ON_2 are employed total product is $(ON_1 \cdot a_1N_1) + (N_1N_2 \cdot a_2N_2)$, that is, the previous total product plus the newly employed multiplied by the prevailing marginal physical product; when ON_3 are employed, the total product is $(ON_1 \cdot a_1N_1) + (N_1N_2 \cdot a_2N_2) + (N_2N_3 \cdot a_3N_3)$, and so on. It is clear that the total product when ON_n are employed is $(ON_1 \cdot$

FIGURE 4

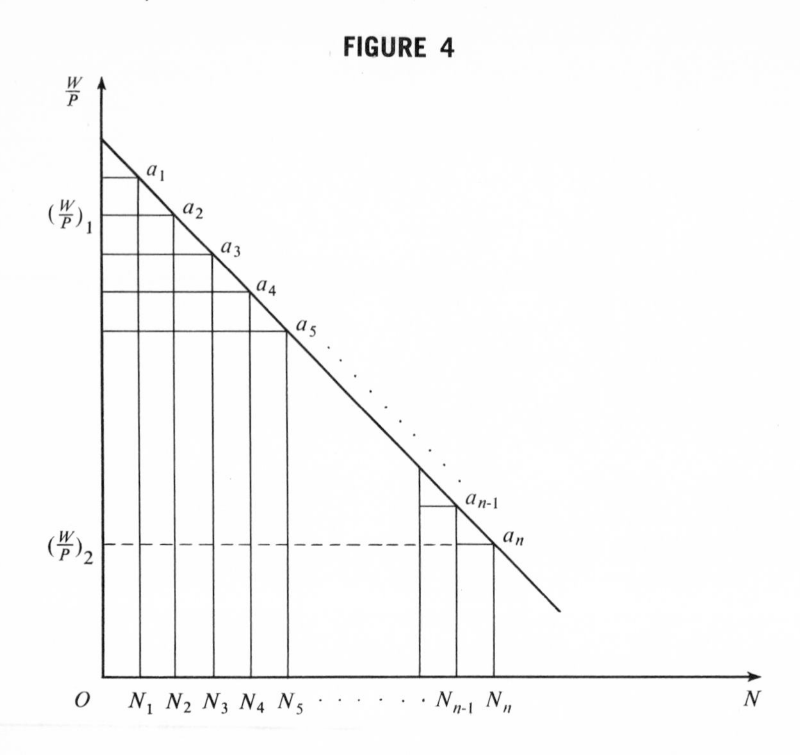

$a_1N_1) + (N_1N_2 \cdot a_2N_2) + \cdots + (N_{n-1}N_n \cdot a_nN_n)$. This expression is the sum of the areas of the tall thin rectangles under the demand curve. When the rectangles are made thin enough, which implies the increments to employment are small enough, this sum is a good approximation to the area under the demand curve, since the missing pieces (the tiny triangles) get smaller and smaller. In the limit (infinitely small increments) the sum gives the area under the curve exactly.

5 Commodity Market Equilibrium, or Savings Equals Investment

We have stressed time and time again in our discussion of this model that macroeconomic equilibrium exists when *all* four markets are clearing; that is, supply is equal to demand. The student may recall from his macroeconomic principles course that national income equilibrium occurs when "planned saving equals planned investment," or more generally, "leakages equals injections."[1] This proposition is demonstrated by reference to what

[1] The more general statement can be made specifically as "planned saving plus taxes" equals "planned investment plus government expenditure" when government is incorporated into the model; or "planned saving plus taxes plus imports" equals "planned investment plus government expenditure plus exports" when government is incorporated into the model and the economy is open to trade. Generically, a *leakage* is any withdrawal from the circular flow of payments to households by domestic firms (such as saving, taxes, or expenditure on imports), and an *injection* is any augmentation of the circular flow of payments to firms by households (such as investment, government expenditure, or foreign expenditure for our exports).

are described as circular flow of income diagrams and by frequent analogy to filling baths, running taps, pulled plugs, constant water level, and so on—the whole being connected by a bewildering maze of pipes and conduits. We believe that economics is about markets, not plumbing. Therefore, although it is certainly true that the commodity market is in equilibrium when leakages equal injections, we feel nothing is to be gained by focusing on the "pipes" and "conduits" to and from markets rather than on the markets themselves in a manner familiar to everyone, namely, through the supply and demand situation in those markets. It is seldom emphasized sufficiently that the flows of dollars (not water) through the pipes are manifestations of supplies and demands. Moreover, the prevailing practice of pointing out that equilibrium occurs when "leakages equal injections" refers only to the commodity market. It implies nothing whatsoever about the situation in the labor, bond, or money markets. If, and when they are considered, these markets are referred to in terms of supply and demand curves, and then it is stated that equilibrium occurs when the two are equal. As far as we are concerned, what is good enough for the labor, bond, and money markets is good enough for the commodity market, so we shall continue to emphasize that equilibrium exists when the demand for commodities is equal to the supply of commodities (we shall also try to deflect your attention from a myopic concentration on leakages and injections). Despite our desire to minimize the use of these expressions, it remains true that when the demand for commodities is equal to the supply of commodities, injections do equal leakages. Consider Figure 2(b) which shows the commodity market in equilibrium, with the supply of commodities equal to the demand for commodities. It also happens that investment (the only injection in the present model which does not include a government sector or trade) is equal to savings (the only leakage). The former is observed directly as being equal to cb; the latter may be inferred to be equal to cb, too. From equation (XIV), we know that savings is equal to the difference between income and consumption. In terms of Figure 2(b) income is equal to Oa which is equal, from the properties of the 45°-line, to ac. However, consumption is equal to ab. Therefore, savings must be equal to cb. In fact, planned saving can always be observed in the commodity market diagram as the vertical distance between the 45°-line and the consumption function. This is true because, through the properties of the 45°-line, the distance to the 45°-line is equal to income. Thus, at points to the right of Y^{s*}, planned savings would exceed planned investment (or leakages exceed injections), since the distance from the consumption function *at such points* to the 45°-line (savings) exceeds the distance from the consumption function to the aggregate demand function (investment) at the same point. We would say, of course, there is excess supply in the commodity market at such points. Conversely, at points to the left of Y^{s*}, planned savings (or leakages) is less than planned investment (or injections), since the distance from the consumption function to the aggregate demand function (investment) is greater than the distance from the consumption function to the 45°-line. We would say excess commodity demand exists at such points.

We need say nothing more about the model until we bring it to bear on some of the problems in Chapter 7. But we should remark about the manner in which the model is assumed to generate the equilibrium or solution values of the endogenous variables.

6 Tâtonnement; Statics and Dynamics

Assume that our model is *not* in equilibrium, that is, there are nonequilibrium prices P, W, and $1/r$ prevailing such that excess demands exist in some markets and excess supplies in the others. How is equilibrium to be brought about? We shall assume that it is brought about by a *tâtonnement* process. What does this mean? The concept is quite simple. The existence of an imaginary personage who is called an *auctioneer* is invoked. The auctioneer announces a random set of prices, which generally are not an equilibrium set (markets will fail to clear). Now the auctioneer has a book for each market and on the left page of each book he records the amounts transactors wish to purchase of each good at the prices he has announced. On the right page he records the amounts of each good transactors wish to sell at the prices he has announced. After he has recorded the intentions of every transactor, the auctioneer totals the demands and supplies in each market and sees if they balance. If they do not balance, he announces a higher price for the markets in which excess demand exists and a lower price for the markets in which excess supply exists. He then calls for, and registers in his books, new bids and offers. When they are all in, he again adds total demand and total supply in each book (or market) and adjusts price upwards if excess demand exists and downwards if excess supply exists. Then he accepts new bids and offers, and the procedure continues. The auctioneer keeps opening his books, taking bids and offers from all transactors, closing his books, and striking a balance. He adjusts price according to whether or not excess demand or supply prevails; up if the former, down if the latter. In this way the auctioneer can grope (there is no better word) his way toward an equilibrium set of prices—a set of prices at which every market clears.

Only when the auctioneer finds such a set do the bids and offers which the transactors have made become binding. Up until this point of equilibrium, all previous demands and supplies have only been expressions of intention, which were not binding. There is built into our tâtonnement process, for that is what we have just described, a *recontracting arrangement*. When demands and supplies are not equal, the bid and offer contracts recorded in the auctioneer's books are not binding. You can recontract without having to carry out your expressed intentions. Only when the auctioneer hits on the equilibrium set of prices are you bound to perform according to your expressed plans.

Why this elaborate charade? Must we inject an element of farce to enliven our dismal science? No. The purpose here is a serious one. Our basic concern in this book is with comparative statics. This means we compare one set of equilibrium values of our endogenous variables with another set after having disturbed the original set by, for example, changing one of the exogenous variables. However, this implies there must be some means of getting from one equilibrium set to the other. We introduce the tâtonnement mechanism, following Walras, for this purpose. When one equilibrium set of prices is no longer an equilibrium set because of a shift, for example, in one of the exogenous variables, then when the auctioneer comes to announce that old set of prices at the beginning of the next period (and the auctioneer cries every period to accommodate the *flow* demand and supplies), he will find his books are not balancing. He therefore starts adjusting prices according to our rule until he hits the new equilibrium set of prices.

The recontracting privilege allowed en route to equilibrium has a special purpose. It is incorporated into the process to prevent the final equilibrium set of prices from being affected by the nonequilibrium sets cried out en route to this happy state. Suppose, for example, the auctioneer announces a commodity price which will not clear the market, but you bid for commodities and you use them to eat, wear, sleep under, or commute in. Then the auctioneer recognizes his error and changes the price. It is almost certain that what *would* have been an equilibrium set of prices had you not obtained some commodities at a nonequilibrium price will no longer be such a set for the very fact that your demand will have changed now that you are semibloated with commodities. It is to prevent the final equilibrium set of prices from being altered by what people do during the transition to the new equilibrium that the recontracting feature was included, at the prompting of Edgeworth, in the tâtonnement process conceived by Walras. "Tâtonnement with recontracting" allows us to hop blithely from one equilibrium set of variables to another new set after some disturbance to the original set with absolutely no concern whatsoever about how we arrive there. If our model of the tâtonnement process is stable (which is not such a big if) we will arrive there as long as the auctioneer follows his price-adjustment rules.

Quite reasonably, one may ask what is the justification for incorporating this tâtonnement process as the economic adjustment mechanism? Is it not pathetic and absurd to suppose that the economy can be assumed to adjust in a manner remotely resembling this process? (We refer you back to §1.6.) The tâtonnement process is a brilliant simplification. It is to macrostatic economic theory what the "frictionless system" is to physics—a beautiful abstraction without which our theorizing would get nowhere.

We stated above that this book is primarily concerned with *comparative static analysis* and explained that this entails looking at equilibrium values of the endogenous variables for a certain set of values of the exogenous variables, changing one (or more) of the exogenous variables' values, and finding the *new* equilibrium values of the endogenous variables that emerge; we then compare these new equilibrium values with the original endogenous values. That is, we *compare* one set of *static* equilibrium values of the endogenous variables with another set of *static* equilibrium values of the same variables after having altered one (or more) exogenous variables, hence the name, comparative statics.

Comparative static analysis is to be contrasted with *dynamic analysis.* In dynamic analysis, the *nonequilibrium* values of the endogenous variables at various instants of time assume primary importance.[1] Except very informally, we eschew any discussion of the dynamic adjustment process—that is, we do not concern ourselves with the values of the endogenous variables between their original and final equilibrium values. This is the reason we rely on the highly artificial device of tâtonnement to take us from one set of equilibrium values to another set. In general, tâtonnement will get us from the original set to the final set without sidetracking us into a consideration of the transition process.

Appendix: The Existence and Uniqueness Problem; Stability

We can expand on the "existence and uniqueness" problem of the solution to a system of simultaneous linear equations (that is, when does one, and only one, solution exist to a system of linear equations) by way of some simple examples. Let m equal the number of equations and n equal the number of unknowns. Now consider the following system:

$$x + y = 10 \tag{2}$$

$$x + y = 11 \tag{3}$$

where $m = n = 2$. Notwithstanding that $m = n$, there is no solution to this system because the equations are *inconsistent.* Next, consider this system where, again, $m = n = 2$:

$$x + 2y = 12 \tag{4}$$

$$2x + 4y = 24 \tag{5}$$

Notwithstanding $m = n$, there is no unique solution to this system either. The reason is that the equations are *functionally dependent.* Equation (5) is simply two times equation (4). Since one equation can be derived from the other by simple scalar multiplication, one equation is redundant and, in effect, we have two unknowns and only one independent equation. Thus, we are confronted with a potentially infinite number of solutions. Finally, consider the following system where $m = 3$ and $n = 2$:

$$x + y = 10 \tag{6}$$

$$y = 6 \tag{7}$$

$$2x + 3y = 26 \tag{8}$$

Notwithstanding that the number of equations exceeds the number of unknowns, this system does have a unique solution, namely, $x = 4$ and $y = 6$.

[1] A good book, at a fairly advanced level, emphasizing macroeconomic dynamics is M. K. Evans, *Macroeconomic Analysis,* Harper & Row, 1969.

In fact, there are only two independent equations in this system, since equation (8) is dependent on the other two. To see this, note that equation (8) is equal to two times equation (6) plus equation (7). This system is again a functionally dependent one.

We now state (without proof) the following rule: if $m = n$, a *necessary and sufficient condition* for a *unique* solution to exist to a *linear* system of equations is that the system's determinant *not equal zero.*

If $m = n$, and the system's determinant *does* equal zero, then there is *either* an infinity of solutions *or* no solution (the system is inconsistent). The determinant of system (2)–(3) is zero, and that system is inconsistent or overdetermined; the determinant of system (4)–(5) is zero, and that system has an infinite number of solutions (e.g., $x = 2$, $y = 5$; $x = 4$, $y = 4$; $x = 6$, $y = 3$; etc.). It is said to be underdetermined. In the case of system (6)–(8), we see that when the dependent equation is discarded, the above rule is applicable.[1]

As Samuelson has observed, "an economic system consists of a designated set of unknowns which are constrained as a condition of equilibrium to satisfy an *equal number of consistent and independent* equations. . . ."[2]

It is worth pointing out that this "existence and uniqueness" question is not only idle mathematics. It can have many substantive implications for economics. Suppose, for example, we develop a theoretical system which implies both full employment and an optimal allocation of resources. Then it would be nice to know that a solution to our model can *exist;* that is, we can prove that these two desiderata are not incompatible. As an empirical matter, if one were to try and estimate the coefficients of a system of equations that was over- or underdetermined, one would find that the matrix of coefficients of the endogenous variables would not invert, since its determinant would be equal to zero.

Having discussed the "existence and uniqueness of equilibrium" problem in a purely formal sense, let us now consider it, and the associated issue of stability, in an economic context. Consider Figure 5, which illustrates the market for a single good with supply and demand curves shaped to intersect three times. In this situation there is no unique equilibrium – instead, we have multiple equilibria. Of these equilibrium positions, those at p_1^* and p_2^* are *locally* (c.f., *globally*) stable, while that at p_3^* is unstable. Let us explain what this means.

If equilibrium was initially at p_3^*, the slightest disturbance which caused price to deviate from p_3^* would lead price to deviate even further from p_3^* and not back to p_3^*. Thus, p_3^* is unstable. If the initiating disturbance drove price above p_3^*, price would rise to p_1^*, since between p_3^* and p_1^* excess demand exists. Conversely, if the initiating disturbance drove price below p_3^*, price would fall to p_2^*, since between p_3^* and p_2^* excess supply exists.

[1] If $m < n$ there is no unique solution (an infinite number of solutions can be generated). If $m > n$ the system is either functionally dependent or inconsistent. For a more complete discussion of linear systems, see M. O'Nan, *Linear Algebra,* Harcourt Brace Jovanovich, 1971.

[2] P. A. Samuelson, *Foundations of Economic Analysis,* Harvard, 1947, pp. 10–20. Emphasis added.

FIGURE 5

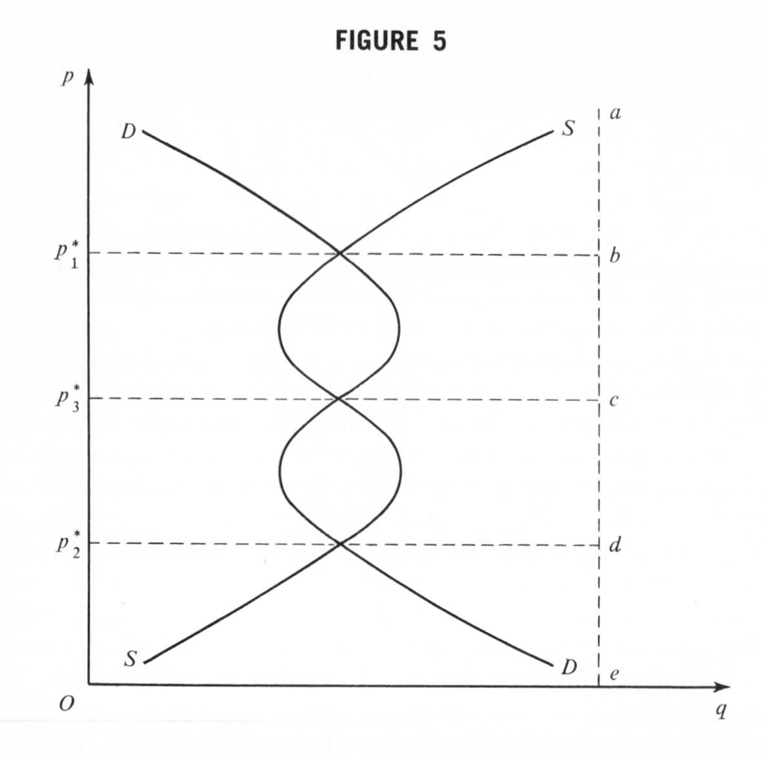

The equilibrium prices p_1^* and p_2^* are *locally* stable, since in the face of *small* deviations in price around these neighborhoods, price goes back to p_1^* or p_2^* as the case may be. For example, if price was originally p_1^* and price was disturbed into the range *ba* or *bc*, price would return to p_1^*. Similarly, if price was originally p_2^* and price was disturbed into the range *dc* or *de*, price would return to p_2^*.

However, p_1^* and p_2^* are not *globally* stable. A *large* enough disturbance in price from either level may cause price to converge to a new equilibrium. For example, if price was originally at p_1^* and it was then disturbed downwards by a large enough amount to throw it into the range *de*, price would not rise to p_1^* again, but would fall to p_2^* instead. Similarly, if price was originally at p_2^* and was disturbed upwards by a large enough amount to throw it into the range *bc*, price would not fall to p_2^* again but would rise to p_1^* instead.

We wish to rule out the possibility of multiple equilibrium and instability in our macroeconomic model. Thus, we shall assume that the supply and demand curves in all four markets are *well behaved,* by which we mean demand curves have negative slopes and supply curves have positive slopes throughout their lengths. This is sufficient to guarantee a unique, and stable, equilibrium in every market. We must be frank, though, and admit that this is a restriction we impose by assumption only. It cannot be established by pure, a priori theoretical reasoning. As the reader may recall, we mentioned in §2.2, that the labor supply curve might slope "backwards" (i.e., have a negative slope) and in §5.2, that the bond supply curve might also have a negative slope.

Summary

In this chapter, the first in Part II of the book, we began by presenting the complete macroeconomic model (excluding government) which had been developed piecemeal throughout Part I. The model consists of sixteen equations and fifteen unknown endogenous variables. However, we showed one equation to be redundant via Walras' law, which states that when $n - 1$ markets in an n-market system are in equilibrium, then the nth market *must* also be in equilibrium. Thus the number of *independent* equations is equal to the number of endogenous variables. (The conditions under which a solution to such a system exists and is unique are discussed in the appendix to this chapter.)

An exogenous variable is one whose value is determined *outside* the system. Such variables are either policy variables like the supply of money or historical faits accomplis like the inherited capital stock. An endogenous variable is one whose equilibrium value is determined *within* the model. The equilibrium value of an endogenous variable depends on both the values of the exogenous variables and the equilibrium values assumed by other endogenous variables. Thus, endogenous variables are said to be "determined and determining."

Next, we were concerned with illustrating the complete model graphically. Each of the four markets (labor, commodities, bonds, and money) is given in a diagram, and the link between the labor market and the commodity market is revealed through the production function. We saw that the equilibrium values of most of the major variables of interest to macroeconomists are illustrated in this five-diagram arrangement; for example, the level of employment (and unemployment), the real wage, labor's absolute income (the product of the real wage and the level of employment), the level of total output (real income or GNP), consumption, investment, saving, aggregate demand, and the interest rate. The only major variable not illustrated *directly* is the commodity price level. However, we shall find when we begin to use the model in succeeding chapters that we can *always* infer what happens to the price level when an initial equilibrium is disturbed.

We emphasize that the model is in full equilibrium when demand is equal to supply in every market. However, equilibrium in the commodity market (only) can be, and commonly is, stated in another way. Commodity market equilibrium also prevails when planned saving equals planned investment (in a model which excludes a government sector and which is closed to foreign trade). Thus, there are two (equivalent) equilibrium conditions for the commodity market: aggregate commodity demand is equal to aggregate commodity supply ($Y^d = Y^s$), and planned saving is equal to planned investment ($S = I$).

The major portion of this book is concerned with *comparative macroeconomic statics*. This means we observe an *original* set of equilibrium values of the endogenous variables, *disturb* this equilibrium is some way (for example, by changing the money supply), find the *new* set of equilibrium values of the endogenous variables, and then *compare* the new set with the old. In general, we shall be able to tell whether the disturbance (or shock) causes the equilibrium value of an endogenous variable to increase, decrease, or remain unchanged. Because we only compare *equilibrium* values of endogenous variables before and after a disturbance is imparted to the model, we are engaged in *comparing static equilibrium positions*. And since the model is macroeconomic in nature, our subject matter is said to be *comparative macroeconomic statics*.

To enable us to go from an original set of equilibrium values of the endogenous variables to a new set without being concerned about the values the variables assume between the two equilibrium positions, we appeal to Walras' famous tâtonnement process augmented by Edgeworth's recontracting device. In a tâtonnement process with recontracting arrangements, an *auctioneer* adjusts prices in the light of the offers to supply and demand he receives (raising price in a market where there is excess demand and lowering it in a market where there is excess supply) until he strikes on a set of prices which clear *all* markets. Then, and only then, are offers to supply and demand made binding.

Questions

1. Discuss the difference between exogenous and endogenous variables.
2. Recall the difference between stock variables and flow variables. In light of this, classify each of the following variables as a stock or flow variable: the supply of money, the national debt, the total supply of old houses, the supply of new houses produced this year, saving, the accumulation of past saving (referred to as saving*s*), investment, the economy's total physical capital.
3. Prove Walras' law.
4. Define *separability*. Show that one, and only one, market in the model presented in this chapter is separable.
5. What is meant by the functional distribution of income? Show that, for any level of employment, total income is equal to the area under the demand for labor curve up to that level of employment. How is total income, interpreted as such an area, allocated between labor and the other factors of production?
6. Prove that when the aggregate demand for commodities is equal to the aggregate supply of commodities and, thus, the commodity market is in equilibrium, planned saving is equal to planned investment (in a model which excludes a government sector).
7. Explain what is meant by *comparative macroeconomic statics*.
8. Explain what is meant by "Walras' tâtonnement process augmented by Edgeworth's recontracting arrangement." Why is the latter necessary?

SELECTED READINGS

1. W. J. Baumol, *Economic Theory and Operations Analysis,* Prentice-Hall, 1961, chapter 12. A good, clear, and elementary discussion of general equilibrium and Walras' law.
2. A. Chiang, *Fundamental Methods of Mathematical Economics,* McGraw-Hill, 1967, chapter 4. A clear and simple account of the "existence and uniqueness" problem.
3. R. W. Clower, "The Keynesian Counterrevolution: A Theoretical Appraisal," in F. H. Hahn and F. P. R. Brechling (eds.), *The Theory of Interest Rates,* London, 1965. The authoritative statement of Walras' and Says' laws. Also a major reinterpretation of Keynes which we shall have occasion to refer to later.
4. A. Leijonhufvud, *On Keynesian Economics and the Economics of Keynes,* Oxford, 1968, chapter 2, sections 1 and 2. Another major reinterpretation of Keynes which, in part, develops the ideas put forth by Clower [3]. The sections referenced here deal with Walras and tâtonnement.
5. F. Modigliani, "Liquidity Preference and the Theory of Interest and Money," *Econometrica,* January, 1944. A path-breaking article. The first attempt to bring the ideas Keynes developed in the *General Theory* into a coherent quasi-general equilibrium framework. Clarified many of the disputes between Keynes and the Classics. Modigliani [6] is an updated version.
6. F. Modigliani, "The Monetary Mechanism and Its Interaction with Real Phenomena," *Review of Economics and Statistics,* February, 1963. Our model is strictly analogous to the one presented in this article. A revised version of his earlier article, [5].
7. D. Patinkin, *Money, Interest, and Prices,* 2nd ed., Harper & Row, 1965, chapter 9. Our model is also strictly analogous to the one presented here. Part I provides an extended discussion of the microeconomic theoretical foundations of the model Patinkin presents quite briefly. See also note B on Walras and tâtonnement.

FURTHER READINGS

8. F. Y. Edgeworth, *Mathematical Psychics,* London, 1881. Where Edgeworth added the recontracting refinement to Walras' tâtonnement process.
9. M. K. Evans, *Macroeconomic Analysis,* Harper & Row, 1969. A good book, at a fairly advanced level, which emphasizes macroeconomic *dynamics*. The student might wish to read Evans' book after finishing the present text, which emphasizes macroeconomic *statics*.
10. L. Walras, *Elements of Pure Economics,* trans. by W. Jaffé, Irwin, 1954. Walras' full general equilibrium model and the introduction of the tâtonnement device.

7

The Influence of Monetary Phenomena

1 Neoclassical and Neo-Keynesian Macroeconomics

The macroeconomic model outlined in the previous chapter could not possibly have been formulated prior to the publication in 1936 of John Maynard Keynes' epochal work, *The General Theory of Employment, Interest, and Money*. To be quite blunt, macroeconomics did not exist as a mode of analysis before that date. Here was one of the true turning points in the history of economic analysis.

As the reader is no doubt aware, the *General Theory* and its implications were highly controversial. In fact, the book was deliberately provocative and one of Keynes' expressed intentions was to wreak havoc in the analytical establishment of the then-received economic theory. In this, he was markedly successful, and in the years following the publication of the *General Theory,* economists were divided into camps. There were the old-guard economists, who identified with the *Classical economists,* and the young Turks, or *Keynesian economists*. The latter group soon held the high ground. With the passage of time, however, a modus vivendi, a rapprochement, between the two schools slowly emerged. Time, here, is measured in decades.

The model we have presented in Chapter 7 did not spring full grown from the mind of Keynes. Both camps took Keynes' own original analytical blueprint to their own drawing boards, where they modified and refined it to fit the design we have created. In the modifying and refining process, the intransigence between the two camps began slowly to dissolve. The old guard evolved into what are now called neoclassical economists, and the young Turks evolved into what may be called neo-Keynesian economists. The two camps both work with the sort of model we have developed in the previous chapter. But they do still differ vitally in respect to the assumptions they make before they run the model through its paces.

Neoclassical economists make a set of assumptions which enables them to take our macroeconomic model and prove all the classical macroeconomic propositions (we will describe what these are as we go through Part II); neo-Keynesian economists make different assumptions, which enable them to take the same macroeconomic model and prove all of Keynes' macroeconomic propositions (these will emerge in Part III). You will appreciate, then, that not much separates neoclassical and neo-Keynesian economists. They both accept the same basic theoretical apparatus, differing only in the assumptions they make before they operate it. We would define a neoclassical macroeconomist as an economist who takes Keynes' basic model refined and modified into the form presented in Chapter 6 and operates it with those assumptions necessary to validate classical macroeconomic propositions; and a neo-Keynesian economist is one who takes the same model and operates it with the assumptions necessary to validate Keynes' macroeconomic propositions. Again, we cannot emphasize too strongly that both sides use the same model. This is good—it is a relief to find that there is not one macroeconomic apparatus applicable to a classical economic world and another macroeconomic apparatus applicable to a Keynesian economic world. The same model yields different results depending upon how it is applied. This point is worth repeating because there is a tendency to believe, for example, that classical economic conclusions are conditional on the use, say, of some sort of Fisherian Equation of Exchange (something which we shall disprove very shortly), and Keynesian economic conclusions are conditional on the use, say, of some IS/LM apparatus (which we shall disprove in Part III). The macroeconomic model we have developed is quite, quite general and it works for both neoclassical and neo-Keynesian schools. This is the reason why Milton Friedman (who is, by every standard, an archetypal neoclassical economist) has been known to say, in an act of only seeming apostasy, "we are all Keynesians now."

Let us examine the points on which the two groups differ.

Prices

The neoclassical assumption about the three prices in our model is that they are *all* flexible in *both* directions. This means that, within the time period for which the model is relevant, all three prices may adjust to levels such that equality of demand and supply in all markets is obtained. In contrast, the neo-Keynesian assumption is that one, or more, of the three prices is rigid within the time period for which the model is relevant. The nominal wage rate W may, for example (example *only*), be pegged at a certain fixed level by a collectively bargained union agreement, or the interest rate r may not be capable of being bid below some minimum level due to the existence of a "liquidity trap." This difference of assumptions concerning the flexibility or rigidity of prices is probably the most important factor distinguishing neoclassical from neo-Keynesian economists.

Money Illusion

First, we must define what is meant by freedom from money illusion. A transactor is free of money illusion if the amounts he supplies and demands of any real good (labor, commodities, real money, and real bonds) do not change *unless* some *real* variable affecting those supply and demand function changes. Consider, for example, our labor supply function, equation (II) $N^s = N^s(W/P)$. This states that the real supply of labor N^s is a function of the real wage. Thus, an equiproportionate change in W and P would leave the real wage and, thus, the supply of labor unchanged. This equation is free of money illusion. Even though two nominal variables (W and P) have changed, there has been no change in a real variable (W/P) and, consequently, the real supply of labor remains unchanged.

Money illusion exists if the contrary is true. A transactor suffers from money illusion if the amounts he supplies and demands of any real good change with a change in some nominal variable, even though all the real variables are unchanged. Suppose, for example, the real supply of labor was written $N^s = N^s(W)$. Now if there were an equiproportionate change in W and P, even though the real wage (W/P) were constant, the real supply of labor would change simply because the nominal variable W had changed.

We take our final definition from Patinkin:

> An individual is free of money illusion if the amount he demands [and supplies] of any real good . . . remains invariant under any change which does not affect relative prices, the rate of interest, . . . real incomes, and the real value of initial bond and money holdings.[1]

Now neoclassical economists assume the absence of money illusion from *all* supply and demand functions. Neo-Keynesian economists frequently believe that it exists in one, or more, of them; usually, the labor or bond supply functions.[2]

Price Expectations

The elasticity of price expectations of any good is defined as the ratio of the proportional rise in the expected future price of that good to the proportional rise in its current price. Price expectations may be inelastic (less than unity), unit-elastic, or elastic (greater than unity). For example, if a current price rises by 10 percent and the expected future price only rises by 5 percent, the elasticity of expectations would be less than unity (inelastic expectations). However, if the current price of a good rises by 10 percent and the expected future price of that good also rises by 10 percent, the elasticity of expectations would be unity (unit-elastic expectations). Finally, if the current price of a good rises by 10 percent and the expected future

[1] D. Patinkin, *Money, Interest, and Prices*, 2nd ed., Harper & Row, 1965, p. 72.

[2] On money illusion in the bond and labor supply functions see "An Aside on Money Illusion" in §5.2.

price of that good rises by 20 percent, the elasticity of expectations would be greater than unity (elastic expectations).

In general, then, when current prices change, if expected future prices change in the same proportion, the elasticity of expectations is unity; if expected future prices change in a smaller proportion, expectations are inelastic. Characteristically, neoclassical economists assume that expectations are unit-elastic in all markets while neo-Keynesian economists assume that expectations may be inelastic in some markets—particularly, the bond market.

Distribution Effects

The demand and supply functions comprising our macroeconomic model assume that the endogenous variables depend only on the totals of the other endogenous and exogenous variables. For example, in equation (V) consumption depends only on the interest rate (which, since it is a market price, is obviously the same for everybody) and *total* income and *total* wealth. In particular, consumption does *not* depend on the *distribution* of income and wealth among the individual transactors. Neoclassical economists assume that *either* the distribution of income and wealth does not affect anything *or* when income and wealth change the existing distributions are maintained (that is, everybody's income and wealth changes in the same proportion). Neo-Keynesian economists assume that the distribution of income and wealth affects the endogenous variables (like consumption) and than when income and wealth change the existing distribution of income and wealth is, in general, changed.

These, then, are the assumptions that distinguish neoclassical macroeconomists from neo-Keynesian macroeconomists. They are summarized in Table 1. Now we must enter a caveat. Macroeconomists do *not* have to fall into one camp or another. They can, for example, straddle the field. As a matter of fact, most of them do. There are very few, if any, pure neoclas-

TABLE 1

ASSUMPTIONS CONCERNING	NEOCLASSICAL	NEO-KEYNESIAN
Prices (W, r, and P)	All are flexible.	One, or more, is rigid.
Money illusion	All supply and demand functions are free of money illusion.	One, or more, supply or demand functions contains money illusion.
Price expectations (W, r, and P)	All are unit-elastic.	One, or more, is inelastic.
Distribution effects of price changes	Do not occur (or are unimportant).	Do occur (and are important).

sical or pure Keynesian economists left nowadays—certainly far fewer than there were a generation ago. In macroeconomics, at least, there has been a coming together. Eclecticism is now the order of the day. One economist might believe that prices are flexible (neoclassical) and also that distribution effects are important (neo-Keynesian). Or another economist might believe that wages are inflexible in the short run (neo-Keynesian), but flexible in the long run (neoclassical). Thus, our classification has erected straw men to a large extent. It has been adopted for pedagogic reasons. However, our intentions are honorable. What we mean to convey is that to derive the classical macroeconomic propositions you must adopt *all* the neoclassical assumptions. On the other hand, to derive "Keynesian" macroeconomic predictions you must drop *at least one* of the neoclassical assumptions and adopt its neo-Keynesian counterpart.

In the rest of Part II we operate our macroeconomic model according to neoclassical assumptions. In Part III we operate the model with one, or more, neo-Keynesian assumptions.

2 The Neutrality of Money

To the classical economists money is *neutral,* or, as they frequently express it, *money is a veil.* What do these two statements mean (and they both mean the same thing)? In saying that money is neutral or a veil, classical economists meant that none of the real variables in the macroeconomic system depended on the nominal quantity of money in the system after full adjustment to the new quantity of money had occurred. The nominal quantity of money *only* affected the nominal variables. In fact, the classical economists went even further. They said that all the real variables in the system are independent of the nominal supply of money and all the nominal variables in the system are *proportional* to the nominal supply of money. This implies that when the supply of money is, for example, doubled, none of the real variables (such as consumption, investment, employment, the interest rate, real income) will change at all, but all the nominal variables (such as the nominal wage rate, the nominal demand for money and, in particular, the nominal price level) will double. Moreover, they will exactly double—no more and no less. This is a strong proposition. Nonetheless, using our macroeconomic model we can show that it is true as long as we operate with the full set of neoclassical assumptions outlined in §1.

The assertion is, then, that doubling the stock of money will exactly double the equilibrium values of the nominal variables while leaving the equilibrium values of the real variables unchanged. To demonstrate the validity of this statement let us come upon our system when it is resting in equilibrium with the original level of the money supply equal to $\bar{M}^s$. This situation is illustrated graphically in Figures 1(a)–(e) by the solid lines. All the markets are clearing and the equilibrium values of the variables are indicated by asterisks as usual. Now we shall disturb this equilibrium by doubling the

FIGURE 1

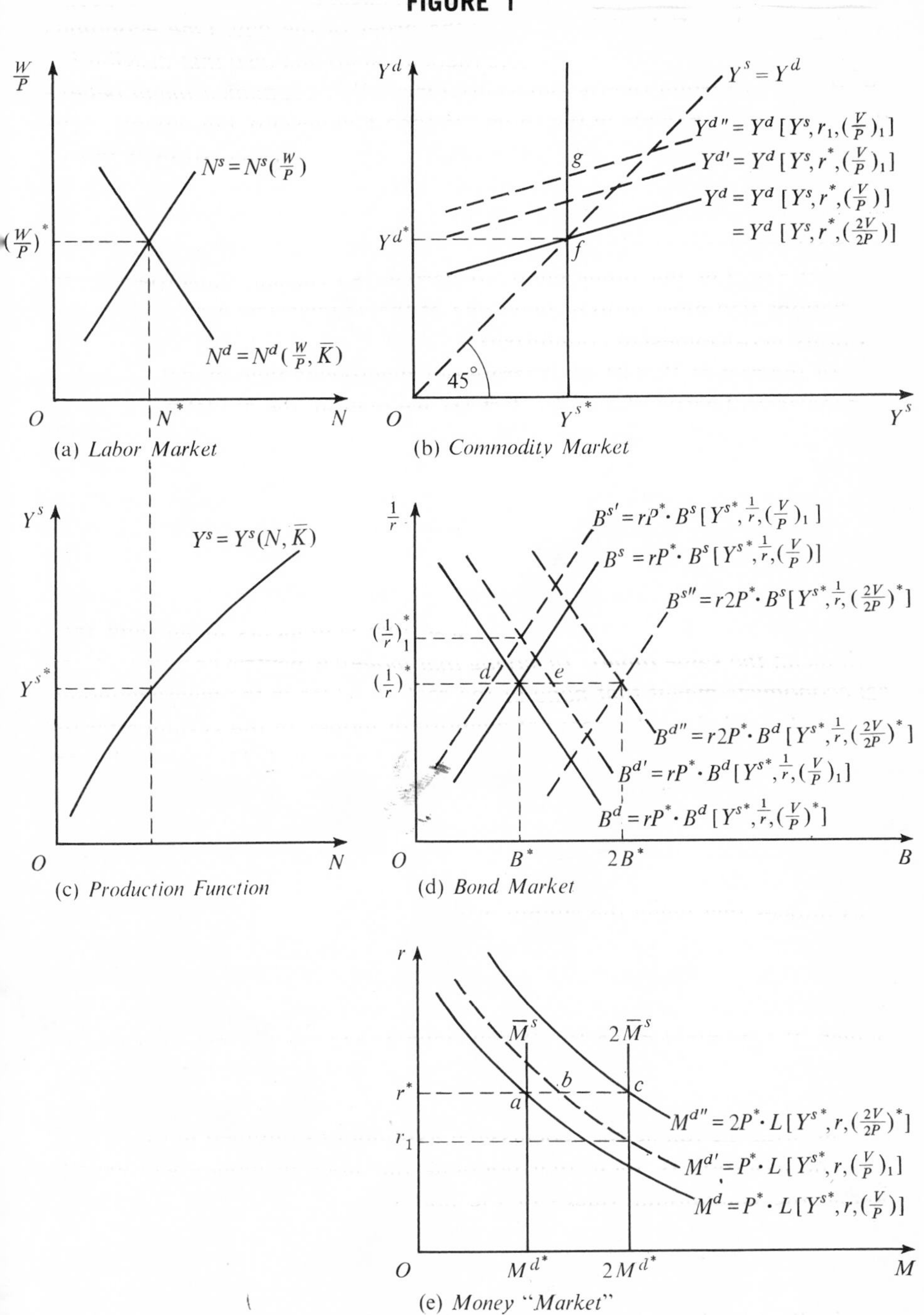

(a) *Labor Market*

(b) *Commodity Market*

(c) *Production Function*

(d) *Bond Market*

(e) *Money "Market"*

stock of money to $2\bar{M}^s$. Furthermore, assume that *everybody's stock of money is doubled*, that is, the doubled money stock is *evenly distributed*. This means that we are abstracting from distribution effects—effects brought about by some people being made relatively better off, and others relatively worse off, by the manner in which the change in the money supply is brought about. Clearly, if when the overall money stock is doubled, my stock of money goes from 10 dollars to 30 dollars and yours stays constant at 10 dollars (even though the total stock of money has doubled from 20 dollars to 40 dollars), the outcome of the conceptual experiment we are about to perform may be different from the outcome if both our stocks of money went up from 10 dollars to 20 dollars. In the latter case, the increase in the stock of money is evenly distributed, in the former case unevenly distributed. At the moment we are concerned with an evenly distributed increase in the stock of money, but not with *how* this is brought about. Economists usually advise you to imagine a munificent monetary authority calling in all your money and reissuing you exactly twice what you had before. It does not really matter how the money gets into peoples' hands. We are interested in the outcome of a conceptual experiment and not *how* it is performed.

So, one way or another, we have doubled everybody's money balances. Real wealth has been increased from $(V/P)^* = \bar{K} + (\bar{M}^s/P^*)$ to $(V/P)_1 = \bar{K} + (2\bar{M}^s/P^*)$. What effect is this going to have? The answer is that all markets will be thrown out of equilibrium. In general, there will be excess supply in the money market and excess demand in the others. Let us be more specific about the situation in each market.

In the money market two things have happened. The supply of money has increased to $2\bar{M}^s$. By itself, this would generate an excess supply of money equal to *ac*. But, in addition, real wealth has been increased to $(V/P)_1$. This increases the demand for money to $M^{d'}$. Thus, the actual excess supply of money after the joint impact of these two events is *bc*.

It might prove helpful here to present in table form using an arithmetic example, the behavior of nominal and real wealth (1) at the original money stock and price level, (2) after the money stock has doubled but before the price level has changed, and (3) after both the money stock and the price level have doubled. This is done in Table 2 where it is assumed that the prevailing level of real capital wealth $\bar{K}$ is equal to 10 (commodities comprising the capital stock) and the original stock of money $\bar{M}^s$ is equal to 50 dollars and the original price level P is 100 dollars.

In the bond market two things have happened also. The supply of bonds has decreased to $B^{s'}$ because of the increase in wealth to $(V/P)_1$ and the demand for bonds has increased to $B^{d'}$ for the same reason. Recall that the supply of bonds B^s and the demand for bonds B^d are, respectively, inversely and directly related to real wealth (V/P). Thus, the actual excess demand for bonds is equal to *de* after these two curves have shifted. As a result, let the price of bonds rise to $(1/r)_1$ in Figure 1(d) which implies the interest rate r_1 in Figure 1(e). This is only a transitional equilibrium interest rate.

In the commodity market aggregate demand will increase for two rea-

TABLE 2 Real and Nominal Wealth

	Before $\bar{M}^s$ increased; $\bar{M}^s = \$50$ $P = \$100$	After $\bar{M}^s$ increased but before P increased; $2\bar{M}^s = \$100$ $P = \$100$	After both $\bar{M}^s$ and P increased; $2\bar{M}^s = \$100$ $2P = \$200$
Nominal wealth (dollars) $V = P\bar{K} + \bar{M}^s$	$V = P\bar{K} + \bar{M}^s$ $= \$100 \cdot 10 + \$50$ $= \$1050$	$V_1 = P\bar{K} + 2\bar{M}^s$ $= \$100 \cdot 10 + \$100$ $= \$1100$	$2V = 2P\bar{K} + 2\bar{M}^s$ $= \$200 \cdot 10 + \$100$ $= \$2100$
Real wealth (commodities) $\frac{V}{P} = \bar{K} + \frac{M^s}{P}$	$\frac{V}{P} = \bar{K} + \frac{\bar{M}^s}{P}$ $= 10 + \frac{\$50}{\$100}$ $= 10\frac{1}{2}$	$\left(\frac{V}{P}\right)_1 = \bar{K} + \frac{2\bar{M}^s}{P}$ $= 10 + \frac{\$100}{\$100}$ $= 11$	$\left(\frac{V}{P}\right) = \bar{K} + \frac{2\bar{M}^s}{2P}$ $= 10 + \frac{\$100}{\$200}$ $= 10\frac{1}{2}$

sons. First, wealth increases from $(V/P)^*$ to $(V/P)_1$. This, we know, will increase the consumption component of aggregate demand and thus, we assume, raise aggregate demand to $Y^{d'}$. Second, aggregate demand increases because the interest rate declines to r_1, raising both the consumption and investment components of aggregate demand, since both react inversely to changes in the interest rate. With this decline in the interest rate, we assume that aggregate demand is raised from $Y^{d'}$ to $Y^{d''}$. Thus, the shift in the aggregate demand curve to $Y^{d'}$ is determined by the real wealth effect alone, while the shift in the aggregate demand curve to $Y^{d''}$ is due to the real wealth effect *and* the interest rate reduction (brought about by the real wealth effect in the bond market discussed in the preceding paragraph). If the aggregate supply curve does not shift, the total excess demand in the commodity market is equal to fg. Naturally enough, this excess demand means that commodity price P will begin to rise.

In the labor market the increase in real wealth does not affect either the supply or demand. Thus, the increase in the money supply does not throw this market out of equilibrium on impact. However, we have just seen that commodity price P will begin to rise. By itself, this would lower the real wage (W/P) and create an excess demand for labor. This excess demand for labor would raise the nominal wage W as firms compete against each other for workers and tend to raise the real wage (W/P) back up again. Hence, there are two forces at work in the labor market: rising commodity prices, which tend to lower the real wage, and rising nominal wages, which tend to raise the real wage. We shall make a special assumption here; we shall assume that the rise in the commodity price level P and the rise in the nominal wage W are *proportional* to each other. This means that their effects on the real wage (W/P) exactly offset each other. When the nominal wage W and the commodity price level P move in proportion to each other (for example, a 10 percent rise in one means a 10 percent rise in the other, and so on), the real wage (W/P) will remain constant throughout. This special assumption has a tremendous pedagogic advantage. If the real wage is constant, then the level of employment N will be constant and, through the production function, so will the level of real income Y^s. This means, of course, that the aggregate supply curve for the commodity market in Figure 1(b) remains fixed where it is. To summarize, then, the special assumption that prices and nominal wages move proportionately will keep the real wage constant; this means the labor market will continue in equilibrium and clear all the time, employment and real income will be unchanged throughout, and aggregate supply will remain constant throughout. In short, we can ignore for all practical purposes Figures 1(a) and 1(c). An assumption with such a massive pedagogic payoff clearly ought to be made, and we shall make it until further notice. However, we assure the reader that none of the conclusions in what follows depends on us having made this special assumption en route. All our conclusions are independent of this special assumption and can be proved, somewhat more tediously, without it.

We have now covered the proximate, or immediate, effects of the doubling of the money stock. The excess demand in the bond market drove up the price of bonds and drove down the rate of interest. The decline in the interest rate and the rise in real wealth generated excess demand in the commodity market equal to fg because aggregate demand rose to $Y^{d''}$ and aggregate supply remained fixed at Y^{s*} (because of the special assumption of proportional changes in prices and nominal wages). This assumption also kept the labor market clearing throughout.

Now what happens? Clearly, our position is not one of equilibrium, since there is excess commodity demand. That means rising prices, which are going to disrupt the transitory equilibrium enjoyed by the bond and money markets. The rising price level feeds into the bond and money markets, thus changing the price of bonds and the interest rate, which will have feedback effects on the commodity market. Let us discuss this process in more detail.

In the commodity market prices will rise under the impact of the excess demand of fg. This rise in prices will have an important effect on the level of aggregate demand. As prices rise real wealth decreases (because of the decline in real money balances). Thus aggregate demand will begin to fall below $Y^{d''}$. The excess demand in the commodity market, initially fg, begins to be eliminated. In the bond market the rise in the price level will affect both the supply and demand for bonds. We showed in Chapter 4 that when the price level increases, the nominal demand and the nominal supply of bonds both increase but the latter increases more than the former. This means both $B^{s'}$ and $B^{d'}$ in Figure 1(d) are shifting to the right, but $B^{s'}$ is shifting right more rapidly. Thus their point of intersection will be at a progressively lower bond price than $(1/r)_1$. In the money market the rise in the price level will cause the demand for nominal money balances to increase. In terms of Figure 1(e) this means $M^{d'}$ is shifting to the right and the interest rate will begin to rise above r_1. Of course, this rise in the interest rate in the money market is a mirror reflection of the decline in bond prices occurring in the bond market; Walras' law sees to that. The rise in interest rates above r_1 brought about by the impact of the rise in the price level on the bond market now has feedback effects on the commodity market. As interest rates rise aggregate demand falls, so the rise in the interest rate helps push aggregate demand in the commodity market down further below $Y^{d''}$. Thus, excess demand originally equal to fg in the commodity market is being eliminated by two forces. First, the rise in prices is, itself, reducing real wealth and, therefore, aggregate demand. Second, the rise in prices through its effects on the bond market is raising interest rates again, which helps lower aggregate demand further.

We now come to the crucial question. When will prices stop rising in the commodity market and, thus, stop the interest rate rising in the bond market? The answer is when the price level has *exactly* doubled. Why? We reason as follows.

Throughout (because of our special assumption about proportional changes in the nominal wage level and prices), the level of aggregate commodity supply has been constant. This means inevitably that for the commodity market to be in equilibrium again, aggregate demand must fall to its old level. This will occur if the interest rate returns to its old level and the price level doubles, because the doubling price level will reduce real wealth to the level which prevailed before the increase in the money stock. But can the interest rate be relied upon to return to its old level after the price level has doubled? Yes, it can. When the price level has doubled, real wealth, we have seen, will be exactly what it was before, but the demand for nominal bonds and the supply of nominal bonds will exactly double. In terms of Figure 1(d), after prices have doubled the demand for nominal bonds will be $B^{d''}$ and the supply of nominal bonds $B^{s''}$. Obviously, if B^d and B^s both double to $B^{d''}$ and $B^{s''}$, they will intersect at the same level as before. Thus, when the price level doubles, the price of bonds will return to $(1/r)^*$.

In the money market the same pattern is repeated. When prices double, real wealth goes back to its previous level, but the demand for nominal money balances is twice what it used to be. So, in Figure 1(e), the demand for nominal money will shift to $M^{d''}$.

So far so good, but is it not possible that there exists some other price level and interest rate combination ("other" than a doubled price level and unchanged interest rate) at which all markets will be in equilibrium after the supply of money has doubled? The answer is no. For example, suppose prices have *less* than doubled. Then two phenomena prevail, which means that the commodity market cannot possibly be clearing. First, if prices have not doubled real wealth cannot be back to its original level, which means that aggregate demand cannot have fallen back to its original level. Second, if prices have not doubled the demand for nominal bonds and supply of nominal bonds curves, $B^{d'}$ and $B^{s'}$, cannot have shifted to $B^{d''}$ and $B^{s''}$. Hence, the price of bonds cannot have fallen to $(1/r)^*$, which means that the interest rate is still *below* r^*. By itself, this would mean that aggregate demand is still above its original level. Thus, if prices less than double both a real wealth effect and an interest rate effect would keep aggregate demand above its original level. Since aggregate supply has not changed it follows that excess demand would still prevail in the commodity market.

The opposite can be easily proved also; if prices more than just double, the commodity market will not clear. Reasoning as above, we see that if prices more than double, real wealth would be reduced below what it was to begin with. By itself, this would lower aggregate demand below its original level. Moreover, if prices more than double, both the nominal bond demand curve and nominal bond supply curve would move beyond $B^{d''}$ and $B^{s''}$, but the nominal bond supply curve would move further. Therefore, the point of intersection would be below $(1/r)^*$, indicating an interest rate *above* r^*. That by itself would imply aggregate demand was below its original level. Thus, if prices more than double both a real wealth effect and an interest rate effect keep aggregate demand below its original level. However, aggregate supply is not changed. Therefore, excess supply in the commodity market exists.

The conclusion is inevitable. If the stock of money is doubled, then the price level must double. Moreover, all the other nominal variables exactly double, while none of the real variables change at all. This is easily demonstrated. Go through the equation system one by one. In (I) and (II), $\bar{K}$ and (W/P) are unchanged because $\bar{K}$ is constant by assumption and W and P move proportionately. Thus the real wage is constant. Hence the equilibrium level of employment N is unchanged. From (IV) this means real income is constant. We have just shown at great length that when the price level doubles the interest rate remains unchanged. Thus, since real income, the interest rate, and real wealth are unchanged, aggregate demand is unchanged and so are its components, consumption and investment [see equations (V), (VI) and (VII)]. Exactly analogous reasoning applies to the other variables: real bond demand and supply and the demand for real money balances [see equations (IX), (X) and (XII)]. If real income and real consumption are unchanged then so is real saving [equation (XIV)]. Finally, money income will have doubled, since the same real income is now multiplied by $2P$ instead of P [see equation (XV)].

Ball players who can only go to their right are a dime a dozen. Good players can go both ways. See then, if you can describe how a halving of the money stock will half the value of all the nominal variables and leave the real variables invariant (this is an obvious examination question).

3 The Strict Quantity Theory

The outcome which we have just analyzed (changes in the price level being proportional to changes in the supply of money) is what may be described as the strict version of the *quantity theory of money*. This theory was a basic tenet of the classical economists—under the conditions of complete price flexibility, no money illusions, unit-elastic price expectations, and an evenly distributed change in the money supply. We have just verified the rectitude of their proposition in a post-Keynesian macroeconomic framework. It is frequently demonstrated on their behalf via the so-called Cambridge equation or, alternatively, Fisher's Equation of Exchange. We shall sketch such alternative presentations briefly. The Cambridge equation is

$$\frac{M^d}{P} = kY^s \tag{1}$$

In effect, (1) states that people demand to hold in the form of real money balances M^d/P a certain proportion k of their real income Y^s. It is, then, in the nature of a demand function for real money balances. It follows that

$$M^d = kY^sP \tag{2}$$

It was then asserted that k and Y^s are constant for all practical purposes over the period for which the model is assumed to be relevant. The former is assumed constant, so the rationalization ran, because it is determined by the institutional structure (used in its most general way) of the economy, that is, by such things as the length of the payment period, the state of financial technology (e.g., the existence or nonexistence of credit cards), and so on. As the institutional structure was assumed to be constant during the period for which the model was applicable, k was also assumed to be constant. Real income was assumed constant because the assumption of completely flexible prices guaranteed full employment (which, we have seen, it does, since everyone offering labor services can find a purchaser). Thus, the real income is equal to the constant level of real output that is generated at full employment. The period during which the model was applicable was assumed too short to allow for capital accumulation to affect output or for technological innovation to occur such that a higher level of output could be produced with the same levels of employment and capital stock.

Now this model comprises one equation in two unknowns, the demand for nominal balances and the price level. It may be completed by an equilibrium condition:

$$M^d = \bar{M}^s \tag{3}$$

which states that the demand for money to hold must equal the supply of money available to hold. The latter is determined exogenously. (This completion of the model to provide two equations for the two unknowns is usually elided. The supply of money, exogenously determined, is normally substituted directly into equation (2) to give one equation in the one unknown, the price level.) It follows from this that if M^d is equal to $\bar{M}^s$ and k and Y^s are constant, P is proportional to $\bar{M}^s$.

Next, let us consider Fisher's Equation of Exchange, which is

$$\bar{M}^sV = Y^sP \tag{4}$$

Equation (4) is given a subtly different interpretation from the Cambridge equation which, you will recall, was a statement about the demand for money. Fisher's equation may be interpreted as follows. The money received for goods sold is equal to the quantity produced (and sold) Y^s times their average price P. This is the right-hand side of (4). The left-hand side says that the money *spent* for goods during the period must equal the (average) supply of money $\bar{M}^s$ multiplied by V, the number of times each dollar was used in the period; V is known as the *income velocity of money*. These two propositions—what is received for sales is equal to PY^s and what is spent for purchases is equal to M^sV—are certainly faultless. Equation (4) states the obvious fact that, in equilibrium, they must be equal; what someone spends, someone receives; and what someone receives, someone must have spent.

To demonstrate proportionality between the price level and the money supply using the Equation of Exchange, real income Y^s and the velocity of circulation V are assumed to be constant during the time period for which the model is relevant on the same grounds that Y^s and k are assumed constant in the Cambridge equation. The exact argument used to justify the constancy of k may be used to justify the constancy of V, since, if both sides of (4) are divided by V, we obtain

$$M^s = \frac{1}{V} Y^s P \qquad (5)$$

Comparing (2) with (3) and (5) yields $k = 1/V$; hence, what is true for k also is true for V.

It is worth drawing attention here to the fact that k has a time dimension. This may be seen by dividing both sides of (2) by money income. Then

$$\frac{M^d}{Y^s_m} = k \qquad (6)$$

where Y^s_m is money income. This also reveals that k is the fraction of money income which the community wishes to hold in the form of nominal money balances. For example, if money income was 100 dollars per year and nominal money balances were 25 dollars, then k would equal 1/4 per year. It would signify that, on the average and in the aggregate, the community wished to hold 1/4 of its flow of money income in the form of nominal money balances. Naturally, if k is equal to 1/4, then velocity V is equal to 4; interpreted, this means each one of the dollars comprising the 25 dollars in money must have been used, on the average, four times per year to finance a flow of money income equal to 100 dollars.

Returning now to Fisher's equation (4), it is quite clear by inspection that if velocity and real income are constant, the price level must be proportional to the money supply. Hence, we reach the same conclusion whether we use the Cambridge equation or Fisher's Equation of Exchange.

The simple algebra of equations (2) and (4) tells us that if real income and k (or V) are constant, the price level will be proportional to the supply of money. What, though, is the substantive economic content of the quantity theory? Quantity theorists reason as follows. An increase in the supply of money to $\bar{\bar{M}}^s$ disturbs the optimum relation between nominal money balances and money income; actual money balances exceed desired money balances, or $\bar{\bar{M}}^s > M^d$. In an attempt to reduce actual money balances $\bar{\bar{M}}^s$ to desired money balances M^d, expenditure is raised. This is the real wealth (or balance) effect of an increase in the money supply. But real income is constant via the full employment assumption. Therefore, the excess demand for goods (reflecting the excess supply of money) manifests itself in rising prices. It is clear from (2) that the rise in prices will raise the demand for nominal money balances. Eventually, the demand for nominal money balances M^d will rise to some level $M^{d'}$ where it equals the supply of nominal money balances $\bar{\bar{M}}^s$. (Note that carefully.) Individual attempts to reduce actual money balances to desired money balances, in fact, eventually raise desired money balances up to the level of actual money balances available. The increase in desired money balances is due to the rise in prices. Actual money balances are constant at $\bar{\bar{M}}^s$ because individual acts of spending do *not* reduce the available supply of money. They merely redistribute the constant stock of money among the individuals in the economy. The final result of individual attempts to lower actual money balances to desired levels is, paradoxically perhaps, to eventually cause desired money balances to rise to the actual level available.

Prior to the advent of the post-Keynesian macroeconomic model that we have developed, equations (2) and (4) were the apparatus with which the classical propositions about the quantity theory were demonstrated. Notwithstanding that these propositions were, and are, true (given the full set of neoclassical assumptions), this apparatus is decrepit. It is not wrong, just passé (somewhat like deciding to go via Model T when a Cadillac waits at the door). Let us explain why we are so harsh.

Both the Cambridge approach and the Equation of Exchange approach involve, albeit implicitly, a truly massive degree of aggregation. They were, in effect, a first thrust at macroeconomics. The economy has been reduced to just two markets—goods and money—and one of these has been thrown out through appeal to Walras' law. This is quite legitimate, of course. In a two-market economy, if one market is clearing the other must be too. The Cambridge equation approach brings to the forefront the money market. Recall that equation (2) [with (3)] involves equating the supply and demand for money. The goods market is dismissed. On the other hand, Fisher's Equation of Exchange brings the goods market into sharp focus downstage while the money market is upstaged via Walras' law.

But who is to say that a macroeconomic approach with two markets is any worse, in principle, than the one we have adopted with four markets? In fact, unless there are compelling reasons to the contrary, a two-market analysis is to be preferred to a four-market analysis on grounds of simplicity. However, we feel there are compelling reasons to the contrary, since the two-market approach conceals some crucial matters. First, the factor market (for labor in our model), from which important macroeconomically disruptive forces can emanate, disappears entirely. Second, both the Cambridge equation and the Equation of Exchange ignore the bond market (which gets washed out in the massive process of aggregation undergone) and thus give the *impression* that the aggregate demand for *goods* has to be proportional to the supply of money if the quantity theory propositions are to hold. If this were true, it would be a very restrictive condition. There seems no a priori reason for such an assumption, and it happens that the quantity theory propositions are not dependent on this objectionable restriction. To illustrate that this is so, consider, within the context of our model, the extreme case where the demand for commodities is completely and entirely independent of the supply of money; that is to say, there is no real balance effect in the commodity demand function at all. Given this assumption, what will happen if the supply of money is doubled? Consider Figures 2(a) and 2(b) representing the commodity and bond markets, respectively. (We omit the money market this time through appeal to Walras' law and the labor market through our assumption that price and wage changes will be proportional, so that this market will always be clearing.)

The increase in the supply of money will have an impact effect only on the bond market. The demand curve will shift right to $B^{d'}$ and the supply curve left to $B^{s'}$. This will lower interest rates to r_1—a reduction which will prove to be transitory. This reduction in the interest rate will affect the commodity market and raise aggregate demand to $Y^{d'}$. Consequently, the price level will begin to rise. The crucial question is when will the price level stop rising? The short answer is when there is no longer any excess demand in the commodity market; this will occur when the interest rate returns to its original level r^*. The interest rate will return to its original level when the supply and demand for bonds intersect at the same interest rate as they did before. This will happen when the curves have shifted, under the impact of the rising price level, to $B^{d''}$ and $B^{s''}$. But that (as we have seen when we went through our earlier example) will occur when the price level has just doubled. This is precisely what we were trying to show; that even though the demand for commodities is quite independent of the supply of money, the price level will still change in proportion to the supply of money. Thus, the impression left by the Cambridge and Fisher equations that the demand for commodities is proportional to the supply of money (and, indeed, must be if the quantity theory propositions are to be validated) is false.

This discussion leads naturally into what is perhaps the most fundamental criticism of the Cambridge and Fisher equation approaches to macroeconomics. By ignoring the bond market they leave themselves open to the charge that they are quite impotent to analyze the forces determining the interest rate. This is certainly true. Moreover, the famous quantity theory proposition that the interest rate (which they take to be a real variable) is independent of the money supply cannot be demonstrated by these two alternative approaches to the quantity theory. They have nothing whatsoever to say about interest rates so they certainly cannot be invoked to elucidate such an argument. In contrast, the four-market, post-Keynesian macroeconomic model which we have been discussing is quite capable of demonstrating the fundamental classical proposition on the invariance of interest rates to changes in the supply of money.

FIGURE 2

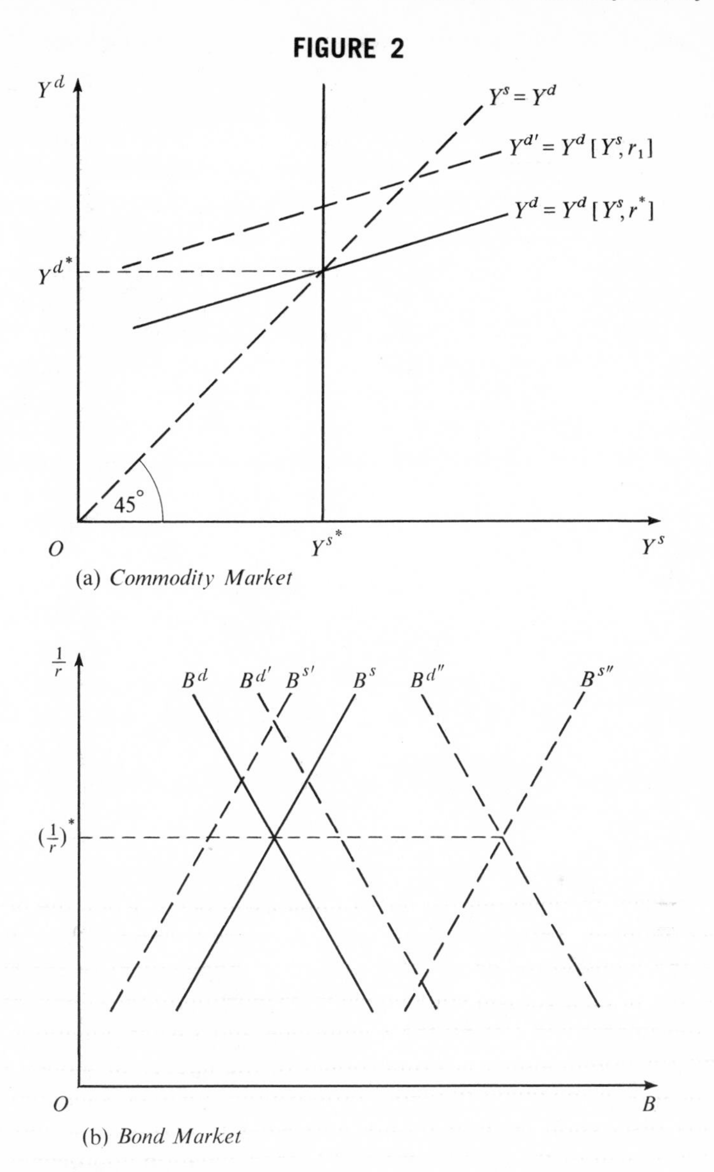

(a) *Commodity Market*

(b) *Bond Market*

This ignoring of interest rate phenomena by the Cambridge and Fisher equations is unfortunate in another respect. It tends to imply, in the former particularly, that the demand for money is independent of the interest rate. Refer back to equation (2)—does it not give the impression that the demand for nominal money balances is proportional to money income (and that is all)?

This type of thinking led many economists to infer that the classical proposition about proportionality between the supply of money and the price level which other economists customarily demonstrated via these equations was crucially dependent on the assumption that the demand for money was independent of the interest rate. This inference was dead wrong, but one sympathizes with the economists who made it because there was no indication to the contrary in the Cambridge and Fisher approaches. We know this inference is wrong from the operations we have performed with our more fully articulated macroeconomic model. Our model includes a demand for money function which is indubitably dependent on the rate of interest. However, the equilibrium interest rate, as we have shown in the previous section, is independent of the money supply—which conforms with the classical assertion. There is a certain amount of perverse appeal in a situation where the demand for money is a function of the interest rate, while the equilibrium interest rate is independent of the supply of money. Our discussion in the previous section revealed where the solution to this paradox lies. The demand curve for nominal money balances shifts as the price level rises because of the increase in the supply of money. Moreover, the shift in the demand curve will be proportional to the rise in prices which, itself, is proportional to the increase in the supply of money. Therefore, the demand for money is proportional to the supply. As a result, the two curves continue to intersect at the same interest rate.

It is these various shortcomings which persuade us to eschew the Cambridge and Fisher equations as analytical devices for the elucidation of the classical propositions about the quantity theory of money. It can be done that way—it is just inefficient and less informative than within the context of the macroeconomic model we have adopted. We emphasize that adoption of a Keynesian-type macroeconomic model does not mean that quantity theory propositions are foreclosed. In spite of any impression you may have picked up elsewhere to the contrary, you do *not* have to use one sort of analysis if you are a so-called quantity theorist and another sort of analysis if you are a so-called Keynesian. The propositions of *both* schools are demonstrable through a post-Keynesian macroeconomic model.[1] The *outcome* will either be that predicted by the strict quantity theory (money is neutral, money is a veil) if the full set of neoclassical assumptions are fed in, or the outcome will be Keynesian if Keynesian-type assumptions are the basis. If you believe that "money matters," as we do, you do not have to nail yourself to the mast of the Cambridge or Fisher equations.

Appendix: The Neutrality of Money; Changes in the Demand[1]

We showed in §2 of this chapter that a change in the supply of money would be neutral under certain circumstances. It is equally possible to show that a change in the demand for money (what is also commonly described as a change in liquidity preference) is neutral as well—under certain circumstances. These circumstances are that (1) all prices are flexible, (2) no trans-

[1] We are reminded again of Friedman's obiter dictum that "we are all Keynesians now." Notwithstanding, Friedman is a passionate exponent of a refined version of the quantity theory of money.

[1] This appendix may be omitted without loss of continuity. It is quite difficult.

actor suffers from any form of money illusion, (3) price expectations are unit-elastic, (4) there are no distribution effects, (5) the change in liquidity preference is uniform (that is, *every* transactor's increased desire to hold money is of the same intensity), and (6) the change in liquidity preference is *unbiased.* The first five sets of circumstances are already quite familiar. They are exactly the same circumstances required for a change in the supply of money to be neutral. However, the sixth condition in the present case is new. What does it mean to say that the change in liquidity preference is unbiased? For expository purposes, let us discuss an increase in liquidity preference. (The discussion for a decrease in liquidity preference would merely be the reverse of what follows.)

When there is an increase in liquidity preference, or an increase in the demand for money, it means that, given the existing real wealth and real money balances, people now want to hold *more* money, *fewer* bonds, and use *fewer* commodities. We may say that their tastes have changed in favor of money and against bonds and commodities. When there is a change in tastes, there is an associated shift in supply and demand curves (as we saw in §4.3 and §5.3). When there is an increase in liquidity preference the demand for money curve will shift to the right, the demand for bonds curve will shift to the left, and the aggregate demand for commodities curve will drop. There will also be a shift in the supply of bonds curve to the right. When peoples' tastes alter in favor of money and against bonds, they become less prone to lend (the leftward shift in the demand for bonds) *and* more disposed to borrow money (the rightward shift in the supply of bonds curve). Consider Figure 3. The initial equilibrium positions of the curves are shown by the solid curves. After the shift in liquidity preference, the new curves are shown dashed and are labeled $M^{d'}$, $B^{d'}$, $B^{s'}$, and $Y^{d'}$. Notice that in our equations, a change in tastes is represented by a change in the *functionals.* There is a change in the demand for money, bonds, and commodities and a change in the supply of bonds, even though none of the *variables* in the equations has changed in value. Such changes, then, must stem from a change in the nature or form of the function. This is represented by the functional. For convenience, we summarize the relevant demand and supply equations before and after the change in liquidity preference in Table 3 (page 181). The changes in demand and supply to the primed values are brought about *solely* by changes in the functionals; all the variables within the brackets remain the same.

So far we have only explained what a shift in liquidity preference amounts to in general. What is the special characteristic of an *unbiased* shift in liquidity preference? An unbiased shift in liquidity preference is a change in preferences in favor of money and against bonds and commodities *without* there being a change in preferences between bonds and commodities, too. Prior to the shift in liquidity preference, in equilibrium the community maintained certain ratios between their real money holdings and real bond holdings, between their real money holdings and real commodity use, and, by implication, between their real bond holdings and real commodity use. After the increase in liquidity preference, the community wants, by definition, to

FIGURE 3

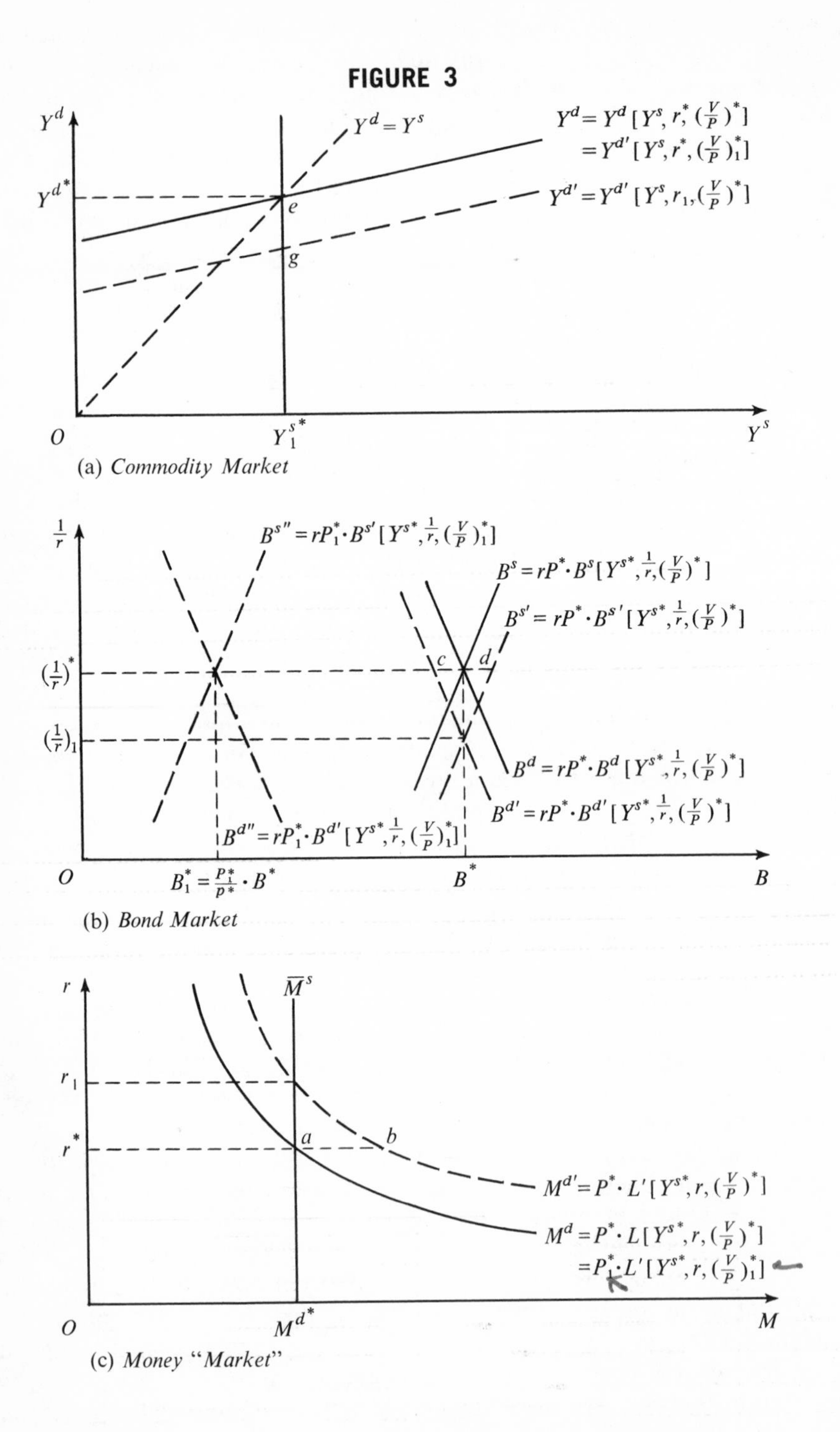

(a) *Commodity Market*

(b) *Bond Market*

(c) *Money "Market"*

TABLE 3 The Effect of a Shift in Liquidity Preference on the Equations

	BEFORE CHANGE IN LIQUIDITY PREFERENCE	AFTER CHANGE IN LIQUIDITY PREFERENCE
DEMAND FOR MONEY	$M^d = P \cdot L\left[Y^{s*}, r, \left(\frac{V}{P}\right)^*\right]$	$M^d = P \cdot L'\left[Y^{s*}, r, \left(\frac{V}{P}\right)^*\right]$
DEMAND FOR BONDS	$B^d = rP \cdot B^d\left[Y^{s*}, \frac{1}{r}, \left(\frac{V}{P}\right)^*\right]$	$B^{d'} = rP \cdot B^{d'}\left[Y^{s*}, \frac{1}{r}, \left(\frac{V}{P}\right)^*\right]$
SUPPLY OF BONDS	$B^s = rP \cdot B^s\left[Y^{s*}, \frac{1}{r}, \left(\frac{V}{P}\right)^*\right]$	$B^{s'} = rP \cdot B^{s'}\left[Y^{s*}, \frac{1}{r}, \left(\frac{V}{P}\right)^*\right]$
DEMAND FOR COMMODITIES	$Y^d = Y^d\left[Y^{s*}, r^*, \left(\frac{V}{P}\right)^*\right]$	$Y^{d'} = Y^{d'}\left[Y^{s*}, r^*, \left(\frac{V}{P}\right)^*\right]$

establish a higher ratio between its real money and bond holdings, and real money and commodity use. But if the increase in liquidity preference is unbiased, the *ratio* between real bond and real commodity use after the increase must be the same as it was before. This situation is summarized in Table 4.

These preliminaries behind us, we are now in a position to analyze the effects of an unbiased increase in liquidity preference. Consider Figures 3(a), 3(b), and 3(c). (The labor market and the production function are omitted because we shall continue to assume that changes in W and P are proportional as we did in §2. This means the labor market always clears at N^* and, thus, real income is always constant at Y^{s*}. Consequently, we can ignore these two diagrams without loss.) The solid curves are the initial positions prior to the increase in liquidity preference and the variables with an asterisk are initial equilibrium values.

Immediately after the increase in liquidity preference, the demand for

TABLE 4 An Unbiased Increase in Liquidity Preference

RATIOS BEFORE INCREASE IN LIQUIDITY PREFERENCE	RATIOS AFTER INCREASE IN LIQUIDITY PREFERENCE
(1) $\dfrac{\text{real money}}{\text{real bonds}}$	(2) $\dfrac{(\text{real money})'}{\text{real bonds}}$
(3) $\dfrac{\text{real money}}{\text{real commodities}}$	(4) $\dfrac{(\text{real money})'}{\text{real commodities}}$
(5) $= \dfrac{(1)}{(3)} = \dfrac{\text{real commodities}}{\text{real bonds}}$	(6) $= \dfrac{(2)}{(4)} = \dfrac{\text{real commodities}}{\text{real bonds}}$

money curve shifts to $M^{d'}$. This creates an excess demand for money equal to *ab*. Opposed to this excess demand for money there is an excess supply of bonds (equal to *cd*) brought about by the decrease in demand for bonds to $B^{d'}$ and increase in supply of bonds to $B^{s'}$, and an excess supply of commodities (equal to *eg*) brought about by the decrease in demand for commodities to $Y^{d'}$. The aggregate demand for commodities is reduced to $Y^{d'}$ by the direct effect of the increased liquidity preference in the commodity market *and* the rise in the interest rate (itself, of course, the direct effect of the increased liquidity preference in the bond market).

This total excess supply of commodities equal to *eg* causes commodity prices to fall. By itself, this decline in price P raises the real wage W/P and creates an excess supply of labor. This excess supply of labor lowers the nominal wage W as unemployed workers compete against each other for the available jobs, thus tending to reduce the real wage again. Once more we observe two forces at work in the labor market – a rise in the price level P tending to raise the real wage W/P, and a fall in W tending to lower it. We shall again invoke the special assumption that we made in §2; namely, that the decreases in price level P and the nominal wage W are proportional to each other, so that the real wage remains constant. If the real wage remains constant, then so does the level of employment at N^* and, via the production function, the level of real output (income) at Y^{s*}. Thus, the aggregate supply of commodities remains the same and the vertical curve Y^{s*} in Figure 3(a) does not shift. Again, we stress that the outcome we derive does not depend on this special assumption of proportional changes in the price level and nominal wage rate. What it does is allow us to turn our backs on the labor market with full confidence that it will remain in equilibrium.

We now focus our attention on the commodity and bond markets and examine what repercussions the fall in commodity prices has there. The fall in price P will raise real wealth $V/P = \bar{K} + (M/P)$. Thus, aggregate demand will begin to rise from $Y^{d'}$ and the deflationary gap *eg* will begin to close because of this direct wealth effect. In addition, the fall in the price level P will shift both $B^{d'}$ and $B^{s'}$ to the left; the latter more than the former for oft-repeated reasons. Thus the price of bonds will again begin to rise, which implies that the rate of interest will begin to fall. This fall in the rate of interest will provide additional impetus to closing the deflationary gap *eg* that existed in the commodity market. Now we know that the price level P will decline and the interest rate move back towards its original level. The question is at which level will they stabilize?

Let the new equilibrium price level be P_1^*, such that the new, and now higher, level of real wealth provides the same degree of stimulation to commodity demand *after* the increase in liquidity preference as the old, lower level of real wealth did *before* the increase in liquidity preference. It follows that if the commodity market is to be in equilibrium, the same interest rate must prevail after the increase in liquidity preference as before the increase. Why? Look at the determinants of commodity demand. They are Y^{s*}, which is constant, $(V/P_1)^*$, which is providing the same degree of stimulation to commodity demand as the old $(V/P)^*$, and the interest rate r. The interest rate must be equal to its old level of r^* if all the determinants of commodity demand *together* are to produce the same level of commodity demand after the increase in liquidity preference as they did before. If a *lower* interest rate than r^* prevailed, commodity demand after the increase in liquidity preference would exceed commodity demand before the increase (Y^{s*} and $(V/P)_1^*$ are providing the same stimulus to commodity demand) and, thus, excess commodity demand would exist, since the supply of commodities is constant. Conversely, if a *higher* interest rate than r^* prevailed, commodity demand after the increase in liquidity preference would be less than commodity demand before the increase and, thus, excess commodity supply would exist, since the supply of commodities is constant. We conclude, then, that the rate of interest does not change when there is an unbiased change in liquidity preference.

When we last discussed the bond market the supply and demand curves were shifting left under the impact of the fall in prices. Since the supply curve was shifting more rapidly than the demand curve, the interest rate was falling from its transitionally high level of r_1 back towards its equilibrium level of r^*. These curves will stop moving when the *nominal* supply and demand for bonds have fallen in proportion to the price level and assume the positions of $B^{s''}$ and $B^{d''}$, respectively, in Figure 3. These curves intersect at r^* and B_1^*. Now, it must be true that these curves have shifted left in proportion to the fall in the price level, since an unbiased increase in liquidity preference means that the ratio of real commodities to real bonds remains constant. As the equilibrium supply and demand for commodities has not changed, then the equilibrium supply and demand for real bonds cannot have changed if this ratio is to be preserved. Thus, in the new equilibrium the new real supply and demand for bonds must equal the original real supply and demand for bonds. That is,

$$\frac{B_1^*}{r^*P_1^*} = \frac{B^*}{r^*P^*}$$

from which it is clear that

$$B_1^* = \frac{P_1^*}{P^*} B^* \tag{7}$$

The expression in (7) is a statement to the effect that the new equilibrium *nominal* supply and demand for bonds must change in proportion to the change in the price level. If the new equilibrium price level is 80 percent of the old equilibrium price level, then the new equilibrium supply and demand for nominal bonds must be 80 percent of the old equilibrium supply and demand for nominal bonds.

It is legitimate to ask whether the new curves for supply and demand for bonds could not intersect at the appropriate nominal quantity B_1^* but, say, at a higher interest rate than r^* (for example, like those labeled $B^{d'''}$ and $B^{s'''}$ in Figure 4)? The answer is they could not. At an interest rate such as

FIGURE 4

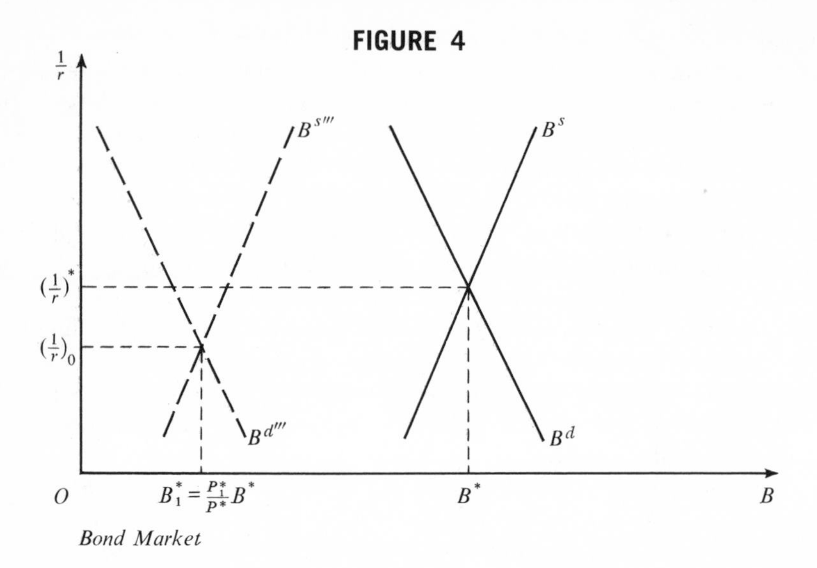

Bond Market

r_0, the commodity market would not be in equilibrium. Because of the higher-than-equilibrium interest rate, there would be an excess supply of commodities and prices would continue to fall. This in turn would cause $B^{d'''}$ and $B^{s'''}$ to move to the left resulting in a violation of the condition that they intersect at B_1^* (the nominal quantity which implies an unchanged real quantity). Thus, preservation of an unchanged real quantity of bonds supplied and demanded would be lost. The converse holds, too. If $B^{d'''}$ and $B^{s'''}$ intersected at B_1^* for a lower interest rate than r^*, excess commodity demand would prevail, the price level would rise, and $B^{d'''}$ and $B^{s'''}$ would move to the right and, therefore, away from B_1^*. We may conclude, then, that bond and commodity market equilibria will only occur after an increase in liquidity preference when the interest rate remains unchanged and the nominal supply and demand for bonds falls in proportion to the fall in the price level.

In this discussion we have concentrated on the reestablishment of equilibrium in the commodity and bond markets, assumed that it prevailed in the labor market throughout, and largely ignored direct discussion of the money market. This, through Walras' law, is forgiven us. If the commodity, bond, and labor markets are followed back into equilibrium, then the money market will find its way there automatically. However, it may be a good thing to look briefly at what happens there. The initial increase in liquidity preference shifts the M^d curve to $M^{d'}$, and the transitory interest rate r_1 emerges. But the excess supply of commodities generated by the increase in liquidity preference and the rise in the interest rate causes prices to fall. The fall in prices then causes the demand for nominal money curve $M^{d'}$ to start shifting left. It will stop shifting left when it *overlays exactly* the original curve M^d. This will occur at the old interest rate r^* and the new, lower price level P_1^*. Notice what has happened. The *same nominal* quantity of money is demanded (equal to the constant nominal quantity of money supplied).

However, the *real* quantity of money demanded has risen from $\bar{M}^s/P^*$ to $\bar{M}^s/P_1^*$. The increased demand for real money balances, which is what an increase in liquidity preference *means*, has been accomplished by a fall in the price level while the nominal quantity available remains unchanged. The increased real money wealth that the community now wishes to hold has been created *automatically*. As Patinkin is provoked to exclaim, "the wonders of the 'invisible hand' never cease."[2]

To this limited extent, a change in the demand for money does affect one real variable in the system, namely, real money wealth. However, all the other real variables such as the real wage, employment, income, and consumption investment remain the same. Thus, we conclude that the purely *monetary phenomenon* of an increase in liquidity preference is neutral in its effects (just as a change in the supply of money is neutral) when the circumstances outlined in the first paragraph of this appendix prevail.

This conclusion was a basic tenet of classical economists. Although we have arrived at it using a distinctly post-Keynesian macroeconomic model, neoclassical economists would have reached it via the Cambridge or Fisher equations. Referring to the latter, for example, if the money supply and real output are constant, it is inevitable that velocity and prices change proportionally. Finally, recall that a decrease in velocity is equivalent to an increase in the demand for money (liquidity preference), since each is the inverse of the other. It is all very simple—one might even say *simpliste*. Certainly, the demonstration somehow does not carry the analytical conviction of the adjustment we described using a post-Keynesian macroeconomic model. Particularly disturbing again, as in our discussion of the effect of changes in the money supply in a neoclassical context, is the absence of any formal mention of the place of the interest rate. What is important to grasp, though, is that we have been able to confirm both the classical and neoclassical assertions about the influence of purely monetary phenomena using a post-Keynesian apparatus. Given the assumptions they made, our analytical apparatus corroborates, and does not refute, their hypotheses.

This concludes our discussion of the influence of purely monetary phenomena on the economic variables when the full set of neoclassical assumptions is made. In the next chapter we investigate the impact of purely "real" phenomena.

Summary

We began this chapter by defining a *neoclassical purist* (who is largely a straw man) as one who believes all three prices are flexible, all demand and supply functions are free of money illusion, all price expectations are unit-elastic, and distribution effects do not exist (or are unimportant). This is in contrast to the *neo-Keynesian* who does not accept one, or more, of these "neoclassical assumptions."

[2] D. Patinkin, *Money, Interest, and Prices,* 2nd ed., Harper & Row, 1965, p. 191.

By accepting the full complement of neoclassical assumptions, we were able to show that money is *neutral* (or a veil). That is, changes in the money supply have no effect on the equilibrium values of the *real* variables (including the interest rate), and the equilibrium values of the *nominal* variables change in *proportion* to the change in the money supply. Thus, the *strict quantity theory* of money is valid. Next, we examined the quantity theory in light of the *Cambridge equation* and *Fisher's Equation of Exchange.* However, in several respects these equations were found wanting as convincing macroeconomic analytical devices. (In the appendix we demonstrated that another purely monetary phenomenon, an *unbiased change in liquidity preference,* was also without any *real* repercussions. Once more, only the equilibrium values of the nominal variables change in response to such a disturbance.)

The model used in this chapter, and throughout the book, is impeccably Keynesian in its antecedents. Nonetheless, we have been able to employ it to prove some famous classical and neoclassical propositions about the neutrality of money and the quantity theory of money. We must infer, therefore, that the implications of the model depend *crucially* on the basic assumptions fed into the model. If the full set of neoclassical assumptions is entered, neoclassical implications will emerge in spite of the fact that the basic structure of the model is due to Keynes and his post-Keynesian followers. We shall see in Part III that when *any* of the neoclassical assumptions are relaxed, the model generates neo-Keynesian implications; for example, money is no longer neutral, unemployment becomes a distinct possibility, and so on.

Questions

(Questions marked with an asterisk are of a higher order of difficulty. They assume that the Appendix has been studied.)

1. Compare and contrast the basic assumptions made by neoclassical macroeconomists and neo-Keynesian macroeconomists.
2. Define *money illusion.* Give two examples of functions which contain money illusion and explain carefully why they do.
3. Define *elasticity of expectations.*
4. What is meant by the neutrality of money? Granted the full complement of neoclassical assumptions, show that money is neutral.
5. Granted the full complement of neoclassical assumptions, explain what happens when the supply of money is halved. Be sure to *prove* that the interest rate remains unchanged.
6. "The [rate of interest] . . . is totally independent of the quantity of money." (D. Ricardo, *Principles of Political Economy,* Everyman's Library, 1935, p. 511). Prove Ricardo's assertion being careful to indicate the assumptions on which your analysis is based.
7. Explain the strict version of the quantity theory of money. Using the Cambridge

equation approach, show under what circumstances the theory is valid. Do the same using Fisher's approach.

8. Develop the Cambridge equation and Fisher's Equation of Exchange. Examine them critically as macroeconomic analytical devices.
9. Define an *unbiased change in liquidity preference*. Show that an unbiased *decrease* in liquidity preference is neutral. Be careful to *prove* that the interest rate remains unchanged.
10. What changes in *either* the Cambridge equation *or* Fisher's equation when there is a change in liquidity preference?

SELECTED READINGS

1. W. J. Baumol, R. W. Clower and M. L. Burstein, F. H. Hahn, R. G. Ball and R. Bodkin, G. C. Archibald and R. G. Lipsey, "A Symposium on Monetary Policy," *Review of Economic Studies,* October, 1960. A symposium on Archibald and Lipsey's earlier critique of Patinkin's real balance effect; also includes discussion of the neutrality question.
2. G. S. Becker and W. J. Baumol, "The Classical Monetary Theory: The Outcome of the Discussion," *Economica,* November, 1952. An early attempt to rescue classical monetary theory from the disrepute it fell into in the early days of the Keynesian juggernaut.
3. J. G. Gurley and E. S. Shaw, *Money in a Theory of Finance,* Brookings, 1960. Introduces the notion of inside and outside money and, for present purposes, mounts an attack on the "rarefied set of assumptions,"—to use Johnson's description—required by neoclassical theory to establish the neutrality of money.
4. H. G. Johnson, "Monetary Theory and Policy," *American Economic Review,* June, 1962, parts I and II. A now-classic survey article on monetary theory and policy which summarizes the outcome of the neutrality debate.
5. F. Modigliani, "The Monetary Mechanism and Its Interaction with Real Phenomena," *Review of Economics and Statistics,* February, 1963. Includes an excellent modern discussion of neutrality.
6. D. Patinkin, *Money, Interest, and Prices,* 2nd ed., Harper & Row, 1965, chapter 10. The authoritative statement on the neutrality of money.
7. A. C. Pigou, *The Veil of Money,* Macmillan, 1949.

8

The Influence of Real Phenomena

In Chapter 7 we discussed the impact of essentially monetary phenomena on the equilibrium values of the variables of our macroeconomic model; our findings were that a change in either the supply of or demand for money is neutral, if we reason from the full set of neoclassical assumptions. In this chapter we shall elucidate the influence of real phenomena on the equilibrium values of the variables in similar circumstances. The changes in real phenomena that we shall study are

1. A change in the marginal productivity of labor.
2. A change in preferences vis-à-vis leisure and income.
3. A change in entrepreneurial expectations about the profitability of investment.
4. A change in the propensity to save (consume), or what is called a change in "thrift."

1 The Productivity of Labor

We showed at some length in Chapter 2 that a profit-maximizing firm will hire labor until the marginal product of labor is equal to the real wage. It was also shown that a firm's demand curve for labor was identical to the marginal physical product curve of labor. We now wish to inquire into the effects of a change in the marginal physical product of labor on the equilibrium values of the variables of the macroeconomic model.

To begin, let us assume for the sake of argument that there is an increase in the marginal physical product of labor. Suppose a smart commodity-maker discovers, quite spontaneously, that by doing something differently, he is able to coax far more output from the existing capital stock than previously. Word gets around, and how to achieve this greater output with the *same* quantities of capital and labor inputs is soon common knowledge. It should be immediately apparent that the marginal physical product of labor is now a higher figure than it was before this discovery. The addition to total output obtained by employing one more worker used to be so much; the addition to total output obtained by employing one more worker is now higher.

Consider Figure 1. Prior to the increase in productivity, if the real wage $(W/P)_1$ prevailed firms employed N_1. After the increase in productivity, however, the marginal physical product when N_1 are employed has risen to $(W/P)_2$. Equivalently, after the increase in productivity the firm can hire as many as N_2 workers before the marginal physical product falls to $(W/P)_1$. In short, the demand curve for labor has shifted to the right.

These preliminaries behind us, we can now trace the impact of an increase in the marginal physical product of labor on the complete model. Consider Figure 2 where, as usual, the solid curves and variables with an asterisk indicate the initial equilibrium values. In Figure 2(a) the initial effect of the increase in the marginal physical product of labor is to shift the demand curve for labor to $N^{d'}$. The prime on the functional is again an indication that the *form* of the function has changed. *That* is what has led to the shift; $\bar{K}$ is constant. Not only has the marginal physical product of labor curve changed but the total product curve has changed as well. Any given level of employment now produces a larger level of real output than before. Hence, in Figure 2(c), the total physical product curve has been moved up to $Y^{s'}$. This is again due to a change in the *form* of the production function, which is denoted by the prime on the functional. The *same* quantities of labor N and capital $\bar{K}$ combine to produce higher levels of output.

At the prevailing wage rate $(W/P)^*$ there is an excess demand for labor equal to *ab*. Firms compete against each other for labor and, in the process,

FIGURE 1

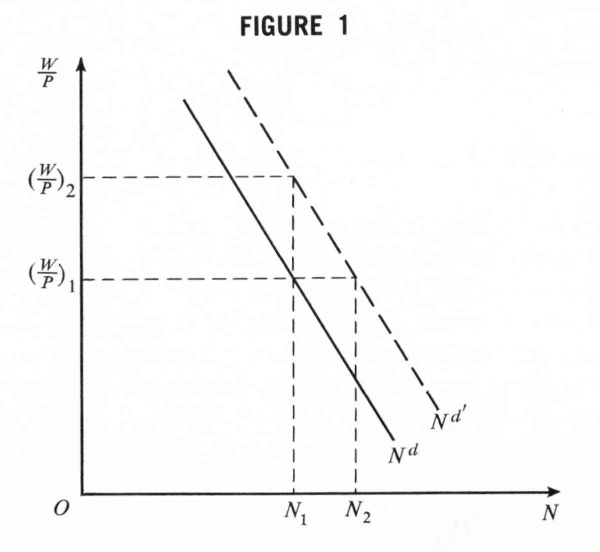

FIGURE 2

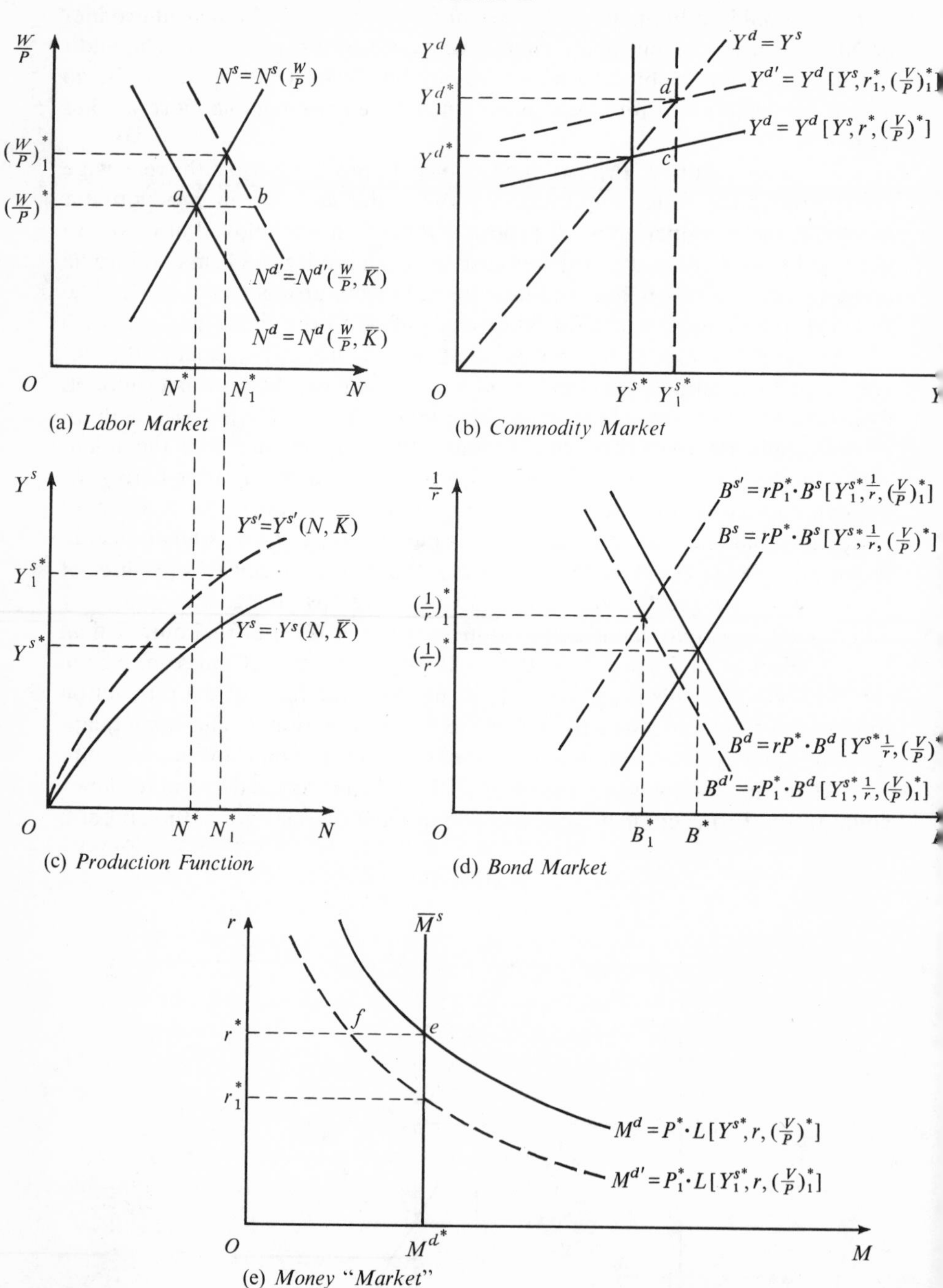

(a) *Labor Market*

(b) *Commodity Market*

(c) *Production Function*

(d) *Bond Market*

(e) *Money "Market"*

bid up the nominal wage W. Employment rises to N_1^* and the real wage rises to $(W/P)_1^*$. The rise in W is not the only reason that the real wage rises. The higher level of employment N_1^* increases the supply of commodities to Y_1^{s*}. Thus, an excess supply equal to cd is created in the commodity market. This causes the price level P to fall, which also tends to raise the real wage. Thus, the real wage rises to $(W/P)_1^*$ because of a rise in W *and* a fall in P.

The fall in P also eliminates the excess supply of commodities in the commodity market. First, it increased the real money balance component of real wealth which raises Y^d. Second, it shifts B^d and B^s left; the latter moves more than the former, thus causing the curves to intersect at a higher bond price (lower interest rate). This fall in the interest rate also causes Y^d to rise. (We remind the reader of the assumption we made in Chapter 5: when Y^s changes, B^d and B^s change equally in the same direction, having no effect on the interest rate. Thus, the fall in the interest rate only occurs because prices have fallen. The increase in income has no effect on the interest rate.) A sufficiently large decrease in P will, as a result of these two effects, eventually cause Y^d to rise to $Y^{d'}$, where equilibrium is once more established in the commodity market.

The decline in the interest rate allows us to conclude unequivocally that both consumption and investment will rise. *All* the determinants of these two variables will have changed so as to induce an increase in them; real income has risen, the interest rate has declined, and real money balances have risen.

Consider finally the money market as shown in Figure 2(e). The fall in the price level to its new equilibrium level of P_1^* would, at the initial equilibrium interest rate r^*, have generated an excess supply of nominal money balances equal to ef. But the decrease in the interest rate, rise in real income, and the rise in real money balances, are jointly responsible for raising the quantity of nominal money demanded to equality with the constant nominal quantity of money being supplied $\bar{M}^s$. This occurs at interest rate r_1^*, real income level Y_1^{s*}, and real money balance holdings $(V/P)_1^*$.

Manifestly, then, the impact of this first real (as opposed to purely monetary) phenomenon has certainly been to change the equilibrium values of the variables in our macroeconomic model; this time both the nominal variables *and* the real variables have been affected. Table 1 summarizes these changes; it indicates the variables whose equilibrium values increase and the variables whose equilibrium values decrease as a result of an increase in the marginal physical product of labor.

Most of Table 1 merely restates information which we have already arrived at by deductive logical argument and which has already been displayed in Figure 2 or mentioned in the text above. However, there are some new results—namely, the variables whose direction of change is not known. For example, we do not know what has happened to real bond holdings. There has been a fall in B, r, and P, so the outcome for the ratio B/rP is indeterminate and depends on the relative changes in these variables, about

TABLE 1 The Effects of an Increase in the Marginal Physical Product of Labor

VARIABLE	INITIAL VALUE	FINAL VALUE	OUTCOME
Employment N	N^*	N_2^*	Increased
Real income Y^s	Y^{s*}	Y_1^{s*}	Increased
Real consumption C	C^*	C_1^*	Increased
Real investment I	I^*	I_1^*	Increased
Real saving S	S^*	S_1^*	Increased
Real bonds B/rP	B^*/r^*P^*	$B_1^*/r_1^*P_1^*$	Not known
Real money M^d/P	M^d/P^*	M^d/P_1^*	Increased
Price level P	P^*	P_1^*	Decreased
Nominal wage W	W^*	W_1^*	Increased
Real wage W/P	$(W/P)^*$	$(W/P)_1^*$	Increased
Interest rate r	r^*	r_1^*	Decreased
Capital stock $\bar{K}$	$\bar{K}$	$\bar{K}$	No change
Money supply $\bar{M}^s$	$\bar{M}^s$	$\bar{M}^s$	No change
Money income Y_m^s	Y_m^{s*}	$Y_{m_1}^{s*}$	Not known
Real wealth V/P	$(V/P)^*$	$(V/P)_1^*$	Increased
Labor's share $N(W/P)/Y^s$	$N^*(W/P)^*/Y^{s*}$	$N^*(W/P)_1^*/Y_1^{s*}$	Not known
Others' share $(B/P)/Y^s$	$(B/P)^*/Y^{s*}$	$(B/P)_1^*/Y_1^{s*}$	Not known

which we do not have any information. The same is true for money income, which is the product of real income and the price level. The former has risen, the latter fallen. Hence, the outcome depends on which factor changed most in relative terms. With respect to the shares in income, we are also uncertain. Labor's *absolute* income (the numerator in labor's share ratio) clearly has risen, but so has real income (the denominator). Therefore, the outcome for the ratio of the two is ambiguous. The same is true for the "others' share." The quantity of nominal bonds outstanding and, therefore, the number of dollars paid in interest has fallen. But the price level has also fallen. This means we do not know whether the total real income paid in interest has increased or decreased, since the result again depends on the relative changes. If we do not know whether real interest payments have risen or fallen, then the share of real income paid to bond holders is ambiguous.

Naturally enough, the outcome (increase or decrease) for each variable is reversed for a decrease in the marginal physical product of labor. The reader may wish to follow the adjustment process and verify the outcomes for such a case as an exercise.

2 The Real Supply of Labor

Let us assume that our macroeconomic model is in equilibrium, then an ingrate commodity-maker throws some locoweed in the communal water supply (a "good" *freely* available to all), which causes all commodity-makers to become more slothful. Basically what has happened is that the indifference curves representing a typical commodity-maker's income/leisure preference map (see §2.2) have rotated clockwise. Thus, at an unchanged real wage rate, one of these *new* indifference curves will be tangent to the constraint line to the right of the point where one of the original curves was tangent to the same constraint. Commodity-makers now desire more leisure and less income. Hence, a decrease in the supply of labor is immediately implied.

What effect will this increased preference for leisure time have on the equilibrium values of the variables? Consider Figure 3(a). The aggregate supply of labor will shift left to $N^{s'}$ (a prime is attached to the functional to indicate that this shift results from a change in the form of the function). The proximate impact, then, will be felt in the labor market. What will the other repercussions be?

At the prevailing real wage rate $(W/P)^*$ there will clearly be an excess demand for labor equal to *ab*. Firms will bid against each other for the available supply and, thus, the nominal wage W and, consequently, the real wage W/P will begin to rise. As the real wage rises, the profit-maximizing level of employment and output will decline. When the real wage reaches its new equilibrium level $(W/P)_1^*$, the optimum level of employment is N_1^*, which gives the optimum level of real output (income) Y_1^{s*}. This reduction in aggregate supply is seen in Figure 3(b) to open up an inflationary gap in the commodity market equal to *cd*. Thus, the price level P will begin to rise, and this upward movement will have crucial repercussions. First, it will shift the supply and demand for bonds right to $B^{s'}$ and $B^{d'}$, respectively; the former shifts more than the latter so the interest rate rises.[1] The rise in the interest rate *plus* the direct reduction in real money balances brought about by the price rise both work to reduce consumption, investment, and aggregate demand. The joint effect of the rise in interest rates and fall in real money balances will eventually shift aggregate demand down to $Y^{d'}$, where the inflationary gap is closed.

[1] The fall in real income Y^s will reduce both the supply and demand for bonds. As in the previous section, we shall assume that these effects are precisely offsetting, so that they leave the interest rate unchanged.

FIGURE 3

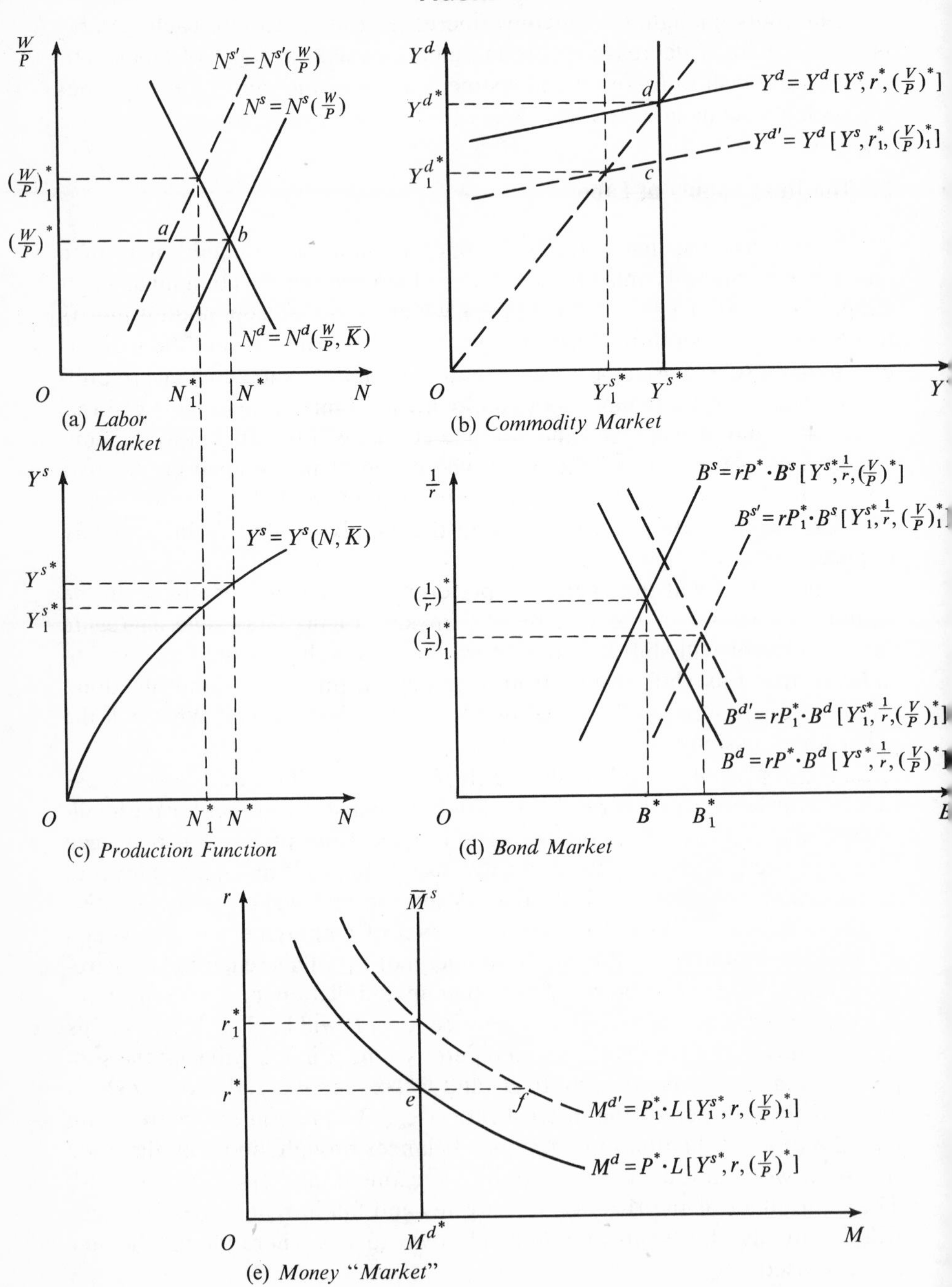

W/P
N^s' = N^s'(W/P)
N^s = N^s(W/P)
(W/P)*_1
(W/P)*
a
b
N^d = N^d(W/P, K̄)
O
N*_1
N*
N
(a) Labor Market
Y^d
Y^d*
Y^d*_1
d
c
Y^d = Y^d [Y^s, r*, (V/P)*]
Y^d' = Y^d [Y^s, r*_1, (V/P)*_1]
O
Y^s*_1
Y^s*
Y
(b) Commodity Market
Y^s
Y^s*
Y^s*_1
Y^s = Y^s(N, K̄)
O
N*_1
N*
N
(c) Production Function
1/r
(1/r)*
(1/r)*_1
B^s = rP*·B^s [Y^s*, 1/r, (V/P)*]
B^s' = rP*_1·B^s [Y^s*_1, 1/r, (V/P)*_1]
B^d' = rP*_1·B^d [Y^s*_1, 1/r, (V/P)*_1]
B^d = rP*·B^d [Y^s*, 1/r, (V/P)*]
O
B*
B*_1
B
(d) Bond Market
r
M̄^s
r*_1
r*
e
f
M^d' = P*_1·L[Y^s*_1, r, (V/P)*_1]
M^d = P*·L[Y^s*, r, (V/P)*]
O
M^d*
M
(e) Money "Market"

In the money market, the rise in the price level creates an excess demand for nominal money balances equal to *ef*. This excess demand is removed by the rise in the interest rate to r_1^*, at which point the nominal demand is equal to the constant nominal supply available. Clearly, the demand for real money balances will be lower in equilibrium, since real income and real money balances have fallen while the interest rate has risen.

Finally, note that although both the nominal wage W and the price level P have risen, the former must have risen relatively more otherwise the labor market would not come into equilibrium. Table 2 summarizes the outcomes for the equilibrium values of the variables.

The reasons for the ambiguity of the direction of change in real bonds, labor's share, and others' share are analogous to those which led to similar

TABLE 2 The Effects of an Increase in the Marginal Rate of Substitution of Leisure for Income

VARIABLE	INITIAL VALUE	FINAL VALUE	OUTCOME
Employment N	N^*	N_1^*	Decreased
Real income Y^s	Y^{s*}	Y_1^{s*}	Decreased
Real consumption C	C^*	C_1^*	Decreased
Real investment I	I^*	I_1^*	Decreased
Real saving S	S^*	S_1^*	Decreased
Real bonds B/rP	B^*/r^*P^*	$B_1^*/r_1^*P_1^*$	Not known
Real money M^d/P	M^d/P^*	M^d/P_1^*	Decreased
Price level P	P^*	P_1^*	Increased
Nominal wage W	W^*	W_1^*	Increased
Real wage W/P	$(W/P)^*$	$(W/P)_1^*$	Increased
Interest rate r	r^*	r_1^*	Increased
Capital stock $\bar{K}$	$\bar{K}$	$\bar{K}$	No change
Money supply $\bar{M}^s$	$\bar{M}^s$	$\bar{M}^s$	No change
Money income Y_m^s	Y_m^{s*}	$Y_{m_1}^{s*}$	Not known
Real wealth V/P	$(V/P)^*$	$(V/P)_1^*$	Decreased
Labor's share $N(W/P)/Y^s$	$N^*(W/P)^*/Y^{s*}$	$N_1^*(W/P)_1^*/Y_1^{s*}$	Not known
Others' share $(B/P)/Y^s$	$(B/P)^*/Y^{s*}$	$(B/P)_1^*/Y_1^{s*}$	Not known

ambiguity in the previous section. Now, however, there is an additional ambiguity. We cannot even determine if the absolute level of labor income has risen or fallen, since employment has fallen to N_1^* and the real wage has risen to $(W/P)_1^*$. Whether or not this product is larger or smaller than the product of N^* and $(W/P)^*$ clearly depends on the elasticity of demand for labor. If the demand for labor is elastic, then labor's absolute income will decline; if the demand is inelastic, absolute income will rise.

Manifestly, the cause of the reduction in the supply of labor in the case just analyzed was for example only. Similar effects would also arise because of a decline in population, a more restrictive immigration policy, or, in short, from anything which causes the real supply of labor to decrease. The analysis of the effects of an increase in the labor supply is entirely analogous and is left as an exercise.

3 Entrepreneurial Expectations about Investment

We showed in §3.2 that the aggregate level of planned investment I was directly related to income, indirectly related to the interest rate, and dependent on entrepreneurial expectations. Algebraically,

$$I = I(Y^s, r) \tag{VI}$$

The influence of expectations in equation (VI) is subsumed in the *form* of the function as represented by the functional I preceding the parentheses. If entrepreneurial expectations concerning the profitability of acquiring more capital change, planned investment changes to I' notwithstanding that Y^s and r are unchanged. We would write, therefore, $I' = I'(Y^s, r)$. A more optimistic view of the future would raise I; a more pessimistic view would lower I. Let us assume for our discussion that expectations become more optimistic.

Obviously, the impact of this change will be felt in the commodity market. Investment demand and, therefore, aggregate demand will increase—the latter to $Y^{d'}$. With the *same* interest rate, real income, and real wealth, aggregate demand is now higher due to the change in expectations. (You will recall that aggregate commodity demand is equal to consumption plus investment. The form of the aggregate commodity demand function has changed because the form of the investment function has changed.) Excess commodity demand, an inflationary gap, equal to *ab* exists. Commodity prices will rise. On its own, this rise in prices will reduce real wealth and, thus, the aggregate demand curve will begin to sink down again. However, this is not all that happens. The rise in prices also has repercussions in the bond market. Both the supply of and demand for bonds shift to the right and, it goes without saying now, the former moves more than the latter (specifically, to $B^{s'}$ and $B^{d'}$). Thus, the interest rate r will rise to r_1^*. This rise in interest rates will help to lower aggregate demand too, since both investment and consumption are decreasing functions of the interest rate. We can rest assured, then, that the inflationary gap *ab* will be closed via the joint effects of a decrease in real wealth and a rise in the interest rate. Eventually, the new curve will overlay the original Y^d curve and there will be equilibrium in the commodity market. The equation of this *new* final equilibrium aggregate demand curve is given below the original one, namely,

$$Y^d = Y^{d'}\left[Y^s, r_1^*, \left(\frac{V}{P_1}\right)^*\right]$$

What has been going on in the labor market all this time? The rise in the price level P has been tending to lower the real wage (W/P). However, there has also been an excess demand for labor as firms bid against each other for workers in an attempt to produce the extra output being demanded. This raises the nominal wage rate W, which tends to raise the real wage. Again, let us make explicit the assumption we have been using up to this point, namely, that the increases in the two nominal variables have been proportional so that the real variable is constant. Thus, employment will remain constant at its original level N^*, and real income will remain constant at its original level Y^{s*}. Nothing has happened to alter the situation in the labor market and the production function, so we omit these parts from Figure 4. It is for this reason that the aggregate commodity supply curve is kept constant in the commodity market in Figure 4(a).

In the money market, there was initially excess demand for nominal money (equal to cd) brought about by the rise in prices. This was removed by a decrease in real wealth and a rise in the interest rate until the nominal demand once again became equal to the nominal supply available.

We have summarized the outcome of this experiment on the equilibrium values of the variables in Table 3. (This time there are no ambiguous cases.) A few of the conclusions in this table not already explained demand attention. First, we note that consumption must have decreased because real wealth has fallen and the interest rate has risen, both of which reduce consumption. It follows that if consumption has decreased and real income is the same, investment must have risen. In equilibrium, we know saving equals investment. As the latter has unequivocally risen, so must the former. The increase in saving necessary to match the increased investment is brought about by the rise in the interest rate and the fall in real money balances. (This is a *very* classical explanation. In Part III we shall examine situations where this is not true.)

Money income has increased because real income is constant and the price level has risen. Labor's share is constant because employment, the real wage, and real income are all constant. This implies that the "others'" share is constant. Hence, we may conclude that the numerator (B/P) in the "others'" share has remained constant. Therefore, since the interest rate has risen, real bonds outstanding must have declined.

To conclude this section, we now enter a massive caveat. We have just analyzed the outcome that will precede the commodity bonanza which will be forthcoming when the new investment commodities which have been added to the capital stock start producing more consumption commodities.

FIGURE 4

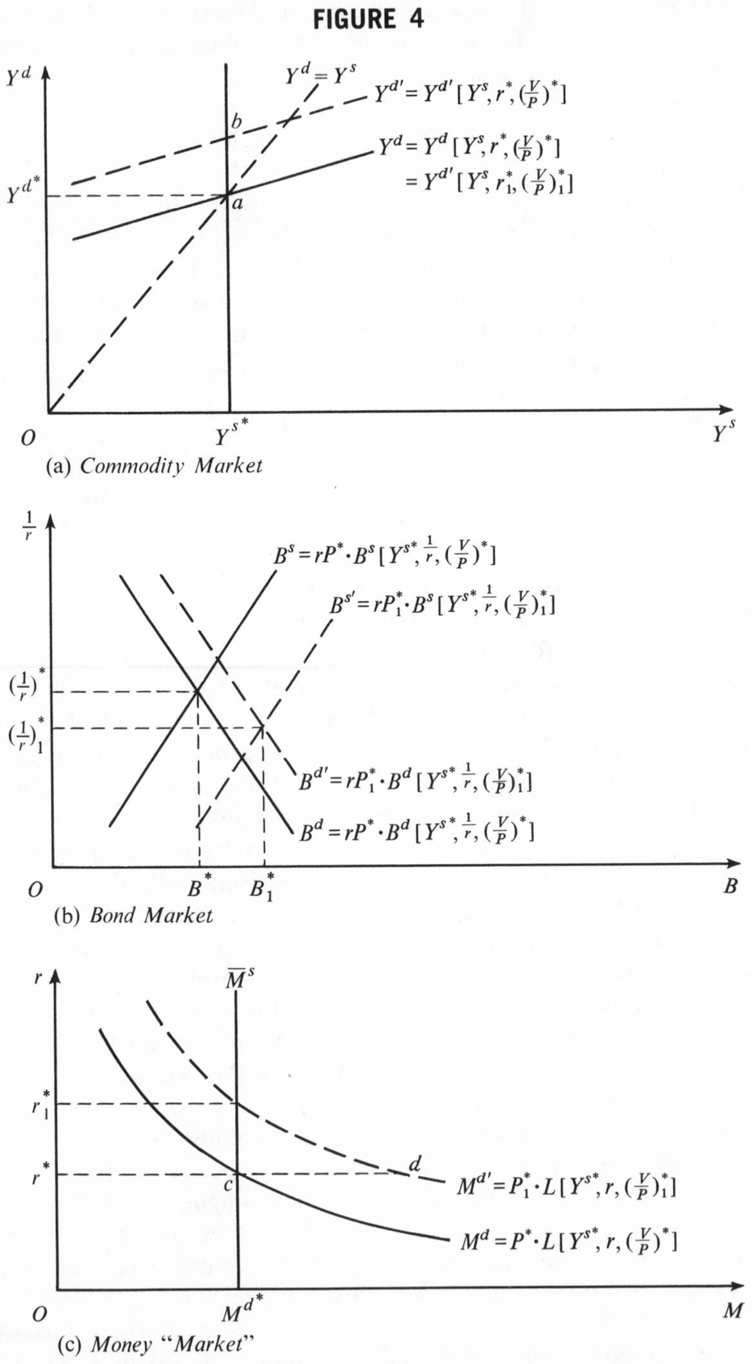

Y^d
$Y^d = Y^s$
$Y^{d'} = Y^{d'}[Y^s, r^*, (\frac{V}{P})^*]$
b
$Y^d = Y^d[Y^s, r^*, (\frac{V}{P})^*]$
$= Y^{d'}[Y^s, r_1^*, (\frac{V}{P})_1^*]$
Y^{d^*}
a
O
Y^{s^*}
Y^s
(a) *Commodity Market*
$\frac{1}{r}$
$B^s = rP^* \cdot B^s[Y^{s^*}, \frac{1}{r}, (\frac{V}{P})^*]$
$B^{s'} = rP_1^* \cdot B^s[Y^{s^*}, \frac{1}{r}, (\frac{V}{P})_1^*]$
$(\frac{1}{r})^*$
$(\frac{1}{r})_1^*$
$B^{d'} = rP_1^* \cdot B^d[Y^{s^*}, \frac{1}{r}, (\frac{V}{P})_1^*]$
$B^d = rP^* \cdot B^d[Y^{s^*}, \frac{1}{r}, (\frac{V}{P})^*]$
O
B^*
B_1^*
B
(b) *Bond Market*
r
$\overline{M}^s$
r_1^*
r^*
c
d
$M^{d'} = P_1^* \cdot L[Y^{s^*}, r, (\frac{V}{P})_1^*]$
$M^d = P^* \cdot L[Y^{s^*}, r, (\frac{V}{P})^*]$
O
M^{d^*}
M
(c) *Money "Market"*

Our *present* level of commodity consumption has been reduced. We were induced to do this by a reduction in wealth and a rise in the rate of interest. The *constant* level of real income was reallocated away from *present* consumption in favor of investment. This is the measure of our current sacrifice; however, our abstinence will be rewarded in the *future*. When the augmented capital stock pays off later on, there will be an avalanche of new commodities and future income will rise. But that is another story—a story called growth. We can say, very unrigorously, that the following sequence of events will unfold: aggregate supply (real income) will increase, prices will fall, the rate of interest will fall, investment and consumption will rise, and, at last, we will be enjoying a higher *future* level of consumption *and* investment.

TABLE 3 The Effects of an Increase in Entrepreneurial Investment Expectations

VARIABLE	INITIAL VALUE	FINAL VALUE	OUTCOME
Employment N	N^*	N^*	No change
Real income Y^s	Y^{s*}	Y^{s*}	No change
Real consumption C	C^*	C_1^*	Decreased
Real investment I	I^*	I_1^*	Increased
Real saving S	S^*	S_1^*	Increased
Real bonds B/rP	B^*/r^*P^*	$B_1^*/r_1^*P_1^*$	Decreased
Real money M^d/P	M^d/P^*	M^d/P_1^*	Decreased
Price level P	P^*	P_1^*	Increased
Nominal wage W	W^*	W_1^*	Increased
Real wage W/P	$(W/P)^*$	$(W/P)_1^*$	No change
Interest rate r	r^*	r_1^*	Increased
Capital stock $\bar{K}$	$\bar{K}$	$\bar{K}$	No change
Money supply $\bar{M}^s$	$\bar{M}^s$	$\bar{M}^s$	No change
Money income Y_m^s	Y_m^{s*}	$Y_{m_1}^{s*}$	Increased
Real wealth V/P	$(V/P)^*$	$(V/P)_1^*$	Decreased
Labor's share $N(W/P)/Y^s$	$N^*(W/P)^*/Y^{s*}$	$N^*(W/P)_1^*/Y^{s*}$	No change
Others' share $(B/P)/Y^s$	$(B/P)^*/Y^{s*}$	$(B/P)_1^*/Y^{s*}$	No change

4 Increased Thrift

How will the equilibrium values of the variables be affected if we become more thrifty? That is to say, suppose we plan to save more (at the *same* levels of real income, interest rates, and real wealth) than we did previously. This new attitude could arise from a change in our preferences or tastes for *future* consumption relative to *current* consumption. As a result, there would be a decrease in our propensities to consume and an increase in our propensities to save (see §3.2).

If the above change occurred, the aggregate consumption function would decline (and the aggregate saving function would rise). In Figure 5 we show this by shifting the aggregate demand function down to $Y^{d'}$. As usual, the prime on the *functional* indicates that the *form* of the aggregate demand function has changed (because of a change in the *form* of the consumption function). There emerges an excess supply of commodities equal to *ab*, which is paralleled by an excess demand for bonds equal to *ef*. The increase in the propensity to save implies an increase in the desire to hold bonds, hence, the shift in the demand curve of bonds to $B^{d'}$ in Figure 5(b). [We have assumed that the increased propensity to save is reflected *only* in an increase in the demand for bonds and not by an increase in the demand to hold money (i.e., to "hoard").]

We see, then, that the rate of interest will fall to r_1 on impact. By itself, this will help to close the deflationary gap *ab* in the commodity market, since both investment and consumption react positively to a decline in the interest rate. But, as usual, there is still more to come. The excess supply of commodities will lower the price level P which will raise real wealth. This, we know, will raise the consumption function even higher. Moreover, the impact decline in the rate of interest to r_1 will not be the final effect there either. The fall in the price level will shift both the supply and demand curves for bonds to the left. The former moves more than the latter to $B^{s'}$ and $B^{d''}$, respectively. The final equilibrium value of the price of bonds is $(1/r)_2^*$. The joint effects of the decrease in the interest rate r and price level P will continue until the aggregate demand curve has risen to overlay exactly the original aggregate demand curve Y^d. The equation of this final equilibrium aggregate demand curve appears beneath the original, namely,

$$Y^d = Y^{d'}\left[Y^s, r_2^*, \left(\frac{V}{P}\right)_1^*\right]$$

Once again we have invoked the special assumption of proportional changes in the nominal price level P and nominal wage rate W (on which, of course, there will be downward pressure as commodity-makers compete among themselves to maintain their jobs as entrepreneurs find the real wage rising and are, thus, tempted to cut back on employment). Since the real wage rate, employment, and real output (income) are, in fact, kept constant, we suppress the labor market and production function from Figure 5. In the money market, the excess supply of nominal money brought about by

FIGURE 5

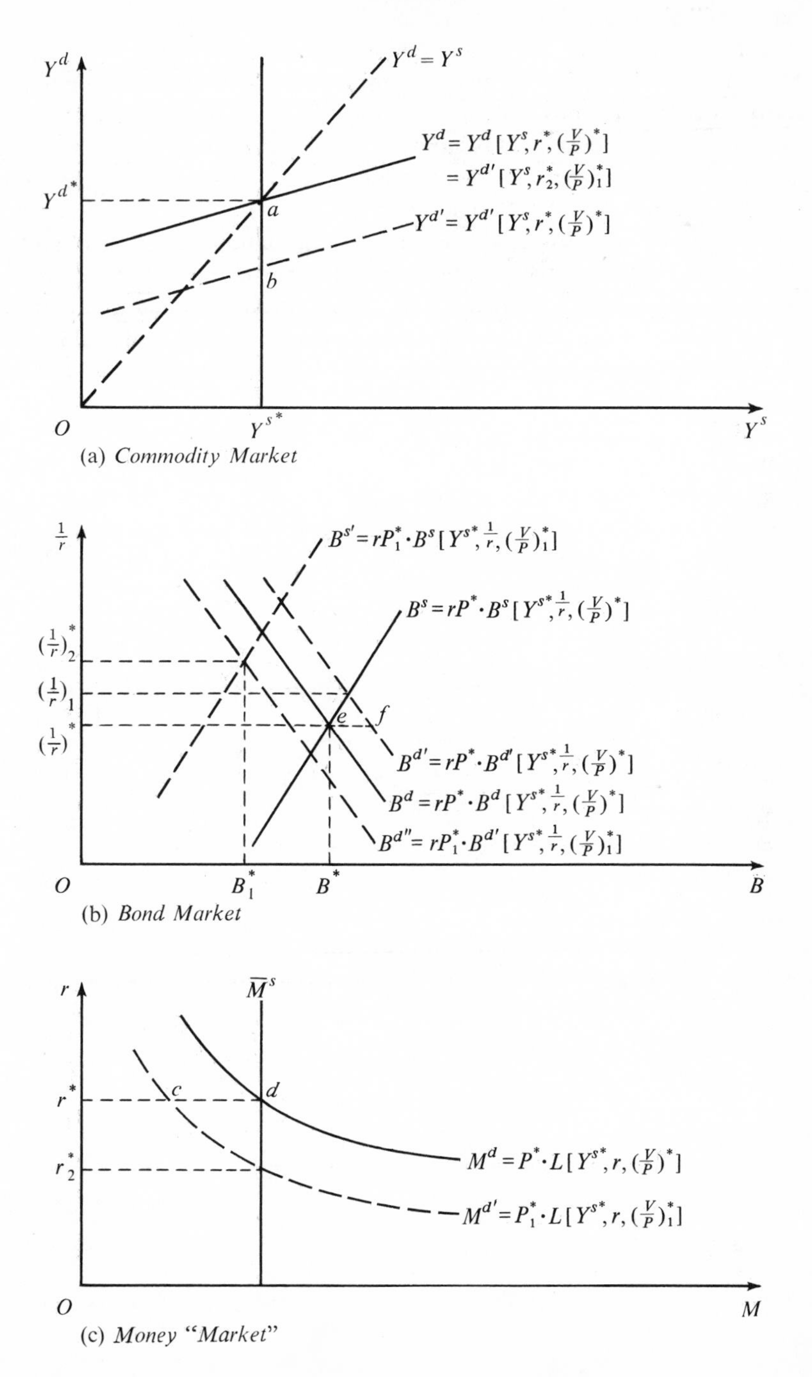

Y^d
$Y^d = Y^s$
$Y^d = Y^d[Y^s, r^*, (\frac{V}{P})^*]$
$= Y^{d'}[Y^s, r_2^*, (\frac{V}{P})_1^*]$
Y^{d*}
a
$Y^{d'} = Y^{d'}[Y^s, r^*, (\frac{V}{P})^*]$
b
O
Y^{s*}
Y^s
(a) *Commodity Market*
$\frac{1}{r}$
$B^{s'} = rP_1^* \cdot B^s[Y^{s*}, \frac{1}{r}, (\frac{V}{P})_1^*]$
$B^s = rP^* \cdot B^s[Y^{s*}, \frac{1}{r}, (\frac{V}{P})^*]$
$(\frac{1}{r})_2^*$
$(\frac{1}{r})_1$
$(\frac{1}{r})^*$
e
f
$B^{d'} = rP^* \cdot B^{d'}[Y^{s*}, \frac{1}{r}, (\frac{V}{P})^*]$
$B^d = rP^* \cdot B^d[Y^{s*}, \frac{1}{r}, (\frac{V}{P})^*]$
$B^{d''} = rP_1^* \cdot B^{d'}[Y^{s*}, \frac{1}{r}, (\frac{V}{P})_1^*]$
O
B_1^*
B^*
B
(b) *Bond Market*
r
$\overline{M}^s$
r^*
c
d
r_2^*
$M^d = P^* \cdot L[Y^{s*}, r, (\frac{V}{P})^*]$
$M^{d'} = P_1^* \cdot L[Y^{s*}, r, (\frac{V}{P})_1^*]$
O
M
(c) *Money "Market"*

the decline in the price level is removed by the fall in the interest rate and rise in real wealth until the nominal quantity of money demanded is equal to the constant nominal quantity of money being supplied.

The entire outcome is summarized in Table 4. A few words of explanation are in order. Investment must have increased, since income is unchanged and the interest rate has fallen. If investment has increased, then saving must also have increased. It is *not* obvious that saving increases because in addition to the increase in thrift (which raises saving), there has been a fall in the interest rate (which lowers saving). However, in equilibrium, saving equals investment, and the fact that the latter has risen unambiguously is enough to insure that saving *must* have risen overall. Since income is constant and investment has risen, consumption must have fallen. The outcomes for the variables labor's share, "others'" share, and real bonds—

TABLE 4 The Effects of an Increase in Thrift

VARIABLE	INITIAL VALUE	FINAL VALUE	OUTCOME
Employment N	N^*	N^*	No change
Real income Y^s	Y^{s*}	Y^{s*}	No change
Real consumption C	C^*	C_1^*	Decreased
Real investment I	I^*	I_1^*	Increased
Real saving S	S^*	S_1^*	Increased
Real bonds B/rP	B^*/r^*P^*	$B_1^*/r_2^*P_1^*$	Increased
Real money M^d/P	M^d/P^*	M^d/P_1^*	Increased
Price level P	P^*	P_1^*	Decreased
Nominal wage W	W^*	W_1^*	Decreased
Real wage W/P	$(W/P)^*$	$(W/P)_1^*$	No change
Interest rate r	r^*	r_2^*	Decreased
Capital stock $\bar{K}$	$\bar{K}$	$\bar{K}$	No change
Money supply $\bar{M}^s$	$\bar{M}^s$	$\bar{M}^s$	No change
Money income Y_m^s	Y_m^{s*}	$Y_{m_1}^{s*}$	Decreased
Real wealth V/P	$(V/P)^*$	$(V/P)_1^*$	Increased
Labor's share $N(W/P)/Y^s$	$N^*(W/P)^*/Y^{s*}$	$N^*(W/P)_1^*/Y^{s*}$	No change
Others' share $(B/P)/Y^s$	$(B/P)^*/Y^{s*}$	$(B/P)_1^*/Y^{s*}$	No change

not dealt with explicitly in the analysis above—are as indicated for exactly the reasons explained at the end of §3.

If we reason from the full set of neoclassical assumptions, thrift is indubitably a good thing. Present real income is constant, but it has been reallocated away from present consumption to saving and investment. The concomitant augmentation of the capital stock means we shall experience a deluge of new commodities in the *future*. Hence, our current parsimony will lead to more enjoyment of the commodity later. As these commodities spill forth, the price level will decline, the rate of interest will decline, investment will rise, income will rise, and, moreover, consumption and saving will rise. Clearly, in the future we shall enjoy the best of everything—a constantly rising capital stock and a constantly rising level of consumption. In a neoclassical context, Ben Franklin's praise of thrift in *Poor Richard's Almanac* is justified. In that context, there is no *paradox of thrift*. When we plan to save more, we do save more. However, we shall see later that, in a neo-Keynesian context, thrift may be paradoxical in the sense that when we plan to save more we actually finish up saving less.

5 The Dynamics of Deflation

At several points in this chapter and in Chapter 7 we have analyzed the comparative static properties of our model in deflationary situations brought about by decreasing the money stock, increasing liquidity preference, increasing thrift, and so on. No matter what caused the deflationary situation, we always found wage and price flexibility was sufficient to guarantee full employment. We must conclude, then, that *in a comparative static analysis*, Keynes was simply wrong when he asserted that "there is . . . no ground for the belief that a flexible wage policy is capable of maintaining a state of continuous full employment. . . ."[1] Having excoriated Keynes on this point, we hasten to draw attention to the emphasis we have put on the phrase "in a comparative static analysis."

Although it is indisputable that in a comparative static framework wage flexibility will guarantee full employment, this does *not* mean that one should, therefore, rely on wage flexibility to produce full employment. In the real world we do not have the privilege of sitting back while an auctioneer grinds through the tâtonnement process and eventually gropes his way to the equilibrium values of the variables which produces full employment. In practice, the grinding deflation of wages and prices that might be necessary before full employment emerges after, for example, an increase in thrift may take so long that society would be swept away in the process. Full employment is only inevitable *in time*. There is the rub. The adjustment might be so slow in actuality that none of us would be around to enjoy the results.

[1] J. M. Keynes, *The General Theory of Employment, Interest, and Money*, Macmillan, 1936, p. 267.

Consider, for example, the following sequence of events. Let thrift increase and assume that

1. Investment and consumption are unresponsive to changes in the interest rate, that is, they are interest-inelastic;
2. Wages and prices are inflexible downwards (not, observe, rigidly fixed – merely inflexible). This might be due, for example, to institutional factors such as trade unions or government-imposed minimums on the wages' side, and long-term binding commodity contracts on the prices' side.

Increased thrift opens a deflationary gap in the commodity market and lowers the interest rate. Because of the low interest elasticities of consumption and investment, however, the lower interest rate will not cause this gap to be closed by very much. Large decreases in the interest rate hardly raise aggregate demand at all. Consequently, we need a large increase in real wealth to raise aggregate demand. This means that a large fall in prices (and wages) is necessary. But wages and prices are inflexible downwards, and, hence, they only adjust slowly. Unless entrepreneurs do something, unsold output will pile up in their warehouses. The action they take, therefore, should be to reduce output by cutting back on employment. Unemployment emerges. Disaffection spreads and the masses begin to march. Moreover, the position can be compounded. The large fall in wages and prices that is necessary immediately, but which is only occurring slowly, could set up adverse expectation effects. As prices and wages fall, consumers and entrepreneurs hold off on their purchases of goods and labor, respectively, in anticipation of further reductions (expectations elasticities are greater than unity). This would worsen an already dangerous situation. With unemployment and bankruptcy rampant, society could conceivably collapse before equilibrium is reestablished. What can be done to overcome these potentially damaging dynamic problems is discussed in Chapter 10.

Keynes, who was an intensely practical man, had these thoughts of dynamic complication at the forefront of his mind. The reader should consult chapter 19 of *The General Theory*, "Changes in Money-Wages," for Keynes' complete position. He is led to the conclusion (with which, as a practical matter, we concur), that "having regard to human nature and our institutions, it can only be a foolish person who would prefer a flexible wage policy to a flexible money policy . . . a method which it is comparatively easy to apply should be deemed preferable to a method which is probably so difficult as to be impracticable."[2] Essentially, the point is this: given a deflationary situation, you can either wait for prices and wages to fall to create the necessary increase in real money balances and reduction in interest rates to raise aggregate demand (a flexible wage policy) or you can create the real money balances and lower the interest rate to raise aggregate demand by increasing the supply of money (a flexible money policy). Given the dynamic

[2] *Ibid.*, p. 268.

properties of the economy, the latter is to be preferred to the former. We analyze the use of a flexible money policy to counteract unemployment caused by wage rigidities in §10.3.

Summary

Previously, we discussed the impact of purely *monetary* phenomena on the equilibrium values of the endogenous variables reasoning from the full set of neoclassical assumptions. We found that only *nominal* variables were affected while *all* the *real* variables were unaffected by such events. In this chapter we considered the impact on the equilibrium values of the endogenous variables of selected *real* phenomena; in particular, we examined the effects of a change in the marginal productivity of labor brought about by some (exogenous) technological innovation, a change in household income/leisure preferences, a change in entrepreneurial expectations, and a change in households' preferences for present consumption vis-à-vis future consumption (a change in thrift). In general, such *real* disturbances result in new equilibrium values for *all* the endogenous variables, both *nominal* and *real*. It is especially interesting to note that unemployment is an impossibility in the model and that there is no such thing as a "paradox of thrift." If we plan to save more, we actually finish up saving more. We cannot emphasize strongly enough, however, that both these latter conslusions are absolutely critically dependent on the incorporation of the neoclassical assumption of price flexibility. We shall see in Part III that rigidity in any *one* of our price variables can lead to permanent unemployment.

Finally, we pointed out that although unemployment is not possible in a comparative static sense when all prices are flexible, one still might be reluctant to wait upon such price adjustments in the real dynamic world in which we live because *time* is of the essence.

Questions

[In all these questions (especially in number 6) consider as given the full set of neoclassical assumptions. (What are they?)]

1. Discuss what happens to the equilibrium values of all the variables in our model if there is an (exogenous) technological improvement in the productivity of capital. (*Hint:* The impact effect will be felt in the production function.)
2. Assume that there is a nationwide revival of the Puritan ethic such that the community's work/leisure preferences switch in favor of more work. Discuss the impact on the equilibrium values of all the variables in our model.
3. Assume that an administration with an antibusiness tinge is returned to Washington, and entrepreneurs' investment expectations become less sanguine. Discuss the impact on the equilibrium values of all the variables in our model.
4. Show that there is no such thing as a "paradox of thrift" in the given neoclassical context.

5. Assume that the community is swept by a mood of Rabelaisian hedonism so that consumption today suddenly seems much better than consumption tomorrow. Show that we will get more consumption today and less tomorrow. (Recall that if there is a paradox of thrift such a change in community preferences would lead to more consumption today *and more* tomorrow. Clearly Rabelaisianism would have a lot to recommend it!)
6. Show that *in a comparative static analysis* Keynes was wrong to assert that "there is . . . no ground for the belief that a flexible wage policy is capable of maintaining a state of continuous full employment" (*General Theory,* p. 267). Nonetheless, explain why, in the real world, one might be reluctant to rely on downward wage adjustments to reestablish full employment in the face of a deflationary disturbance.

SELECTED READINGS

1. J. M. Keynes, *The General Theory of Employment, Interest, and Money,* Macmillan, 1936, chapter 19. Keynes' discussion of wage flexibility and the dynamics of deflation.
2. F. Modigliani, "The Monetary Mechanism and Its Interaction with Real Phenomena," *Review of Economics and Statistics,* February, 1963.
3. D. Patinkin, *Money, Interest, and Prices,* 2nd ed., Harper & Row, 1965, chapter 11. A discussion of the impact of selected real phenomena in a neoclassical context.

9

Government; Monetary and Fiscal Policy

1 The Equations and the Variables including Government

The time is ripe to formally incorporate the government into our macroeconomic model. The economic raison d'être of government (as opposed to its political function of providing a stable society) is to buy, and make available to us collectively, commodities with public-good characteristics. The properties of public goods, and why the government is invoked to provide them, were explained in Chapter 1. The public-good commodities which the government does buy in our collective behalf are made available to us "free," that is, we hasten to add, without *direct* charge. The government finances the commodity purchase program by either taxing or borrowing—which is to say, *indirectly*. Apart from providing the community with collectively consumable commodity services, the government can employ its fiscal (i.e., tax and expenditure) policy to bring about changes in the equilibrium values of other economic variables in a manner which it (we) deems (deem) desirable.

The introduction of this new transactor on the economic stage requires that we modify the equations of our macroeconomic model in the following ways.

Aggregate Demand

The Consumption Function Prior to the advent of government, *all* real income Y^s was available to households. However, the government collects taxes, all of which, we shall assume, come from households. This means that the real disposable income available to households on which to base their consumption decisions is also affected by the government's real tax collections. When real taxes go up, real consumption will decline, and vice versa. Thus we introduce the modified consumption function

$$C = C\left(Y^s, T, r, \frac{V}{P}\right), \qquad C_1 > 0, C_2 < 0, C_3 < 0, C_4 > 0 \qquad \text{(V')}$$

where T is equal to real tax receipts.

Real tax receipts has the dimension "commodities per time period." Clearly, real tax receipts is a *flow* variable.[1] We should mention that, with some slight degree of complication, we could have the government collect taxes from firms, too. However, no substantial modification of our results would ensue, so we shall adopt the simpler alternative.

Government Expenditure Since the government does not make the public-good commodities itself, it must buy a certain real quantity $\bar{G}$ from private firms. Thus, the government does not affect the total supply of commodities (real income available) directly; it only affects the demand for them. The real quantity of commodities $\bar{G}$ that the government purchases is decided as a policy matter. Hence, $\bar{G}$ is an exogenously determined variable.

When government purchases are added to private consumption and investment, we obtain the modified aggregate demand for commodities equation

$$Y^d = C + I + \bar{G} \qquad \text{(VII')}$$

where consumption C is now given by (V′).

In our familiar commodity market diagram, the fixed, exogenously determined quantity of real government purchases $\bar{G}$ is added vertically to the private consumption and investment functions (see Figure 1).

Demand for Bonds

Before we decided to include government in the model, private demand for real bonds was an increasing function of real income. However, now the relevant income variable on which households base their bond purchase decisions is real private disposable income. This is clearly affected by the government's tax collections. When the latter increases, ceteris paribus, the private sector's real disposable income and, therefore, its planned bond purchases, decrease. Hence, in the real bond demand function we include tax receipts, which will affect that demand inversely. Thus,

$$\frac{B^d}{rP} = B^d\left(Y^s, T, \frac{1}{r}, \frac{V}{P}\right), \qquad B_1^d > 0, B_2^d < 0, B_3^d < 0, B_4^d > 0 \qquad \text{(IX')}$$

The argument here is clearly analogous to that presented to justify the inclusion of tax collections T in the consumption function.

[1] To see the dimension, note that nominal taxes are so many dollars per time period (\$/time period) and the price level P is so many dollars per commodity (\$/commodity). Therefore, real taxes T, which is nominal taxes divided by the price level, is equal to

$$T = \frac{\dfrac{\$}{\text{time period}}}{\dfrac{\$}{\text{commodity}}} = \text{commodities/time period}$$

FIGURE 1

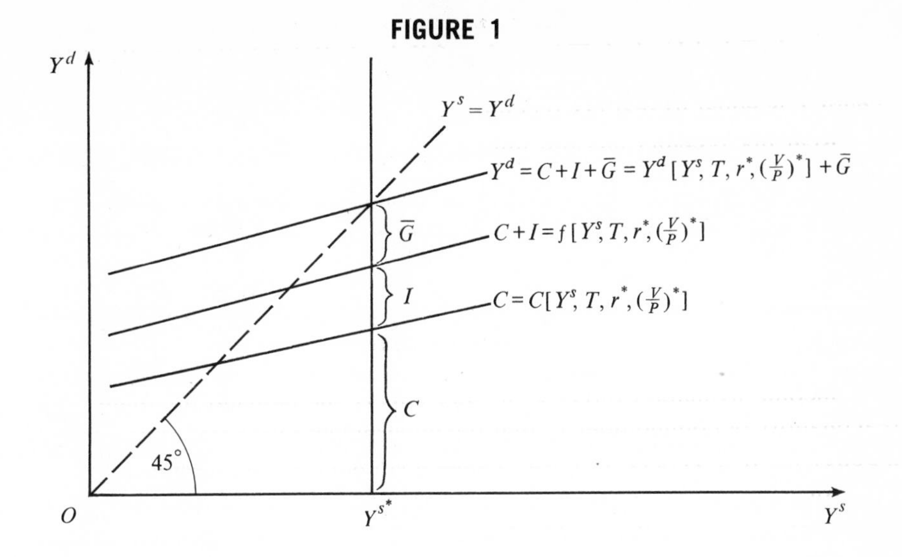

The Supply of Bonds

Private Basically the real supply of private bonds (X) remains unchanged. However, now private and government bonds are being supplied. To acknowledge this we put a subscript p on the private bond supply function to obtain

$$\frac{B_p^s}{rP} = B_p^s\left(Y^s, \frac{1}{r}, \frac{V}{P}\right), \qquad B_1^s > 0,\ B_2^s > 0,\ B_3^s < 0 \qquad \text{(X}'\text{)}$$

Government Apart from being involved in taxing and spending, the government is also involved in borrowing, or debt redemption. When the government's total expenditure on commodities exceeds its tax receipts, the government has a budget *deficit*. It obtains the money to finance the excess of its expenditure over its tax receipts by borrowing—that is, by issuing new bonds. When the government's total expenditure is less than its tax receipts, the government has a budget *surplus*. It uses the surplus of its receipts over expenditure to redeem some of its own debt outstanding in the form of bonds. To do this, it buys back its own bonds on the bond market (and tears them up). Its motivation is, of course, to save the interest payments. (In fact, the government could also issue additional fiat money when it has a deficit or redeem outstanding fiat money when it has a surplus. However, we will assume the government does not exercise this option. When it has a deficit, it issues only bonds; when it has a surplus, it retires only bonds.)

Bonds issued by the government are exactly like the privately issued bonds with which we are familiar; namely, they are perpetuities promising to pay the holder 1 dollar per annum. Qualitatively, then, there is no difference between debt issued by firms and debt issued by the government. (For clarity, we denote the supply of government bonds by B_g^s.) Households are indifferent about who issues these bonds. Therefore, *all* bonds, government and private, command the same price $1/r$.

At any moment there will be a certain number of government bonds $\bar{B}_g^s$ outstanding due to *past* government budget deficits. This is a fait accompli—it is inherited from the past (just as the capital stock K is inherited). Hence, $\bar{B}_g^s$ is an exogenous variable. In saying that a certain number of government bonds is outstanding due to the cumulative impact of past budget deficits we implicitly assume that the government, unlike the private sector, is not concerned about the real value of its outstanding bonds. In diagrammatic terms the inherited number of bond liabilities would be a fixed quantity $\bar{B}_g^s$, unresponsive to changes in both the price of bonds and the commodity price level. To represent $\bar{B}_g^s$ we would use a vertical, perfectly inelastic, straight line.

In the *current period,* the government has to issue (retire) new bonds whose monetary value is equal to the money value of the government's deficit. The monetary receipts the government obtains from issuing new bonds is equal to the quantity of new bonds the government issues ΔB_g^s times the price per bond $1/r$ it receives. That is

$$\frac{\Delta B_g^s}{r} \tag{1}$$

The money value of the government's deficit is equal to

$$P\bar{G} - PT \tag{2}$$

that is, the government's real commodity purchases times the price of commodities minus the government's real tax receipts times the price of commodities. Since (1) is equal to (2) we obtain the identity

$$\frac{\Delta B_g^s}{r} = P\bar{G} - PT \tag{3}$$

Dividing through by the price level we obtain

$$\frac{\Delta B_g^s}{rP} = \bar{G} - T \tag{Xa}$$

which states that the real value of new government bond issues is equal to its real purchases of goods minus its real taxes. An alternative formulation of (Xa) is

$$\Delta B_g^s = rP(\bar{G} - T) \tag{4}$$

From (4) we see that the supply of *new* government bonds issued (retired) is inversely related to the price of bonds; as this price falls the government has to supply more bonds to cover its current deficit. Thus, the supply of new bonds has an atypical slope compared with the usual run of supply curves (see Figure 2). It slopes down from left to right.

It is also apparent from (4) that the supply of *new* government bonds is proportional to the commodity price level P. For example, if the general price level P doubles, so does the number of new government bonds supplied. Such a situation is illustrated by the dashed curve in Figure 2.

FIGURE 2

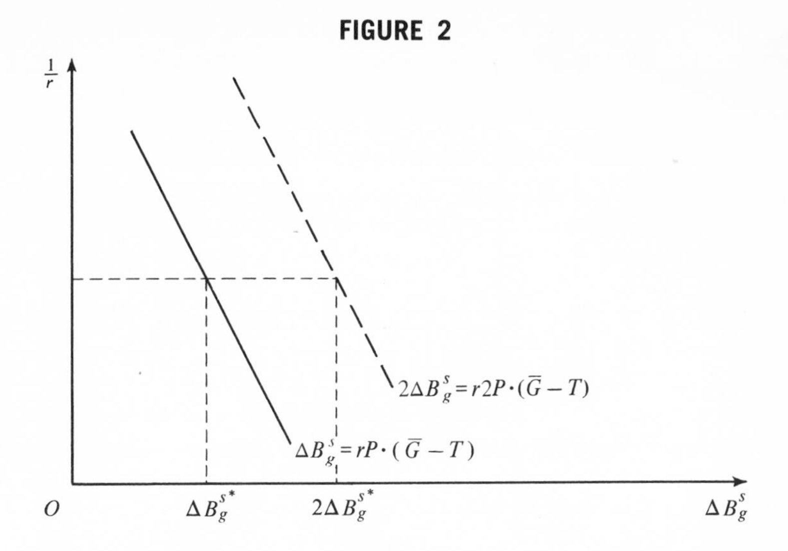

Given the number of government bonds outstanding because of past deficits $\bar{B}^s_g$, the total number of bonds, both private and government, supplied to the market in the current period is equal to

$$B^s = B^s_p + \Delta B^s_g + \bar{B}^s_g \tag{Xb}$$

It goes without saying, of course, that the second term in this sum, the number of *new* government bonds issued, can be negative; in particular, this will be the case when the government has a budget surplus.

Figure 3 shows the situation diagrammatically; the total supply of bonds, both private and government, to be held in the current period is equal to the horizontal sum of the private supply [Figure 3(a)], the supply of new government bonds [Figure 3(b)], and the supply of government bonds already outstanding [Figure 3(c)]. Thus, gh in Figure 3(d) is equal to $ab + cd + ef$. The downward slope of the curve for new supply of government bonds indicates that the *total* supply curve no longer inevitably slopes upwards, as we have hitherto assumed [and have continued to assume in Figure 3(d)]. We shall ignore this complication, however.

Demand for Money

By assumption, only the private sector holds a money balance. The government sector is understood to get by without one. Just as the private sector's commodity demand and bond demand functions had to be amended on the inclusion of government, the demand for money function must be amended to acknowledge that real private disposable income is the relevant variable on which households now base their decisions. Hence,

$$\frac{M^d}{P} = L\left(Y^s, T, r, \frac{V}{P}\right), \quad L_1 > 0, L_2 < 0, L_3 < 0, L_4 > 0 \tag{XII'}$$

FIGURE 3

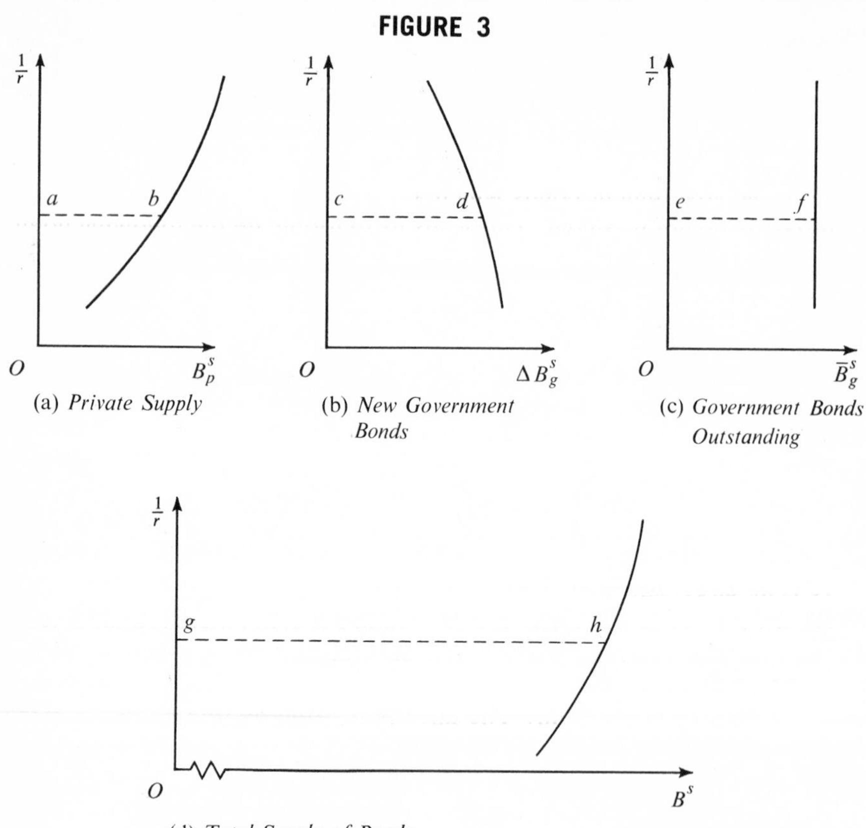

(a) *Private Supply* (b) *New Government Bonds* (c) *Government Bonds Outstanding*

(d) *Total Supply of Bonds*

It follows that, ceteris paribus, an increase in tax receipts T will decrease the demand for money, and vice versa.

Saving

After incorporation of the government, private saving is defined as the differences between private disposable income and consumption. Thus, we immediately obtain

$$S = Y_d^s - C \tag{XIV'}$$

where Y_d^s is real private disposable income defined by (XVII) below.

Wealth

In the simplified model, nominal net wealth was equal to the nominal value of the capital stock plus the nominal supply of outside (fiat) money. Now, after the incorporation of government, the private sector of the economy has a new form of asset in which to hold its wealth, namely, government bonds. You will recall that privately issued bonds do not appear as part of the private sector's wealth; private bonds held as an asset by some household are an outstanding liability of some firm and we assumed that the positive increment to wealth felt by the household sector was exactly offset by the negative wealth effect incurred by the issuing firms. As a result, private bonds wash out when the consolidated wealth of the private sector is calculated. Within the private sector there is no direct and immediate offset to the government bonds which are held as an asset. Hence, government bonds do not wash out. This leads us to formulate the following nominal wealth equation

$$V = P\bar{K} + \bar{M}^s + \frac{(\bar{B}_g^s + \Delta B_g^s)}{r} \tag{XVI'}$$

where we have added the nominal value of government bonds to the nominal value of the capital stock and supply of outside money. To obtain real wealth, divide through by the price level P:

$$\frac{V}{P} = \bar{K} + \frac{\bar{M}^s}{P} + \frac{(\bar{B}_g^s + \Delta B_g^s)}{rP} \tag{5}$$

What we have just said may be subject to some qualification. Although there is no direct and immediate offsetting liability to the government bonds which the private sector tucks into its wealth portfolio, there is undoubtedly an indirect and delayed offset. When governments incur a liability in the form of bonds, they also incur a liability to pay interest on them. Where does this money come from? The answer is, from us (the private sector). Assuming that other conditions are constant, if the government issues more bonds, then it also incurs the obligation to levy taxes to pay the interest on them. If the private sector recognized this and fully discounted the future tax liability implied by the government's issuing more bonds, the people would not regard these bonds as an augmentation of its own wealth. The new government bonds would be washed out by the *prospective* taxes. You may be wondering why the government does not enrich us all by issuing vast quantities of bonds, since (XVI') seems to indicate that such a move would make us all wealthy. The answer lies in the prospective taxes we would thereby incur. Otherwise, surely, everyone would clamor for the government to deliver us into Utopia on a carpet of government bonds. In (XVI') we have assumed that even though the private sector does not discount the implied future taxes, the government does not issue bonds with abandon, but solely in response to its fiscal position.

Later in the text we shall assume that the private sector completely discounts the future tax liabilities implied by government bond issues. Although we regard this as an unrealistic assumption, we shall do it as an exercise.

Disposable Income

Disposable income has been defined previously as the difference between total real income and that quantity collected as taxes. Hence, all that remains is to provide it with a formal equation:

$$Y_d^s = Y^s - T \tag{XVII}$$

The Tax Function

We have talked about tax receipts, but have failed to mention how this variable is determined. We are of two minds in this situation. Sometimes we shall treat tax receipts as a quantity exogenously determined by government and denote it T. More often, however, we shall regard it as an endogenous variable which is an increasing function of real income and the tax *rate*. Consider Figure 4 where real tax receipts are shown to be an increasing function of real income.

We see from the figure that if real income is Y_1^s, real tax receipts will be T_1; if real income is Y_2^s, real tax receipts will be T_2, and so on. Here, Y_0 is the *minimum* level of taxable income. If income falls *below* this level the government pays *us*. (The government gives a *subsidy* or *transfer payment*.) The *average tax rate* is defined as tax receipts divided by real income. When real income is Y_1^s, the average tax rate is the slope of the ray $OR(OT_1/OY_1^s)$; when it is Y_2^s, the average tax rate is equal to the slope of the ray OS (OT_2/OY_2^s). The *marginal tax rate* is defined as the change in taxes divided by the change in income, $\Delta T/\Delta Y^s$. Thus, when income rises from Y_1^s to Y_2^s, taxes increase from T_1 to T_2. The marginal tax rate is $(T_2 - T_1/Y_2^s - Y_1^s)$, which is equal to SU/RU, which in the limit is equal to the slope of the tax function over the range of income Y_1^s to Y_2^s. The slope of the illustrated function increases as income increases; the curve is convex from below. This implies that there is an *increasing marginal tax rate*. The tax structure is progressive as illustrated. Usually, it is not harmful to assume that marginal tax rates are constant. Geometrically, this means a linear tax function. Fre-

FIGURE 4

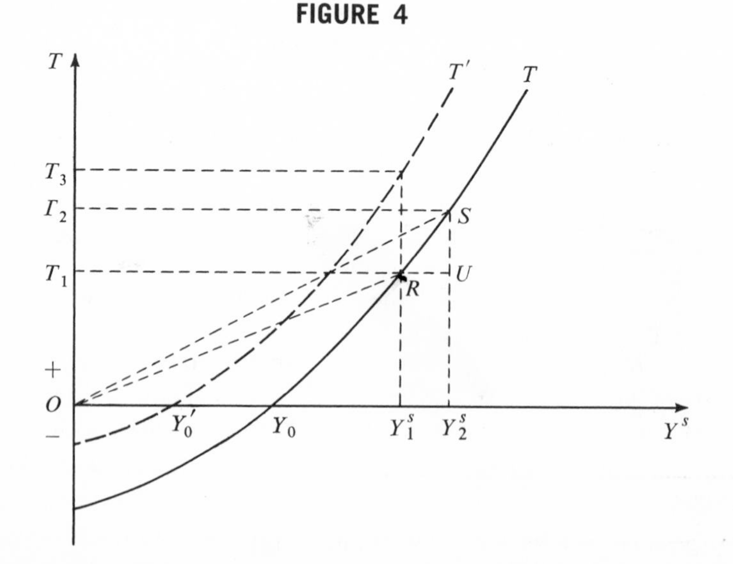

quently, we resort to this simplification. When the government changes tax rates, the slope and/or the intercept of the tax function changes. If, for example, the government increased tax rates we would get a function like T'. Now, at the same level of income Y_1^s, tax receipts would no longer be T_1 but T_3. Similarly, tax receipts would be higher for any level of real income. With the new tax rate, the minimum level of taxable income falls to Y_0'.

This discussion may be summarized by the following general tax function:

$$T = t(Y^s, \bar{t}_0), \qquad t_1 > 0, t_2 > 0 \tag{XVIII}$$

where $\bar{t}_0$ stands for the tax rate. By assumption, T increases when $\bar{t}_0$ increases, and vice versa. The tax rate is a variable set by the government; therefore, it is classified as exogenous.

We are now in a position to summarize our macroeconomic model after the formal inclusion of a government sector. All the equations we have discussed are listed in Table 1. In addition, without going into lengthy statements concerning the dimensions of the variables, we classify them as we did in Chapter 6—first, according to whether they are endogenous or exogenous and then as flow, stock, price, or pure policy variables (a new classification).

I. Endogenous Variables
  A. Flow variables: N^d, N^s, Y^s, Y_d^s, C, I, Y^d, S, Y_m^s, T, ΔB_g^s.
  B. Stock variables: B^d, B_p^s, B^s, V, M^d.
  C. Price variables: P, W, $1/r$.
II. Exogenous Variables
  A. Flow variables: $\bar{G}$.
  B. Stock variables: $\bar{K}$, $\bar{M}^s$, $\bar{B}_g^s$.
  C. Policy variables: $\bar{t}_0$.

This time we have nineteen endogenous variables and twenty equations (notice equations (Xa) and (Xb) as well as the other eighteen). But we know, through Walras' law, that one of these equations is otiose. Hence, we do have the same number of independent equations as endogenous variables. We mentioned earlier that we shall occasionally make real tax receipts T (normally, an endogenous variable) into an exogenous variable $\bar{T}$. When we do so, we lose one endogenous variable and its corresponding equation (XVIII); thus, equality between equations and unknowns is still preserved.

2 The Nonneutrality of Money; Money Illusion in the Bond Market[1]

In this section we continue to work with the full set of neoclassical assumptions *except* that now we introduce money illusion in the bond supply function.

[1] The reader may omit this section on a first reading without loss of continuity.

TABLE 1 The Complete Macroeconomic Model including Government

EQUATION		NAME	MARKET
(I)	$N^d = N^d\left(\frac{W}{P}, \bar{K}\right)$	Labor demand function	Labor market
(II)	$N^s = N^s\left(\frac{W}{P}\right)$	Labor supply function	
(III)	$N^d = N^s$	Labor market clearance condition	
(IV)	$Y^s = Y^s(N, \bar{K})$	Production (or commodity supply) function	Commodity market
(V′)	$C = C\left(Y^s, T, r, \frac{V}{P}\right)$	Commodity demand function for consumption (the consumption function)	
(VI)	$I = I(Y^s, r)$	Commodity demand function for investment (the investment function)	
(VII′)	$Y^d = C + I + \bar{G}$	Total (or aggregate) commodity demand function	
(VIII)	$Y^d = Y^s$	Commodity market clearance condition	
(IX′)	$\frac{B^d}{rP} = B^d\left(Y^s, T, \frac{1}{r}, \frac{V}{P}\right)$	Bond demand function	Bond market
(X′)	$\frac{B_p^s}{rP} = B_p^s\left(Y^s, \frac{1}{r}, \frac{V}{P}\right)$	Private bond supply function	
(Xa)	$\frac{\Delta B_g^s}{rP} = \bar{G} + T$	New government bond supply function	
(Xb)	$B^s = B_p^s + \Delta B_g^s + \bar{B}_g^s$	Total bond supply function	
(XI)	$B^d = B^s$	Bond market clearance condition	

TABLE 1 (continued)

EQUATION		NAME	MARKET
(XII)	$\frac{M^d}{P} = L\left(Y^s, T, r, \frac{V}{P}\right)$	Money demand function	Money market
(XIII)	$M^d = \bar{M}^s$	Money market clearance condition and (exogenous) money supply function	
(XIV′)	$S = Y_d^s - C$	Definition of saving	Definitions of useful supplementary variables
(XV)	$Y_m^s = PY^s$	Definition of money income	
(XVI′)	$V = P\bar{K} + \bar{M}^s + \frac{(\bar{B}_g^s + \Delta B_g^s)}{r}$	Definition of money wealth	
(XVII)	$Y_d^s = Y^s - T$	Definition of real private disposable income	
(XVIII)	$T = t(Y^s, \bar{t}_0)$	Tax function	

But why, you may ask, draw attention to this case in particular? Surely, if money illusion exists anywhere in the system, a change in the supply of money will affect things (almost by definition of *money illusion*). Why is it of special significance in the bond market? The answer to this very legitimate question is that there is a transactor whose activities in the bond market are typically characterized by a money illusion response. That transactor is the government. It is usually, and quite reasonably, assumed that the government has accumulated a certain amount of debt $\bar{B}_g^s$ whose real value outstanding is of little concern. The actual amount outstanding is the cumulative outcome of the government's past fiscal policies. When it had a budget deficit, it issued debt; when it had a budget surplus, it retired debt. Moreover, the government does not issue or retire debt in any other circumstances. This is in stark contrast to the behavior we have assumed for the private sector. The private sector, you will recall, is very concerned about the real value of its debt—both what it wishes to hold (demand) and have outstanding (supply). When economic conditions change, the private sector responds by changing its demand for and supply of outstanding bonds (see Chapter 5). However, as a result of its past budget deficits, the government has outstanding a fixed nominal quantity of bonds $\bar{B}_g^s$, which is unresponsive to both the interest rate and the commodity price level. This is the essence of a money illusion reaction. It is sufficient, as we shall soon see, to make changes in the money supply nonneutral, so that money ceases to be a veil. A change in the supply of money *will* disturb the equilibrium values of real variables in the ways we shall now discover. Consider Figure 5 and assume that the supply of money is doubled to $2\bar{M}^s$.

Initially, excess supply in the money market will be equal to *ab*. The demand for money has shifted on impact to $M^{d'}$ because of the increase in wealth to $(V/P)'$. This excess supply of money manifests itself in the bond market as an excess demand equal to *cd*. At first, the interest rate declines to r_1. This, *plus* the real balance effect caused by the doubled nominal supply of money, makes the aggregate demand curve shift to $Y^{d'}$. Excess commodity demand equal to *ef* ensues, and commodity prices begin to rise.

Resorting to our usual assumption of proportional changes in commodity prices P and nominal wages W (because of the excess demand for labor), we may consider the real wage $(W/P)^*$ as constant; thus, so is employment N^* and real income Y^{s*} (once more, we omit the corresponding parts of the figure). The problem then reduces to the reestablishment of equilibrium in the commodity, bond, and money markets.

The problem can be resolved in the following way. Ask yourself rhetorically, what would be the position if (since we have doubled the money supply) the price level P doubled and the real variables remained constant? The key is the wealth variable. Nominal wealth was originally (that is, before the doubling of $\bar{M}^s$) equal to

$$V = P\bar{K} + \bar{M}^s + \frac{\bar{B}_g^s}{r} + \frac{\Delta B_g^s}{r}$$

After the doubling of $\bar{M}^s$ and the doubling of the price level while all the real variables remained constant, it would be equal to

$$V' = 2P\bar{K} + 2\bar{M}^s + \frac{\bar{B}_g^s}{r} + \frac{2\Delta B_g^s}{r}$$

It may be helpful to explain the final term in this sum. If the *real* budget deficit is to be held constant when the price level is doubled, the quantity of *new* securities issued by the government must also be doubled [see equation (4), which shows proportionality between ΔB_g^s and P]. Clearly, $V' < 2V$ and, thus, nominal wealth has not doubled. It follows that $V'/2P < V/P$, that is, real wealth has *declined*. And, consequently, real aggregate demand must have fallen from $Y^{d'}$ to Y^d and *beyond*. Excess supply would emerge in the commodity market. Obviously, the culprit here is $\bar{B}_g^s$, which has not changed in response to the change in the price level. This is what causes real wealth to be less than it was originally when the price level doubles while all the real variables remain constant.

It is apparent, then, that a "neutral outcome" would not provide equilibrium. At the very least, there would be excess commodity supply. What can we rely on to close this incipient deflationary gap in the commodity market? The answer is a decline in the rate of interest. But can we be certain this will occur? We can. On impact, the interest rate declines to r_1. In the earlier examples we discussed, this transitory interest rate gave way to r^* again when the supply and demand curves for bonds shifted to the right

FIGURE 5

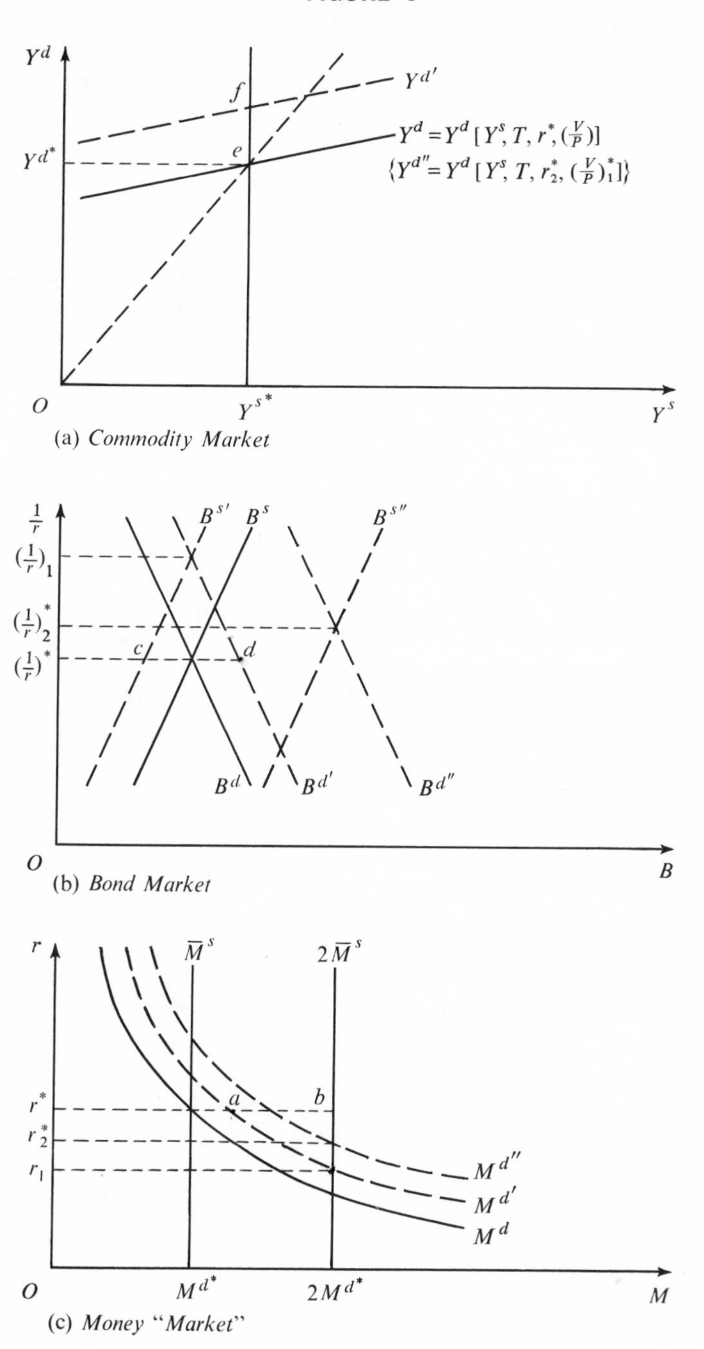

(a) *Commodity Market*

(b) *Bond Market*

(c) *Money "Market"*

(as commodity prices rose) to finally intersect at the same level. But now, at twice the commodity price level, the total number of bonds supplied would not be twice the number supplied at the original price level. The $\bar{B}^s_g$ component of the total bond supply curve is constant no matter what the price level. Refer to Figure 6. What would happen in the bond market if the price level doubled? Consider the supply situation first.

The original supply curve is labeled B^s and its associated equation is

$$B^s = rP^* \cdot B^s\left[Y^{s*}, \frac{1}{r}, \left(\frac{\bar{M}^s}{P} + \frac{\bar{B}^s_g}{rP} + \frac{\Delta B^s_g}{rP}\right)\right] + \bar{B}^s_g + \Delta B^s_g$$

If there were no money illusion in this supply curve, after the supply of money and the price level had doubled, all the real variables would be the same and the nominal supply of bonds would double. This situation is represented by the curve $2B^s$, whose equation is

$$2B^s = r2P^* \cdot B^s\left[Y^{s*}, \frac{1}{r}, \left(\frac{2\bar{M}^s}{2P} + \frac{2\bar{B}^s_g}{r2P} + \frac{2\Delta B^s_g}{r2P}\right)\right] + 2\bar{B}^s_g + 2\Delta B^s_g$$

But there *is* money illusion in this supply curve. The quantity $\bar{B}^s_g$ does *not* double. Therefore, the actual supply curve which would prevail is found to the left of $2B^s$. This curve has been labeled $B^{s''}$, and it has the equation

$$B^{s''} = r2P^* \cdot B^s\left[Y^{s*}, \frac{1}{r}, \left(\frac{2\bar{M}^s}{2P} + \frac{\bar{B}^s_g}{r2P} + \frac{2\Delta B^s_g}{r2P}\right)\right] + \bar{B}^s_g + 2\Delta B^s_g \qquad (6)$$

Next, consider the demand side. The original curve, labeled B^d, does not contain any money illusion. It has the equation

$$B^d = rP^* \cdot B^d\left[Y^{s*}, T, \frac{1}{r}, \left(\frac{\bar{M}^s}{P} + \frac{\bar{B}^s_g}{rP} + \frac{B^s_g}{rP}\right)\right]$$

FIGURE 6

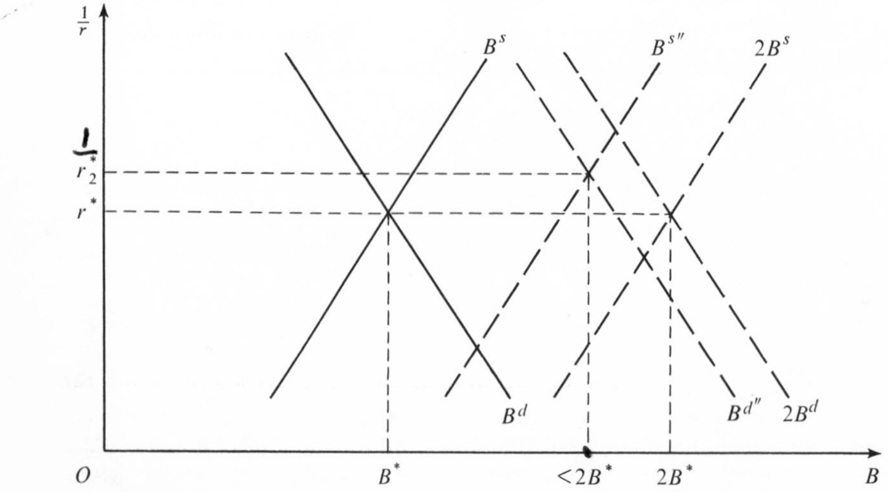

The demand for nominal bonds would be doubled if all the nominal variables doubled when the money supply doubled. Then we would obtain the curve $2B^d$, whose equation is

$$2B^d = r2P^* \cdot B^d\left[Y^{s*}, T, \frac{1}{r}, \left(\frac{2\bar{M}^s}{2P} + \frac{2\bar{B}_g^s}{r2P} + \frac{2\Delta B_g^s}{r2P}\right)\right]$$

However, because $\bar{B}_g^s$ does not double, the demand for nominal bonds after the money supply and the price level have doubled and all the other real variables remained constant would be less than $2B^d$; this is represented by the curve labeled $B^{d''}$ with the equation

$$B^{d''} = r2P^* \cdot B^d\left[Y^{s*}, T, \frac{1}{r}, \left(\frac{2\bar{M}^s}{2P} + \frac{\bar{B}_g^s}{r2P} + \frac{2\Delta B_g^s}{r2P}\right)\right] \tag{7}$$

This curve is to the left of $2B^d$.

Thus, in the situation we are discussing, both the supply and demand curves for bonds are to the left of $2B^s$ and $2B^d$, respectively. As yet, there is no reason to suppose these curves will intersect at a rate of interest higher than r^*. But we have drawn them doing so. Why? The shift from $2B^s$ to $B^{s''}$ is a measure of the decrease in wealth we have experienced by the nonincrease in $\bar{B}_g^s$. This decrease in wealth affects the demand for bonds and puts $B^{d''}$ to the left of $2B^d$. Since the marginal propensity to spend wealth on bonds is assumed to be less than unity, the curve $B^{d''}$ is not as far to the left of $2B^d$ as the curve $B^{s''}$ is to the left of $2B^s$. Thus, $B^{d''}$ and $B^{s''}$ must intersect at a higher interest rate r_2^*. (The complicated equations in the bond market have been omitted in Figure 5. However, in that diagram $B^{s''}$ and $B^{d''}$ correspond to the curves in Figure 6 which have the equations (6) and (7) respectively.)

In this example, then, the equilibrium interest rate has declined from r^* to r_2^*. The rise in the price level has brought the aggregate demand curve down from $Y^{d'}$ until it overlays exactly the original aggregate demand curve Y^d. The real wealth effect and the decline in the interest rate jointly ensure that this occurs and commodity market equilibrium is reestablished. The new aggregate demand curve $Y^{d''}$ has the equation

$$Y^{d''} = Y^d\left[Y^s, T, r_2^*, \left(\frac{V}{P}\right)_1^*\right]$$

and appears in curly brackets below the original curve Y^d. In the money market, the rise in the price level and the fall in the interest rate has raised the quantity of nominal money demanded until it is equal to the nominal quantity being supplied.

The outcome of this example for the equilibrium values of the variables is summarized in Table 2. Some additional discussion is in order. Investment has increased because of the decline in the interest rate while real income and the capital stock remain constant. Since real government expenditure is constant, this means that consumption must have fallen because the sum of consumption, investment, and government expenditure is un-

TABLE 2 The Effects of an Increase in the Quantity of Money with Money Illusion in the Bond Market

VARIABLE	INITIAL VALUE	FINAL VALUE	OUTCOME
Employment N	N^*	N^*	No change
Real income Y^s	Y^{s*}	Y^{s*}	No change
Real consumption C	C^*	C_1^*	Decreased
Real investment I	I^*	I_1^*	Increased
Real government expenditure G	$\bar{G}$	$\bar{G}$	No change
Real saving S	S^*	S_1^*	Increased
Real taxes T	T^*	T^*	No change
Real bonds B/rP	B^*/r^*P^*	$B^*/r_2^*P_1^*$	Increased
Real money M^d/P	M^d/P^*	$2M^d/P_1^*$	Not known
Price level P	P^*	P_1^*	Increased
Nominal wage W.	W^*	W_1^*	Increased
Real wage W/P	$(W/P)^*$	$(W/P)_1^*$	No change
Interest rate r	r^*	r_2^*	Decreased
Capital stock $\bar{K}$	$\bar{K}$	$\bar{K}$	No change
Money supply $\bar{M}^s$	$\bar{M}^s$	$2\bar{M}^s$	Increased
Money income Y_m^s	Y_m^{s*}	$Y_{m_1}^{s*}$	Increased
Disposable income Y_d^s	Y_d^{s*}	Y_d^{s*}	No change
Real wealth V/P	$(V/P)^*$	$(V/P)_1^*$	Decreased
Labor's share $N(W/P)/Y^s$	$N^*(W/P)^*/Y^{s*}$	$N^*(W/P)_1^*/Y^{s*}$	No change
Others' share $(B/P)/Y^s$	$(B/P)^*/Y^{s*}$	$(B/P)_1^*/Y^{s*}$	No change

changed (because the supply of commodities is unchanged). But, looking at the consumption function, we see that if real income is constant and taxes are constant (which they will be, since real income and tax rates are constant), the fall in interest rates will raise consumption. This rise, then, must have been offset by the decrease in real wealth.

Labor's absolute and relative share of real income is constant, since employment, the real wage, and real income are constant. It follows immediately that the others' absolute and relative share is constant, too. For this to occur, the ratio B/P must remain constant. However, within the B total there is a restructuring—government bonds become a smaller fraction, private bonds a larger fraction. This is because $\bar{B}_g^s$ is constant and fewer new government bonds need be issued because the interest rate has fallen (recall that this supply curve is "perverse"). More private bonds will be issued because the interest rate has fallen and, in addition, because the real liquidity provided by holding government bonds is declining.

Since the ratio B/P is constant and the interest rate r has fallen, total real bonds outstanding will rise. It is not known whether real money balances rise or fall since it is not clear how the price level has increased relative to the supply of money.

3 Fiscal Policy with Price Flexibility; A Balanced Budget

We now switch our attention from monetary policy when all prices are flexible to fiscal policy under the same circumstances. First, we shall analyze a situation in which the government would meet any financial Neanderthal's criteria of "fiscal responsibility." The government has never run a budget deficit so there are no outstanding government bonds ($\bar{B}_g^s = 0$); moreover, it is not about to change its policy (so $\Delta B_g^s = 0$). However, the government does have a mandate to provide more public-good commodities. Therefore, it plans to increase government expenditure $\bar{G}$ and also raise its taxes $\bar{T}$ to finance the increased expenditure. The government always increases $\bar{T}$ in step with $\bar{G}$ to keep its budget balanced. Effectively, then, tax receipts is an exogenous variable. All the other neoclassical assumptions hold.

Consider Figure 7. We start with the model in equilibrium. The government then raises $\bar{G}$ and $\bar{T}$ equally to $\bar{\bar{G}}$ and $\bar{\bar{T}}$, respectively, which throws the commodity market out of equilibrium and introduces excess demand. The rise in government expenditure is not matched by an equal fall in consumption (due to the higher taxes). Disposable income, it is true, will decrease by the amount that taxes increase. However, the marginal propensity to consume from disposable income is less than unity. So consumption will fall, but by less than the increase in taxes (equals government expenditure). The excess commodity demand caused by the shift in aggregate demand to $Y^{d\prime}$ will raise the price level P. The decline in real money balances will reduce real wealth, and aggregate demand will begin to sink back down. This reduction in aggregate demand will be reinforced by a rise in the interest rate.

The increase in taxes reduces disposable income. Thus, the demand for bonds will shift left to $B^{d\prime}$ and the interest rate will rise to r_1 initially. However, the rise in prices emanating from the commodity market also has repercussions on the supply and demand curves for bonds. We know that both curves will shift to the right and, for familiar reasons, the former will move more rapidly than the latter. Thus, the interest rate will eventually rise to r_2^*. This rise in the interest rate and the reduction in real wealth induce the

FIGURE 7

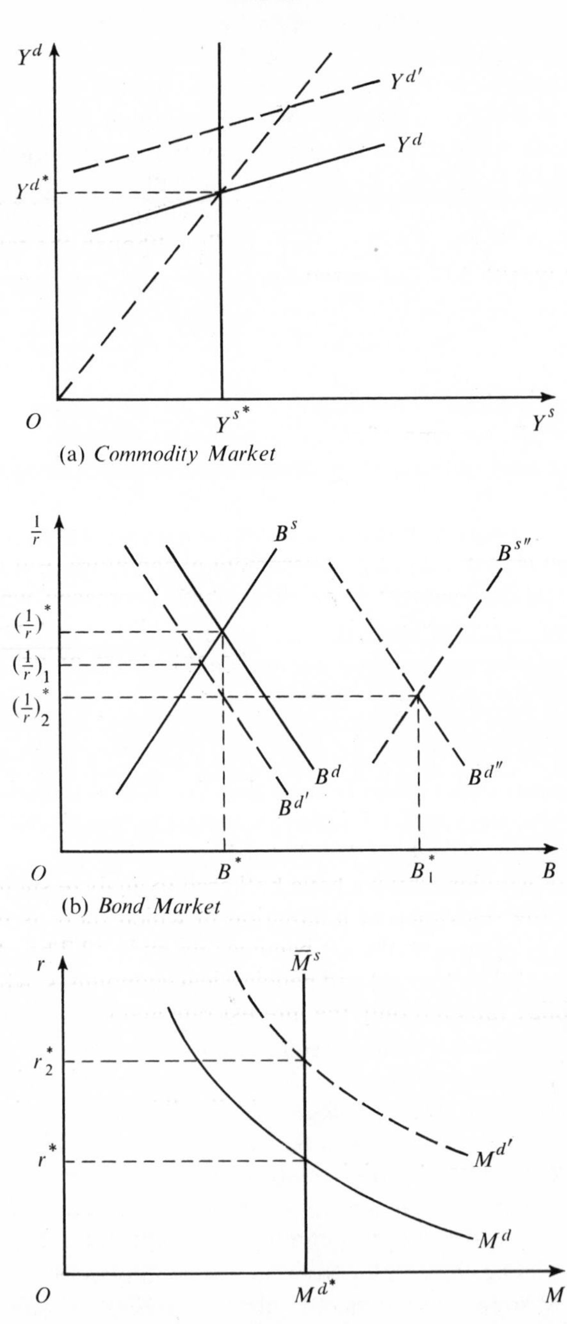

(a) *Commodity Market*

(b) *Bond Market*

(c) *Money "Market"*

private sector to release commodities (from both consumption and investment) to the government sector. We assume once more that the price level P and the nominal wage rate W increase proportionately, thus keeping the real wage, employment, and real income constant (and allowing us to omit the corresponding figures). Although real income is constant (and, therefore we observe in passing, there is no real income multiplier in this world), the income mix has changed; it has shifted away from private commodities in favor of collective commodities. In this particular version of a neoclassical world, fiscal policy affects the *structure* of income and the interest rate; it does not affect the *level* of income. Finally, although the fall in disposable income and wealth has decreased the real demand for money, the nominal demand curve has shifted to $M^{d'}$ because of the rise in the price level. The nominal quantity of money demanded is kept equal to the nominal supply available by a combination of a fall in disposable income, a fall in real wealth, and a rise in the rate of interest.

The overall outcome of this experiment is summarized in Table 3. A few remarks are in order. The reason we know that real saving must have decreased is as follows. We have already discussed the fact that, in equilibrium, "leakages" must equal "injections," that is, planned saving plus taxes must equal planned investment plus government expenditure. But in this example both taxes and government expenditure have increased while investment has decreased. It follows that saving must have decreased, too. In this case, where there is no government debt, the only form of financial wealth is money, whose quantity is constant. Thus, since the price level rose, real wealth must have declined. As employment, the real wage, and real income are constant, we may conclude that labor's absolute and relative share of earned income is constant. It follows that the others' share is constant, too. This means that the ratio B/P is constant. Therefore, since the interest rate increased, real bonds outstanding have decreased.

You may wonder why we have bothered to analyze such an odd example. What is the relevance of a situation in which there is no government debt and the government always balances its budget? The idea was to test the assertions of the classical and neoclassical economists, who used to state that fiscal policy affected only the interest rate and the income mix, not real income. If we want to test their assertions, we must play the game according to their ground rules. In what some people might regard as the good old days of the neoclassicists, governments typically did not run substantial budget deficits (by current standards) and, thus, the quantity of government debt outstanding was minimal—minimal, not zero, as we have assumed, because deficits were run, and debt was issued, to finance periods of stress such as wars. By and large, though, the quantity of government debt outstanding was relatively much less important in their day than it is in ours (perhaps because we fight world wars, while they specialized in gunboat activities). Whatever the cause, if budgets are balanced (and, thus, government debt is unimportant) and the other neoclassical assumptions hold then we have seen that classical and neoclassical assertions concerning fiscal policy are correct. We

TABLE 3 The Effects of Fiscal Policy with a Balanced Budget and No Government Debt

VARIABLE	INITIAL VALUE	FINAL VALUE	OUTCOME
Employment N	N^*	N^*	No change
Real income Y^s	Y^{s*}	Y^{s*}	No change
Real consumption C	C^*	C_1^*	Decreased
Real investment I	I^*	I_1^*	Decreased
Real government expenditure G	$\bar{G}$	$\bar{\bar{G}}$	Increased
Real saving S	S^*	S_1^*	Decreased
Real taxes T	$\bar{T}$	$\bar{\bar{T}}$	Increased
Real bonds B/rP	B^*/r^*P^*	$B_1^*/r_2^*P_1^*$	Decreased
Real money M^d/P	M^d/P^*	M^d/P_1^*	Decreased
Price level P	P^*	P_1^*	Increased
Nominal wage W	W^*	W_1^*	Increased
Real wage W/P	$(W/P)^*$	$(W/P)_1^*$	No change
Interest rate r	r^*	r_2^*	Increased
Capital stock $\bar{K}$	$\bar{K}$	$\bar{K}$	No change
Money supply $\bar{M}^s$	$\bar{M}^s$	$\bar{M}^s$	No change
Money income Y_m^s	Y_m^{s*}	$Y_{m_1}^{s*}$	Increased
Disposable income Y_d^s	Y_d^{s*}	Y_d^{s*}	Decreased
Real wealth V/P	$(V/P)^*$	$(V/P)_1^*$	Decreased
Labor's share $N(W/P)/Y^s$	$N^*(W/P)^*/Y^{s*}$	$N^*(W/P)_1^*/Y^{s*}$	No change
Others' share $(B/P)/Y^s$	$(B/P)^*/Y^{s*}$	$(B/P)_1^*/Y^{s*}$	No change

have been able to corroborate their predictions using a post-Keynesian analytical apparatus, which serves to show once again that our macroeconomic model is quite general. If you work with one set of assumptions (for example, the neoclassical set), you get one set of results; if you use other assumptions (say, a neo-Keynesian set), as we shall do in Part III, then your results are different.

4 The Irrelevance of Say's Law to Classical Economic Conclusions

It has been asserted that Say's law is an essential prerequisite for the classical conclusions to hold. For example, Keynes stated that "[Say's law] underlies the whole classical theory, which would collapse without it."[1] We have seen that this is wholly false. We have been able to establish classical conclusions without even mentioning Say's law. Now, though, we shall digress to discuss it.

J. B. Say was a French economist (1767–1832) who is most famous for the statement, freely translated, "supply creates its own demand." This distillation is derived from the inaccurate observation that people supply factors of production only in order to demand goods. The argument is that people supply factors of production only to earn income so that they may demand the output produced by their original decision to supply more factors. Supplying factors generates output, or real income, which generates an equal amount of spending (demand). In terms of our analytical apparatus, this implies a marginal propensity to spend out of income equal to unity. The result in our commodity market would be that the total spending curve would have a slope of unity and, therefore, exactly overlay the 45°-line (see Figure 8). It is blindingly obvious that in such circumstances real income (aggregate supply) and aggregate demand must always intersect on the 45°-line (since the latter *is* the 45°-line); and, thus, it would be impossible for a deflationary gap (or, for that matter, an inflationary gap) to appear. Manifestly, deficient aggregate demand and, therefore, any sort of unemployment is an impossibility.

If Say's law prevailed it would be sufficient to sustain the conclusions of classical economics. However, it is certainly not *necessary*. When the marginal propensity to spend is less than unity causing the aggregate demand curve to cut across the 45°-line from above, any deflationary gap that might appear will be closed by the fall in prices, which, by raising real wealth and lowering the interest rate, would raise aggregate demand. Prices only need to fall far enough for aggregate demand eventually to rise to equal aggregate supply. It is this real wealth and interest rate effect caused by price flexibility in our macroeconomic model, and not Say's law, which guarantees that the demand for commodities will always equal the supply of commodities.

In an economy comprising commodities, bonds, and money, we would expect the marginal propensity to spend on commodities to be less than unity and, thus, Say's law not to hold. Hence, if Say's law were needed to validate classical economic theory, we would regard that as a very debilitating restriction. We have seen, though, that while sufficient to validate classical theory, Say's law is not necessary. Keynes' stricture must be rejected.

Having shown that Say's law is not necessary to validate classical and

[1] J. M. Keynes, *The General Theory of Employment, Interest, and Money*, Macmillan, 1936, p. 19.

FIGURE 8

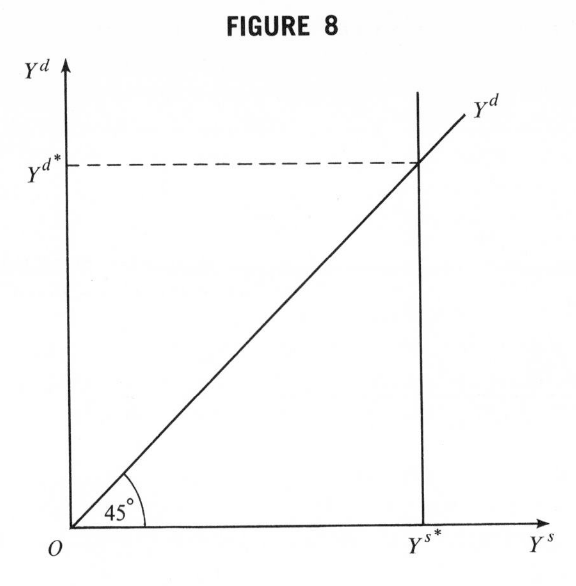

neoclassical macroeconomic conclusions, let us see what is implied by Say's law. Consider an n-good economy; $n-2$ commodities, bonds, and money. Say's law states that, *regardless of the interest rate or the level of prices,* total planned expenditures *on* commodities and bonds are always exactly equal to total expected income *from* selling commodities and bonds. This is merely a precise way of expressing the popular translation we mentioned above—"supply creates its own demand." Algebraically,

$$\sum_{i=1}^{n-2} P_i S_i + \frac{B^s}{r} \equiv \sum_{i=1}^{n-2} P_i D_i + \frac{B^d}{r} \tag{8}$$

where B^s/r and B^d/r equal the value of bonds offered for sale and demanded for purchase, respectively. The left-hand side shows total income expected to accrue from selling commodities and bonds; the right-hand side shows planned total expenditure on commodities and bonds. Say's law states that these two magnitudes are equal. Equation (8) is Say's identity. Notice it implies that transactors *never* plan to change the amount of money they hold. The reason for this will become apparent shortly. Say's law holds only in a barter economy where, by definition, the demand for money is identically zero.

Let us assume that this economy is in equilibrium—all markets are clearing with certain levels of the $n-2$ commodity prices and a particular interest rate. Now *arbitrarily* change one of the $n-2$ commodity prices. Then juggle the remaining $n-3$ commodity prices and the interest rate to clear the $n-2$ commodity markets again. This is, in general, possible. But, by Say's identity, if the commodity markets are all clearing so must the bond market [see equation (8) above]. Now *every* market—commodity, bond, and money—is clearing again. (Notice that the money market has never stopped clearing. The supply of money is fixed and Say's identity implies that transactors never plan to change the amount of money they hold.)

What have we proved? In effect, we have shown that the economy can be in equilibrium at *any* set of money prices. The number of equilibrium-generating money price levels is infinite and any level can be chosen arbitrarily. We have uncovered an incipient inconsistency; if you have Say's identity you cannot have a determinate money price level, but having a determinate money price level is the only thing which gives meaning to the concept of a "money economy." Consequently, if you insist on retaining Say's law you must do without a money economy; and, as a corollary, if you are happy with a barter economy you get Say's identity as a bonus. This seems reasonable, since in a barter economy it is manifestly impossible to "sell" (i.e., trade) a commodity or bond without simultaneously "buying" (i.e., accepting in trade) another commodity or bond.

The implication of Say's identity which we mentioned earlier—that transactors never plan to change the amount of money they hold—should not be so surprising now. Say's identity only holds in a barter economy and in such an economy the demand for money is *always* identically equal to zero (since, by definition, goods are traded directly for goods).

It may be useful to emphasize some of the conclusions we have reached in operating our model according to neoclassical assumptions. First, we have found that money is neutral: purely monetary events, such as a change in the supply of money or an unbiased change in liquidity preference, affect only nominal variables while leaving the real variables undisturbed. Second, the real variables' equilibrium values are disturbed only by some real phenomenon. The examples we detailed were changes in (1) the marginal productivity of labor, (2) the community's work/leisure preferences, (3) entrepreneurs' expectations, and (4) thrift. Third, fiscal policy only affects the *mix* of income (the relative extent to which it is comprised of consumption, investment, and government expenditure) and *not* the level of income. This finding immediately implies there is no such thing as a real income multiplier in a classical environment. Fourth, a factor which we have not remarked upon explicitly but which has constantly been implied, unemployment in a classical environment is unknown. Flexibility of nominal wages W and prices P guarantee a real wage at which everyone who wants a job can find one.

In a neo-Keynesian world *all* these conclusions are false. The examination of such a world is what we undertake next in Part III.

Summary

In this chapter we formally amended the basic model presented in Chapter 6 to incorporate a government sector. Most of the modifications required are relatively simple. The first four equations of the model representing the labor market and the production function are unaffected. Given that the government now levies taxes which reduce households' disposable income, these taxes must be entered in the consumption function, the demand for bonds, and the demand for money; in each case, the effect of taxes is inverse. Since the government demands commodities for collective consumption, aggregate commodity demand is redefined to include government demand $\bar{G}$ (which is *always* assumed to be exogenous). The most complicated modifications occur in the bond supply function. This now consists of the supply of private bonds (which remains unchanged) *plus* the already outstanding supply of government bonds which is denoted $\bar{B}_g^s$ (and is equal to the cumulative value of past government budget *deficits*) *plus* the new supply of government bonds ΔB_g^s (which is a function of the government's *current* budget deficit). The value of $\Delta \bar{B}_g^s$ can, of course, be negative, when the government is running a budget *surplus*. The government's *fiscal position* is defined as the difference between its expenditure $\bar{G}$ and its tax receipts T; when $\bar{G}$ exceeds T the government has a budget *deficit,* and when the reverse is true it has a budget *surplus*. Finally, given the existence of government bonds (which do *not* wash out in the balance sheet consolidation process required to calculate the private sector's net wealth), the private sector's net wealth is equal to the physical capital stock, plus the real value of its outside money holdings, plus the real value of its government bonds (which we assume the private sector does *not* discount for their implied future tax liabilities). The government's tax receipts are, alternatively, assumed to be either exogenously determined *or* an increasing function of real income and the (exogenously determined) tax rate.

The model now consists of nineteen endogenous variables and twenty equations. However, only nineteen of the latter are independent, since one of the market clearance conditions can be shown to be otiose through Walras' law.

The commodity market still clears when the aggregate demand for commodities is equal to the aggregate supply. An *alternative* condition for commodity market clearance when government is included in the model, however, is now that "planned saving plus taxes must equal planned investment plus government expenditure."

Using the model amended to incorporate a government sector, we demonstrated that money is no longer neutral. The underlying reason is that one of the crucial neoclassical assumptions is explicitly relaxed. The total bond supply function now contains *money illusion,* since the government is unconcerned about the real supply of its outstanding debt obligations accumulated through past budget deficits $\bar{B}_g^s$. And *absence* of *money illusion* from *every* demand and supply function is *necessary* for money to be *neutral*. Even though money is no longer neutral, *some* crucial real variables, such as real income and the level of employment, *are* independent of the supply of money.

Next, we used the model to analyze a specific problem in *fiscal policy,* namely, an increase in government expenditures and taxes so that a *balanced budget* is maintained. Such an *equal* increase in government expenditures and taxes *does* disturb equilibrium in the commodity market, since the decrease in consumption caused by the increase in taxes is less than the increase in government expenditure (because the *mpc* is less than unity). Thus, on net, aggregate demand increases. The final outcome of this fiscal policy exercise is that the *mix* of income changes in favor of collective consumption, but the *level* of total *income* does *not* change. In a model in which all prices are flexible there is, therefore, *no* real income multiplier. Income is *always* at the full employment level.

Finally, we discussed *Say's law* (a loose translation is "supply creates its own demand"). We argued that Say's law is *not* crucial to classical and neoclassical theory. Full employment is maintained in such systems by price flexibility. As it turns out, Say's law is inconsistent with a determinate price level, and it can only hold in a barter economy.

Questions

(*Note:* Questions marked with an asterisk are more difficult. They assume that §2 has been read.)

1. Show that only when the commodity market is in equilibrium, with aggregate commodity demand equal to aggregate commodity supply, is it also true that "planned saving plus taxes equal planned investment plus government expenditure."
2. Explain why an equal increase in government expenditure and taxes disturbs equilibrium in the commodity market.
3. Assuming price flexibility, show that if there is an increase in government expenditure there is no change in real income (i.e., that the real income multiplier is zero).
4. Assuming price flexibility, show that *any* change in fiscal policy does not affect the level of income, but only its composition, or mix.
5. Show that the supply curve of *new* government bonds required by the government's current fiscal position (a) *may* be in the negative quadrant and (b) *will* have a perverse slope compared with a normal supply curve.
6. Derive the expression for the private sector's net real assets (or real wealth) when the model includes a government sector.
7. Indicate how the tax function will shift if (a) the minimum level of taxable income is raised, but marginal tax rates are kept constant (what happens to the average tax rate?); (b) the marginal tax rate is increased, but the minimum level of taxable income is held constant (what happens to the average tax rate?); (c) *all* average and marginal tax rates are increased (what happens to the minimum level of taxable income?).

*8. Show that when government is included in the model a decrease in the supply of money is *not* neutral. Which neoclassical assumption is being relaxed?

9. Show that Say's law is not a prerequisite for the neoclassical conclusion that full employment is guaranteed in a world of flexible prices.
10. Show that Say's law is inconsistent with a monetary economy and must hold in a barter economy.

*11. Exclude government from the model. Assume an increase in the money supply. Show that money is *not* neutral if we assume that *firms* have money illusion in their bond supply function. (In particular, assume that when prices rise entrepreneurs do *not* have their firms write up the value of their capital equipment *pari passu,* issue an equivalent amount of bonds, and take the proceeds as a capital gain. See §5.2, "An Aside on Money Illusion," for background.)

SELECTED READINGS

1. W. J. Baumol, *Economic Theory and Operations Analysis,* Prentice-Hall, 1961, chapter 12. A clear and simple discussion of Say's and Walras' laws.
2. R. W. Clower, "The Keynesian Counterrevolution: A Theoretical Appraisal," in F. H. Hahn and F. P. R. Brechling (eds.), *The Theory of Interest Rates,* Institute of Economic Affairs, 1965. The authoritative discussion of Say's and Walras' laws.
3. J. M. Keynes, *The General Theory of Employment, Interest, and Money,* Macmillan, 1936, chapter 3. Keynes' attack on Say's law and his assertion that it is crucial to classical and neoclassical theory.
4. F. Modigliani, "The Monetary Mechanism and Its Interaction with Real Phenomena," *Review of Economics and Statistics,* February, 1963.
5. D. Patinkin, *Money, Interest, and Prices,* 2nd ed., Harper & Row, 1965, chapter 12; chapter 13, section 4; and note L. An examination of the model including a government sector and discussions of Say's law.

FURTHER READINGS

6. G. C. Archibald and R. G. Lipsey, "Monetary and Value Theory: A Critique of Lange and Patinkin," *Review of Economic Studies,* October, 1958.
7. G. S. Becker and W. J. Baumol, "The Classical Monetary Theory: The Outcome of the Discussion," *Economica,* November, 1952.
8. O. Lange, "Say's Law: A Restatement and Criticism," in O. Lange (ed.), *Studies in Mathematical Economics and Econometrics,* University of Chicago Press, 1942.
9. J. B. Say, *Traité d'Économie Politique,* Paris, 1817. The original source for his law.

Part III

Neo-Keynesian Macroeconomics

10

Complications in the Labor Market; Illusions and Rigidities

In Part II we concluded that when wages and prices were flexible involuntary unemployment was an impossibility. The demand for labor was always equal to the supply of labor. By inference, everyone who wanted a job could find one if he were prepared to accept the equilibrium real wage. In such a world, people without a job are either voluntarily unemployed (they *choose* not to work at the going real wage) or frictionally unemployed (they are "between jobs"). Pigou summed up the classical position in the following manner: "With perfectly free competition among work people . . . everyone will actually be employed." [1] This, more than anything, was what incensed Keynes about classical economics. At that time in England, about 20 percent of the labor force was pounding the pavement looking for work.

> Who will deny [involuntary unemployment]? [he cried.] The classical theorists resemble Euclidean geometers in a non-Euclidean world who, discovering that in experience straight lines apparently parallel often meet, rebuke the lines for not keeping straight. . . . Yet, in truth, there is no remedy except to throw over the axiom of parallels and to work out a non-Euclidean geometry. Something similar is required today in economics. We need to . . . work out the behavior of a system in which involuntary unemployment . . . is possible.[2]

Keynes, and those who came after him, discarded classical axioms right and left. What happens when one does so now occupies us in Part III. The results will be startling.

1 Money Illusion in the Labor Market

Keynes asserted that "ordinary experience tells us, beyond doubt, that a situation where labor stipulates (within limits) for a *money-wage* rather

[1] A. C. Pigou, *Theory of Unemployment,* A. M. Kelley, 1968 (reprint of 1933 ed.), p. 252.

[2] J. M. Keynes, *The General Theory of Employment, Interest, and Money,* Macmillan, 1936, pp. 16–17.

than a real wage, so far from being a mere possibility, is the normal case. This leaves the question of what the actual level of employment will be quite indeterminate."[1]

Given Keynes' assumption, we can show that his conclusion is correct. In effect, his assumption is that the labor force suffers from money illusion. The supply of labor is a function of the nominal money wage and *not* the real wage. If the nominal money wage increases (no matter what is happening to the price level and, therefore, the real wage), the supply of labor will increase, and vice versa.

The only modification to the model we shall make is the introduction of money illusion into the labor supply function. All the other neoclassical assumptions such as price and wage flexibility, no money illusion in any other functions, unit-elastic price expectations, and no distribution effects will be retained. Notwithstanding, our macroeconomic model's predictions become totally non-neoclassical. The labor supply function becomes

$$N^s = N^s(W), \qquad N_1^s > 0 \tag{II'}$$

with N^s directly related to the nominal wage W. It is worth noting that, prior to this modification, the labor market was self-contained, or separable. There were the three equations (I), (II), and (III) and three endogenous variables N^d, N^s, and W/P. This market could generate the equilibrium values of employment N^* and the real wage $(W/P)^*$ by itself which is why it was said to be separable. After we substitute (II′) for (II), this is no longer true. Then there are three equations (I), (II′) and (III), but *four* endogenous variables N^d, N^s, W/P, and W. Notice that the real wage and the nominal wage are two separate variables. The labor market is no longer self-contained, or separable. What happens in the rest of the macroeconomic model now affects the labor market. This, in essence, is what Keynes meant when he said that "actual employment will be quite indeterminate." To illustrate this situation we shall revert to the simple model which excludes the government sector. Nothing substantive will be lost thereby. Geometrically, it is also convenient to present the labor market somewhat differently. Instead of plotting the real wage W/P on the vertical axis, we shall plot the nominal wage W (see Figure 1). In such a diagram, the supply of labor function is not a problem. It is an increasing function of the nominal wage and it is stable. In particular, the function is not affected by the price level. However, the demand for labor, which is *still* a function of the real wage, will be downward sloping with respect to the money wage for a *given* price level, but will shift left when the price level falls and right when the price level rises. For example, when the price level is held constant (other things being equal) at P_1, the demand for labor curve will be N^d and the equilibrium money wage and level of employment W^* and N^*, respectively. If the price level should rise to P_2, this would mean a lower real wage for any given nominal wage and, thus, the demand for labor in Figure 1 would increase to

[1] J. M. Keynes, *The General Theory of Employment, Interest, and Money,* Macmillan, 1936, p. 8. Emphasis added.

FIGURE 1

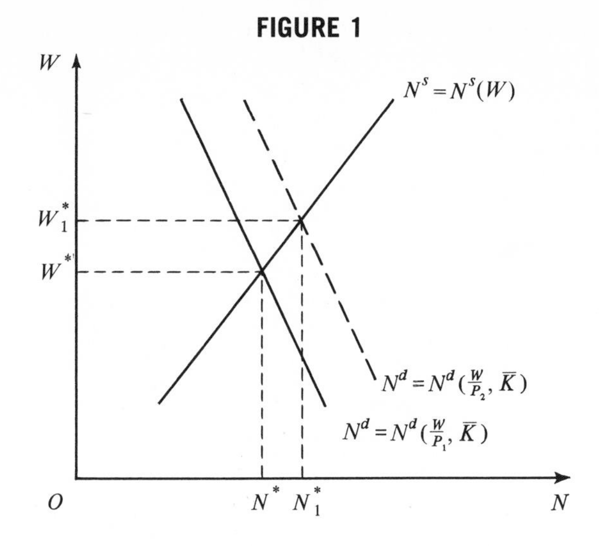

$N^{d'}$ and the equilibrium money wage and level of employment to W_1^* and N_1^*, respectively. Analogously, this demand for labor curve would shift left of N^d for any price level below P_1.

As usual, let us begin with our model in equilibrium and introduce some disturbance by changing the value of one of the exogenous variables. Specifically, let the supply of money be doubled from $\bar{M}^s$ to $2\bar{M}^s$. You will recall from §7.1 that the outcome of this experiment with the full set of neoclassical assumptions was neutral. No real variables altered, while all the nominal variables increased in proportion to the supply of money. What will happen now that we have money illusion in the labor supply function? Consider Figure 2. Note that in Figure 2(a) the nominal wage W is now plotted on the vertical axis.

When the supply of money is doubled from $\bar{M}^s$ to $2\bar{M}^s$ the impact increase in real wealth will shift the bond supply and demand curves to $B^{s'}$ and $B^{d'}$, respectively. Excess demand equal to *ab* is created in the bond market [Figure 2(d)], lowering the interest rate to r_1. This reduction in the interest rate *and* the impact increase in real wealth raises the aggregate demand curve to $Y^{d'}$. Excess demand equal to *cd* is created in the commodity market [Figure 2(b)], and commodity prices P begin to rise.

Suppose prices rise to P_1^*. This rise lowers the real wage. The fall in the real wage shifts the demand curve for labor to the right. Excess demand equal to *ef* is created in the labor market [Figure 2(a)] and, as employers bid against each other for labor, the nominal wage rises to W_1^*. Both the nominal wage and the price level rise, but the latter rises more than the former. The fall thus implied in the real wage leads to more employment, namely, N_1^*, being offered.

When employment rises, though, so does real output (income)—to Y_1^{s*}. This rise in real income alters the situation in the commodity market. If equilibrium is to be reestablished when aggregate supply has shifted to Y_1^{s*},

FIGURE 2

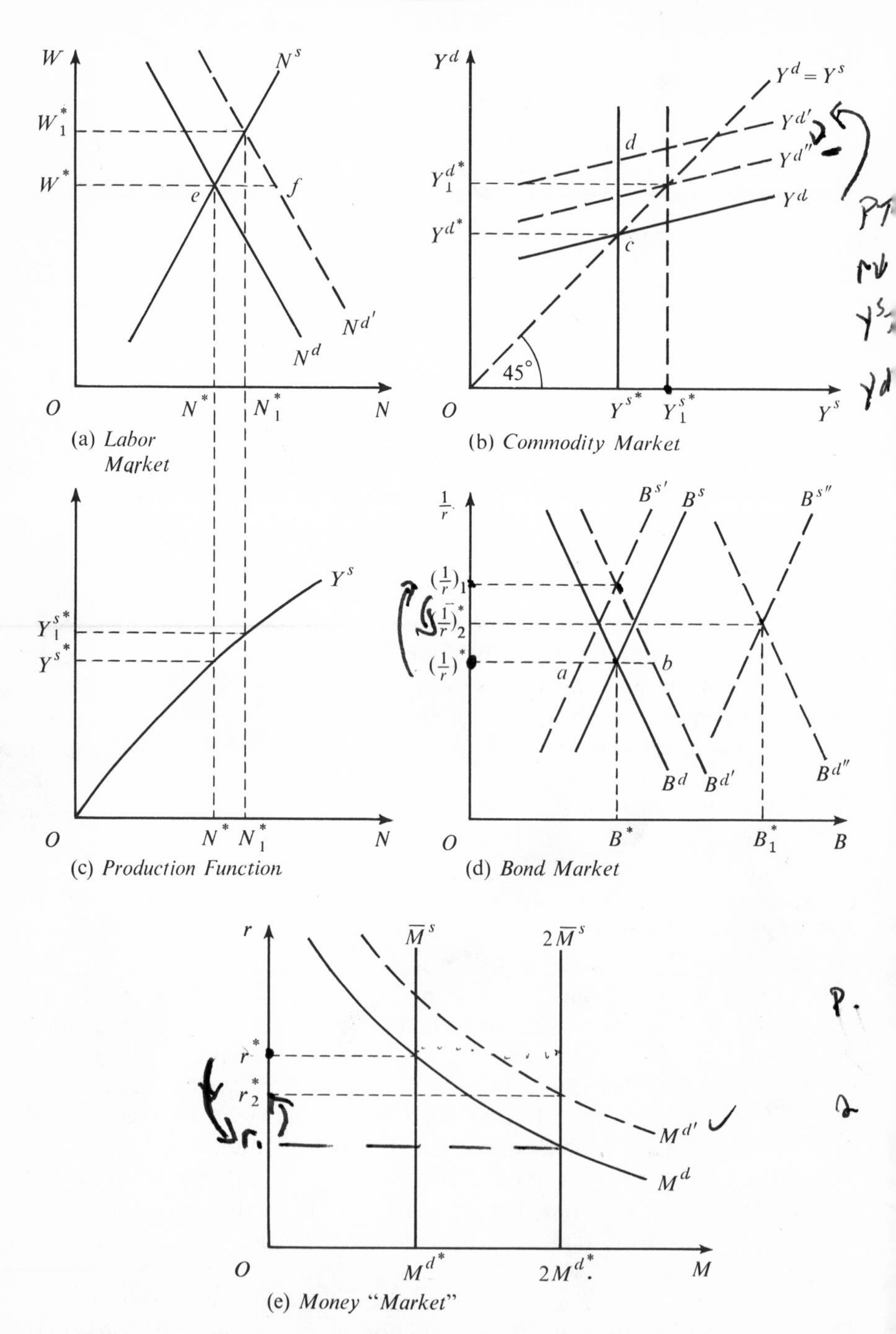
W
W_1^*
W^*
N^s
e
f
$N^{d'}$
N^d
O
N^*
N_1^*
N
(a) Labor Market
Y^d
$Y^d = Y^s$
$Y^{d'}$
$Y^{d''}$
Y^d
d
Y_1^{d*}
Y^{d*}
c
45°
O
Y^{s*}
Y_1^{s*}
Y^s
(b) Commodity Market
Y^s
Y_1^{s*}
Y^{s*}
O
N^*
N_1^*
N
(c) Production Function
$\frac{1}{r}$
$B^{s'}$
B^s
$B^{s''}$
$(\frac{1}{r})_1$
$(\frac{1}{r})_2^*$
$(\frac{1}{r})^*$
a
b
B^d
$B^{d'}$
$B^{d''}$
O
B^*
B_1^*
B
(d) Bond Market
r
$\overline{M}^s$
$2\overline{M}^s$
r^*
r_2^*
$M^{d'}$
M^d
O
M^{d*}
$2M^{d*}$
M
(e) Money "Market"

the aggregate demand curve $Y^{d'}$ cannot fall back to its *original* position. There are now more commodities being supplied, so aggregate demand permanently must remain higher than it was originally if equilibrium is to prevail again in the commodity market. This is shown by the curve $Y^{d''}$. What can we rely on to ensure that aggregate demand is permanently increased? The answer is a permanent increase in real wealth and a permanent reduction in the rate of interest. The first results from the fact that, although prices increase, they do not double. Therefore, whereas real wealth was originally equal to $(V/P)^* = \bar{K} + (M^s/P^*)$, when equilibrium is reestablished real wealth equals $(V/P)_1^* = \bar{K} + (2M^s/P_1^*)$. As P_1^* is less than twice P^*, real wealth has clearly increased.

Rising prices feed into the bond market and shift both the supply of bonds and demand for bonds to the right away from the impact supply and demand curves $B^{s'}$ and $B^{d'}$. As we well know, the supply curve shifts more rapidly than the demand curve; therefore, the interest rate falls from its impact level r_1 back toward r^*. However, it will not fall all the way back, since that would only occur if the price level had doubled (which it does not). Hence, the interest rate will only fall to r_2^*, where the supply and demand curves $B^{s''}$ and $B^{d''}$ prevail.

In the money market, the excess supply of money originally created is eliminated by a combination of events. The nominal demand for money is increased to equal the doubled nominal supply available by a rise in the price level, an increase in real income, a fall in the interest rate, and a rise in real wealth. The final situation is shown by the demand curve labeled $M^{d'}$ in Figure 2(e).

It is quite obvious that in the situation we have just analyzed, money is anything but neutral. The veil has dropped. All the real variables have new equilibrium values and *none* of the nominal variables has increased in proportion to the money supply. It is a classic (a bad word) example of the non-neutrality of money which shows splendidly how the alteration of one ground rule in our game (the substitution of money illusion in the supply curve of labor), while the rest of the model is kept inviolate, alters the outcome completely. The overall result is summarized in Table 1.

We conclude that real consumption must have increased because real income and real wealth have increased while the interest rate decreased. Similarly, real investment must have increased because real income increased and the interest rate decreased. If real investment increased, real savings must have increased, too. Real money increased because the supply doubled while prices less than doubled. This is also sufficient to explain the increase in real wealth. Money income increased because both real income and prices increased. We do not know what happened to the functional distribution of income. Because the real wage declined while employment rose the change in the numerator of labor's share is ambiguous. The others' share is similarly ambiguous. The outcome for real bond holdings is indeterminate because although real income and real wealth have increased (which would raise real bond holdings), their price has risen which would

TABLE 1 The Impact of Increased Money Supply with Money Illusion in the Labor Supply Function

VARIABLE	INITIAL VALUE	FINAL VALUE	OUTCOME
Employment N	N^*	N_1^*	Increased
Real income Y^s	Y^{s*}	Y_1^{s*}	Increased
Real consumption C	C^*	C_1^*	Increased
Real investment I	I^*	I_1^*	Increased
Real saving S	S^*	S_1^*	Increased
Real bonds B/rP	B^*/r^*P^*	$B_1^*/r_2^*P_1^*$	Not known
Real money M^d/P	M^d/P^*	$2M^d/P_1^*$	Increased
Price level P	P^*	P_1^*	Increased
Nominal wage W	W^*	W_1^*	Increased
Real wage W/P	$(W/P)^*$	$(W/P)_1^*$	Decreased
Interest rate r	r^*	r_2^*	Decreased
Capital stock $\bar{K}$	$\bar{K}$	$\bar{K}$	No change
Money supply $\bar{M}^s$	$\bar{M}^s$	$2\bar{M}^s$	Increased
Money income Y_m^s	Y_m^{s*}	$Y_{m_1}^{s*}$	Increased
Real wealth V/P	$(V/P)^* = \bar{K} + (\bar{M}^s/P^*)$	$(V/P)_1^* = \bar{K} + (2M^s/P_1^*)$	Increased
Labor's share $N(W/P)/Y^s$	$N^*(W/P)^*/Y^{s*}$	$N_1^*(W/P)_1^*/Y_1^{s*}$	Not known
Others' share $(B/P)/Y^s$	$(B/P)^*/Y^{s*}$	$(B/P)_1^*/Y_1^{s*}$	Not known

have the opposite effect. We cannot, therefore, reach a conclusion one way or the other.

2 Money Illusion in the Labor Market and Rigid Money Wages

An interesting variation on the theme we have just explored is to introduce downward rigidity in the money wage. We assume the labor force resists cuts in the money wage below the prevailing level. Workers will accept the quantity of employment offered at the prevailing money wage rate, but they will not accept money wage reductions.

Geometrically, this gives us a labor supply function with a kink in it at the prevailing money wage like that illustrated in Figure 3. Let the original demand for labor be represented by the curve N^d. The quantity of employ-

FIGURE 3

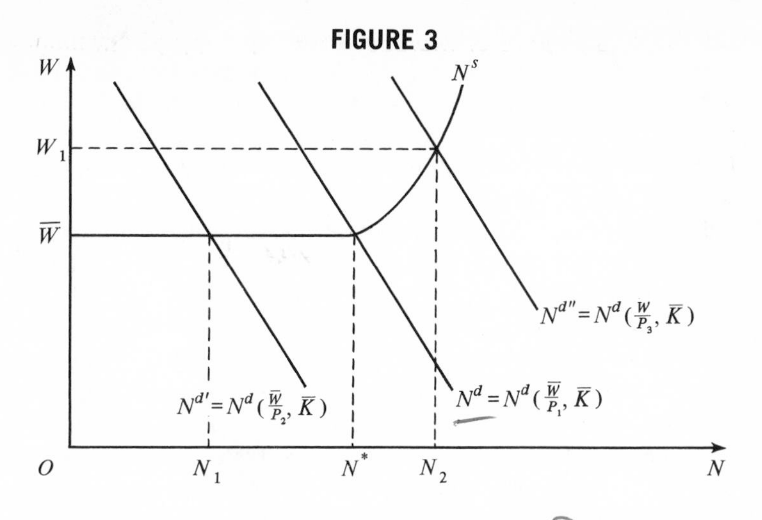

ment would be N^*. If, for example, the price level fell to P_2, the increase in the real wage would shift the demand curve left to $N^{d'}$. Labor resists wage cuts and insists on the money wage $\overline{W}$. It must, therefore, accept the quantity of employment N_1, which is all that employers are offering at the prevailing real wage $\overline{W}/P_2$. As a result, $N^* - N_1$ workers are without jobs because they would like to work at $\overline{W}$, but are not offered employment at that wage. If the price level should rise above P_1 to P_3, thus reducing the real wage, the demand for labor would shift to $N^{d''}$ and the money wage would be bid up to W_1. Here we are on the upward-sloping part of the supply curve. Keynes did think that money wages were inflexible downwards from the prevailing level. For example, he said, "workers will usually resist a reduction in money wages" and "Every trade union will put up some resistance to a cut in money-wages, however small."[1] Or consider his remark, "more labor would, as a rule, be forthcoming at the existing money-wage if it were demanded."[2] In effect, the formal modification we have made in our macroeconomic model is to change the labor supply equation (II) to

$$N^s = \begin{cases} N^d & N^d < N^* \\ N^s(W) & N^d > N^* \end{cases} \qquad \text{(II')}$$

The first of these equations is operative when the demand for labor is less than the original equilibrium level. Actually, in this situation we have lost one equation entirely (the labor supply equation) and one endogenous variable, namely, W. The money wage is now exogenously fixed at $\overline{W}$. When the demand for labor exceeds the original equilibrium level the second of these two equations is operative and we are back in exactly the same situation analyzed in §1.

When a fixed nominal wage is incorporated into our model, what hap-

[1] J. M. Keynes, *The General Theory of Employment, Interest, and Money,* Macmillan, 1936, pp. 9, 15.

[2] *Ibid.*, p. 7.

pens if an initial equilibrium situation is disturbed by some deflationary impulse? Assume that the disturbance is due to a decline in entrepreneurs' expectations. Entrepreneurs now plan to invest less at the prevailing levels of income and interest rates. Referring to Figure 4(b), we see that aggregate demand drops to $Y^{d'}$. Excess commodity supply equal to *ab* emerges and prices begin to fall to, let us say, P_1^*.

The fall in prices reacts on the bond market [see Figure 4(d)]. Both curves shift left; since the supply curve moves less rapidly than the demand curve, the interest rate falls to r_1^*. This fall in the interest rate *plus* the rise in real wealth brought about by the fall in prices cause consumption to increase. The decline in the interest rate also leads to some rise in investment above the level entrepreneurs had planned after the original collapse of their expectations. Both the rise in consumption and the rise in investment cause aggregate demand to rise from $Y^{d'}$ to $Y^{d''}$. Thus, the deflationary gap created in the commodity market is closed from one direction by a rise in aggregate demand from its low level of $Y^{d'}$ and from the other direction by a reduction in aggregate supply.

The fall in commodity prices to P_1^* raises the real wage because the nominal wage is rigid at $\bar{W}$. This shifts the demand for labor curve left to $N^{d'}$. The quantity of employment offered is N_1^* which, via the production function, means real output (income) falls to Y_1^{s*}. Thus, in the commodity market, the aggregate supply curve shifts left from Y^{s*} to Y_1^{s*}. This decrease in aggregate supply to Y_1^{s*} and the increase in aggregate demand to $Y^{d''}$ are sufficient to reestablish equilibrium in the commodity market; the two curves intersect on the 45°-line.

In the money market the falls in the price level and in real income reduce the demand for nominal money balances. However, the quantity of nominal money demanded is made equal to the fixed nominal supply available by the reduced interest rate and the rise in real wealth. The results of this experiment are given in Table 2.

Technically, we are not certain what happens to consumption and investment (and, therefore, saving). We *are* sure that aggregate demand has decreased, but whether either component has declined is ambiguous. For example, income has declined, which tends to reduce consumption, but the interest rate has also declined and real wealth has risen. Both these latter factors tend to raise consumption. Consequently, the actual outcome depends on the income, interest rate, and wealth elasticities of consumption. We would *expect* (we cannot say more) the former elasticity to dominate and consumption to decline on balance. If consumption declined, it would be *possible* (in a remote way, we expect) for investment to actually rise. The decrease in the interest rate, which tends to increase investment, could have swamped the effects of the decrease in income and more pessimistic entrepreneurial expectations. The outcome for investment depends on the relative strength of this interest elasticity, which we would, again, *not* expect to be strong enough to cause investment to rise. All in all, then, we would

FIGURE 4

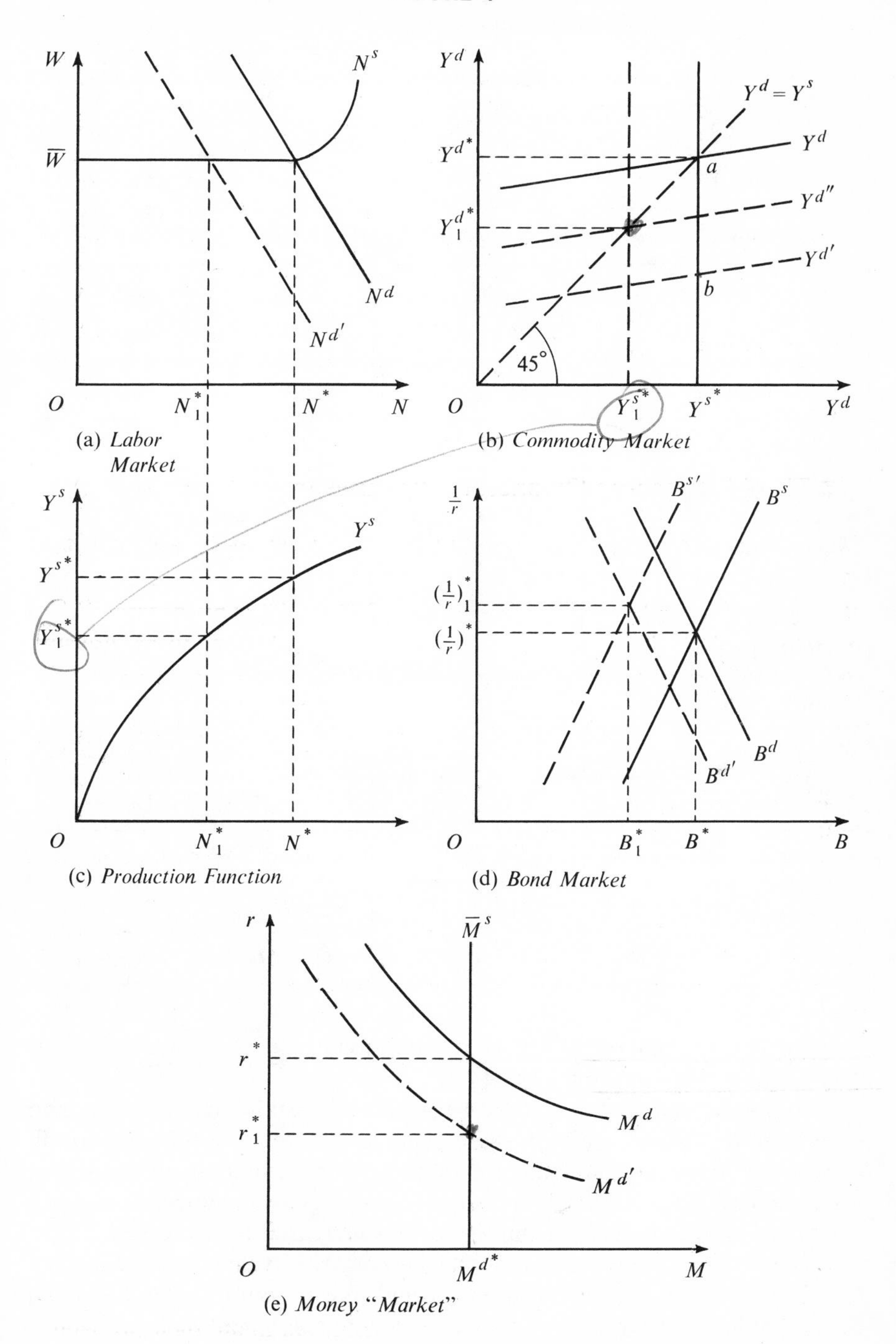
W
$\overline{W}$
N^s
N^d
$N^{d'}$
O
N_1^*
N^*
N
(a) Labor Market
Y^d
$Y^d = Y^s$
Y^{d*}
Y_1^{d*}
$Y^{d''}$
$Y^{d'}$
a
b
45°
O
Y_1^{s*}
Y^{s*}
(b) Commodity Market
Y^s
Y^{s*}
Y_1^{s*}
O
N_1^*
N^*
(c) Production Function
$\frac{1}{r}$
$B^{s'}$
B^s
$(\frac{1}{r})_1^*$
$(\frac{1}{r})^*$
B^d
$B^{d'}$
O
B_1^*
B^*
B
(d) Bond Market
r
$\overline{M}^s$
r^*
r_1^*
M^d
$M^{d'}$
O
M^{d*}
M
(e) Money "Market"

TABLE 2 A Decrease in the Marginal Efficiency of Investment with Money Illusion in the Labor Market and Downward Money Wage Rigidity

VARIABLE	INITIAL VALUE	FINAL VALUE	OUTCOME
Employment N	N^*	N_1^*	Decreased
Real income Y^s	Y^{s*}	Y_1^{s*}	Decreased
Real consumption C	C^*	C_1^*	Not known
Real investment I	I^*	I_1^*	Not known
Real saving S	S^*	S_1^*	Not known
Real bonds B/rP	B^*/r^*P^*	$B_1^*/r_1^*P_1^*$	Not known
Real money M^d/P	M^d/P^*	M^d/P_1^*	Increased
Price level P	P^*	P_1^*	Decreased
Nominal wage W	$\bar{W}$	$\bar{W}$	No change
Real wage W/P	$(\bar{W}/P)^*$	$(\bar{W}/P)_1^*$	Increased
Interest rate r	r^*	r_1^*	Decreased
Capital stock $\bar{K}$	$\bar{K}$	$\bar{K}$	No change
Money supply $\bar{M}^s$	$\bar{M}^s$	$\bar{M}^s$	No change
Money income Y_m^s	Y_m^{s*}	$Y_{m_1}^{s*}$	Decreased
Real wealth V/P	$(V/P)^*$	$(V/P)_1^*$	Increased
Labor's share $N(W/P)/Y^s$	$N^*(\bar{W}/P)^*/Y^{s*}$	$N_1^*(\bar{W}/P)_1^*/Y_1^{s*}$	Not known
Others' share $(B/P)/Y^s$	$(B/P)^*/Y^{s*}$	$(B/P)_1^*/Y_1^{s*}$	Not known

guess that consumption, investment, and saving all would decrease. But keep in mind that we *are* guessing.

Money income has decreased because both real income and the price level have decreased. Labor's share is uncertain because the direction in which the numerator has changed is ambiguous; employment has fallen while the real wage has risen. The others' share is also ambiguous because we do not know whether the numerator has increased or decreased.

The result of this experiment in the labor market is unemployment equal to $N^* - N_1^*$. Although N^* workers would like to work at the prevailing wage, employers only offer N_1^* jobs. This unemployment is due *solely* to the rigid money wage that labor demands. The reader may refer back to

§8.3, where we performed *exactly* the same experiment except that money wages were flexible and no permanent unemployment resulted. Wage rigidity can produce unemployment; wage flexibility will guarantee full employment in a comparative static analysis. We stress again, though, that this does *not* necessarily imply that one would advocate a policy of wage flexibility in the real world in a deflationary situation. In the real world, the dynamic problems introduced in §8.5 can be of the essence.

3 Monetary Policy To Cure Unemployment

We have just seen that when our macroeconomic model is appropriately specified (namely, by introducing money wage rigidity), unemployment may certainly emerge in a deflationary situation. We know that *in the long run* wage flexibility would cure this. However, the dynamic adjustment process could be so painful that we would not survive to witness the final full employment equilibrium. This is why Keynes advocated a flexible money policy (rather than a flexible wage policy) to cure the unemployment of a deflationary situation. How does the process work?

Let us start from a position where unemployment exists. In particular, suppose we pick up the story where we left it at the end of the previous section. Consider Figure 5. Unemployment equal to $N_f^* - N_1^*$ prevails because the real wage is above the labor market–clearing level. The essential solution of this problem is to increase the money stock (which will raise prices, thus lowering the real wage) and increase employment. The increased output resulting from increased employment will be demanded because of increased real money balances and lower interest rates – both of which are also brought about by the increase in the supply of money.

In detail, the analysis runs as follows (we assume the initial equilibrium position is the same as the final equilibrium position reached in §2). The monetary authority wants to establish full employment at N_f^* and a level of aggregate demand sufficient to absorb the supply of commodities Y_f^{s*} forthcoming at that level of employment. What happens when it increases the money supply to, say, $\bar{M}^{s\prime}$? There will be an excess supply of money in the money market.

This excess supply of money generates excess demand for bonds equal to *cd*, since the increase in real money balances shifts the supply curve of bonds left to $B^{s\prime}$ and the demand curve for bonds right to $B^{d\prime\prime}$. The interest rate falls to r_1 and, in combination with the increase in real money balances, raises aggregate demand to $Y^{d\prime\prime}$. Excess commodity demand equal to *ef* has been created. Note that the impact aggregate demand curve aimed for in this situation must exceed the final aggregate demand curve desired because the rise in prices and the rise in the interest rate from its interim low level of r_1 will cause the *impact* aggregate demand curve to sink. The excess commodity demand *ef* raises prices to P_1^*. The rise in prices feeds into the labor and bond markets. We deal with the former first. The decline in the real wage to

FIGURE 5

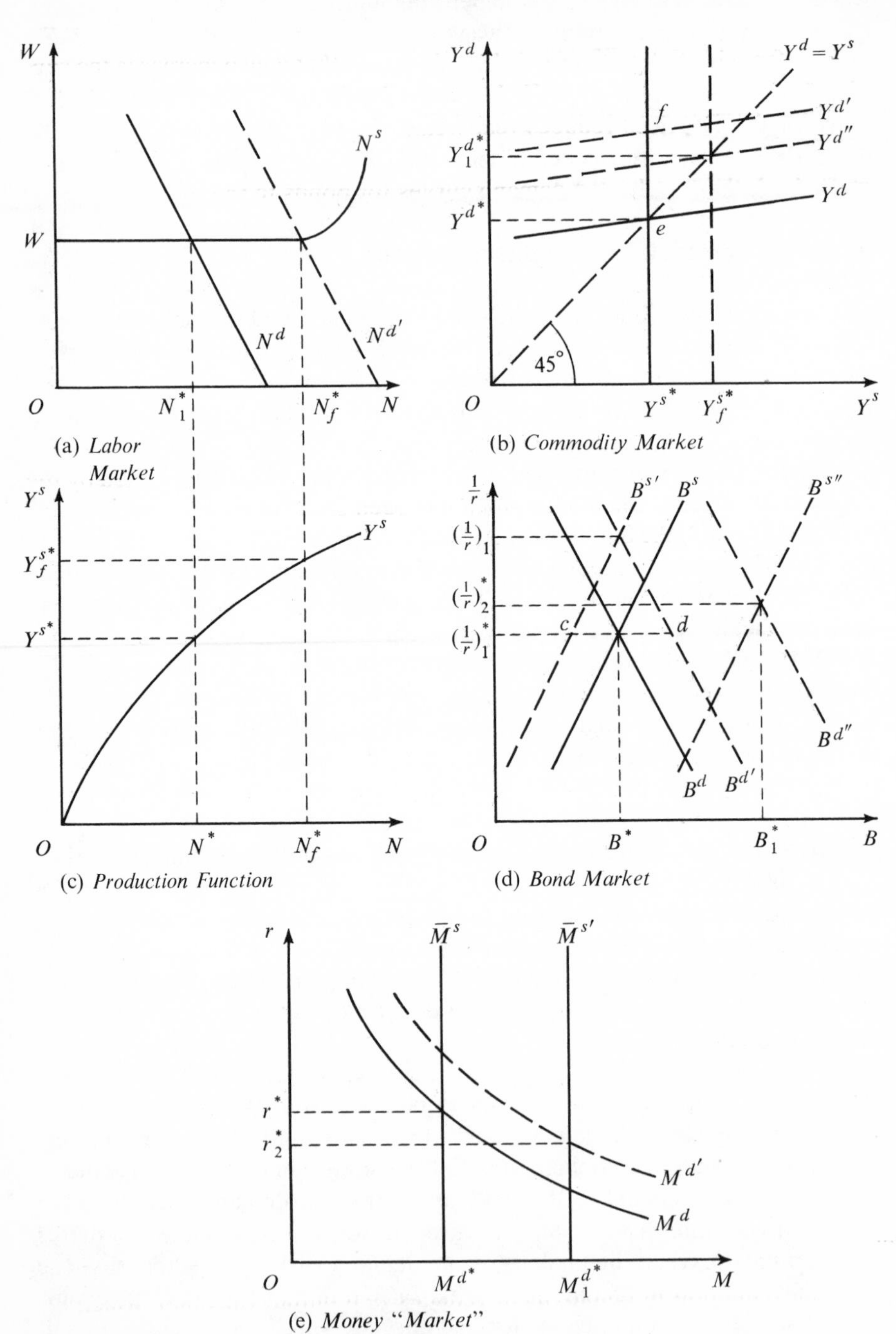

(a) *Labor Market*

(b) *Commodity Market*

(c) *Production Function*

(d) *Bond Market*

(e) *Money "Market"*

$(\bar{W}/P)_1^*$ causes the demand for labor to increase to $N^{d'}$. Employment rises to N_f^* and output (income) rises to Y_f^{s*}.

The rise in the price level closes the excess demand in the commodity market from both directions. We have just seen that it also increases the supply of commodities to Y_f^{s*}; and it decreases the demand. This is due to the fact that the rise in prices reduces real wealth from $(V/P)^*$ to $(V/P)_1^*$ and also raises the interest rate to r_2^*. This, in turn, occurs because a rise in prices shifts both the supply and demand curves for bonds to the right (the former more rapidly than the latter), specifically, to $B^{s''}$ and $B^{d''}$, respectively. Although the interest rate rises, it will not reach r^* again because the increase in prices is not proportional to the increase in the money supply. Therefore, real money balances after the increase in the money supply and the rise in prices will be greater than they were before. The combination of the decrease in real money balances to $(V/P)_1^*$ and the rise in the interest rate to r_2^* lowers the aggregate demand curve to $Y^{d''}$, where it is equal to full employment aggregate supply.

Finally, in the money market, the excess supply of money created by the decision to increase the money stock has been eliminated, too. The increase in the price level, the increase in real income, and the decrease in the interest rate have increased the nominal demand to equal the nominal supply available. This is shown by the demand curve $M^{d'}$ in Figure 5(e). Equilibrium has been established in all markets.

You will note that we have, in effect, inflated our way out of a deflationary situation. In this example, the deflationary situation was triggered by a decline in entrepreneurial expectations. However, let us now consider an alternative approach.

4 Cost-Push Inflation I; A Collectively Bargained Money Wage

We start with our macroeconomic model in equilibrium at full employment; the situation is represented by the solid curves in Figure 6. Now let our workers combine collectively to extract a higher nominal money wage $\bar{\bar{W}}$. The unionized workers will not work for any money wage below this level. Clearly, the horizontal part of the labor supply curve in Figure 6(a) is raised from $\bar{W}$ to $\bar{\bar{W}}$. This rise in the real wage reduces the demand for labor, so that employment falls from N^* to N_1. Hence, the difference $N^* - N_1$ of *previously* employed labor services is no longer required. However, in addition, at a real wage of $(\bar{\bar{W}}/P)^*$, $N_0 - N^*$ labor services which were not previously offered will be offered. So, in total, at the real wage $(\bar{\bar{W}}/P)^*$, $N_0 - N_1$ labor units are looking for jobs without being able to find them. This, then, is the extent of unemployment.

The reduction in employment reduces real output (income), which reduces the aggregate supply of commodities to Y_1^s. Manifestly, excess demand now emerges in the commodity market equal to *ab*. Commodity prices rise to, say, P_1^*. This rise in commodity prices has several repercussions. First,

FIGURE 6

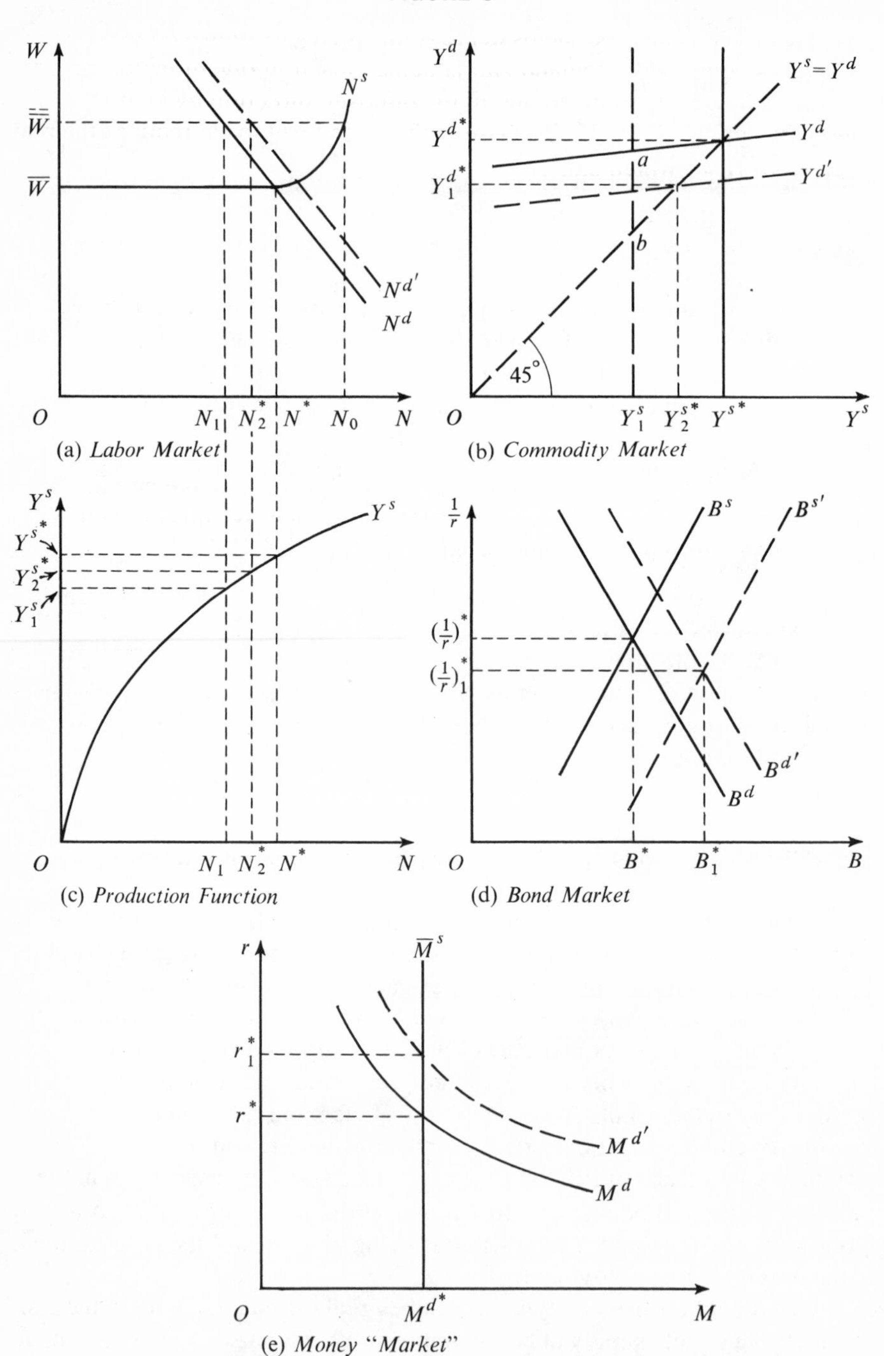
W
$\overline{\overline{W}}$
$\overline{W}$
N^s
$N^{d'}$
N^d
O
N_1 N_2^* N^* N_0 N
(a) Labor Market
Y^d
Y^{d*}
Y_1^{d*}
$Y^s = Y^d$
Y^d
$Y^{d'}$
a
b
45°
O
Y_1^s Y_2^{s*} Y^{s*} Y^s
(b) Commodity Market
Y^s
Y^{s*}
Y_2^{s*}
Y_1^s
O
N_1 N_2^* N^* N
(c) Production Function
$\frac{1}{r}$
$(\frac{1}{r})^*$
$(\frac{1}{r})_1^*$
B^s
$B^{s'}$
$B^{d'}$
B^d
O
B^* B_1^* B
(d) Bond Market
r
$\overline{M}^s$
r_1^*
r^*
$M^{d'}$
M^d
O
M^{d*} M
(e) Money "Market"

it reduces real wealth, which causes the aggregate demand curve to begin to sink from Y^d. Moreover, the rise in the price level shifts the bond supply and demand curves right (the former more than the latter), so that the interest rate rises to r_1^*. This, too, helps depress the aggregate demand curve. Thus, the excess commodity demand gap is being closed in one direction by a reduction in aggregate demand and in the opposite direction by an increase in aggregate supply above Y_1^s. The rise in the price level to P_1^* reduces the real wage to $(\bar{W}/P)_1^*$, which shifts the demand for labor curve right to $N^{d'}$. Employment rises to N_2^* and output (income) rises to Y_2^{s*}. Unemployment will then amount to $N_0 - N_2^*$. In the money market, the excess demand for nominal money balances brought about by the rise in prices is eliminated by a fall in real income, a rise in the interest rate, and a fall in real wealth; see the curve labeled $M^{d'}$ in Figure 6(e). The overall outcome is summarized in Table 3.

Both consumption and investment must have decreased because real income and real wealth have decreased while the interest rate has increased. Since investment has decreased, saving must also have decreased. Real money (and, therefore, real wealth) has decreased because the nominal supply of money is constant while the price level has risen. We do not know what has happened to money income because real income is down and the price level is up. Furthermore, we cannot determine what has happened to labor's share, others' share, or real bonds for the now familiar reason that we do not know in which direction the numerators of these ratios have moved.

It is apparent that we have experienced an unholy mixture of deflation and inflation. Employment, output, income, consumption, and investment are all down (deflationary manifestations), but commodity and labor prices have both increased (inflationary phenomena).

Now the Employment Act of 1946 states that "it is the continuing policy and responsibility of the Federal Government to use all practicable means . . . to promote maximum employment."[1] How might the government meet this obligation? One solution would be to pursue an easy money policy. That is, it could increase the supply of money. If it did so, the analysis, starting from the final equilibrium position of Figure 6, would then follow exactly the analysis we just discussed in §3. You will recall that in effect the increase in the money supply increases prices further above P_1^*. This lowers the real wage which increases employment and output. The increased output will be demanded because of the increase in income and wealth and the reduction in interest rates. Full employment can be reestablished in this manner. The cost, however, is more inflation. The price level must be raised enough to lower the real wage to a level where all who want a job can find one. Many economists feel that this is *the* dilemma of modern industrial societies. Labor is well organized and full employment puts it in a position to demand higher nominal money wages. The government then experiences the pressure of the unemployment that emerges; it feels obliged to do something about the situation and what it does is to inflate its way out of the problem.

[1] Employment Act of 1946, section 2.

TABLE 3 The Effect of a Collectively Bargained Increase in the Money Wage

VARIABLE	INITIAL VALUE	FINAL VALUE	OUTCOME
Employment N	N^*	N_2^*	Decreased
Real income Y^s	Y^{s*}	Y_2^{s*}	Decreased
Real consumption C	C^*	C_1^*	Decreased
Real investment I	I^*	I_1^*	Decreased
Real saving S	S^*	S_1^*	Decreased
Real bonds B/rP	B^*/r^*P^*	$B_1^*/r_1^*P_1^*$	Not known
Real money M^d/P	M^d/P_2^*	M^d/P_1^*	Decreased
Price level P	P^*	P_1^*	Increased
Nominal wage W	$\bar{W}$	$\bar{\bar{W}}$	Increased
Real wage W/P	$(\bar{W}/P)^*$	$(\bar{\bar{W}}/P)_1^*$	Increased
Interest rate r	r^*	r_1^*	Increased
Capital stock $\bar{K}$	$\bar{K}$	$\bar{K}$	No change
Money supply $\bar{M}^s$	$\bar{M}^s$	$\bar{M}^s$	No change
Money income Y_m^s	Y_m^{s*}	$Y_{m_1}^{s*}$	Not known
Real wealth V/P	$(V/P)^*$	$(V/P)_1^*$	Decreased
Labor's share $N(W/P)/Y^s$	$N^*(\bar{W}/P)^*/Y^{s*}$	$N_2^*(\bar{\bar{W}}/P)_1^*/Y_2^{s*}$	Not known
Others' share $(B/P)/Y^s$	$(B/P)^*/Y^s$	$(B/P)_1^*/Y_2^{s*}$	Not known

In this case, the government is said to *validate* the cost-push inflation. It is crucial to note that the collectively bargained increase in money wages pushes the price level up from P^* to P_1^*. If the government sat on its hands (ignored the injunctions of the 1946 Employment Act) that would be the end of the matter. Prices would *not* continue to rise. There would be a one-shot rise in the price level (and permanent involuntary unemployment equal to $N_0 - N_2^*$). *By itself*, collective bargaining would not lead to continuously rising prices. If the union raised nominal wages above $\bar{W}$ to, say, $\bar{\bar{W}}$ there would be another increase in the price level. However, there would also be more unemployment and, sooner or later, the union membership would not tolerate any further wage claims by the leaders. If the leaders persisted, workers would leave the union. Because workers would rather work at a wage rate below $\overline{\overline{\overline{W}}}$ than be unemployed, there is some ceiling on the money wage unions can impose and, therefore, also on the rise in prices they can inflict.

A *continuous* rise in the price level results because government undoes the work of the unions by raising the price level further (through an easy money or fiscal policy) which leads to a reduction in the real wage and the reemergence of full employment. The union is back at where it started from. The real wage is back to its original level. What do the unions do? The answer usually is they submit another wage claim. Prices rise, employment falls, the government inflates, the real wage falls, employment rises again, unions submit another wage claim, and so on. This is what makes cost-push inflation a *continuous* process—it is the interaction of collective bargaining and government actions to undo the effects of such bargaining. We cannot emphasize too strongly that collective bargaining *by itself* will not generate *continuously* rising prices.

Whether it is good or bad to validate a cost-push inflation depends on the burden of unemployment as opposed to the burden of inflation. Unemployment means that the actual output produced is below the economy's potential production. We actually forego real income. If an inflationary solution to the unemployment problem is adopted, output is raised back to its maximum potential. We do not forego real income. However, *if the inflation is unanticipated,* there will be a redistribution of the available income—away from creditors, since the real value of their assets and their interest receipts will decline, and in favor of debtors, since the real value of their debts and interest payments will decline. If you believe that the cost of income redistribution is less than the loss of real income, you would urge governments to validate cost-push originated inflations; on the other hand, if you feel that the income redistribution cost is more burdensome than the loss of real income, you would urge governments not to validate cost-push originated inflations.

At a different level, one might argue why not do something about the cost-push itself. One suggestion might be to constrain the employees' power of collective bargaining. That, however, takes us outside the field of macroeconomics and is too wide and controversial a topic to be dealt with here.

5 Cost-Push Inflation II; A Collectively Bargained Real Wage

We have just seen in the above discussion that collectively bargaining for a money wage may be a thankless task. You cannot secure a permanent increase in real wages. Your best hope is that the inflationary process instituted by the government to combat the effects of collective bargaining is unanticipated, so the redistribution of income and wealth resulting from the inflation is in favor of your members. Do union leaders have an alternative? Let us consider the so-called escalator clause.

As part of the collective bargaining agreement, unions can include an *escalator clause,* which ties the money wage rate to the price level. When

FIGURE 7

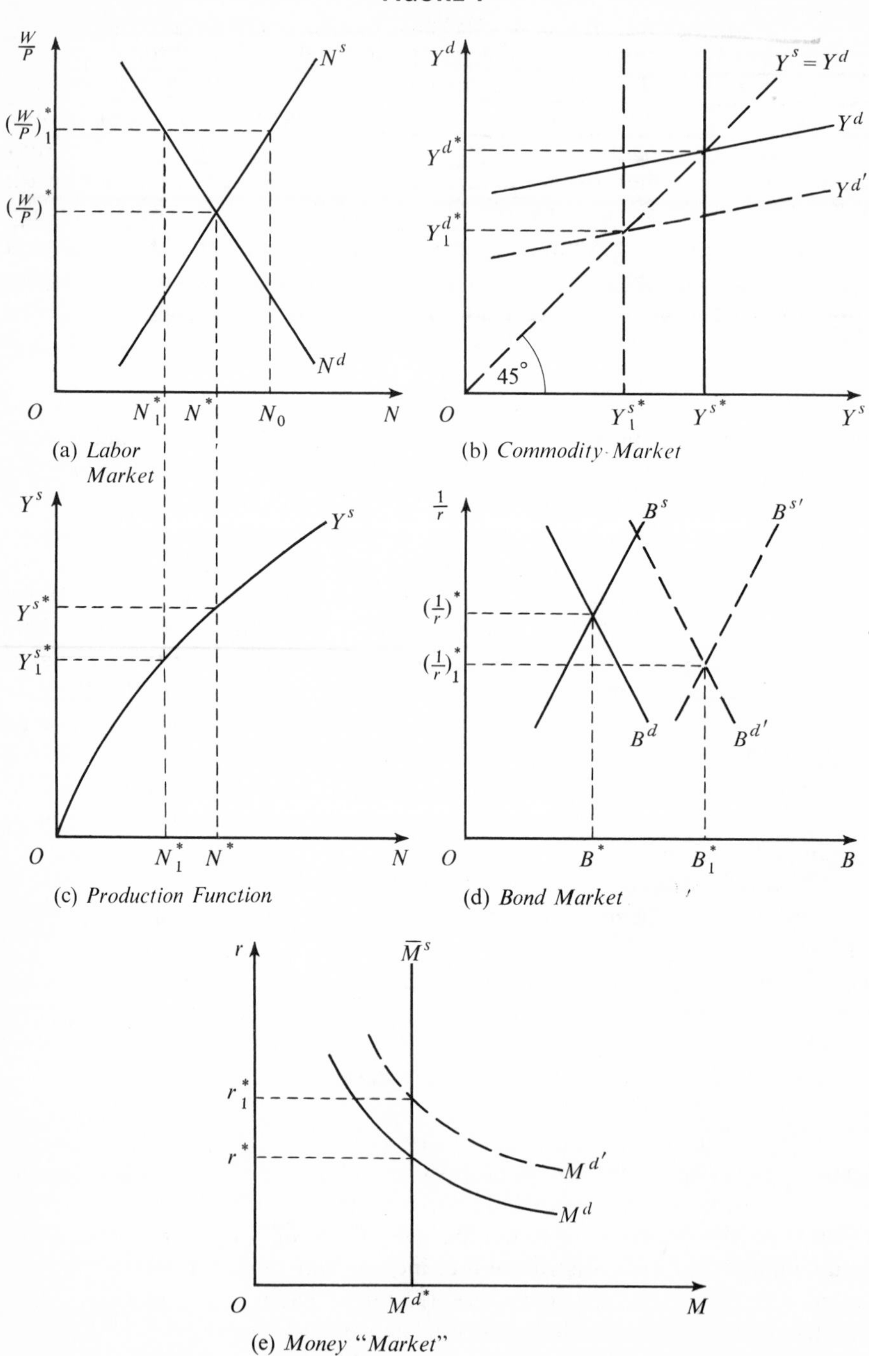

(a) *Labor Market*

(b) *Commodity Market*

(c) *Production Function*

(d) *Bond Market*

(e) *Money "Market"*

prices rise, so does the money wage rate. (The reverse is not usually true.) Effectively, then, the union is able to bargain for a certain real wage because if the price level rises, the money wage rises in tandem and, hence, the real wage remains unchanged. How does this affect things?

Start with the model in equilibrium as shown by the solid curves in Figure 7 (where, note, we have reintroduced the labor market with the supply and demand curves in terms of the real wage). By exploiting the escalator clause in the contract, the union now collectively bargains for the real wage $(W/P)_1^*$. Employment falls to N_1^* and real income falls to Y_1^{s*}. Excess demand prevails in the commodity market, so prices rise to P_1^*. This shifts the supply and demand curves for bonds to the right (the former more rapidly than the latter), so that the interest rate rises to r_1^*. This rise in the interest

TABLE 4 The Effect of a Collectively Bargained Increase in the Real Wage via an Escalator Clause

VARIABLE	INITIAL VALUE	FINAL VALUE	OUTCOME
Employment N	N^*	N_1^*	Decreased
Real income Y^s	Y^{s*}	Y_1^{s*}	Decreased
Real consumption C	C^*	C_1^*	Decreased
Real investment I	I^*	I_1^*	Decreased
Real saving S	S^*	S_1^*	Decreased
Real bonds B/rP	B^*/r^*P^*	$B_1^*/r_1^*P_1^*$	Not known
Real money M^d/P	M^d/P^*	M^d/P_1^*	Decreased
Price level P	P^*	P_1^*	Increased
Nominal wage W	W^*	W_1^*	Increased
Real wage W/P	$(W/P)^*$	$(W/P)_1^*$	Increased
Interest rate r	r^*	r_1^*	Increased
Capital stock $\bar{K}$	$\bar{K}$	$\bar{K}$	No change
Money supply $\bar{M}^s$	$\bar{M}^s$	$\bar{M}^s$	No change
Money income Y_m^s	Y_m^{s*}	Y_m^{s*}	Not known
Real wealth V/P	$(V/P)^*$	$(V/P)_1^*$	Decreased
Labor's share $N(W/P)/Y^s$	$N^*(W/P)^*/Y^{s*}$	$N_1^*(W/P)_1^*/Y_1^{s*}$	Not known
Others' share $(B/P)/Y^s$	$(B/P)^*/Y^{s*}$	$(B/P)_1^*/Y_1^{s*}$	Not known

rate plus the reduction in real wealth brought about by the rise in prices lower Y^d to $Y^{d'}$, where commodity market equilibrium prevails once again. The rise in prices also shifts the demand for nominal money curve to $M^{d'}$. The excess demand in this market is removed by the rise in interest rates, fall in real income, and fall in the real wealth already discussed. The extent of unemployment is $N_0 - N_1^*$, which represents the people clamoring for jobs at $(W/P)_1^*$, but unable to find them. The overall outcome is summarized in Table 4. You should by now be able to supply the reasons why an increase, decrease, no change, or unknown change has occurred in the equilibrium values of the variables.

In this situation, the government is powerless to use its *macroeconomic* policy tools (monetary or fiscal) to implement its mandate under the Employment Act of 1946 "to promote maximum employment." The government can only increase employment to the old level N^* by lowering the real wage to $(W/P)^*$ again. But if it attempts to do this by raising the price level through, for example, increasing the money supply it will be unsuccessful. The escalator clause guarantees that as prices rise, money wages also rise; thus, the real wage and employment will remain unchanged. In fact, if the government is foolish enough to attempt a macroeconomic solution it will only make the situation even more dire for the $N_0 - N_1^*$ unemployed workers. Not only will they fail to become employed but the real value of any unemployment compensation they are receiving (which in the real world is normally fixed in *nominal* amount whether it comes from the government or their union) will be debased. An attempted macroeconomic solution to this problem will give inflation without reducing unemployment.

Clearly, if this problem is going to be tackled at all, microeconomic policy tools must be used. We must resort to tactics such as retraining, relocation, putting more people on the government payroll, and so on.

Summary

In Part II we operated our model using the full set of neoclassical assumptions (except that, in Chapter 9, we did allow money illusion to creep into the real supply of bonds function). This chapter begins Part III, where we shall work with the model in a neo-Keynesian context. What we do is relax one or more of the neoclassical assumptions; for example, we introduce price expectations that are not unit-elastic, price rigidities, money illusion, and distribution effects. These modifications will usually be inserted one at a time and *not* simultaneously.

As our first step, we introduced *money illusion* into the labor supply function by making the supply of labor depend on the *nominal* wage instead of the *real* wage. We found that although full employment will always still prevail in equilibrium as long as money wages are flexible, the actual level of employment is no longer strictly determinate in the sense that *any* disturbance to the model (such as a change in the money supply or government expenditure, or taxes or entrepreneurial expectations or attitudes towards thrift) will change the equilibrium level of employment.

Next, we combined money illusion in the labor supply function with downward *wage rigidity*. With these specifications, it turns out that *any* deflationary impulse not only reduces the level of employment but also leads to persistent *unemployment*. (As we proceed through the rest of this book it will become apparent that rigidity in *any* of the three prices—the price of labor *or* commodities *or* bonds—is *necessary and sufficient* to create persistent unemployment in the presence of a deflationary impulse. In fact, rigidity in one of these prices is the *only* thing that can lead to persistent unemployment in the presence of such an impulse.)

If unemployment does exist, it can, generally, be removed through either an antideflationary monetary policy or fiscal policy. The key is to create excess demand in the commodity market, which, by raising the price level and reducing the real wage, will create an increase in the demand for labor.

We then discussed the problem of cost-push inflation in two different situations. First, we examined what happens when organized labor bargains for a certain money wage increase. We found that collective bargaining increases unemployment and raises the *level* of prices. However, it does *not* lead to *continuously rising prices* (inflation) unless the government "validates" the cost-push by pursuing an easy money or fiscal policy to remove the unemployment caused by the rise in wages. Second, we looked at the cost-push inflation problem when labor collectively bargains effectively for a real wage. The result is again a rise in the level of unemployment and prices (rather than a *persistent* rise in prices). In this case, however, the government is powerless to remove the unemployment through a macroeconomic policy. Any attempt to do so using either fiscal or monetary means will not end unemployment and will lead to further increases in the price level.

Questions

1. Assume money illusion exists in the labor supply function but that the nominal wage is flexible. Show that a decrease in government expenditure will reduce the level of employment without creating unemployment.
2. Assume money illusion exists in the labor supply function and that the nominal wage rate is rigid downwards. Show that *any* deflationary impulse (select from a decrease in the supply of money, a decrease in government expenditure, an increase in tax rates, an increase in thrift, and so on) will lead to a reduction in the level of employment and persistent unemployment.
3. Assume unemployment in an initial equilibrium position due to money illusion in the labor supply function and downward money wage rigidity. Devise a *fiscal policy* to remove this unemployment and explain how your model works.
4. Assume an initial equilibrium position. What is the effect on the endogenous variables of a collectively bargained increase in money wages? Devise a *fiscal*

policy to remove the unemployment explaining how it does so and what its effects are on the endogenous variables.

5. Assume that organized labor successfully bargains collectively for an increase in *real* wages. Explain why it might be inadvisable for the government to pursue its obligation "to promote maximum employment" through *macroeconomic* (monetary or fiscal) policy. What alternative (microeconomic) policy might the government consider to eliminate the resultant unemployment?
6. Assume that organized labor bargains collectively for increased *money* wages. If the government does nothing, do you think this will lead to continuously rising prices? If so, why? If not, why not?

SELECTED READINGS

1. M. Bronfenbrenner and F. D. Holzman, "Survey of Inflation Theory," *American Economic Review,* September, 1963. Contains extensive references to the literature on the theory of inflation.
2. D. C. Hague (ed.), *Inflation,* St. Martin's, 1962.
3. H. G. Johnson, "The General Theory after Twenty-five Years," *American Economic Review, Proceedings,* May, 1961.
4. J. M. Keynes, *The General Theory of Employment, Interest, and Money,* Macmillan, 1936, chapters 2, 19, and 20.
5. D. Patinkin, *Money, Interest, and Prices,* 2nd ed., Harper & Row, chapter 12, sections 1–4.
6. A. C. Pigou, *Theory of Unemployment,* A. M. Kelley, 1968 (reprint of 1933 ed.).
7. W. L. Smith, "A Graphical Exposition of the Complete Keynesian System," *Southern Economic Journal,* October, 1956.
8. W. Thorp and R. Quandt, *The New Inflation,* McGraw-Hill, 1959. By "new" the authors mean "cost-push."
9. J. Tobin, "Money Wage Rates and Employment," in S. E. Harris (ed.), *The New Economics,* Knopf, 1947.

FURTHER READINGS

10. J. Duesenberry, "Mechanics of Inflation," *Review of Economics and Statistics,* May, 1950.
11. W. Fellner, "Demand Inflation, Cost Inflation, and Collective Bargaining," in P. Bradley (ed.), *The Public Stake in Union Power,* University Press of Virginia, 1959.
12. A. P. Lerner, "The Inflationary Process—Some Theoretical Aspects," *Review of Economics and Statistics,* August, 1949.
13. F. Machlup, "Another View of Cost-Push and Demand-Pull Inflation," *Review of Economics and Statistics,* May, 1960.
14. J. D. Pitchford, "Cost and Demand Elements in the Inflationary Process," *Review of Economics Studies,* February, 1957.
15. C. Schultze, "Study Paper Number 1," in Joint Economic Committee, *Recent Inflation in the United States,* Washington, 1959.
16. R. T. Selden, "Cost-Push versus Demand-Pull Inflation," *Journal of Political Economy,* February, 1959.
17. C. G. F. Simkin, "Notes on the Theory of Inflation," *Review of Economic Studies,* no. 52, 1952–1953.

11

Complications in the Commodity Market; Rigidities, Illusions, and Inelasticities

In Chapter 10 we discovered that permanent unemployment can emerge when appropriate money illusions and rigidities are incorporated in the labor market of our macroeconomic model. In this chapter we will find that similar problems arise when analogous characteristics are injected into the commodity market. In addition, the situation may be complicated by crippling inelasticities in the relevant components of the commodity demand function.

We shall now make an interesting generalization about the adjustment process assumed by neoclassical macroeconomists and contrast it with the adjustment process assumed by neo-Keynesian macroeconomists. Neoclassical macroeconomists are essentially *price-adjusters*. When equilibrium is disturbed, it is reestablished by *price changes* in all three variables (commodities, labor, and bonds). In contrast, neo-Keynesian macroeconomists are essentially *quantity-adjusters*. When equilibrium is disturbed, it is reestablished, wholly or in part, by *quantity adjustments*. One, or more, of the three price variables is assumed to be inflexible, and, as a result, macroeconomic equilibrium is regained only partially through price adjustments of the flexible variables and partially through changes in the *quantities* of the goods traded (commodities, labor, real bonds, and real money). In §10.2 we saw how the assumption of wage inflexibility implied quantity adjustments in all four markets if equilibrium were to be reestablished in them after some initial disturbance. Here we shall assume commodity price inflexibility and find that the results are analogous; that is, equilibrium can only be reestablished with different quantities of commodities, labor, real bonds, and real money traded and held in the respective markets.

1 Commodity Prices Inflexible Downwards I

Downward inflexibility in commodity prices is to the commodity market what downward inflexibility in wages is to the labor market. Just as workers may be reluctant to accept wage cuts in a deflationary situation, firms may be loathe to reduce prices. In effect, the price level has become an exogenous variable $\bar{P}$. Firms would rather sell a lower output at the same price level than the same output at a lower price level. This is very similar to the workers' willingness to sell less labor services at the going wage rather than sell the same quantity of labor services at a lower wage (the situation discussed in §10.2). What happens when entrepreneurs react in this manner? Consider Figure 1.

Assume that there is an increase in thrift. The implied decrease in consumption will, by itself, reduce aggregate demand. However, the increase in thrift also implies an increase in the demand for bonds to $B^{d'}$. (The additional saving finds its way into bonds, we assume, not money or "hoarding.") Thus, the interest rate falls to r_1^*, raising investment and also raising consumption somewhat above the new, low level the community planned on when it decided to be more thrifty. Aggregate demand falls to $Y^{d'}$ as a result of the joint impact of the increase in thrift *and* the fall in the interest rate. A deflationary gap appears in the commodity market—excess commodity supply equal to *ab* exists. In previous situations we relied on this excess supply of commodities to lower the price level. A lowered price level then increases real wealth and decreases the interest rate further, so that the aggregate demand curve eventually rises to cross the 45°-line at *a* and to eliminate the deflationary gap. Now, however, firms do not reduce prices when faced with an excess supply of commodities. Thus, no increase in the community's real wealth or further reduction in the rate of interest is forthcoming. Consequently, the aggregate demand curve stays where it is at $Y^{d'}$.

This is not the end of the matter, though. If firms continued to produce Y^{s*}, which implies employment N^*, they would soon be buried in inventories of unsold commodities. At the prevailing price level, which firms refuse to cut, the community would no longer buy Y^{s*} commodities. If firms will not cut prices in order to move their output and they do not want their inventories to mount up, they must reduce their output to a level which *can* be sold at the going interest rate and real wealth level. This level is Y_1^{s*}.

However, to produce Y_1^{s*}, only N_1^* labor is required. Therefore, firms must cut back employment to that level. Let us assume that wages are inflexible downward, too. This may arise either from reluctance on the part of workers or their unions to accept money wage cuts or from an attack of conscience by firms. Given that they are resisting commodity price reductions, firms may not wish to assume the mantle of ogre by imposing money wage cuts on their work force in the face of an excess supply of labor. If both prices and money wages are fixed at the going levels, the real wage remains constant at $(\bar{W}/\bar{P})$. But now because firms only want to employ N_1^* labor to produce the Y_1^{s*} output that they can sell, their demand curve for labor must shift back to $N^{d'}$, where it goes through point *c* in Figure 1(a). This is a peculiar sort of demand curve. Normally, at the real wage $(\bar{W}/\bar{P})$ firms would employ N^* and produce Y^{s*}. However, since they insist on

FIGURE 1

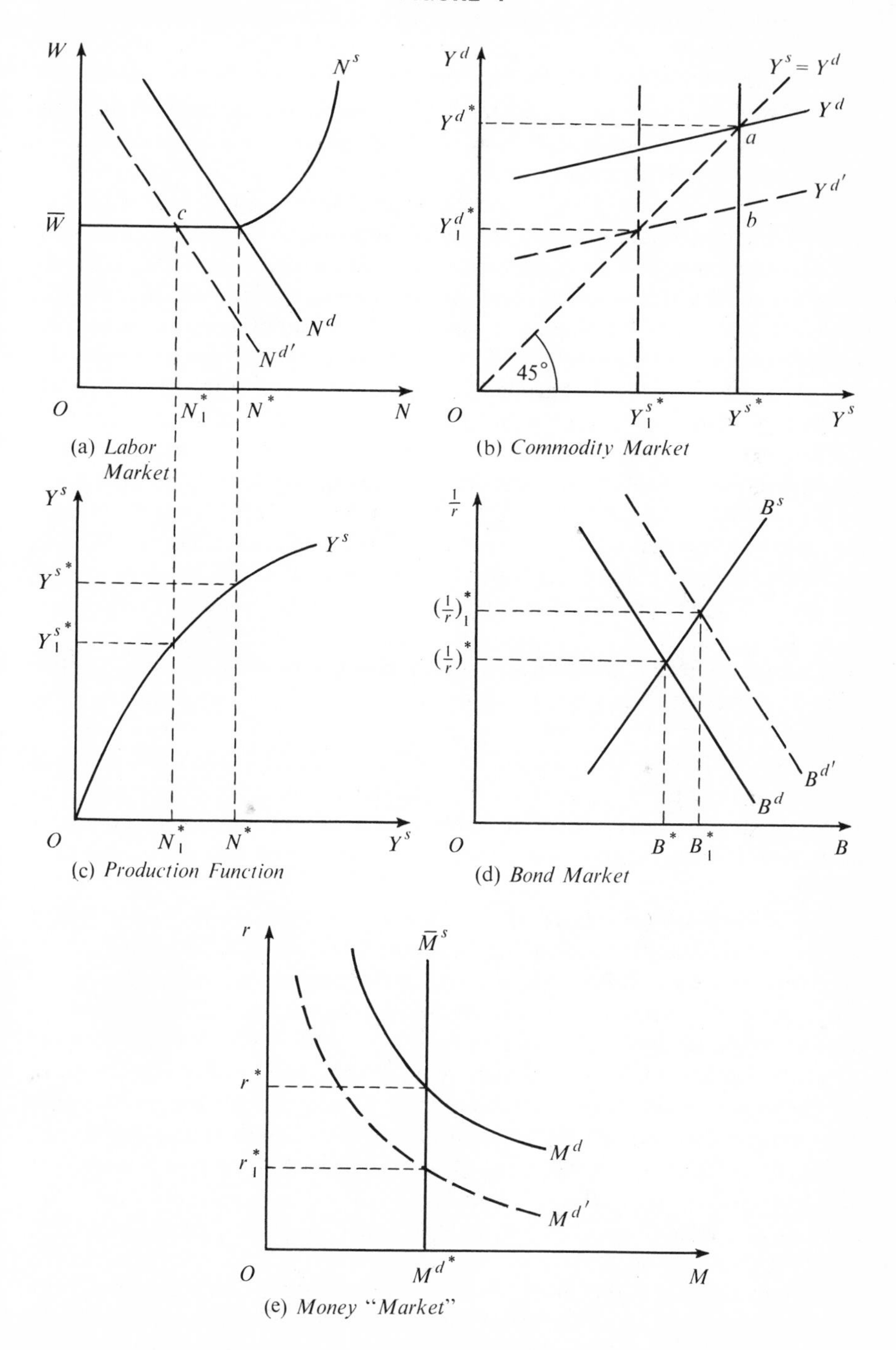

(a) *Labor Market*

(b) *Commodity Market*

(c) *Production Function*

(d) *Bond Market*

(e) *Money "Market"*

maintaining prices at $\bar{P}$ they cannot sell such a high output in the face of the decreased demand. Firms' "irrational" behavior in the face of excess commodity supplies (reducing output rather than prices) forces them to behave "irrationally" in the labor market. The firms move off their true, permanent demand for labor curve N^d onto the ersatz, transitional demand curve $N^{d'}$. $N^{d'}$ is a money illusion–type demand curve for labor imposed on firms by their money illusion–dominated behavior in the commodity market. This is such a mongrel demand curve that we are reluctant to describe it as a curve at all. It probably only amounts to the point *c*. Be that as it may, permanent unemployment equal to $N^* - N_1^*$ appears.

In the money market, the decrease in real income to Y_1^{s*} shifts the demand for money curve to $M^{d'}$. The nominal quantity of money demanded is made equal again to the fixed nominal supply of money by a decline in the interest rate.

The results of this experiment are summarized in Table 1. A few remarks are appropriate here. Aggregate commodity demand has unambiguously decreased, since aggregate commodity supply has decreased. Thus, the *sum* of consumption and investment must have decreased. But, technically, we do not know for *sure* that either has declined. The problem is this. Income is down and thrift is up (recall that the latter changes the form of the consumption function). Both tend to lower consumption. However, the interest rate is down and that tends to raise consumption. Real balances are unchanged. If, as we expect, the thrift increase and income decrease dominate the interest rate's effect on consumption, consumption will decline overall. Hence, we have put a "decreased" with a question mark in Table 1 for consumption. The same problem arises with investment. Income is down, which lowers investment, but the interest rate is also down, which raises investment. However, we expect the former effect to dominate. Thus, again, we insert a "decreased" in Table 1 for investment, but with a question mark, too. If investment has decreased (with a question mark), so must have saving.

In Figure 1(d) we have shown that there has been an unambiguous *increase* in real bonds outstanding. The number of bonds held has increased, the interest rate has fallen, and the price level remains constant. However, this description is misleading. Income has fallen, which, we *always* assume, decreases the demand for and supply of bonds equally and, thus, does not affect the interest rate. But it clearly reduces the number of bonds outstanding and it is *this* effect that is not shown in Figure 1(d). If this reduction is greater than the increase in demand for bonds caused by the original increase in thrift, then the number of bonds held will decline; and we do not know what has happened to real bonds held, since both B, in the numerator, and r, in the denominator, are down. We admit our ignorance in Table 1 by inserting "not known."

When operating the model in the present context, we take the commodity price level to be an exogenous variable fixed at $\bar{P}$. Since W is also fixed at $\bar{W}$, the real wage is constant at $\bar{W}/\bar{P}$. Money income is down because

TABLE 1 The Effect of Thrift when Prices (and Wages) are Inflexible Downwards

VARIABLE	INITIAL VALUE	FINAL VALUE	OUTCOME
Employment N	N^*	N_1^*	Decreased
Real income Y^s	Y^{s*}	Y_1^{s*}	Decreased
Real consumption C	C^*	C_1^*	Decreased (?)
Real investment I	I^*	I_1^*	Decreased (?)
Real saving S	S^*	S_1^*	Decreased (?)
Real bonds B/rP	$B^*/r^*\bar{P}$	$B_1^*/r_1^*\bar{P}$	Not known
Real money M^d/P	$M^{d*}/\bar{P}$	$M^{d*}/\bar{P}$	No change
Price level P	$\bar{P}$	$\bar{P}$	No change
Nominal wage W	$\bar{W}$	$\bar{W}$	No change
Real wage W/P	$\bar{W}/\bar{P}$	$\bar{W}/\bar{P}$	No change
Interest rate r	r^*	r_1^*	Decreased
Capital stock $\bar{K}$	$\bar{K}$	$\bar{K}$	No change
Money supply $\bar{M}^s$	$\bar{M}^s$	$\bar{M}^s$	No change
Money income Y_m^s	Y_m^{s*}	$Y_{m_1}^{s*}$	Decreased
Real wealth V/P	$V/\bar{P}$	$V/\bar{P}$	No change
Labor's share $N(W/P)/Y^s$	$N^*(\bar{W}/\bar{P})/Y^{s*}$	$N_1^*(\bar{W}/\bar{P})/Y_1^{s*}$	Not known
Others' share $(B/P)/Y^s$	$(B^*/\bar{P})/Y^{s*}$	$(B_1^*/\bar{P})/Y_1^{s*}$	Not known

the price level is constant and real income has declined. With respect to shares of income, we are also uncertain. Both the numerator and denominator of labor's share is down and, from what we said in the previous paragraph, we do not know which way the numerator of the others' share has gone.

2 Commodity Prices Inflexible Downwards II

In §1 we assumed that commodity prices were inflexible downwards through entrepreneurs' irrational reluctance to lower them. Businessmen were either stupid, disagreeable, or both. Can such downward inflexibility be accounted for more reasonably by an explanation which is more firmly grounded in received economic theory? Consider the following rationale in which downward inflexibility of the commodity price level reflects *rational* entrepreneurial behavior.

Assume that the production function exhibits constant returns to scale (at least over a large range of outputs). This implies that there is no diminishing marginal physical product of labor; output is always proportional to labor input. Therefore, we are giving up our assumption of diminishing returns. Some crucial geometric implications emerge from this. The production function now appears as in Figure 2. Up to N_0, output is proportional to labor input as revealed by the fact that the production function is a straight line going through the origin.

Since we know that the slope of the production function is equal to the marginal physical product of labor, the constant slope of this function up to N_0 reflects a constant marginal physical product of labor up to that point. Diminishing returns do not set in until we go beyond N_0. Since we know that labor's demand curve is identical to its marginal physical product curve, we obtain the peculiar demand curve for labor illustrated in Figure 3. It is a horizontal straight line up to N_0 at a level equal to the marginal physical product of labor.

It will be convenient to discuss the labor market demand curve in terms of the money wage, so in Figure 4(a) we have redrawn the curve with the money wage plotted on the vertical axis. This curve is drawn on the assumption of a *given* price level. If the price level should rise (real wages fall), the curve would shift up, and vice versa.

With this groundwork, we are now in a position to see what these modifications imply for the macroeconomic model as a whole. Consult Figure 4. We have included in Figure 4(a) a money illusion–type supply curve of labor. The supply of labor is perfectly elastic up to N_0 at the going money wage. This supply curve, then, overlays exactly the demand curve up to N_0. The money wage is assumed rigid downwards.

FIGURE 2

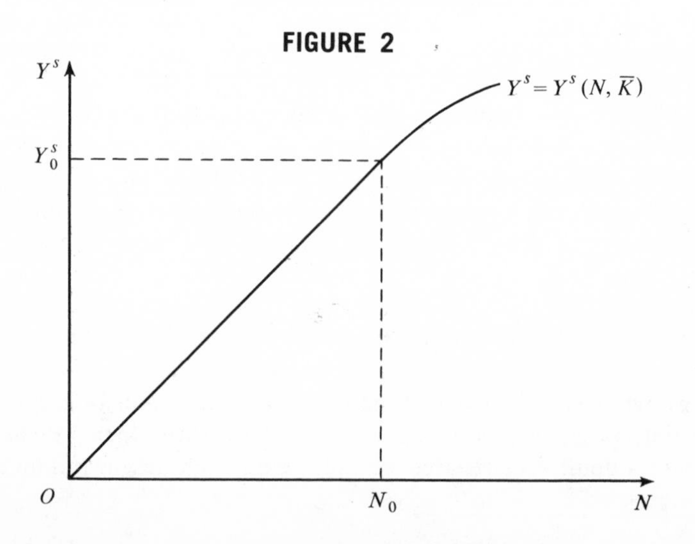

FIGURE 3

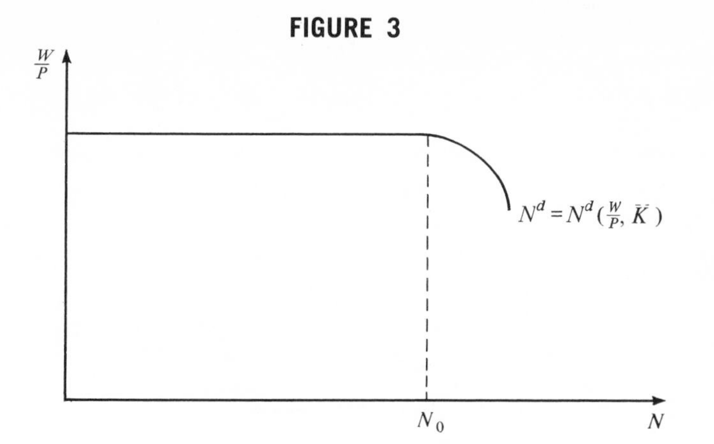

It is quite obvious that the labor market is not going to generate a unique level of output (real income) as it does when diminishing returns prevail. You will recall from Chapter 2 that a firm maximizes its profits by hiring labor until the marginal physical product of labor is equal to the real wage. However, in this case there is no *unique* level of employment at which this equality occurs. The marginal physical product of labor is equal to the real wage at *all* levels of employment (up to N_0). As there is no unique profit-maximizing level of employment for firms, there is, analogously, no unique profit-maximizing level of output. Profits are maximized at *any* level of output between 0 and Y_0^s. (The reader interested in the microsituation of individual firms should conceive of total revenue and total cost functions for output which overlay each other exactly up to each firm's share of Y_0^s. Total revenue is proportional to output because of perfect competition in the product market; total cost is proportional to output because there is no diminishing return.)

The causality of our model is reversed. Up to Y_0^s, output will be determined by aggregate commodity demand (Y_0^s is an upper limit to output because all firms incur losses at a higher output). To begin, let us assume that demand has settled down to Y^d. Thus $Y_0^s = Y^{s*}$ output and $N_0 = N^*$ labor are demanded. Notice how demand determines output which determines employment.

Now let there be an increase in thrift. Demand falls to $Y^{d'}$, and this level prevails after the increase in thrift has had its *direct* impact in the commodity market *and* after the interest rate has fallen to r_1^* because of the increased demand for bonds $B^{d'}$ (a result of increased thrift). This effect has been detailed in §1. A deflationary gap equal to *ab* emerges in the commodity market. In the previous section only the irrationality of entrepreneurs prevented them from lowering prices in the face of this excess supply. However, now the smart, rational thing to do is hold the price line. If they were to lower prices with the money wage fixed at $\bar{W}$, the real wage of labor would rise above its marginal physical product for *any* level of employment. The profit-maximizing levels of employment and output would be *no* employ-

FIGURE 4

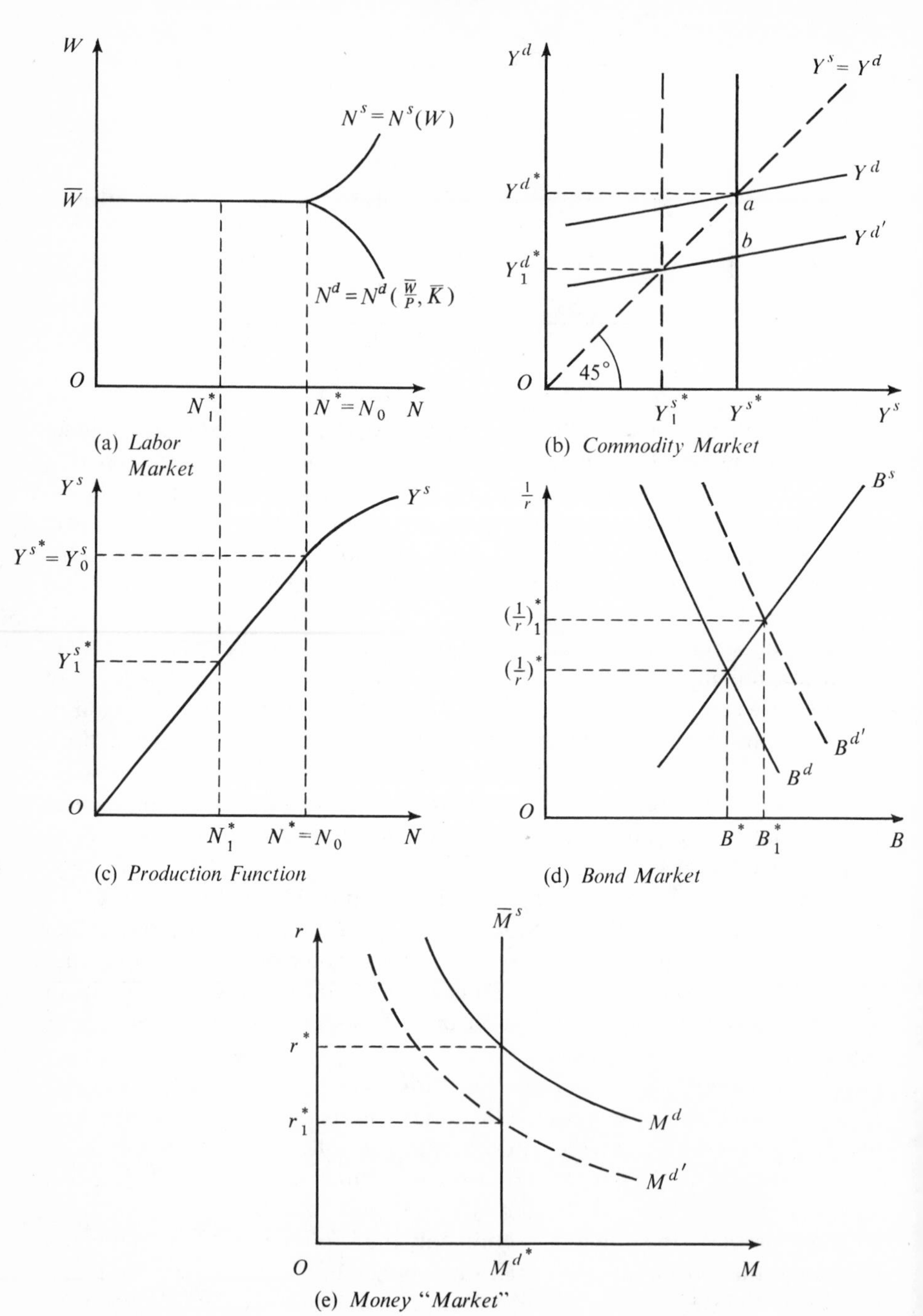

W
$\overline{W}$
O
$N^s = N^s(W)$
$N^d = N^d(\frac{\overline{W}}{P}, \overline{K})$
N_1^*
$N^* = N_0$
N
(a) Labor Market
Y^d
$Y^s = Y^d$
Y^{d*}
Y_1^{d*}
Y^d
$Y^{d'}$
a
b
45°
O
Y_1^{s*}
Y^{s*}
Y^s
(b) Commodity Market
Y^s
$Y^{s*} = Y_0^s$
Y_1^{s*}
O
N_1^*
$N^* = N_0$
N
(c) Production Function
$\frac{1}{r}$
$(\frac{1}{r})_1^*$
$(\frac{1}{r})^*$
B^s
$B^{d'}$
B^d
O
B^*
B_1^*
B
(d) Bond Market
$\overline{M}^s$
r
r^*
r_1^*
M^d
$M^{d'}$
O
M^{d*}
M
(e) Money "Market"

ment or output. However, if entrepreneurs keep prices constant, the real wage remains constant and they maximize their profits by selling whatever output is demanded. This action is clearly rational—it is the profit-maximizing decision to keep present prices constant. As only Y_1^{s*} output is now demanded, only N_1^* employment will be offered by firms. Unemployment equal to $N^* - N_1^*$ is created, and it does not disappear. This permanent unemployment is basically due to the fact that with rigid prices real wealth will not increase nor will the interest rate decline below r_1^* to raise aggregate demand above $Y^{d'}$. Notice that we are still on the demand for labor curve.

The outcome here is exactly the same as in §1 (including the outcome in the money market which we have not bothered to discuss again). This time we have, however, been able to reach these conclusions with an analysis somewhat more firmly grounded in received economic theory. In particular, we did not have to resort to "off-curve" analysis and assume irrational entrepreneurial behavior. However, we did have to forego the assumption of diminishing returns.

The overall outcome for all the variables in the present case is exactly the same as before and, therefore, is also summarized by Table 1. The reasons advanced in §1 for the direction of the changes in the variables apply equally here.

The unemployment $N^* - N_1^*$ which exists is permanent because the real balance increase and the decrease in interest rate necessary to raise the aggregate demand curve up from Y^{d*} to Y^d again are not forthcoming automatically. The fixed price level sees to that. A way out is clearly indicated—create the real balances and decrease in the interest rate as a matter of policy. This can be done by increasing the supply of money. A sufficiently easy monetary policy will certainly create a real balance increase and an interest rate decrease strong enough to raise $Y^{d'}$ back to Y^d. That rise will increase output to Y^{s*} again, raise employment to N^* again, and, thus, solve the problem.

The reader may, with a certain amount of justification, still be dissatisfied with the explanations of price inflexibility offered in this section and the preceeding one. These explanations do, after all, either assume entrepreneurial irrationality or require us *not* to assume diminishing returns, which is a serious step. However, in Chapter 16 we return to the problem of wage-price inflexibility. There the inflexibility is assumed to result from *inelastic wage and price expectations* (based on lack of perfect information). The reader may find that analysis more palatable (realistic).

3 Secular Stagnation

After the appearance of the *General Theory* it was commonly held that the level of investment forthcoming at full employment income would not be large enough to absorb the saving planned at that level of income.

There would be, it was argued, a chronic deflationary gap in the commodity market. Consider Figure 5.

The level of output (income) at full employment is, we assume, Y_0^s. However, at this level of income, planned investment would be only I_0, although the level of saving planned would be S_0. Clearly, there would be a painful excess of planned saving over planned investment. In other words, a chronic state of excess supply equal to *ab* would appear in the commodity market. This deficiency of commodity demand was variously attributed to satiation of consumer wants (believe it or not) and, partly as a result, to the meagerness of profitable investment opportunities.

In past examples when prices were flexible (and price rigidities were *not* a crucial part of the secular stagnation argument), we relied upon the decrease in prices which resulted from the excess commodity supply to raise real wealth and lower the interest rate until aggregate demand was raised from Y^d to pass through point *a* and, thus, reestablish commodity market equilibrium. For this sequence of events *not* to occur here, a real balance effect must be clearly excluded from the commodity demand function. That is why we have purposely omitted real wealth from the aggregate demand functions in Figure 5. If this omission were not made, the secular stagnation case would fall apart right here. Remember, though, that this is not necessarily a severe limitation if the supply of money is predominantly of the inside variety, which does not generate a real balance effect. On the other hand, if government (and its attendant debt) is included in the model we unavoidably get a real financial asset effect.

Another implication of the secular stagnation hypothesis is that at full employment income the interest rate cannot fall low enough for planned investment to rise and planned saving to fall until they are equal. This occurrence would reestablish commodity market equilibrium and turn back

FIGURE 5

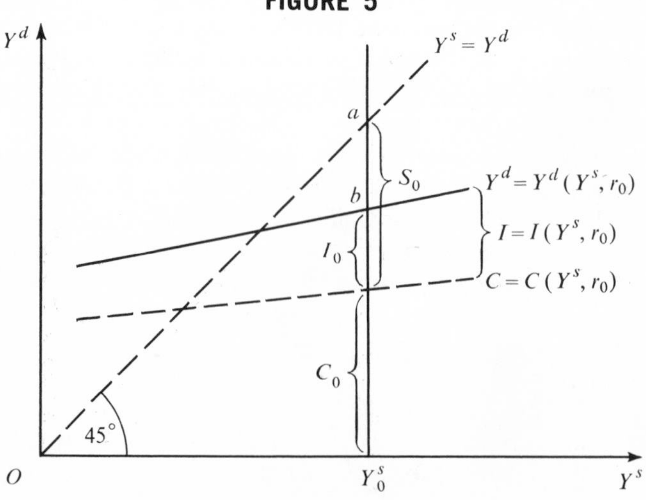

FIGURE 6

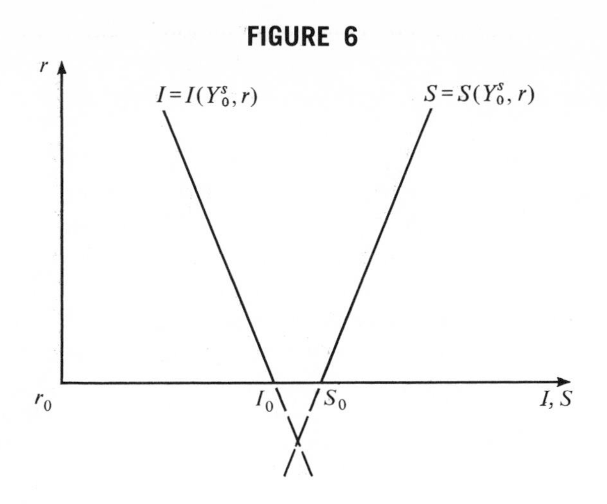

the threat of secular stagnation; so the situation illustrated in Figure 6 is asserted to prevail.

At the full employment income level Y_0^s, even if the interest rate fell to r_0 (zero), planned investment would never rise above I_0 and planned saving would never fall below S_0. Manifestly, there is no positive or zero interest rate (the only set of feasible interest rates) at which planned investment and planned saving can be equal and the commodity market, thus, clear.

Essentially, what secular stagnationists formally assert is that our macroeconomic model has *no solution*. The chronic excess supply of commodities will reduce prices, wages, and the interest rate. But even when prices, wages, and the interest rate have hit zero, excess commodity supplies will still exist at full employment. Saving and investment are insufficiently interest elastic. Basically, this is what cripples the commodity market. Again we emphasize that for this argument to stand a chance of being valid, real balances must be clearly excluded from the aggregate commodity demand function. If they were not, when prices approached zero, real wealth would be infinite—and it is implausible that with infinite wealth we would not be willing to buy everything produced.

One must admit that it is *possible* that there is no positive or zero interest rate at which planned investment equals planned saving at full employment income. Is it, however, very *probable?* M. J. Bailey has advanced arguments to indicate that it is not.[1] Bailey asserts that at very low interest rates the optimal capital stock would be enormous and, thus, we would be faced with a veritable plethora of profitable investment opportunities—far more than the minimum required to guarantee full employment. He cites the following example. Fill in the Gulf of Mexico from the Rio Grande to Miami to a distance of 50 miles seaward and top it off with dredgings from the Mississippi in order to create land with a yield at least comparable to the

[1] M. J. Bailey, *National Income and the Price Level,* McGraw-Hill, 1962, pp. 111–112, 130.

best agricultural land now available in this country. In §3.2 we saw that the price of capital services decreases when the interest rate decreases. Thus, at a low enough interest rate, an investment such as we are discussing would become profitable.

Now, what would such a project cost? Bailey calculates the cost at 450,000 dollars *per acre* at present prices. It is 1500 miles from the Rio Grande to Miami, so a 1500 × 50 mile strip is 75,000 square miles, or 48 million acres. Thus, the total cost of the project would be 21,600 *billion* dollars. But in the 1960s a mere 100 billion dollars of investment would assure full employment. (*Total* gross national product in this era averaged about 800 billion dollars.) If it is assumed that the investment necessary to provide full employment in a growing economy increases at 3.5 percent per annum, when 100 billion dollars is compounded at this rate it takes about sixty years to reach the figure of 21,600 billion dollars. That means this *one* landfill project alone would provide enough profitable investment opportunity for sixty years at an interest rate low enough to guarantee full employment. And after that, you could start work on the Atlantic coast from Miami to Boston.

Basically, Bailey's example shows that if the interest rate fell low enough, the investment schedule would become very elastic, having a shape like the curve I' shown in Figure 7. If such a curve is transplanted to Figure 6, there is clearly some positive interest rate at which planned saving will equal planned investment, even if the planned saving curve in Figure 6 is retained.

These arguments are enough, then, to indicate that at low enough interest rates planned investment will increase sufficiently to close the chronic deflationary gap secular stagnationists feared in the commodity market. There are also arguments to the effect that at a low enough (but still positive) interest rate, planned saving would become very small or even negative. Negative saving (dissaving or consuming capital) *is* a feasible value in our model. This argument proceeds as follows. Consider one of the perpetual

FIGURE 7

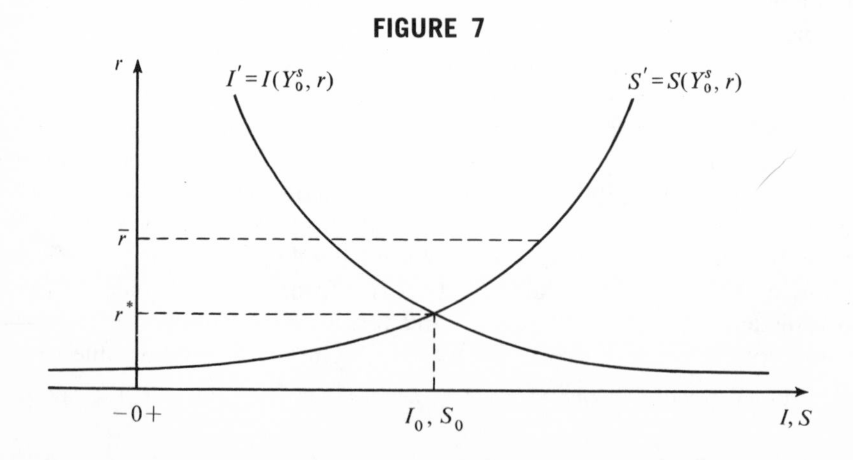

bonds in our model paying 1 dollar interest per annum. At an interest rate of 5 percent, this would be worth 20 dollars. If the interest rate fell to 1 percent, the price of bonds would rise to 100 dollars; if the interest rate fell to 0.00001 percent, bonds would be worth 10 *million* dollars each; if the interest rate fell to 0.000000000004 percent, the bonds would be worth 25 *trillion* dollars each. What does this latter figure mean? For one thing, it means that if you sold just one bond *you* could buy the complete United States gross national product for the next twenty-five years! And, note, the only cost to you, your heirs and assigns, is the annual interest payment of 1 dollar you would forego for each bond you sold. The temptation to sell some of these bonds (that is, to dissave) might prove overwhelming. Diagrammatically, what we are saying in Figure 7 is that the saving function would become very elastic, and even negative, at low but still positive interest rates such as S'. If such a curve were transplanted to Figure 6, there would clearly be some positive interest rate at which planned saving would equal planned investment, even if the investment curve in that diagram were retained. In all honesty, we should point out that the bonds we have been talking about must be government bonds undiscounted for their implied tax liability. As usual, a private bond would wash out. At very low interest rates a holder of a privately issued bond might feel very wealthy, but the issuer would feel an equally crushing burden of debt. To this extent, we have infringed on the ground rules of our model by slipping government in.

You may think we are out of the woods now, having shown that the saving and investment schedules appear like those in Figure 7, which clearly intersect at a positive interest rate. If this is true, the secular stagnation hypothesis does not seem to stand a chance even when real balances are excluded from the aggregate demand function because there is a positive interest rate at which planned saving equals planned investment at full employment income Y_0^s (namely, r^* in Figure 7). However, one problem remains. We are still in the secular stagnation bind if the interest rate will not fall to r^*. We shall discover in the next chapter, "Complications in the Bond and Money Markets," that this is a distinct possibility. There may be a floor to the interest rate at an $\bar{r}$ which is above r^*. In such circumstances, the interest rate is prevented from falling to r^*, which means that at the *lowest* possible interest rate $\bar{r}$, there will be an excess of planned saving over planned investment at full employment (the commodity market would fail to clear), and secular stagnation would remain a *theoretical issue*. We stress "a theoretical issue" because the basic premise on which the hypothesis is constructed—fulfillment of consumer needs and lack of profitable investment opportunities—does not seem the problem it was thought to be when secular stagnation arguments were all the rage. Rather, the situation has been quite the opposite. Some argue though, it should be reported, that we would face a secular stagnation problem if the military-industrial complex were not constantly filling the incipient deflationary gap with military hardware or if Madison Avenue were not filling it by generating spurious demands for basically worthless, useless, and unwanted products. The claim is that if both these loads on the commodity market demand curve were removed, secular stagnation would become a real, practical problem.

4 Distribution Effects

So far we have assumed that when the model is subjected to a disturbance and moves from one equilibrium position to another, either the change in prices and wages has no effects on the distribution of income and wealth or, if such a redistribution has occurred, it has no effect on the demand and supply functions. None of these assumptions, you will notice, includes a term involving the *distribution* of income and wealth. They only contain the *levels* of these variables.

What happens if adjustment to a disturbance *does* involve distribution effects on income and wealth and the redistribution which occurs does affect some of the demand and supply functions? Let us suppose that the consumption function, for example, depends not only on the level of income and wealth but also on their distribution. In particular, assume that the rich (measured in terms of income and wealth) have a lower propensity to consume out of income and wealth than the poor. Thus, if income and wealth are redistributed in favor of the rich by the adjustment to a disturbance, the level of consumption for given levels of income and wealth will be reduced.

We shall continue to make all the other neoclassical assumptions, namely, flexibility of all three prices, unit-elastic expectations, and no money illusions. The model is originally in equilibrium, as shown by the solid curves in Figure 8. (We omit the labor market and production function diagrams, since price and wage flexibility will ensure full employment and, thus, a constant level of real income.) Now assume that the money supply is doubled and that the rich are the recipients of this increase in the supply of money. The demand and supply curves for bonds will shift to $B^{d'}$ and $B^{s'}$ creating an excess demand for bonds equal to *cd*. At first, the price of bonds will rise to $(1/r)_2$. This fall in the interest rate plus the direct effect of the increase in real balances will raise aggregate demand to $Y^{d'}$ and create an inflationary gap in the commodity market equal to *ab*.

In Chapter 7 we saw that with the full set of neoclassical assumptions changes in the money supply were neutral. A doubling of the money supply, for example, doubled all the nominal variables and left the real variables unchanged. Now, however, we are incorporating a distribution effect. Hence, if the price level doubles now and the interest rate returns to its original level, an excess supply of commodities will result. This follows since the aggregate commodity demand curve will have fallen *below* its original level Y^d because at any level of income Y^s there is a lower level of consumption. Real balances before and after the doubling in the price level will be the same, but we are assuming they will be redistributed in favor of the rich (whose propensity to consume out of real balances is lower than that of the poor). Thus, commodity market equilibrium will be reached (the $Y^{d'}$ curve would sink to

FIGURE 8

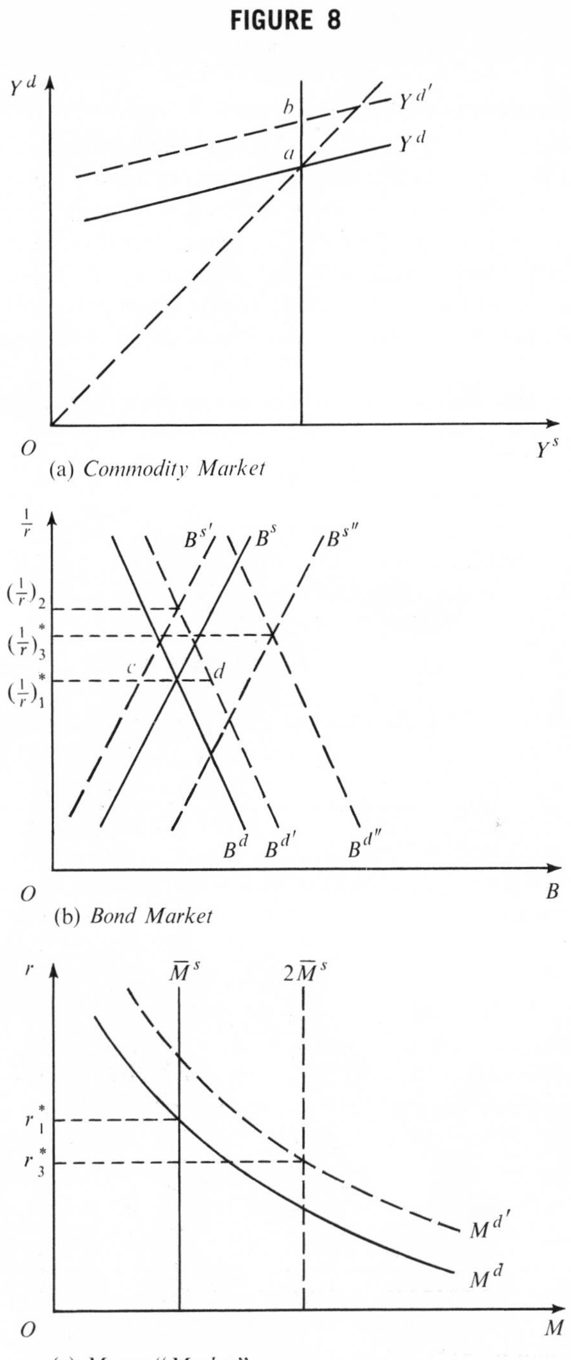

(a) *Commodity Market*

(b) *Bond Market*

(c) *Money "Market"*

overlay the Y^d curve) *before* the price level has doubled. The price level will rise, but it will not double; the $B^{d'}$ and $B^{s'}$ curves will move to the right (the latter more than the former), but not enough to intersect at the original price of bonds. Thus, equilibrium will be reestablished with a higher bond price (and lower interest rate r_3). Equilibrium will be reestablished in the money market by the rise in the price level, the rise in real balances, and the fall in the interest rate. The original demand for money curve shifts left from M^d to $M^{d'}$.

The results of this experiment are summarized in Table 2. The following comments are in order. Investment must have risen, since the interest rate has fallen and real income is constant. If investment has risen then so must saving. If real income is constant and investment has risen, consumption

TABLE 2 The Effects of a Change in the Supply of Money when Distribution Effects Exist

VARIABLE	INITIAL VALUE	FINAL VALUE	OUTCOME
Employment N	N^*	N^*	No change
Real income Y^s	Y^{s*}	Y^{s*}	No change
Real consumption C	C^*	C_1^*	Decreased
Real investment I	I^*	I_1^*	Increased
Real saving S	S^*	S_1^*	Increased
Real bonds B/rP	$B^*/r_1^*P^*$	$B_1^*/r_3^*P_1^*$	Increased
Real money M^d/P	M^d/P^*	$2M^d/P_1^*$	Increased
Price level P	P^*	P_1^*	Increased
Nominal wage W	W^*	W_1^*	Increased
Real wage W/P	$(W/P)^*$	$(W/P)_1^*$	No change
Interest rate r	r_1^*	r_3^*	Decreased
Capital stock $\bar{K}$	$\bar{K}$	$\bar{K}$	No change
Money supply $\bar{M}^s$	$\bar{M}^s$	$2\bar{M}^s$	Increased
Money income Y_m^s	Y_m^{s*}	$Y_{m_1}^{s*}$	Increased
Real wealth V/P	$(V/P)^*$	$(V/P)_1^*$	Increased
Labor's share $N(W/P)/Y^s$	$N^*(W/P)^*/Y^{s*}$	$N^*(W/P)_1^*/Y^{s*}$	No change
Others' share $(B/P)/Y^s$	$(B/P)^*/Y^{s*}$	$(B/P)_1^*/Y^{s*}$	No change

must have fallen. Real money balances have risen, since the supply of money doubled and the price level less than doubled. Labor's share is constant since employment, the real wage, and real income are all constant. If labor's share is constant so is the others' share. This means B and P in the numerator have increased in proportion, since Y^s is constant. Finally, consider real bonds. If B/P is constant and r has fallen, real bonds have increased.

5 Fixed Coefficients of Production

In our studies so far, we have never witnessed a situation in which disturbance of the model from an equilibrium position by a deflationary impulse leads to *capital* being unemployed. The existing stock of capital $\bar{K}$ is always fully utilized. Given $\bar{K}$ and a certain real wage, entrepreneurs adjust the level of employment they offer until the marginal physical product of labor (when the capital stock is fixed at $\bar{K}$) is equal to that real wage. As a result, only the quantity of labor employed responds to any disturbance imparted to the model. The basic reason why capital is *never* left unemployed is that we have assumed a flexible production function in which capital and labor are always substitutable and, moreover, the firm's capital service charges represent a fixed, or sunken, cost. The capital stock $\bar{K}$ has been acquired and, whether it is utilized or not, its service charges have to be met. Since entrepreneurs must meet the charges associated with the capital input, it pays them never to underutilize and waste this resource.

Our model, then, is not capable of explaining either transitory or permanent unemployment of capital. However, even the most casual observation of deflationary situations reveals that both labor and capital become unemployed. In recession and depression longshoremen *and* ships are idle, steelworkers *and* blast furnaces go unutilized, auto workers *and* their factories are underemployed. One might legitimately ask, therefore, how can the model be modified to generate underutilization of capital? One answer is by modifying our previous assumption about the nature of the production function.[1] Instead of assuming *continuous* substitutability of capital and labor in the production function, we shall now assume that capital and labor are only substitutable *before* a given production process is adopted. *After* a particular production process has been adopted, the two factors must be used in fixed proportions.

The issue is conveniently illustrated by Figure 9(c). Suppose that firms are deciding what factor combination to employ to produce the level of output Y^{s*}. The factor combinations they may choose from are given by the solid isoquant labeled Y^{s*} in Figure 9(c). The actual process they select will depend on the factor-price ratio, or the slope of the isocosts (which are not

[1] There are *other* possible explanations; for example, those which invoke the concept of *user-cost*. (See J. M. Keynes, *The General Theory of Employment, Interest, and Money*, Macmillan, 1936, chapter 6.) However, these are somewhat more complicated than the case we shall examine in this section and are not discussed.

FIGURE 9

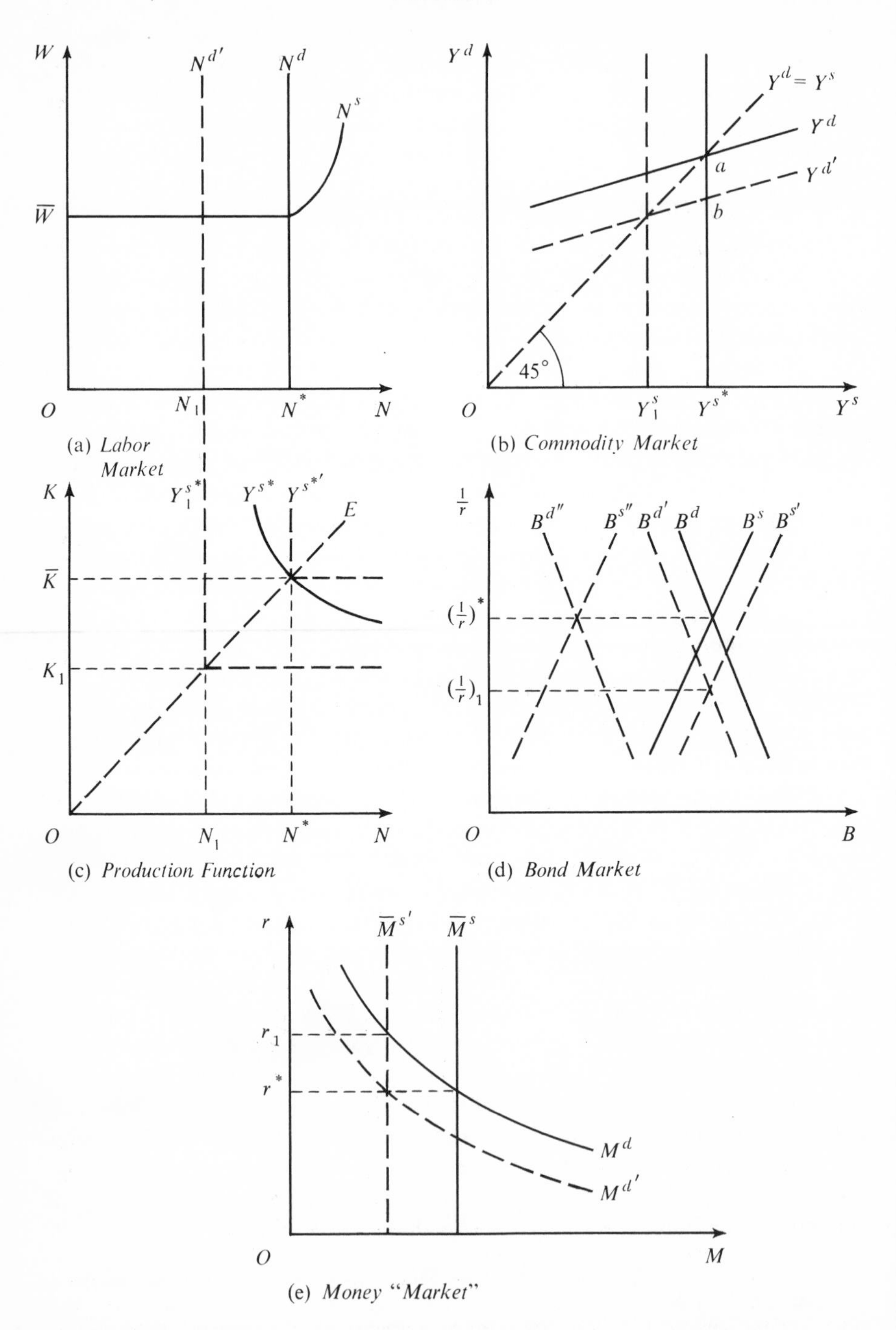

(a) *Labor Market*

(b) *Commodity Market*

(c) *Production Function*

(d) *Bond Market*

(e) *Money "Market"*

shown in the diagram). Assume that the factor-price ratio at planning time is such that firms choose to produce Y^{s*} with $\bar{K}$ capital (services) and N^* labor (services). *After* this decision is made, we shall assume that firms are "locked into" this particular production process and must *always* use capital and labor in the ratio $\bar{K}/N^*$. The relevant isoquant becomes the right-angled line $Y^{s*'}$. The rationale is that once a unit of capital (machine) is installed, it must be worked by a fixed labor crew because it has been designed that way. After installation, capital and labor must be used in the *fixed proportion* indicated by the ray OE through the origin with slope equal to $\bar{K}/N^*$.

Thus, if planned output were to fall to Y_1^s, this output must be produced with K_1 capital and N_1 labor. *This is true no matter what the ratio of factor prices is.* Now the operational isoquant is the right-angled dashed line Y_1^s. It is apparent that this production process is independent of the slope of the isocosts, since an infinite number of isocosts with different slopes (but all representing the same total cost) can just touch Y_1^s at its right angle. Thus, the ratio of factor prices has nothing to do with choosing the capital-labor ratio K_1/N_1 to produce Y_1^s. This choice is predetermined by the machine's design. K_1 capital requires a crew of N_1 labor to produce it, and that is that. Capital and labor are not substitutable *after* a given type of capital has been installed.

E. S. Phelps introduced some descriptive terminology with which to classify production functions.[2] Substitution between capital and labor both before *and* after installation gives what is called a *putty-putty* production function. This is the sort of production function we have worked with until now. When substitution between capital and labor before installation is followed by fixed labor requirements after installation, we have a *putty-clay* production function. This is the sort of production function we are working with now.

putty-putty

putty-clay

We get an unusual demand for labor curve with a putty-clay production function. The putty-putty production function, used so far, produced a demand for labor curve identical to the marginal physical product of labor curve. Now, with a putty-clay production function, the marginal physical product of labor is zero. This is easy to see. If firms are producing any level of output with the required capital-labor ratio and they add another unit of labor there is zero increase in output. Thus, there can be no question of firms adjusting employment until the marginal physical product of labor is equal to the real wage. In fact, the demand for labor is completely independent of the real wage and is, instead, simply a function of the level of planned output. If Y_1^s is to be produced, N_1 labor is required; if Y_2^s is to be produced, N_2 labor is required; and so on. Graphically, the demand for labor is completely inelastic with respect to the real wage. Such demand curves are illustrated in Figure 9(a) by N^d and $N^{d'}$. Algebraically, the demand for labor equation in our model becomes

$$N^d = N^d(Y^s)$$

[2] E. S. Phelps, "Substitution, Fixed Proportions, Growth, and Distribution," *International Economic Review*, September, 1963.

With these preliminaries behind us, let us see what the implications of a deflationary impulse are for the model. The initial full employment equilibrium position is illustrated by the solid curves in Figure 9. Observe that the labor market in Figure 9(a) incorporates a money illusion–type supply curve with the money wage rigid downwards at $\bar{W}$. This type of labor supply curve has been included because we shall discover that *in this model* the existence of a rigid money wage does *not* lead to permanent unemployment in a deflationary environment. This is somewhat surprising. Our previous findings that rigidity in the wage rate inevitably leads to permanent unemployment are not valid here. Thus, this is a very interesting special case—special in that it occurs only when the production function is one with fixed coefficients.

Now let us disturb the initial equilibrium in a deflationary direction by reducing the supply of money to $\bar{M}^{s\prime}$. This decreases the demand and increases the supply of bonds to $B^{d\prime}$ and $B^{s\prime}$, respectively. Thus, at first, the interest rate rises to r_1. This rise in the interest rate and the reduction in real balances which has occurred reduce aggregate commodity demand to $Y^{d\prime}$. An excess supply of commodities equal to *ab* emerges. Hence, if firms do nothing, inventories will accumulate at the rate *ab*. Let us assume that to forestall such an unintended inventory accumulation, firms reduce output to what can be sold, namely, to Y_1^s. This output *must* be produced with N_1 labor and K_1 capital. Thus, the demand for labor curve shifts to $N^{d\prime}$. Unemployed labor equal to $N^* - N_1$ and unemployed capital equal to $\bar{K} - K_1$ emerge. This will prove to be transitory as we shall now explain.

At this point, entrepreneurs are faced with excess capacity which they would like to bring back into use. To this end, we assume that they start asking lower prices for their product in an attempt to increase sales. (Commodity price rigidity is not a feature of the present model.) As the price level falls, the bond demand and supply curves shift left—the latter more rapidly than the former. Consequently, the interest rate begins to fall below r_1. This reduction in the interest rate and the increase in real balances brought about by the falling price level both work to raise aggregate demand above $Y^{d\prime}$. It is apparent that the price level need only fall far enough for the interest rate to fall and real balances to rise sufficiently for Y^d to pass through point *a* once more. When this occurs, output will again equal Y^{s*} and the demand curve for labor will shift back to N^d. Employment of labor is N^* once more and the whole existing capital stock $\bar{K}$ is being utilized. It can, in fact, be shown (though we do not prove it here) that the interest rate and real balances return to their original levels. That is why in Figure 9(d) we have drawn the final bond demand and supply curves $B^{d\prime\prime}$ and $B^{s\prime\prime}$ intersecting at the original equilibrium price of bonds $(1/r)^*$. Of course, for real balances to remain unchanged, the fall in the price level must be proportional to the reduction in the supply of money.

We wish to draw attention to two features of this model. First, during the adjustment to the deflationary disturbance, capital is temporarily unemployed. So far no other model we have discussed has exhibited this feature.

Its appearance in this model is *solely* due to the assumption of a putty-clay production function. Second, the distribution of income has unambiguously shifted in favor of labor, since real income and the level of employment are constant. However, the real wage has risen because the money wage is fixed at $\bar{W}$ and the price level has fallen. It follows that $N(W/P)/Y^s$ must have increased. The reader can supply the other results for himself.

6 Markup Inflation; Monopolization of the Commodity Market

Until now we have assumed that our firms sell their product in perfectly competitive markets. What would happen if monopoly was substituted for this assumption?

Consider Figure 10. The curve D is the total market demand curve for the product and the curve S the total market supply curve of the product. Under perfect competition, it is well known that S is the horizontal sum of the individual firms' marginal cost curves. Hence, we write $S = MC$. If conditions are *perfectly competitive,* the equilibrium quantity produced and price of the product would be Y_1^{s*} and P_1^*, respectively. In such circumstances marginal revenue is equal to the price of the product. Therefore, marginal costs are equal to marginal revenue (profits are maximized) when Y_1^{s*} is produced, and this output can be sold for P_1^*.

Now though, suppose that a commodity-maker with robber baron proclivities acquires sole control of all firms and monopolizes the market for commodities. We shall assume that this action does not affect the production functions and, therefore, the cost structure of the individual firms. Our man merely accepts the present industrial apparatus and plans to exploit the

FIGURE 10

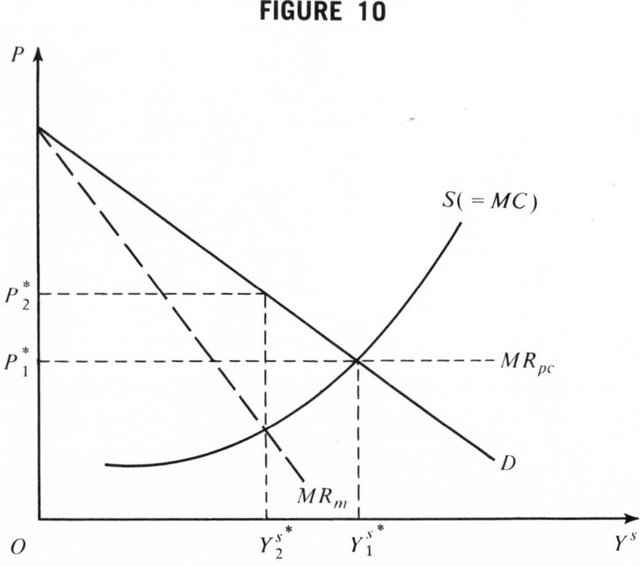

power of his monopolistic position. Since the cost picture has not changed the marginal cost curve remains the same. However, a monopolist can only sell more by lowering his price. To a monopolist, then, marginal revenue is always less than price. The marginal revenue curve is below the demand curve (the one labeled MR_m in Figure 10) everywhere. To maximize profits, a monopolist, like anyone else, will produce the output at which marginal cost equals marginal revenue. Given the monopolist's marginal revenue curve MR_m, this clearly means he will produce the output Y_2^{s*}, at which the marginal revenue curve MR_m and the marginal cost curve MC intersect. The demand price for that output is P_2^*. Thus, effectively, monopolization of the product market leads to reduced output from Y_1^{s*} to Y_2^{s*} and increased price from P_1^* to P_2^*. Hence, we know what has happened in the commodity market.

Monopolization of the product market will also affect the labor market. Consider Figure 11. We explained in Chapter 2 that a profit-maximizing, perfectly competitive firm will hire labor until the cost of an additional unit of labor services W equals the addition to revenue that the additional unit of labor services contributes to total revenue (which is equal to its marginal physical product MPP multiplied by the price of each unit of the product P). That is to say, profit will be maximized when

$$W = MPP \times P \tag{1}$$

Dividing through by P we obtain

$$\frac{W}{P} = MPP \tag{2}$$

which states that labor services will be hired until their marginal physical product is equal to the real wage, or, in other words, until the real product they produce is equal to the real purchasing power that has to be turned over

FIGURE 11

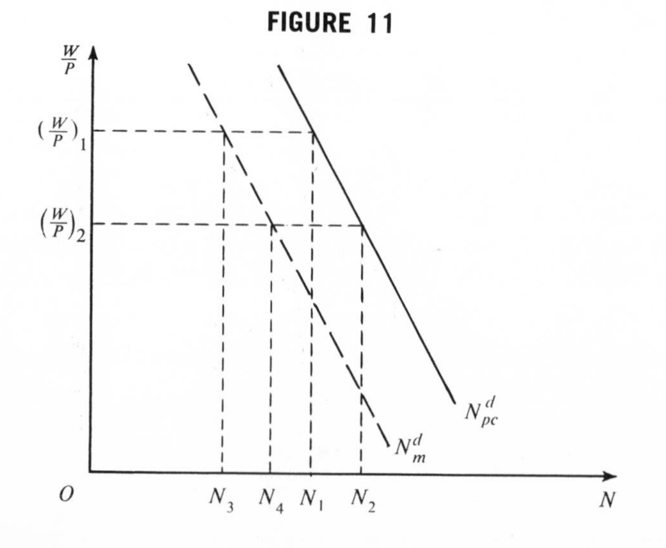

to them. We see that at the real wage $(W/P)_1$, N_1 will be employed. This many labor services need to be hired before the marginal physical product falls to $(W/P)_1$. At a lower real wage $(W/P)_2$, N_2 will be employed, since that many labor services are required before the marginal physical product falls to $(W/P)_2$. Using this reasoning, we were able to conclude that under perfect competition the demand curve for labor is identical to the marginal physical product of labor curve. The curve N^d_{pc} in Figure 11 is the demand for labor curve as a function of the real wage under perfect competition.

Things are slightly different under monopoly conditions, however. A monopoly, just like a perfectly competitive firm, will hire labor until the cost of an additional unit of labor services W equals the addition to revenue that the additional unit of labor services contributes to total revenue. But the latter is now equal to that unit's marginal physical product times the *marginal revenue* obtained from selling the additional product. Note that we say "marginal revenue," and *not* "price." Under monopolistic conditions, the additional output (MPP) cannot be sold at the same price. Price has to be reduced. Hence, we multiply by marginal revenue. Thus, a monopolist maximizes profits when

$$W = MPP \times MR \tag{3}$$

Divide both sides of (3) by the price level to obtain

$$\frac{W}{P} = MPP \times \frac{MR}{P} \tag{4}$$

The monopoly, just like the perfectly competitive firm, hires labor until the real purchasing power it receives [the left-hand side of (4)] is equal to the real product it produces.[1] At any real wage W/P, the monopolist adds workers until the right-hand side of (4) falls to equal the real wage. Since MR/P is less than unity (marginal revenue is always less than price for a monopoly; see Figure 10), you can see by comparing (2) and (4) that the monopoly will stop hiring labor at any given real wage before a perfectly competitive firm will. As workers are added the right-hand side of (4) will equal its left-hand side before such equality is attained in equation (2). This occurs because the right-hand side of (4) includes a fraction less than unity. Thus, in Figure 11, at the real wage $(W/P)_1$, the monopolist hires only N_3 workers, whereas the perfect competitor hired N_1. A similar argument applies to any real wage. At $(W/P)_2$ the competitive firm hired N_2, but the monopolist hires only N_4. By such reasoning, we can generate the monopolist's demand for labor curve. It will be like N^d_m in Figure 11—always to the left of the competitive factor demand curve N^d_{pc}.

[1] Note that the dimension of the right-hand side of (4) is in real terms, namely, commodities per time period. On the right-hand side of (4) we have

$$\text{Commodities per time period} \times \frac{\dfrac{\$}{\text{commodity}}}{\dfrac{\$}{\text{commodity}}} = \text{commodities per time period}$$

Now that we have examined these basic issues, let us see what effects the emergence of monopoly forces in our macroeconomic model has. The solid curves in Figure 12 represent the initial equilibrium positions under perfectly competitive conditions. As Figure 12(b) illustrates, real output (income) is reduced to Y_1^{s*} as the monopolist restricts supply. Excess commodity demand equal to *ab* prevails. The excess demand is removed when the aggregate demand curve falls from Y^d to $Y^{d'}$. This fall is brought about, first, by the rise in prices to P_1^* (which reduces real wealth) and, second, by the rise in the interest rate to r_1^*. The second change ensues because the rise in prices shifts the bond supply and demand curves right to $B^{s'}$ and $B^{d'}$, respectively (the supply curve shifts more than the demand curve for familiar reasons). In the money market the rise in the price level shifts the nominal demand curve to $M^{d'}$. The nominal demand for money is held down to the nominal supply available by the rise in interest rates, fall in real income, and fall in real wealth. In the labor market, the demand curve shifts left to N_m^d with resulting decreases in real wages to $(W/P)_1^*$ and employment to N_1^*. The fall in the real wage is due to the rise in the price level *and* a fall in the nominal wage as the workers compete among themselves for the fewer jobs the monopolist makes available.

The outcome of this experiment is summarized in Table 3. Consumption has decreased because income and wealth have decreased and the interest rate has risen. Investment has decreased, since income has decreased and the rate of interest has risen. This means saving must have decreased. Real money is down because its nominal quantity is constant and the price level has risen. Money income is ambiguous because real income is down while the price level is up. Oddly enough, the functional distribution of income is ambiguous, too. Intuitively, one would expect monopolization of the commodity market to unambiguously hurt labor. However, although labor's absolute income is certainly down, since both employment and the real wage are down, so is real income. Therefore, the ratio of labor's income to total income remains uncertain. Similarly, the others' share is obscure. Both *B* and *P* have increased, so their ratio may have increased or decreased. If we do not know which way the numerator has moved, we do not know which way the others' share ratio has moved. Analogous reasoning leaves the real bond holding situation unclear. Although we do not know what has happened to the others' share, we do know what has happened to one component of it, namely, profits. A monopolist can earn permanent, above-normal profits—and our monopolist will. Thus, profits have increased from normal, under perfect competition, to above normal after the introduction of monopolization.

Note that prices have undergone a one-shot increase from P^* to P_1^*. This is the extent of markup inflation—prices do *not* continue to rise. Is this not reminiscent of cost inflation? You will recall from the previous chapter that a collectively bargained increase in wages led to a one-shot increase in prices. By itself, a cost-induced increase in prices was *not* self-perpetuating. Prices did not continue to rise. We stress this, since it is a widespread

FIGURE 12

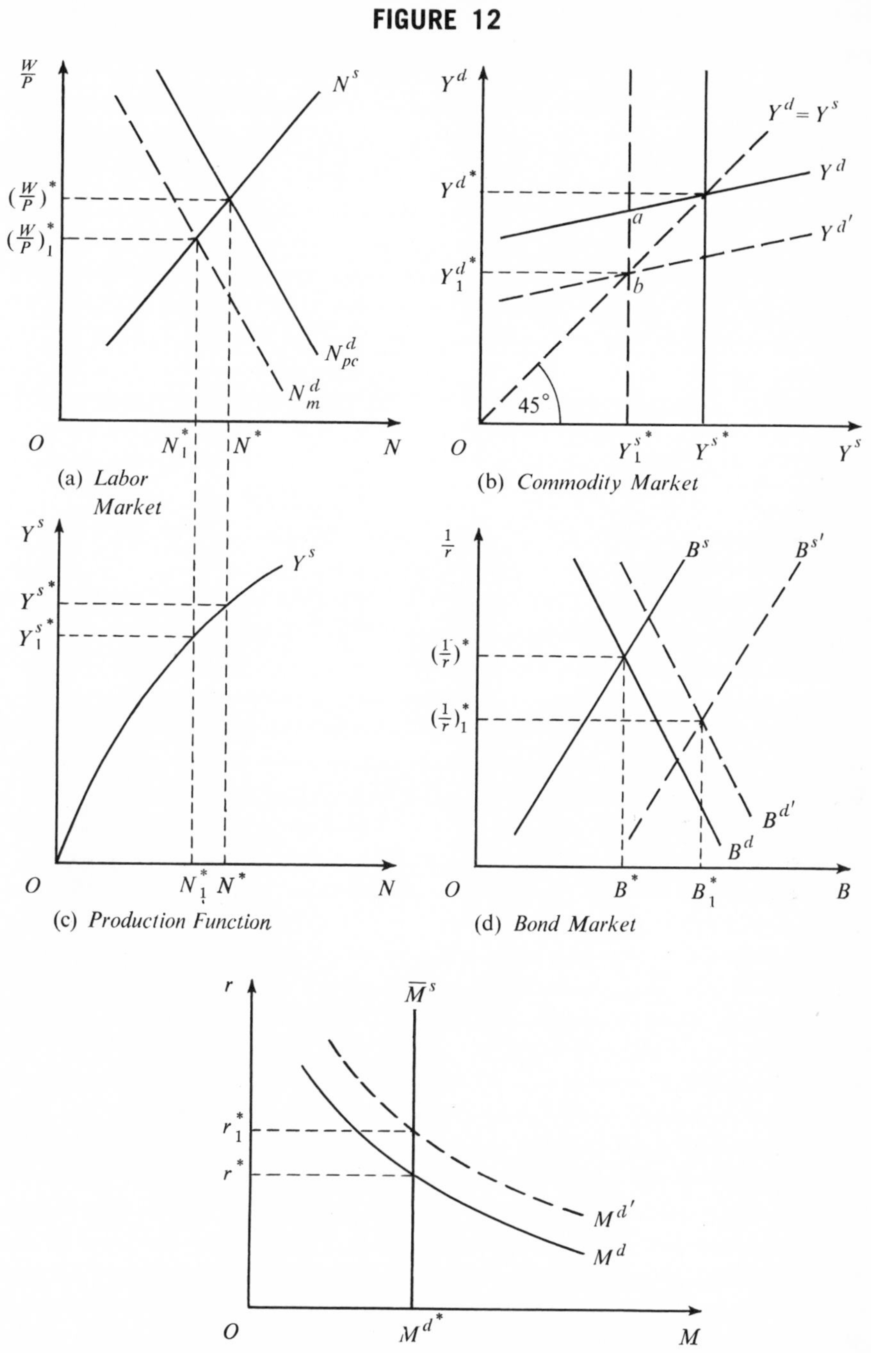

(a) *Labor Market*

(b) *Commodity Market*

(c) *Production Function*

(d) *Bond Market*

(e) *Money "Market"*

TABLE 3 The Effects of Monopolization of the Commodity Market; Markup Inflation

VARIABLE	INITIAL VALUE	FINAL VALUE	OUTCOME
Employment N	N^*	N_1^*	Decreased
Real income Y^s	Y^{s*}	Y_1^{s*}	Decreased
Real consumption C	C^*	C_1^*	Decreased
Real investment I	I^*	I_1^*	Decreased
Real saving S	S^*	S_1^*	Decreased
Real bonds B/rP	B^*/r^*P^*	$B_1^*/r_1^*P_1^*$	Not known
Real money M^d/P	M^d/P^*	M^d/P_1^*	Decreased
Price level P	P^*	P_1^*	Increased
Nominal wage W	W^*	W_1^*	Decreased
Real wage W/P	$(W/P)^*$	$(W/P)_1^*$	Decreased
Interest rate r	r^*	r_1^*	Increased
Capital stock $\bar{K}$	$\bar{K}$	$\bar{K}$	No change
Money supply $\bar{M}^s$	$\bar{M}^s$	$\bar{M}^s$	No change
Money income Y_m^s	Y_m^{s*}	$Y_{m_1}^{s*}$	Not known
Real wealth V/P	$(V/P)^*$	$(V/P)_1^*$	Decreased
Labor's share $N(W/P)/Y^s$	$N^*(W/P)^*/Y^{s*}$	$N_1^*(W/P)_1^*/Y_1^{s*}$	Not known
Others' share $(B/P)/Y^s$	$(B/P)^*/Y^{s*}$	$(B/P)_1^*/Y_1^{s*}$	Not known

fallacy that either unions or monopolies can, *by themselves,* cause prices to *continuously* spiral up. It is just not true. Our model showed that government action in the form of an increase in the money supply (to counteract the unemployment caused by collective bargaining) was required to generate a continuous upward spiral of wages and prices.

The same holds true for markup inflation. After monopolization, prices have *stabilized* at P_1^*. There will be no further price increases. However, employment has fallen from N^* to N_1^*. (Notice that, in a technical sense, there is no unemployment. Everyone who wants to work at the new, lower real wage is working.) Suppose the government decides to try to reestablish the old level of employment N^* by an easy money policy. It may try, but it will not succeed.

Increasing the supply of money will create excess commodity demand through an increase in real balances and a transitory decline in the interest rate. Prices will begin to rise, but so will wages and, therefore, costs. If the rises in prices and wages are proportional, the real wage and employment will not be affected. In effect, the demand curve, marginal revenue curve, and marginal cost curve are all rising and the latter two continue to intersect at the same output. Thus, the monopolist is not induced to change output or, therefore, employment. In the end prices and costs will increase in proportion to the money supply while output and employment will remain constant. Nothing will be gained. Money proves to be a veil again. Nominal variables move proportionately while real variables remain unchanged. The government is powerless to undo the evil of monopoly via its macroeconomic (either monetary *or* fiscal) tool kit.

What is the alternative? Do we unleash the attorneys-at-law in the Justice Department? Bust the commodity-makers trust? Flush out the smoke-filled motel rooms at the commodity-makers' convention and jail any recalcitrant commodity-maker entrepreneur price-fixers? In short, the government must utilize its microeconomic equipment to impose competitive conditions in the commodity market. It is worse than useless to tackle a microeconomic problem such as monopolization with macroeconomic weapons.

Summary

In this chapter we continued our analysis of the model's properties in a neo-Keynesian context. *Commodity price rigidity* was introduced (arbitrarily at first and then with a somewhat more sound theoretical foundation, namely, a constant returns-to-scale aggregate production function). We showed that no matter what the cause of downward price rigidity, *persistent unemployment* will emerge in the presence of *any* deflationary impulse. Such unemployment can, in general, be *removed* by an appropriately devised *monetary* or *fiscal policy.*

The theory that at full employment the level of planned investment would fall chronically short of the level of planned saving is referred to as the *secular stagnation* hypothesis. This hypothesis relies on two things: first, when prices are flexible, a real wealth effect must be excluded from the aggregate demand function; second, either there is no positive interest rate at which planned investment will equal planned saving (which we showed to be improbable) or, if such a positive interest rate exists, actual interest rates cannot (for a reason to be explained in the next chapter) fall to this level.

The properties of the model were then analyzed in another neo-Keynesian context, namely, when *distribution effects* exist. If, during inflation, income and wealth are redistributed in favor of those with relatively high income and wealth (individuals who are assumed to have a relatively low *mpc*), money is not neutral.

Next, we analyzed a model with a *putty-clay* production function, wage rigidity, and price flexibility in the presence of a deflationary impulse. This model is capable of explaining unemployment of capital during deflations (which our previous models with the *putty-putty* production functions were not).

The final problem we discussed was that of *markup inflation*. We saw that monopolization of previously competitive producers leads to a *one-shot* increase in the price level (and *unemployment*). It does *not* lead to continuously rising prices. Moreover, this unemployment cannot be removed by macroeconomic (monetary or fiscal) policy. Microeconomic policy must be brought to bear.

Questions

1. Explain why commodity prices may be inflexible downwards.
2. Assume commodity prices are inflexible downwards. Select a deflationary impulse and explain what happens to the equilibrium values of the endogenous variables. Pay particular attention to the level of unemployment and gross national product.
3. Assume that unemployment because of downward commodity price rigidity exists. Devise a monetary or fiscal policy to remove it and explain carefully how your policy does so.
4. What is the secular stagnation hypothesis? Explain why a real wealth effect must be excluded from the aggregate demand function if this hypothesis is to hold. Why does this hypothesis also imply that there is no positive interest rate at which planned saving equals planned investment at full employment real income?
5. It is *possible* that there is no positive interest rate at which planned saving and planned investment are equal at full employment. Explain why this is not *probable*.
6. Explain what is meant by *distribution effects*. Assume that a distribution effect exists in the consumption function (specify its nature appropriately yourself). What happens to the equilibrium values of the endogenous variables when an expansionary fiscal policy is pursued?
7. Show that money is not neutral if a distribution effect exists in the bond demand function.
8. Explain the difference between a putty-putty production function and a putty-clay production function. Show that a macroeconomic model containing a putty-clay production function is capable of explaining the emergence of unemployed capital in the face of a deflationary fiscal policy. Why do models with a putty-putty production function not generate such an implication?
9. Explain why monopolization of previously competitive producers will lead to a one-shot increase in the price level (and unemployment), but not to continuously rising prices.

SELECTED READINGS

1. G. Ackley, "Administered Prices and the Inflationary Process," *American Economic Review, Proceedings,* May, 1959.
2. G. Ackley, *Macroeconomic Theory,* Macmillan, 1961, chapter 16. Emphasis on markup aspects of inflation.
3. M. J. Bailey, *National Income and the Price Level,* McGraw-Hill, 1962, chapter 4, sections 7 and 8. Argues convincingly that at some positive interest rate full employment saving will equal investment.
4. M. Bronfenbrenner and F. D. Holzman, "Survey of Inflation Theory," *American Economic Review,* September, 1963. Contains extensive references to the literature on markup or administered-price inflation.
5. J. Cornfield, W. D. Evans, and M. Hoffenberg, "Full Employment Patterns, 1950: Part I," *Monthly Labor Review,* February, 1947. An alarming forecast of the investment required in the postwar period if full employment was to be maintained. Proved false largely because the authors underforecast consumption.
6. D. C. Hague, *Inflation,* St. Martin's, 1962.
7. A. H. Hansen, "Economic Progress and Declining Population Growth," *American Economic Review,* March, 1939. Discusses the secular stagnation question.
8. J. M. Keynes *The General Theory of Employment, Interest, and Money,* Macmillan, 1936, chapter 11. Keynes' views on the influence of interest rates on investment.
9. W. I. King, "Are We Suffering from Economic Maturity?" *Journal of Political Economy,* October, 1939. Discusses the secular stagnation hypothesis.
10. A. Leijonhufvud, *On Keynesian Economics and the Economics of Keynes,* Oxford, 1968, chapter 3, section 3. Makes the case that Keynes himself was *not* an interest-elasticity pessimist. (For other literature on the interest elasticity of investment see the references under *Investment* in the Selected Readings of Chapter 3.)
11. D. Patinkin, *Money, Interest, and Prices,* 2nd ed., Harper & Row, 1965, chapter 12; chapter 14, section 5; and note L. Discusses wage and price rigidity, distribution effects, and secular stagnation.

12

Complications in the Bond and Money Markets; The Liquidity Trap

In Chapters 10 and 11 we saw that permanent unemployment can result from the existence of rigidities in the wage rate or in the commodity price level. In this chapter we shall find that downward inflexibility in the interest rate—a floor to the interest rate—can raise the same problem. Thus, we shall conclude that permanent unemployment is associated with rigidities in any, or all, of the three prices in our model: the price of labor W, the price of commodities P, and the price of bonds $(1/r)$.

1 The Liquidity Trap

During the discussion of the secular stagnation question in §11.3, we saw that it is highly probable that there is some positive interest rate at which the commodity market will clear. This invites another question: Is there some minimum interest rate which the bond and money markets will tolerate? The answer is very important because if this minimum tolerable interest rate is above the (perhaps very small) interest rate necessary to make the commodity market clear, we will not get clearance. Referring back to Figure 7 in Chapter 11, we are concerned with the existence of a minimum tolerable interest rate $\bar{r}$ (a floor to the interest rate), which could conceivably be above r^* (the interest rate at which the commodity market clears). When this minimum interest rate is reached we have a *liquidity trap*.

We draw specific attention to the omission of real balances from the aggregate commodity demand functions. What follows depends crucially on this assumption. It is impossible to get caught in a liquidity trap if real balances are included in the aggregate demand function (as we explain in §2 below).

The problem arises in the bond market. Consider Figures 1(a) and 1(b) showing the bond and money markets, respectively. The crucial feature in Figure 1(a) of the bond market is that the demand curve intersects the vertical axis at $(1/\bar{r})$. This implies that at such a high bond price (low interest rate) the demand for bonds is zero. Potential lenders are not willing to lend because the running yield on bonds is very low and, more importantly, the prospect of capital losses on bond holdings is very high. Lenders reason that such high bond prices cannot last and will probably fall in the future; so they feel that if they bought bonds now they would be stuck with a capital loss later. Notice we are asserting that bond price (interest rate) expectations are *inelastic* – a particularly Keynesian assumption. The risk of a capital loss on bonds when their price is as high as $(1/\bar{r})$ is very large and the low yield of $\bar{r}$ is not sufficient to induce lenders to undertake such a risk. Consequently, they will not lend. Their demand for bonds is zero.

Given this feature, what happens now if there is (for a reason which we need not inquire into yet) a decrease in commodity prices? As we well know, a decrease in the commodity price level shifts both the bond supply curve and the bond demand curve to the left – with the supply curve decreasing more than proportionally to the price level and the demand curve decreasing less than proportionally to the price level. Thus, the supply curve shifts to $B^{s'}$, $B^{s''}$, and so on and the demand curve shifts to $B^{d'}$, $B^{d''}$, and so on. At the same time, the interest rate falls progressively from r_1 to r_2 to $\bar{r}$ [see Figure 2(a)]. Notice that *all* the bond demand curves $B^{d'}$, $B^{d''}$, and so on emanate from $(1/\bar{r})$. Under no circumstances will people lend at a lower interest rate.

In the money market [Figure 2(b)], the decline in the price level shifts the demand for nominal balances curve progressively left to $M^{d'}$, $M^{d''}$. The demand for nominal balances is kept equal to the fixed nominal quantity supplied by the decrease in the interest rate.

When the bond price level has declined sufficiently to generate the $B^{d''}$ and $B^{s''}$ curves, the bond market becomes inoperative. No one will lend. If

FIGURE 1

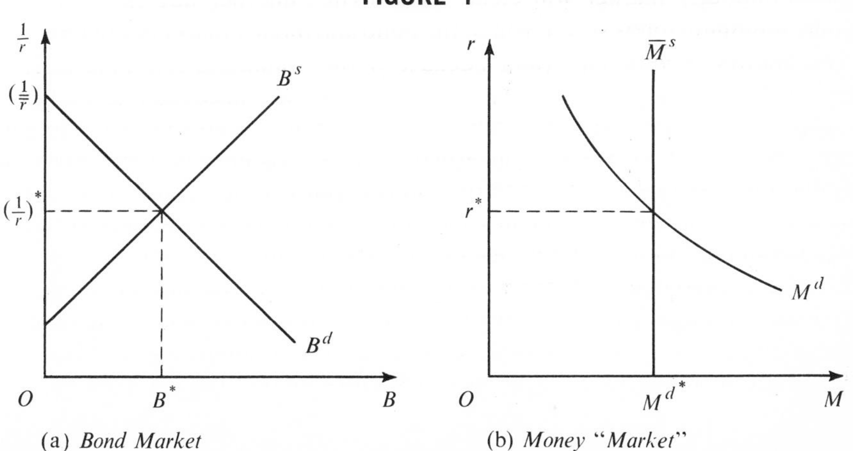

(a) *Bond Market* (b) *Money "Market"*

FIGURE 2

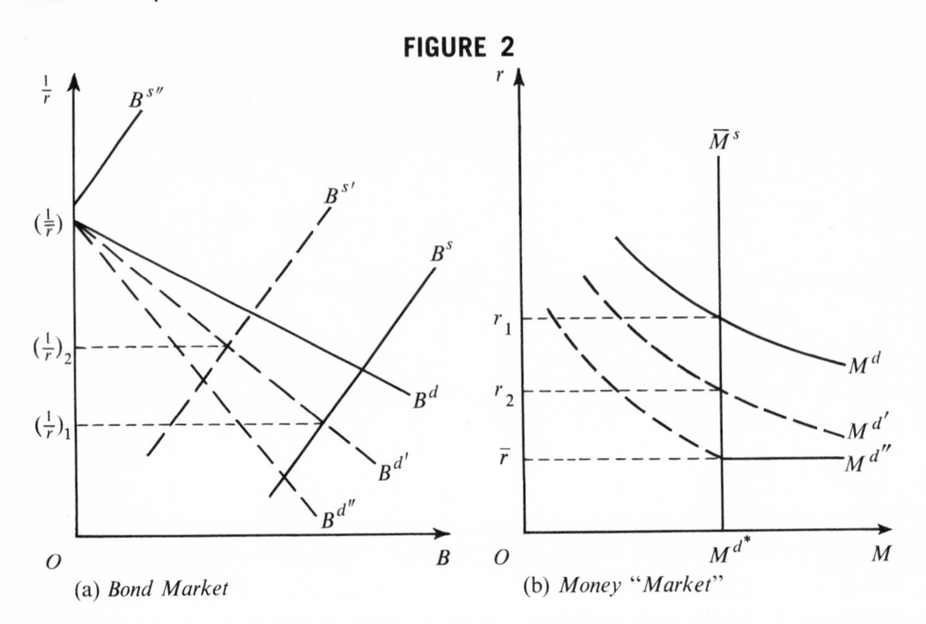

the price level continues to fall, the resulting increase in real money balances is held idle; it is hoarded. The demand for real money balances to hold increases exactly with the supply of real money balances being generated by the decline in prices. The demand for real money balances becomes a bottomless pit.

This phenomenon of a minimum tolerated interest rate by the bond market is usually approached in the following manner. Assume that prices are fixed (ceteris paribus) and the increase in real balances is brought about by an increase in the nominal supply of money. Consider Figure 3. In the bond market demand curves shift right to $B^{d'}$ and $B^{d''}$, rotating around $(1/\bar{r})$. This is because the increase in the money supply raises real balances while prices are constant. The same increase in real balances shifts the supply curves left to $B^{s'}$ and $B^{s''}$. In the money market, the decrease in the interest rate from r_1 to r_2 to $\bar{r}$ causes the nominal quantity of money demanded to increase equally with the increasing nominal supply available $\bar{M}^{s'}$ and $\bar{M}^{s''}$.

When the interest rate has been driven down to $\bar{r}$, no one will lend again. All increases in the nominal supply of money beyond $\bar{M}^{s''}$ do not find their way into the bond market, but into idle money balances. The demand for money balances increases dollar for dollar with the supply. Again, we see that the demand for real money balances has become a bottomless pit. These money balances will remain idle, hoarded, as long as the bond market remains so unpropitious. The two cases we have just gone over demonstrate Keynes' assertion that "we can . . . produce precisely the same effects on the rate of interest by reducing wages (and prices), whilst leaving the quantity of money unchanged, that we can produce by increasing the quantity of money whilst leaving the level of wages (and prices) unchanged."[1]

[1] J. M. Keynes, *The General Theory of Employment, Interest, and Money,* Macmillan, 1936, p. 266.

FIGURE 3

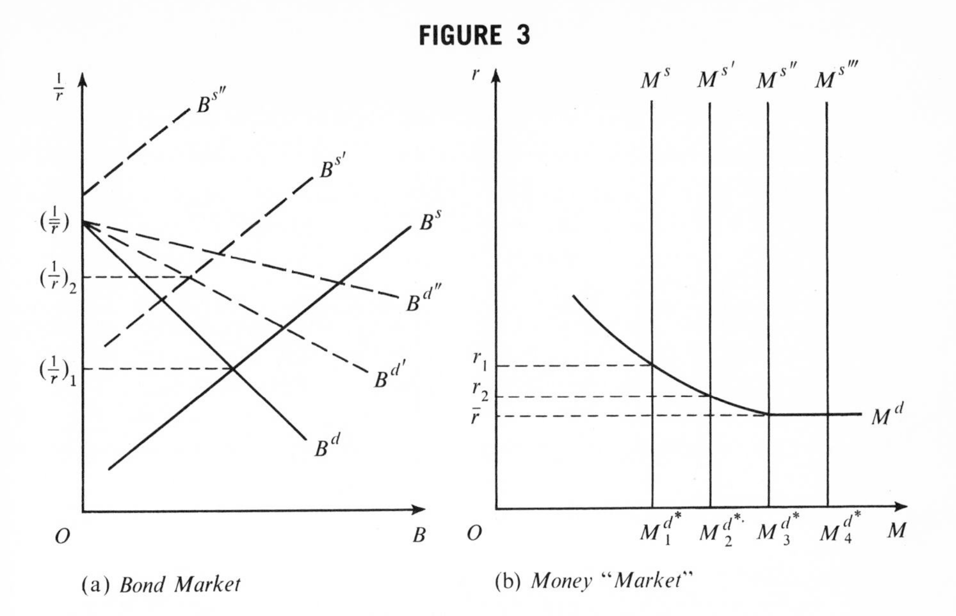

(a) *Bond Market* (b) *Money "Market"*

Given the possibility of a minimum tolerable interest rate the bond market might stand, what bearing might this have on the overall characteristics of our macroeconomic model?

2 The Possibility of Unlimited Deflation or Permanent Unemployment

If we incorporate a liquidity trap into our model and exclude a real balance effect from the aggregate commodity demand function, we make possible unlimited deflation, given a sufficiently large initial deflationary impulse to our model. We assume in this experiment that prices and wages are flexible. It is the interest rate which is rigid (eventually) at $\bar{r}$.

Consider Figure 4. Assume that there is an increase in thrift.[1] This is the initial deflationary impulse. The aggregate demand for commodities is reduced to $Y^{d'}$ and the demand for bonds is increased to $B^{d'}$. The two curves shift because of changes in the *form* of these relations. There is an excess supply of commodities equal to *ab* and an excess demand for bonds equal to *de*. Both commodity prices and the rate of interest begin to fall. The fall in the rate of interest causes the aggregate commodity demand curve to begin to rise toward Y^d again; the deflationary gap tends to close. Note that the fall in prices is not helpful in this regard. The commodity demand function includes no real balance effect, although in the past we relied on such an effect to help close the deflationary gap. Now this aid is denied us.

[1] With very slight modification, the discussion presented below can also be applied when the initial deflationary impulse is a decrease in entrepreneurial expectations. After you have seen how the argument runs, you may wish to work this case out as an exercise.

However, the real balance effect does go to work in the bond market [Figure 4(d)]. It shifts the demand curve right, rotating it around $(1/\bar{r})$, and the supply curve left. Once these curves have reached $B^{d''}$ and $B^{s'}$, which they do when prices fall to P_1, no more lending will occur. The minimum interest rate lenders will quote is $\bar{r}$ and there are no borrowers at that rate. The interest rate has reached its floor. When this floor (or trap) rate prevails the aggregate demand curve has, we assume, risen only to $Y^{d''}$. Excess commodity supply equal to *ac* still exists. We are in real trouble. The auctioneer responsible for achieving equilibrium values of the variables via the tâtonnement process is faced with an impossible task. He can continue to announce lower prices and wages until he is blue in the face, but he cannot get rid of the excess supply of commodities that would be forthcoming at full employment. The spectrum of limitless, unbounded deflation emerges. In effect, there is no equilibrium price or wage level. This is why we have omitted the usual asterisk on P_1 – it is not an equilibrium price level. In the money market [Figure 4(e)], the demand curve shifts left to $M^{d'}$ when the price level falls to P_1.

As long as firms continued to employ N^* workers – and, if we assume proportionate decreases in prices and wages keep the real wage constant in the labor market, there is no reason why they should not – this excess supply of unsold commodities would prevail. Firms would soon be buried in their own inventories. What can be done?

The disequilibrium which is presently manifesting itself in the commodity market can be shifted into the labor market. How? Firms can convert the excess supply of commodities into an excess supply of labor by employing only N_1^* workers. These workers produce the Y_1^{s*} output that *can* be sold. The limitless deflation with which we are faced when an excess supply of commodities equal to *ac* exists is converted into $N^* - N_1^*$ unemployment when the demand curve for labor is shifted left to pass through point *f*. The curve $N^{d'}$ which passes through that point is of the transitory type discussed in §11.1. Moving to this curve (point) reduces the aggregate supply of commodities to Y_1^{s*}, the quantity that can be sold. In doing so, permanent disequilibrium in the labor market is substituted for permanent disequilibrium in the commodity market. Disequilibrium is still with us, nonetheless. If one assumes entrepreneurs would rather contemplate a permanent pool of unsold labor than a continuously growing pile of unsold inventories, one can easily imagine that they would take the former option.

Moreover, there is nothing that labor can do to extricate itself from this fix. If the unemployed compete with each other and bid down the money wage to lower the real wage in an attempt to find employment, they will not be successful. Labor's lot will only be made worse. Entrepreneurs will not increase employment beyond N_1^* because they cannot sell more than Y_1^{s*} output under any circumstances. Thus, the best that labor can hope for is that the money wage will be bid down to W_2 and the real wage, therefore, to W_2/P_1. When this has happened, we are at point *g* in Figure 4(a) (on the sec-

FIGURE 4

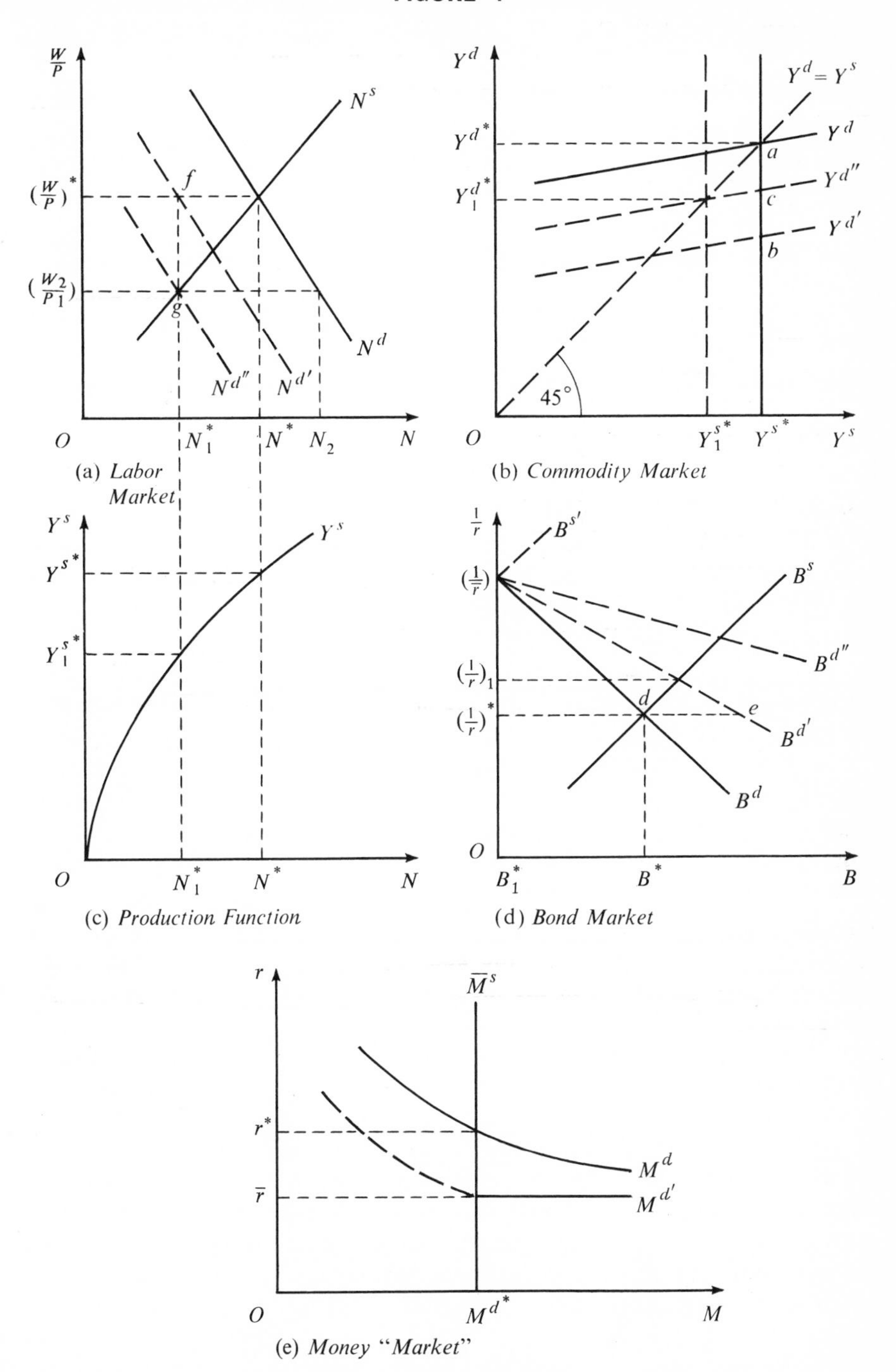

(a) *Labor Market*

(b) *Commodity Market*

(c) *Production Function*

(d) *Bond Market*

(e) *Money "Market"*

ond transitory demand for labor curve labeled $N^{d''}$). At point g, there is no excess supply of labor, so there is no further downward pressure on the money wage. And, technically, there is no longer any unemployment since g is on the supply curve of labor; everyone who wants a job at the real wage (W_2/P_1) has a job. Notice, though, that labor is indubitably worse off. Its absolute income and its share of total income have decreased, since employment is constant, the real wage has declined (which reduces absolute income), and real income is constant (which reduces labor's share).

If labor does bid down the money wage and real wage in this way—and, since we assume wage flexibility, there is no reason why it should not—it will remove the unemployment. However, we are not in any real equilibrium. Entrepreneurs are not happy with their lot. Instead, they are burdened with frustration. At the real wage W_2/P_1, they would *like* to employ N_2 labor, which is their "true" demand for labor according to the permanent demand for labor curve N^d. But, if they did employ this number, they could not sell the resulting output. We have seen that Y^{s*} output cannot be sold no matter how low the price of commodities, so the larger output which would be forthcoming if N_2 were employed could not possibly be sold either. Presumably, entrepreneurs find frustration a lesser evil than bankruptcy to bear, and we may assume they would accept the discontent of staying at point g.

Whichever way you look at this example, somebody is not going to be happy. There is either excess commodity supply, unemployment, or entrepreneurial frustration. This disequilibrium can be rattled around from place to place, but it cannot be eliminated. When our macroeconomic model is specified in this way, then, we cannot rely on it to generate equilibrium values of *all* the variables. It was with such a model in mind that Keynes reached the conclusion, "there . . . is no ground for the belief that a flexible wage (and price) policy is capable of maintaining a state of continuous full employment. . . . The economic system cannot be made self-adjusting along these lines."[2] Keynes was correct. But note, however, that his correctness is crucially dependent upon the exclusion of a real balance effect from the commodity demand function. This, of course, may not be a severe limitation if our money is predominantly of the inside variety and, thus, not the type that generates a real balance effect.

We are now in a position to assert the following important conclusion based on material presented in Chapters 10, 11, and 12: *permanent unemployment is possible within a macrostatic analytical framework if, and only if, one or more of the three price variables in our model is rigid.* In Chapter 10 we saw that a rigid money wage can lead to permanent unemployment, in Chapter 11 we saw that a rigid price level can do the same, and in this chapter we have seen that a rigid interest rate can do the trick, too (when real balances are omitted from the aggregate demand function). This list is *exclusive.* There are no other ways in which permanent unemployment can arise.

[2] Keynes, *op. cit.*, p. 267.

3 The Emasculation of Monetary Policy by a Liquidity Trap

Earlier, we demonstrated how it is always possible to eliminate any unemployment that may arise due to wage or price rigidity by the judicious use of monetary policy. However, the existence of a liquidity trap prevents monetary policy from being used to this end. We shall now indicate why.

Consider Figure 5. In Figure 5(a) we have plotted the money wage on the vertical axis. Examination of the labor market shows unemployment equal to $N^* - N_0$ prevails. Full employment real income is Y_0^s, while the actual level of real income is Y^{s*}. The unemployment is assumed to be the result of money wage rigidity at $\bar{W}$. However, the analysis which follows is independent of the cause of the unemployment.[1] What happens when the monetary authorities increase the money stock in the face of this unemployment? As a result of the real balance effect on these curves, the increase in the money stock will shift the demand for bonds right, rotating it around $1/\bar{r}$, and the supply of bonds left. What are the curves' positions when the money stock is increased to $\bar{M}^{s'}$? The demand for bonds shifts to $B^{d'}$ and the supply of bonds to $B^{s'}$. The interest rate reaches its minimum level $1/\bar{r}$.

This fall in the interest rate increases the aggregate commodity demand curve in Figure 5(b) to $Y^{d'}$. Note that this increase in commodity demand is due *solely* to the decline in the interest rate. There is no real balance effect in the commodity demand function. Given the aggregate supply of commodities Y^{s*}, this increase in aggregate demand creates excess demand equal to *ab*. Commodity prices rise, we assume, to P_1^*. This increase in prices reduces the real wage from $(\bar{W}/P)^*$ to $(\bar{W}/P)_1^*$ shifting the demand for labor curve right to $N^{d'}$ and raising employment to N_1^*. These changes increase output to Y_1^{s*}, at which the excess commodity demand is eliminated; and, hence, there is no further upward pressure on the price level.

In the money market, the excess supply of money created by the original increase in the money supply to $\bar{M}^{s'}$ has been eliminated by the rise in the price level to P_1^*, the rise in real income to Y_1^{s*}, and the fall in the interest rate to $\bar{r}$. The demand for nominal money curve has shifted right to $M^{d'}$.

When the money supply is increased to $\bar{M}^{s'}$ we hit the liquidity trap interest rate $\bar{r}$. What happens if the money supply is increased further? The short answer is nothing. The interest rate will not decline any further, since no one will lend at an interest rate below $\bar{r}$. Any further increase in money balances is hoarded. Since the interest rate cannot be reduced and there is no real balance effect in the commodity demand function, aggregate commodity demand is fixed at $Y^{d'}$. If $Y^{d'}$ cannot be increased, there is no way to create excess commodity demand in order to drive up the price level and, thus, drive down the real wage. This must happen if the demand for labor curve is to shift further right and additional employment be generated. Effectively,

[1] The cause could just as well be price rigidity or the existence of a liquidity trap. Only marginal changes in the following analysis would be required to accommodate such cases and you may wish to work them out as an exercise.

FIGURE 5

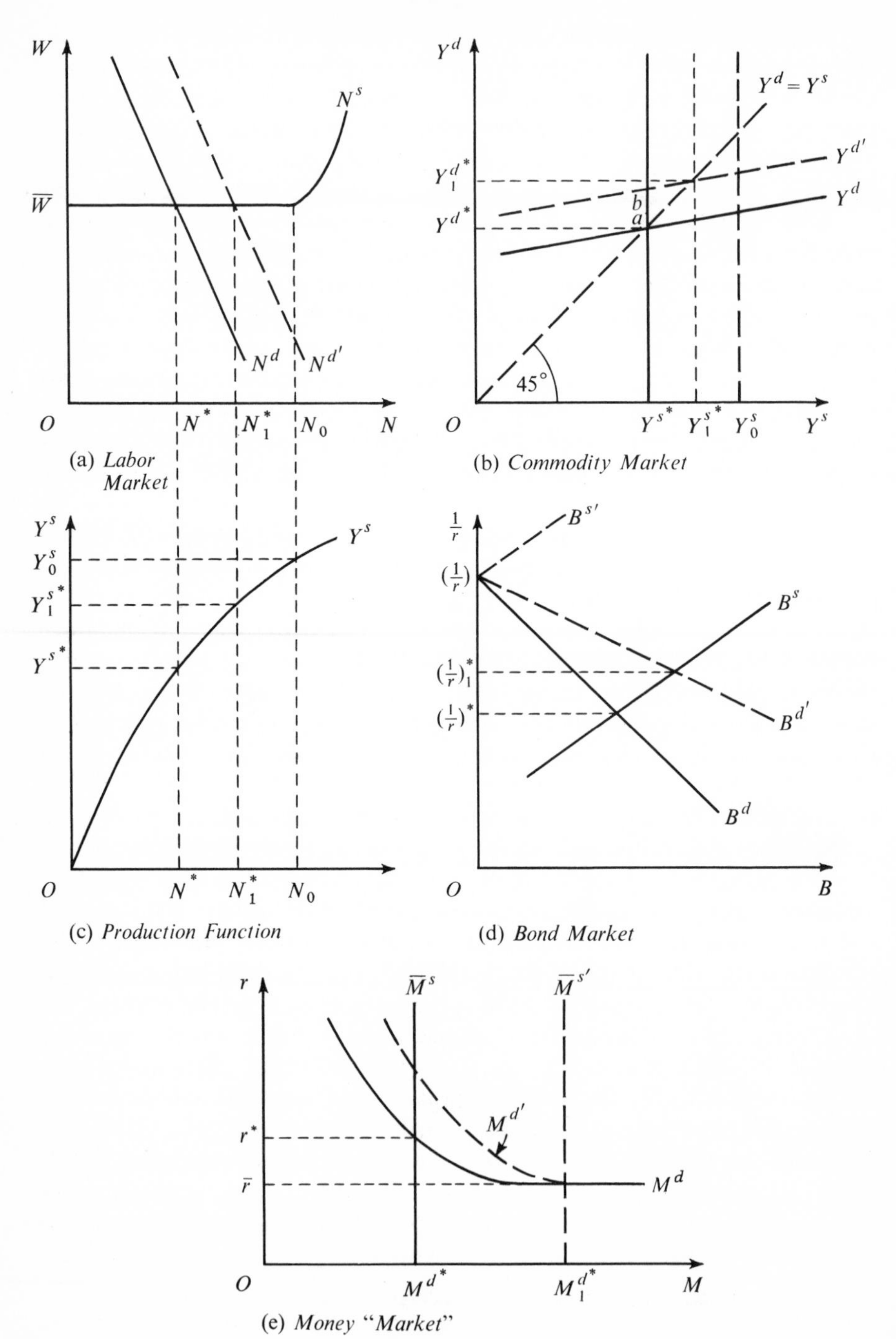

W
$\overline{W}$
N^s
N^d
$N^{d'}$
O
N^*
N_1^*
N_0
N
(a) Labor Market
Y^d
$Y^d = Y^s$
$Y^{d'}$
Y^d
Y_1^{d*}
Y^{d*}
b
a
45°
O
Y^{s*}
Y_1^{s*}
Y_0^s
Y^s
(b) Commodity Market
Y^s
Y_0^s
Y_1^{s*}
Y^{s*}
O
N^*
N_1^*
N_0
(c) Production Function
$\frac{1}{r}$
$B^{s'}$
$(\frac{1}{r})$
B^s
$(\frac{1}{r})_1^*$
$(\frac{1}{r})^*$
$B^{d'}$
B^d
O
B
(d) Bond Market
r
$\overline{M}^s$
$\overline{M}^{s'}$
$M^{d'}$
r^*
$\bar{r}$
M^d
O
M^{d*}
M_1^{d*}
M
(e) Money "Market"

then, an increase in the money supply beyond $\bar{M}^{s'}$ is of no use. Monetary policy is emasculated.

We have just seen that circumstances can arise in which it is at least theoretically possible that monetary policy may be incapable of counteracting any unemployment that may emerge. (Recall that this is not true unless there is a liquidity trap. In previous chapters we have seen that unemployment caused by wage or price rigidities can be overcome by an expansionary monetary policy.)

This theoretical innovation has had a tremendous impact on the development of economics. Prior to the Keynesian revolution, economists assumed, more or less universally, that a government's tax and expenditure policies should be tailored to meet the community's public-good requirements. This usually meant that once the decision to appropriate a certain amount for public-good consumption had been made, the appropriate taxes would be levied to meet that expenditure exactly (in peace time). There was no call for budget deficits. If anything, there was pressure to run budget surpluses so that the outstanding government debt could slowly be reduced by redemption. This all changed in the wake of the Keynesian revolution. If monetary policy is useless in bringing about full employment, what can be done instead? The answer in this particular case is for the government to pursue an active fiscal policy—spending more and taxing less.

The original impetus for work toward a more detailed understanding of fiscal policy issues arose from the problem of the liquidity trap and the problem of secular stagnation discussed in Chapter 11. There, you will recall, no matter how low the interest rate was driven through monetary policy, commodity market equilibrium could not be reestablished because saving and investment were held to be interest inelastic. The ensuing inquiry soon became more widespread, however, with a great explosion of activity in the field of fiscal policy analysis. It is no exaggeration to say that this area soon usurped monetary policy as *the* major economic stabilization technique. Fiscal policy was advocated for use in both directions—as an expansionary and a contractionary instrument. "Money does not matter" became a catch phrase among economists throughout the 1940s and even into the 1950s. Fiscal policy was all the rage. Monetary policy was completely upstaged.

By the mid 1950s, however, a reaction set in. There may be a liquidity trap, the skeptics allowed, but has anyone ever seen one? Does the theoretical possibility that monetary policy may lack expansionary thrust in a limited set of circumstances justify discarding this policy for all time and for all economic conditions? Moreover, accumulating research on monetary policy indicated that "money does matter." In this respect the contributions of Friedman, his collaborators, students, and other followers of the *Chicago School* have been particularly important. The University of Chicago's Department of Economics has long been associated with the intellectual tradition of the quantity theory of money.[2] In the wake of the publication of

[2] Oddly enough, there used to be a similar tradition at Keynes' own institution—Cambridge University (where he was a Fellow of Kings College). Recall the famous Cambridge equation

Keynes' *General Theory,* however, from which the implication that "money does not matter" was derived and emphasized, the quantity theory fell on hard times. For almost exactly twenty years, the Chicago school's voice was muted, or, when it was raised, ignored.[3] However, in 1956 Friedman and some of his students published a collection of essays which refocused attention on both the theoretical and empirical relevance of money.[4] It would not be too far wrong to date the revival of interest in money, the notion that "money does matter," with the publication of these essays. Interest in money has persisted to the present day and has engaged the energies of those well outside the group defined by the Chicago School. In the field of monetary theory and policy, research has proceeded apace, including theoretical and empirical inquiries into the demand for money, the supply of money, the influence of money on prices and incomes, the theory of inflation, the term structure of interest rates, the lag in effect of monetary policy, and so on. This is not a book in monetary theory and policy, so it would be inappropriate here to provide detailed references. However, it would be remiss not to mention Friedman and Schwartz's monumental *Monetary History of the United States*.[5] This is a landmark study whose main thesis is that money *does* matter—very much. In all, then, monetary policy has now regained parity with fiscal policy as an area of concern and field of research. Monetary policy has crept back towards center stage where it is now, in most circles, given equal billing with fiscal policy as an economic stabilization technique. In the next chapter we move on to discuss fiscal policy and how it operates.

Summary

This chapter discussed the implications for the model of upward rigidity in bond prices (which is equivalent to *downward rigidity in the interest rate*). Such rigidity is conditional upon *inelastic bond price expectations*. If there

approach to the quantity theory discussed in §7.3. But that tradition was killed at Cambridge by the macroeconomic revolution sparked by Keynes and fanned by his followers, many of whom emphasized the revolution's implication that "money does not matter." The Cambridge quantity theory tradition died only at Cambridge, however. It was co-opted by Chicago where Friedman's restatement of the quantity theory of money is supported by a basically Cambridge equation approach to the demand for money. (See M. Friedman, "The Quantity Theory of Money; A Restatement," in M. Friedman (ed.), *Studies in the Quantity Theory of Money,* University of Chicago Press, 1956). Ironically enough, if one had to single out an event which indicated the beginning of the revival of interest in monetary economics, it would be this collection of essays by Friedman and his students.

[3] To inject a personal note here may provide some historical perspective on the economic disrepute into which the Chicago School had fallen. In 1956 I was an undergraduate at the London School of Economics, where in a course on monetary theory the instructor (who, although no longer there, shall remain nameless) mentioned in a casual aside and with ill-concealed contempt that the Chicago School simply amounted to a coterie of quantity theorists with a passionate devotion to madcap schemes for the reform of the banking system such as the imposition of 100 percent reserve requirements.

[4] *Ibid.*

[5] M. Friedman and A. J. Schwartz, *A Monetary History of the United States, 1867–1960,* National Bureau of Economic Research, 1963.

is some minimum interest rate which the bond and money markets will tolerate, then when this minimum interest rate is reached we have a *liquidity trap*. Even when wages and commodity prices are flexible, this interest rate rigidity can lead to either persistent *deflation* (*continuously* falling prices) *or* persistent *unemployment* (given a sufficiently large *initial* deflationary impulse and no real wealth effect in the aggregate commodity demand function). This chapter, in combination with Chapters 10 and 11, allows us to arrive at the supremely important conclusion that within a macrostatic context unemployment will be permanent if, and only if, one or more of the three price variables in our model is rigid.

In previous chapters, we showed that unemployment caused by wage or price rigidities could always be removed by fiscal *or* monetary policy. However, when the interest rate is rigid, *monetary* policy is emasculated (as long as there is no real balance effect in the aggregate commodity demand function).

Questions

1. Assume that the price level falls indefinitely, ceteris paribus. Show, nonetheless, that if bond price expectations are inelastic, there is a minimum below which the interest rate will not fall.
2. Assume that the supply of money is increased indefinitely, ceteris paribus. Show that if bond price expectations are inelastic, there is a minimum below which the interest rate will not fall.
3. Show that if there is some minimum below which the interest rate will not fall and there is no real wealth effect in the aggregate commodity demand function, secular stagnation might occur.
4. Show that if a liquidity trap exists and there is no real wealth effect in the aggregate commodity demand function, a sufficiently large decrease in entrepreneurial expectations could lead to persistent unemployment. Why would this not occur if a real wealth effect exists in the aggregate commodity demand function?
5. Show that monetary policy is incapable of eliminating unemployment caused by a liquidity trap. Devise a fiscal policy to eliminate such unemployment.

SELECTED READINGS

1. J. M. Keynes, *The General Theory of Employment, Interest, and Money,* Macmillan, 1936, chapter 13.
2. D. Laidler, *The Demand for Money,* International, 1969. Excellent survey of the various theories of the demand for money and the pertinent empirical evidence. Contains a comprehensive bibliography. Concludes that the evidence for the existence of a liquidity trap is tenuous.
3. A. Leijonhufvud, *On Keynesian Economics and the Economics of Keynes,* Oxford, 1968, chapter 5, section 3. Makes the point that although Keynes recognized the theoretical possibility of a liquidity trap, he did not think it important from a practical point of view.
4. D. Patinkin, *Money, Interest, and Prices,* 2nd ed., Harper & Row, 1965, chapter 14, section 3. The authoritative theoretical discussion of the liquidity trap.

FURTHER READINGS

5. M. Friedman (ed.), *Studies in the Quantity Theory of Money,* University of Chicago Press, 1956. A collection of theoretical and empirical essays on the quantity theory. Marked the revival of interest in money after the field had laid largely dormant for almost a generation.
6. M. Friedman and A. J. Schwartz, *A Monetary History of the United States, 1867–1960,* National Bureau of Economic Research, 1963. A monumental scholarly discussion of the influence of money on economic events in the United States over almost a century. Makes the case that "money always matters." Hostile critics would say that it implies "money *only* matters."
7. H. G. Johnson, "Monetary Theory and Policy," *American Economic Review,* June, 1962. Masterly summary of the research in this area during the revival of interest in monetary theory and policy.

13

Hicksian IS/LM Analysis

There exists an extremely fruitful analytical apparatus for the elucidation of macroeconomic relationships known as *IS/LM analysis*. Originally developed by Hicks,[1] this apparatus comes into its own when unemployment prevails and, thus, real income is less than full employment real income. Although the technique has been extended to cover full employment situations as well, it loses much of its simplicity and elegance by this. Thus, we shall not attempt to use the *IS/LM* analysis for such cases.

Essentially, *IS/LM* analysis concentrates on the conditions that must prevail if both the money and commodity markets are to clear under less than full employment conditions. The unemployment that prevails is usually attributed to the existence of a rigid money wage. Thus, the wage rate is fixed at $\bar{W}$. Moreover, prices at $\bar{P}$ are also assumed to be rigid. This may be the result of either short-run price inflexibility (§11.1) or constant returns to scale (§11.2). With both wages and prices fixed, the real wage is fixed at $\bar{W}/\bar{P}$. In such a model, you will recall that output (income) and employment are determined solely by aggregate commodity demand. The labor market implied by this setup is like that discussed in §11.2. Thus, we operate the model with a nonclearing labor market and then concentrate on the conditions necessary to make the commodity and money markets clear. The bond market is *assumed* to clear when the money market clears and is, therefore, excluded from the discussion. We also assume throughout this chapter that money is of the inside variety and, thus, that no real balance effect exists.

1 The LM Curve

An *LM* curve is defined to be a locus of combinations of interest rates and real income levels at which the supply of money (the *M* part of *LM*) is

[1] J. R. Hicks, "Mr. Keynes and the 'Classics'; A Suggested Interpretation," *Econometrica*, April, 1937.

FIGURE 1

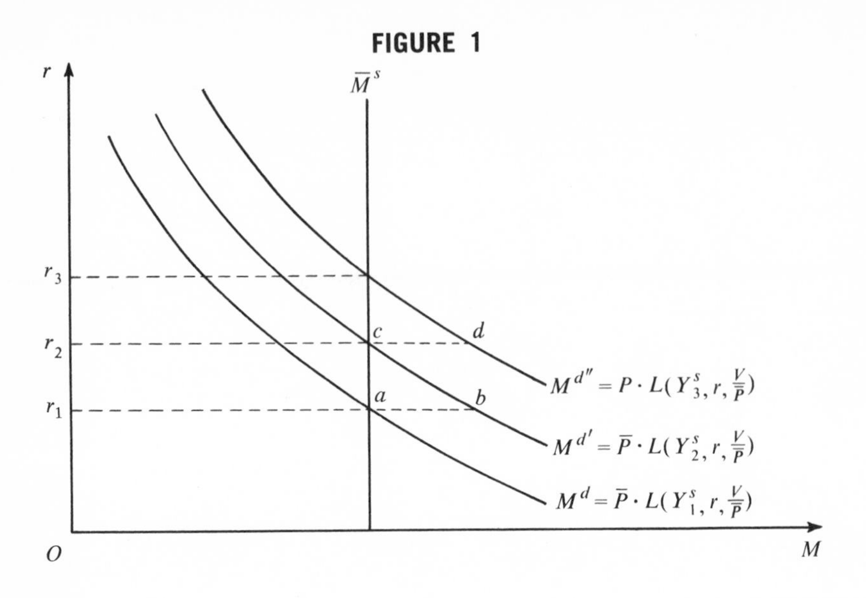

equal to the demand for money (the L part of LM). How is an LM curve derived and what sort of shape may it be expected to have? Consider Figure 1. The supply and demand for money are equal at an interest rate of r_1 and a real income level of Y_1^s. Thus, r_1 and Y_1^s define one point on an LM curve, since they are an interest rate and real income level at which money supply and demand are equal (and an LM curve is the locus of *all* such points). This is the point marked A in Figure 2.

Now suppose there was a rise in real income (for some reason) to Y_2^s; then the demand for money would shift right to $M^{d'}$ and there would be an excess demand for money equal to ab in Figure 1. For this excess demand to be removed, the interest rate must *rise* to r_2. Thus, when real income rises to Y_2^s, the interest rate must rise to r_2 if the supply of and demand for money are to remain equal. Hence, another point on the LM curve is the point B, corresponding to Y_2^s and r_2, in Figure 2. Analogously, should real income rise to Y_3^s, the demand for money would shift right to $M^{d''}$ and an excess demand for money equal to cd in Figure 1 would exist at r_2. For this to be eliminated, the interest rate must rise to r_3. Thus, the combination Y_3^s and r_3 is another point on the LM curve—the point C in Figure 2. It is clear from the foregoing discussion that when real income rises the interest rate must rise too, if the supply of and demand for money are to remain equal. It follows that the LM curve generally has a positive slope (although we shall soon discuss some exceptions to this rule).

2 Shifts in the LM Curve I; Changes in the Money Supply

The curve LM in Figure 2 was derived for a *given* supply of money $\overline{M}^s$ (see Figure 1) and a *given* state of liquidity preference or *form* of the demand

FIGURE 2

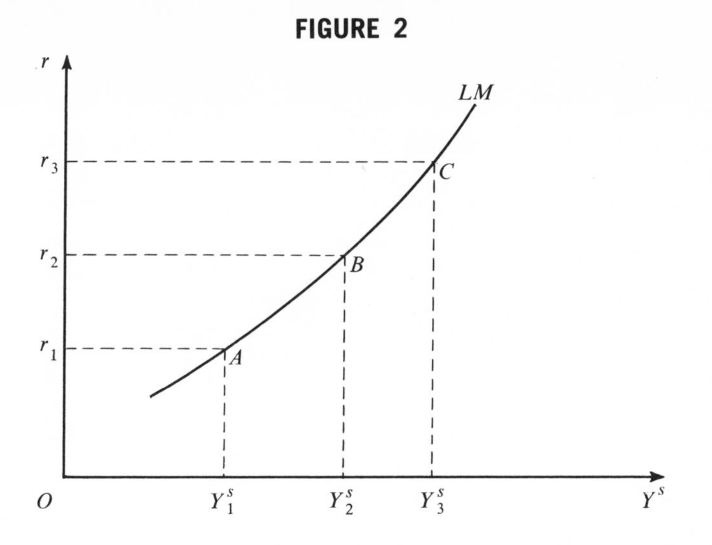

for money function (that is, the community's tastes for money to hold vis-à-vis other assets were held constant). If either the supply of money is different from $\bar{M}^s$ or the form of the demand for money function is different from L, we would obtain a different LM curve.

For example, assume that the supply of money is not $\bar{M}^s$, but some higher quantity $\bar{M}^{s\prime}$ (see Figure 3). If the level of real income is Y_1^s, the demand for money curve is M^d. In order that the demand for money equals the supply when real income is Y_1^s, the interest rate now must be r_1'—a lower interest rate than r_1. The point A' in Figure 4 corresponds, then, to Y_1^s and r_1' and is one point on a *new LM* curve, labeled LM', obtained when the supply of money has been increased to $\bar{M}^{s\prime}$. Similarly, if the supply of money is $\bar{M}^{s\prime}$ and the level of real income is Y_2^s the supply and demand for money will be

FIGURE 3

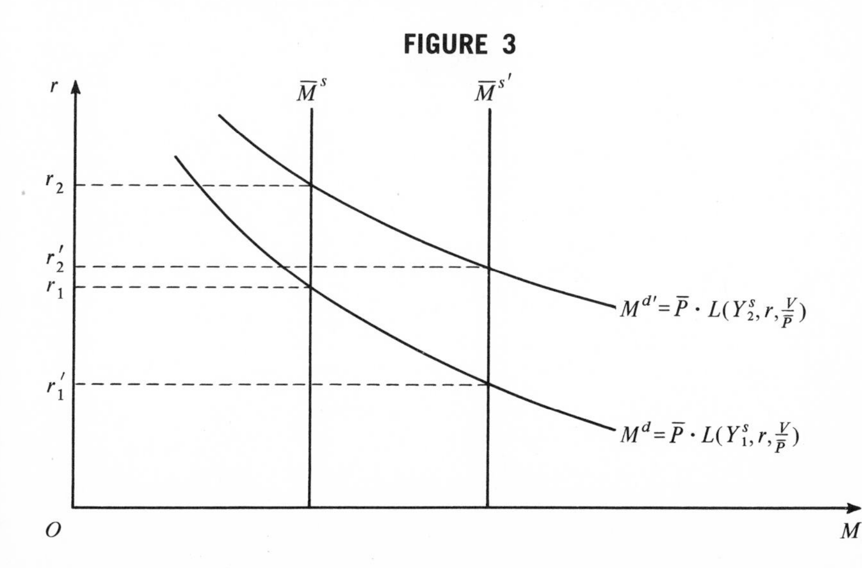

FIGURE 4

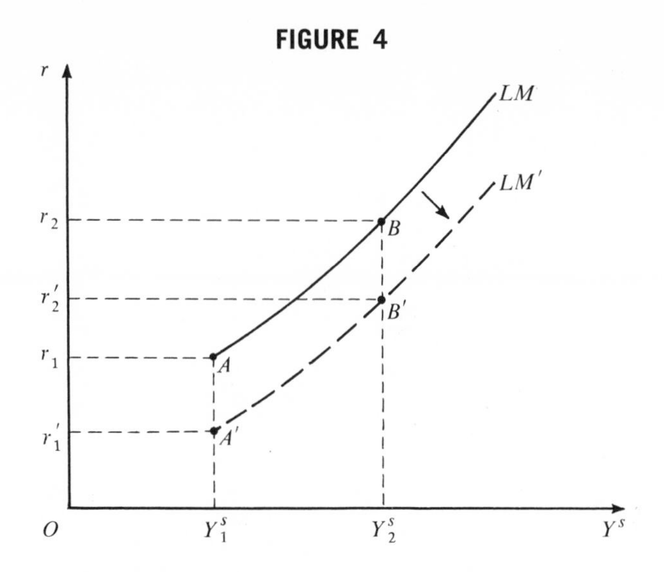

equal at r_2' (and not r_2 as was true before), which corresponds to point B' in Figure 4. It is apparent that an increase in the supply of money has shifted the *LM* curve downward toward the right (in the direction of the arrow in Figure 4). Basically, the reason for this is quite simple. If the supply of money is increased, then there must be a decrease in the interest rate and a rise in income for the demand for money to become equal to the supply again.

Manifestly, a decrease in the supply of money will have the opposite effect. Consult Figures 5 and 6. When the supply of money is decreased to $\overline{M}^{s''}$ and if the level of income is Y_2^s, the interest rate which must prevail to equate money supply and demand is r_2''; this corresponds to point B'' in Figure 6. Obviously, a decrease in the supply of money shifts the *LM* curve upward toward the left. Once more the reasoning is simple. If the supply of

FIGURE 5

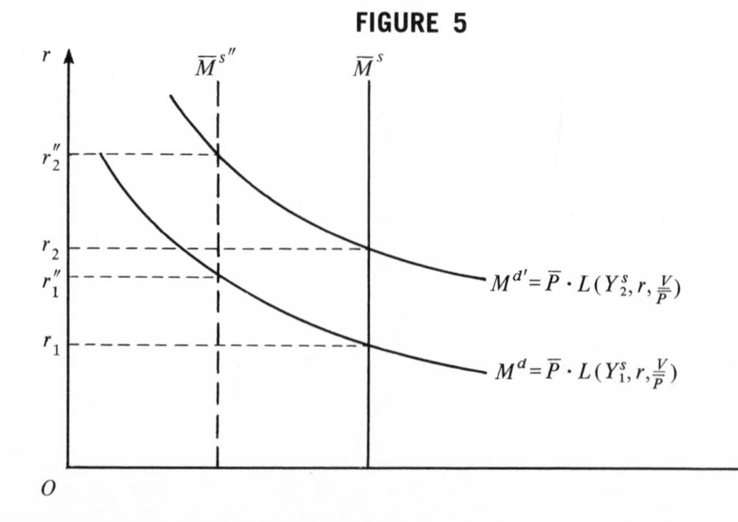

FIGURE 6

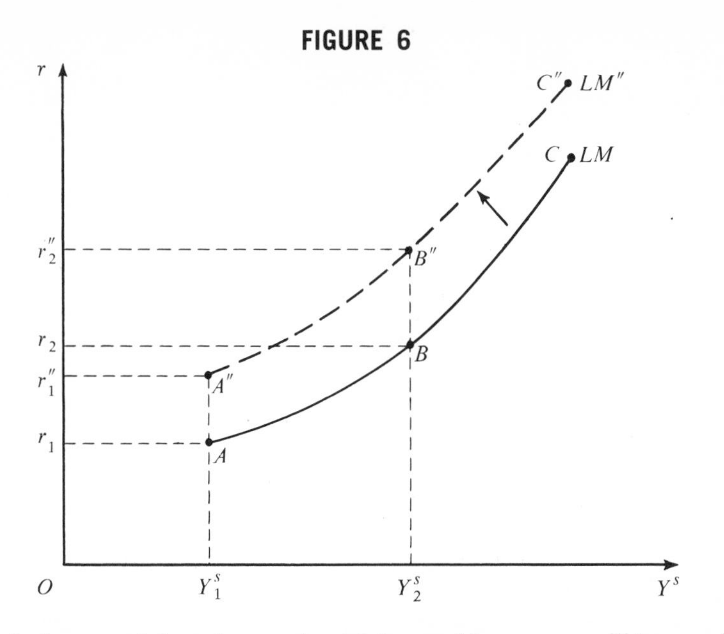

money is decreased then the supply and demand for money will be equal only at a higher rate of interest and lower level of real income.

We conclude that an increase in the supply of money shifts the *LM* curve right and a decrease in the supply of money shifts the *LM* curve left.

3 Shifts in the LM Curve II; Changes in Liquidity Preference

Next, we want to examine what happens to the *LM* curve if there is a change in the community's preferences (or tastes) for money vis-à-vis other assets (a so-called change in liquidity preference). Consider Figures 7 and 8. Assume, first, that there is a decrease in liquidity preference; that is, the *form* of the demand for money function has changed so that for any given interest rate and real income level the community now wishes to hold less money than before. If the original demand for money was M^d (with form L) then, after the decrease in liquidity preference, the new demand for money will be $M^{d'}$ (with form L'). It is clear that if income remains constant at Y_1^s, then the interest rate must fall to r_1' in order for the demand for money to again equal the supply. So, with decreased liquidity preference, r_1' and Y_1^s are an interest rate–real income combination which now equates money supply and demand. This combination corresponds to A' in Figure 8. If the level of income were Y_2^s, then, with the original degree of liquidity preference, the demand for money curve would be $M^{d''}$ and the supply and demand for money would be equal for Y_2^s and r_2, respectively (point B in Figure 8). When liquidity preference decreases, the *new* demand for money curve $M^{d'''}$ prevails and the interest rate and income level at which the supply of money equals the demand are r_2' and Y_2^s (point B' in Figure 8). Clearly, then, a decrease in

FIGURE 7

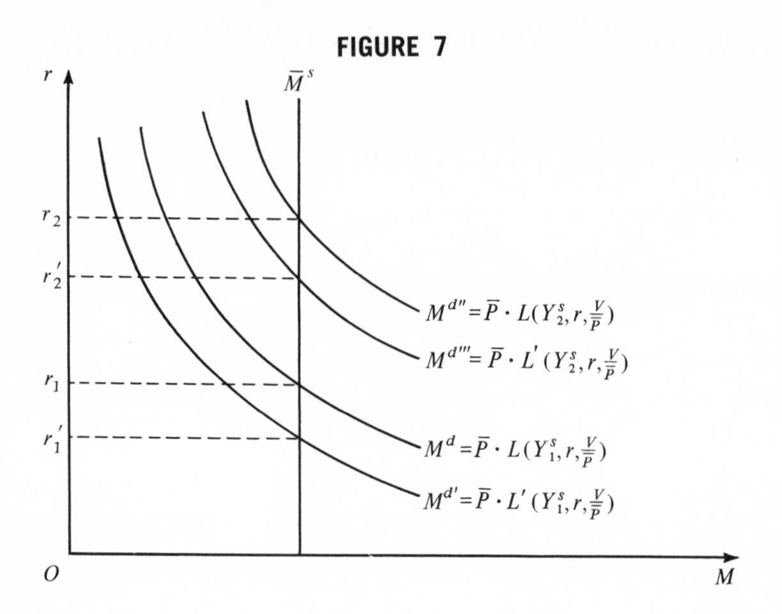

liquidity preference has shifted the *LM* curve right to *L'M*. The explanation is straightforward. When the supply of money is fixed and there is a decrease in the demand for money because liquidity preference has fallen, the quantity of money demanded can rise only to equal the fixed quantity supplied through a fall in the interest rate and a rise in income. Naturally, we obtain the opposite result when liquidity preference increases. Consider Figures 9 and 10. With the original degree of liquidity preference, M^d is applicable and the supply of money equals the demand at r_1 and Y_1^s. With increased liquidity preference, $M^{d'}$ prevails (because of the changed *form* of the demand for money function revealed by L'') and, thus, the supply of money will

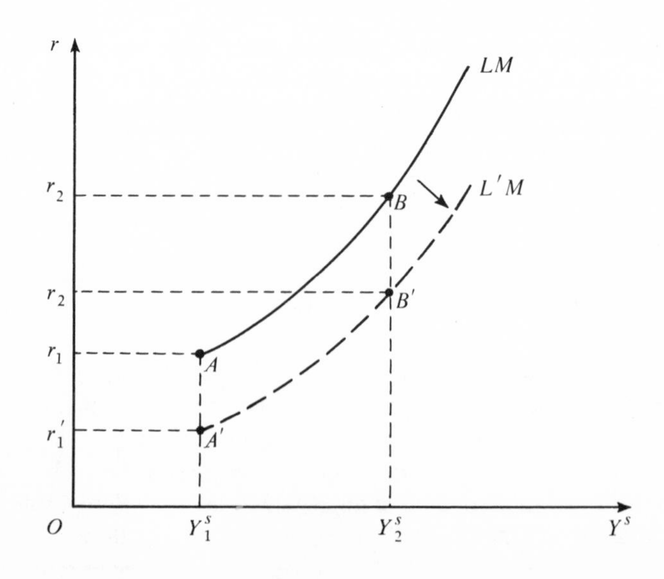

FIGURE 9

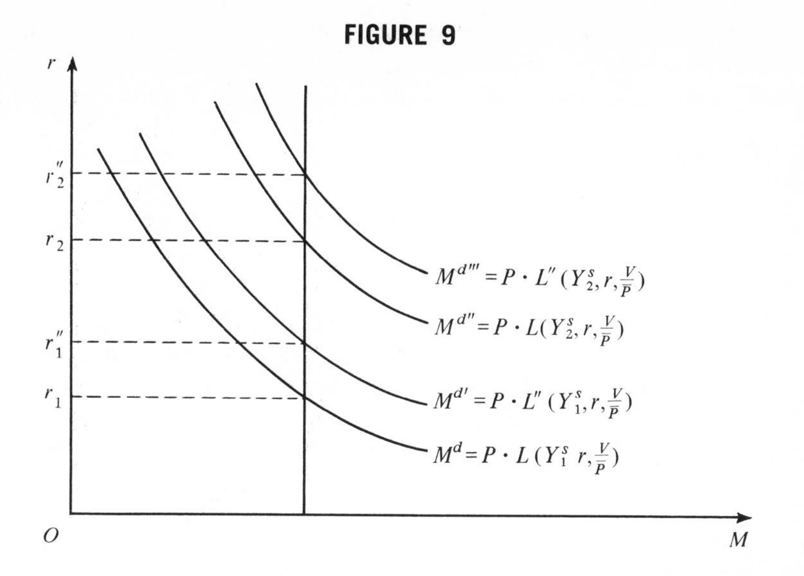

equal the demand at r_1'' if income remains constant at Y_1^s. This corresponds to A'' in Figure 10. Similarly, if income happens to be Y_2^s, after the increase in liquidity preference the demand for money will shift from $M^{d''}$ to $M^{d'''}$ and money supply and demand will be equal only at r_2'' as long as income remains constant at Y_2^s. This corresponds to B'' in Figure 10. Clearly, the *LM* curve has shifted left to $L''M$. Generally, then, when there is an increase in liquidity preference while the supply of money is constant, the quantity of money demanded can only be made equal to the fixed supply available by a rise in the interest rate and a fall in income.

We may conclude that a decrease in liquidity preference shifts the *LM*

FIGURE 10

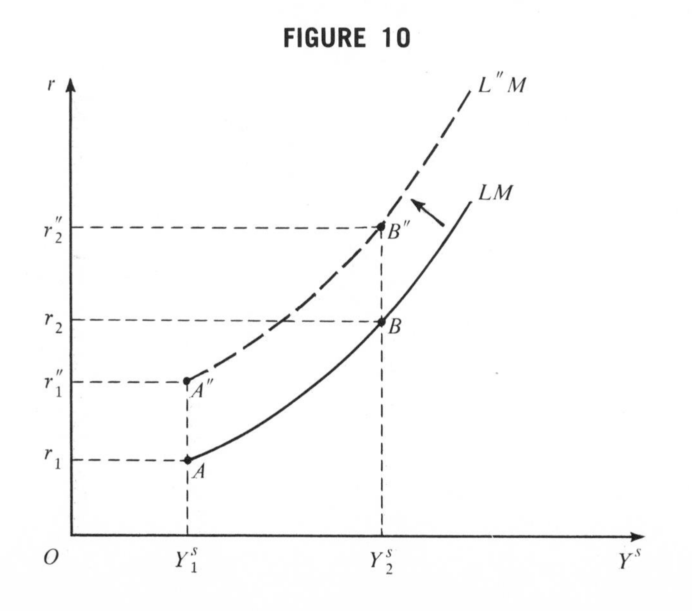

curve right, while an increase in liquidity preference shifts it left. Clearly, a decrease in liquidity preference has the same effect on the *LM* curve as an increase in the supply of money, while an increase in liquidity preference has the same effect as a decrease in the supply of money. (These results are quite reasonable if you think about them.)

4 The Situation Off an LM Curve

We have still to show what the situation is *off* an *LM* curve. Consider Figure 11. We know that the supply of money equals the demand at point *A* (namely, when income is Y_1^s and the interest rate is r_1) because *A* is on the *LM* curve—the locus of income and interest rate combinations at which this equality prevails. What, though, is the case at some point off the *LM* curve such as *B*, *C*, *D*, or *E*? Consider point *B* first. We have just noted that at point *A* there is equality between money supplied and demanded. Point *B* corresponds to the same level of income Y_1^s, but a *higher* interest rate r_2. Since the quantity of money demanded *declines* when the interest rate rises, at point *B* the supply of money $\bar{M}^s$ (which is fixed) must exceed the demand for money M^d. Next, look at point *C*. Supply and demand for money are equal at *A* where income is Y_1^s and the interest rate is r_1. But point *C* corresponds to the same interest rate r_1 and a *lower* level of income Y_2^s. Since the demand for money *decreases* when the level of income decreases, at point *C* the supply of money must exceed the demand. Similar reasoning for *any* point to the left of *LM* will reveal that the supply of money to be held exceeds the demand for money to hold, that is, there is an excess supply of money. Hence, we enter the notation $\bar{M}^s > M^d$ in that space.

As you might expect, the opposite is true to the right of *LM*. Consider

FIGURE 11

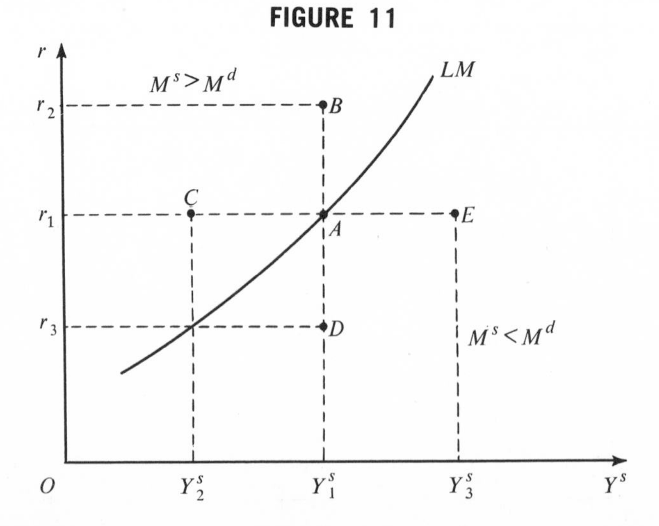

point D; it corresponds to the same level of income Y_1^s as point A, but has a lower rate of interest r_3. Since the quantity of money demanded increases when the interest rate declines, the quantity of money demanded at D must exceed the fixed supply. Finally, consider point E. If supply and demand for money are equal at r_1 and Y_1^s (point A), the demand must exceed the supply at point E, which corresponds to the same interest rate and a higher level of income Y_3^s (since the demand for money increases when income increases). Thus, $M^d > \bar{M}^s$ at points such as D and E, and similar reasoning reveals that this is the case at *all* points to the right of LM. Hence, the notation $M^s < M^d$ has been entered in this space.

5 The IS Curve

We define an IS curve as the locus of all interest rate and real income levels at which the supply of commodities is equal to the demand for commodities—that is, the commodity market is clearing, or in equilibrium. How is an IS curve derived and what shape can it be expected to have?

Consider Figure 12. The investment and saving functions, labeled I and S, respectively, are drawn for a *given* level of income Y_1^s. We know that the commodity market clears when planned investment ("injections") is equal to planned saving ("leakages"). For the level of income Y_1^s, this occurs when the interest rate is r_1. Thus, we have identified one combination of income and interest rate at which the commodity market clears. This combination is the point A in Figure 13. Now suppose that the level of income rises to Y_2^s. In general, this will shift both the S curve and the I curve to the right, since both saving and investment are increasing functions of the level of income.

FIGURE 12

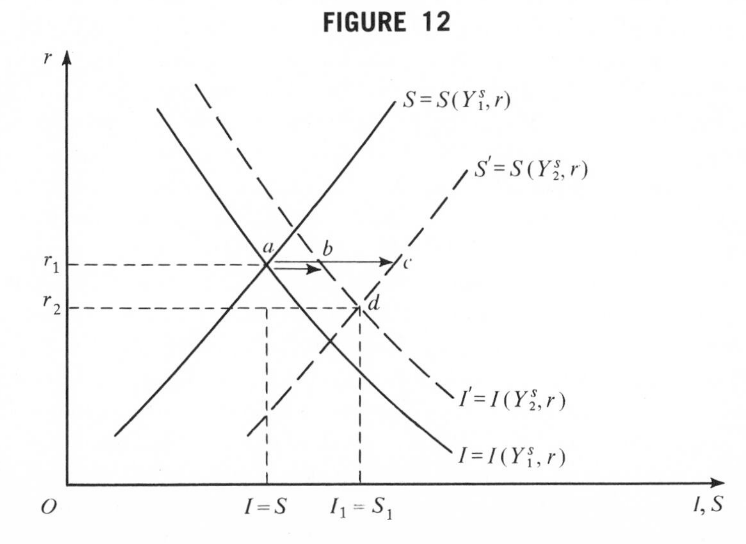

FIGURE 13

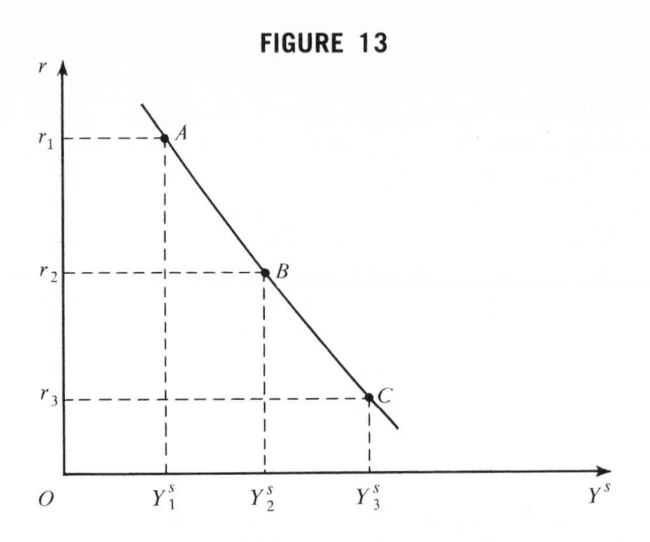

The new curves are labeled I' and S'. You will notice immediately that the saving curve has shifted right more than the investment curve. This is intentional and is the result of assuming that the marginal propensity to save (out of income) is greater than the marginal propensity to invest (out of income). [This is not a new assumption; it is one that we have made throughout this book (see §3.3). It is this assumption that makes the slope of the aggregate demand curve less than unity and, thus, causes the aggregate demand curve to cut the 45°-line in our basic commodity market diagram from above when moving from left to right.]

When the marginal propensity to save exceeds the marginal propensity to invest, a given increase in income from Y_1^s to Y_2^s will naturally shift the saving curve further to the right than it will shift the investment curve (in Figure 12) by *ac* and *ab*, respectively. After these shifts have occurred, the commodity market will not clear at the old rate of interest r_1. There will be an excess supply of commodities equal to *bc*. For the commodity market to clear at the *higher* level of income Y_2^s, the interest rate must *decline* to r_2. The excess supply of commodities at r_1 and Y_2^s is eliminated by an increase in the investment component of aggregate demand (the movement from *b* to *d* along I' in Figure 12) and an increase in the consumption component of aggregate demand (i.e., *decrease* in saving—the movement from *c* to *d* along S' in Figure 12). The combination of r_2 and Y_2^s is plotted as point *B* in Figure 13. Point *B* represents another combination of income and interest rate at which the commodity market will clear. It becomes apparent that the *IS* curve slopes downwards. We need only consider what would happen if there were another *increase* in income to Y_3^s. This would shift the *S* and *I* curves in Figure 12 to the right again to S'' and I'' (not shown)—and the former more than the latter. Thus for planned saving to equal planned investment (alternatively, for the commodity market to clear), the rate of interest would have to decline to, say, r_3. Hence, we obtain point *C* in Figure 13.

6 Shifts in the IS Curve I; Changes in Entrepreneurial Expectations

The *IS* curve just derived in Figure 13 is based on a given set of entrepreneurial expectations and a given attitude toward thrift. What happens when either of these changes? We treat the effects of changes in entrepreneurial expectations on the *IS* curve in this section and consider the effects of changes in thrift in the following section. Look at Figures 14 and 15. As Figure 14 shows, with the original set of entrepreneurial expectations, saving and investment were equal at Y_1^s and r_1; however, if entrepreneurial expectations become more optimistic the investment curve shifts from I to I''. Note that more investment is planned at the same levels of income and interest rate. The shift from I to I'' is due to a change in the *form* of the investment function, hence, the prime on the functional. With more optimistic entrepreneurial expectations and the same level of income Y_1^s, the interest rate has to rise to r_1' if the commodity market is to clear. Thus, the new combination of income and interest rate levels at which the commodity market will clear is Y_1^s and r_1', which corresponds to point A' in Figure 15.

If we had started with the original set of expectations, and a higher level of income such as Y_2^s, then the commodity market would have cleared at Y_2^s and r_2, since the relevant saving and investment curves would be S' and I', respectively. After expectations became more optimistic the new investment schedule would be I''' and now the commodity market would clear when income was Y_2^s and the interest rate was r_2'. This combination corresponds to point B' in Figure 15. Therefore, we see that when expectations become more optimistic the whole *IS* curve shifts upwards toward the right. Basically, the reasoning here is quite simple—the excess commodity demand created by the rise in planned investment (brought about by improvement in expecta-

FIGURE 14

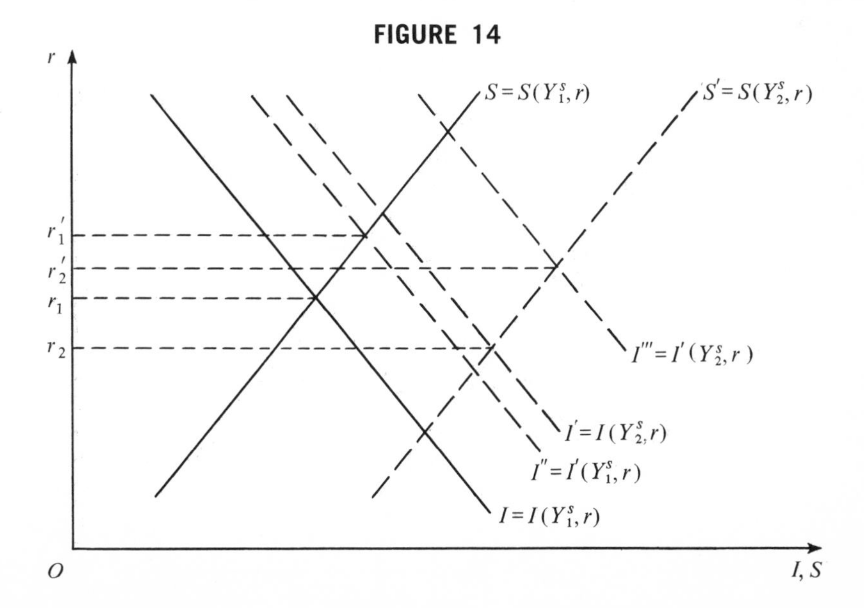

FIGURE 15

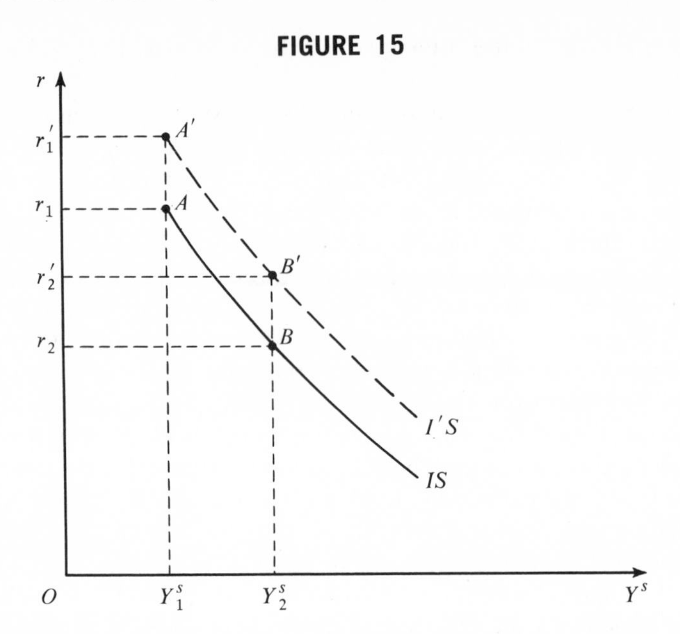

tions) can be eliminated by a combination of a rise in the interest rate and a rise in income. (A rise in income helps to remove the excess demand by causing the supply of commodities to increase more than the demand; this effect occurs because the marginal propensity to spend is assumed to be less than unity.)

On the other hand, when entrepreneurial expectations become more pessimistic, the *IS* curve shifts downwards to the left. Consider Figures 16 and 17. As Figure 16 shows, with the original set of expectations, the commodity market clears when the interest was r_1 and the level of income Y_1^s. After expectations become worse, the investment curve shifts left to I' (note that this is because of a change in the *form* of the function, as indicated again by the prime on the functional). This means that the interest rate must de-

FIGURE 16

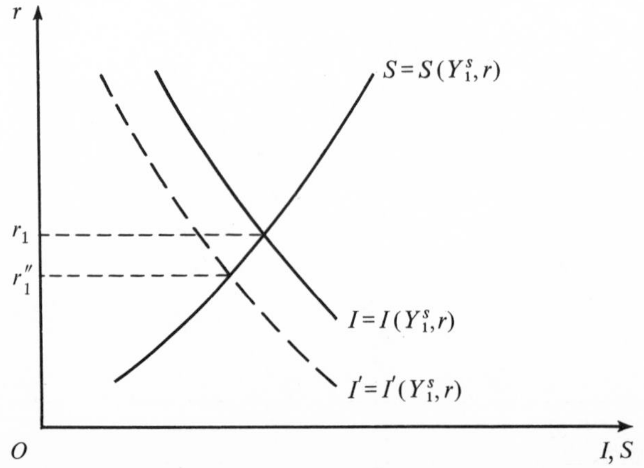

FIGURE 17

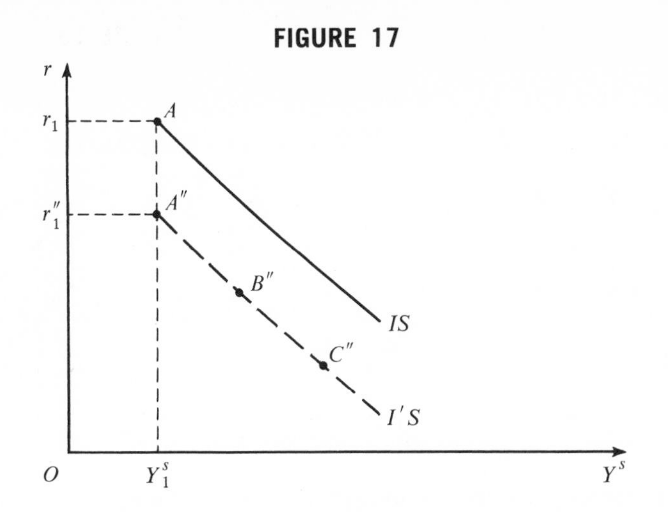

cline to r_1'' if the commodity market is to clear now at the same level of income Y_1^s. The combination of r_1'' and Y_1^s corresponds to point A'' in Figure 17. The other points B'' and C'', respectively indicating interest rate and income levels at which the commodity market will clear when expectations become more pessimistic, may be developed by analogous reasoning. In general, then, poorer expectations cause the *IS* curve to shift downward to the left to $I'S$, indicating that the excess supply of commodities (brought about by the more pessimistic expectations) can be removed by a decline in the interest rate (which raises investment and consumption) combined with a decrease in income (which reduces the supply of commodities more than the demand).

7 Shifts in the IS Curve II; Changes in Attitudes towards Thrift

The *IS* curve will shift if the community's tastes for present goods (consumption) versus future goods (saving) undergo any change. Two options exist: the community can become either more or less thrifty, that is, change its tastes in favor of future goods vis-à-vis present goods or against future goods vis-à-vis present goods.

Consider Figures 18 and 19, which illustrate the impact of increased thrift on the *IS* curve. Originally, the commodity market clears at an income level of Y_1^s and interest rate r_1, point A in Figure 19. When thrift increases, the community plans to save more at the same interest rate and income level. The change which occurs in the form of the saving function is shown in Figure 18 by the dashed curve S'. For the commodity market to clear now at the same level of income Y_1^s, the interest rate that must prevail is r_1'; this combination is point A' in Figure 19. Had we started out with a higher level of income Y_2^s we would have saving and investment curves in Figure 18 to the right of S and I and intersecting at some lower interest rate, such as r_2. Such curves would have generated point B in Figure 19. If thrift had increased

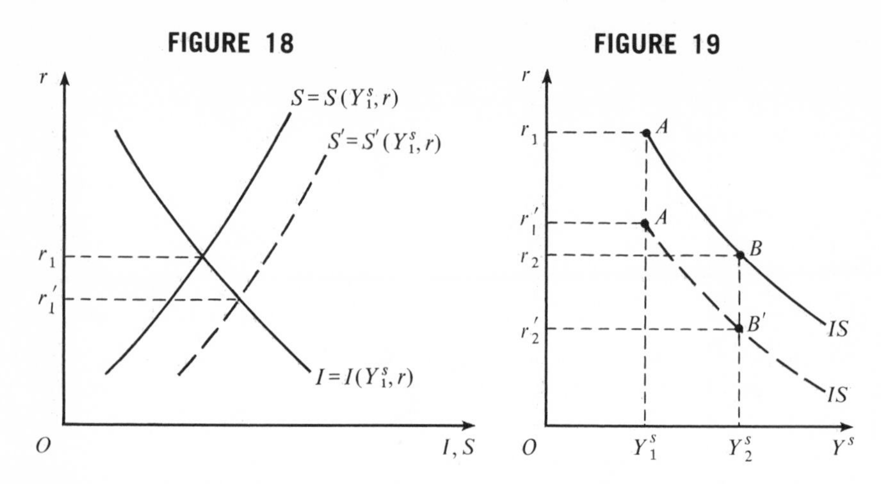

FIGURE 18

FIGURE 19

from that position, then the commodity market would only have cleared again at the same level of income Y_2^s for a lower interest rate, say, r_2'. Hence, we obtain the point B' in Figure 19. Clearly, increased thrift shifts the IS curve left to IS'. The rationale is clear—when a decrease in aggregate demand for commodities is brought about by an increase in thrift, aggregate commodity demand and aggregate commodity supply are reequalized by a fall in both the interest rate and income. This removes the *excess* supply of commodities, since a fall in income reduces supply more than demand and a fall in the interest rate raises demand (both investment and consumption).

The reverse outcome occurs if there is a decrease in thrift. Consider Figures 20 and 21. With the old attitude towards thrift, the commodity market cleared at Y_1^s and r_1 (point A in Figure 21). With the more profligate attitude, the saving curve in Figure 20 shifts to S' and now at the same level of income Y_1^s the commodity market will clear only at a higher interest rate r_1'' (point A'' in Figure 21). If we had begun with some higher level of income such as Y_2^s, there would have been two different curves in Figure 20, S'' and I'' to the right of S and I and intersecting at an interest rate below r_1, say, r_2. We would

FIGURE 20

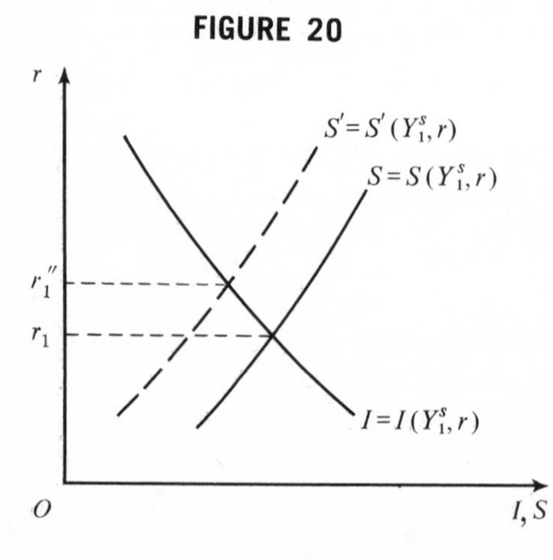

FIGURE 21

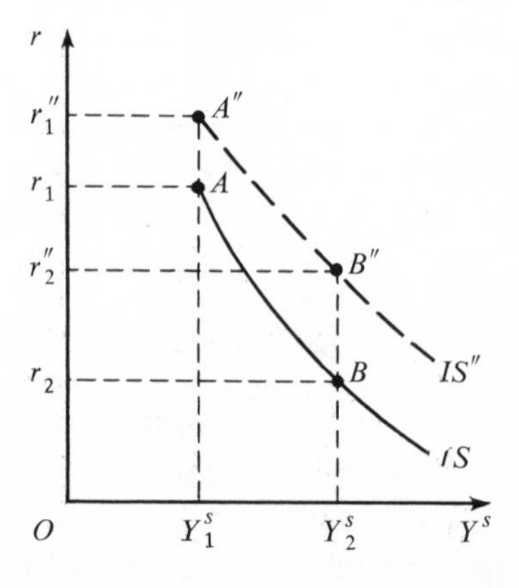

have used these values to locate point B in Figure 21. Then, when the urge to spend overcame the community, the S'' curve would have shifted left; and when income was Y_2^s, commodity market clearance would occur only at a higher interest rate than r_2, say, r_2''. This is the reasoning used to generate point B'' in Figure 21.

Obviously, decreased thrift moves the IS curve right to IS''. The logic is that any excess demand injected into the commodity market by decreased thrift is eliminated by a rise in the interest rate and an increase in income. The former decreases demand (both investment and consumption) and the latter increases supply more than demand. Jointly, both effects lead to the elimination of the excess demand for commodities.

Summarizing, we may conclude that an increase in the marginal efficiency of investment *or* a decrease in thrift will shift the IS curve right; a decrease in the marginal efficiency of investment *or* an increase in thrift will shift the IS curve left. The excess demand for commodities injected into the system by a disturbance of the former type is eliminated by a rise in both income and the interest rate; the excess supply of commodities created by a disturbance of the latter type is eliminated by a fall in both income and the interest rate.

8 The Situation Off an IS Curve

We know that on an IS curve (at a point such as A in Figure 22) the demand for commodities is equal to the supply of commodities. What is the situation at points *off* an IS curve such as B, C, D, or E? Let us consider point B first.

The commodity market clears at Y_1^s and r_1. Therefore, at Y_1^s and a *higher* interest rate such as r_2 there must be an excess supply of commodities. Now

FIGURE 22

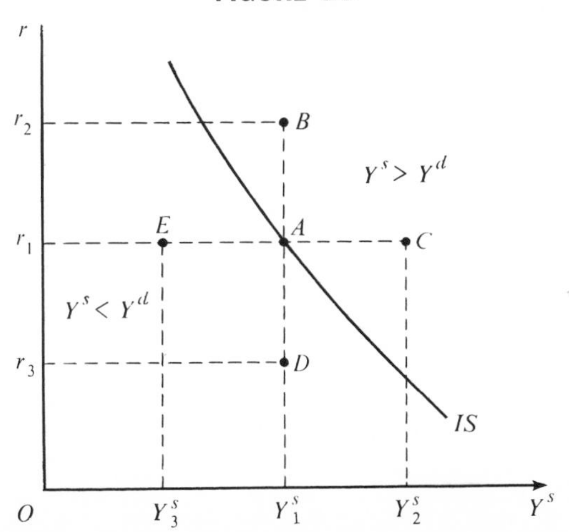

consider point C. If the commodity market clears at Y_1^s and r_1, then at the same rate of interest and a *higher* level of income such as Y_2^s there must be an excess supply of commodities (since when income increases the supply of commodities increases more than the demand). Thus, we may conclude that the space to the right of an *IS* curve involves an excess supply of commodities, and we enter the notation $Y^s > Y^d$ there to signify such a state of affairs.

At point D there must be an excess demand for commodities. We know the commodity market clears at Y_1^s and r_1. Therefore, an excess demand would appear at the same level of income and a *lower* interest rate such as r_3. The same holds true at point E. If the commodity market clears at Y_1^s and r_1, at that interest rate and a lower level of income such as Y_3^s an excess demand will result (since a decrease in income reduces supply more than demand). Thus, we conclude that all points to the left of an *IS* curve involve an excess demand for commodities, and we enter the notation $Y^s < Y^d$ in this space to indicate just that.

9 Equilibrium in the Money and Commodity Markets

An *LM* curve is the locus of interest rate and income levels at which the supply of money equals the demand for money; an *IS* curve is the locus of interest rate and income levels at which commodity supply and demand are equal. It follows that a point where an *LM* and an *IS* curve intersect identifies an interest rate and income level at which *both* money supplied equals money demanded *and* commodities supplied equals commodities demanded. In Figure 23, this occurs at r^* and Y^{s*}. From our preceding discussion about

FIGURE 23

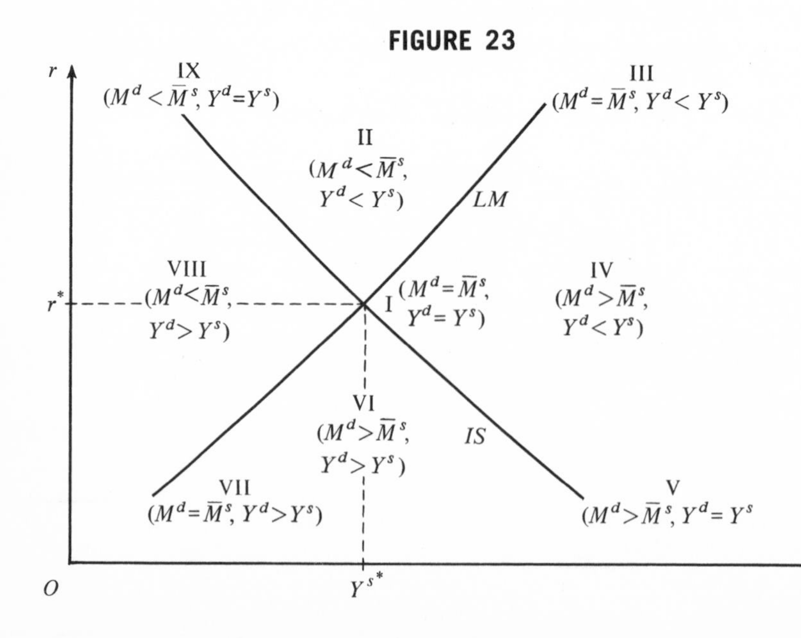

FIGURE 24

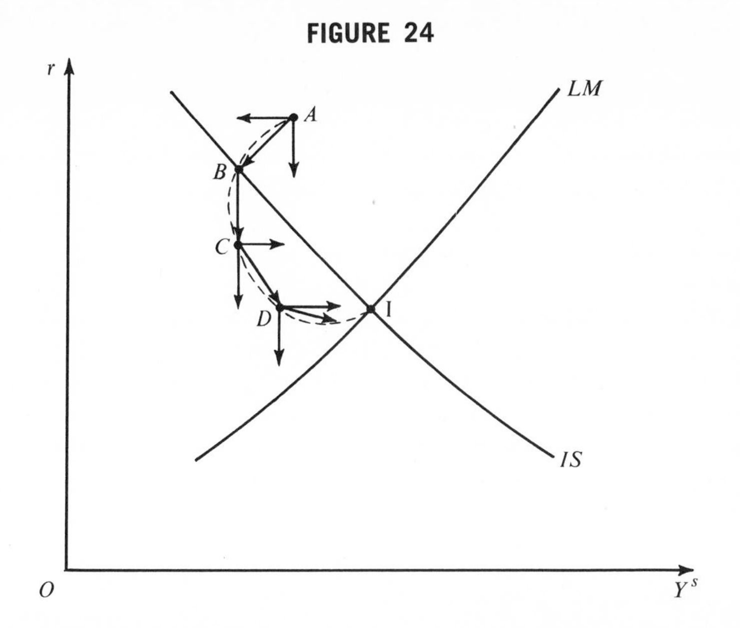

the situation existing *off* these curves (see, especially, §4 and §8 of this chapter and Figures 11 and 22), we can immediately enter the conditions which prevail at any point in this figure.

1. At I, the demand for money equals the supply of money and the demand for commodities equals the supply of commodities ($M^d = \bar{M}^s$, $Y^d = Y^s$).

2. At II, there is an excess supply of both money and commodities ($M^d < \bar{M}^s$, $Y^d < Y^s$).

3. Along *LM* from I to III, the supply of money equals the demand for money and there is an excess supply of commodities ($M^d = \bar{M}^s$, $Y^d < Y^s$).

4. At IV, there is an excess demand for money and an excess supply of commodities ($M^d > \bar{M}^s$, $Y^d < Y^s$).

5. Along *IS* from I to V, there is an excess demand for money, but the commodity market clears ($M^d > \bar{M}^s$, $Y^d = Y^s$).

6. At VI, there is an excess demand for both money and commodities ($M^d > \bar{M}^s$, $Y^d > Y^s$).

7. Along *LM* from I to VII, the demand for money equals the supply of money, but there is an excess demand for commodities ($M^d = \bar{M}^s$, $Y^d > Y^s$).

8. At VIII, there is an excess supply of money and an excess demand for commodities ($M^d < \bar{M}^s$, $Y^d > Y^s$).

9. Along *IS* from I to IX, there is an excess supply of money, but the commodity market clears ($M^d < \bar{M}^s$, $Y^d = Y^s$).

A relevant question to ask now is the following: if we are *not* at I (that is, we do not have equilibrium) but are at some other point in Figure 23, do forces exist that would take us towards I (and equilibrium)? We shall now indulge in some very casual dynamics. Consider a point such as *A* in Figure 24. At *A* we know there are excess supplies of both money and commodities. The excess supply of money imposes downward pressure on the interest rate; this is represented by the vertical vector pointing down at A. The excess supply of commodities imposes downward pressure on the level of income; this is represented by the horizontal vector at A. Let us assume that both these forces are resolved by the vector $\boldsymbol{AB}$ and that, as a consequence, both the interest rate and the level of income will decline. What happens when we move to B? Here, the excess commodity supply has been eliminated but there is still an excess supply of money exerting downward pressure on the interest rate; this is represented by the vertical vector $\boldsymbol{BC}$. Suppose we go down to C—what is the situation there? At C we find an excess demand for commodities tending to raise income (represented by the horizontal vector at C) and an excess supply of money tending to lower the interest rate (represented by the vertical vector at C). We can resolve these two forces using the vector $\boldsymbol{CD}$. At D forces similar to those at C exist and they have been resolved in a similar manner. Observe that we are converging on money and commodity market equilibrium at I. The movement from A to B to C . . . to I just outlined is the result of a discrete (steplike) analysis. In a continuous process one can easily imagine income and the interest rate following a path like that indicated by the dashed line $ABCD$.

Before we turn the reader loose on his own to experiment with other situations, it might be worthwhile to look at one more example. Consider point E in Figure 25. At E an excess demand for money tends to raise the interest rate (the vertical vector) and an excess demand for commodities tends to raise income (the horizontal vector). Assume these vectors are resolved by $\boldsymbol{EF}$. What is the position at F? The excess commodity demand has been eliminated, but an excess demand for money is still imposing upward

FIGURE 25

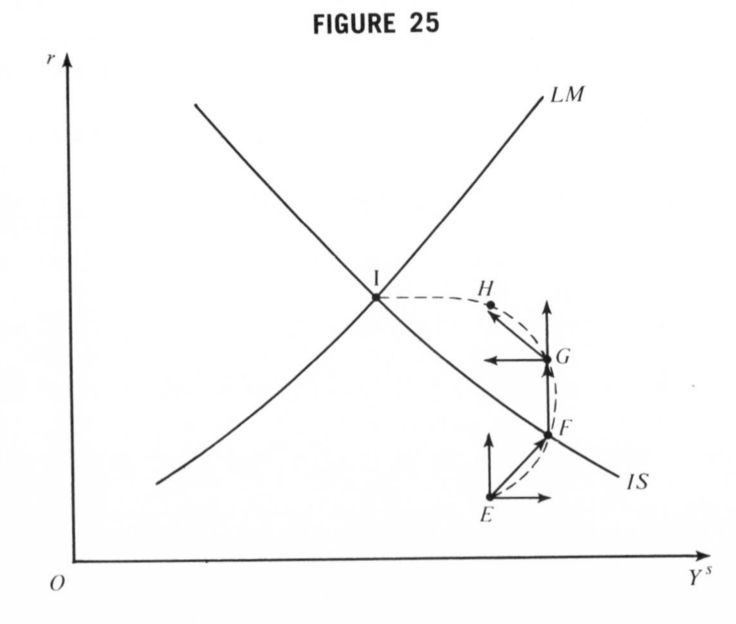

FIGURE 26

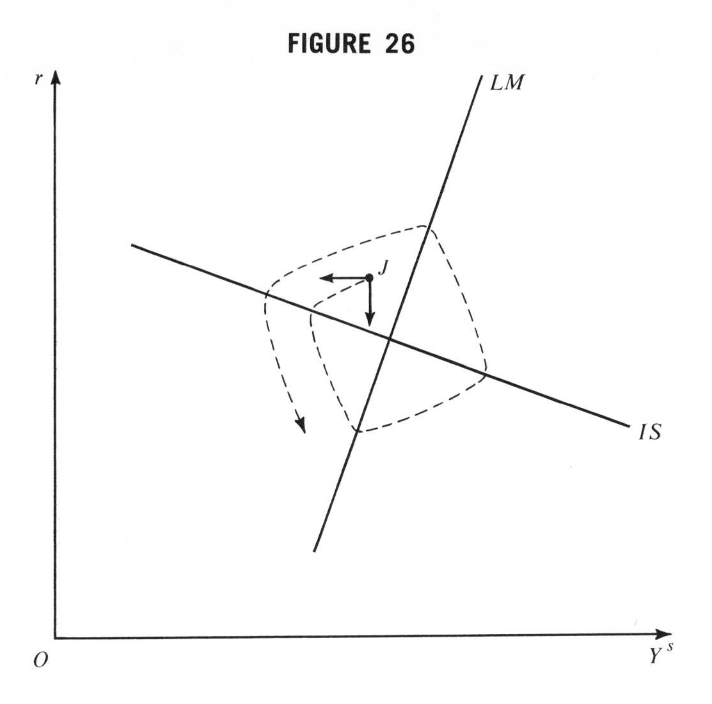

pressure on the interest rate (represented by the vector ***FG***). When we move up to G, there is an excess supply of commodities, which tends to lower income (the horizontal vector at G), and an excess demand for money (the vertical vector at G) whose resolution, we have assumed, is the vector ***GH***; at H . . . , and so on. Clearly, in a continuous process one can visualize income and the interest rate converging on I according to the dashed path *EFGH*.

The reader will find it instructive to work out other convergence paths toward I (equilibrium) starting from some other disequilibrium points in Figures 24 and 25. They will prove completely analogous to the two examples just analyzed. Nonetheless, in all honesty we again stress that this dynamic analysis is, *strictly* speaking, illegitimate. However intuitively appealing it may be, our model is simply not capable of generating *actual* convergence paths of the income and interest rate variables towards these equilibrium values. Our model is completely static. Moreover, since it is completely static, we do not even know whether the model is *stable* (that is, if we start at somewhere other than equilibrium, do we move towards equilibrium or further away from it?). Consider the initial disequilibrium situation represented by point J in Figure 26. It is *possible* that the excess supply of commodities, initially imposing downward pressure on income at J, resolves continuously into the dashed vector. As illustrated, this diverges from equilibrium instead of converging on it. Clearly, such a model, which moves further and further from equilibrium, is *unstable*. Having drawn attention to this problem, we shall *assume* in all that follows that our models are stable like those in Figures 24 and 25 and not unstable like the one in Figure 26.

10 The Effects of Changes in the Money Supply and Liquidity Preference

With this *IS*/*LM* analytical apparatus now in hand, it is trivially easy to elucidate the impact of changes in the money supply or liquidity preference on income and the interest rate.

Consider Figure 27 where *LM* is the curve associated with the original money supply $\bar{M}^s$ and *LM*′ is the new curve associated with the increased money supply $\bar{M}^{s\prime}$. Initially, equilibrium is at I where r^* and Y^{s*} prevail. After the increase in the money supply, the new equilibrium point is I′, where r_1^* and Y_1^{s*} prevail. Clearly, the increase in the money supply is not neutral. Two real variables, the interest rate and real income, have responded to a change in it. This is consistent with what we found earlier, given rigid wages and prices (see §11.2). When the *LM* curve shifted from *LM* to *LM*′, the point I, which used to be one of equilibrium, becomes a disequilibrium point. An excess supply of money exists which exerts downward pressure on the interest rate and this, in turn, creates excess commodity demand which exerts upward pressure on real income. That is why the dashed trajectory between I and I′ has been inserted to indicate, casually, a plausible transition path from I to I′.

Decreasing the supply of money would have had the opposite effect. The new equilibrium level of income Y_2^{s*} would turn out to be lower and the new equilibrium interest rate r_2^* higher. Money is again not neutral. This time an excess demand for money would prevail at I after the *LM* curve shifted to *LM*″. This would raise the interest rate which would create an excess supply of commodities and, thus, cause income to decline. The trajectory from I to I″ suggests this sequence of events.

The same figure may be employed to illustrate the impact of a change in liquidity preference. You will recall that a decrease in liquidity preference

FIGURE 27

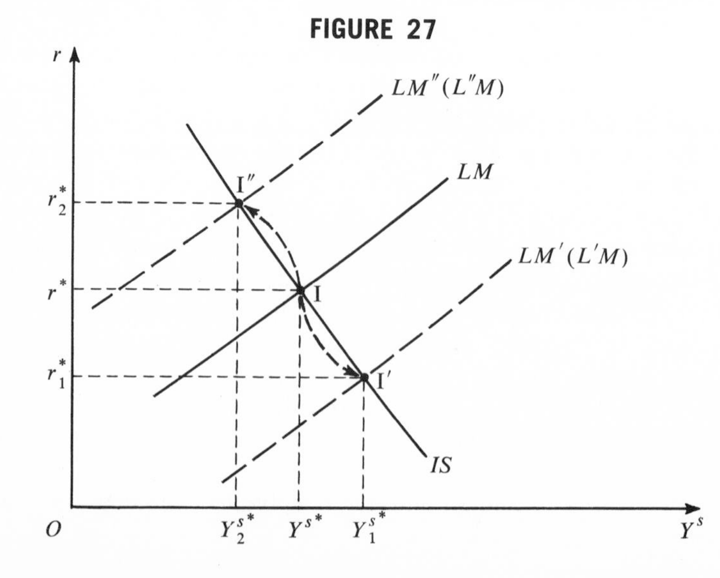

shifts the *LM* curve right (to, say, *L'M*). After such a shift, an excess supply of money exists at I. It is eliminated by a rise in income to Y_1^{s*} and a fall in interest to r_1^*. Note here that changes in liquidity preference are not neutral either (whether it is *unbiased* or not), since they affect at least two real variables, r and Y^s.

An increase in liquidity preference shifts the *LM* curve left to, say, *L''M*. After such a shift, excess demand for money, which raises the interest rate, exists at I. This creates an excess commodity supply, which lowers income. A path such as that indicated by the trajectory II'' might be traced. The excess demand for money caused by the increase in liquidity preference is eliminated by a rise in the interest rate and a decrease in income.

In summary, we may state that an increase in the supply of money or a decrease in liquidity preference will raise income and lower the interest rate; a decrease in the supply of money or an increase in liquidity preference will lower income and raise the interest rate. These conclusions are exactly the same as those we arrived at earlier when manipulating the model in a neo-Keynesian environment (where either of the price variables W or P is inflexible). However, they drop out of the *IS*/*LM* analysis very elegantly.

11 The Effects of Changes in Entrepreneurial Expectations and Attitudes towards Thrift

Let us begin by imagining a collapse in entrepreneurial expectations. This, we know, shifts the *IS* curve left to *I'S* (see Figure 28). When the expectations become more pessimistic, I becomes a position of excess commodity supply. Income falls and as a result an excess supply of money which reduces the interest rate emerges. A trajectory such as that shown between I and I' might be followed with income and the interest rate both falling. Be

FIGURE 28

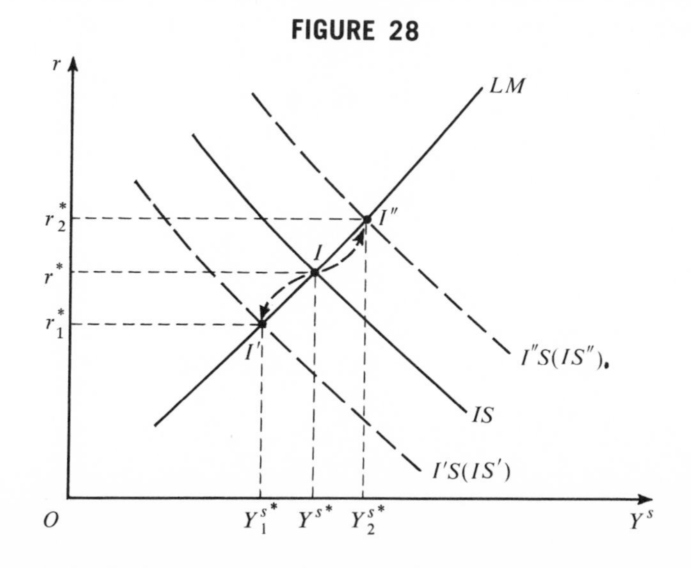

that as it may, it is certain that we end up with a lower interest rate r_1^* and lower level of real income Y_1^{s*}.

An exactly similar outcome would ensue if there had been an increase in thrift. This also shifts the *IS* curve left (to *IS'*). Again, an excess supply of commodities emerges at I which is eventually removed by the decrease in both income and the interest rate to Y_1^{s*} and r_1^*, respectively.

Should there be an improvement in entrepreneurial expectations (or a decrease in thrift), the *IS* curve moves right to *I''S* (or *IS''*). In both cases, an excess demand for commodities appears at I. This excess raises income which, in turn, creates an excess demand for money which raises the interest rate. Whether the initial impetus was an improvement in expectations or a decrease in thrift, the result is the same. Income rises to Y_2^{s*} and the interest rate rises to r_2^*. Both increases are sufficient to eliminate the excess commodity supply at I while maintaining equilibrium in the money market, too.

In summary, we may state that either more pessimistic expectations or an increase in thrift will lower both income and the interest rate; an improvement of expectations or a decrease in thrift will raise both income and the interest rate.

12 Some Limiting Cases

In this section we explore three special limiting cases in the context of an *IS*/*LM* analysis: secular stagnation, a liquidity trap, and an income- and interest-inelastic investment function.

Secular Stagnation

You will recall from § 11.3 that the secular stagnation hypothesis implies there is no positive interest rate which at the level of real income required to generate full employment will clear the commodity market (or, equiva-

FIGURE 29

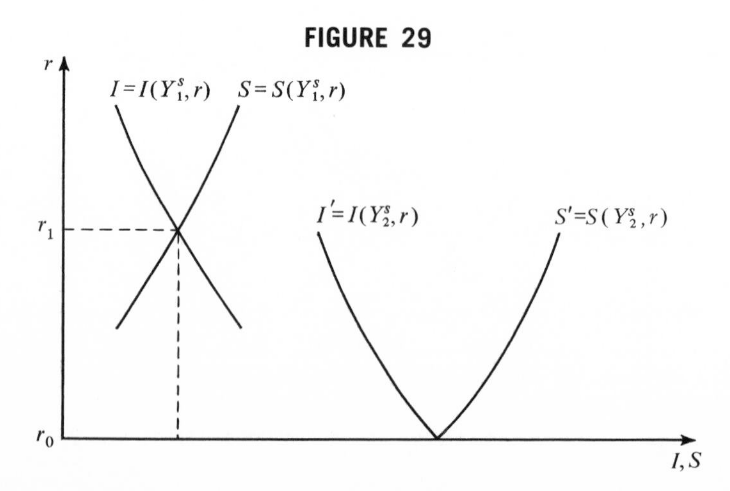

FIGURE 30

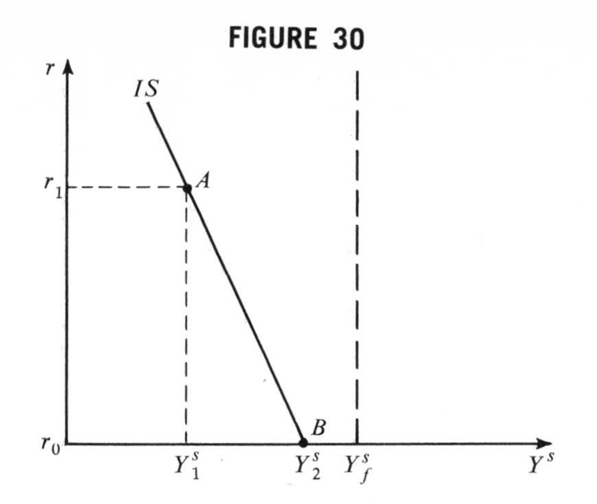

lently, equalize planned investment and planned saving). In terms of an *IS* curve, this calls for a curve that cuts the horizontal axis to the left of the full employment real income level (Y_f^s in Figure 30). How do we know this? Point *A* in Figure 30 is the interest rate and income combination r_1 and Y_1^s at which planned saving equals planned investment; it is obtained from the *I* and *S* curves in Figure 29. Now, when income increases to Y_2^s, these curves both shift right to I' and S' and saving and investment are equal at the interest rate and income combination r_0 and Y_2^s, or point *B* in Figure 30. As long as Y_2^s is less than Y_f^s, point *B* will lie to the left of Y_f^s. With the type of *IS* curve implied by the secular stagnation hypothesis, it is manifestly impossible to generate full employment real income Y_f^s via *monetary policy*. No *LM* curve, however large the quantity of money, will intersect this *IS* curve at Y_f^s. This is obvious from Figure 31, where the supply of money has been increased progressively from $\bar{M}^s$ to $\bar{M}^{s'}$ to $\bar{M}^{s''}$ without creating complete joy in the commodity market. The best that *could* be attained is an interest rate of r_0 and an income level of Y_2^s. The cause of this dilemma is, of course,

FIGURE 31

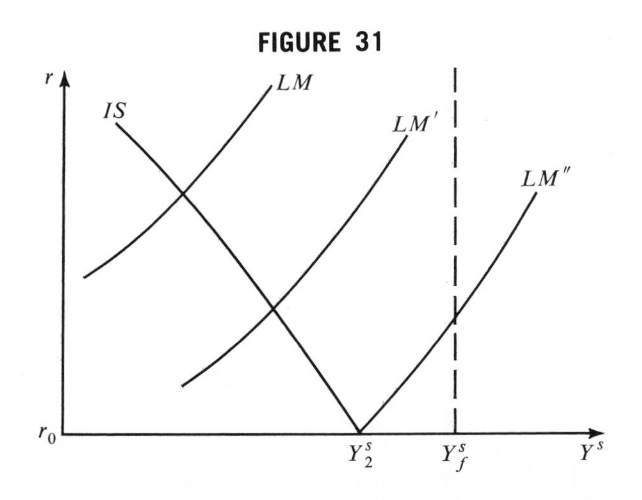

FIGURE 32

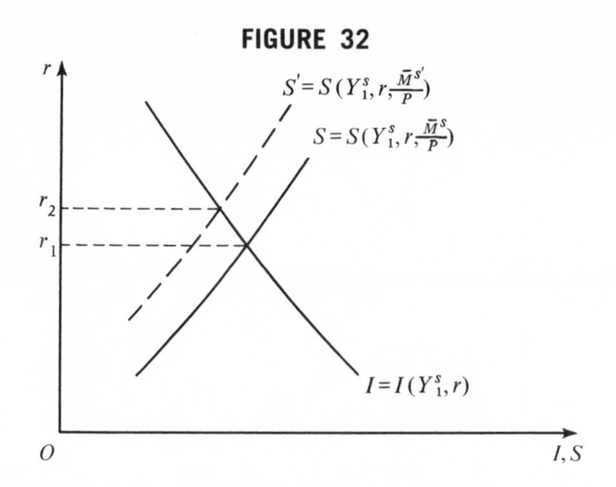

a relatively interest-inelastic investment schedule and a marginal propensity to save out of income which is greatly in excess of the marginal propensity to invest out of income. A moment's reflection will indicate that if the I curves in Figure 29 were significantly more interest-elastic *or* if, when income rose, the I curve shifted right almost as much as the S curve, then an IS curve like that in Figure 30 would not result—it would be much flatter throughout.

What happens when a real balance effect is included in the commodity market? It makes the positions of both the IS curve and the LM curve dependent on the supply of money. Consider Figure 32. When the supply of money is $\bar{M}^s$, saving and investment are equal at r_1 and Y_1^s (point A in Figure 33). When, however, the supply of money is $M^{s'}$ the S curve shifts left to S' in Figure 32 and, now, saving and investment are equal at r_2 and Y_1^s (point B in Figure 33). Clearly, in general, increased real money balances shifts the IS curve upward to the right to IS'. What implications does this have for the

FIGURE 33

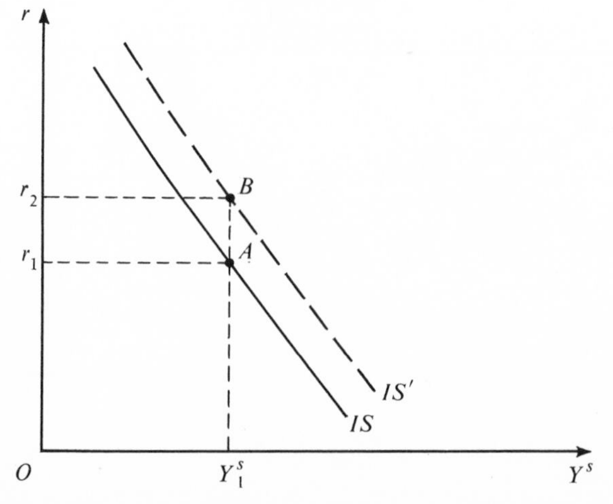

FIGURE 34

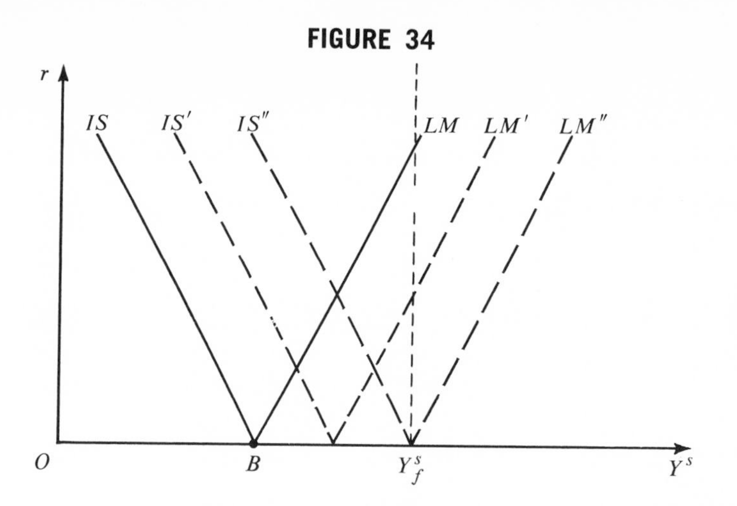

secular stagnation hypothesis? It means that monetary policy will no longer be emasculated by this phenomenon. Consider Figure 34 and start off at point B where secular stagnation is upon us. Now when the supply of money is increased to $\bar{M}^{s'}$, $\bar{M}^{s''}$, and so on, generating the LM curves LM', LM'', and so on, the IS curves *also* shift right to IS', IS'', ... Obviously it is only a matter of increasing the money supply enough before we hit Y_f^s.

We may conclude, therefore (as we did in §11.3), that the exclusion of a real balance effect from the commodity market is required for the secular stagnation hypothesis to hold. Of course, if our money supply is of the inside variety this is *not* a strong restriction.

The Liquidity Trap

A liquidity trap generates a horizontal tail to an LM curve such as that shown in Figure 36. To understand why this is so, examine Figure 35. The

FIGURE 35

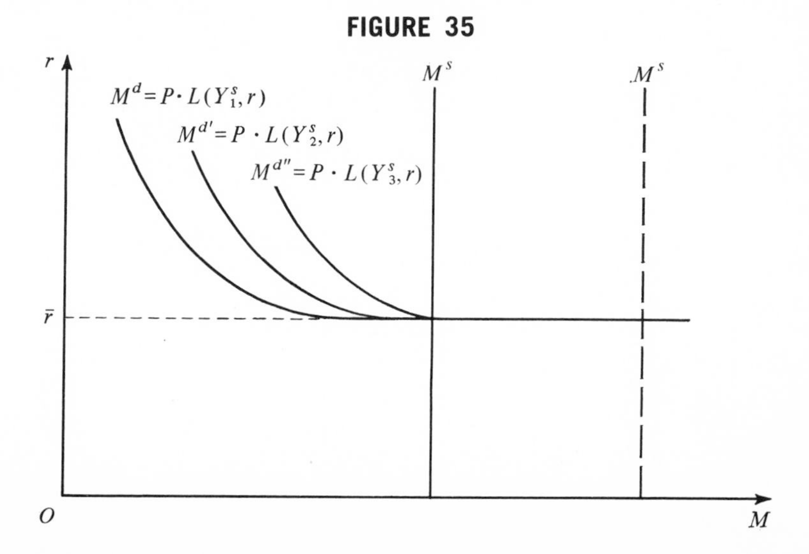

FIGURE 36

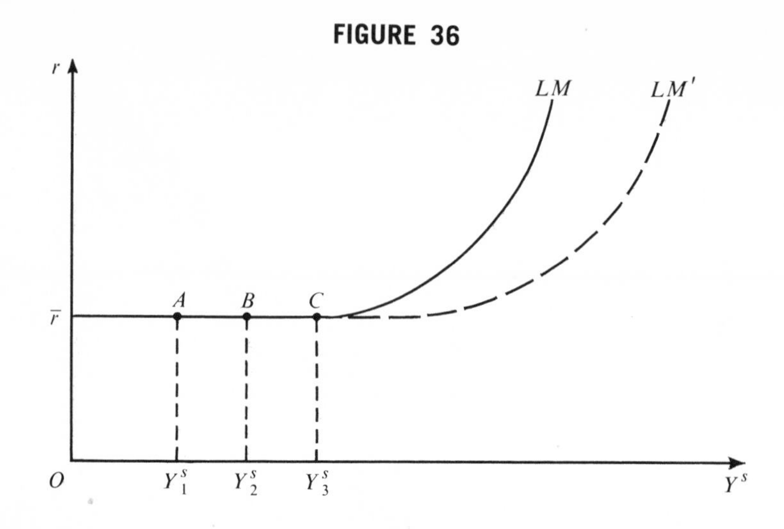

M^d, $M^{d'}$, $M^{d''}$ curves in that figure are, respectively, associated with the levels of income Y_1^s, Y_2^s, and Y_3^s. Hence, when the supply of money is $\bar{M}^s$ the supply and demand for money are equal at $\bar{r}$ and Y_1^s (point A in Figure 36), $\bar{r}$ and Y_2^s (point B), and $\bar{r}$ and Y_3^s (point C); thus, part of LM is horizontal. Moreover, all LM curves converge into this horizontal segment. For example, look what happens when the supply of money is $\bar{M}^{s'}$—the dashed curve in Figure 35. Once more, the supply of money equals the demand at $\bar{r}$ and Y_1^s (M^d and $\bar{M}^{s'}$), $\bar{r}$ and Y_2^s ($M^{d'}$ and $\bar{M}^{s'}$), and $\bar{r}$ and Y_3^s ($M^{d''}$ and $\bar{M}^{s'}$); these coordinates are identical with points A, B, and C again.

This is sufficient to negate monetary policy once we are in a liquidity trap position. Consider Figure 37. The money and commodity markets are clearing at $\bar{r}$ and Y_1^{s*}. The latter, however, is less than the full employment level of income Y_f^s. But no matter how much the money supply is increased and, thus, the LM curve is shifted right to LM', LM'', and so on, we do not

FIGURE 37

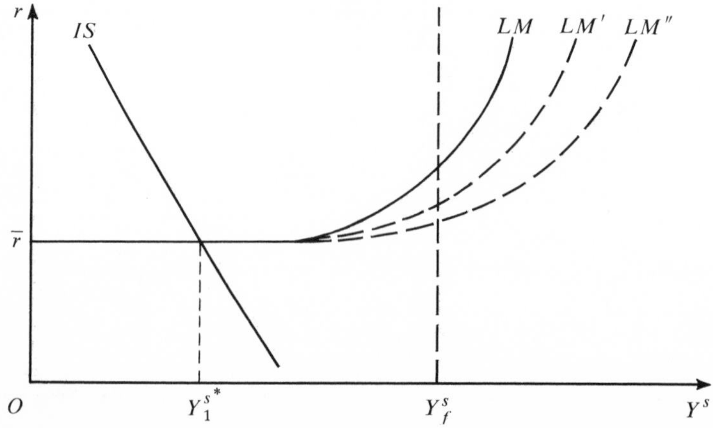

get off the point determined by $\bar{r}$ and Y_1^{s*}. The interest rate just cannot be reduced below $\bar{r}$ to generate any additional investment or consumption expenditure.

The emasculation of monetary policy by a liquidity trap is again conditional upon the exclusion of a real balance effect from the commodity market. We saw above (when discussing secular stagnation) that a real balance effect in the commodity market makes the *IS* curve shift right when the *LM* curve shifts right. This being so, as the *LM* curve shifts to *LM'*, *LM''*, and so on, it is only a matter of time before the *IS* curve would have shifted right far enough to get us out of the liquidity trap. Once more, though, we point out that the exclusion of a real balance effect is not a strong restriction if our money supply is predominantly of the inside variety

An Income- and Interest-inelastic Investment Function.

An investment function that is inelastic with respect to income and the interest rate generates a very steep *IS* curve like the one shown in Figure 39 by *IS*. To understand why this is, consider the limiting case where investment is completely independent of the level of income and the interest rate. Therefore, instead of the investment function $I = I(Y^s, r)$, we have $I = \bar{I}$ – a certain level of investment $\bar{I}$ is planned *no matter what* the levels of income and interest rate are. In effect, investment is an exogenous variable here. Such an investment function is shown in Figure 38 by $\bar{I}$. When income is Y_1^s, investment and saving are equal at r_1 and Y_1^s (point *A* in Figure 39). When income is Y_2^s, they are equal at Y_2^s and r_2 (point *B* in Figure 39).

Had investment been more income and interest elastic, instead of $\bar{I}$ in Figure 38 we would have had the curve *I*. Then, saving and investment would have been equal at r_1 and Y_1^s (point *A*). But at a higher level of income we would obtain the curves *I'* and *S'*, which would be equal at r_3 and Y_2^s (point *C* in Figure 39). Clearly, then, in general, the more income- and interest-inelastic the investment function, the steeper is the *IS* curve. This has impor-

FIGURE 38

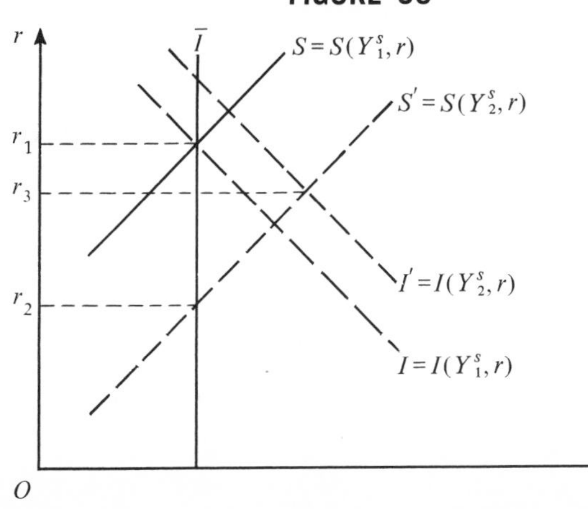

FIGURE 39

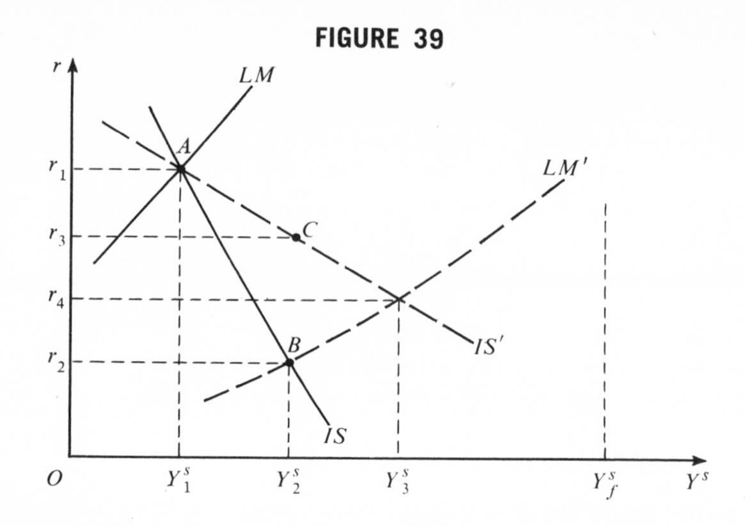

tant implications for the sensitivity of monetary policy. Look closely at Figure 39. Assume that *LM* and *IS* originally prevail and then the money supply is increased so that *LM* shifts to *LM'*. The effect is to reduce the interest rate a great deal to r_2 and raise income a little to Y_2^s. If, however, *IS'* prevailed an equal increase in the money supply would reduce the interest rate a little (to r_4) and raise the level of income a lot (to Y_3^s). Obviously, the more income- and interest-elastic the investment schedule the more responsive is the level of income to given monetary policy maneuvers.

We conclude this section by putting these limiting cases in perspective. Very few economists believe in the secular stagnation hypothesis any longer and only a few more are concerned with liquidity trap phenomena. These theoretical details are now only curios, although they exercised economists a great deal in the past. Many economists can still be found, however, who take an interest-inelastic investment function seriously and, thus, have serious reservations about the sensitivity of income to monetary policy manipulations. Even so, it is our *impression* that their numbers are dwindling from the majority who once believed in this. A generation ago, a majority of economists probably felt that "money does not matter" either because the economy was locked in a liquidity trap or, if not, because manipulation of the money supply caused gyrations in the interest rate with hardly any effect on income because investment was income- and interest-inelastic. Nowadays, many more economists believe "money does matter."

13 The Inclusion of Government in the IS/LM Model

The inclusion of government in the model manifests itself in the *IS* curve. (It does not affect the *LM* curve.) In what manner, one might ask. Consider Figure 40. At the equilibrium income level $Y_1^s = OY_1^s = ab$, consumption is equal to *ac*. The unconsumed income is either saved or, now that

FIGURE 40

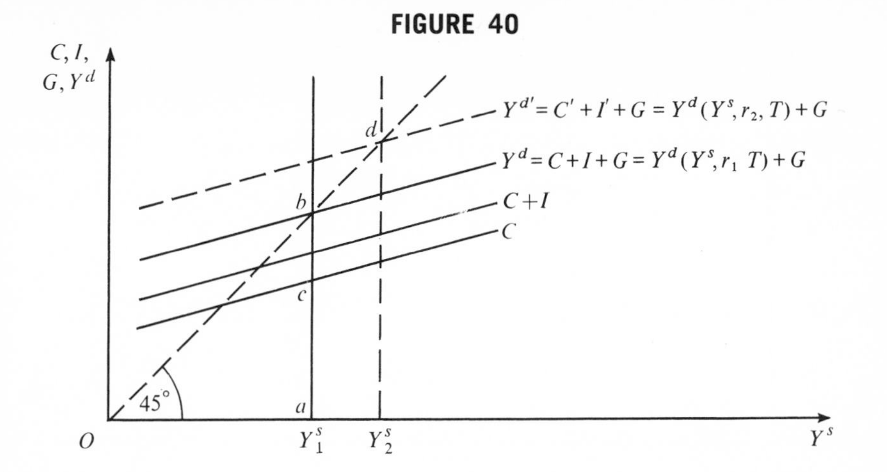

government exists, used to pay taxes. Thus, *bc* is equal to saving *plus* taxes. But, looking at things from the commodity demand side, we see that *bc* is also clearly equal to investment plus government expenditure. We come, therefore, to the well-known commodity market equilibrium condition after government exists; namely, $S + T = I + G$. It is clear from Figure 40 that one income level and interest rate combination at which the commodity market will clear is Y_1^s and r_1. This is point *A* in Figure 41. If income rises to Y_2^s, the interest rate will have to *fall* so that Y^d can rise to $Y^{d'}$, where it passes through *d* and the commodity market clears again. Thus, for the commodity market to clear, the interest rate must be lower if the level of income is higher. This gives point *B* in Figure 41. Manifestly, the *IS* curve is still retaining its downward slope.

Changes in Government Expenditures

How do changes in *G* and *T* affect the position of an *IS* curve? Consider Figure 42 which shows government expenditure originally equal to $\bar{G}$. With

FIGURE 41

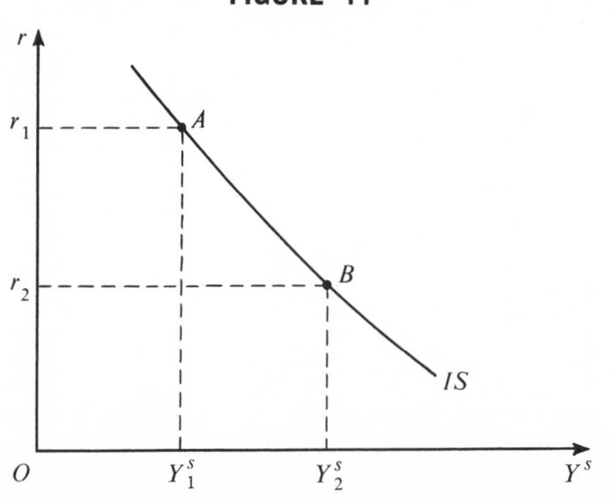

FIGURE 42

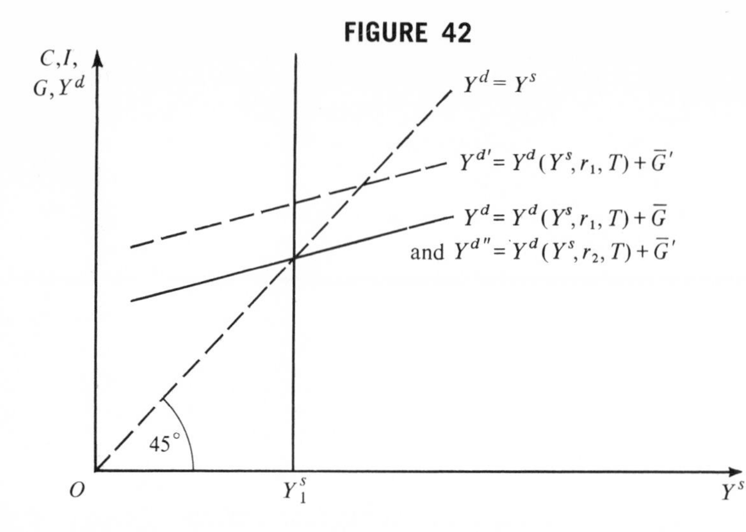

this level of government expenditure, commodity market equilibrium occurs at r_1 and Y_1^s (point A in Figure 43). If government expenditure rose to $\bar{G}'$ then, ceteris paribus, there would be excess commodity demand at Y_1^s. For this to be removed, the interest rate would have to *rise* to, say, r_2. As a result, there would be a new commodity demand curve $Y^{d''}$ overlaying Y^d (involving lower consumption and investment, C' and I', respectively). Thus, with higher government expenditure, the commodity market at the same level of income will only clear at a higher rate of interest r_2 (point C in Figure 43). Similar reasoning will persuade the reader that a *reduction* in government expenditure will require a *reduction* in the interest rate if the commodity market is to clear at the same level of income. A point such as D (corresponding to the lower rate r_3) in Figure 43 is obtained. Since this reasoning can be pursued at *any* level of income, it follows that a rise in government expenditure shifts the IS curve to the right (IS' in Figure 43). The explanation is

FIGURE 43

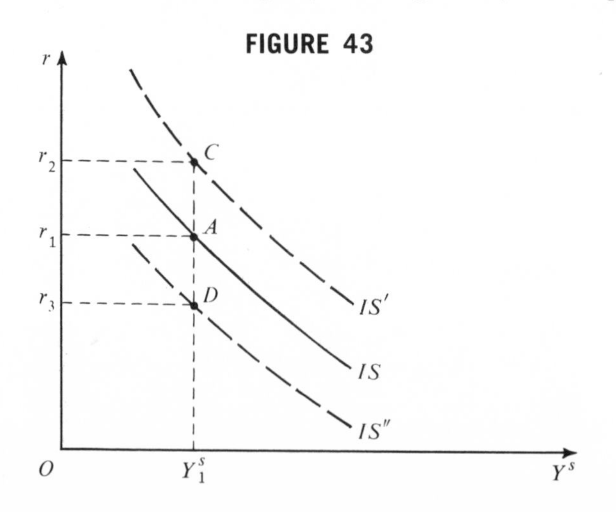

still quite straightforward. When government expenditure rises, the excess commodity demand thereby created is removed by a rise in both interest rates and income (which increases the supply of commodities more than the demand); when government expenditure falls, the excess supply of commodities is removed by a fall in both interest rates and income (which reduces the supply of commodities more than the demand).

Changes in Taxes

We may dispense with additional diagrams in elucidating the impact of a change in taxes on the position of an *IS* curve. The principles are now so familiar that they are practically redundant. If the commodity market is originally in equilibrium at Y_1^s, a rise in taxes will, by reducing consumption demand, create excess commodity supply. For that excess to be removed at the same level of income Y_1^s, the interest rate must *fall* (which will raise consumption and investment). Thus, with higher taxes, we must have a lower interest rate to clear the commodity market at any particular level of income. Clearly, then, raising taxes shifts the *IS* curve left. The opposite is true for a reduction in taxes. At any level of income, such a reduction will create excess commodity demand through increased consumption. This must be removed by a *rise* in interest rates, which will lower consumption and investment until commodity market equilibrium is reestablished. In summary then, a rise in G or a fall in T shifts the *IS* curve to the right; a fall in G or a rise in T shifts it to the left.

Fiscal Policy in an IS/LM Model

The road to fiscal policy application is now open. The government now has another tool that it can use for stabilization purposes in addition to monetary policy. Consider Figure 44. The economy has settled down in equilibrium at Y_1^{s*} which is less than full employment income Y_f^s. The alternative

FIGURE 44

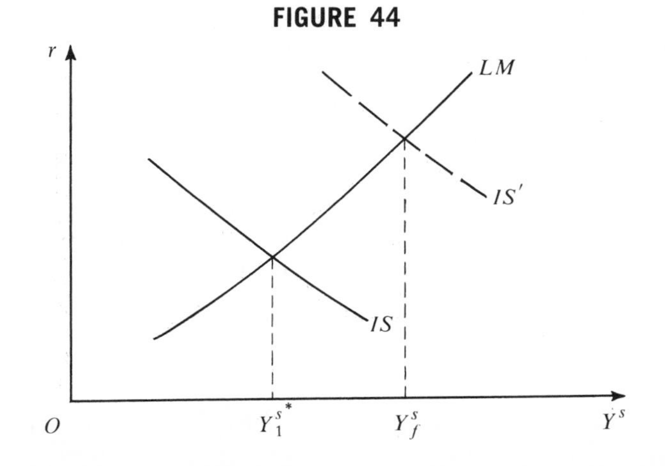

routes to full employment via fiscal policy are clear. The *IS* curve must be shifted right to *IS′*, where it will intersect the *LM* curve at Y_f^s. This shift to the right may be achieved through an increase in government expenditure and/or a reduction in taxes.

Which road to full employment should one take – increased government expenditure or reduced taxes? There is no objective reason to choose one over the other. However, personal philosophy about the role of government in private affairs may guide one's choice. Lowering taxes to regain full employment reduces the relative importance of government as a provider of collective commodities. This must be so, since G is held constant and the output of commodities rises from Y_1^s to Y_f^s. Thus, *private* consumption and investment must have risen relative to collective consumption. Raising government expenditures has the opposite effect. At full employment, real income is the same at Y_f^s, but G is higher. Therefore, the ratio of collective consumption to private consumption and investment must be higher when G is raised than when T is lowered.

Fiscal policy has interesting implications for the model whenever it labors under any of the pathological conditions discussed above in §13. Under conditions of secular stagnation, for example, the reader will recall (see Figure 31 and the corresponding discussion) that an increased money supply could not make the *LM* curve intersect the *IS* curve at Y_f^s, no matter how far right the *LM* curve was shifted. The maximum level of income obtainable through monetary policy was Y_2^s. Now with fiscal policy available, income can be raised beyond Y_2^s. All it takes is a reduction of taxes or an increase in government expenditure of the required size to shift the *IS* curve right until it intersects the prevailing *LM* curve at Y_f^s.

Under liquidity trap conditions (see Figure 37 and the corresponding discussion), no increase in the money supply, however large, was capable of raising income above Y_1^{s*}. With fiscal policy the *IS* curve itself can be shifted right to intersect the prevailing *LM* curve at Y_f^s.

Finally, we saw that with an interest-inelastic investment schedule (see Figure 39 and the corresponding discussion), monetary policy has a great impact on interest rates and very little impact on the level of income. This problem, too, may be sidestepped by fiscal policy. Instead of trying to bring about full employment through monetary policy, which is inefficient in this context, the *IS* curve itself can be shifted right by raising G or lowering T until full employment is attained.

In this chapter we have applied Hicks' geometric technique of *IS/LM* analysis to the determination of the equilibrium level of national income. In Chapter 14 we approach the same problem using simple algebraic methods.

Summary

In this chapter we derived the *IS/LM* analytical apparatus of Hicks in a context of wage and price rigidity. An *LM* curve is defined to be the locus of interest rate and income combinations at which the money market is in equilibrium. In general, the curve will slope up from left to right. When the demand for money is infinitely elastic with respect to the interest rate (the liquidity trap), however, a section of the *LM* curve will be horizontal; when the demand for money is completely independent of the interest rate, the *LM* curve will be vertical. These are two limiting cases for the *LM* curve. An *LM* curve shifts right (except in a liquidity trap) when the money supply increases or liquidity preference decreases; it shifts left when the money supply decreases or liquidity preference increases. *Off* an *LM* curve, there is an excess demand for money to the right and an excess supply of money to the left.

Similarly, we define an *IS* curve to be the locus of interest rate and income combinations at which the commodity market is in equilibrium. (That is, planned saving is equal to planned investment in a model excluding a government sector or planned saving plus taxes is equal to planned investment plus government expenditure in a model including a government sector.) In general, the *IS* curve will slope down from left to right. An *IS* curve shifts right when there is an increase in entrepreneurial expectations, a decrease in thrift, an increase in government expenditure, or a decrease in taxes; it shifts left when there is a decrease in entrepreneurial expectations, an increase in thrift, a decrease in government expenditure, or an increase in taxes. *Off* an *IS* curve, there is an excess supply of commodities to the right and an excess demand for commodities to the left.

The money and commodity markets are *both* in equilibrium only where the *IS* and *LM* curves intersect. Their intersection indicates the equilibrium interest rate and level of real income. An increase in the supply of money or a decrease in liquidity preference will lower the equilibrium interest rate and increase the equilibrium level of income, since the *LM* curve shifts to the right, and vice versa. An increase in entrepreneurial expectations, a decrease in thrift, an increase in government expenditure, or a decrease in taxes will raise both the equilibrium interest rate and the equilibrium level of income, and vice versa. (These conclusions are, of course, all predicated on our assumption of dynamic stability.)

There are some limiting cases which we discussed. Under conditions of secular stagnation, the *IS* curve cuts the income axis short of full employment income. When a real balance effect is excluded from the aggregate commodity demand function, monetary policy is powerless to bring about full employment. Under liquidity trap conditions, the *LM* curve is horizontal and, again, monetary policy is powerless to bring about full employment real income. When investment is independent of the interest rate, the *IS* curve is relatively steep. Thus, monetary policy hardly affects the equilibrium level of income. [When both investment and saving (consumption) are functions of income *only,* the *IS* curve is vertical and monetary policy does not affect income at all.]

Questions

1. Define an *LM* curve and show how it is derived. Explain the relationship between the supply and demand for money off an *LM* curve (a) to the right and (b) to the left.
2. Explain why (a) an *LM* curve will be horizontal when the demand for money is infinitely elastic with respect to the interest rate, (b) an *LM* curve will be vertical when the demand for money is completely independent of the interest rate.
3. Explain in which direction, and why, an *LM* curve shifts when there is (a) an increase in the supply of money, (b) a decrease in the supply of money, (c) an increase in liquidity preference, (d) a decrease in liquidity preference.
4. Define an *IS* curve and show how it is derived when a government sector is included in the model. Explain the relationship between the supply of and demand for commodities (a) off an *IS* curve to the right, (b) off an *LM* curve to the left.
5. Explain in which direction, and why, an *IS* curve shifts when there is (a) an increase in entrepreneurial expectations, (b) a decrease in thrift, (c) an increase in government expenditure, (d) a decrease in taxes, (e) a decrease in entrepreneurial expectations, (f) an increase in thrift, (g) a decrease in government expenditure, (h) an increase in taxes.
6. What is the shape of an *IS* curve under secular stagnation conditions? Why is monetary policy powerless to establish full employment income in such circumstances? How would you amend your analysis and conclusions if a real balance effect were included in the aggregate commodity demand function?
7. Explain why monetary policy is incapable of generating full employment (a) when liquidity trap conditions prevail, (b) when investment is independent of both income and the interest rate and saving is independent of the interest rate.
8. Devise a fiscal policy to establish full employment under the conditions of question 7.

SELECTED READINGS

1. M. J. Bailey, *National Income and the Price Level,* McGraw-Hill, 1962, chapters 1–3. An excellent presentation of the *IS/LM* technique for an economy with flexible prices.
2. J. R. Hicks, "Mr. Keynes and the 'Classics'; A Suggested Interpretation," *Econometrica,* April, 1937. Where Hicks introduced his *IS/LM* technique.
3. D. Patinkin, *Money, Interest, and Prices,* 2nd ed., Harper & Row, 1965, chapter 13.
4. W. L. Smith, "A Graphical Exposition of the Complete Keynesian System," *Southern Economic Journal,* October, 1956. A useful expository article.

14

Successive Approximations to Income Determination

In the previous chapter we concentrated exclusively on the geometric approach to Hicksian *IS*/*LM* analysis. Much of what we said there can be stated more economically by resort to some simple algebra. This is what we propose to do now; we shall start with an extremely simple model of income determination, then complicate it progressively. Throughout this chapter (as in the previous one), we shall continue to assume that the nominal wage rate is fixed at $\bar{W}$ and the nominal price level is fixed at $\bar{P}$. Thus, output (income) and employment are determined solely by aggregate demand. The labor market does not (necessarily) clear, since the real wage rate is fixed at $\bar{W}/\bar{P}$. Thus, we concentrate only on the conditions necessary to clear the commodity and money markets.

1 Model I; The Multiplier

Let us begin with the simplest possible model, excluding a government sector. This comprises

$$Y^s = Y^d \tag{1}$$

which is the commodity market clearance condition;

$$Y^d = C + \bar{I} \tag{2}$$

which is the definition of aggregate demand; and

$$C = b_0 + b_1 Y^s \tag{3}$$

which is the consumption function. Equations (1)–(3) comprise the commodity market equations. We also have

$$\frac{M^d}{\bar{P}} = m_0 + m_1 Y^s - m_2 r \tag{4}$$

which is the demand for money function, and

$$M^d = \bar{M}^s \tag{5}$$

which is the money market clearance condition. Equations (4) and (5) comprise the money market equations, which turn out to be supremely uninteresting in the present model. The reader will notice that all relationships are assumed to be linear—a simplification retained throughout this chapter. Model I comprises five equations in five endogeous variables—namely, Y^s, Y^d, C, M^d, and r. We assume, therefore, that a solution exists. The other two variables—namely, $\bar{I}$ and $\bar{M}^s$—are exogenous.

Another feature of model I is that the commodity market is *separable*. That is to say, the commodity market equations by themselves can determine the equilibrium (or solution) values of all the variables they contain. If you examine equations (1)–(3), you will see these three equations contain three endogenous variables (Y^s, Y^d, and C) and one exogenous variable ($\bar{I}$). Thus, it is immediately obvious that the level of real income is independent of the supply of money. "Money does not matter" in model I. Of course, this is because aggregate demand is completely independent of monetary variables. You will note that both consumption and investment are independent of the interest rate and real balances. Consequently, no matter what the values of r and $\bar{M}^s/\bar{P}$, they do not affect aggregate demand one way or the other. This model is represented graphically in Figures 1(a) and 1(b). Notice that if $\bar{M}^s$ is increased, which would lower the interest rate, no repercussion occurs in the commodity market. Aggregate demand is independent of both real balances and the interest rate. This illustrates that money does not matter in model I. Note, also, that the money market is *not* independent of the commodity market. If the level of income changes, the demand for money curve shifts right, raising the equilibrium interest rate. But there is no feedback into the commodity market when this change occurs. Essentially, model I works like this. Equations (1)–(3) determine Y^{s*}. When the value thus determined is introduced into equations (4) and (5) they become two

FIGURE 1

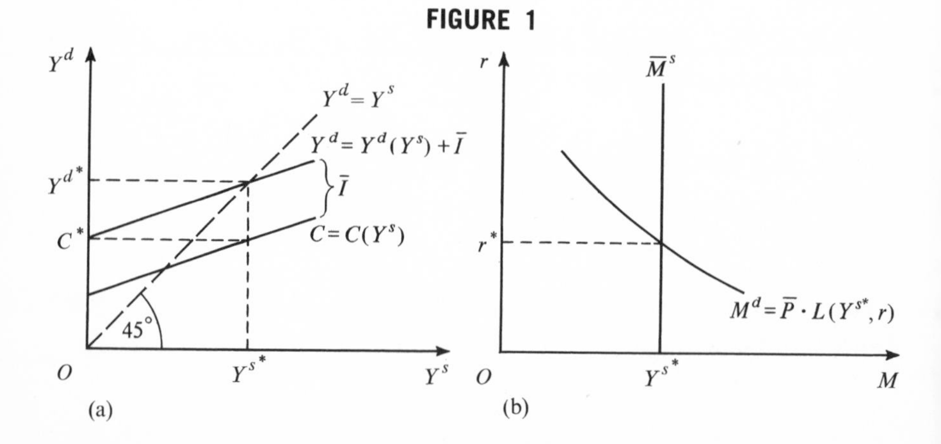

FIGURE 2

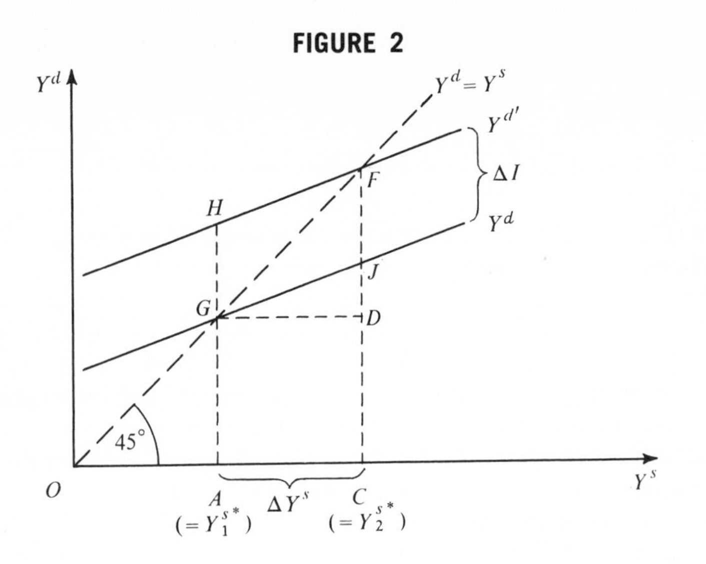

equations in two unknowns (M^d and r). Therefore, they may then be solved for these variables.

We shall be particularly concerned in this chapter with *multipliers*. The multiplier is a many-splendored thing. It is misleading, in fact, to talk about *the* multiplier. Multipliers are not unique—there are thousands of them. Each model has its own. The multiplier varies from model to model according to the manner in which the specifications of the models differ.

What, then, is a multiplier? The question may be answered in general terms as follows. Given the initial position illustrated in Figure 1, introduce a permanent change in expenditure ΔI and, when the economy is in equilibrium again, compare the initiating change in expenditure with the change in real income ΔY^s that finally occurred. In particular, find the ratio

$$\frac{\Delta Y^s}{\Delta I} = \text{the multiplier} = k \tag{6}$$

where, we emphasize, the changes in Y^s and I are between *equilibrium* values of these variables.

It is now reasonable to ask how is the multiplier related to the parameters of our model? An important relationship does exist and can be derived as follows. Consider Figure 2. The initial real income level when aggregate demand is Y^d is Y_1^{s*} (point A). If we increase investment by ΔI, aggregate demand rises by an equal amount to $Y^{d'}$. In Figure 2, $\Delta I = GH = JF$. The new equilibrium level of real income is Y_2^{s*} (point C). Hence, income has increased by AC. Now we know that, by definition

$$k = \frac{\Delta Y^s}{\Delta I} = \frac{AC}{GH}$$

Is the ratio AC/GH equal to anything in particular? We shall see that it is. Divide numerator and denominator by AC. Then

$$k = \frac{1}{\frac{GH}{AC}} = \frac{1}{\frac{JF}{AC}} = \frac{1}{\frac{DF - DJ}{AC}} = \frac{1}{1 - \frac{DJ}{AC}}$$

But DJ/AC is equal to the slope of the consumption function b_1 or the marginal propensity to consume *mpc*. So we obtain

$$k = \frac{1}{1 - b_1} = \frac{1}{1 - mpc} = \frac{1}{mps}$$

since $mpc + mps = 1$. In words, in this simple model, the multiplier is equal to either the reciprocal of 1 minus the marginal propensity to consume *or* the reciprocal of the marginal propensity to save. It is clear by inspection that as the *mpc* increases, so does the multiplier, and vice versa.

For example, if the *mpc* is 0.8 then the multiplier k equals $1/(1 - 0.8)$, or 5. Since $\Delta Y^s = k \times \Delta I$, this means a 1-unit change in investment would give rise to a 5-unit change in income. Alternatively, if the *mpc* was 0.9 then the multiplier k would equal $1/(1 - 0.9)$, or 10. And since $\Delta Y^s = k \times \Delta I$, a 10-unit change in investment would give rise to a 100-unit change in income. (In the appendix to this chapter, we examine some of the reasons why observed multipliers are often much smaller than those predicted by our simple model.)

At first glance, the multiplier process appears to give something for nothing—like a sort of economic perpetual motion machine. Does it not appear that expenditure has risen by a certain amount ΔI and real income has risen by a larger amount ΔY^s? That is true but this real income is not obtained without cost. If such a mistaken impression arises, it comes from ignoring the other markets in the model, particularly the labor market. We know that an increase in real income entails an increase in employment. The cost of the higher real income is the lost leisure, or increased work. Nothing is for nothing—in economics, especially.

Putting aside the geometry for a moment, what is the intuitive, heuristic, common-sense explanation of the multiplier process? Why, when expenditure increases by a certain amount, does income increase by a larger amount? The rationale is quite simple. When more commodities are purchased for investment purposes, these purchases lead to additional employment and real income. The newly employed find their income has increased. What do they do? They spend part of it on consumption. More commodities are purchased. This leads to more employment and more real income. Again, the newly employed find their income has increased. And what do they do with it? They spend part of it on consumption, and so it goes. In essence, the permanent injection of primary expenditure *induces a chain of secondary consumption expenditure* among the newly employed, and the new expenditure generates new employment.

If we think of this process as being discrete, then the multiplier as a function of the *mpc* can be obtained, alternatively, as follows. The initial injection of expenditure ΔI raises real income by an equal amount. This is the "first-round" increase in income [see equation (7)]. Of this new income, the amount spent on consumption by the newly employed workers is equal to $mpc\Delta I$. This spending in the "second round" raises income by that amount. The newly employed workers whose income has gone up by $mpc\Delta I$ themselves spend a proportion equal to *mpc* times their increase in income on consumption; i.e., the "third-round" increase in spending is equal to $mpc[mpc]\Delta I = (mpc)^2\Delta I$. The process continues. New income induces new consumption, which induces new income, which induces new consumption, and so on. Clearly, the *total* increase in income ΔY^s is equal to the sum of the increases which occurred in each round and is given by equation (7).

$$\underset{\text{Round 1}}{\Delta Y^s = \Delta I} + \underset{\text{Round 2}}{mpc\Delta I} + \underset{\text{Round 3}}{(mpc)^2\Delta I} + \cdots + \underset{\text{Round } n \text{ (last)}}{(mpc)^{n-1}\Delta I} \tag{7}$$

This is obviously a geometric series. When the powered factor (in this case, *mpc*) is between zero and unity, it is well known that such series have finite sums equal to the constant ΔI times the reciprocal of 1 minus the powered factor.[1] Hence, (7) is equal to

$$\Delta Y^s = \frac{1}{1 - mpc}\Delta I$$

From which it follows that

$$k = \frac{\Delta Y^s}{\Delta I} = \frac{1}{1 - mpc}$$

which is exactly what we found the multiplier to equal before. This alternative approach reveals more clearly why the ultimate increase in income resulting from a given permanent injection of primary expenditure depends on the *mpc*. When the *mpc* is large, the new consumption expenditure induced at each round is clearly going to be larger than if the *mpc* were small. Therefore, the total increase in income will be larger when the *mpc* is large than

[1] This result is easily proved. We have

$$\Delta Y^s = \Delta I + mpc\Delta I + (mpc)^2\Delta I + \cdots + (mpc)^{n-1}\Delta I \tag{7}$$

Multiply (7) by *mpc* to obtain

$$mpc\Delta Y^s = mpc\Delta I + (mpc)^2\Delta I + (mpc)^3\Delta I + \cdots + (mpc)^n\Delta I \tag{7'}$$

Next, subtract (7′) from (7) to obtain

$$\Delta Y^s - mpc\Delta Y^s = \Delta I - (mpc)^n\Delta I \approx \Delta I$$

since *mpc*, which is a number between zero and unity, when raised to the *n*th power will be virtually equal to zero. So,

$$\Delta Y^s(1 - mpc) = \Delta I$$

and

$$k = \frac{\Delta Y^s}{\Delta I} = \frac{1}{1 - mpc}$$

when it is small. With a large *mpc* a sizable part of any new income is spent; with a small *mpc* only a little is spent. Therefore, in the former case, there is a great deal of induced income, spending, and employment; in the latter case, only a little. [This chain of induced secondary consumption expenditure which produces the multiple increase in real income can only come into play when unemployed resources exist. If there is no unemployment real output (income) cannot be increased. Consequently, an initial increase in expenditure could have no multiplier effect. It would merely lead to a rise in prices.]

The multiplier notion is so basic to neo-Keynesian macroeconomic theory that it bears examination from two other diagrammatic perspectives. First, consider Figure 3, where time t is measured horizontally, income Y^s is measured vertically, and b equals *mpc*. From $t = 0$ to $t = t - 1$, equilibrium income is Y^{s*}. In the tth period, however, investment increases by ΔI. (Investment is exogenous and we may assume this increase is due to entrepreneurs' expectations becoming more sanguine.) This injection of primary expenditure is assumed to be permanent, so expenditure is increased by this amount in all periods from t to $t + n$. In $t + 1$, therefore, we have an expenditure of ΔI *plus* the increment of induced consumption expenditure $b\Delta I$ (resulting from the fact that income in the previous period increased by ΔI). Thus, by $t + 1$, income has increased to $Y^{s*} + \Delta I + b\Delta I$. In $t + 2$, additional consumption equal to $b^2\Delta I$ will be induced, since income rose in the previous period by $b\Delta I$. So, by $t + 2$, income has increased to $Y^{s*} + \Delta I + b\Delta I + b^2\Delta I$. Continuing in this fashion, by $t + n$, income will have risen

FIGURE 3

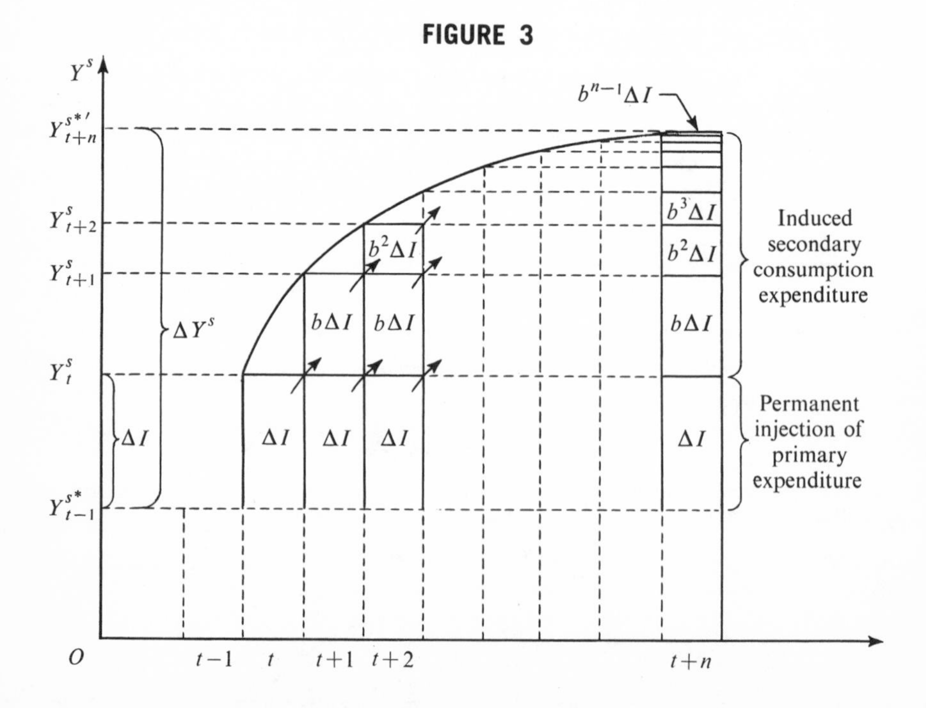

FIGURE 4

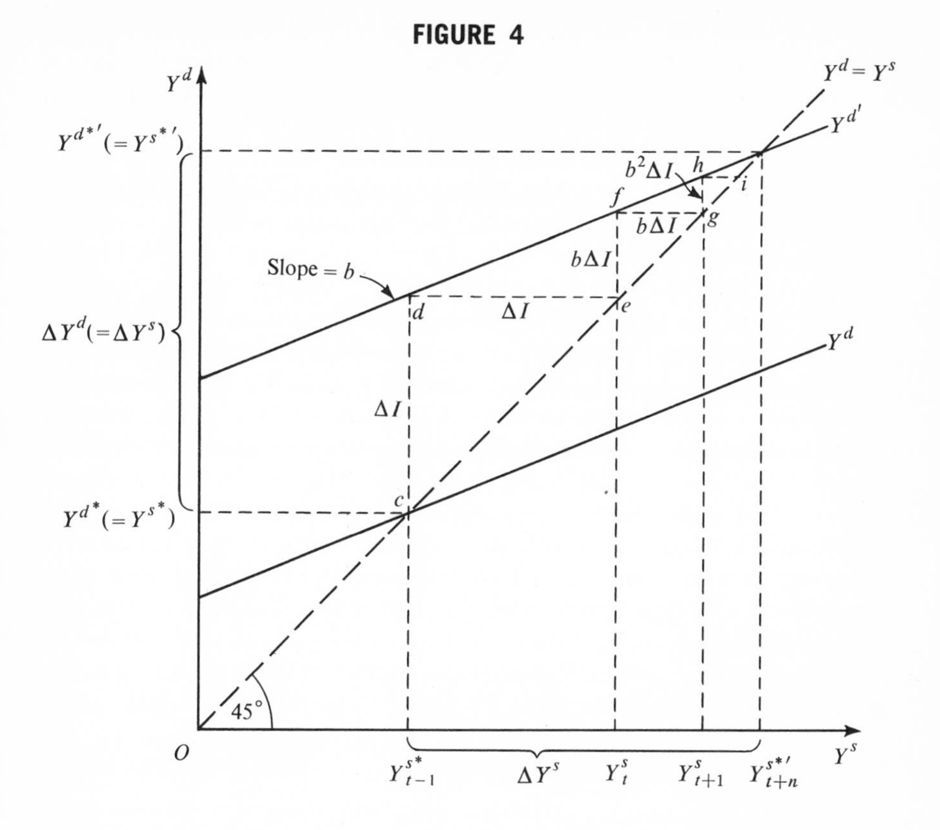

to $Y^{s*'}$, which is equal to $Y^{s*} + \Delta I + b\Delta I + b^2\Delta I + \cdots + b^{n-1}\Delta I$. Clearly, $Y^{s*'} - Y^{s*} = \Delta Y^s = \Delta I + b\Delta I + b^2\Delta I + \cdots + b^{n-1}\Delta I$, which is (7) and from which we have already seen the multiplier can be calculated as $1/(1-b) = 1/(1-mpc)$.

Second, consider the version of the familiar commodity market diagram in Figure 4. Until time $t-1$, aggregate demand is given by Y^d and equilibrium income by Y^{s*}_{t-1}. In period t, investment increases by ΔI, which generates the new aggregate demand curve $Y^{d'}$. Since investment is assumed to be exogenous, the *slopes* of Y^d and $Y^{d'}$ are identical and equal to the $mpc = b$. This increase in aggregate demand in period t of ΔI, which is equal to cd, increases aggregate supply (income) in period t by the *equal* amount de. (Note that $cd = de$ from the properties of the 45°-line.) This first-period increase in income is due to the (permanent) primary injection of expenditure ΔI.

When income increases by ΔI in t, additional consumption and, therefore, aggregate demand are induced in period $t+1$; this induced consumption and aggregate demand equal $b\Delta I$. Notice that $b\Delta I$ equals ef, since the *slope* of the hypotenuse of triangle def equals b, and base (ΔI) times slope (b) equals height ($b\Delta I$). This increase in aggregate demand in $t+1$ equal to ef raises aggregate supply (income) in $t+1$ by an equal amount fg, which raises aggregate demand in $t + 2$ by gh, which is equal to $b^2\Delta I$ (since the base of triangle fgh is $b\Delta I$ and the slope of its hypotenuse is b), and so on.

It is clear that the ultimate increase in aggregate demand and aggregate supply after n periods will be equal to $cd + ef + gh + \ldots$, or, equivalently, $de + fg + hi + \ldots$. These series are both equal so we have $\Delta Y^d = \Delta Y^s = \Delta I + b\Delta I + b^2\Delta I + \cdots + b^{n-1}\Delta I$ by inspection (and inference). This is again equal to (7), from which we know that the multiplier can be calculated to be $1/(1 - mpc) = 1/(1 - b)$.

How would model I appear in an *IS*/*LM* context? If you examine Figure 1(a) again you will notice that there is only one level of income Y^{s*} at which the commodity market clears no matter what the level of the interest rate. Thus, the *IS* curve, which (you will recall) is the locus of interest rates and income levels at which the commodity market clears, is a vertical line. The *LM* curve has an upward slope. If real income increases, the interest rate must rise if the money market is to clear. Thus, the *IS*/*LM* situation is as shown in Figure 5, which again makes it clear that money does not matter in this model. If the *LM* curve shifts (as a result of changes in the supply of money or liquidity preference), the only change is in the interest rate. There is no effect on income whatsoever. The only way income can be affected is through changes in the *IS* curve.

We shall now develop an algebraic treatment of model I. In particular, we are interested in the equilibrium value of real income Y^{s*}. This can be obtained solely from the commodity market equations by substituting (3) in (2) and the result into (1). We have

$$Y^s = b_0 + b_1 Y^s + \bar{I} \tag{8}$$

This is now one equation in one unknown. By simple algebraic manipulation, we can solve for Y^s:

$$Y^s = \frac{1}{1 - b_1} b_0 + \frac{1}{1 - b_1} \bar{I} \tag{9}$$

FIGURE 5

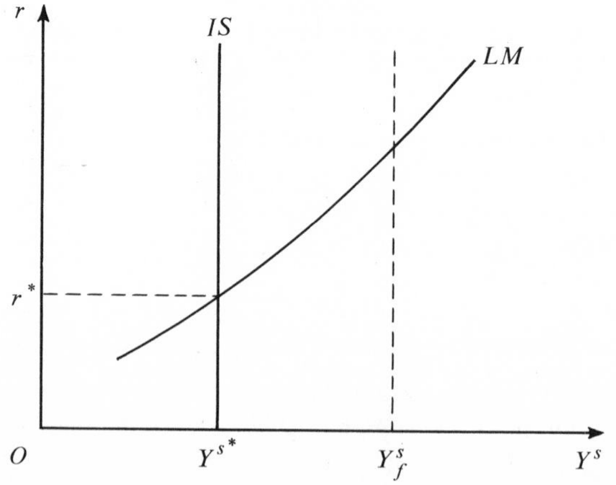

which implies that the level of income depends only on the parameters of the consumption function (its intercept b_0 and its slope b_1) and the level of investment $\bar{I}$.[2]

Now the multiplier is the change in income resulting from a given change in expenditure. Mathematically, it is the partial derivative of income with respect to changes in various categories of expenditure. In model I, the categories of expenditure which can change are investment and consumption (via a shift in the intercept of the consumption function b_0). If we take the partial derivative of (9) with respect to these two categories of expenditure we obtain

$$\frac{\partial Y^s}{\partial I} = \frac{\partial Y^s}{\partial b_0} = \frac{1}{1 - b_1} = \text{the multiplier}$$

which, of course, is what we found the multiplier to be in the geometric analysis. Notice that a change in b_0 is equivalent to a change in thrift. Thrift increases when b_0 falls, and vice versa. Thus, when thrift increases, equilibrium income declines.

2 Model II; Induced Investment

The principles by which various models may be handled should be apparent from the extended discussion of model I. Succeeding models can be treated more succinctly.

Model II is identical to model I except that we now allow for induced investment with the restriction that the sum of the *mpc* and the marginal propensity to invest (*mpi*) is less than unity; that is, $0 < b_1 + i_1 < 1$. We have

[2] It is worth drawing closer attention to equation (9). This is a special type of equation known as a *reduced-form* equation. A reduced-form equation is one in which an endogenous variable is expressed as a function of exogenous variables and parameters only. See how in (9) Y^s is a function only of $\bar{I}$ (which is an exogenous variable) and the parameters b_0 and b_1 (the intercept and slope of the consumption function).

There is a reduced-form equation for *every* endogenous variable in the model. The one for Y^d is the same as the one for Y^s, since (1) tells us that $Y^d = Y^s$. However, what is the equation for consumption, the third endogenous variable in our model? Substitute (1) in (2) and the result in (3). This yields

$$C = b_0 + b_1(C + \bar{I})$$

Solving for C we get

$$C = \frac{1}{1 - b_1} b_0 + \frac{b_1}{1 - b_1} \bar{I}$$

This is consumption's reduced-form equation; consumption is a function of the exogenous variable $\bar{I}$ and the parameters b_0 and b_1. In general, the reduced-form equation for any endogenous variable is obtained by solving the system for the value of that endogenous variable.

If this were a textbook on econometrics, we would have a great deal more to say about reduced-form equations, since they comprise a crucial part of the theory of that subject. Since this is not the case, however, we stop here.

$$\text{Commodity market} \begin{cases} Y^s = Y^d & (10) \\ Y^d = C + I & (11) \\ C = b_0 + b_1 Y^s & (12) \\ I = i_0 + i_1 Y^s & (13) \end{cases}$$

$$\text{Money market} \begin{cases} \dfrac{M^d}{\bar{P}} = m_0 + m_1 Y^s - m_2 r & (14) \\ M^d = \bar{M}^s & (15) \end{cases}$$

The commodity market in model II is still separable. It contains four endogenous variables (Y^s, Y^d, C, and I) and four equations. We can, therefore, obtain values for these variables without reference to the money market. Money continues not to matter. There is only one level of income at which the commodity market will clear no matter what the interest rate is. The *IS* curve remains vertical. Changes in the monetary variables do not affect the level of income, only the interest rate.

To solve for Y^s, substitute (13) and (12) in (11), and use the result in (10). After rearrangement, we obtain

$$Y^s = \frac{1}{1 - b_1 - i_1}(b_0 + i_0) \tag{16}$$

The multipliers of this model which indicate the responsiveness of income to shifts in the level of the consumption and investment functions, are

$$\frac{\partial Y^s}{\partial b_0} = \frac{\partial Y^s}{\partial i_0} = \frac{1}{1 - b_1 - i_1}$$

This multiplier is larger than the one in model I. The intuitive reason is quite obvious. In model II, any change in expenditure induces not only secondary consumption expenditure but secondary investment expenditure as well. Thus, one would expect the ensuing change in income to be larger than when this does not occur (as in model I).

3 Model III; Incorporation of Government

To obtain model III, we incorporate government into model I. The government is assumed to set both its expenditure $\bar{G}$ and tax receipts $\bar{T}$ exogenously. With government in the model, we relate consumption to disposable income, which is defined as income minus taxes. Notice that investment reverts to the status of an exogenous variable. Thus,

$$\text{Commodity market} \begin{cases} Y^s = Y^d & (17) \\ Y^d = C + \bar{I} + \bar{G} & (18) \\ C = b_0 + b_1(Y^s - \bar{T}) & (19) \end{cases}$$

$$\textit{Money market}\begin{cases} \dfrac{M^d}{\bar{P}} = m_0 + m_1 Y^s - m_2 r & (20) \\ M^d = \bar{M}^s & (21) \end{cases}$$

The commodity market in model III is still separable. It contains three equations and three unknowns (Y^s, Y^d, and C). Here too, money does not matter for familiar reasons. The IS curve remains vertical, since there is only one level of income at which the commodity market will clear no matter what the level of the interest rate. Substituting (19) in (18) and the result into (17) and rearranging, we obtain

$$Y^s = \frac{1}{1 - b_1}(b_0 + \bar{I} + \bar{G}) - \frac{b_1}{1 - b_1}\bar{T}$$

Differentiating the above yields the expenditure multipliers

$$\frac{\partial Y^s}{\partial b_0} = \frac{\partial Y^s}{\partial \bar{I}} = \frac{\partial Y^s}{\partial \bar{G}} = \frac{1}{1 - b_1}$$

and the tax multiplier

$$\frac{\partial Y^s}{\partial \bar{T}} = -\frac{b_1}{1 - b_1}$$

The expenditure multipliers in model III are identical to those of model I. However, we now have a tax multiplier. The negative sign indicates that when taxes rise income falls. The tax multiplier is also smaller in absolute value than the expenditure multipliers, since b_1 is less than unity.

An interesting fiscal experiment is traditionally performed on this model. Let the government increase its expenditure and its taxes by equal amounts. That is, government raises its expenditures while keeping its budget balanced. The injection of additional expenditure will tend to increase income by

$$\frac{1}{1 - b_1}\Delta\bar{G}$$

The increase in taxes will tend to lower income by

$$-\frac{b_1}{1 - b_1}\Delta\bar{T}$$

Thus, the total change in income will equal

$$\Delta Y^s = \frac{1}{1 - b_1}\Delta\bar{G} - \frac{b_1}{1 - b_1}\Delta\bar{T}$$

But $\bar{G}$ is equal to $\bar{T}$ by assumption so we can substitute either one for the other. Let us substitute $\bar{G}$ for $\bar{T}$ to obtain

$$\Delta Y^s = \frac{1}{1 - b_1}\Delta\bar{G} - \frac{b_1}{1 - b_1}\Delta\bar{G} = \frac{1 - b_1}{1 - b_1}\Delta\bar{G} = \Delta\bar{G}$$

This implies that when government expenditure and taxes are increased by equal amounts, the resulting increase in income is exactly equal to the increase in government expenditure. The multiplier is equal to 1 (unity). This is the famous *balanced budget multiplier* theorem.

The reader may wish to consider the following heuristic explanation. The government raises its expenditure by $\Delta\bar{G}$. In the first round, expenditure rises by that amount; in the second round, expenditure rises by $b_1\Delta\bar{G}$; in the third round, by $b_1^2\Delta\bar{G}$; and so on. The total increase in aggregate demand brought about by the increase in government expenditure will tend to be

$$\Delta\bar{G} + b_1\Delta\bar{G} + b_1^2\Delta\bar{G} + b_1^3\Delta\bar{G} + \cdots$$

But the government also raises its taxes by $\Delta\bar{T}$. This will lower disposable income by that amount, but the first-round decrease in aggregate demand because of this decline in income will be only $-b_1\Delta\bar{T}$; in the second round it will be $-b_1^2\Delta\bar{T}$; and so on. The total decrease in aggregate demand because of the rise in taxes will tend to be

$$-b_1\Delta\bar{T} - b_1^2\Delta\bar{T} - b_1^3\Delta\bar{T} - \cdots$$

The overall change in aggregate demand will, therefore, be equal to the sum of these two series. Remembering that $\Delta\bar{G}$ is equal to $\Delta\bar{T}$ by assumption, this sum is immediately seen to be equal to $\Delta\bar{G}$. As real income is determined by aggregate demand in this model, $\Delta Y^s = \Delta\bar{G}$, which is what we found above.

4 Model IV; Endogenous Taxes

In model IV we shall continue to include a government sector making exogenously determined expenditures, but we shall now allow its tax receipts to be a function of the level of income. We have

$$\text{Commodity market}\begin{cases} Y^s = Y^d & (22)\\ Y^d = C + I + \bar{G} & (23)\\ C = b_0 + b_1(Y^s - T) & (24)\\ I = i_0 + i_1Y^s & (25)\\ T = t_0 + t_1Y^s & (26)\end{cases}$$

$$\text{Money market}\begin{cases} \dfrac{M^d}{\bar{P}} = m_0 + m_1Y^s - m_2r & (27)\\ M^d = \bar{M}^s & (28)\end{cases}$$

The commodity market consists of five equations in five unknowns (Y^s, Y^d, C, I, and T). It is, therefore, separable and independent of monetary events. Money still does not matter because none of the commodity market relationships depend on the rate of interest or real balances. The commodity market will clear at only one level of income, no matter what the rate of interest is. The *IS* curve continues to be vertical.

The equilibrium level of income can be obtained by substituting (26) into (24) and the result into (23) along with (25). This result is then substituted into (22) to yield

$$Y^s = \frac{1}{1 - b_1 + b_1 t_1 - i_1}(b_0 + i_0 + \bar{G} - b_1 t_0) \tag{29}$$

From this we see that the expenditure multipliers are

$$\frac{\partial Y^s}{\partial b_0} = \frac{\partial Y^s}{\partial i_0} = \frac{\partial Y^s}{\partial \bar{G}} = \frac{1}{1 - b_1 + b_1 t_1 - i_1}$$

and the tax multipliers are

$$\frac{\partial Y^s}{\partial t_0} = -\frac{b_1}{1 - b_1 + b_1 t_1 - i_1}$$

$$\frac{\partial Y^s}{\partial t_1} = -\frac{b_1(b_0 + i_0 + \bar{G} - b_1 t_0)}{(1 - b_1 + b_1 t_1 - i_1)^2} = -\frac{b_1 Y^s}{(1 - b_1 + b_1 t_1 - i_1)}$$

The first tax multiplier indicates how income responds to a change in *average* tax rates; the second tax multiplier indicates how income responds to a change in *marginal* tax rates. With the exception of the marginal tax multiplier, these multipliers are smaller than those obtained in previous models when government either did not exist or set its tax receipts exogenously. The reason for this is that in these multipliers, the product $b_1 t_1$ enters positively in the denominator. The intuitive explanation of why these multipliers should be smaller is obvious. With the tax function we have assumed, when income rises in each round some part of that increase is creamed off in the form of taxes. Hence, the residual amount on which induced, secondary consumption expenditure is based is smaller than it otherwise would be. Also note that the marginal tax multiplier is a function of the level of income. Essentially, this is because the change in tax revenues and, consequently, the change in disposable income and consumption will depend on the original level of income.

It is interesting to note that in models III and IV, which incorporate a government sector, how the government handles its budget deficit or surplus position has no effect on the real sector. By definition, the government has a budget deficit when its expenditure exceeds its taxes. It must obtain the funds to finance the excess of its expenditure over its tax receipts from somewhere. In our model it has three alternatives. It can (1) print new fiat money or (2) it can borrow money from its creature the monopoly bank by issuing more bonds or (3) it can borrow money from the public by issuing more bonds. Printing new fiat money increases the supply of money and lowers the rate of interest. But in models III and IV money does not matter. The commodity market is independent of changes in the rate of interest and real balances. Thus, there are no repercussions in the commodity market if the government finances its deficit in this way. If the government chooses its other options and borrows the money by issuing more bonds to the monopoly bank or the public, this increases the supply of bonds, which lowers their price and, thus, increases the rate of interest. But this, too, has no effect in the commodity market. Thus, the method the government chooses to finance its deficit has no bearing on the commodity market. Of course, this holds in reverse, too. If the government has a surplus it can use its tax receipts in excess of its expenditure to (1) redeem fiat money or (2) redeem some of its outstanding bonds held by the monopoly bank or (3) redeem some of its outstanding bonds held by the public. The first option would raise the interest rate; the second and third options would lower it. Either way, the commodity market is not affected, since it is independent of changes in both the interest rate and real balances.

5 Model V; "Money Only Matters"

Until now we have developed models in which money does not matter. Consequently, if the government is going to influence the level of real income it *must* use fiscal policy. It is reasonable to ask if there is a class of models in which *fiscal policy* does not matter. Indeed there is. If the demand for money is independent of the rate of interest while the commodity demand is dependent, then the result is that "money *only* matters" and fiscal policy does not matter. Consider model V:

$$\text{Commodity market} \begin{cases} Y^s = Y^d & (30) \\ Y^d = C + I + \bar{G} & (31) \\ C = b_0 + b_1(Y^s - T) - b_2 r & (32) \\ I = i_0 + i_1 Y^s - i_2 r & (33) \\ T = t_0 + t_1 Y^s & (34) \end{cases}$$

$$\text{Money market} \begin{cases} \dfrac{M^d}{\bar{P}} = m_0 + m_1 Y^s & (35) \\ M^d = \bar{M}^s & (36) \end{cases}$$

Both the consumption and investment functions have been made inversely dependent on the interest rate, but the interest rate has been excluded from the demand for money function. Model V consists of seven equations in seven endogenous variables (Y^s, Y^d, C, I, r, T, and M^d), so we assume a solution exists. The significant point is that the commodity market is no longer separable, since it contains five equations and six endogenous variables (Y^s, Y^d, C, I, r, and T). However, the money market *is* separable, since it contains two equations and two endogenous variables (M^d and Y^s).

Consequently, we can solve for the equilibrium level of real income Y^s in the money market. Simply substitute (36) in (35) and rearrange to obtain

$$Y^s = \frac{1}{m_1}\left(\frac{M^s}{\bar{P}} - m_0\right) \tag{37}$$

The impact of changes in the supply of money on the level of income is given by

$$\frac{\partial Y^s}{\partial(M^s/\bar{P})} = \frac{1}{m_1}$$

There are no expenditure or tax multipliers in this model. How could there be when the level of income is *completely* determined in the monetary sector of the model? The only thing that changes when expenditure variables or tax rates change is the rate of interest.

The reader might find a geometric analysis of model V helpful. Consider Figure 6. Looking at the money market in Figure 6(b) first, we see that originally the supply of money is $\bar{M}^s$. The demand for money is independent of the rate of interest so it, too, is a vertical line. Equilibrium between money demanded and supplied is obtained by changes in the level of income. Equality is reached when the supply of money $\bar{M}^s$ is at the level of income Y_1^{s*}, where the demand for money curve M^d overlays the supply curve. This uniquely determined level of income Y_1^{s*} is then transferred to the commodity market. Commodity demand is brought into equality with the already determined supply by appropriate changes in the rate of interest.

What happens if the supply of money increases to $\bar{M}^{s'}$? The demand for money and the larger supply are equalized by an increase in income to Y_2^{s*}. Equilibrium in the money market is indicated by the dashed curve in Figure 6(b), where $M^{d'}$ exactly overlays $\bar{M}^{s'}$. The uniquely determined higher level of income Y_2^{s*} may now be transferred to the commodity market diagram. Commodity demand is raised to $Y^{d'}$, where it equals Y_2^{s*}, by a fall in the rate of interest to r_2^*.

To illustrate that the expenditure and tax multipliers are nonexistent in model V consider, for example, what would happen if there were an increase in government expenditure $\bar{G}$ when we started in equilibrium at Y_2^{s*} and $Y^{d'}$. The commodity demand curve would shift up to $Y^{d''}$ (not shown), creating excess commodity demand. How would this be removed? Commodity supply is uniquely determined from the money market at Y_2^{s*}. Thus, commodity demand would have to fall until it overlays $Y^{d'}$ again. This would occur through a rise in the rate of interest, which reduces consumption and investment. We see, therefore, that a change in $\bar{G}$ would have no effect on the level of real income and, thus, conclude that the multiplier is zero. The result would be the same if any other category of expenditure or taxes had been changed.

Finally, it is useful to examine model V in an *IS*/*LM* context. Consider Figure 7. The *IS* curve has its usual downward slope, since the commodity market will clear at several different combinations of real income and in-

FIGURE 6

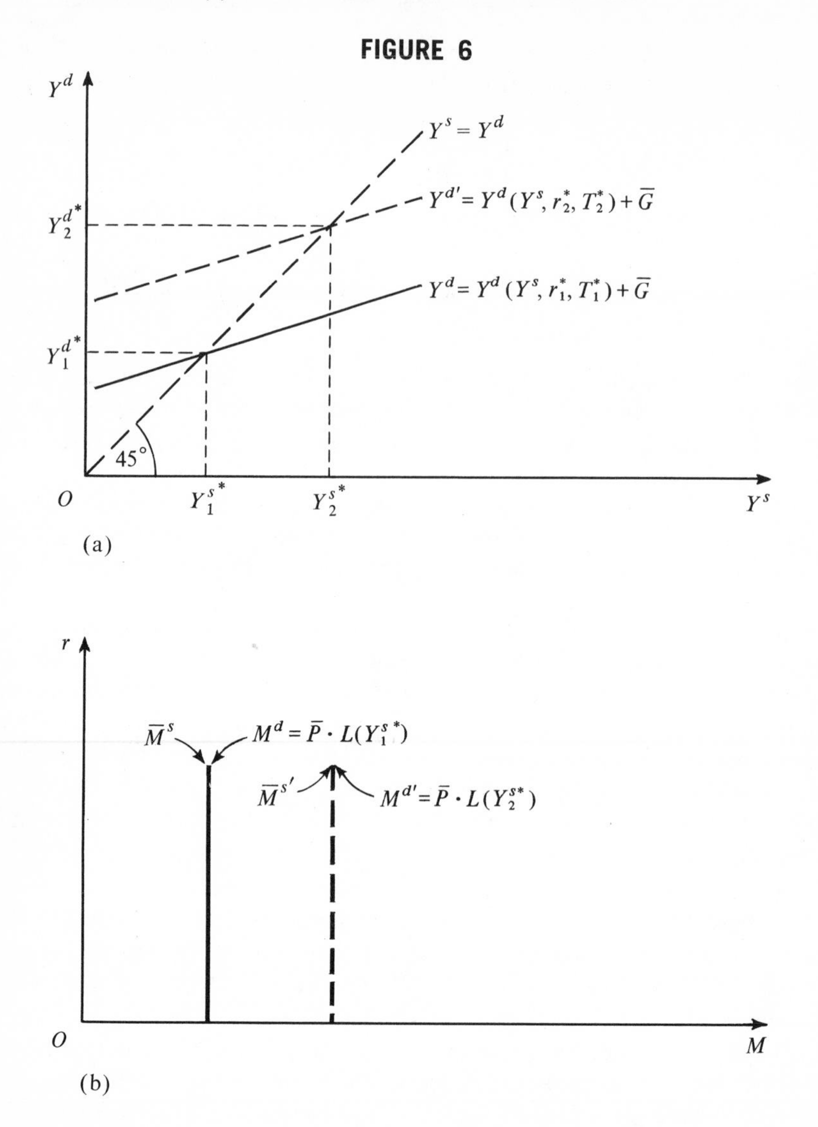

terest rates. However, the *LM* curve is vertical. There is only one level of income which equates the supply of money with the demand, no matter what the interest rate is. It will now be obvious from Figure 6 why only money matters, and not fiscal policy. An increase in the money supply shifts the *LM* curve to *LM'*, raising income from Y_1^{s*} to Y_2^{s*} and causing the interest rate to fall to r_2^*. However, if the money supply is kept constant and there is an increase in government expenditure, for example, the *IS* curve shifts to *IS'*. But this only raises the interest rate to r_3^* and has no effect on real income, which remains constant at Y_2^{s*}.

The foregoing discussions of models I through V make it quite clear why economists have devoted so much effort to empirical studies of the re-

FIGURE 7

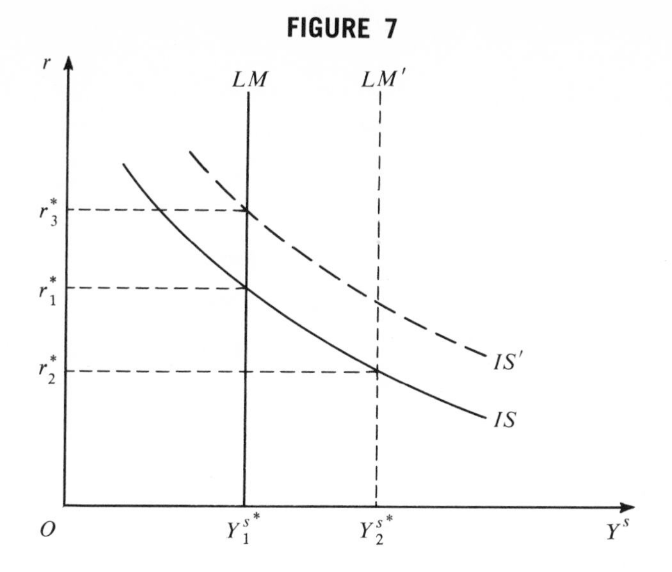

sponsiveness of commodity demand and the demand for money to changes in the interest rate. Their findings have crucial policy implications. If commodity demand is unresponsive to changes in the interest rate (and real balances), money does not matter a whit and changes in the level of income can only be accomplished through fiscal policy. Alternatively, if the demand for money is unresponsive to changes in the rate of interest, fiscal policy is worthless and changes in the level of income can only be achieved through monetary policy.

What is the box score on these empirical studies? It has been definitely established that the demand for money *is* a function of the rate of interest. Thus, fiscal policy does matter.[1]

The responsiveness of commodity demand to changes in the interest rate is also fairly well established. To be more precise, we should, perhaps, say the responsiveness of one component of that demand—namely, long-term investment. The evidence on the responsiveness of consumption and short-term investment is less conclusive. Nonetheless, as long as *some* commodity demand is responsive to interest rate changes, money matters.[2] Thus, we come to the eclectic conclusion that money and fiscal policy both matter. Neither is a paper tiger. We are obliged, then, to set up an appropriate model.

[1] In this case it is also assumed that wages and prices have some inflexibility. You will recall from §9.3, that with *flexible* prices and wages, fiscal policy had no effect on real income, even though the demand for money was interest responsive. Thus, we have two conditions: fiscal policy matters when prices and wages are imperfectly flexible *and* the demand for money is interest responsive.

[2] In this case it is also assumed that wages and prices have some inflexibility. We saw throughout Part II that when wages and prices were flexible, money had *no* effect on real income. It only affected prices. Thus, we again have two conditions: money matters when wages and prices are imperfectly flexible *and* commodity demand is interest responsive (or responsive to changes in real balances).

6 Model VI; The General IS/LM Model

Model VI is the general *IS*/*LM* model. The interest rate appears in both the commodity demand functions and the demand for money function. We have

$$\text{Commodity market}\begin{cases} Y^s = Y^d & (38)\\ Y^d = C + I + \bar{G} & (39)\\ C = b_0 + b_1(Y^s - T) - b_2 r & (40)\\ I = i_0 + i_1 Y^s - i_2 r & (41)\\ T = t_0 + t_1 Y^s & (42)\end{cases}$$

$$\text{Money market}\begin{cases} \dfrac{M^d}{\bar{P}} = m_0 + m_1 Y^s - m_2 r & (43)\\ M^d = \bar{M}^s & (44)\end{cases}$$

Model VI contains seven equations and seven endogenous variables (Y^s, Y^d, C, I, r, T, M^d) in addition to three exogenous variables ($\bar{P}$, $\bar{G}$, and $\bar{M}^s$). This model is not separable in any way. The commodity market contains five equations and six endogenous variables (Y^s, Y^d, C, I, r, and T), while the money market contains two equations and three endogenous variables (M^d, Y^s, and r). Thus, the complete system is interdependent and must be solved simultaneously.

The variable of primary interest to us is, as usual, real income Y^s. We wish to express it as a function only of the exogenous variables and the parameters of the relationships. We proceed in three stages.

First, substitute (42) in (40); then substitute the result in (39) along with (41); finally, substitute the result in (38) and isolate r on the left-hand side.

$$r = \frac{1}{b_2 + i_2}(b_0 + i_0 - b_1 t_0 + \bar{G}) - \frac{(1 - b_1 - b_1 t_1 - i_1)}{b_2 + i_2} Y^s \qquad (45)$$

This is one equation in two unknowns (r and Y^s) and is the equation of the *IS* curve. We see by inspection how this curve shifts under varying circumstances. For example, an increase in entrepreneurial expectations *raises* i_0 and, thus, the intercept. Hence, the curve would shift right. An increase in thrift *lowers* b_0 (the intercept in the consumption function) and, thus the intercept in (45) falls, causing the curve to shift left. Obviously, an increase in $\bar{G}$ increases the intercept in (45) and shifts the whole curve right. Similarly an increase in the *average* tax rate t_0 lowers the intercept in (45), and the whole curve shifts left. Note that an increase in the *marginal* tax rate t_1 changes the *slope* of the curve, ceteris paribus, raising it in absolute value (making it steeper) if t_1 increases and lowering it in absolute value (making it shallower) if t_1 decreases.

As b_2 and i_2 tend towards zero (consumption and investment become interest inelastic), both the intercept and the slope (in absolute value) approach infinity. That is, the *IS* curve tends to the vertical. This is what we found in the geometric analysis. As b_2 and i_2 tend towards infinity the slope of the *IS* curve approaches zero. That is, the curve tends towards the horizontal.

Continuing our algebraic manipulations, we next substitute (44) in (43) and isolate r on the left-hand side. This yields

$$r = \frac{1}{m_2}\left(m_0 - \frac{\bar{M}^s}{\bar{P}}\right) + \frac{m_1}{m_2} Y^s \tag{46}$$

which is one equation in two unknowns (r and Y^s) and is the equation of the *LM* curve. We can also see how this curve shifts under various circumstances. If $\bar{M}^s$ increases, the intercept in (46) is reduced and the curve shifts right, and vice versa for a decrease in $\bar{M}^s$. If there is an increase in liquidity preference (indicated by an increase in m_0), the intercept rises and the curve shifts left; of course, the opposite is true for a reduction in liquidity preference.

As m_2 approaches infinity (the demand for money becomes highly interest elastic), the slope of the *LM* curve approaches zero. That is, the *LM* curve tends towards the horizontal. On the other hand, if m_2 tends towards zero (the demand for money becomes interest inelastic), the intercept and slope tend towards infinity. That is, the *LM* curve approaches the vertical. This, too, confirms our earlier geometric analysis.

Finally, to complete our work, we see that equations (45) and (46) are two equations in two unknowns (r and Y^s). As it is Y^s that interest us, we reduce them to one equation in one unknown by equating their right-hand sides and then isolate Y^s. We obtain

$$\begin{aligned} Y^s = {} & \frac{m_2}{m_1(b_2 + i_2) + m_2(1 - b_1 + b_1 t_1 - i_1)} (b_0 + i_0 - b_1 t_0 + \bar{G}) \\ & - \frac{m_0(b_2 + i_2)}{m_1(b_2 + i_2) + m_2(1 - b_1 + b_1 t_1 - i_1)} \\ & + \frac{b_2 + i_2}{m_1(b_2 + i_2) + m_2(1 - b_1 + b_1 t_1 - i_1)} \frac{\bar{M}^s}{\bar{P}} \end{aligned} \tag{47}$$

Equation (47) allows us to investigate the effects of changes in such variables as government expenditure, average and marginal tax rates, the money supply, liquidity preference, thrift, and entrepreneurial expectations on the equilibrium level of income. All we need do is take the partial derivative of (47) with respect to the relevant variable. Doing this, we obtain

$$\frac{\partial Y^s}{\partial \bar{G}} = \frac{\partial Y^s}{\partial i_0} = \frac{\partial Y^s}{\partial b_0} = \frac{m_2}{m_1(b_2 + i_2) + m_2(1 - b_1 + b_1 t_1 - i_1)} \geqslant 0 \tag{48}$$

These multipliers are generally positive, as indicated. However, they are zero if m_2 is equal to zero (that is, if the demand for money is interest inelastic). This we should expect because we concluded earlier that fiscal policy does not matter in such circumstances.

The impact on income of a change in average and marginal tax rates is shown by the partial derivatives of Y^s with respect to t_0 and t_1. Thus,

$$\frac{\partial Y^s}{\partial t_0} = -\frac{m_2 b_1}{m_1(b_2 + i_2) + m_2(1 - b_1 + b_1 t_1 - i_1)} \leqslant 0 \tag{49}$$

$$\frac{\partial Y^s}{\partial t_1} = -\frac{m_2 b_1 Y^s}{m_1(b_2 + i_2) + m_2(1 - b_1 + b_1 t_1 - i_1)} \leqslant 0 \tag{50}$$

In general, these tax multipliers are negative as shown. However, if m_2 is zero, then so are the tax multipliers. Again, this confirms that fiscal policy does not matter in such circumstances.

We turn now to the impact of monetary phenomena on the level of income. Taking the partial derivative of (47) with respect to liquidity preference m_0 and the supply of money, we obtain

$$\frac{\partial Y^s}{\partial m_0} = -\frac{b_2 + i_2}{m_1(b_2 + i_2) + m_2(1 - b_1 + b_1 t_1 - i_1)} \leqslant 0 \tag{51}$$

$$\frac{\partial Y^s}{\partial (M^s/\bar{P})} = \frac{b_2 + i_2}{m_1(b_2 + i_2) + m_2(1 - b_1 + b_1 t_1 - i_1)} \geqslant 0 \tag{52}$$

The first of these multipliers is generally negative: income rises when liquidity preference falls, and vice versa. The second of these multipliers is generally positive: income rises when the money supply rises, and vice versa. However, both are zero if b_2 and i_2 are zero (consumption and investment are interest inelastic). That is the result we would expect, since we concluded earlier that money does not matter in such circumstances.

The final special case worth examining (which has interested us earlier) is when the demand for money becomes infinitely interest elastic—that is, m_2 approaches infinity. It is immediately obvious that money does not matter because both money multipliers (51) and (52) tend towards zero. To see how the expenditure and tax multipliers are affected, first divide the top and bottom of (48), (49), and (50) by m_2.

$$\frac{\partial Y^s}{\partial \bar{G}} = \frac{\partial Y^s}{\partial i_0} = \frac{\partial Y^s}{\partial b_0} = \frac{1}{\dfrac{m_1}{m_2}(b_2 + i_2) + (1 - b_1 + b_1 t_1 - i_1)} \tag{53}$$

$$\frac{\partial Y^s}{\partial t_0} = -\frac{b_1}{\dfrac{m_1}{m_2}(b_2 + i_2) + (1 - b_1 + b_1 t_1 - i_1)} \tag{54}$$

$$\frac{\partial Y^s}{\partial t_1} = -\frac{b_1 Y^s}{\dfrac{m_1}{m_2}(b_2 + i_2) + (1 - b_1 + b_1 t_1 - i_1)} \tag{55}$$

Now it can easily be seen that as m_2 becomes infinite

$$\frac{\partial Y^s}{\partial \bar{G}} = \frac{\partial Y^s}{\partial i_0} = \frac{\partial Y^s}{\partial t_0} = \frac{1}{1 - b_1 + b_1 t_1 - i_1} \tag{56}$$

$$\frac{\partial Y^s}{\partial t_0} = -\frac{b_1}{1 - b_1 + b_1 t_1 - i_1} \tag{57}$$

$$\frac{\partial Y^s}{\partial t_1} = -\frac{b_1 Y^s}{1 - b_1 + b_1 t_1 - i_1} \tag{58}$$

These are the simple fiscal policy multipliers obtained in principles courses when changes in income are assumed to have no effect on the interest rate which, therefore, cannot in turn change consumption and investment. It is quite obvious that the simple fiscal multipliers (56), (57), and (58) are larger than their respective counterparts (48), (49), and (50) for general fiscal policy.

We have now completed our exploration of the comparative static properties of our macroeconomic model when it is operated with neo-Keynesian (rather than neoclassical) assumptions. It is time now to stand back and look at the debate between Keynes and the Classics in the perspective of this discussion. This we shall do in the following chapter.

Appendix: Why Is the Multiplier So Small? [1]

Most estimates of the marginal propensity to consume b_1 obtained from time series studies are approximately 0.9. This would seem to imply a government expenditure multiplier of about 10. However, most estimates of the government expenditure multiplier itself are around 2 – well below 10. How can we explain this apparent inconsistency? There are several reasons. Some of these reasons are already familiar, but it will do no harm to recap them briefly. (Note that what we shall say to rationalize the smallness of the government expenditure multiplier applies with only marginal differences to the tax multiplier as well.)

In model IV, which incorporates taxes as an endogenous variable, we find our first reason. The appearance of the marginal propensity to tax t_1 in the denominator of that model's multiplier indubitably means that the multiplier must be smaller than when t_1 does not appear. The intuitive reason is obvious and has been mentioned earlier. The induced secondary consumption expenditure (which is the engine of the multiplier) is less in each round because part of each round's increment in income is creamed off in taxes.

When we proceed to model VI we are dealing with a model in which, for the first time, the real sector is not separable. The equilibrium level of income cannot be solved for without reference to the monetary sector. We found that the government expenditure multiplier in model VI is given by

[1] This appendix can be omitted without loss of continuity.

equation (48) and, for our present purposes the more convenient form, equation (53). If you compare (53) with the multiplier of model IV, which is $1/(1 - b_1 + b_1t_1 - i_1)$, you can see that in general (53) is the smaller, since it also includes in its denominator the term $(m_1/m_2)(b_2 + i_2)$ which will be positive as long as consumption *or* investment is interest responsive *and* the demand for real money balances is income responsive *and* the demand for money is not perfectly interest elastic. Since empirical studies indicate that i_2 (if not b_2) is positive, m_1 is positive, and m_2 is a good deal less than infinite, we may safely conclude that the expression $(m_1/m_2)(b_2 + i_2)$ in the denominator of (53) is positive and, thus, give it as a second reason why observed multipliers are less than the naive model I would permit.

The intuitive explanation for this lower-valued multiplier is quite simple, too. A rise in government expenditure begins to induce a chain of secondary consumption and investment expenditure. However, the rise in income also increases interest rates and this chokes off some consumption and investment. In terms of a 45°-line diagram, visualize an aggregate demand curve pushed up by an increase in government expenditure to $Y^{d'}$, which indicates proximately a new equilibrium level of income. However, as the interest rate rises the consumption and investment curves *fall,* dragging $Y^{d'}$ with them. Thus, the *ultimate* new aggregate demand curve $Y^{d''}$ is lower than the *proximate* one $Y^{d'}$ and, consequently, the final equilibrium level of income is lower than was first indicated.

Let us open our model to foreign trade for the first (and only) time. Elaborating on model VI, we obtain model VII

Commodity market

$$Y^s = Y^d \tag{59}$$

$$Y^d = C_d + I + \bar{G} + \bar{X} \tag{60}$$

$$(C_d + J) = b_0 + b_1(Y^s - T) - b_2r \tag{61}$$

$$I = i_0 + i_1Y^s - i_2r \tag{62}$$

$$T = t_0 + t_1Y^s \tag{63}$$

$$J = j_0 + j_1(Y^s - T) \tag{64}$$

Money market

$$\frac{M^d}{\bar{P}} = m_0 + m_1Y^s - m_2r \tag{65}$$

$$M^d = \bar{M}^s \tag{66}$$

Now, C_d is consumption expenditure on domestically produced goods and J is consumption expenditure on foreign (imported) goods and $\bar{X}$ is foreign expenditure on our goods (exports). Some comment is called for. In (60) notice that aggregate commodity demand has been amended. Now we must include only consumption expenditure on domestic goods instead of all consumption. Obviously, consumption expenditure on foreign goods does not affect *our* aggregate demand for commodities. However, we must include in our aggregate demand for commodities what foreigners demand. This is our exports of commodities $\bar{X}$. We assume that $\bar{X}$ is an exogenous variable. Our total consumption expenditure (on both domestic and imported goods) is given by (61). Equation (64) states that our expenditure on imports is a function of our disposable income. The parameter j_1 is the marginal propensity to import. Notice, finally, that we do not need a market clearance equation for the foreign trade sector. Our imports and exports do not have to be equal.

Model VII contains eight equations and eight endogenous variables (Y^s, Y^d, C_d, I, r, J, T, and M^d) as well as four exogenous variables ($\bar{P}$, $\bar{G}$, $\bar{X}$, and $\bar{M}^s$). This model is not separable in any way. Both the commodity market and the money market contain more endogenous variables than they do equations: six equations and seven endogenous variables (Y^s, Y^d, C_d, I, r, J, and T) for the commodity market and two equations and three endogenous variables (M^d, Y^s, and r) for the money market. Thus, the complete system is interdependent and must be solved simultaneously.

We wish to express real income Y^s as a function of the exogenous variables and parameters of the various relationships only. We proceed, as for model VI, in three stages.

First, substitute (63) in (61) and isolate C_d; then substitute (63) in (64) and substitute this into the equation in C_d; then substitute the latter with (62) into (60). Finally, substitute this result in (59) and isolate r on the left-hand side.

$$r = \frac{1}{b_2 + i_2}(b_0 + i_0 - j_0 - b_1t_0 + j_1t_0 + \bar{G} + \bar{X}) - \frac{(1 - b_1 + b_1t_1 + j_1 - j_1t_1 - i_1)}{b_2 + i_2} Y^s \tag{67}$$

(67) is one equation in the two unknowns r and Y^s, and it also happens to be the equation of the *IS* curve when the model incorporates foreign trade. Very briefly, we can point out that the *IS* curve shifts right when exports increase and left when they decrease; this can be seen from the appearance of $\bar{X}$ in the intercept of (67) with a positive sign. Similarly, the *IS* curve shifts right when the average propensity to import decreases and left when the average propensity to import increases; this can be seen from the appearance of j_0 (the intercept of the import function) in the intercept of (67) with a negative sign. The other properties of this *IS* curve are similar to the *IS* curve of model VI discussed in §6 immediately following its equation (45).

Second, substitute (66) in (65) and isolate r on the left-hand side.

$$r = \frac{1}{m_2}\left(m_0 - \frac{M^s}{\bar{P}}\right) + \frac{m_1}{m_2} Y^s \tag{68}$$

which is the familiar equation of the *LM* curve and is exactly the same as equation (46) in model VI.

Equations (67) and (66) are two equations in two unknowns. We are interested in Y^s, so, as our third step, we equate their right-hand sides and isolate Y^s.

$$Y^s = \frac{m_2}{m_1(b_2+i_2)+m_2(1-b_1+b_1t_1+j_1-j_1t_1-i_1)}$$
$$(b_0+i_0-j_0-b_1t_0+j_1t_0+\bar{G}+\bar{X})$$
$$-\frac{m_0(b_2+i_2)}{m_1(b_2+i_2)+m_2(1-b_1+b_1t_1+j_1-j_1t_1-i_1)}$$
$$+\frac{(b_2+i_2)}{m_1(b_2+i_2)+m_2(1-b_1+b_1t_1+j_1-j_1t_1-i_1)}\frac{\bar{M}^s}{\bar{P}} \tag{69}$$

Taking the partial derivative of (69) for $\bar{G}$ to obtain the government expenditure multiplier, we find

$$\frac{\partial Y^s}{\partial \bar{G}} = \frac{m_2}{m_1(b_2+i_2)+m_2(1-b_1+b_1t_1+j_1-j_1t_1-i_1)} \geqslant 0 \tag{70}$$

Now compare this multiplier with the multiplier of model VI in equation (48). They are similar in every respect except that (70) includes $(j_1 - j_1t_1)$ in the second term of the denominator. Since j_1 is the marginal propensity to import and t_1 is the marginal propensity to tax (both restricted between zero and unity) the inclusion of the term $(j_1 - j_1t_1)$ in the denominator of (70) must make that denominator larger than the denominator of (48). Inevitably, then, (70) as a whole is smaller than (48) as a whole. We may conclude, therefore, that opening the economy up to trade decreases the multiplier further.

Once more, there is an obvious intuitive reason. When government expenditure is increased and triggers off secondary induced consumption and investment expenditure, the eventual rise in income will be larger when *all* the induced expenditure is on domestic goods. When the economy is open to trade, part of the secondary induced expenditure is on foreign goods. And this, of course, does nothing to raise domestic income. Like saving and taxes, imports are a leakage from the circular flow of income.

Next, let us make some different suppositions about the household sector's attitude towards government activity and see what implications this has for the government expenditure multiplier.

In all previous models, households disregarded the government's expenditure. This is the usual assumption; the government is cast in a separate role. Its expenditure is ignored by households when arriving at their own expenditure decisions. When, for example, the government provided a public-good commodity for collective consumption, households ignored this and planned to consume the same quantity of commodities privately as they did before the government made more commodities available for collective consumption. Let us see what happens if we change this assumption. Now we suppose that households include government expenditure on commodities as part of their real income and collective consumption of commodities in their own consumption. Consequently, if more commodities are provided collectively, this will affect private commodity consumption. Essentially, we are suggesting modifications to the consumption function. Instead of the usual simple version when government is included, namely,

$$C = b_0 + b_1(Y^s - T)$$

we are now proposing the following consumption function:

$$C + \bar{G}_c = b_0 + b_1(Y^s - T + \bar{G}_c + \bar{G}_I) \tag{71}$$

where $\bar{G}_c$ is government expenditure on commodities for collective consumption and $\bar{G}_I$ is government expenditure on commodities for collective investment. Total government expenditure $\bar{G} = \bar{G}_c + \bar{G}_I$. The left-hand side of (71) implies that households now regard collectively consumed commodities as part of household consumption. The inclusion of $\bar{G} = \bar{G}_c + \bar{G}_I$ in the parentheses on the right-hand side of (71) reflects the fact that households now include government expenditure as part of their own real income. Is this completely asinine, or is there some justification for this procedure?

Consider the following rationale. If the government buys milk and "gives" it away to children is not the household sector's real income thereby raised? Moreover, would this not affect the household sector's private milk purchases? And, remember, the government does "give" away (i.e., without *direct* charge) lots of commodities such as roads, schools, and sanitation. Look at it the other way—would not our real income be lower without them?

Now let us incorporate this sort of consumption function in a simple income determination model. We shall use model IV except we substitute (71) for (24) to obtain the following model VIII:

Commodity market

$$Y^s = Y^d \tag{72}$$

$$Y^d = C + I + \bar{G}_c + \bar{G}_I \tag{73}$$

$$C + \bar{G}_c = b_0 + b_1(Y^s - T + \bar{G}_c + \bar{G}_I) \tag{74}$$

$$I = i_0 + i_1 Y^s \tag{75}$$

$$T = t_0 + t_1 Y^s \tag{76}$$

Money market

$$\frac{M^d}{\bar{P}} = m_0 + m_1 Y^s - m_2 r \tag{77}$$

$$M^d = \bar{M}^s \tag{78}$$

There are four exogenous variables ($\bar{G}_c$, $\bar{G}_I$, $\bar{M}^s$, and $\bar{P}$) and seven equations in seven endogenous variables (Y^s, Y^d, C, I, T, M^d, and r). In addition, the model is separable in that the commodity market contains five equations in five endogenous variables (Y^s, Y^d, C, I, and T). A solution for real income Y^s can, therefore, be obtained without reference to the money market. We proceed as follows.

Substitute (76) in (74), the result with (75) in (73), and, finally, this result in (72). After solving for Y^s we obtain

$$Y^s = \frac{1}{1 - b_1 + b_1 t_1 - i_1}[b_0 - b_1 t_0 + i_0 + b_1 \bar{G}_c + (1 + b)\bar{G}_I] \tag{79}$$

From this we see that the government expenditure multipliers are

$$\frac{\partial Y^s}{\partial \bar{G}_c} = \frac{b_1}{1 - b_1 + b_1 t_1 - i_1} \tag{80}$$

$$\frac{\partial Y^s}{\partial \bar{G}_I} = \frac{1 + b_1}{1 - b_1 + b_1 t_1 - i_1} \tag{81}$$

Notice that there are now two different government expenditure multipliers: a government consumption expenditure multiplier (80) and a government investment expenditure multiplier (81). Comparing the former with the (single) government expenditure multiplier of model IV, we see that (80) is smaller, since $b_1 < 1$ by assumption. However, the government investment expenditure multiplier (81) in the present model is *larger* than the equivalent multiplier in model IV; in fact, it is nearly twice as large. We are concerned, however, with why observed multipliers are so small. Perhaps part of the reason is that the private sector's consumption function is represented by an equation such as (74) and the private sector interprets much government expenditure to be collective consumption.

Finally, if a consumption function like (74) were incorporated in model VII the government consumption expenditure multiplier would appear like (70) except that the numerator would be $b_1 m_2$ instead of m_2. Clearly, such a multiplier would be less than (70), which we have suggested may already be quite small.

In the above discussion, we assumed that the private sector was cognizant of the government's expenditure activities and, thus, adopted the consumption function (74). We shall continue with this approach, while we make the additional assumption that the household sector is also cognizant of the government's deficit position.

Previously, we operated as if the private sector completely ignores the government's debt position. Households are not affected by the government's debt. Government may be of, for, and by the people, but the people do not regard the government's debt as its own. When their own private debt goes up, households are always assumed to be painfully aware of the interest obligation they incur (and, when their bonds are *not* consols, of the eventual obligation to redeem their debt). This is not the case with their government's debt—they completely ignore the interest burden incurred in their behalf by government.

Now, we change this and assume that households regard government debt as their own. Hence, when government debt goes up households recognize that they incur an additional tax burden (to pay the interest on the government's debt). Government, we might say, is of, for, by, and just like the people.

The import of this change is that households now regard deficit financing as equivalent to taxation. The explanation runs as follows. Suppose the government's budget was originally balanced, that is, it was financing all its expenditure out of current taxation. Now let it reduce taxation while maintaining the same expenditure. It must, therefore, begin to borrow by issuing more bonds—it begins to deficit finance. From the *long-run* point of view this reduction in taxation does *not* change the household sector's total resources. Why? Interest must be paid on the new government debt (and, if the debt is not a consol, at some time it will have to be redeemed). How can the household sector prepare itself to make such interest payments (and, finally, to redeem the debt)? The answer is for the household sector to *save* the amount made available to it when the government switches from taxation to deficit financing. Thus, the interest on these savings will be available to pay the interest on the debt (and the principal will be available to finance its final redemption). If households do this, in effect, they recognize that such a switch in government financing operations does not change their own lifetime resources so they will not change their lifetime consumption pattern. The government's financing operations would, therefore, be without effect. In other words, the household sector is fully *discounting* the future tax liability incurred in its behalf by its government.

Instead of the consumption function (74) we have

$$C + \bar{G}_c = b_0 + b_1 Y^s \tag{82}$$

Government taxation and expenditure are both eliminated from the right-hand side because the household sector does not regard its *resources* Y^s as being affected one way or the other by the particular tax-expenditure posture adopted by its government. Note, though, that the household sector continues to regard collectively consumed goods as equivalent to privately consumed goods. If (82) is substituted for (74) in model VIII (while all the other equations remain the same) we obtain model IX. This model has four exogenous variables ($\bar{G}_c$, $\bar{G}_I$, $\bar{M}^s$, and $\bar{P}$) and seven equations in seven endogenous variables (Y^s, Y^d, C, I, T, M^d, and r). The commodity market is separable, since it still consists of five equations in five endogenous variables (Y^s, Y^d, C, I, and T). Real income in terms of the exogenous variables and parameters may be found by simply substituting (82) and (75) in (73) and the result in (72), then isolating Y^s.

$$Y^s = \frac{1}{(1 - b_1 - i_1)}(b_0 + i_0 + \bar{G}_I) \tag{83}$$

from which the government consumption expenditure and investment expenditure multipliers are, respectively,

$$\frac{\partial Y^s}{\partial \bar{G}_c} = 0 \tag{84}$$

$$\frac{\partial Y^s}{\partial \bar{G}_I} = \frac{1}{1 - b_1 - i_1} \tag{85}$$

We see that the government consumption expenditure multiplier is zero. This is generally true when the household sector regards government activities in the way we have assumed. If, for example, the consumption function represented by (82) were included in model VII the government consumption expenditure multiplier would no longer be given by (70). It would also be zero. The intuitive, commonsensical explanation is again obvious. When the government provides one more commodity for collective consumption the household sector merely reduces its private consumption of commodities by one.

The smallness of observed government expenditure multipliers *could* (we say no more), therefore, be due to the fact that households regard collective consumer goods just like private consumer goods, households interpret much government expenditure to be of a collective consumption nature, *and* the household sector *completely* discounts its future liabilities for taxation when the government engages in deficit financing. Clearly, however, these sets of circumstances cannot all prevail, or, as we have seen, government expenditure multipliers would be zero (and they are not observed to be *that* small). Perhaps the household sector only partially, instead of fully, discounts the future tax liability implied by deficit financing.

Summary

In this chapter we developed several successively more complicated models of income determination. Our basic strategy was to present the equations of each model and then solve for the equilibrium value of real income Y^s in terms of the model's parameters and exogenous variables. From this *reduced-form* equation, it was a simple matter to calculate the expenditure, tax, and money multipliers by partial differentiation. In models I through IV we found that "money does not matter" because the commodity market equations are separable and, thus, the equilibrium level of income can be expressed in terms of the parameters of the commodity market equations and exogenous commodity market variables *only*. This separability occurs so long as the commodity market equations are independent of all monetary variables, namely, the interest rate and real balances.

We constructed model V to illustrate a situation where "fiscal policy does *not* matter" and "money *only* matters." In that model the demand for real money balances is made independent of the interest rate. This implies that the equilibrium level of income is determined *solely* by the money market equations.

Model VI is the *general IS/LM* model for a closed economy in which "*both* fiscal policy and money matter." The commodity market is not separable, since consumption and investment are made functions of the interest rate. Therefore, the complete model must be solved simultaneously. By examining the expenditure, tax, and money multipliers in this general model, we saw it was relatively easy to demonstrate the algebraic equivalents of the limiting cases (the liquidity trap phenomenon, a completely interest-inelastic investment and saving function, and so on) analyzed geometrically in Chapter 13.

Model VII (presented in the Appendix) is the general *IS/LM* model for an economy open to trade. Opening the economy to trade influences the *IS* curve, which will shift right when exports increase or imports decrease, and left when exports decrease or imports increase.

Finally, we discussed some of the reasons why empirically estimated multipliers are so much smaller than the naive multiplier $1/(1 - mpc)$ obtained from the simplest model I of income determination.

Questions

(*Note:* Questions marked with an asterisk assume the appendix has been read.)

1. Explain why "money does not matter" in model I. Assume the following parameters and values for the exogenous variables in that model: $b_0 = 30$, $b_1 = 0.9$, $\bar{I} = 20$. Find (a) the size of the multiplier, (b) equilibrium income, (c) equilibrium consumption.
2. Given the data of question 1, suppose an increase in thrift decreased b_0 to $b_0' = 20$.
   (a) Find the new equilibrium level of income.
   (b) Find the new equilibrium level of consumption.
   (c) What has happened to saving?
   (d) Sketch an *IS/LM* diagram illustrating your answers to questions 1 and 2.
   (e) What has happened to the interest rate and why?
3. Prove that in model I the multiplier is equal to $1/(1 - mpc)$.
4. Explain why, when both government expenditure and taxes are exogenous, equal increases in government expenditure and taxes (i.e., "a balanced budget increase in expenditure") increase equilibrium income by the amount that government expenditure has increased. (In short, prove the "balanced budget multiplier theorem.")
5. Does "money matter" in model IV? If so, why; if not, why not? Sketch an *IS/LM* diagram illustrating this model.
6. Assume the following values for the parameters and exogenous variables in model IV: $b_0 = 20$, $b_1 = 0.8$, $i_0 = 10$, $i_1 = 0.1$, $\bar{G} = 30$, $t_0 = -10$, $t_1 = 0.125$. Find (a) the expenditure multiplier and the *average* tax multiplier, (b) equilibrium income, (c) equilibrium saving, (d) equilibrium investment, (e) the government's *fiscal position* in equilibrium (i.e., the size of its surplus or deficit), (f) the *marginal* tax multiplier.
7. Assume that as entrepreneurs become more sanguine i_0 in question 6 increases to 20. Find the answers to question 6(a)–(f) now.
8. Does "fiscal policy matter" in model V? If so, why; if not, why not? Sketch an *IS/LM* diagram illustrating this model.
9. Assume the following (relevant) values for the parameters and exogenous variables in model V: $m_0 = 0$, $m_1 = 0.25$, $t_0 = -10$, $t_1 = 0.125$, $\bar{G} = 25$, $\bar{P} = \$2$, $\bar{M}^s = \$200$.
   (a) Find the values of the expenditure, average tax, and marginal tax multipliers.
   (b) What is the money multiplier equal to?
   (c) Find equilibrium income.

(d) Does the government have a surplus or deficit in equilibrium? What is its size?
(e) Is planned saving equal to, less than, or more than planned investment in equilibrium?

10. Assume that the monetary authority increases the money supply in question 9 by 20 dollars. Find the answers to 9(a)–(e) now.
11. Explain why a large amount of professional empirical research effort has been devoted to trying to establish whether or not the demand for real money balances is responsive to the interest rate.
12. Referring to model VI:
    (a) Derive the equation for the *IS* curve and sketch the curve roughly. Now indicate whether the *IS* curve will shift left or right for each of the following changes: an increase in thrift, an increase in entrepreneurs' expectations, a decrease in average tax rates, an increase in government expenditure.
    (b) Derive the equation for the *LM* curve and sketch the curve roughly. Resketch it if the demand for money is very unresponsive to changes in the interest rate (i.e., m_2 is small). Resketch it if the demand for money is highly responsive to changes in the interest rate (i.e., m_2 is large). How will the curve look if the supply of money increases?
    (c) Derive the reduced-form equation for income by solving the equations for the *IS* and *LM* curves [from (a) and (b)] simultaneously. Now calculate the expenditure, average tax rate, and marginal tax rate multipliers. What do these reduce to, respectively, as the demand for money becomes infinitely elastic with respect to the interest rate?

*13. Give as many arguments as you can for why empirically estimated expenditure multipliers are *much* smaller than the naive multiplier $1/(1 - mpc)$ derived from the simplest income determination model (model I) commonly presented in courses on the principles of macroeconomics.

*14. Assume model VII for an economy open to trade.
    (a) Derive the equation of the *IS* curve. List the factors which would cause the curve to shift right (for example, an increase in entrepreneurial expectations, and so on).
    (b) Derive the equation of the *LM* curve. List the factors which would cause the curve to shift left.
    (c) Find the reduced-form equation for national income.
    (d) Calculate the expenditure, average tax rate, and marginal tax rate multipliers.
    (e) Assume that the equilibrium level of income does not generate full employment. Suggest a *trade* policy to Congress that would raise income (for example, more or fewer tariffs, and so on).

*15. Assume that households regard government expenditure on collective commodities $\bar{G}_c$ as an integral part of household consumption and that households also regard *all* government expenditure (on consumption goods $\bar{G}_c$ *and* investment goods $\bar{G}_I$) as part of their own real income.
    (a) If total consumption is only a linear function of income, what would this special type of consumption function look like?
    (b) Substitute this function in model IV for the usual consumption function and calculate both the government consumption and investment expenditure multipliers.

SELECTED READINGS

1. M. J. Bailey, *National Income and the Price Level,* McGraw-Hill, 1962, chapter 3. An excellent discussion of the multiplier in variously specified national income models. Relevant to this chapter's appendix.
2. D. Laidler, *The Demand for Money,* International, 1969. A survey of the empirical evidence on the demand for money, which concludes that there is little doubt it *is* a function of the interest rate. Therefore, model V of this chapter in which "fiscal policy does *not* matter" and "money *only* matters" would *not* seem to be a particularly useful model.
3. D. Patinkin, *Money, Interest, and Prices,* 2nd ed., Harper & Row, 1965, chapter 14, section 2.
4. P. A. Samuelson, "The Simple Mathematics of Income Determination," in L. A. Metzler, (ed.), *Essays in Honor of Alvin H. Hansen,* Norton, 1948. Some elementary Keynesian models presented algebraically. Also discusses the balanced budget multiplier.

FURTHER READINGS

5. W. J. Baumol and M. H. Peston, "More on the Multiplier Effects of a Balanced Budget," *American Economic Review,* March, 1955. Discusses the balanced budget multiplier theorem and contains detailed references to the literature on this topic.
6. R. A. Musgrave, *The Theory of Public Finance,* McGraw-Hill, 1955, p. 430. Lists the literature on the balanced budget multiplier theorem.

15

Keynes versus the Classics

The time has come when we must try to resolve *in a comparative static context* some of the disputes which arose between Keynes and the Classics.[1] In the last analysis, these disputes can be reduced to essentially two controversies.

1. The *unemployment controversy* centers on whether permanent involuntary unemployment can exist in equilibrium in a competitive free-enterprise economy. The classical answer is no; Keynes answered yes.
2. The *interest rate controversy* revolves around several points of dispute. First, is money neutral? The classics replied affirmatively, Keynes negatively. Second, is the interest rate determined by the supply of and demand for *loanable funds*, or by *liquidity preference* (and the supply of money)? The classics chose the former explanation, Keynes the latter. Finally, is interest a *real* phenomenon, determined by such fundamental factors as thrift and the marginal productivity of capital, or is interest basically a *monetary* phenomenon? The classics answered real; Keynes answered monetary.

We shall try to resolve these two controversies as well as a third which is not part of the "Keynes versus the Classics" debate, but arises from the classical view of money.

3. The *dichotomy* (*separability or decomposability*) *controversy* arises because the Classics argued that "money is a veil" (neutral) which changes only the equilibrium values of the nominal variable proportionately, but leaves the equilibrium values of the *real* variables

[1] We emphasize that we are appraising Keynes and the Classics here as *only comparative static theorists*. It has been argued that Keynes should really be judged as a *macroeconomic disequilibrium* theorist—that he was not really interested in what Mrs. Robinson has described, in her own inimitable way, as "the soft soil of static equilibrium analysis." We defer our discussion of Keynes as a macroeconomic *disequilibrium* theorist to the next chapter.

(output, employment, the real wage, the interest rate, and so on) unchanged. The equilibrium values of these real variables are determined solely and exclusively in the real sector (the labor and commodity markets). Thus, the real sector can be *dichotomized* from (*separated* or *decomposed* from) the financial sector of the model and, implicitly, run through its *own* tâtonnement to determine the equilibrium values of the real variables.

Before we attempt a detailed resolution of these issues, let us lavish praise on Keynes. His contribution to economics was at least the equal of Galileo's contribution to astronomy. The quasi-general equilibrium analysis which we have employed throughout this book has proved to be as fruitful a device to economists as Galileo's telescope was to astronomers. Certainly Keynes' macroeconomic model had many crudities and rough edges – but so did Galileo's telescope. Just as it is unimaginable that anyone could have conceived and put into operation the 200-inch telescope at Mount Palomar without benefit of Galileo's simple version, it is inconceivable that the tremendous advances that have taken place within macroeconomics over the last generation could have occurred without Keynes' original pioneering effort. Thus, even though we have been critical of Keynes at several points earlier in this book and will again take issue with him in this chapter, we do not mean to undervalue Keynes' achievement. In quasi-general equilibrium analysis, Keynes had the vision to advance a whole new way of looking at economics. That, perhaps, is enough to ask of any economist. Keynes' signal contribution was the provision of a new analytical apparatus, sophisticated versions of which are now universally used by economists who deal with macroeconomic problems. Hence, we see why Friedman, who is a savage critic of the *use* to which administrations and their economic advisers put this apparatus, is still prepared to say "we are all Keynesians now."[2] Even though the apparatus Keynes conceived was incomplete in places, imperfect in others, and used by him to draw some wrong inferences, these only marginally diminish the spectacular nature of his achievement.

When forced in the periodic appraisals made of Keynes' contribution to name his major theoretical innovation, one eminent economist will opt for the consumption function, another the multiplier, a third for the liquidity preference function, and so on. We feel that such an approach misses the essential nature of Keynes' originality. It is not the individual pieces that are original (in fact, the historians of economic thought have found antecedents for practically all the components of the Keynesian model). What puts the stamp of genius on Keynes is the insight which led him to unite all the in-

[2] Perhaps this admission should not have raised as many eyebrows as it did. After all, Friedman himself has contributed important refinements to some of the components of Keynes' basic apparatus. We have in mind his theories of the consumption function and the demand for money. See, for example, M. Friedman, *A Theory of the Consumption Function,* Princeton University Press, 1957; and "The Demand for Money: Some Theoretical and Empirical Results," *Journal of Political Economy,* August, 1959. As we have said so often, neoclassical economists are not precluded from using the Keynesian apparatus. In fact, it is the most elegant device for demonstrating their propositions once their assumptions are fed into it.

dividual components and thus create a different technique for looking at economics via an operational quasi-general equilibrium apparatus. Adam Smith and Leon Walras were equipped with similar vision, and Keynes ranks with them as one of the truly original economic thinkers of all time.

1 The Controversy over Unemployment

The disagreement over unemployment is whether or not it will exist in equilibrium in a competitive, free-enterprise economy. Keynes argued that permanent, and involuntary, unemployment was to be expected in the normal course of events. The classical economists disagreed.[1]

We have seen throughout this book that *in a comparative static analysis* unemployment can exist *only* if one or more of the three price variables in the model is rigid. The classical economists did not dispute this. They would have readily agreed that if, for example, the nominal wage was fixed institutionally by trade union bargaining power or minimum wage laws, there would be no reason to suppose that the real wage could adjust to clear the labor market. But classical economists would argue that Keynes' prediction of permanent unemployment is only valid when the *special* assumption of wage rigidity is made. Classical economists were probably not as aware that rigidity in the commodity price or in the interest rate could also lead to permanent unemployment and would concede that Keynes had, to that extent, revealed new circumstances under which unemployment might appear in a comparative static context. On the other hand, they might respond that Keynes had only uncovered two new *special* cases, not the sort of *general* theory that he claimed. Theirs was the general theory; only in the special cases that Keynes unearthed was his conclusion of permanent unemployment warranted.

It is necessary to agree that *rigidity* in any of the three price variables is a special assumption. However, consider the intermediate problem. The classical theory of no significant unemployment implies *very (infinitely) fast adjustment* in the three prices to their new equilibrium levels. Keynes' theory of permanent unemployment implies *rigidity*. What about the middle ground where the three prices adjust *slowly?*[2] This is, perhaps, the most frequent case encountered in practice. In such a situation, unemployment, although not permanent, can be large, widespread, and of long duration. Everything depends on the *speed* with which the price variables adjust. The

[1] A. C. Pigou was, perhaps, the last in the line of the great classical economists. J. M. Keynes credits him with producing "the only detailed account of the classical theory of employment which exists" (*General Theory of Employment, Interest, and Money,* Macmillan, 1936, p. 7). Thus, Keynes devoted the eight, somewhat erratic, pages of his appendix to chapter 19 of the *General Theory* to an attack on Pigou. For Pigou's detailed account of the classical theory of employment see his *The Theory of Unemployment,* London, 1929; and *Employment and Equilibrium,* London, 1941 – both of which contain references to other classical economists.

[2] In Chapter 16 "Macroeconomic Disequilibrium," we cite arguments to the effect that it *is rational* for transactors to adjust prices *slowly*.

classical economists worked out the implications of their model when prices were assumed, at least implicitly, to adjust quickly and, thus, *quantities* did not have to be adjusted. The most sympathetic interpretation of Keynes is that he derived the implications of the model when this fast adjustment process was reversed. Prices adjust slowly, making quantity adjustments inevitable. Keynes asked what the implications of the model were when quantity adjustments occurred. He found that unemployment could be large (if the initial disturbance from equilibrium was large), widespread, and of long duration. We conclude that rapid adjustments in prices and wages and rigidity in prices and wages are both special cases, while time-consuming adjustments in prices and wages are the norm. Keynes, in analyzing the implications of the model in the latter context, justifies his claim to having provided the most general theory.

2 The Controversy over the Interest Rate

Keynes and the Classics were at odds over the interest rate on several counts. They disputed whether the interest rate was affected by the supply of money, whether the interest rate was determined by liquidity preference or loanable funds, and whether interest was a real or a monetary phenomenon. We shall discuss these issues in turn.

Money and Interest; The Neutrality Question

To Keynes, the supply of money and the rate of interest were inversely related: an increase in the former reduced the latter, and vice versa. To the Classics, the interest rate was independent of the supply of money, except for a *transitory* inverse relationship. In short, money was neutral to the Classics. All the real variables were invariant against changes in the supply of money while the nominal variables changed in proportion.

We have laid the groundwork for the resolution of this dispute in the earlier chapters of this book. Our conclusion has been that in the long run money *is* neutral when

1. All three prices are flexible.
2. No money illusion exists in *any* supply or demand function.

(Remember that an example of a supply function with de facto money illusion is a bond supply function containing a fixed supply of previously issued government bonds, which does not change when the general price level changes.)

3. No distribution effects exist.
4. Expectations are unit-elastic.

When one or more of these restrictions is relaxed, money is not neutral. On these theoretical issues, Keynes and neo-Keynesians now agree with classical and neoclassical economists. Whether, in practice, money is neutral is an empirical question. Do the restrictions 1–4 hold or not? Obviously, this cannot be decided a priori, but only empirically. A very casual interpretation of the historical record would seem to imply that even if they do not hold in the short run, they are likely to hold in the long run. There has been a manifold increase in the supply of money over the last century *without* a progressive decline in the interest rate.

Our conclusion on the neutrality or nonneutrality of money dispute between Keynes and the Classics is, then, eclectic. If the full set of neoclassical assumptions 1–4 hold, money is neutral; if one or more does not hold, money is not neutral. Moreover, in the short run assumptions 1–4 probably do *not* hold and, therefore, Keynes and the neo-Keynesians are correct in saying money is not neutral; in the long run assumptions 1–4 are more likely to hold and, therefore, Classics and neoclassics are correct in saying money is neutral.

A Loanable Funds or Liquidity Preference Explanation of Interest

Keynes introduced the notion of liquidity preference into macroeconomic theory and asserted that the interest rate was determined by the interaction of supply and demand in the *money market.* The Classics and neoclassics, on the other hand, held what is described as a *loanable funds* theory of the determination of the interest rate. According to this theory, the interest rate is determined in the loan market (which is identical with the *bond market*). A clear statement of the Classics' position is provided by J. S. Mill: "the interest rate . . . depends essentially and permanently on the comparative amount of real capital offered and demanded in the way of loan [so that] fluctuations in the interest rate arise from variations either in the demand for loans or in the supply."[1] If we identify "loans offered" with our bonds demanded and "loans demanded" with our bonds supplied, Mill is clearly implying that the interest rate is determined in the loan, or bond, market.

In order to resolve this dispute and make sense of this controversy, we must try to pin down what "determined in the loan (or money) market" means. It *cannot* mean three things.

First, it cannot mean that the interest rate affects only one of these markets—that is, either the bond market alone or the money market alone. This would signify that the interest rate appears only as an argument in the supply and demand for bonds functions *or* it appears only as an argument in the demand for money function, and it does not appear as an argument in any of the other supply or demand functions. In general, this is not true. We argued in Chapters 3, 4, and 5 on the microfoundations of the commodity, money, and bond markets that, in general, the interest rate affects the commodity demand function (for both consumption and investment), the demand for money function, and both the supply and demand for bond functions. In general, then, we cannot correctly conclude that the interest rate influences either the bond market *or* the money market and no other.

Second, it cannot mean that the supply and demand functions in the

[1] *Principles of Political Economy,* W. J. Ashley (ed.), London, 1909, pp. 647, 641.

bond market are *solely* dependent on the interest rate or, alternatively, that the demand for money function is *solely* dependent on the interest rate. If this were true, then a tâtonnement process in the bond market alone or the money market alone would determine the equilibrium interest rate. However, we have seen that, in general, both the bond supply and demand functions and the money demand function depend on other variables besides the interest rate. Thus, as these variables change during the tâtonnement process there will be feedback effects in the bond and money markets. Consequently, the interest rate cannot be determined in isolation in either of these markets. It is worth noting that if the interest rate were determined in isolation in one of these markets, we would have the very antithesis of general equilibrium analysis. The latter implies the simultaneous determination of the variables in all markets.

Finally, it cannot mean that the market "dropped" through the license of Walras' law makes any substantive difference. For example, it has been suggested that if one drops the money market he believes in a loanable funds theory of the determination of the interest rate; and if one drops the bond market he believes in a liquidity preference theory. But we know that Walras' law is quite general; you can drop any market. As a consequence, Abba Lerner is reputed to have abruptly halted this erroneous line of reasoning by asking rhetorically, and tongue in cheek, what theory of interest would a person hold if he dropped the peanut market?

We come to an eclectic conclusion again in this dispute between Keynes and the Classics – namely, that there is no substantive difference between their two theories (except that the Classics took a longer view than Keynes). If the model is consistent, an interest rate which equates supply and demand for bonds and for money will emerge. The interest rate is simultaneously determined by the mutual interaction of all the system's variables.

Here, we emphasize again that it is strictly illegitimate to talk about a "market" for money at all. Perhaps, therefore, in talking about the money market as though it has explicit existence, Keynes gave an unfortunate slant to the subject.

In another respect, however, Keynes had a permanent and more beneficial effect on the theory of interest. He introduced a third margin on which it operated; namely, *liquidity preference,* or how the interest rate influences the optimal size of money and bond holdings in a given portfolio of assets. This was a fundamental contribution; and interest rate theory will never be the same. The Classics were clear about how interest operated on two other margins; namely, *time preference,* or the optimal consumption pattern between present and future goods, and the *marginal productivity of capital,* or the optimal capital stock (both discussed in Chapter 3). But the Classics ignored the influence of the interest rate on the demand for money and, thus, the effect its changes had on the composition of the optimum asset portfolio. This question, discussed in Chapter 4, is strictly a consequence of the contribution of Keynes and the neo-Keynesians.

Is Interest a Real or a Monetary Phenomenon?

Another dispute which flared up in the debate between Keynes and the Classics involves the nature of interest. Is interest essentially a *monetary* phenomenon as Keynes' analysis implied or a *real* phenomenon as the Classics insisted? There is no unequivocal answer. Consider these arguments.

Just as the price of shoes is matched with the shoe market, so the price of bonds $1/r$ is matched with the bond market or the interest rate is matched with the money market. The bond and money markets compose the financial sector of our macroeconomic model, so, through this analogy, interest is obviously a monetary phenomenon. On the other hand, the interest rate is the quotient of two money prices. We know that the present value A_v of A dollars due one period hence is $A_v = A/(1 + r)$, so that $r = (A - A_v)/A_v$. This expression has the dimensions of a *relative* price (like, for example, the real wage) which seems to imply that interest is a real phenomenon. Clearly, although both these classifications of the interest rate are correct, they are also empty of any *analytical* significance.

What happens if we try to seek operational relevance? Suppose we say that if the interest rate affects only commodity markets, call it real; if it affects only the bond and money markets, call it monetary. This seems reasonable, too. But, in general, we have seen that the interest rate affects the bond, money, and commodity markets. Recall the *threefold* margin – interest influences the optimum asset portfolio, consumption pattern, and capital stock. Thus, this approach must be rejected.

How about this alternative? If the interest rate is determined in the commodity market, call it real; if it is determined in the bond or money market, call it monetary. This also seems reasonable. However, it restricts the interpretation of the interest rate's realness to the special cases when the model is separable, or dichotomizable. Some dichotomizable models were discussed in Chapter 14. They were models, you will recall, where the real markets (labor and commodities) were separable in that the solution values of the real variables could be obtained from the subset of equations comprising the real sector, and the financial markets (money and bonds) were then sufficient to determine the values of the nominal variables. However, these models were all special cases. We shall have more to say about the dichotomy problem in §3, which follows. Suffice it to say here that, in general, the macroeconomic model is *not* dichotomizable. Usually, it is impossible to break off a subset of markets, run them through a self-contained tâtonnement, and determine the equilibrium values of the subset of variables. Normally, everything depends on everything else. Consequently, everything becomes monetary (to some extent at least), including, of course, the interest rate.

Finally, consider an alternative suggested by Patinkin. The interest rate is real if its long-run equilibrium value is *not* affected by exogenous changes which do not affect relative prices, but is only affected by exogenous changes which affect relative prices; the interest rate is monetary if its long-run equilibrium value is affected by exogenous changes whose only other influence is on nominal variables. If these criteria are adopted with all the now-familiar neoclassical assumptions, the interest rate would be regarded as real. In Chapter 8 we saw that in such a context, exogenous changes in thrift, work/leisure attitudes, productivity, and so on which cause relative prices to vary also cause the interest rate to vary and in Chapter 7 we saw that changes in the supply of money and unbiased changes in liquidity preference which leave relative prices undisturbed also leave the interest rate's long-run equilibrium value unchanged. Once any one of the neoclassical assumptions is relaxed, however, and we operate the model in a neo-Keynesian context, *any* exogenous change (including changes in the supply of money and liquidity preference) alters relative prices and the long-run equilibrium value of the interest rate. Thus, according to Patinkin's suggested criteria, it seems that if the model is operated in a neoclassical context the interest rate is real, while if it is operated in a neo-Keynesian context the interest rate is monetary. Once more, then, we find that there is no unequivocal answer to whether the interest rate is real or monetary. The Classics and neoclassics were correct to regard interest as real in the context of their model; Keynes and the neo-Keynesians were correct to regard it as monetary in the context of their model.

3 Neutrality and Dichotomy

The classics and the neoclassics frequently asserted that

1. Money is neutral, or, equivalently, "money is a veil." That is, a change in the supply of money only changes the nominal variables proportionately, while leaving the real variables unchanged.[1]

2. The real variables (output, employment, interest rate, real wage, and so on) are determined entirely in the real sector, and the monetary elements (especially the absolute price level and the nominal wage) are determined in the financial sector. This is the famous *neoclassical dichotomy*. It implies that the real sector (the labor and commodity markets) can be separated from the financial sector (the bond and money markets) and, when the real markets are run through a separate tâtonnement, they are capable of determining the equilibrium values of all the real variables. The real sector is supposed to consist of a self-contained subset of equations from which the solution of all the real variables can be obtained. Hence, the model is separable, or dichotomizable.

We have already seen that neutrality does not exist when any one of the neoclassical assumptions is relaxed. This is not the purpose of our discussion now. We wish to find out when the two claims of neutrality and dichot-

[1] To quote an example from I. Fisher (who was a famous classical economist of later vintage like Pigou), "If there is no change in the quantities sold . . . , the *only* possible effect of doubling M . . . will be a doubling of the p's . . ." (*Purchasing Power of Money*, New York, 1911, p. 154. Emphasis added).

omy are justified if we conduct the inquiry according to neoclassical ground rules. Accordingly, we shall assume throughout that all three prices are flexible, expectations are unit-elastic, no distribution effects exist, and no money illusion exists in any of the functions; *however,* we shall assume government to have a fixed supply of bonds outstanding (because of past deficits) which is invariant against changes in the price level; hence, we introduce money illusion into the bond supply function.

We shall discuss the neutrality and dichotomy properties for three different specifications of the model. We have, then, three cases to consider.

Case 1 In the first case we assume all money is of the outside variety and there is no government debt. This is as classical a specification as one can have. Money, in classical times, was predominantly of the fiat or commodity variety (therefore, clearly of the outside type) and governments were not fiscally active except in times of war (thus, the quantity of outstanding government debt was minimal).

The influence of a change in the quantity of money in such circumstance was examined in great detail in §7.2. We found that money was, indeed, neutral. Moreover, we also discovered that the strict version of the quantity theory of money held—namely, that the change in prices is *proportional* to the change in the supply of money. However, the macroeconomic model will not dichotomize. The reason is quite straightforward. The nine equations of the model which comprise the real sector (from §6.1) are

$$N^d = N^d(W/P, \bar{K}) \tag{I}$$

$$N^s = N^s(W/P) \tag{II}$$

$$N^d = N^s \tag{III}$$

$$Y^s = Y^s(N, \bar{K}) \tag{IV}$$

$$C = C(Y^s, r, M/P) \tag{V}$$

$$I = I(Y^s, r) \tag{VI}$$

$$Y^d = C + I \tag{VII}$$

$$Y^d = Y^s \tag{VIII}$$

$$S = Y^s - C \tag{IX}$$

This system of *nine* equations contains *ten* endogenous variables (N^d, N^s, W/P, Y^s, Y^d, C, r, I, S, and M/P). In general, therefore, we cannot determine the equilibrium values of the real variables from the subsystem of equations which make up the real sector. Such equilibrium values can be determined only when the equations of the financial sector are added. In so doing, we obtain a complete system which is determinate. We may conclude, then, that when money is of the outside variety and no government debt exists money is neutral, it is invalid to dichotomize, and the quantity theory of money holds. These conclusions are summarized in Table 1.

TABLE 1

SPECIFICATION OF MODEL	DOES NEUTRALITY PREVAIL?	IS IT VALID TO DICHOTOMIZE?	DOES THE STRICT QUANTITY THEORY HOLD?
Case 1 All M outside, $B_g = 0$	Yes	No	Yes
Case 2 All M inside, $B_g > 0$	No	No	No
Case 3 All M inside, $B_g = 0$	Yes	Yes	Yes

Case 2 In the second case we assume all money is of the inside variety and there is government debt outstanding. The model is, thus, a modern one in that nowadays most money is bank money (clearly of the inside type) and a large government debt is not at all unusual.

We examined the influence of changes in the supply of money in such circumstances in detail in §9.2. There we saw that money was not neutral and that the strict version of the quantity theory of money did not hold. In this case prices respond to changes in the supply of money, but not *proportionally*. Moreover, when the model is specified in this way, it will not dichotomize. In case 2, just as in case 1, the real sector is comprised of fewer equations than there are endogenous variables. The equations (from §9.1) are

$$N^d = N^d(W/P, \bar{K}) \tag{I}$$

$$N^s = N^s(W/P) \tag{II}$$

$$N^d = N^s \tag{III}$$

$$Y^s = Y^s(N, \bar{K}) \tag{IV}$$

$$C = C(Y^s, T, r, V/P) \tag{V}$$

$$I = I(Y^s, r) \tag{VI}$$

$$Y^d = C + I + \bar{G} \tag{VII}$$

$$Y^d = Y^s \tag{VIII}$$

$$Y^s_d = Y^s - T \tag{XVII}$$

$$S = Y^s_d - C \tag{XIV}$$

$$T = t(Y^s, \bar{t}_0) \tag{XVIII}$$

These eleven equations contain twelve endogenous variables (N^d, N^s, W/P, Y^s, C, T, r, V/P, I, Y^d, Y^s_d, and S). Thus, under case 2 in Table 1, we have indicated that money is not neutral, the model will not dichotomize, and the strict version of the quantity theory is not valid.

Case 3 In the third case we engineer a model in which money is neutral, the model dichotomizes, and the strict version of the quantity theory prevails. The model is, necessarily, hybridized and *not* very realistic. It requires that all money be inside money (a basically modern monetary system) and that no government debt exist (a basically classical fiscal position). With these specifications the equations of the real sector are exactly the same as the nine equations listed under case 1, *except* that the consumption function [equation (V)] does not include the variable real money balances M/P. This is because with inside money collective wealth is not affected by changes in the supply of money and, thus, neither is consumption affected.[2] Consequently, we are left with nine equations and nine endogenous variables and, presumably, can determine the equilibrium values of the real variables from the real equations alone. The system does dichotomize.

When the system dichotomizes in this way, its graphical representation is quite elegant. Equations (I), (II), and (III) determine $(W/P)^*$ and N^* as shown in Figure 1(a). Given N^*, equation (IV) then determines Y^{s*} as shown in Figure 1(b). Given Y^{s*}, we can now solve for r^*, I^*, and S^*. We know that

$$S = S(Y^s, r)$$

$$I = I(Y^s, r)$$

and in commodity market equilibrium,

$$I = S$$

This is a system of three equations in three unknowns (r, I, and S) because Y^s has already been determined at Y^{s*}. Thus, the system can be solved. The equilibrium interest rate r^* is that which equates saving and investment. This is illustrated in Figure 1(c).

Once we have Y^{s*} and r^* we can solve for C^* from equation (V). Then, using C^* and I^* we can find Y^{d*} from equation (VII). Thus, we have obtained the equilibrium values of all the real variables without reference to the financial sector and, hence, the model is dichotomizable. Let us proceed a step further and plunge into the now separate monetary sector, since this is where the absolute price level is determined. The money market equations are

$$M^d = P \cdot L(Y^s, r)$$

$$M^d = \bar{M}^s$$

These are two equations in two unknowns (M^d and P) because we already know the equilibrium values of Y^{s*} and r^*. Hence, with Y^s and r determined, the first of these equations is equivalent to

$$M^d \frac{1}{P} = \text{constant}$$

[2] Recall that inside money does not affect collective wealth because it washes out (see §5.4).

FIGURE 1

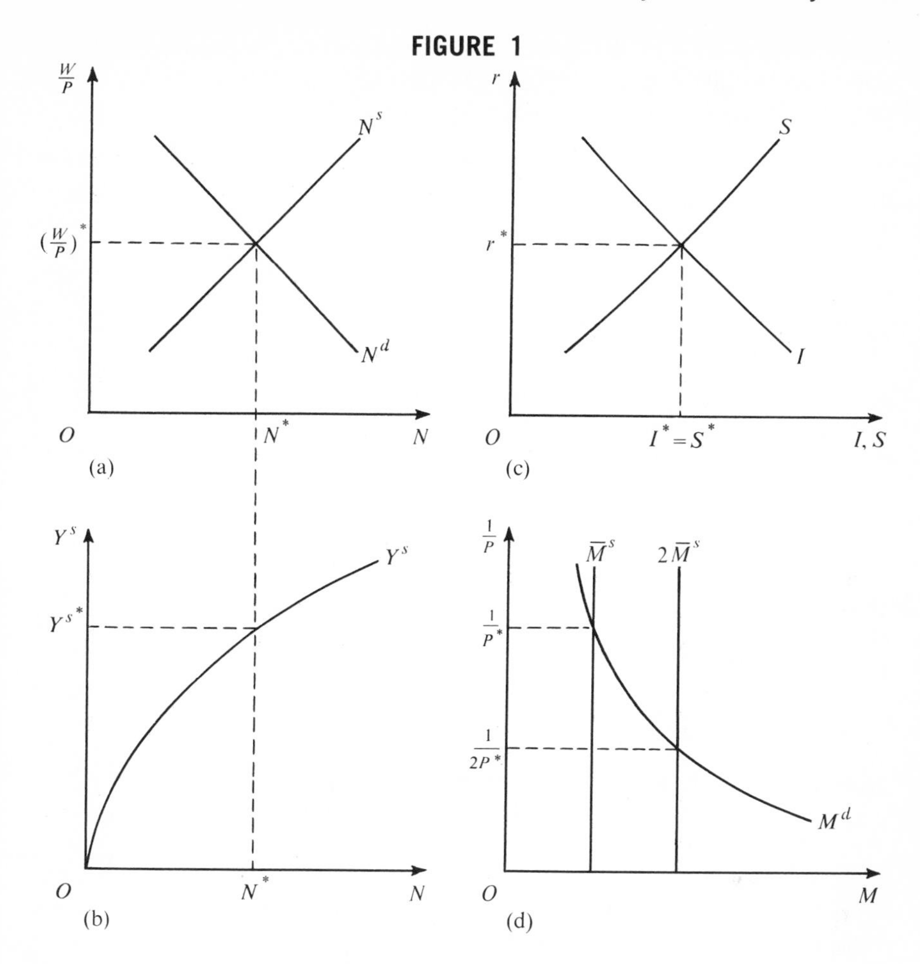

which is the equation of a rectangular hyperbola. Thus, if we plot $1/P$ against M^d we obtain the rectangularly hyperbolic curve M^d, illustrated in Figure 1(d). Introducing the exogenously determined supply of money, we see that doubling the money supply from $\bar{M}^s$ to $2\bar{M}^s$ doubles the absolute price level from P^* to $2P^*$. That is, the strict quantity theory holds. [Of course, once P^* is determined so is W^*, in such a way as to make W^*/P^* equal $(W/P)^*$.] Therefore, for case 3, money is neutral, the model is dichotomizable, and the strict quantity theory holds. (Money must be neutral—that is, without effect on the interest rate—because the equilibrium value of the interest rate was obtained in the real sector without any reference to the money supply.) These conclusions are summarized in Table 1.

By now it should be clear that the validity of divorcing real economic analysis from monetary economic analysis (to dichotomize) depends solely on whether or not some form of real balance variable appears among the equations of the real sector. This variable can be either real outside money or real government debt (undiscounted for implicit future taxes) or a mixture of the two. As long as the real balance variable appears in any of these three forms, dichotomization is not valid; when there is no real balance variable in the real markets, dichotomization is valid and real economics can be studied separately from monetary economics.

4 The Real Balance Effect

The real balance effect has appeared ubiquitously throughout this book. It is now appropriate to pull together the threads of the analytical points which have revolved around this variable.

First, Keynes asserted that a competitive, free-enterprise economy did not necessarily guarantee full employment. However, we have seen that in a regime where all prices are flexible, a real balance effect is sufficient to bring about full employment. This comparative static theoretical proposition was established through the work of Pigou, Scitovsky, and Haberler.[1] It should be noted, though, that although neoclassical economists wanted to demonstrate the theoretical rectitude and consistency of the classical macroeconomic assertion that full employment was guaranteed in a world of price flexibility, they did *not* necessarily recommend that when some deflationary disturbance occurred, the fall in prices which would bring about the rise in real balances and eventually reestablish full employment should be waited for passively. The required increase in real balances could be created by an active money policy rather than by merely standing idly by and letting the price level fall while keeping the money supply constant.

Second, we have just seen in §3 that the existence of a real balance effect in the real sector is what integrates monetary and real economic analysis (or, equivalently, monetary and value theory). When such an effect is present, separating real from monetary analysis is not valid. This implication of the real balance effect is particularly associated with the work of D. Patinkin and is the theme (and subtitle) of his magnum opus *Money, Interest, and Prices; An Integration of Monetary and Value Theory*.[2]

The third point is that if a real balance effect is completely absent from the system, we become involved in a contradiction. To demonstrate this, we exclude a real balance effect from *all* functions. This can be done by assuming a model in which all money is the inside type and government debt is zero.

The initial equilibrium position of the model is shown by the solid curves in Figure 2. Notice that in Figure 2(c) we have plotted the demand for nominal balances as a function of $1/P$ using the approach to the money market discussed in §3. Now increase the supply of money. With completely inside money, this can occur only if the monopoly bank buys more bonds. The increased demand for bonds lowers the interest rate to r_1, which, in turn,

[1] A. C. Pigou, "The Classical Stationary State," *Economic Journal,* December, 1943; T. Scitovsky, "Capital Accumulation, Employment, and Price Rigidity," *Review of Economic Studies,* VIII, 1940–1941; G. Haberler, *Prosperity and Depression,* Geneva, 1941.

[2] 2nd ed., Harper & Row, 1965.

FIGURE 2

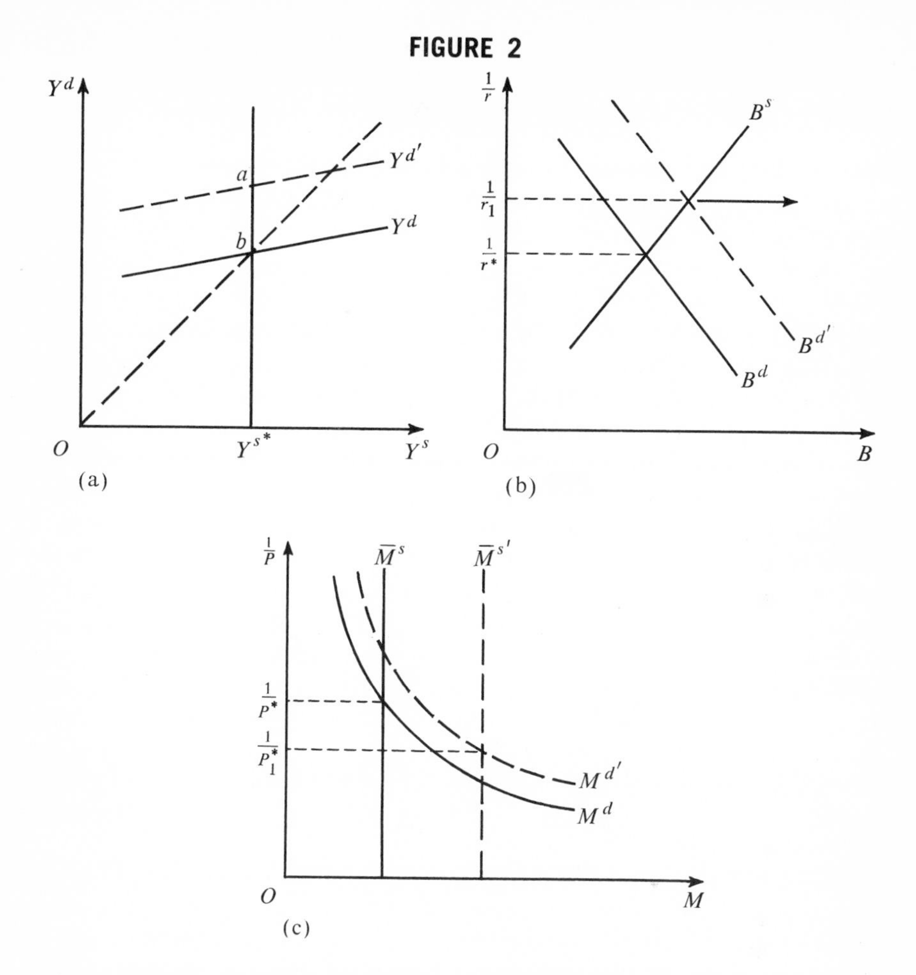

raises aggregate demand to $Y^{d'}$. Thus, an inflationary gap equal to *ab* appears in the commodity market and commodity prices begin to rise. The interesting point here is that nothing within the commodity and bond markets can stop the rise in commodity prices from going on indefinitely. There is no new equilibrium level. The reason is quite straightforward. With no real balance effect in the bond demand and supply functions, *both* curves move to the right *in proportion* to the rise in the price level. Thus, they continue to intersect at the same interest rate r_1 as indicated by the horizontal arrow in Figure 2(b). (The reader will recall that we have usually relied upon the real balance variable in the bond demand and supply functions to make the bond supply curve shift to the right more rapidly than the bond demand curve when P increases and, thus, cause the interest rate to rise. This is now denied us.) With the interest rate remaining at r_1 and no real balance effect in the aggregate demand function, there is absolutely no reason for the aggregate demand curve to sink below $Y^{d'}$ as prices rise. Consequently, the inflationary gap remains equal to *ab* and rises indefinitely.

Now let us consider the money market. When the interest rate fell to r_1, the demand for nominal balances curve M^d shifted to $M^{d'}$. Given the increase in the supply of money, the money market diagram implies that the price level rises to $1/P_1^*$. Here we see the contradiction. The commodity and bond markets imply that commodity prices rise indefinitely; the money market implies they rise to P_1^*. Since both implications cannot be true, it follows that we have forced a contradiction.

Finally, we should note that at present the appropriate definition of real balances is the subject of spirited controversy. The debate was provoked by Pesek and Saving's book.[3] Until now we have only included outside money and government debt in the community's real balances and have excluded inside money on the grounds that it washes out when the community's collective real net worth is calculated (see §5.4). Pesek and Saving's thesis is that *all* money, outside *and* inside, is part of the community's wealth and, thus, outside money should also be included in real balances. Their argument is extended, subtle, and is itself the subject of great current dispute. Having drawn the reader's attention to the controversy, we propose to leave it at that and wait until the verdict is in.

Summary

In this chapter we attempted to resolve the controversies between Keynes and the Classics over unemployment and the interest rate as well as to discuss the *dichotomy question* (whether *real* and *monetary* economics can be validly separated).

The Classics argued that unemployment would *not* occur in equilibrium in a competitive, free-enterprise economy. When wages, prices, and the interest rate are all flexible, the Classics are correct. However, when either of these three prices are inflexible, permanent involuntary unemployment can prevail and Keynes may be said to be correct. Because *slow* adjustment of prices in the real world is probably the most usual case, unemployment may be large, widespread, and of long duration as the economy adjusts to a new equilibrium after an initial deflationary impulse. (The economy's behavior in *disequilibrium* is discussed in the next chapter.)

In the controversy over the interest rate, the Classics believed that the interest rate was independent of the supply of money (money was neutral), the interest rate was determined by *loanable funds*, and that interest is essentially a *real*, and not a *monetary*, phenomenon. Keynes, on the contrary, argued that the supply of money affected the interest rate, the interest rate was determined by *liquidity preference*, and interest was, essentially, a monetary phenomenon.

If all four neoclassical assumptions are granted, then, in the *long run*, money *is* neutral and the interest rate *is* independent of the money supply (see also Chapter 7). Hence, given their ground rules, we must judge the

[3] B. P. Pesek and T. R. Saving, *Money, Wealth, and Economic Theory*, Macmillan, 1967.

Classics to be correct. However, if any *one* of the neoclassical assumptions is relaxed money is *not* neutral. Moreover, in the *short run,* the interest rate is inversely related to the supply of money. Thus, if prices are inflexible, or money illusion exists anywhere, or expectations are not unit-elastic, or distribution effects exist, and always in the short run, money is not neutral and we must say that Keynes was correct.

The question of whether the interest rate is determined by loanable funds (that is, in the bond market as the Classics thought) or by liquidity preference (in the money market as Keynes thought) must, after all is said and done, be judged "no contest." The equilibrium value of the interest rate, like the equilibrium value of every other variable in the model, is determined by the *simultaneous* interaction of *all* the system's variables. Keynes did, however, make a unique contribution to interest rate theory. He showed that the interest rate influenced the optimal asset portfolio. (The Classics had already shown that it influenced the optimal present/future consumption pattern and the optimal capital stock.)

As to whether interest is basically a real or monetary phenomenon, if we adopt Patinkin's suggestion that it should be regarded as real if its long-run equilibrium value is *not* affected by exogenous changes which do not also affect relative prices, and *is* only affected by exogenous changes which do affect relative prices, then, when we make the usual four neoclassical assumptions, interest is real. Once any of these assumptions is relaxed, *any* exogenous change (including changes in the money supply) affects the long-run equilibrium value of the interest rate, so that interest can be said to be monetary.

Finally, we discussed the famous neoclassical dichotomy question which asks if the real markets can be separated from the financial markets and the former run through a separate tâtonnement, which by itself will generate the equilibrium values of all the *real* variables. We found that, generally, it is not valid to dichotomize. This procedure is only justified in the special case when all forms of real balance effect are excluded from the equations of the real sector. Hence, we see why the real balance effect is said to integrate monetary and value theory (the financial and real sectors). Moreover, it turns out that when a real balance effect is *completely* excluded from the model, the model involves a contradiction.

Questions

1. What do you think is Keynes' major contribution to *comparative static* macroeconomic theory? Justify your answer.
2. In the last analysis, what were the two major disputes between Keynes and the Classics over static macroeconomic theory? Who, in your opinion, won these disputes and why?
3. Appraise critically the loanable funds versus liquidity preference debate over the determination of the interest rate.
4. What was Keynes' major contribution to the theory of interest?

5. Try to resolve the question of whether interest is basically a real or a monetary phenomenon.
6. What is meant by the "neoclassical dichotomy"?
7. Show that (a) "neutrality does not imply dichotomy"; (b) "dichotomy does imply neutrality."
8. Devise a model in which money is neutral, the strict quantity theory holds, and in which dichotomization is valid.
9. What problem arises if a real balance effect is excluded from *every* supply and demand function?
10. Write an essay on the real balance effect.

SELECTED READINGS

1. G. Haberler, *Prosperity and Depression,* 3rd ed., Geneva, 1941.
2. H. G. Johnson, "*The General Theory* after Twenty-five Years," *American Economic Review, Proceedings,* May, 1961. A superb appraisal of Keynes' contribution to economics.
3. H. G. Johnson, "Monetary Theory and Policy," *American Economic Review,* June, 1962, parts I and II. Excellent survey of the neutrality, dichotomy, and integration of monetary and value theory questions.
4. M. Kalecki, "Professor Pigou on the 'Classical Stationary State' – A Comment," *Economic Journal,* LIV, 1944.
5. J. M. Keynes, *The General Theory of Employment, Interest, and Money,* Macmillan, 1936, chapters 13–20. Keynes on interest and employment.
6. D. Patinkin, *Money, Interest, and Prices,* 2nd ed., Harper & Row, 1965, chapters 8 and 15, and notes I, J, K, and M. Excellent material on the issues separating Keynes and the Classics.
7. B. P. Pesek and T. R. Saving, *Money, Wealth, and Economic Theory,* Macmillan, 1967. Argues that inside money does not wash out and is a legitimate component of the community's wealth. Thus, it should be included in real money balances as well as outside money.
8. A. C. Pigou, "The Classical Stationary State," *Economic Journal,* December, 1943. Points out that a real balance effect will guarantee full employment when commodity prices are flexible. See also [1], [4], and [9].
9. T. Scitovsky, "Capital Accumulation, Employment, and Price Rigidity," *Review of Economic Studies,* VIII, 1940–1941.

FURTHER READINGS

(Probably, the less said about the loanable funds versus liquidity preference debate the better. However, if the student wishes to delve into this more deeply, the following three articles survey the recent literature on this topic.)

10. W. J. Baumol, "Stocks, Flows, and Monetary Theory," *Quarterly Journal of Economics,* LXXVI, 1962.
11. L. R. Klein, "Stocks and Flows in the Theory of Interest," in F. H. Hahn and F. P. R. Brechling (eds.), *The Theory of Interest Rates,* Institute of Economic Affairs, 1965.
12. G. L. S. Shackle, "Recent Theories Concerning the Nature and Rate of Interest," *Economic Journal,* June, 1961.

16

Macroeconomic Disequilibrium

In Chapter 15 we appraised the disputes between Keynes and the Classics in a *comparative static* context. While praising Keynes for his creative vision in literally inventing the apparatus of quasi-general equilibrium analysis, we found his predictions that (1) a competitive, free-enterprise economy can generate permanent involuntary unemployment is dependent on the existence of a rigidity in one or more of the three price variables in the model, and (2) money is not neutral applies only if such rigidities exist or money illusion is present or price expectations are not unit-elastic or distribution effects exist and are important. In essence, we concurred with the following appraisal of Keynes: "(1) the model which Keynes had the gall to call his 'general theory' is but a special case of the Classical theory, obtained by imposing certain restrictive assumptions on the latter, and (2) the Keynesian 'special case,' while theoretically trivial, is nonetheless important because it so happens that it is a better guide in the real world. . . ."[1] In effect, such a conclusion "represents the final rejection of Keynes' every claim to being a major theoretical innovator."[2]

These conclusions leave Keynes in a very poor light. He had set out to overturn classical economic theory in its entirety, but apparently had hardly made a dent. All he did was include various ad hoc assumptions such as price rigidities and money illusion (which were not well founded in theory) and then analyze the model in these circumstances.

Until recently, these were the terms of the truce between neoclassical and orthodox Keynesian economists. The former had carried off the theoretical honors, while conceding to Keynes and his followers the policy rele-

[1] A. Leijonhufvud, *On Keynesian Economics and the Economics of Keynes,* Oxford, 1968, p. 7. It cannot be stressed too strongly that Leijonhufvud is merely presenting a succinct summary of the outcome of the debate, not his own opinion.

[2] *Ibid.,* p. 8.

vance of his special case. Lately, however, Keynes' contribution has undergone a major reinterpretation as a result of the work of Clower and Leijonhufvud. It is now argued that Keynes was not interested in treading the "soft soil of static equilibrium analysis," but was first and foremost a macroeconomic *disequilibrium* theorist.

In the first section of this final chapter we discuss this reinterpretation of Keynes. In succeeding sections we examine the lags in monetary and fiscal policy and the debate whether our economic authorities should be allowed to take discretionary economic stabilization actions or, alternatively, should be constrained by fixed rules. Finally, we take a brief look at the theory of economic policy.

1 Keynes Reinterpreted

Keynes claimed that his *General Theory* showed that in a competitive, free-enterprise economy large-scale and widespread involuntary unemployment would commonly follow a deflationary shock from any source. *If* this prediction by Keynes rests solely on the inclusion of some price rigidity in the model, then Keynes' claim to theoretical originality does, indeed, stand on pretty weak ground. Neither the Classics nor their supporters would be particularly impressed by someone claiming to have advanced a more *general* theory than their own, if all this new theory did was change their assumption of price flexibility everywhere to the assumption of a price rigidity somewhere. After all, the Classics were well aware that wage rigidity would lead to the emergence of unemployment in the face of a deflationary shock—that was how *they* explained unemployment. To be told by Keynes that rigidity in either of the other two price variables would lead to the same result might have forced from some mythical Classic the admission, "Yes, I see now and I apologize for overlooking these two possibilities. Thank you for drawing them to my attention." However, he might be forgiven for adding, with the utmost justification, "Nonetheless, I think that your claim to have advanced a more *general* theory on the strength of these two gems is somewhat brash." Moreover, if these rigidities were introduced without solid theoretical foundations, but simply on the basis of *institutional* arrangements (such as wage minimums because of collective bargaining by unionized labor) or *legal* restrictions (such as minimum wage laws or fair trade laws) or, worse yet, ad hoc considerations (entrepreneurs "prefer" to reduce output and employment rather than prices and wages when demand falls), then Keynes' claim that he had made a significant *theoretical* contribution to the involuntary unemployment question would not have much merit.

However, the Keynesian counterrevolution spearheaded by Clower and Leijonhufvud provides a major new interpretation which saves Keynes from this sort of damning criticism. His defenders maintain that the *neoclassical* propositions are derived from a system based on a very special assumption—that of a tâtonnement process with recontracting conducted by an auctioneer (see §6.6). If this assumption is relaxed, Clower and Leijonhufvud argue, then *imperfect price flexibility in all markets is the predictable outcome of rational decision making by transactors* (and not an ad hoc special assumption). With no auctioneer, prices are less than perfectly flexible and transactions inevitably take place out of equilibrium. There is what is called "false trading" at "false prices." Clower and Leijonhufvud suggest that Keynes was concerned primarily, if not exclusively, with such macroeconomic disequilibrium problems. We shall show that in the absence of an auctioneer false trades are made at false prices, and this is sufficient to trigger a Keynesian multiplier process. The new interpretation of Keynes, then, is that his claim to have advanced a more *general* theory is justified in that his model does not rely on tâtonnement. Conversely, it is the neoclassical theory and its implications which are *special* because they rely on the highly special assumption of tâtonnement with recontracting and the ubiquitous auctioneer.

In this section we shall examine our model for the first time in a non-tâtonnement context. Hence, now we are out of the field of comparative macroeconomic statics and into the region of macroeconomic disequilibrium analysis. As we shall see, a Keynesian adjustment process will emerge. Consider Figure 1, where, as usual, we start with our model in equilibrium as shown by the solid curves and the asterisked values of the variables. Note that the vector of prices which is consistent with original equilibrium is P^*, W^*, and $(1/r)^*$. What happens when a deflationary shock is imparted to the model? Let us assume entrepreneurial expectations take a turn for the worse. (The analysis below only requires marginal amendment to embrace different deflationary impulses.)

Aggregate demand falls to $Y^{d'}$ and an excess supply of commodities equal to ab emerges. We know that in a tâtonnement context and with no price rigidities anywhere in the model, the auctioneer would search for new equilibrium values of the variables. In particular, he would lower the price of commodities and nominal wages. The lower price of commodities would lead to lower interest rates and higher real balances, which would raise $Y^{d'}$ towards Y^d again and, thus, tend to eliminate the deflationary gap. The auctioneer would eventually find a new equilibrium vector of prices P_1^*, W_1^*, and $(1/r)_1^*$ at which the deflationary gap was eliminated, full employment was restored, and full employment real income was enjoyed once more. (See §8.3 for a complete analysis of this case.) Of course, while the auctioneer is searching for the appropriate vector of price variables, all transactors are assumed to be sitting on their hands. In a tâtonnement model no transactions take place at disequilibrium values of the prices—that is, there is no false trading at false prices. You will recall from §6.6, where we first discussed tâtonnement, that such false trading at false prices was avoided by resort to the process of recontracting. The auctioneer received offers of supplies and demands at various prices, but these offers were made binding only when he had found price variables which cleared all markets.

Now, however, we are without benefit of an auctioneer who will find the equilibrium values of the price variables for us. Transactors are not con-

FIGURE 1

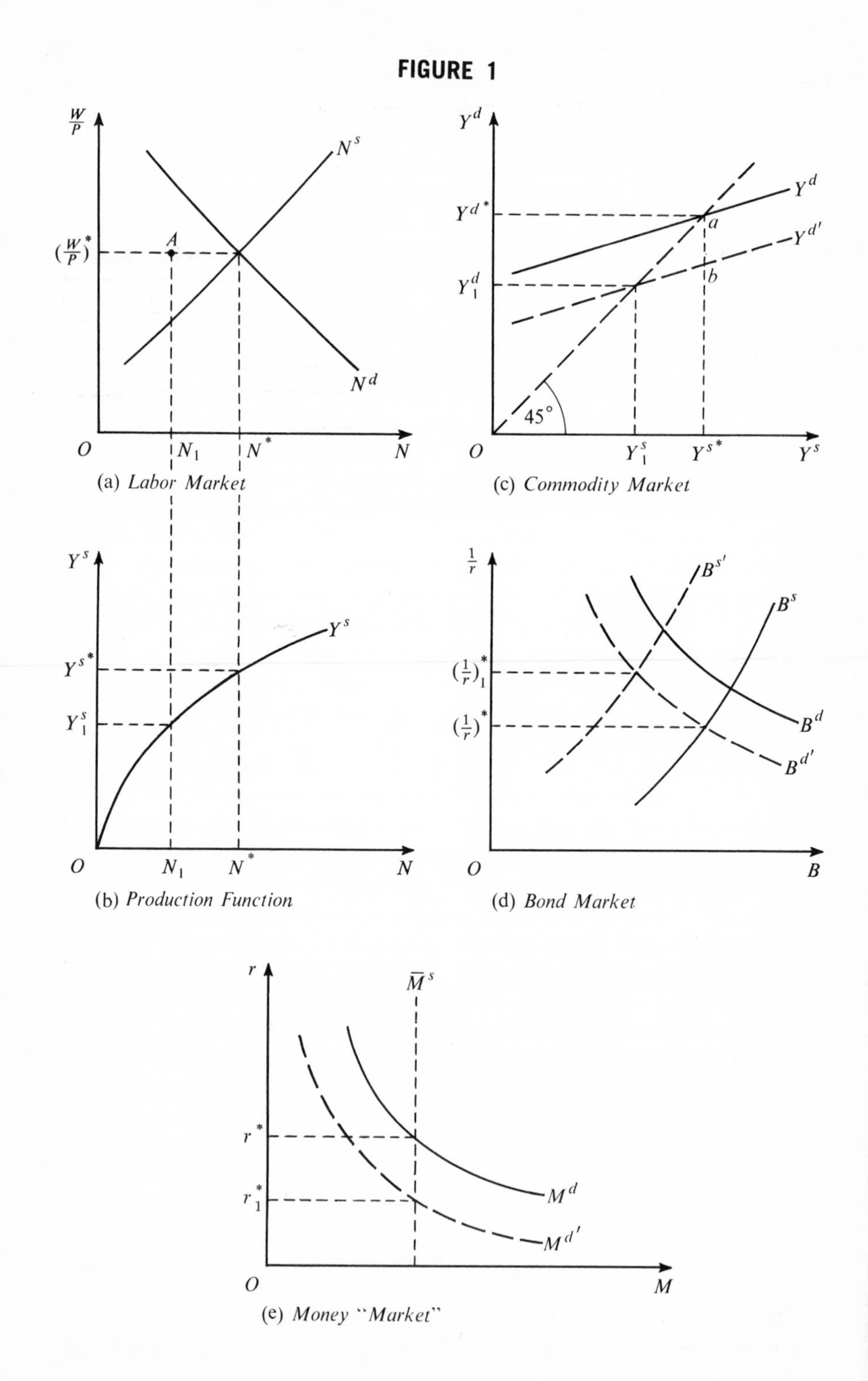

(a) *Labor Market*

(c) *Commodity Market*

(b) *Production Function*

(d) *Bond Market*

(e) *Money "Market"*

fronted with a new set of prices which will make all markets clear. These prices must now be *searched* for by transactors themselves.

If we all had perfect information like the auctioneer, the new equilibrium values of the price variables would be established immediately. However, in our nontâtonnement world, information is far from perfect. Ignorance and uncertainty abound. No one knows the new equilibrium values of the price variables, and so we must try to search them out. But this searching is a time-consuming process during which transactions will perforce occur. That is, there will be false trading at false prices. This leads to complications, as we shall see.

First, we should explain why when information is not perfect, prices may be expected to adjust to their new equilibrium values with something less than infinite speed. Consider an entrepreneur who had experienced a decline in sales (as some of them must) when aggregate demand for commodities fell to $Y^{d'}$. Presumably, he could *immediately* quote a price low enough to raise his sales again to the previous level. But is this necessarily a wise thing to do? It need not be. For example, perhaps demand is only temporarily decreased and it will soon return to its previous level. Clearly, the entrepreneur would be ill advised to lower his price to maintain his sales during this temporary decline if, very soon after, he would simply have to raise it again when demand picks up. Since the entrepreneur cannot be certain whether the decline in demand is temporary (he has no information), the only way he can find out is to await developments. Thus, at least until he has confirmed that the decrease in demand is more than transitory, he will hold to his previous price.

We know that the decrease in demand is a basic one; however, the entrepreneur is unaware of this fact. While he waits for information to come in, as it will in the form of persistently lower sales, his inventories will begin to pile up. Since he will regard this as undesirable, he may be expected to reduce his production to stop this untoward accumulation of inventories. But reduced production implies a smaller demand by the entrepreneur for the factors of production. Hence, he will lay off some of his work force. Then, the decreased demand for commodities leads to unemployment.

What will an unemployed worker do? Presumably, he can immediately offer his services at a low enough wage to find employment again. But is that a shrewd move on his part? Again the answer is no. The worker does not know whether the decline in demand for his services at his prevailing wage is temporary or permanent, just as the entrepreneur does not know at first whether the decline in demand for his product at the prevailing price is temporary or permanent. Therefore, it would be unwise for the worker to offer his services at a lower wage to keep himself employed if, had he waited a short time, he would have been reemployed at his old wage rate. Here again the worker cannot be sure whether the decline in demand for his services at the prevailing wage rate is temporary or permanent. Since he has no information, he must wait and see what happens. Until he is sure that the demand for his services at the prevailing wage rate is permanent he will not change the asking price for his labor (what is called his *labor reservation price*). As time passes, if no one offers him a job at the prevailing wage, the worker will know that the decrease in the demand for his services at that wage is permanent.

Now let us assume that both entrepreneur and worker are persuaded that the decreased demand they face at the going prices is, indeed, permanent. What should they do? Consider the worker first. Should he drastically lower his asking price so that the first employer he approaches will hire him and he will be back in a job? Again, this is not necessarily the best move. It is one option open to him, but if he is willing to wait a while and invest some time and energy searching the job market he could easily do better. Consider Figure 2 where the nominal wage W is measured vertically and time t horizontally. If the worker drops his asking (or reservation) price to W_0 he would find a job immediately at t_0. But if he searches the job market, by t_1 the best offer he would generate is W_1; if he searched further, by t_2 he would have uncovered an offer of W_2. We have drawn the curve sloping upward, since it seems reasonable to assume that if more time is spent on the search process better wage offers will be generated. We have also shown the curve sloping upward at a diminishing rate on the assumption that the further the search has already proceeded, the more difficult it will be to generate a given increment in the wage offered. If the best offer the worker can generate (by t_θ) is W_θ, should he, therefore, search until t_θ to obtain the highest possible wage? In general, the answer is no. If the worker is a maximizer, as we assume, it is only rational for him to search the job market as long as the *marginal* benefit of additional search exceeds the *marginal* cost of search. When the two become equal, he stops searching and takes a job. The marginal cost of searching for a given period of time is equal to the best wage which he has so far received in that time period (but not accepted and, therefore, foregone); the marginal benefit of additional search for an equivalent period of time is the *present value* of the *increase* in the wage rate that he expects to generate in that time period by further exploration. Let us look at this in terms of Figure 2. At t_1, the best wage offer the worker has uncovered is W_1. If he does not accept this offer but continues to search for the unit period from t_1 to t_2 the marginal cost of this additional search is the wage W_1 that he foregoes. By searching from t_1 to t_2, he expects to generate a wage offer of W_2. He therefore expects to increase the wage at which he will work by $W_2 - W_1$. The marginal benefit to him of the additional search is the present value of $W_2 - W_1$; that is, $W_2 - W_1$ for the rest of his working life discounted by the current interest rate. If W_1 is less than the present value of $W_2 - W_1$, he continues to search; if W_1 is more than the present value of $W_2 - W_1$, he takes a job at W_1. While he searches, the job-seeker withholds his services from the labor market; that is, he remains unemployed. For all intents and purposes, the job-seeker originally places the reservation price of W^* on his services, but as he searches he discovers that he will not become reemployed at W^*. Gradually, as this new information becomes available to him, he reduces his reservation price. The important point is that the generation of the

FIGURE 2

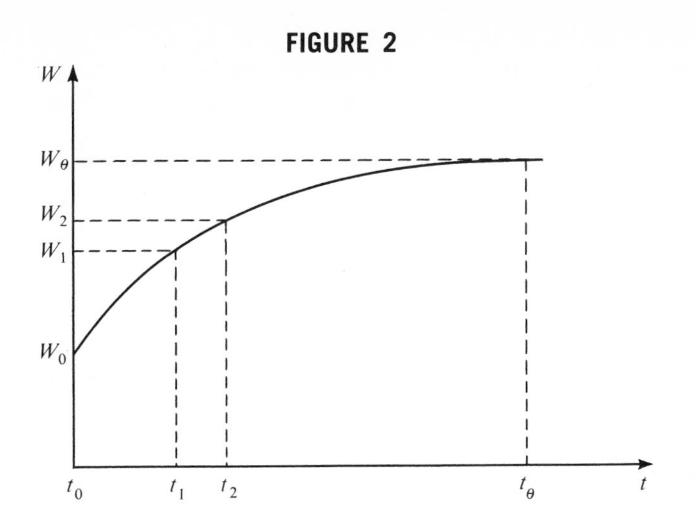

new information takes time during which the job-seeker is not employed.

There is an extremely important implication in this piece of analysis; namely, the rational worker does *not* necessarily react to a reduction in the demand for his services by reducing his reservation price low enough so that he is immediately reemployed. He adjusts this reservation price downwards in the light of the information generated by his search activities in the job market. While these labor reservation prices slowly crumble, however, the quantity of labor services demanded is reduced to the level which produces the output entrepreneurs can still sell. When disequilibrium prevails in the labor market, adjustments in the quantity of employment appear more rapidly than adjustments in prices. According to this analysis, efficient markets in which transactors are optimizing "will *not* be characterized by prices that instantly fluctuate so as always to clear the market . . ."[3] We have, then, what we alluded to at the beginning of Chapter 11 as a typically Keynesian phenomenon, namely, quantity adjustments emerging in a market which is out of equilibrium before price begins to adjust to the changed circumstances. (Contrast this with the characteristic neoclassical assumption that price adjustments remove any disequilibrium in a market, making quantity adjustments unnecessary.)

Now let us return to the entrepreneur's problem. We left him facing a decrease in demand which he initially responded to by cutting back output (and employment) rather than his price, since he hoped that the reduced demand was temporary. However, the decreased demand proves to be fundamental. He could now cut his price wildly and keep his sales from falling, just as his employees could have reduced their reservation prices to a level low enough to make sure they kept their jobs. But just as hasty reductions in the employees' reservation wage were not optimal from their point of view,

[3] A. A. Alchian, "Information Costs, Pricing, and Resource Employment," *Western Economic Journal*, June, 1969. This is an excellent article which presents a more comprehensive analysis of the topic we are discussing.

hasty price reductions by the entrepreneur are not optimal from his point of view either. Before cutting the reservation price he places on the commodities he produces, the entrepreneur will want to explore the market himself in an attempt to ascertain what, given the changed conditions, is the best bargain he can now strike. Since price revisions are costly, the entrepreneur is being quite rational when he chooses to adapt to the disequilibrium in the commodity market by adjusting the quantity he produces first and *then*, in the light of the information he discovers, adjusting his prices later. Thus, in the commodity market, just as in the labor market, disequilibrium elicits an adjustment in the quantity sold before there is any adjustment in the price at which the commodity is offered for sale; this is again the characteristically Keynesian ordering of the disequilibrium adjustment mechanism.[4]

Having explained why we may reasonably expect wages and prices to react only relatively sluggishly to a deflationary disturbance, we can now pursue the complete macroeconomic adjustment process. Referring back to Figure 1, we see that aggregate demand originally fell to $Y^{d'}$. With wages and prices holding at W^* and P^* for the reasons just explained, no reduction in the interest rate or increase in real balances occurs to raise $Y^{d'}$ back toward Y^d. On the contrary, a downward multiplier process takes charge and aggregate demand and supply decrease to Y_1^d and Y_1^s, respectively. Output of Y_1^s can be produced with N_1 labor, so the *effective demand* for labor falls to this level—point A in Figure 1(a). In this disequilibrium situation, the effective demand for labor passing through point A diverges from the usual (what Clower calls *notional*) demand for labor curve N^d.

The situation will remain this way as long as wages and prices stay at W^* and P^*. However, we have involuntary unemployment equal to $N^* - N_1$ and involuntary underproduction equal to $Y^{s*} - Y_1^s$, since, at the real wage $(W/P)^*$, entrepreneurs would like to produce Y^{s*} (their notional supply), but do not because they could not sell that output. However, these unemployed workers and underproducing entrepreneurs are not idle. They are searching their respective markets for jobs and sales. As this search uncovers a generalized decrease in demand, they will lower the reservation prices they have placed on their services and commodities. As prices decline, B^d and B^s in Figure 1(d) move left and, since the former shifts less than the latter, the interest rate declines. This decrease in the interest rate combined with the increase in real balances (brought about by the fall in prices) increases aggregate demand from $Y^{d'}$. Output and employment rise in step. If W crumbles in proportion to P (which is a simplifying assumption without substantive implications), even though both W and P are falling, the real

[4] Here we should pause to note that Keynes in using a *quantity*, instead of a price, adjusting theory of exchange, merely postulated a slow "reacting" price, without showing that slow price responses were consistent with utility or wealth maximizing behavior in open, unconstrained markets (*ibid.*, p. 117). The theoretical rationalization we are now providing for a Keynesian adjustment process related to the search costs of information is the result of work done by Stigler and Alchian; see G. J. Stigler, "Information in the Labor Market," *Journal of Political Economy*, October, 1962; and A. A. Alchian, "Information Costs, Pricing, and Resource Employment," *Western Economic Journal*, June, 1969.

wage remains constant. Thus, in Figure 1(a) the effective demand for labor will shift from A towards the intersection of the two notional curves N^d and N^s. *Eventually,* the fall in prices and wages will proceed far enough for the aggregate demand to coincide once more with Y^d, and full employment will again prevail. This will occur when transactors have searched out the new vector of market-clearing prices W_1^*, P_1^*, and $(1/r)_1^*$.

The essential point is that although the *final* outcome is consistent with neoclassical predictions, the *disequilibrium transition* is very, very Keynesian. There is widespread unemployment of potentially long duration and extensive excess capacity. Thus, it seems reasonable to concur with the "new interpretation" put forth by Clower and Leijonhufvud that Keynes really comes into his own as a macroeconomic disequilibrium theorist.

2 The Dynamic Multiplier

In Chapter 14 we discussed *comparative static* multipliers at great length. In this section we wish to examine the *dynamic,* or *period, multiplier.* Recall that a comparative static multiplier is defined to be the ratio of the change in income and the associated change in expenditure or taxes *when the change in expenditure or taxes is permanent.* In contrast, a dynamic multiplier is defined to be the ratio of the total *accumulated* change in income over and above its initial level and the associated change in expenditure or taxes *when the change in expenditure or taxes is a one-shot (or one-period) event.*

Figure 3 will assist us in our discussion of the dynamic multiplier. Income is plotted vertically and time horizontally. Let the level of income from t_0 to t_1 be Y_0, which is, we assume, below the full employment level of income; thus, unemployment prevails and excess productive capacity exists. In period t_1 let us assume that government expenditure is increased by ΔG, *after which it reverts to its original level.*[1] In other words, there is a change in government expenditure for one period. Now we ask what will happen to income.

In t_1, income rises to $Y_0 + \Delta G$. We might conjecture that income in t_2 would fall to Y_0 again, since government expenditure in that period falls back to its original level. This, however, would be a false conjecture. Since income in t_1 increases by ΔG, a fraction of this increase (dependent on the $mpc = b < 1$) will be spent in t_2. Thus, income in t_2 does *not* fall to Y_0, but only to $Y_0 + b\Delta G$. Similarly, since income in t_2 was $b\Delta G$ above its original level, a fraction b of this increase will be spent in t_3. Consequently, income in t_3 will be $Y_0 + b^2\Delta G$. By analogous argument, income in t_n will be $Y_0 + b^{n-1}\Delta G$. Since b is less than unity, as n tends towards infinity, Y in t_n converges on the initial level of income Y_0.

We have established, then, that the level of income in each period after

[1] Our analysis can easily be adapted to a one-shot change in any other type of expenditure or taxes.

FIGURE 3

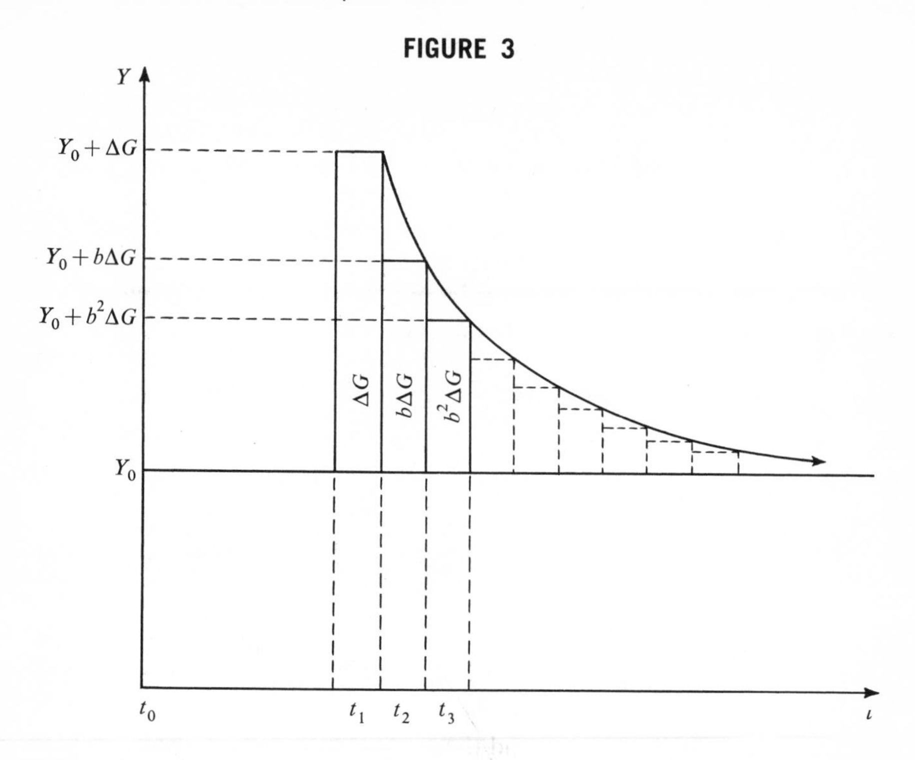

a one-shot increase in government expenditure ΔG in period t_1 is as shown in the second column of Table 1. If we now subtract the initial level of income Y_0 from the level in each succeeding period, we shall find the resulting *change* in income. These changes are shown in the third column of Table 1. The total accumulated change in income ΔY over all periods in excess of the initial level of income is simply the sum of the entries in column three. Clearly,

$$\Delta Y = \Delta G + b\Delta G + b^2\Delta G + \cdots + b^{n-1}\Delta G$$

The right-hand side of this equation is a geometric series similar to the one we came across in §14.1. We showed there that geometric series have a finite sum equal to $[1/(1 - b)]\Delta G$. Thus,

$$\Delta Y = \frac{1}{1-b}\Delta G \quad \text{and} \quad \frac{\Delta Y}{\Delta G} = \frac{1}{1-b}$$

Hence, we conclude that the ratio of the total *accumulated* change in income over and above its initial level when there is a one-shot change in expenditure (which is, by definition, a dynamic multiplier) is equal to $1/(1 - b)$.

The dynamic multiplier is particularly relevant to the kind of problem we discussed in the previous section. There, you will recall, an initial full employment level of income was disturbed by a deflationary shock. While transactors groped for information about the new vector of market-clearing prices, a downward multiplier process emerged and income initially declined.

TABLE 1

PERIOD	LEVEL OF INCOME	CHANGE IN INCOME IN EXCESS OF INITIAL INCOME
t_1	$Y_0 + \Delta G$	ΔG
t_2	$Y_0 + b\Delta G$	$b\Delta G$
t_3	$Y_0 + b^2\Delta G$	$b^2\Delta G$
.	.	.
.	.	.
.	.	.
t_n	$Y_0 + b^{n-1}\Delta G$	$b^{n-1}\Delta G$

However, as reservation wages and prices crumbled in the light of the information that transactors uncovered during their search process, income eventually rose back towards its full employment equilibrium level. The time path followed by income might be like that illustrated by the solid curve AFG in Figure 4. Starting at t_1, when the deflationary shock hits, until t_θ, when full equilibrium is finally reestablished, income is far below full employment real income Y^*. In the process of transition we forego income which is then lost forever. This income loss in the adjustment process could be reduced by a timely fiscal policy relying on the dynamic multiplier. When the deflationary shock hits, a judicious one-shot increase in government expenditure (or a tax reduction) would cause real income to follow a path like the dashed curve ABG instead of the solid curve AFG. As a result, the accumulated gain in income (over what it would have been without fiscal intervention) would be equal to the shaded part of Figure 4. Clearly, this fiscal program is not op-

FIGURE 4

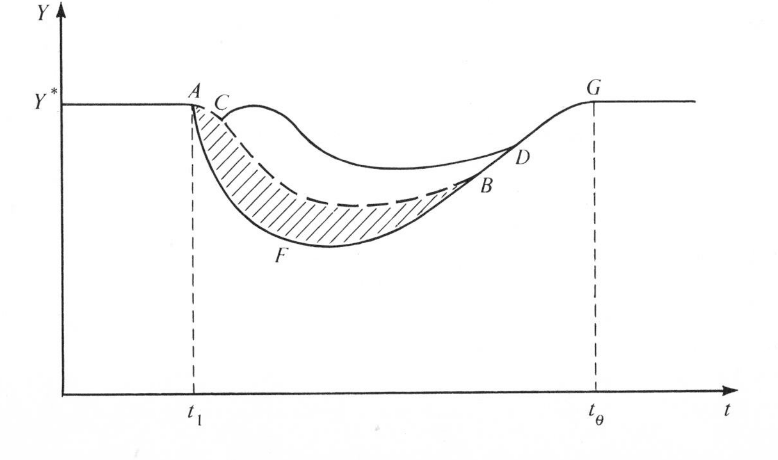

timal. It is easy to imagine that additional doses of fiscal policy could be designed for later periods so that the total loss of income during the transition would be reduced even further. For example, a one-shot dose of fiscal policy in the second period (on top of the first-period dose) might cause income to follow the path *ACDG*. In theory, an ideal program of successively smaller one-shot fiscal doses could be designed which would practically wipe out the downward plunge in income which would otherwise accompany the deflationary shock.

3 Lags in Monetary and Fiscal Policy

At the end of §2 we alluded to a theoretically optimal fiscal policy. In fact, throughout this book we have always taken for granted that our monetary and fiscal authorities were capable of diagnosing precisely what ailed the economy and implementing the curative dose of monetary or fiscal policy necessary to achieve such desirable goals as full employment and price stability. In all our earlier work we assumed that the corrective disturbance imparted to the model by the monetary or fiscal authorities was handled by the auctioneer and its effects adjusted through the process of tâtonnement with recontracting in a timeless environment. In the real world, of course, these assumptions are far from true. The effects of monetary and fiscal policies do not work themselves out instantaneously. On the contrary, monetary and fiscal policy actions are subject to lags in time. We now wish to discuss the lag problems associated with monetary and fiscal policies.

Consider a time scale such as that illustrated in Figure 5. We shall assume the economy is initially in full equilibrium, but at t_1 a shock is imparted to the model by a change in entrepreneurial expectations, a change in household attitudes towards thrift, or any one of the other myriad events that can throw the economy out of equilibrium. Thus, the need for corrective action arises at t_1. However, the fact that the economy's equilibrium has been disturbed will not be apparent immediately. The evidence which policy decision-makers require if they are to make informed decisions is not immediately available. This evidence takes the form of statistics on GNP, personal in-

FIGURE 5

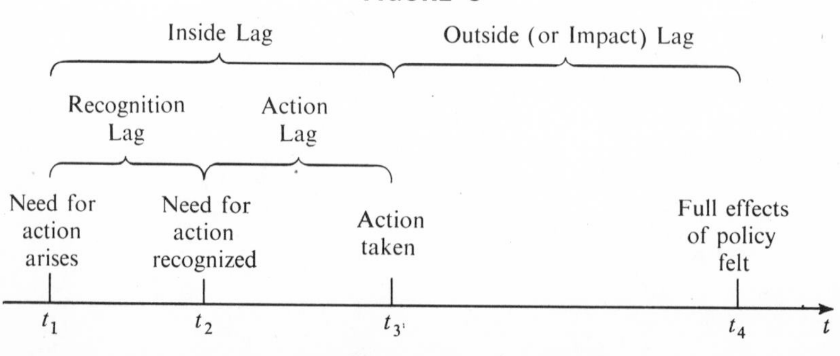

come, employment, unemployment, industrial production, prices, and so on; and these statistics are published only at discrete time intervals. Some data are available on a weekly basis, others appear monthly, and yet others are available only quarterly. For example, GNP, which is certainly one of the most important indicators of the economy's health is only estimated by the Department of Commerce on a quarterly basis. Consequently, up to three months can easily elapse before the policy-makers recognize, at t_2, that the economy is in trouble. Moreover, one swallow does not make a spring. It is often inadvisable to infer something on the basis of one observation. Consequently, before policy-makers are willing to agree that an obvious need for action has arisen they would be wise to wait for corroboratory evidence to appear. This, of course, implies that they must be willing to lose more time. The time between the need for action arising (t_1) and being recognized with certainty (t_2) is described as the *recognition lag.* It is only fair to mention that the recognition lag may be shorter than we have suggested because some economic statistics, called *leading indicators, anticipate* changes in other fundamental economic variables such as GNP, industrial production, and prices. These leading indicators include such statistics as the average work-week; the rate of hiring; new orders for durable goods, machinery, and equipment; and stock market prices. These indicators appear in *Business Cycle Developments* (published by the Department of Commerce, Bureau of the Census) and are available to assist policy-makers in recognizing changes in economic conditions as early as possible.

Having recognized the need for action, policy-makers must decide what to do; they must debate what action to take and how much. In a system where responsibility for monetary and fiscal policy decisions is diffuse, the process of debate and compromise takes time. We have indicated that agreement is reached and action taken at t_3. The time between the recognition of the need for action and action actually being taken (t_2 to t_3) is described as the *action lag*. Together, the recognition and action lags are described as the *inside lag* (t_1 to t_3).

When action is taken at t_3, the effects of the policy implemented are not felt immediately. Those affected by the change in monetary or fiscal policy take time to react to the new policy and reorganize their economic plans accordingly. The extent of the policy change has to be gauged, its implications discussed, and the appropriate response decided upon. The changes induced in transactors' plans themselves generate further economic repercussions; and it is likely to be some time before the complete chain of actions and reactions works itself out and the full effects of the initial change in monetary or fiscal policy are finally felt at t_4, as we have indicated in Figure 5. The period between policy action being taken and the full effects of that policy change finally being felt is described as the *outside,* or *impact,* lag.

Our discussion of the lag in effect of monetary and fiscal policy has been quite general so far. What are some of the specific lag problems associated with these policies? Clearly, both monetary and fiscal authorities face the same sort of recognition lag problems, since both have the same economic data available. However, the time required for the appropriate action to be taken differs for the two types of policy. Authority for monetary policy decisions is somewhat diffused—but nowhere near as diffused as authority for fiscal policy decisions. The de facto power for decision making on monetary policy actions rests with the Federal Reserve System's seven-member Board of Governors which has full authority over changes in reserve requirements, "reviews and determines" discount rates established by the individual Reserve banks, and comprises a majority of the twelve-member Open Market Committee. The latter committee meets about every three weeks, and since open market operations are the monetary authority's most operationally significant policy instrument, the action lag for monetary policy is potentially quite short. This, of course, assumes that the individuals who comprise the monetary authority all divine the same message from the ongoing flow of economic statistics and agree immediately on the appropriate response—which is frequently not the case. The data available often mean different things to different people, and it is not unusual for the process of debate and compromise to go on for several months before a majority (if not consensus) view of the problem with the required response emerges and is translated into action.

Although the inside lag for monetary policy is potentially quite short, the outside lag appears very long. The transmission mechanism of monetary policy between actions being taken and the final full effects of those actions being felt is beset by delays. Suppose, for example, the Federal Reserve sees deflationary forces at work and, wishing to lean against this wind, strikes an expansionary stance by increasing bank reserves and lowering its own discount rate. Banks must then translate these reserves into an increase in the money supply via a multiple-credit expansion. Credit becomes more readily available and the interest rate falls. This induces consumers to change their consumption plans and to start to reappraise their investment intentions. However, such reappraisals take time. New investment projects take a particularly long time to get going. Alternative proposals need to be drawn up, discussed, and decided upon; bids must be solicited and contracts let; appropriations must be allocated; and, finally, the construction process itself is time consuming. It is not surprising, therefore, that the outside lag in monetary policy is quite long. By empirical estimate, its *minimum* length appears to be six months. There is, however, still a great deal of disagreement among economists on this issue and some researchers argue that the lag is substantially greater. Rasche and Shapiro, for example, argue that it may be as long as three years.[1]

Two other points are worth mentioning. First, some research indicates that the lag in effect of monetary policy is not only long but also variable.[2] The significance of this issue on stablization policy is discussed in the fol-

[1] R. H. Rasche and H. T. Shapiro, "The F.R.B.–M.I.T. Econometric Model: Its Special Features," *American Economic Review*, May, 1968, p. 145. This is an extreme estimate.

[2] See, for example, M. Friedman and A. J. Schwartz, "Money and Business Cycles," *Review of Economics and Statistics*, February, 1963.

lowing section. Second, the lengths of both inside and outside lags are different depending on whether an expansionary or a contractionary monetary policy is adopted.

Let us now discuss the action lag and the outside lag in fiscal policy. Because all significant tax and expenditure changes in the United States require Congressional legislation, the action lag for fiscal policy is both long and variable. Although we cannot describe the actual legislative process surrounding fiscal policy decisions in detail, it is so cumbersome and time consuming as to render fiscal policy a wholly inappropriate stabilization instrument for economic "fine tuning."[3] At best, in present circumstances, it can be used only when some gross disturbance requires corrective action. Presidents Kennedy and Johnson sought to shortcircuit this action lag in fiscal policy by requesting from Congress standby power to introduce temporary tax cuts and public works programs. These Presidential requests fell on deaf ears, however, and the supplicants came away from Congress empty-handed. Congress is very jealous of its control over the economy's purse strings and argues that such authorizations would amount to a self-abnegating delegation of its authority to the executive.

The empirical evidence suggests that the full effects of fiscal actions are felt by the economy significantly more quickly than the full effects of monetary policy actions are felt. In other words, the outside lag in fiscal policy is shorter than the outside lag in monetary policy. Rasche and Shapiro have estimated that 75 percent of the full effect of changes in federal defense expenditures is realized in three quarters and of changes in federal personal income taxes in two quarters.[4]

In summary, then, both monetary and fiscal policy decisions are associated with serious time lags. The outside lag is longest for monetary policy while the inside lag is longest for fiscal policy. For both policies, the most sanguine estimate would put the total lag at three or more quarters.

4 Rules versus Discretion

Meaning

As we shall see shortly, the problem of the lag in effect of monetary policy just discussed is one of the issues which has given rise to the contemporary debate among economists whether the monetary authorities in their efforts to maintain economic stability should have free and unfettered discretion in the use of the instruments at their disposal or whether their use of these instruments should be constrained by certain well-defined rules. At present the authorities can exercise discretion. A small, though perhaps growing, number of economists now suggest that this discretion be removed and that

[3] The budget process is described in all its gory detail by D. J. Ott and A. F. Ott, *Federal Budget Policy*, rev. ed., Brookings, 1969, chapter 3.

[4] *Op. cit.*, p. 145. Notice that the expenditure and tax lags are different.

the authorities' behavior be prescribed by rule. The rule most widely advocated is that the monetary authorities should increase the supply of money at a certain rate, say, between 3 percent and 6 percent annually. These suggested minimum and maximum rates of increase vary from advocate to advocate depending, usually, on the particular definition of money adopted. We shall see below, however, that certain more complicated rules of behavior have been suggested in an attempt to meet some of the objections raised against the simple rules of monetary expansion just mentioned.

History

The debate over rules versus discretion has a long intellectual history. Academic proponents of a monetary rule in the 1920s and 1930s included such diverse economists as J. R. Commons, I. Fisher, and H. C. Simons. Academicians were not the only proponents, either. In 1934 Representative Wright Patman (Democrat, Texas) introduced a bill in the House calling for the adoption of a monetary rule. Interest in the debate waned during the late 1930s, the 1940s, and the early 1950s. This loss of interest paralleled the widespread contempt into which monetary policy as a whole fell in this period due to the feeling that "money does not matter anyway," deduced by many economists from their interpretation of Keynesian macroeconomic theory. As the belief that "money does matter" began to reassert itself, academic interest in the rules versus discretion debate revived. The case for a monetary rule was made again almost simultaneously, but independently, by E. S. Shaw and M. Friedman in 1959.[1] Since then there has been a steady stream of academic contributions to the subject and a resurgence of official interest.[2]

The Disagreements

Economic Stability The proponents of discretion argue that a predominantly competitive, free-enterprise economy is inherently unstable and prone to recurrent bouts of expansion and contraction if left to its own devices. Consequently, a competent authority well armed with discretionary powers is necessary to keep the economy on an even keel. Advocates of such powers might point to the catastrophic depression of the 1930s and argue that this sort of massive contraction is endemic to a competitive economy and that another depression has been averted since then only because we have a well-equipped authority that has been ready, willing, and able to take wise and judicious discretionary action to prevent the reces-

[1] E. S. Shaw, "Money Supply and Stable Economic Growth," in *United States Monetary Policy,* The American Assembly, Columbia, 1958. M. Friedman, "The Goals and Criteria of Monetary Policy," in N. H. Jacoby (ed.), *A Program for Monetary Stability,* Fordham, 1959.

[2] Witness, for example, these two official sources: Hearings before the Joint Economic Committee, Congress of the United States, *Standards for Guiding Monetary Action,* U.S. Government Printing Office, 1968; Subcommittee on Domestic Finance, Committee on Banking and Currency, Congress of the United States, *Compendium on Monetary Policy and Guidelines,* U.S. Government Printing Office, 1968.

sions that we have experienced in the postwar period from snowballing into a major depression. Marked economic instability is the unwelcome, but inevitable, bedfellow of a competitive, free-enterprise economy. Fortunately, he can be kept in his place by shrewd and timely doses of discretionary medicine. This, the proponents argue, is demonstrated by the improvement in the record of economic stability in the postwar period.

The supporters of rule take the opposite position. They assert that the economy is basically stable. To be sure, various shocks or impulses (such as, for example, those imparted from economic disturbances originating abroad) may throw it into temporary, short-run disequilibrium, but left to its own devices it will soon find its way automatically back to equilibrium. Hence, those in favor of rules feel that *major* economic fluctuations do not just happen, they are caused. Moreover, they are caused by inappropriate official discretionary policies which could not have been pursued if a monetary rule was being followed. Furthermore, proponents of rules argue, small economic fluctuations, although inevitable, are often, in fact, exacerbated by ill-advised discretionary activities. Proponents of rules believe that these small disturbances would quickly iron themselves out and that a monetary authority armed with discretionary powers is more likely to destabilize the situation further than to get the economy back to equilibrium more rapidly than would happen under its own self-corrective powers. Advocates of a monetary rule would blame the Great Depression on an inappropriate discretionary monetary policy and, likewise, place a large measure of the blame for the smaller postwar recessions in the same place. In sum, they would argue that under a regime of rules major fluctuations would be impossible and minor ones would not be compounded.

The Optimal Policy in a World of Uncertainty Given that the economy will be periodically thrown into disequilibrium (on which both parties to the debate agree), what is the optimum policy to pursue? If the monetary authority had perfect knowledge, i.e., it was an economic superman, clearly one must support discretionary action. The authority would know precisely the extent and nature of the disequilibrium and take appropriate discretionary action to reestablish equilibrium exactly. On occasion, the appropriate action might correspond to the monetary rule—so the authority would adopt that policy.

But, the real world is full of the dark forces of ignorance and uncertainty. What is the optimal policy in this context? Advocates of rules place more emphasis on our ignorance and uncertainty than do advocates of discretion, who tend to emphasize the quality and extent of our economic knowledge. One does not want to make the supporters of a rule sound like know-nothing economists, but they are people who question the accuracy of our forecasting ability and the alleged stability of certain important economic relationships. Of particular importance in this regard is the lag in effect of monetary policy. Rule supporters argue that this lag is both long *and* variable. The asserted variability is important to their position. If the lag was merely long and we could forecast well enough in advance, discretion might be justifiable. But if the lag is variable, as well as long, one does not know in a particular situation what the impact of any discretionary action will be and when it will occur. Thus, proponents of rules conclude that the policy which will do least harm is a constant rate of monetary expansion. This is what will minimize uncertainty and maximize predictability for the community. In fact, they argue that discretion *contributes* to uncertainty and weakens predictability. The community is forced to guess, first, what discretionary action the authorities will take; second, how much; and third, when its impact will be felt.

Holding a more sanguine opinion about our economic knowledge, advocates of discretion contend that the community's uncertainty about the future is reduced by its knowledge that the monetary authority stands ready to intervene appropriately to forestall any adverse economic developments. If this discretion is wisely exercised, of course, uncertainty *is* reduced. But if it is not—if the situation is misjudged—and the authorities overreact (moving too forcefully) or act too late (when the self-corrective forces of the economy are already struggling to overcome the disequilibrium), then the exercise of discretion will compound the economy's residual instability and increase the uncertainty of the community's predictions. This is the position taken by advocates of rule.

The Functions of Authority Although supporters of a rule will agree that those responsible for our monetary affairs are as able, far-sighted, and public-spirited as mortal man can be, they insist that these authorities are as ignorant, too. They may have the will to do good, but they do not have the capacity. The monetary authority is not malevolent, it is merely as uninformed as everyone else. Rather than leave it free to attempt good deeds, which it may on occasion do, we would be better off to constrain it so that it can do the least amount of harm—which is frequently the unintended consequence of its actions. This reveals the classical (nineteenth- as opposed to twentieth-century) liberal philosophical streak in the position of most supporters of a rule. In their opinion, authority is a necessary evil that has to be accepted in many areas (and they would acknowledge that some governmental authority is particularly necessary in monetary affairs), but, nonetheless, that authority should be firmly shackled. It should be enjoined to do the least harm rather than to do the most good, the latter being a task for which it is ill equipped and in which it is almost certain to fail.

The twentieth-century liberal takes the opposite view. He is much more tolerant of governmental activism and is prone to see a large and increasing role for government in our affairs—especially, perhaps, in our economic affairs. He is, therefore, likely to advocate discretion in the area of monetary policy.

A danger that the classical liberal sees in the emergence of an authority which can take important discretionary actions is that power inevitably accrues to it. Since the authority has the capacity to help and to harm important groups, these groups will surely try to exert pressure on its judgment. Although the authority may try to remain objective, it will be exposed to a biased sample of opinion. Those with most to gain or lose will exhibit a more vital interest in its actions. The views of these pressure groups may loom disproportionately large when the monetary authority has to make decisions, and, as a result, the decisions may not be optimal from the point of view of the community as a whole. The advocates of a rule contend that the harm resulting from undue exposure to special-interest or pressure groups would be avoided if the capacity for discretionary action was revoked. Notice that the advocates of a rule do not impugn the authority's motives nor do they accuse it of corruption or malfeasance. There is agreement that these are upright men possessed of probity and sobriety. However, the problem is that there is no way in which they can be insulated from exposure to groups who declare their personal interest to be consistent with the community's interest when that may be very far from the case.

Some Alternative Rules and Their Critics

The case for a rule of monetary expansion can be made in the context of the familiar Cambridge equation:

$$\frac{M^d}{P} = kY \tag{1}$$

where M^d is the demand for nominal money balances, P is the price level, and Y is real income. Essentially, this equation states that the community demands to maintain in the form of real money balances an amount which bears the proportion k to its real money income. This may be rewritten as

$$M^s = kYP \tag{2}$$

if it is assumed that the demand for nominal money is equal to the supply of nominal money M^s. From (2) it is apparent that

$$\frac{\Delta M^s}{M^s} = \frac{\Delta k}{k} + \frac{\Delta Y}{Y} + \frac{\Delta P}{P} \tag{3}$$

As an example, Friedman, who is, perhaps, the most forceful exponent of a simple rule, wants to make $\Delta P/P$, the rate of change of prices, equal to zero.[3] He believes that the long-run rates of growth in k and Y are 1 percent and 3 percent, respectively, thus he would recommend the rate of growth in the money supply be 4 percent, which should result in P being unchanged. This is the essence of Friedman's case for his rule of a constant rate of monetary

[3] The early advocates of a rule tended to make price stabilization the specific objective of official policy and criterion by which its performance should be judged. See, for example, H. C. Simons, "Rules versus Authorities in Monetary Policy," *Journal of Political Economy*, February, 1936. This approach has fallen out of favor largely because, first, it is difficult to get agreement on which particular index to stabilize and, second, but more important, the connection between price changes and changes in the money supply in the short run is not stable enough to be made the objective of the authorities' actions and standard by which their performance can be fairly measured. Of course, the money supply rule discussed in the text is designed to give broad, general, price stability.

expansion. He believes that k and Y do increase at the indicated rates and, thus, that an increase in M^s to match them would generate stability in the overall level of prices. He allows for a band of expansion between 3 percent and 5 percent (as opposed to the unique value 4 percent) primarily because our banking system is ill designed for much greater precision. However, a band does allow the monetary authorities some residual degree of discretion which they can exploit to lean against the economic winds, if they are capable of judging these correctly, without allowing them any room to overreact. Friedman regards overreaction by the monetary authorities as one of their major weaknesses.

Supporters of discretion are not persuaded that either k or Y exhibit the behavior attributed to them by Friedman. They argue that these variables are not particularly stable in the short run and that there is no reason to suppose they would behave as Friedman suggests in the long run. In this context, one might note that the average long-run increase in k observed by Friedman is based on estimates obtained from data stretching back from the present into the late nineteenth century. However, if only the postwar period is examined, there has been a marked *fall* in k. Conceivably, then, the trend in k may have changed; it has, after all, been falling for nearly twenty-five years. Consequently, proponents of discretion appeal for discretionary powers to manipulate the supply of money over a broader band of values than Friedman would condone in order to counteract untoward developments in k and Y.

Partially in response to this argument, Bronfenbrenner has advanced a more sophisticated rule.[4] Since the average productivity of labor Π is defined to be equal to Y/N, the income term in (2) can be divided into two components; namely, the labor force N times the average productivity of labor Π. Thus (2) is equivalent to

$$M^s = kN\Pi P \tag{4}$$

It is clear that (4) can be rewritten as

$$\frac{\Delta M^s}{M^s} = \frac{\Delta k}{k} + \frac{\Delta N}{N} + \frac{\Delta \Pi}{\Pi} + \frac{\Delta P}{P} \tag{5}$$

The purpose of the rule is to stabilize prices. Therefore, by setting $\Delta P/P$ equal to zero we obtain

$$\frac{\Delta M^s}{M^s} = \frac{\Delta k}{k} + \frac{\Delta N}{N} + \frac{\Delta \Pi}{\Pi} \tag{6}$$

which, in words, implies that the percentage change (growth) in the money supply should match the full employment growth of the economy plus any growth in the demand for money. In practice, the growth in M^s in the current period is adjusted to the observed growth in the variables on the right-hand side of (6) that took place in the previous period. Bronfenbrenner's

[4] M. Bronfenbrenner, "Monetary Rules: A New Look," *Journal of Law and Economics*, October, 1965.

rule has much greater flexibility than Friedman's. The latter's rule calls for a year-in, year-out increase in the money supply between 3 and 5 percent. The rate of monetary expansion called for by Bronfenbrenner's rule is adjusted to new economic circumstances which change the rate of growth of the work force and its average productivity and the community's demand to hold money.

Opponents of fixed rules of monetary expansion such as those just described base their arguments on the tenet that "money does not matter." This opinion is grounded in the belief that (1) changes in the level of real money balances brought about by changes in the supply of money do not affect aggregate demand; (2) if monetary policy is to work, it works through changes in the interest rate, but both consumption and investment are unresponsive to changes in the interest rate; and (3) on occasion, the interest rate itself is not reducible due to a liquidity trap. For those who hold these opinions, monetary policy is ineffective as an economic stabilization technique and the whole question of whether a monetary rule or discretionary policy should be followed is relatively meaningless. Such beliefs were widespread among economists in the 1940s and early 1950s. Paradoxically, though, if one believes that money does not matter because it does not affect anything, the appropriate position to support is a fixed rule of one sort or another because such a rule of thumb would be the easiest policy to implement and all the energy expended by the authorities on making the money supply and the interest rate assume this or that value would be conserved. It is probably true to say, however, that since then the notion that "money does matter" once more has become widely held and, thus, that the debate of rules versus discretion is a meaningful one.

Naturally, advocates of a fixed rule of monetary expansion believe that "money does matter." They assign an important role to money in the way the economy performs. Moreover, when they look at the long-run record of discretionary use of monetary policy they conclude a fixed rule would have performed better. They are on the strongest ground when they point to the record of the years between the First and Second World Wars. The rate of change of monetary expansion during this period was especially variable and the economic record was very spotty. They pay particular attention to the great contraction of 1929–1933. This, they argue, was largely attributable to the unwise policy of allowing the money supply to contract by more than 20 percent; if a fixed rule had been followed such a reduction would not have occurred and, as a result, the great economic contraction would have amounted to, at worst, only a recession. In stating that an inappropriate monetary policy was followed then, the advocates of a rule are probably correct. Supporters of discretion point to the low level of interest rates established during this period and respond that monetary policy was powerless to counteract the massive contractionary forces at work. But they are probably wise to divert attention from this episode and concentrate on the postwar period, where they are on firmer ground. Agreement is fairly widespread that the exercise of discretion has been more judicious since the war than before it. Perhaps the relevant question now is not whether a rule would have done better in the dim and distant past, but whether it would do better than the discretionary record in more recent times when our economic understanding has improved so remarkably. Although most advocates of a rule are prepared to agree that the discretionary record has improved, they are not prepared to concede victory in the debate. They insist that had a rule been adhered to, the postwar experience would have been improved and the economic fluctuations experienced would have been both less frequent and smaller.[5] Moreover, they tend to take the very long view and say that although things have not been too bad for a generation, there is no guarantee error will not creep back into our ways. If discretionary authorities have been influenced, if not bound, by the most faulty economic theories in the past such as the "real bills" doctrine and "the money does not matter" nexus, what guarantee do we have that some other new-fangled, but ill-founded, theory may not capture the minds of our discretionary authorities in the future? Those who assign a significant probability to such an event would recommend adoption of a rule even if they were forced to concede that the contemporary exercise of discretion has not been all that bad.

5 The Theory of Economic Policy

In Chapter 14, "Successive Approximations to Income Determination," we examined various progressively more complicated macroeconomic models and, in the context of a particular model, we then asked what would be the effect of a change in any of the economic *policy instruments* (such as government expenditure, the money supply, etc.) on, for example, the equilibrium level of income. In this final section, we take a slightly different approach. We shall assume a particular model, establish certain desirable goals for selected *policy targets* (such as income and consumption), and then ask what values of the policy instruments should be established to bring about the desired values of the policy targets.

Consider the following macroeconomic model:

$$\textit{Commodity market} \begin{cases} Y^s = Y^d & (7) \\ Y^d = C + \bar{I} & (8) \\ C = b_0 + b_1 Y^s - b_2 r & (9) \end{cases}$$

$$\textit{Money market} \begin{cases} \dfrac{M^d}{\bar{P}} = m_0 + m_1 Y^s - m_2 r & (10) \\ M^d = \bar{M}^s & (11) \end{cases}$$

[5] It is somewhat disheartening to observe that only one substantial empirical study exists on whether discretion has worked better than various rules would have. We refer to F. Modigliani's "Some Empirical Tests of Monetary Management and of Rules versus Discretion," *Journal of Political Economy,* June, 1964. Modigliani's conclusion is that since the Second World War discretion has worked better than the various rules that he considered. While recognizing the difficulties involved in reaching valid conclusions from empirical research in this area, one must lament its dearth since the whole question can only be settled empirically and not through interminable a priori theorizing.

This model is not separable, since the commodity market contains four endogenous variables (Y^s, Y^d, C, and r) and only three equations. Thus, the whole model must be solved simultaneously—this can be done, since there are five equations and five endogenous variables (Y^s, Y^d, C, r, and M^d). There are three exogenous variables ($\bar{I}$, $\bar{P}$, and $\bar{M}^s$). Only one of these ($\bar{M}^s$) is, however, a policy instrument. Both $\bar{P}$ and $\bar{I}$ are exogenous, but they are not subject to control by the authorities in charge of economic policy.

Let us solve for Y^s first. This can be done by expressing (10) in terms of r and substituting in (9). Then substitute this result in (8) and the new equation in (7). After isolating Y^s, we obtain

$$Y^s = \frac{b_0}{1 - b_1 + b_2(m_1/m_2)} - \frac{b_2(m_1/m_2)}{1 - b_1 + b_2(m_1/m_2)} + \frac{\bar{I}}{1 - b_1 + b_2(m_1/m_2)} + \frac{b_2/m_2}{1 - b_1 + b_2(m_1/m_2)} \frac{\bar{M}^s}{\bar{P}} \tag{12}$$

which is the reduced-form equation for Y^s (see §14.1). This can be written in the simplified form

$$Y^s = \alpha_0 + \alpha_1 \bar{M}^s \tag{13}$$

by collapsing the first three terms in (12), which involve only parameters and constants, into the new constant α_0 and writing the coefficient on $\bar{M}^s$ in (12) in the condensed form α_1. By an analogous procedure, the system (7)–(11) can be solved for C and written in the condensed form

$$C = \beta_0 + \beta_1 \bar{M}^s \tag{14}$$

Let us now assume that our economic policy-making authorities decide that they would like to achieve certain values of the target variables Y^s and C. In particular, they would like

$$Y^s = \hat{Y}^s \tag{15}$$

$$C = \hat{C} \tag{16}$$

where $\hat{Y}^s$ and $\hat{C}$, respectively, are the desired target values for Y^s and C. By substitution of (15) and (16) in (13) and (14), respectively, we obtain

$$\hat{Y}^s = \alpha_0 + \alpha_1 \bar{M}^s \tag{17}$$

$$\hat{C} = \beta_0 + \beta_1 \bar{M}^s \tag{18}$$

The question confronting the policy-making authority is what value should be selected for $\bar{M}^s$ to achieve $\hat{Y}^s$ and $\hat{C}$ when these target variables have acquired the status of constants? To achieve $\hat{Y}^s$, (17) implies

$$\bar{M}^s = \frac{\hat{Y}^s - \alpha_0}{\alpha_1} \tag{19}$$

while to achieve $\hat{C}$, (18) implies

$$\bar{M}^s = \frac{\hat{C}^s - \beta_0}{\beta_1} \tag{20}$$

However, in general, $\bar{M}^s$ cannot be set equal to (19) *and* (20). It would be a very fortuitous event indeed if the terms on the right-hand sides of (19) and (20) were such that those right-hand sides were equal. The policy-making authority has overreached itself. It has promised goods it cannot deliver. The problem in this example is that the policy-making authority has selected two policy targets, but it has only one policy instrument. In effect, (17) and (18) amount to two simultaneous equations in only one unknown (the required value of $\bar{M}^s$). Such systems are said to be overdetermined and, in general, do not have a solution. The authority could use (19) to set $\bar{M}^s$ to achieve $Y^s = \hat{Y}^s$ *or* (20) to set $\bar{M}^s$ to achieve $C = \hat{C}$, but it cannot do both. Here we have illustrated an important principle of the theory of economic policy: the authority needs as many policy instruments as policy targets it wishes to achieve.

Let us now amend the equation system (7)–(11) to include one more policy instrument. In particular, substitute

$$Y^d = C + \bar{I} + \bar{G} \tag{8'}$$

for equation (8) where government expenditure $\bar{G}$ is another policy instrument. The reduced-form equations for Y^s and C can now be obtained from this amended system in the same way as they were determined for the original system. The condensed versions of these reduced-form equations would be

$$Y^s = \alpha_0 + \alpha_1 \bar{M}^s + \alpha_2 \bar{G} \tag{13'}$$

$$C = \beta_0 + \beta_1 \bar{M}^s + \beta_2 \bar{G} \tag{14'}$$

Continuing to assume that (15) and (16) give the desired target values for Y^s and C, by substitution in (13′) and (14′), we obtain

$$\hat{Y}^s = \alpha_0 + \alpha_1 \bar{M}^s + \alpha_2 \bar{G} \tag{17'}$$

$$\hat{C} = \beta_0 + \beta_1 \bar{M}^s + \beta_2 \bar{G} \tag{18'}$$

Treating $\hat{Y}^s$ and $\hat{C}$ in (17′) and (18′) as constants, we see that the question confronting the authorities is what values of $\bar{M}^s$ and $\bar{G}$ are consistent with them and, therefore, can be selected to achieve them. In the context of this problem, (17′) and (18′) amount to two simultaneous equations in the two unknown values of the policy instruments $\bar{M}^s$ and $\bar{G}$. They can easily be solved by substitution to give

$$\bar{M}^s = \frac{\alpha_0\beta_2 + \alpha_2\hat{C} - \alpha_2\beta_0 - \beta_2\hat{Y}}{\alpha_2\beta_1 - \alpha_1\beta_2} \tag{21}$$

$$\bar{G} = \frac{-\alpha_0\beta_1 - \alpha_1\hat{C} + \alpha_1\beta_0 + \beta_1\hat{Y}}{\alpha_2\beta_1 - \alpha_1\beta_2} \tag{22}$$

provided that $\alpha_2\beta_1 - \alpha_1\beta_2$ does not equal zero. The policy-making authority faces no inconsistency now. If it sets the values of its policy instruments according to (21) and (22) it will achieve the desired values of its target

FIGURE 6

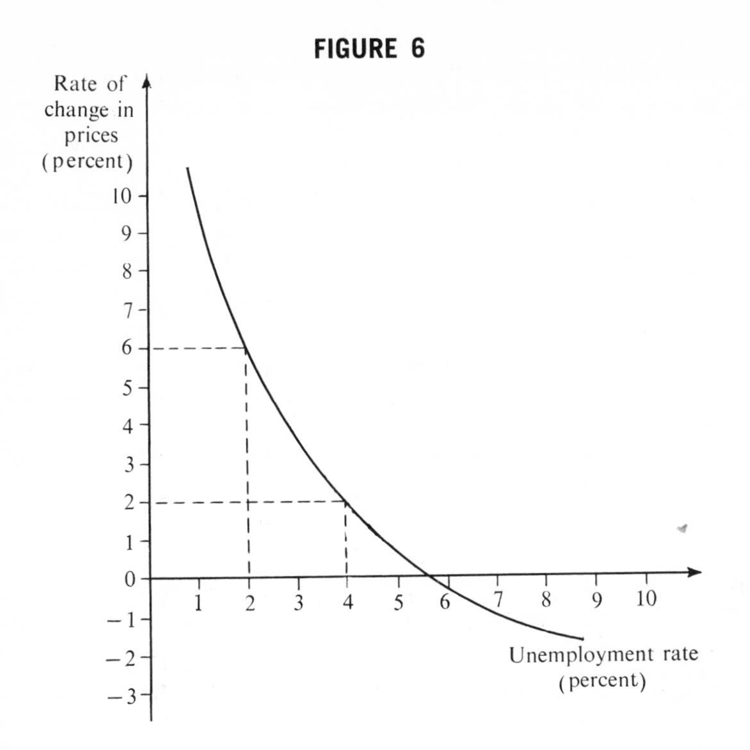

variables $\hat{Y}^s$ and $\hat{C}$ simultaneously. Now that the authority has as many instruments as it has targets, it can achieve its goals.

We must add immediately, however, that equality between the number of instruments and the number of targets is neither a necessary nor a sufficient condition for the policy-making authority to achieve its adopted goals. To illustrate that equality between instruments and targets is not necessary, consider an economic authority which has adopted the goal of full employment and which operates in a neoclassical economy. We know that in such an economy full employment prevails automatically and is completely independent of the authority's monetary or fiscal policy. Hence, the authority can select *any* values for $\bar{M}^s$, $\bar{G}$, and $\bar{T}$, and full employment will always prevail.

An authority might select targets which are incompatible with each other (although each might be attainable individually). In this case, the authority cannot achieve all its targets simultaneously, even though it has the same number of instruments as targets. Thus, equality between the number of instruments and the number of targets is clearly not a sufficient condition for all targets to be attainable. The famous Phillips curve relationship illustrated in Figure 6 is an example of this problem.[1] This figure shows that as the unemployment rate falls, the rate at which prices rise increases; and vice versa. For example, if unemployment is 4 percent, prices rise 2 percent per

[1] See A. W. Phillips, "The Relation between Unemployment and the Rate of Change of Money Wage Rates in the United Kingdom, 1862–1957," *Economica*, November, 1958.

annum; if unemployment is reduced to 2 percent, the rate of price increase rises to 6 percent per annum. We see that price stability requires an unemployment rate of 5.5 percent. Hence, if such a relationship exists (and a good deal of the empirical research indicates that it does), then clearly the twin goals of full employment and price stability are incompatible. In effect, the authority is *constrained* to choose targets for the rate of change in the price level and the (un)employment rate which are consistent with the Phillips curve relationship. Moreover, if this constraint is really bona fide, the authority cannot avoid it simply by adding more policy instruments to its arsenal. It must accept the facts of economic life and recognize that it is involved in a "tradeoff" among its goals. It can have a lower rate of inflation at the expense of a higher rate of unemployment or it can have a lower rate of unemployment at the expense of a higher rate of inflation—but it cannot have both a lower rate of unemployment and a lower rate of inflation.[2]

Finally, economic policy must be coordinated if it is to be efficient. Suppose a fiscal authority was responsible for setting $\bar{G}$ and a monetary authority for setting $\bar{M}^s$. We know that $\bar{M}^s$ and $\bar{G}$ must be set according to (21) and (22) to achieve $\hat{Y}^s$ and $\hat{C}$. It is apparent, then, that an uncooperative monetary authority (just for example's sake) could frustrate the fiscal authority's intentions by selecting $\bar{M}^s$ according to some other criterion. When it comes to policy making, competition between rival governmental agencies is highly undesirable. If policy making is to be effective, there should be agreement on goals and a cooperative (or simultaneous) selection of the values of policy instruments.

Summary

We began this final chapter by discussing the "new interpretation" of Keynes as, first and foremost, a macroeconomic disequilibrium theorist. The essence of this view is that Keynes did, indeed, make a fundamental contribution to macroeconomic theory by analyzing its disequilibrium behavior in a nontâtonnement context. In the absence of an auctioneer, the search costs of acquiring information imply *slow* adjustment of wages and prices by transactors, and this is sufficient to trigger a Keynesian multiplier contraction in the face of a deflationary shock. The *eventual* new equilibrium may be consistent with neoclassical theory, but the disequilibrium *interim* period is distinctly Keynesian in flavor. In the context of such a disequilibrium adjustment process, we showed that fiscal stabilization policy can take advantage of the properties of the *dynamic multiplier*.

Both monetary and fiscal policy are subject to a time *lag*. This lag is divided into an *inside lag* (consisting of a *recognition lag* and an *action lag*) and an *outside lag*. The inside lag is longer for fiscal policy than monetary policy, while the outside lag is longer for monetary policy than fiscal policy.

[2] Unless the *structure* of the economy is changed so that the Phillips curve is shifted closer to the origin.

The *minimum* estimate of the total lag for both types of policy exceeds six months.

The long lag associated with monetary policy together with either its *variability* or the fact that we cannot forecast accurately far into the future has led some economists to argue that the monetary authorities' discretionary behavior should be constrained and that they should be forced to adhere to some *monetary rule*. Here, we considered Friedman's and Bronfenbrenner's rules in some detail.

Our final topic of discussion was the *theory of economic policy* wherein certain *policy targets* are adopted and then *policy instruments* are selected to achieve them. Usually the policy-maker requires as many instruments as there are targets to control, but this equality is neither always necessary nor sufficient to achieve the targets. Some targets may be realized automatically, and other targets may be incompatible with each other, even though there are as many instruments as targets. We illustrated a case of incompatibility of targets using the Phillips curve relationship, which indicates that there is a *trade off* between the rate of change of prices and the unemployment rate.

Questions

1. Explain why Keynes is now held in relatively low esteem as a *comparative static* macroeconomic theorist.
2. What do you understand by the "new interpretation" of Keynes?
3. What makes Keynes' *General Theory* "general" and not a series of "special cases" of neoclassical theory?
4. Suppose you were fired today from your job as clerk at the local supermarket where you earn $2.80 an hour. You know you could get a job as a lemon picker tomorrow at $1.50 an hour. Would you sign on as a lemon picker tomorrow? If so, why? If not, why not?
5. You decide to sell your 1951 Plymouth coupe. Will you accept the first offer you receive? If not, why not? How long will you wait before you do accept an offer?
6. Assume a macroeconomic model originally in equilibrium. Analyze the impact of a reduction in government expenditure (*or* an increase in thrift) in a non-tâtonnement context.
7. Define the *dynamic multiplier*. Show that, in a simple model, it is equal to $1/(1 - b)$ where b is the *mpc*.
8. Explain the way in which the principle of the dynamic multiplier might be advantageously applied to policy when a model in which all prices crumble only slowly is exposed to a deflationary shock.
9. Discuss the lags in effect of monetary or fiscal policy in general.
10. Compare and contrast the lags in effect of monetary and fiscal policy.
11. Make the best case you can in favor of allowing the monetary authority to use discretionary policy.
12. Make the best case you can in favor of constraining the monetary authority to conform to certain rules.
13. Explain Friedman's monetary rule.
14. Explain Bronfenbrenner's monetary rule.

15. Postulate a model including two policy targets and one policy instrument (and which is different from that used in the text) and show that your model is inconsistent.
16. Explain why equality between the number of policy instruments and policy targets is neither necessary nor sufficient to achieve the desired values of the target variables.

SELECTED READINGS

Keynes Reinterpreted

1. A. A. Alchian, "Information Costs, Pricing, and Resource Unemployment," *Western Economic Journal,* June, 1969. Further develops the implications of Stigler's earlier work [5] on the search costs of information.
2. R. J. Barro and H. J. Grossman, "A General Disequilibrium Model of Income and Employment," *American Economic Review,* March, 1971. A lucid and simple analysis of macroeconomic disequilibrium.
3. R. W. Clower, "The Keynesian Counterrevolution: A Theoretical Appraisal," in F. H. Hahn and F. P. R. Brechling (eds.), *The Theory of Interest Rates,* Institute of Economic Affairs, 1965. A superb article which contains the authoritative statements of Say's and Walras' laws and a formal analysis of a Keynesian macroeconomic disequilibrium adjustment process.
4. A. Leijonhufvud, *On Keynesian Economics and the Economics of Keynes,* Oxford, 1968. A monumental scholarly reinterpretation of Keynes building on the pioneering work of Clower [3]. Destined to become a classic.
5. G. J. Stigler, "Information in the Labor Market," *Journal of Political Economy,* October, 1962. An excellent analysis of the implications of search costs for unemployment.

The Dynamic Multiplier

6. D. Patinkin, *Money, Interest, and Prices,* 2nd ed., Harper & Row, 1965.

Lags in Monetary and Fiscal Policy

7. A. Ando, E. C. Brown, J. Kareken, and R. M. Solow, "Lags in Fiscal and Monetary Policy," in Commission on Money and Credit, *Stabilization Policies,* Prentice-Hall, 1963. Finds long outside lags.
8. J. Culbertson, "Friedman on the Lag in Effect of Monetary Policy," *Journal of Political Economy,* December, 1960. A critique of Friedman's analysis of the lag problem.
9. M. Friedman and A. J. Schwartz, "Money and Business Cycles," *Review of Economics and Statistics,* February, 1963. Finds the outside lag in monetary policy to be both long (up to eighteen months) *and* variable.
10. R. H. Rasche and H. T. Shapiro, "The F.R.B.–M.I.T. Econometric Model: Its Special Features," *American Economic Review,* May, 1968. Estimates the outside lags in monetary and fiscal policy. Finds the former may be as much as three years.
11. A. A. Walters, "Monetary Multipliers in the United Kingdom," *Oxford Economic Papers,* November, 1966. Estimates a reasonably short outside lag for the U.K.—namely, two quarters.

Rules versus Discretion

12. M. Bronfenbrenner, "Monetary Rules: A New Look," *Journal of Law and Economics,* October, 1965. Argues the case for his monetary rule.

13. M. Friedman, *A Program for Monetary Stability,* Fordham, 1959, chapter 4. Makes the case for his old (3 percent to 5 percent) rule.
14. M. Friedman, *The Optimum Quantity of Money,* Aldine, 1969, chapter 1. Makes the case for his new (2 percent) rule.
15. L. E. Gramley, "Guidelines for Monetary Policy—The Case Against Simple Rules," in W. L. Smith and R. L. Teigen (eds.), *Money, National Income, and Stabilization Policy,* rev. ed., Irwin, 1970. Argues the case for discretion.
16. F. Modigliani, "Some Empirical Tests of Monetary Management and of Rules versus Discretion," *Journal of Political Economy,* June, 1964. Concludes that since the Second World War discretion has worked better than any other variety of rules would have.
17. E. S. Shaw, "Money Supply and Stable Economic Growth," in *United States Monetary Policy,* The American Assembly, Columbia, 1958. Makes a clear, elementary, and witty case for rules.
18. H. C. Simons, "Rules versus Authorities in Monetary Policy," *Journal of Political Economy,* February, 1936. Makes the case that the monetary authorities' specific objective should be price stability.

The Theory of Economic Policy

19. M. Friedman, "The Role of Monetary Policy," *American Economic Review,* March, 1968. Contains critical remarks about the Phillips curve.
20. B. Hansen, *The Theory of Fiscal Policy,* Harvard, 1958, part 1.
21. R. G. Lipsey, "The Relation between Unemployment and the Rate of Change of Money Wage Rates in the United Kingdom, 1862–1957: A Further Analysis," *Economica,* February, 1960. Provides a theoretical foundation for the purely empirical relationship which Phillips [22] originally estimated.
22. A. W. Phillips, "The Relation between Unemployment and the Rate of Change of Money Wage Rates in the United Kingdom, 1862–1957," *Economica,* November, 1958.
23. J. Tinbergen, *Economic Policy: Principles and Design,* North-Holland, 1956. The classic source on the theory of economic policy by the first Nobel Prize winner in economics (jointly with R. Frisch).

An Epilogue on Wage-Price Policies

In the United States, prices have risen continuously, at varying rates, since the Second World War. Earlier, when discussing cost-push and administered price inflation we showed that, for a given degree of unionization and industrial concentration, neither collective bargaining by labor nor monopolization of the commodity market by entrepreneurs would cause prices to rise continuously.[1] Might it be possible, however, that the continuous increase in prices that we have experienced is due to a progressive increase in the degree of unionization or industrial concentration? The evidence does not support an affirmative answer. To quote briefly some relevant statistics, the percentage of the total labor force that was unionized actually declined from 25 to 23 percent from 1953 to 1968. Moreover, in 1954 the fifty largest manufacturing firms accounted for 23 percent of value added to GNP while the figure was 25 percent in 1966. Alternatively, taking shipments by the largest four firms in an industry as an index of industrial concentration, we find that, for twenty-two selected industries, the share of the largest four firms in total shipments shows little change over this period. (This share increased in half the industries and decreased in the other half.)

Given no substantive change in the degree of unionization and industrial concentration, the continuous rise in prices must, then, be attributable to the pursuit of excessively easy monetary and fiscal policies in the past. Such inappropriate policies may have been followed in an attempt to *validate*[2] the effects of cost-push inflation, but the fact remains that if no such attempt is made prices will stabilize (at a higher level, true, but, nonetheless, they will stabilize). In the last analysis, continuously rising prices

[1] See Chapter 10, Sections 4 and 5, and Chapter 11, Section 6, respectively. The degree of unionization and industrial concentration assumed in those analyses was total since the whole work force became unionized and all firms were monopolized.

[2] *Ibid.*

are the result of overly easy monetary and fiscal policies. Governments are loathe to recognize this point. On the contrary, instead of acquitting their responsibility to implement appropriate policies, they are frequently tempted to try to suppress inflationary forces by adopting "wage-price" or "incomes" policies which amount to the imposition of direct controls on wages and prices. The United States succumbed to this temptation in August, 1971.[3] In this epilogue we shall discuss briefly this new economic policy.

In the first phase of the new policy prices and wages were frozen at their existing levels for a period of ninety days.[4] This wage-price freeze was presided over by the Cost of Living Council (hereafter, the Council), a new institution created expressly for that purpose. At the time of writing (August, 1971) it is not clear what will follow in the second phase of the new economic policy when the first ninety days are over. However, since the option to continue the freeze exists let us examine some of the problems associated with an attempt to freeze wages and prices over any considerable period of time. First, we concentrate on the problems associated with freezing prices.

The quality of most products is not unique. Quality is a variable, not a parameter, with almost all goods. There is an optimum price-quality-output mix which will maximize a firm's profits and there is no reason to suppose that "quality" is in any way sacrosanct. It is widely accepted that price and output are proper variables to alter when it comes to the pursuit of profit. It is not so widely acknowledged, but it is nonetheless true, that product quality is just as important in this decision. By way of example, assume that, if it were not for the freeze, a producer would serve his best interests by selling his product, which has a certain quality, at a 5 percent higher price. Finding this route closed, there is nothing to stop him from lowering the quality of his product to the extent that the frozen price still amounts to an (appropriate) price increase on the now debased product. Hence, quality debasement would become widespread as profit-maximizing entrepreneurs obey the Council de jure but not de facto. The Council was, of course, aware of this in principal and announced that such quality debasement was not to occur.[5] However, the Council seems blind to the scope for quality debasement in practice. It might recognize a chocolate bar shrinking before its eyes, but quality variations can be very subtle and much more difficult to detect than this. An automobile with four coats of paint is of lower quality than one with five coats, but only a very diligent member of the Council or automobile buyer would be able to detect that one coat of paint had dis-

[3] Direct controls had been placed on wages and prices during the Second World War, but 1971 marked the first occasion when they had been used in peacetime.

[4] This promulgation was accompanied by other decisions, the most important of which were to the effect that (1) government expenditure and taxes were both reduced, (2) businesses would receive a tax credit on new investment expenditures, (3) a 10 percent surcharge was imposed on imports, and (4) the United States would no longer convert foreign held dollars into gold. De facto, the latter decision put the United States dollar on a free exchange rate.

[5] Despite the hard line the Council indicated that it planned to take on debasement, it allowed the automobile companies to charge for as optional equipment on their 1972 models some of what had been standard equipment on the 1971 models.

appeared. What about the thickness of carpets? Thinner in this year's models than last year's. But they are artificial fiber this year and not wool. Is that a quality debasement or improvement? Who knows? Certainly not the Council. A little reflection will reveal the tremendous range for obtaining a real price increase by almost undetectable quality debasements in complex manufactured products so that the spirit of the freeze is circumvented even if the letter is not. One other obvious way, of course, is to reduce the amount and/or quality of service available with the product. We might, for example, expect fewer salesclerks per customer or fewer home deliveries. It follows that the real price of something you have to wait around the store to buy or now have to carry home yourself is certainly higher than something immediately thrust into your hands by a smiling salesclerk or delivered to your door. It is clearly beyond the competence of the Council (at least as it is presently conceived) to police such matters.

But let us suppose, for the sake of argument, that producers do not exert their option to make compensating quality variations. What then? Assume conditions are such that a 5 percent price rise is necessary to clear the market for a certain product but that prices are held at the frozen level. At this artificially low price, there will be excess demand. The result must be that some people go without entirely or else the producer puts them on a waiting list and lengthens his order book. What is the *real* price if the former happens? The answer is infinity. The good is not available to some at *any* price. Who actually gets the relatively limited supplies now coming onto the market depends on the particular rationing scheme the producer chooses to introduce given that he is now prevented from rationing by price. Perhaps long-established customers (or personal friends) get preference. The point is some nonpecuniary rationing mechanism must be introduced to ration the limited supply among the competing claimants.

The possibility also exists that, in time, those who were lucky enough to obtain some of the commodity (through one special relationship with the producer or another) would resell some of it at a higher price to those who were not so lucky. These transactions would probably take place through some enterprising middleman. In effect, an "unofficial" (black) market would arise. In effect, the unofficial middleman acts to raise the price to remove the excess demand. Of course, during this process there is a transfer of income from the producers and consumers to these middlemen who are willing to take the risk, or bear the social opprobrium, of operating in an unofficial market. Although such people are frequently condemned, this does not alter the fact that they exist and will always appear where "official" prices are not market-clearing prices. The Council may be satisfied that it has held prices at their frozen levels if its statisticians only collect their price information from official lists. However, the consumer will know otherwise since many of them will have to pay unofficial prices.

Suppose the producer does not impose a rationing mechanism other than price but merely makes his product available on a first-come, first-served basis and you go on the waiting list if you do not get served first. The result is again that even though the nominal price may remain the same, the real price has gone up. A product for which you must wait six months for delivery is more expensive than one you can pick up tomorrow. We simply have queue-pricing as well as money-pricing.

We can predict with confidence, then, that if prices are frozen for a long period, quality debasement, unofficial markets, and queue-pricing will result notwithstanding that producers might continue to post nominal prices that conform to the freeze. Real prices will change though nominal prices may not.

Next, let us examine how the new policy affects wages. There are numerous arguments which suggest that a long-term freeze on wages is also destined to be ineffective.

Employers and employees negotiate compensation rates per time period (wage per week, salary per month, and so on as the case may be). It is these rates which are asked to conform to the Council's freeze. However, even if wage rates conform to the freeze this is no guarantee that *earnings* will. Earnings include overtime and bonuses and these can be substantial enough to cause earnings to diverge from rates markedly. Yet it is earnings which comprise the corporate wage bill and reflect employees' income, not wage rates. Therefore, if the alleged function of the wage freeze is to contain wage-costs so as to avoid cost-push inflation, it will clearly fail if it has only the slippery grasp on earnings which control over rates implies. Either the Council is unaware of what is described as *wage drift* or it has certainly failed to acknowledge the problems it poses for the wage freeze.

There is also the question of fringe benefits. The Council has made it clear that the whole wage "package"—that is, the wage rate plus changes in the working week, fringe benefits, and so on—should be frozen. However, it would be foolish not to recognize that the management community has demonstrated tremendous ingenuity in the past in taking income in *kind* to bypass the impact of progressive income tax rates; stock options, lavish expense accounts, and pension rights along with sundry other items such as a company car, payment of health insurance fees, children's educational expenses, oak-panelled executive dining suites, etc., spring to mind immediately. There seems no reason to suppose that other members of the working community will not demonstrate similar initiative in circumventing a wage freeze when their self-interest so dictates. The myriad ways available are certainly beyond the capacity of the Council to combat as it is presently constituted. How would the Council prevent cleaner and bigger rest-room facilities, more and better recreational facilities, cheaper and quicker canteen facilities? Merely posing the question reveals the impossibility of answering it. It is obvious, then, that even if employees, perhaps through their unions, do conform to the freeze on wage rates and the more obvious fringe benefits like pensions, holidays, etc., the scope for circumvention via less obvious fringe benefit routes (which are nonetheless significant to the employees' overall well-being) remains wide open. If such circumventions do occur, of course, there will have been no real constraint on income—

merely a reversion to a form of "payment in kind" with all that that entails for equity and efficiency. All that the Council will have accomplished is to have induced a change in the labor compensation-mix away from cash and cash-equivalent fringe benefits towards fringe benefits with less obvious pecuniary equivalents. Let us stress that there is nothing immoral about employees bargaining for fringe benefits of this type if they choose to observe the wage freeze. It is merely a case of workers taking part of their income in the form of an improved *quality* of working environment. We should observe, however, that employees would not choose this method if they could obtain equivalent pecuniary compensation, since it is clearly second-best from their point of view.

Finally, there is the equivalent on the labor side to quality variations on the product side. Employers will want to pay more than the frozen wage to their employees only if it is profitable for them to do so. Assuming that it is, they do not have to resort to the sort of working environment quality improvements mentioned in the previous paragraph. Other alternatives are available. Employers can, for example, manage their work force less rigorously so that they get less work out of each employee and make up for this by employing more workers. In effect, the workers here are taking part of their income in the form of on-the-job leisure. Specifically, one might expect management to ignore abuse of coffee-break, lunch, and wash-up time. The net effect of this policy is that the quality of the labor input has declined as far as management is concerned. This policy, let it be noted, is the one which would be in the best interests of both employers and employees given the constraint on free collective bargaining over the wage rate imposed by the Council. In circumstances of free wage rate negotiations, however, it is highly unlikely that this would be the policy which served the best interests of both parties. This is just one more example of a potentially disastrous unintended economic consequence of a wage freeze.

Debasement of the quality of the work force need not be quite so covert. Management can merely promote each worker in a particular job category to a higher job category. This would give the employee the higher wage it is profitable for the employer to pay to the employee which he presently cannot do openly without engaging the wrath of the Council. However, the quality of the work force in each category would be lower. The Council has denounced such stratagems but when it is in both the employers' and the employees' interests, who is going to complain to the Council? If the freeze continues, one can expect to see storekeepers being turned into inventory control officers and keypunch operators becoming data processing assistants. Imagination is the only constraint.

To summarize, then, in the long run a freeze on prices will lead to product quality debasement, unofficial markets, and queue-pricing. Similarly, a freeze in wages will lead to work force quality debasement and to more payment in kind.

We have derived these implications in the content of a wage-price freeze. However, their relevance is not limited to such a policy. They are inferences that can be drawn from the behavior of transactors who are confronted by markets which cannot be cleared by price and wage adjustments. If, in the second phase of the new economic policy, mandatory wage-price guidelines are adopted which specify *some* wage and price flexibility, the above implications will still emerge whenever the wages and prices allowed by the guidelines do not correspond to those which would be established by market forces.

Variations on the theme of a wage-price policy have been played in many Western European countries including Denmark, France, Italy, the Netherlands, Sweden, and the United Kingdom. They have failed and been abandoned or lapsed into disuse and ineffectiveness everywhere. We conjecture that a similar fate awaits the United States' venture. As Frank Paish has observed, the hard fact of the matter is that *if inappropriate monetary and fiscal policies are pursued, a wage-price policy will not work; if appropriate monetary and fiscal policies are pursued, a wage-price policy is not necessary.*

Index of Names

Index of Subjects

1
2
3
4
5
6
7
8
9
0